Corporation Law

CORPORATE COUNSEL GUIDES

►Corporation Law

JAMES D. COX AND
THOMAS LEE HAZEN

AMERICAN BAR ASSOCIATION
General Practice,
Solo & Small Firm
Division

Cover by Jill Tedhams/ABA Publishing.

The materials contained herein represent the opinions and views of the authors and/or the editors, and should not be construed to be the views or opinions of the law firms or companies with whom such persons are in partnership with, associated with, or employed by, nor of the American Bar Association or the General Practice, Solo and Small Firm Division unless adopted pursuant to the bylaws of the Association.

Nothing contained in this book is to be considered as the rendering of legal advice for specific cases, and readers are responsible for obtaining such advice from their own legal counsel. This book is intended for educational and informational purposes only.

Corporate Counsel Guides: Corporation Law is an adaptation of the authors' *Treatise on the Law of Corporations*, 3rd Edition (West: 2010). Used with permission.

Printed in the United States of America

16 15 14 13 12   5 4 3 2 1

Library of Congress Cataloging-in-Publication Data

Cox, James D., 1943-
  Corporation law / by James D. Cox and Thomas Lee Hazen.—1st ed.
      p. cm.—(Corporate counsel guides)
  Includes bibliographical references and index.
  ISBN 978-1-61438-550-9 (print : alk. paper)
  1. Corporation law—United States. I. Hazen, Thomas Lee, 1947–II. Title.
  KF1414.C685 2012
  346.73'066—dc23

                                                                        2012025699

Discounts are available for books ordered in bulk. Special consideration is given to state bars, CLE programs, and other bar-related organizations. Inquire at Book Publishing, ABA Publishing, American Bar Association, 321 North Clark Street, Chicago, Illinois 60654-7598.

www.ShopABA.org

CONTENTS

CHAPTER 10
DIRECTORS' AND OFFICERS' DUTIES OF
CARE AND LOYALTY   159

PART A. DILIGENCE, SKILL, AND CARE;
LIABILITY FOR NEGLIGENCE IN MANAGEMENT   160

PREFACE

This book is designed to be an easy to access reference guide for corporate counsel as well as outside counsel dealing with corporate law. The book is an abridged version of our four-volume treatise on corporate law—James D. Cox & Thomas Lee Hazen, *Treatise on the Law of Corporations* (3rd ed. West 2010).

We have kept references to a minimum in order to promote readability without sacrificing reference to helpful primary sources. Our hope is that this book will provide a useful overview and explanation of key concepts. The complexity of the field of corporate law precludes comprehensive treatment within a readable one-volume book so we have focused on breadth and understanding rather than depth. Once you have gained a basic understanding of the subject from this book, you might want to consult a more comprehensive source such as our four-volume treatise published by West.

We hope that you will find this book useful. We welcome your comments or suggestions for improvement.

James D. Cox
Durham, N.C.

Thomas Lee Hazen
Chapel Hill, N.C.

June 2012

CHAPTER 1

FORMS OF BUSINESS ASSOCIATION— DEFINITIONS AND DISTINCTIONS

TABLE OF SECTIONS

§ 1.1   THE CORPORATION

Corporations made possible much of the industrial and commercial development of the nineteenth and twentieth centuries. Corporate form permits investors to combine their capital and participate in the profits of large- or small-scale business enterprises. Corporations provide centralized management, with owners' risk limited to the capital contributed and without peril to their other resources and business. The capital needed for modern business could hardly have been assembled and combined in any other way.

§ 1.2   THE CONCEPT OF CORPORATE ENTITY OR PERSONALITY

A corporation may be realistically described as a legal unit, a concern separated off with a legal existence, status, or capacity of its own, a legal device or instrument for carrying on some business enterprise or some social, charitable, religious, or governmental activities. Corporation A is a legal person entirely different from individual shareholder X, or, rather, it has a legal capacity that is distinct from X's, even though X organized it, manages it, and owns all or practically all of its shares.

Unlike in an individual enterprise or partnership, in a corporation the maximum loss to shareholders or owners due to the business's debts and torts, with rare exceptions, will not exceed the amount that they have invested in the enterprise. If Y loans money or otherwise extends credit to A corporation, he must look to the corporate assets for repayment; ordinarily he cannot recover from the shareholders or levy on their property.[1] The separateness of the corporation is also generally recognized for tax purposes, the corporation usually being considered a taxable entity.

§ 1.3   THE CORPORATION AND THE CONSTITUTION

When questions arise concerning the right of corporations to invoke constitutional protections, the Supreme Court resolves the question by examining the nature and purpose of the specific articles, clauses, or amendments. Over time, this inquiry has yielded a "corporate personality" for constitutional purposes. Corporations, as artificial persons, are entitled to many, but not all, of the protections and guarantees afforded natural persons.

Citizenship. One significant limitation on a corporation's rights under the Constitution is the Supreme Court's refusal to grant it citizenship status for the purposes of the privileges and immunities clause of Article IV, Section 2, as well as under the Fourteenth Amendment.[2] As a consequence of corporations' being denied citizenship status, states may, as a valid exercise of their police powers, regulate foreign corporations conducting business within their borders, provided the regulations do not impermissibly affect commerce.[3]

On the other hand, a corporation is a citizen for the purposes of determining whether the federal court has jurisdiction based on diversity of citizenship under Article III of the Constitution.[4] Corporations also enjoy First Amendment protections.[5] The corporation's citizenship for jurisdictional purposes and its presence for venue purposes are now controlled by statute.

Person. Various constitutional provisions afford protection to a "person." The Court interprets this language as including artificial persons such as corporations when the provision does not pertain to a "purely personal" guarantee.[6] Thus, a corporation is a person for purposes of the Fourth Amendment's protection against unlawful searches and seizures of its property[7] and the Fifth Amendment's protection against double jeopardy.[8] For example, the Court reasoned that, because a corporation's success depends heavily on its goodwill, it should be protected by the Fifth Amendment from a second, damaging criminal trial. The corporation is also a person protected by the due process clauses of the Fifth and Fourteenth Amendments,[9] as well as the equal protection clause of the Fourteenth Amendment.[10]

A corporation is not a "person" under the self-incrimination clause of the Fifth Amendment. Because that guaranty is intended to prohibit the use of physical or moral compulsion exerted on the person asserting the privilege, its protection is purely personal in nature and therefore applies only to natural persons.[11]

Corporations, while entitled to many Fourth, Fifth, and Fourteenth Amendment freedoms, do not enjoy the same right of privacy as do individuals.[12] Because a corporation exists solely by the grace of the legislature and "[t]here is a reserved right in the legislature to investigate [a corporation's] contracts and find out whether it has exceeded its powers,"[13] the corporation's books and records carry no personal privacy.[14] This position ensures that under appropriate circumstances, the government can have access to the information needed to regulate corporations. While government agencies have a legitimate right to make inquiries to assure the corporation's behavior is consistent with the law and the public interest, the government must be mindful that the Fourth Amendment does protect the corporation from unreasonable searches and seizures.[15]

Liberty. A corporation does not enjoy the full protections of the Fourteenth Amendment's due process guarantees respecting "liberty."[16] The liberties embodied in the Fourteenth Amendment generally are those associated with a natural, not artificial, person. However, in *Grosjean v. American Press Co.*,[17] the Supreme Court held that the Fourteenth Amendment's due process clause accords corporations the protection embodied in the First Amendment.[18] Occasionally, the Court recognizes constitutional protections without having to address the corporation's status. For example, in *First National Bank of Boston v. Bellotti*,[19] the Supreme Court avoided the issue as to whether a corporation is entitled to First Amendment protection by rephrasing the issue. It focused on whether the speech involved itself was constitutionally protected. Reasoning "the Constitution often protects interests broader than those of the party seeking their vindication," the Court there concluded that corporate expenditures to support political activity were constitutionally protected.[20]

Legal Process. In *Ross v. Bernhard*,[21] the Court accepted the position that "a corporation's suit to enforce a legal right was an action at common law carrying the right to a jury trial at the time the Seventh Amendment was adopted."[22] Thus, the corporation enjoys the right to a jury trial where such right existed at common law. And, relying on the Sixth Amendment, corporations have a constitutional right to effective assistance of counsel.[23] To sue or be sued, however, they must be represented by counsel—that is, a corporation cannot proceed pro se.[24]

§ 1.4 NON-TAX ADVANTAGES OF CORPORATIONS

The principal non-tax advantages customarily given for doing business in the corporate form are: (1) exemption of shareholders from personal liability; (2) continuity of the organization's existence despite changes in its members; (3) centralized management by a board of directors; (4) free transferability of a participant's interest; (5) access of the business to additional capital; (6) the organization's capacity to act as a legal unit in holding property, contracting, and bringing suit; and (7) standardized methods of organization, management, and finance prescribed by corporation statutes for the protection of shareholders and creditors, including a more or less standardized system of shareholder relations, rights, and remedies.

A primary advantage of the corporation is the shareholders' limited liability. Shareholders are immune from personal liability for corporate debts and torts beyond the amount of their agreed investments in the corporation's stock.

Limited liability may be less of a factor in selecting corporate form today than it once was, in light of the growing number of alternative business forms that grant limited liability to owners. For example, the limited partnership, the limited liability partnership, and the limited liability company are forms of doing business where the owners can enjoy limited liability. In addition, even in a general partnership, in most states the partners elect to have the business treated as a limited liability partnership to at least some extent. Most states permit a partnership to elect to become a limited liability partnership and thereby eliminate the partners' personal liability for the negligence of the partnership or of the other partners.

A second important advantage gained by incorporation is continuity of existence. Incorporation creates an entity endowed with the capacity to exist either perpetually or for a fixed period, notwithstanding the death or change of its members. When the membership of a common law partnership changes—for example, when a partner's interest is transferred or when a partner dies—the partnership is dissolved. Partnership statutes in many states grant entity status, as do limited liability company statutes.

In publicly held corporations, free alienation of shares is a distinct advantage of the corporate form of doing business. Closely held corporations frequently place contractual restrictions on transferability of shares. A prime requisite for the functioning of the corporation system as a capital-raising device is liquidity for investment. Even with limited liability an investor must still consider the possibility of a change in his own or in corporate circumstances which may affect his investment interest." In a closely held business, however, in which each shareholder often is an active, vital member of the management team and the active participants do not look to outside investors for funds, free transferability of shares may be undesirable.

Great flexibility in financing is available to a corporation. It may issue many different kinds of securities, each with distinct claims and preferences against the corporate income or assets. For instance, a corporation may issue several classes of stock, varieties of bonds, debentures, or notes and hybrid securities having characteristics of both equity securities and debt securities. The great flexibility corporations have in the types of securities they can issue permits corporations to tailor their economic relationships to the demands of particular investors in prevailing market conditions.

Because a corporation is viewed as a legal entity that exists apart from its shareholders, it may sue, be sued, hold property, enter into contracts, and perform most other acts that an individual can perform. Another aspect of the concept of the corporation as a distinct legal person that may prove advantageous is that shareholders, to some extent, can remain anonymous. The corporate name sometimes acts as a mask behind which shareholders can conceal their identities, perhaps even for the purpose of evading their rightful responsibilities. A corporation's list of shareholders is ordinarily a private record, except to the extent that the Securities Exchange Act of 1934[25] and state statutes[26] require disclosure or provide shareholder inspection rights.

At least in large business enterprises, an advantage of corporate organization over some other types of association is the greater standardization of a corporation's organization and operation. Every state statute has detailed provisions on the legal relations of shareholders toward each other and the corporation. Further, an elaborate system of regulation of management and protection of shareholders' and creditors' rights has been established and is constantly under review by the courts.

§ 1.5 DISADVANTAGES OF THE CORPORATE FORM

The corporate form of doing business has a number of distinct disadvantages. A single owner or small group of owners starting a new business has little appetite for the more formal procedures of operation that accompany incorporation. A disadvantage of the corporate form is the necessity of compliance with various statutory formalities, which require considerable legal advice and other expert assistance. Examples include the filing of various reports and documents. Further, a corporation experiences greater difficulty in doing business across state lines. A corporation domiciled in one state that does business in other states is invariably required to "qualify" in the other states— that is, obtain authorization from each of the other states to transact business. A partnership can generally operate in another state without the formality of qualification. In some states a corporation is prohibited from engaging in specific kinds of activity—for example, only recently did the accounting profession agree to permit its professionals to incorporate. Generally, corporate income is subject to a double tax burden—first, to the corporation and, second, when distributed as dividends, as personal income to the shareholders. In sum, the sentiment is frequently expressed: "When in doubt, don't incorporate."[27]

§ 1.6   TAX CONSIDERATIONS IN SELECTING A BUSINESS FORM

[1] Tax Considerations in Selecting a Business Form

A corporate entity can avoid double taxation by electing to be a Subchapter S corporation. Under the tax laws, an S corporation is similar to a partnership in that the business's income and losses are attributed to its owners (whether distributed or not), and the corporation is not a taxable entity. Only a small business corporation may elect to be an S corporation.[28] A "small business corporation" is a corporation with not more than 75 shareholders; it may issue only a single class of stock, which may be owned only by individuals, estates, and certain trusts; and its shares may not be owned by nonresident aliens or certain ineligible corporations, such as financial institutions.[29] The Subchapter S election must be consented to by all the shareholders and must be made no later than by the fifteenth day of the third month of the taxable year in which the election is to take effect. Absent an election, all corporate entities are taxed as C corporations.[30]

In the end, the tax considerations on the type of business to be formed can, in isolated cases, be quite complex. More generally, however, those forming a small business will be sensitive to non-tax considerations as well, such as shielding its owners from the business's debts. In these situations, the disadvantages of double taxation are ameliorated by the availability of Subchapter S. However, this may come at the irritation of losing some fringe benefits that are available to shareholders of a C corporation.

In broad overview, the partnership is not treated as a tax entity under the federal Internal Revenue Code.[31] The partnership is required to file an information return listing the partners and their share of the partnership income. Each partner's share of the partnership income (whether distributed to the partners or not) is taxed to that partner as personal income. A corporation, in contrast, is usually treated as a taxable unit separate and apart from its shareholders. This commonly results in the same income and same assets being taxed twice, once to the corporation and again to its shareholders. For example, the corporation pays a tax on its income, and dividends received by its shareholders are taxed to the shareholders to the extent they represent distributions from the corporation's earnings and profits. Similarly, the corporation pays state and local property taxes on its assets, and the shareholders often pay property taxes on their shares of stock, which represent, among other things, their interests in the corporation's assets. Therefore, double taxation is a common concern in deciding whether to incorporate a business.

[2] The Check-the-Box Rules

Formerly, the tax laws imposed severe restrictions on the attributes of entities opting to be taxed other than as a corporation. The IRS, drawing on the guidelines set down by the Supreme Court in *Morrisey v. Commissioner*,[32] identified six factors that were to be considered in deciding whether an association would be taxable as a corporation: (1) associates engaged in a joint venture, (2) the purpose of transacting business and sharing in its gains, (3) continuity of life, (4) centralized management through representatives of its participants, (5) limited liability, and (6) free transferability of interests.[33] An association would not be classified as a corporation unless the association had more corporate characteristics than noncorporate characteristics.[34]

The foregoing six characteristics meant that planners did not have complete freedom in drafting the internal governance and operational rules for noncorporate forms of doing business. All of that changed in 1997 when the IRS replaced the *Morrisey* test with a "check the box" procedure under which an entity may elect to be taxed as a corporation or not.[35] Under the current approach, all that is required at the outset is that a noncorporate form of doing business elect whether or not to be taxed as a corporation. Entities that select noncorporate tax treatment may at a later date elect corporate tax treatment.

§ 1.7 THE BUSINESS TRUST (MASSACHUSETTS BUSINESS TRUST)

The business trust, often referred to as the "Massachusetts trust" because of its reputed origin in Massachusetts and its frequent use there, is a business organization created by a deed or declaration of trust under which assets suitable for a business enterprise are transferred to trustees to be managed for the benefit and profit of persons holding transferable certificates evidencing the beneficial interests in the trust estate. The trustees have legal title to the property in trust and act as principals for the certificate holders ("shareholders"). Vesting title to the enterprise's assets in trustees and empowering them to act as representatives of the business create a business organization, if not a legal unit.[36] The business trust, therefore, embodies at least three important characteristics of the corporate form of business: limited liability, centralized management, and transferability of ownership. Moreover, continuity of existence is attained by providing for the remaining trustees or the beneficial owners to appoint new trustees as successors in case of vacancies.

The declaration, or deed of trust, somewhat like a corporation's charter or articles of incorporation, establishes the organization, its business purposes, and authorized shares and specifies the powers of the trustees as well as the rights of the certificate holders. The trustees of a business trust perform the same functions as the board of directors of a corporation or joint stock company, although in form they carry on the business in their own names. Trust property is held and conveyed in the names of the trustees, and actions are initiated by and against the trustees. This arrangement gives the enterprise the corporate advantage of centralized management. Incoming shareholders become parties to the trust agreement, or at least claim to be beneficiaries under it. The beneficiaries of the trust are simply passive investors with transferable certificates as shares or units of interest.

One major disadvantage of the business trust is its rather shaky legal status in some jurisdictions. Although a number of state statutes expressly declare that the business trust is a permissible form of association for the conduct of business, and although it would probably be sanctioned by courts in most jurisdictions even in the absence of a statute, the courts in a few states have, in the absence of enabling legislation, treated it like a partnership or joint stock company for purposes of shareholder personal liability.[37]

Recently, there has been a resurgence of interest in business trusts because they are particularly well suited for many investor-oriented products, such as real estate investment trusts and asset-backed securities. Delaware and Wyoming each have taken the lead in enacting modern business trust statutes authorizing unincorporated business trusts.[38] Both statutes accord the trust's organizers unlimited freedom with respect to the powers, selection, and activities of the trustees. However, the fact that this form of doing business is nevertheless a trust limits the ability of the participants to fully contract out of fiduciary norms. More than half the states have adopted business trust statutes.

§ 1.8   Public or Government Corporations

A public corporation is a corporation created and controlled by public authority to perform some government or public function as an agency of the government. Public corporations differ from business corporations and nonprofit corporations in a number of ways. A public corporation is not a voluntary association of individuals. Establishing a public corporation, in contrast to a business corporation or nonprofit corporation, does not create contractual relationships between the state and the corporation, the corporation and the individual shareholders, or among the shareholders themselves. A body of statutory and case law, completely separate from the law applicable to business corporations or nonprofit "private" corporations, now governs the creation and operation of public corporations.

A corporation may be public, even though it does not exercise governmental powers, if it is created for some public purpose and is controlled by the government. Examples of this type of corporation include the Tennessee Valley Authority and state universities. Educational institutions, hospitals, and asylums founded by private benefactors for purposes of general or public charity, however, are not considered public corporations, even though the state may contribute to their support through appropriations and donations and may reserve some control over their affairs.

While there is no universally accepted theory or policy governing the creation and regulation of government corporations, a partial explanation for government use of corporations is the ability of a separate corporation to operate with greater autonomy than could an ordinary government bureau or agency. It has been said that a corporation can more efficiently apply the techniques of modern business management.

§ 1.9 MUNICIPAL CORPORATIONS

"A municipal corporation is a legal institution, formed by charter from sovereign power, erecting a populous community of prescribed area into a body politic and corporate, with corporate name and continuous succession, and for the purpose and with the authority of subordinate self government improvement and local administration of affairs of state."[39] Municipal corporations are thus incorporated cities, towns, and villages created to serve the dual role as agents of the state and local governing entities. Their characteristic feature is the power and right to local self-government.

Municipal corporations derive their legitimacy from the state. They are created either by a special enactment of the legislature, through compliance with the state's general municipal corporations law, or by satisfaction of any existing state constitutional or statutory home rule provision.

An integral part of the incorporation process is the municipal charter. It contains the municipal powers and gives the form of governance the entity will have as well as its boundaries, wards, or other subdivisions, and sets forth any classification of powers and duties of its various departments, boards, and officers.[40] Municipalities adopt in their charter one of three forms of government: (1) the mayor-council plan, (2) the commission plan, or (3) the city manager (or council-manager) plan. The mayor-council form of government is further divided into a "weak mayor" or "strong mayor" system. The choice of the form of government is considered a local concern.[41]

Once validly formed, the municipal corporation enjoys the same characteristics as private corporations, such as a continuous existence, capacity to sue, be sued, and contract in its own name. Additionally, by virtue of state constitution or statute, municipal corporations generally have the power to control development within their incorporated area, to raise revenues through taxes, and to participate in state and federal revenue-sharing and grants. Its power to borrow money, however, generally requires voter approval.

§ 1.10 Charitable and Other Nonprofit Corporations

Virtually all states have statutes providing for the formation of charitable, educational, literary, scientific, social, fraternal, religious, recreational, and other non-profit corporations. The nonprofit corporation statutes grew helter-skelter over the years without reference to any statutory model, and at one time they existed in great variety and astonishing combinations. A number of jurisdictions have adopted the Revised Model Non-profit Corporation Act (RMNPCA) drafted by the Corporation, Banking and Business Law section of the American Bar Association.

Although most recent legislation dealing with nonprofit corporations has been entirely separate from legislation relating to business corporations, provisions in the modern nonprofit corporation acts generally parallel those in the business corporation statutes.[42] Thus, judicial decisions interpreting and applying a nonprofit statute may be helpful in interpreting and applying a business corporation statute, and vice versa.

A corporation does not cease to be classified as "nonprofit" simply because it seeks to make profits from some of its activities. Many nonprofit organizations engage in profit-making activities. For example, a leading law school once owned and reaped profits from a macaroni factory. Similarly, hospitals operate at profit-making rates to subsidize those patients who are unable to pay the full rate. As long as the profits are used to further an organization's educational, charitable, or cultural purposes and are not paid to the members as dividends, the organization is usually classified as "nonprofit," even though its members may reap non-pecuniary or indirect benefits. In recent years, the IRS and the states have increased their scrutiny of profit-making activities of nonprofits and also the obligations of nonprofit directors.[43]

§ 1.11 Publicly Held Corporations and Close Corporations

Perhaps the most significant classifications of business corporations are publicly held corporations (sometimes referred to as "public-issue corporations") and close corporations (often referred to as "closely held corporations"). A publicly held corporation is a business corporation, such as IBM or Microsoft, which has numerous shareholders—perhaps hundreds of thousands scattered all over the world—and whose shares (or some classes of shares) are traded on a national securities exchange or at least are traded regularly in the over-the-counter market maintained by securities dealers. The close corporation, on the other hand, is often defined simply as a corporation with relatively few shareholders. Several statutes determine close corporation status by reference to the number of shareholders the corporation has.[44] Another popular definition describes the close corporation as a corporation whose shares are not generally traded in securities markets.[45]

Although a close corporation is usually a small enterprise, the amount of its assets, the scope of its operations, the number of persons it employs, or the volume of its sales does not determine whether it is "close." Many close corporations have tremendous assets and worldwide operations. For example, Mars Inc., producer of candies and other foods, and Hallmark Cards Inc., a leading manufacturer of greeting cards, are close corporations, and until 1955 the vast Ford Motor Company was also. Most of the incorporated enterprises in this country, perhaps 90 percent or more, are close corporations, but publicly held corporations have far greater economic significance. A few hundred giant, publicly held corporations control the great bulk of this nation's productive property.

Often the number of shareholders in a close corporation gradually increases: Additional shares are issued to friends or relatives of the founding shareholders; shareholders transfer part of their holdings to their children, or a successful close corporation "goes public" by making a public distribution of its shares. Many corporations, of course, are hybrid or intermediate, having characteristics of both publicly held and close corporations. Thus, in many situations some shares in the corporation are rather widely distributed, but a majority of the voting shares—enough for effective control of the corporation—are retained by a single individual, a single family, or a relatively small number of people.

§ 1.12 THE JOINT VENTURE CORPORATION

Individuals engaged in a joint enterprise may incorporate their undertaking, and several corporations may organize a new company to carry out a joint undertaking. When individuals engaged in a joint business or commercial operation decide to conduct their venture in the corporate form, the resulting corporation is sometimes referred to as a "joint venture corporation." The term "joint venture corporation" is ordinarily used, however, to designate a company created by other corporations. Thus, one authority defines "joint venture corporation" as "a corporation whose stock is owned by other corporations and which engages in a business different from that of its parents (even though the difference be only that it sells its products in a foreign territory)."[46] A corporation of this kind is also referred to as a "joint company," a "jointly owned subsidiary," or a "collaborative subsidiary."

§ 1.13 AGENCY—CORE CONCEPTS

Although not a separate business entity, an agency relationship is central to all forms of business association. The rules of agency determine the legal consequences of acts by individuals with respect to the business associations with which those individuals may be associated. As an artificial entity, a corporation or other business entity can act only through its agents.[47] For example, the officers of a corporation in both legal theory and in practice are the agents of the corporation.[48] What follows here is an overview of agency law.

[1] Fiduciary Nature of Agency Relationship

To begin with, agency is a *fiduciary* relationship that permits one person (the agent) to act on behalf of another (the principal).[49] The existence of an agency relationship depends upon the consent of the principal (actual, apparent, or implied) to allow the agent to act on the principal's behalf, as well as the agent's consent to the relationship.[50]

[2] When Does an Agency Relationship Exist?

An agency relationship is based on the mutual consent of the principal and the agent.[51] The existence of the relationship can be based on an express agreement or an inference of such an agreement based on the surrounding facts.[52] Control of the agent by the principle is a key element of an agency relationship. Third parties need not know of the existence of the relationship, although the principal's actions and words vis-à-vis third parties can, in themselves, create apparent authority. It is well established in the law that an agency relationship cannot be recognized without an existing principal.[53] The principal must have a valid existence in order for an agency relationship to exist.[54]

[3] How an Agent Binds the Principal

Within the context of an agency relationship, there are a number of ways in which the principal may be held accountable for the words, acts, or deeds of the agent. The five legal theories for binding a principal are as follows: (1) actual authority,[55] (2) apparent authority,[56] (3) respondeat superior,[57] (4) estoppel,[58] and (5) ratification.[59]

Actual Authority and Apparent Authority

Actual authority refers to any express agreement between the principal and agent as well as any agreement that may be implied from the surrounding circumstances.[60] As defined by the Restatement of Agency, an agent acts with actual authority when "the agent reasonably believes, in accordance with the principal's manifestations to the agent, that the principal wishes the agent so to act."[61] Express authority is found in written or spoken words. Implied actual authority can be found on the basis of circumstantial evidence.[62]

Apparent authority results from manifestations, not from the principal to the agent but from the principal to the third party, that the agent has authority to perform the act in question.[63] An agent cannot create his or her own apparent authority. There must at least be a manifestation of acquiescence or agreement from the principal. The principal can thus create apparent authority in an agent by allowing an agent to conduct business in a particular way and thereby create the impression that actual authority in fact exists.[64]

The difference between actual authority (express or implied) and apparent authority can be seen from the following triangle.

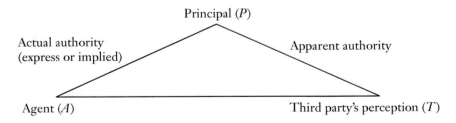

Manifestations routed down the side of the triangle from *P* to *A* result in "authority." The agent is told by these manifestations what the principal consents to the agent doing on the principal's behalf. Often the manifestations from the principal to the agent do not spell out in so many words the acts that the agent is authorized to perform; the agent may not be given "express authority" to do a particular act, such as to employ 10 workers to install specified machinery in a particular plant. The authority to do that act may have to be inferred or implied from either the title or position the principal has given to the agent or the nature and scope of the task the principal has assigned to the agent. The authority is then referred to as "implied authority." If the agent reasonably believes from the principal's manifestations, interpreted in the setting in which they were made, that the principal wants the agent to perform an act on the principal's behalf, the agent is authorized to perform that act and has the same power to affect the principal's legal relations by performing the act as an agent who has been given express authority to perform it.

On the other hand, "apparent authority"—sometimes labeled "ostensible authority"—results from manifestations such as those routed down the side of the triangle from P to T. By these manifestations the principal is telling another party what authority the agent has to act on behalf of the principal. These manifestations create an appearance of authority, which may or may not accurately reflect the authority actually given. Nevertheless, the agent with apparent authority has the power to bind the principal to the third party. A manifestation that creates apparent authority in an agent can be either a direct communication to a third party or a communication to the public in general, such as by advertisement.[65]

Apparent authority ordinarily cannot be created by the agent's own words or actions, such as by falsely representing to a third party that the agent is authorized.[66]

A principal's acquiescence in an agent's performance of unauthorized acts may create authority in the agent insofar as the agent thereafter reasonably believes that the principal consents to performance of similar acts in the future. The principal's acquiescence may also create apparent authority in the agent, because a third party, aware of the agent's performance of the acts, may reasonably believe from the principal's manifestations (apparent acquiescence) that the agent is authorized to perform such acts on the principal's behalf.[67] Furthermore, acquiescence by the principal may be held to constitute ratification of an unauthorized act. In this area the concept of apparent authority and the doctrine of estoppel tend to intertwine.[68]

Respondeat Superior

Respondeat superior is a concept used by the Restatement of Agency and the courts to impose liability on employers for torts committed by employees.[69]

Estoppel

An agent's authority can also be established using general principles of estoppel.[70]

Ratification

Finally, when an act is without authorization, after-the-fact approval by the principal can operate as a ratification of the previously unauthorized act.[71] Related to the ratification is the concept of affirmance, whereby a principal's acquiescence with knowledge of an agent's unauthorized act can operate as a ratification.[72] Ratification operates within the corporation and allows an after-the-fact approval of a previously unauthorized act by a corporate official.

NOTES

1. For a more comprehensive discussion of limited liability and the circumstances in which a court will disregard the separate personality of a corporation and impose liability for the corporation's debts on the shareholder or shareholders, *see* Chapter 7.
2. Asbury Hosp. v. Cass County, 326 U.S. 207, 210–12 (1945); Selover, Bates & Co. v. Walsh, 226 U.S. 112, 126 (1912).
3. *See, e.g.,* Allenberg Cotton Co. v. Pittman, 419 U.S. 20, 32–34 (1974) (state court does not have jurisdiction over corporation incorporated in another state unless there are sufficient intrastate contacts). *Compare to* Eli Lilly & Co. v. Sav-On-Drugs, 366 U.S. 276, 280–81 (1961) (service on foreign corporation upheld where office and 18 employees maintained within state).
4. Bank of United States v. Deveaux, 9 U.S. (5 Cranch) 61, 86–88 (1809).
5. *See* Citizens United v. Federal Election Commission, 130 S. Ct. 876 (2010) (First Amendment precludes laws limiting corporate funding of independent political broadcasts in candidate elections).
6. *See* United States v. White, 322 U.S. 694, 699 (1944).
7. G.M. Leasing Corp. v. United States, 429 U.S. 338, 353 (1977).
8. *See, e.g.,* United States v. Martin Linen Supply Co., 430 U.S. 564, 568–71 (1977).
9. *See, e.g.,* First Nat'l Bank v. Bellotti, 435 U.S. 765, 780 n.15 (1978).
10. Bell v. Maryland, 378 U.S. 226, 262 (1964).
11. *See, e.g.,* United States v. Doe, 465 U.S. 605, 608 (1984) (individual may be entitled to avoid producing document potentially incriminating to him; corporation remains obligated to produce document).

12. *See, e.g.*, California Bankers Ass'n v. Shultz, 416 U.S. 21, 65–67 (1974); United States v. Morton Salt Co., 338 U.S. 632, 651–52 (1950).
13. Hale v. Henkel, 201 U.S. 43, 75 (1906).
14. United States v. White, 322 U.S. 694, 700 (1944).
15. G.M. Leasing Corp. v. United States, 429 U.S. 338, 353 (1977).
16. Northwestern Nat'l Life Ins. Co. v. Riggs, 203 U.S. 243, 255 (1906).
17. 297 U.S. 233 (1936).
18. *Id.* at 243–44.
19. 435 U.S. 765 (1978).
20. *Id. See also* FEC v. Beaumont, 539 U.S. 146 (2003).
21. 396 U.S. 531 (1970).
22. *Id.* at 533–34.
23. *See, e.g.*, United States v. Rad-O-Lite of Philadelphia, Inc., 612 F.2d 740, 743 (3d Cir. 1979).
24. *See, e.g., In re* Las Colinas Dev. Corp., 585 F.2d 7, 11 (1st Cir. 1978).
25. 15 U.S.C. §§ 78a to 78l-1 (2006).
26. Many corporation statutes require production of a list of shareholders at shareholders' meetings. *See, e.g.*, 6 N.Y. Bus. Corp. Law § 607 (McKinney 2003).
27. *See, e.g.*, George C. Seward & W. John Nauss, Basic Corporate Practice 1 (2d ed. 1977):

> When in doubt, do not incorporate. Many small corporations are formed unadvisedly. The corporate form of doing business is probably disadvantageous for a small, new venture. The cost of the privilege of limited liability will probably be very high. To determine whether incorporation is advisable, the cost of establishing and maintaining the corporation and the potential tax disadvantages of corporate status should be measured against the advantages of corporate status, principally those of limited liability and relative ease of raising capital. Hence a basic rule: do not incorporate unless the advantages are worth the cost. Time devoted at the outset to determining whether incorporation is advisable will be well spent.

28. I.R.C. § 1361(a)(1) (2009).
29. I.R.C. § 1361(b)(1), (2) (2009). Although only one class of stock is permitted, voting rights within that class may be varied.
30. The terms "C corporation" and "S corporation" appear only in the world of taxation and distinguish corporations that are governed by the special rules set forth in Subchapter S from the more generally applicable Subchapter C of the Internal Revenue Code.
31. An important exception to the partnership not being a taxable entity arises in the case of a publicly traded partnership. I.R.C. § 7704 (2009).
32. 296 U.S. 344 (1935).
33. *See* Treas. Reg. § 301.7701-2(a) (1988).
34. *Id.* § 301.7701-2(a)(3) (1988).
35. *Id.* § 301.7701-3(a) (2008).

36. *See In re* Vento Dev. Corp., 560 F.2d 2 (1st Cir. 1977); Lafayette Bank & Trust Co. v. Branchini & Sons Constr. Co., 342 A.2d 916 (Conn. Super. 1975).
37. *See, e.g.*, F.D.I.C. v. Slinger, 913 F.2d 7 (1st Cir. 1990) (benefits of business trust status are lost where individual is sole trustee and beneficiary).
38. DEL. CODE ANN. tit. 12, § 3801 (2007); WYO. STAT. ANN., §§ 17-16-1534, 17-23-101 *et seq.* (2007).
39. EMMETT C. YOKLEY, MUNICIPAL CORPORATIONS § 5 (1956 & Cum. Supp. 1987).
40. EUGENE McQUILLIN, MUNICIPAL CORPORATIONS § 9.02 (3d ed. 1987).
41. OSBORNE M. REYNOLDS, JR., LOCAL GOVERNMENT LAW § 18 (1982).
42. *See* ABA–ALI, MODEL NON-PROFIT CORP. ACT vii (rev. ed. 1964).
43. Thomas Lee Hazen & Lisa Love Hazen, *Punctilios and Nonprofit Corporate Governance—A Comprehensive Look at Nonprofit Directors' Fiduciary Duties*, 14 U. PA. J. BUS. L. ---- (2012).
44. *E.g.*, DEL. CODE ANN. tit. 8, §§ 342(a)(1) to (3) (2001) (fewer than 30 shareholders).
45. In the words of a Massachusetts court, a close corporation is "typified by: (1) a small number of stockholders; (2) no ready market for the corporate stock; and (3) substantial majority stockholder participation in the management, direction and operations of the corporation." Donahue v. Rodd Electrotype Co., 328 N.E.2d 505, 511 (Mass. 1975).
46. G. E. Hale, *Joint Ventures: Collaborative Subsidiaries and the Antitrust Laws*, 42 VA. L. REV. 927 (1956). Economically, a joint venture corporation "may differ only slightly from contractual cooperation between two operating companies." *Id.*
47. *See, e.g., In re* Merrill Lynch Trust Co. FSB, 235 S.W.3d 185 (Tex. 2007) (noting that since a corporation can act only through human agents, an arbitration agreement generally includes disputes about their agents' actions).
48. *See, e.g.*, Wasatch Oil & Gas, L.L.C. v. Reott, 163 P.3d 713 (Utah Ct. App. 2007).
49. "Agency is the fiduciary relationship that arises when one person ('a principal') manifests assent to another person ('an agent') that the agent shall act on the principal's behalf and subject to the principal's control, and the agent manifests assent or otherwise consents so to act." RESTATEMENT (THIRD) OF AGENCY § 1.01 (2006).
50. *Id.*
51. *See Id.* ("Agency is the fiduciary relationship that arises when one person (a 'principal') manifests assent to another person (an 'agent') that the agent shall act on the principal's behalf and subject to the principal's control, and the agent manifests assent or otherwise consents so to act").
52. *See, e.g.*, Nichols v. Arthur Murray, Inc., 248 Cal. App. 2d 610, 56 Cal. Rptr. 728 (1967) (finding agency relationship); A. Gay Jenson Farms Co. v. Cargill, Inc., 309 N.W.2d 285 (Minn. 1981) (commercial loan with significant control over the borrower rendered the borrower an agent of the creditor).

53. *See, e.g.*, Warren Abner Seavey, Agency § 34 (1964).
54. *See, e.g.*, P.I.M.L., Inc. v. Fashion Links, LLC, 428 F. Supp. 2d 961, 970 (D. Minn. 2006) ("Instances where several persons associate to promote a business prior to incorporation, and enter into contracts with third parties for the benefit of that business, can trigger promoter liability. Promoter liability exists when a person enters into a contract for a non-existent corporation.").
55. RESTATEMENT (THIRD) OF AGENCY § 3.01 (2006).
56. *Id.* § 2.03.
57. *Id.* § 2.04.
58. *Id.* § 8B.
59. *Id.* § 4.01.
60. *See, e.g.*, Trustees of UIU Health & Welfare Fund v. New York Flame Proofing Co., 828 F.2d 79, 83–84 (2d Cir. 1987) (discussing actual authority stemming from membership in multi-employer bargaining group); *In re* Northwest Airlines Corp., 383 B.R. 283, 295 (Bankr. S.D.N.Y. 2008) ("a party dealing with an agent cannot proceed in reliance on actual authority if it becomes aware of restrictions on that agent's authority").
61. RESTATEMENT (THIRD) OF AGENCY § 2.01 (2006).
62. *E.g.*, Lind v. Schenley Industries, Inc., 278 F.2d 79, 85 (3d Cir. 1960).
63. RESTATEMENT (THIRD) OF AGENCY § 2.03 (2006).
64. *See, e.g.*, Essco Geometric v. Harvard Industries, 46 F.3d 718 (8th Cir. 1995) (Missouri law).
65. The principal's communications to a third party may or may not specify in so many words the act or acts that the agent is authorized to perform. Where the principal does not specify but the third party reasonably infers from the principal's words or actions that the agent has authority to perform an act, it is proper to refer to the agent's "inferred apparent authority" or "implied apparent authority" to perform that act, although those terms are seldom used by the courts.
66. RESTATEMENT (THIRD) OF AGENCY § 6.11 (1) (2006).
67. *See* Foote & Davies, Inc. v. Arnold Craven, Inc., 324 S.E.2d 889 (N.C. App. 1985).
68. RESTATEMENT (THIRD) OF AGENCY §§ 4.01, 4.03 to 4.08 (2006).
69. *Id.* § 2.04.
70. *E.g.*, *In re* Nigeria Charter Flights Contract Litig., 520 F. Supp. 2d 447, 465 (E.D.N.Y. 2007).
71. RESTATEMENT (THIRD) OF AGENCY § 4.01 (2006).
72. Chemical Bank v. Affiliated FM Ins. Co., 169 F.3d 121, 128 (2d Cir. 1999) (affirmance may be inferred from failure to timely repudiate actions of unauthorized agent).

CHAPTER 2

THE EVOLUTION OF CORPORATIONS IN ENGLAND AND AMERICA

TABLE OF SECTIONS

§ 2.1 EARLY AMERICAN CORPORATIONS AND EVOLUTION OF AMERICAN GENERAL INCORPORATION LAWS

State legislatures have plenary powers to create corporations. From the post-Revolutionary War period and into the early nineteenth century, American corporations were created by the enactment of special legislative acts[1]—that is, by acts creating a particular corporation, as distinguished from a general law allowing any persons to organize into and be a corporation by complying with prescribed conditions. To incorporate by special act, a private bill had to be introduced in the state legislature, be considered by the legislative committees, pass both houses, and be signed by the governor. Special acts also were used to grant additional privileges to existing corporations or to make changes in their charters.

Corporations were uncommon prior to the 1800s, and those that existed were specifically chartered by the state to operate banks, insurance companies, and companies to build and operate canals, bridges, and roads.[2] The dominant feature of businesses incorporated in the eighteenth century was their public character.[3] With the charter came the privilege of monopoly status, as well as the power to assess members in the locality for any deficiencies or capital requirements. However, as the concept of private property became more and more a part of American society and jurisprudence, the corporation and its members were viewed less and less as simply instruments of the state. For example, the Supreme Court held the Constitution's contract clause prevented the legislature from altering established property rights embodied in the relationship between the corporation and its members.[4] Further evidence of the decline of the public nature of the corporation was the evolution of the law to the view that members could not be assessed without their assent, and courts began to assume that the corporation's members enjoyed limited liability unless they agreed otherwise.[5] Finally, America's embrace of markets and competition was reflected in the courts' construction of the young country's corporate law by the first half of the nineteenth century. For example, the courts began to hold that the grant of a charter did not carry with it monopoly status.[6] Barely half a century earlier, a major motivating force for incorporation was the monopoly status it conferred for the activity being incorporated.

With the increasing pressures of industrialization, legislatures found themselves deluged with requests for legislation bestowing corporate status. The early reliance on special legislative acts to confer corporate status on individual entities proved not only inefficient but also rife with the opportunity for favoritism and corruption.[7] Ultimately, states adopted constitutional provisions declaring that, with specified exceptions, the legislature should not pass any special act creating a corporation. These constitutional provisions permitted corporations to be formed only by compliance with general incorporation laws.[8] General incorporation legislation has now developed to the extent that almost any legitimate enterprise can be conducted in corporate form upon compliance with simple statutory formalities. In states that do not have a constitutional prohibition, however, corporations can still be created by special act.

The first American general incorporation act—that is, an act allowing any persons to incorporate by compliance with the terms of the statute—apparently was a statute passed in 1811 in the State of New York. In that year, the New York legislature, seeking to encourage the manufacture of various commodities, enacted a law making incorporation available to organizers of concerns that manufactured specified kinds of products.[9] Corporate existence, however, was limited to 20 years, and the capital of such an enterprise could not exceed $100,000.[10]

Soon after New York's pioneer enactment, other states passed acts authorizing the incorporation of manufacturing companies. The more modern general corporation acts were expansive. Having grown out of the old manufacturing company acts, they covered almost every kind of lawful business. The trend toward use of general acts permitting incorporation by signing and filing articles of incorporation began immediately after 1835.[11] With the arrival of general incorporation laws, in contrast to incorporation by special act, businessmen could with certainty and efficiency gain the benefits of corporate status for their businesses.

In 1888, the New Jersey legislature authorized corporations organized under the law of that state to purchase and hold shares of stock in other corporations,[12] thus making possible the creation of holding companies with numerous subsidiaries. Delaware and many other states soon followed New Jersey's lead and authorized corporations to hold stock in other corporations. Growth of holding companies and parent-subsidiary relationships among companies resulted in small groups of persons holding large concentrations of economic power.

In 1896, New Jersey enacted what may be regarded as the first permissive modern incorporation act—that is, a statute that conferred broad powers on corporations, empowered promoters of corporations to set up almost any kind of corporate structure they desired, granted broad powers to corporate directors and managers, and provided great protection against liability for corporate directors and managers. Soon, New Jersey was referred to as "the Mother of Trusts."

In 1913, however, reform-minded then-governor Woodrow Wilson caused New Jersey to amend its more permissive provisions. Delaware, which had borrowed most of its corporation law from New Jersey, seized the opportunity to assume leadership in providing and keeping up-to-date a body of permissive corporate laws. At various times, several states—Maine, West Virginia, and later Nevada—have attempted to "out-Delaware Delaware" in an effort to attract incorporation business and, more specifically, tax revenues and fees. These imitators, however, have had little success in displacing Delaware's preeminence in the race for the rechartering business. Still other states have liberalized their statutes to encourage their local businesses to "stay at home" by incorporating locally rather than organizing in Delaware, New Jersey, or some other permissive jurisdiction.

It can thus be said that, by the end of the nineteenth century, the states had loosened the bonds that once hobbled the corporation's formation and operation. Populist concerns over the concentration of economic powers in large corporations, frequently networked through interlocking ownership or boards of directors, translated into an unending legislative agenda designed to channel or thwart the economic power of corporations.

It is safe to say that the liberalization trend that began toward the end of the nineteenth century continued throughout the twentieth century so that today all states have broadly permissive enabling corporation statutes with very little evidence in any state statute of regulatory or paternalistic provisions. While, in some instances, the changes were prompted by competition for incorporation fees and the accompanying tax revenues, a more compelling explanation of the trend is the increasing belief among legislators and local drafting groups that corporations are not monolithic in their needs or operations; one set of rules is not appropriate for all corporate entities. Legislatures, especially since the 1960s, have consistently embraced the philosophy of allowing corporations, within the broad framework of local law, to tailor their governance structure to accommodate their own special needs and relationships.

§ 2.2 MODERN CORPORATION ACTS

The cumbersome and unartfully drafted corporation acts were overly restrictive in that they imposed burdensome conditions precedent to incorporation, and unreasonable limitations on the scope of the corporate franchise. This unfortunate state of affairs led to efforts by legislative drafting committees and committees of concerned business lawyers to formulate clear and precise legislation.

The Model Act first appeared in completed form in 1950.[13] The Model Act continued the liberalizing trend that originated in New Jersey and Delaware and for a long time has been universally viewed as "'enabling,' 'permissive,' and 'liberal' as distinguished from 'regulatory' and 'paternalistic.'"[14] From time to time, other states have competed for the lead in this type of liberalization (which at times has been referred to as "the race to the bottom" although others view it as a "race to the top").[15] The Delaware legislature, however, continues to be the leader in originating permissive corporate legislation.[16] Delaware's continued popularity among public corporations is documented by the fact that nearly 90 percent of public corporations that change their corporate domicile choose to reincorporate in Delaware.[17] The Model Act was intended not to become a uniform corporation law but rather to serve as a drafting guide for the states. Eventually the Model Act became the pattern for large parts of the corporation statutes in most states (notable exceptions being California, Delaware, and New York). The Committee on Corporate Laws revises the Model Act from time to time, and typically a number of states amend their corporation statutes to adopt the latest revisions.

The first complete revision of the Model Act appears in the Revised Model Business Corporation Act (1984). The Revised Model Act incorporates many simplifying and innovative provisions that the states had experimented with over the years. In addition, the Revised Model Act has through subsequent revisions continued the liberalizing trend that started in Delaware. As of 2008, 33 states had adopted the Model Act as a basic template.[18] Even in those states that have adopted the Model Act, there are many state-by-state variations.

Most states, in addition to a general business corporation act, have more-specialized general chartering acts governing the formation and regulation of corporations in special fields of business such as banking, building and loan associations, insurance, railroads, and public utilities. Similarly, virtually all states now have a separate act for professional corporations.

Modern business corporation statutes are primarily "enabling" acts, which make it easy for businessmen to organize and operate an enterprise, large or small, with the advantages of the corporate mechanism. These enabling acts provide the legal framework and financial structure of the corporate devices by which most modern business is transacted and in which managers' energies and investors' capital can be combined effectively.

Corporation laws deal with such matters as the following: the content of the articles of incorporation; the rights of shareholders; the powers and liabilities of directors; rules governing shareholders' meetings and directors' meetings; restrictions on corporate finance, such as limitations on the withdrawal of funds by way of dividends and share purchases; the keeping and inspection of corporate records; and authorization of organic changes, such as charter amendments, sale of all corporate assets, merger, and consolidation, and dissolution and winding up. Some of these provisions seek to prevent management and majority shareholders from abusing their power to the detriment of minority shareholders and corporate creditors.

North Dakota amended its corporate statute in an attempt to make its chartering provisions the most shareholder-friendly corporate law. The North Dakota provisions include:

- a prohibition on staggered boards of directors—all directors are elected to one-year terms;
- generally, there is no plurality voting—directors must be elected by a majority of the "yes" votes cast;
- shareholders are entitled to a "say on pay";
- 5 percent shareholders who have held their stock for two years have an absolute right to proxy access;

- the board may not be chaired by an executive officer;
- shareholders must be reimbursed proxy expenses for certain successful proposals;
- supermajority provisions are prohibited;
- 10 percent of the shareholders may call a special meeting at any time;
- 5 percent of the shareholders may propose to amend the corporate articles;
- shareholders generally must approve the issuance of shares representing 20 percent or more of the voting power; and
- board-adopted "poison pill" takeover defenses are of limited duration, and the shareholders may prohibit the adoption of a poison pill.

Modern corporation acts became "enabling," "permissive," and "liberal" as a result of state legislative decisions to eliminate or reduce restrictions that earlier incorporation acts had imposed on corporations. Charters granted by the state legislatures and early general incorporation statutes limited the size of corporations, the scope of their business activities, the amount of capital they could assemble by issuing shares, and the size of the indebtedness they could incur by borrowing.

§ 2.3 REFORM EFFORTS, THE AMERICAN LAW INSTITUTE'S CORPORATE GOVERNANCE PROJECT, AND A BRIEF INTRODUCTION TO THE SARBANES-OXLEY ACT OF 2002

Undeniably, there is broad-based dissatisfaction with traditional corporate governance procedures. Many of the recommendations have questioned the "race to the bottom" in corporate legal principles, discussed earlier in this chapter, and recommend either the federal chartering of corporations or that the content of state laws be improved through the imposition of federal minimum standards. Others have invoked a structural approach of healing the corporation from within itself. Among the approaches suggested by this group are mandating that corporate boards have a critical mass of "outside" directors, that outside directors be armed with a professional staff to assist them in discharging their responsibilities, that the boardroom become more diversified, with membership including representatives from labor, consumer, or creditor groups, or that there be significant representation of institutional holders on the board of directors. Of these many suggestions, the one that has the greatest currency is expanding the role of outside directors on the boards of publicly traded corporations. Indeed, the most significant corporate development in the last quarter century has been the rapid evolution from the inside to the outside board. The change in the composition of the American boardroom was stimulated by the popular perception within management that outside directors have much to contribute to the vision and strength of the organization. Further impetus for the managers' acceptance of outside directors is the courts' increasing dependence on outside directors as evidence of the propriety of corporate conduct. One of the most recent and most notable corporate law reform projects, the American Law Institute's Corporate Governance Project, reflects the evolution and thinking of the prominent role that outside directors can and should play in the governance of the American corporation.

The American Law Institute (ALI), after more than a decade of study and fractious debate, adopted in 1992 a voluminous set of principles, recommendations, and commentary titled the Principles of Corporate Governance: Analysis and Recommendations. A core feature of the project is its heavy reliance on outside directors.

Principles of Corporate Governance is different from earlier ALI projects. It is not merely a restatement of prevailing corporate principles that have developed over time. Many of the ALI's positions have scant support in the states, and in some areas the ALI embraces positions that are a matter of popular practice within corporations but are not legally compelled. It thus has been seen as a reform-minded document, driven by academic theory rather than commercial practicality, and it has been attacked without quarter by the representatives of the managerial class. As a result of the firestorm of protest that met its early version in 1980, the document underwent important changes that muffled its more innovative contributions. Nevertheless, the document continues to offer authoritative guidance of where the law may go on many important corporate law questions.

In broad overview, Principles of Corporate Governance has detailed provisions on the functions, powers, and rights of directors as well as recommendations that for certain-sized corporations, outsiders should compose a majority of the board of directors and that the corporations should also have audit, nominating, and executive compensation committees. The project has sought to bring clarity through rigor to the jurisprudence that surrounds director decision-making. The project therefore has chapters devoted to the duty of care and, more generally, to the business judgment rule, the treatment of conflicts of interest, and the role of directors in hostile attempts to acquire their firm. Finally, there is extensive treatment to all aspects of derivative suit litigation, including the manner for initiating the suit, the corporation's participation in the suit, settlement, damages, and indemnification.

In general, Principles of Corporate Governance carefully distinguishes among what it sets forth as an analysis of the present law, what it asserts the law should be, and what it recommends as good corporate practice though not the law. While its provisions are not likely to be adopted in toto by any state, and it was not drafted with this objective in mind, it surely can be expected to have a distinct impact on the direction of corporate law and good corporate practice. For these reasons, its provisions are examined at appropriate locations throughout this book.

More recently, the Sarbanes-Oxley Act of 2002[19] (SOX) reformed corporate governance in response to corporate scandals. SOX affects the conduct of corporations, accountants, attorneys, officers, and directors. It places an emphasis on internal controls, increased public company disclosure requirements, and director independence. CEOs and CFOs must certify that they reviewed their company's financial reports and that the reports are materially accurate and that they comply with sections 13(a) or 15(d) of the Securities Exchange Act of 1934. Signing the reports potentially makes CEOs and CFOs liable in a claim for securities fraud in connection with the sale of a security because there is an inference of scienter if the signers had reason to know of any material misstatements or omissions in the reports. In addition, Section 301 of the Act mandates that independent directors comprise the audit committee. SOX also expands the role of the audit committee, making it a corporate "watchdog."

§ 2.4 FOREIGN CORPORATIONS

As discussed in the next section, the law of the state of incorporation governs the internal affairs of the corporation. Nevertheless, other states in which the corporation does business may regulate a corporation incorporated in another state as a foreign corporation. There are numerous policy reasons a state may wish to regulate a foreign corporation's intrastate activities. Their authority to do so was recognized early in the nineteenth century,[20] and regulatory steps for a foreign corporation to qualify to do business within a state are today fairly standardized. States may exclude a foreign corporation from carrying on intrastate activities when a foreign corporation has not fulfilled the state's qualification requirements for foreign corporations.[21] Nevertheless, the regulation of foreign corporations is not without limits, especially given the strong commitment to the free movement of goods and services that is embodied in the commerce clause of the Constitution. States thus have the power to forbid foreign corporations from conducting business within the state so long as the business does not constitute interstate commerce and the state otherwise conforms with the due process and equal protection clauses of the Constitution.[22]

A foreign corporation seeking to engage in intrastate activities in a state must obtain a certificate of authority by filing certain information with the state.[23] This requirement applies only to foreign corporations that are "doing business" within the state. About the only matters in the application process that approach substantive requirements are the common requirement that the foreign corporation's name be "distinguishable" from that of other corporations doing business within the state[24] and that the foreign corporation designate a registered agent to receive service of process.[25] Once the certificate is obtained, the foreign corporation enjoys the right to do business within the state.[26]

Most states following the Model Business Corporation Act's approach sanction the failure to comply with the requirements for foreign corporations doing business in the state.[27] To wit, the delinquent corporation is barred from maintaining suit in any court within the state until it has obtained a certificate of authority.[28] These provisions are sometimes referred to as "door closing" statutes.

Under the approach taken by door closing statutes, the failure to obtain a certificate of authority does not impair the validity of contracts made within the state. The clear intent of this sanction is to encourage the delinquent corporation to bring itself into compliance, rather than to impose a more harsh sanction. Indeed, the Model Act authorizes the court to stay the proceeding so that a party can obtain a certificate of authority.[29]

§ 2.5 CHOICE-OF-LAW RULE: THE INTERNAL AFFAIRS DOCTRINE

Internal affairs cover all governance and fiduciary issues that arise within the corporation, including relations among stockholders, the rights of stockholders, the duties and obligations of the officers and directors, election and appointment of directors, issuance of shares, meetings, inspection rights, acquisition procedures, dividend regulation, and dissolution. With very limited exceptions discussed below, internal affairs are governed by the law of the state of incorporation. This is customarily referred to as the internal affairs doctrine and is a mainstay of corporate law. Therefore, in a leading case, the Delaware Supreme Court, when called upon to decide whether the Delaware subsidiary of a Panamanian corporation could vote the shares it held in the parent, held that per the internal affairs doctrine, the issue should be resolved according to Panamanian, not Delaware, law.[30] Consequently, the subsidiary was allowed to vote the shares in its parent. Had the court instead opted for Delaware law, the subsidiary would have been barred from voting the shares. Hence, the act of incorporation also involves selecting the body of law that will apply to the corporation's internal affairs. The rigidity of this approach stands in sharp contrast to the revolution in conflicts of law that occurred during the second half of the twentieth century where, under the interest-analysis approach, open-ended standards and flexible methodologies were preferred over rigid, territorially bound principles.

In the United States, the internal affairs doctrine has created a dominant body of corporate law principles—the Delaware corporate law. Over 40 percent of the corporations listed on the New York Stock Exchange are incorporated in Delaware. Delaware's supremacy is easily understood. Indeed, it enjoys an unerodible advantage over other states.[31] First, it has the largest body of precedent interpreting its provisions. To the extent businesspeople like certainty, Delaware provides it. Though its present code bears the date of its enactment in 1967, it carried forward significant portions of the earlier law so that pre-1967 decisions continue to illuminate the Delaware statute. Second,

Delaware's corporate law cannot be easily amended because the state constitution conditions any change in the corporate law upon a two-thirds vote of the legislature. This stability of the legal landscape provides further certainty. Third, Delaware populates its judiciary with those experienced in the trenches of practicing corporate law. Though they have not themselves been captains of industry, members of the Supreme Court and the Court of Chancery have counseled many who were. Fourth, Delaware's Court of Chancery is not only experienced in handling numerous corporate matters, but its procedures facilitate the litigants' securing a hearing and resolution in the most time-bounded disputes, especially issues that arise in the context of takeovers. And finally, though perhaps not uniformly the most permissive and broadly enabling of all corporate statutes, any differences from the statutes of states are at the margins. Overall, Delaware's success in attracting corporate charters is most understandable, and its success is fed by the vitality of the internal affairs doctrine.

As will be seen below, there are some notable departures from the internal affairs doctrine. New York applies a limited set of its corporate provisions to foreign corporations that have two-thirds of their shares, voting shares, or taxable income in New York.[32] A more sweeping application of local laws to "pseudo-foreign" corporations occurs in California, where corporations with half their taxable income or property and half their shareholders within California are subject to a lengthy list of provisions of the California Corporations Code.[33] Neither the New York nor the California provisions apply to companies listed on a national securities exchange, and the California provisions also exempt certain over-the-counter listed securities.[34] Not surprisingly, a California court has upheld the constitutionality of the state's pseudo-foreign corporation provision,[35] whereas the Delaware courts have enshrined the internal affairs doctrine in the Constitution.[36]

NOTES

1. E. Merrick Dodd, Jr., *The First Half Century of Statutory Regulation of Business Corporations in Massachusetts*, in HARVARD LEGAL ESSAYS 65–131 (1934).
2. LAWRENCE M. FRIEDMAN, A HISTORY OF AMERICAN LAW 129–130 (3d ed. 2005).

3. Of special note is that the greater number of incorporations were of churches, cities, boroughs, and charities. *Id.*
4. Trustees of Dartmouth College v. Woodward, 17 U.S. (4 Wheat.) 518 (1819).
5. E. MERRICK DODD, JR., AMERICAN BUSINESS CORPORATIONS UNTIL 1860 75–93 (1954).
6. MORTON J. HORWITZ, THE TRANSFORMATION OF AMERICAN LAW 114–39 (1977).
7. *Id.*
8. *See* William L. Cary, *Federalism and Corporate Law: Reflections Upon Delaware*, 83 YALE L.J. 663, 663–664 (1974).
9. 1811 N.Y. LAWS ch. 67, Act Relative to Incorporations for Manufacturing Purposes.
10. E. Merrick Dodd, Jr., *American Business Association Law a Hundred Years Ago and Today*, in 3 LAW: A CENTURY OF PROGRESS, 1835–1935, 254, 271, 289 (1937).
11. *Id.*
12. 1888 N.J. Laws ch. 269, § 1, *repealed by* 1896 N.J. Laws ch. 190, § 10 (*reprinted in* 1 GEN. STAT. OF N.J., 1709–1893, at 983).
13. 1 MODEL BUSINESS CORP. ACT ANN. §§ 1, 2 (2d ed. 1971 & Supp. 1973, 1977).
14. HARRY G. HENN, HANDBOOK OF THE LAW OF CORPORATIONS AND OTHER BUSINESS ENTERPRISES, 22 n.40 (2d ed. 1970).
15. William L. Cary, *Federalism and Corporate Law: Reflections Upon Delaware*, 83 YALE L.J. 663 (1974).
16. *See generally* ERNEST L. FOLK, THE DELAWARE GENERAL CORPORATION LAW, A COMMENTARY AND ANALYSIS (1972).
17. *See* Note, *Is Delaware Still a Haven for Incorporation?*, 20 DEL. J. CORP. L. 965, 999–1002 (1995); Roberta Romano, *Law as a Product: Some Pieces of the Incorporation Puzzle*, 1 J.L. ECON. & ORG. 225, 244 (1985).
18. Thirty states have adopted all or a substantial part of the Model Business Corporation Act including Alabama, Arizona, Arkansas, Connecticut, Florida, Georgia, Hawaii, Idaho, Indiana, Iowa, Kentucky, Maine, Massachusetts, Mississippi, Montana, Nebraska, New Hampshire, North Carolina, Oregon, Rhode Island, South Carolina, South Dakota, Tennessee, Utah, Vermont, Virginia, Washington, West Virginia, Wisconsin, and Wyoming. Alaska, the District of Columbia, and New Mexico have adopted certain provisions. MODEL BUS. CORP. ACT ANN., at ix (4th ed. & 2008 Supp.).
19. 15 U.S.C.A. §§ 7211 to 7266 (West Supp. 2009).
20. *See* Bank of Augusta v. Earle, 38 U.S. 519 (1839). More recently, the Supreme Court reminds states that equal protection and due process require even-handed treatment of foreign corporations. *See* WHYY, Inc. v. Borough of Glassboro, 393 U.S. 117 (1968) (regarding validity of ad valorem taxes).
21. Wheeling Steel Corp. v. Glander, 337 U.S. 562 (1949).
22. *See* American Motorists Ins. Co. v. Starnes, 425 U.S. 637 (1976).

23. All states follow the basic pattern set out in the Model Business Corporation Act. *See* Model Bus. Corp. Act Ann. § 15.03 (1999).
24. Model Bus. Corp. Act §§ 4.01 & 15.06 (1984).
25. *Id.* § 15.07. Procedures are set forth as well for changing the designation. *See id.* §§ 15.08 & 15.09.
26. *Id.* § 15.05.
27. *Id.* § 15.02(a) ("A foreign corporation transacting business in this state without a certificate of authority may not maintain a proceeding in any court in this state until it obtains a certificate of authority.").
28. *See, e.g.,* Del. Code Ann., tit. 8, §§ 378, 383 (2001).
29. Model Bus. Corp. Act § 15.02(c) (1984).
30. *See* McDermott Inc. v. Lewis, 531 A.2d 206 (Del. 1987).
31. *See generally* Douglas Branson, *Indeterminacy: The Final Ingredient in an Interest Group Analysis of a Corporate Law,* 43 Vand. L. Rev. 85 (1990).
32. N.Y. Bus. Corp. Law §§ 1317 to 1319 (McKinney 2003 & West Supp. 2009).
33. *See* Cal. Corp. Code § 2115 (West 1990 & West Supp. 2009).
34. *Id.* § 2115(e); N.Y. Bus. Corp. L. § 1320 (McKinney 2003 & West Supp. 2009).
35. Wilson v. Louisiana-Pacific Resources, Inc., 187 Cal. Rptr. 852 (Ct. App. 1983).
36. Vantagepoint Venture Partners 1996 v. Examen, Inc., 871 A.2d 1108 (Del. 2005); Draper v. Paul N. Gardner Defined Plan Trust, 625 A.2d 859 (Del. 1993).

CHAPTER 3

THE INCORPORATION PROCESS

§ 3.1 SELECTION OF THE CORPORATE FORM

After considering the relevant business and financial exigencies of a formative business, the attorney must weigh the relative advantages and disadvantages of the corporate form and then must give careful thought to the choice of a suitable business form. If the enterprise is to be publicly held, the corporate form is practically foreordained. A real choice exists, however, in a closely held enterprise, and the decision to be made is an important one. This section discusses in broad outline the preliminary considerations involved in determining whether a particular closely held business can be conducted most effectively as a corporation or in some other business form. These comments, it is believed, are sufficient to put the lawyer on notice regarding areas in which a more detailed exploration may be desirable.

Giving advice on how to choose a business form for a closely held enterprise is extremely difficult. Much of the difficulty arises from the limitless variations in the characteristics of businesses and the circumstances of the business participants, and from the probability of constant change in those variables. Thus, an organizational form may be adapted to a particular business today, but be unsuited to it tomorrow. These changing needs are not a problem, because the entity can transform itself into the type of entity best suited for its contemporary needs.

Beginning in the last quarter of the twentieth century, new forms of business entities developed that have dramatically changed the choice of entity decision. The Wyoming legislature in 1977 enacted the first statute authorizing the limited liability company.[1] The limited liability company form of doing business in essence allows the participants to establish what formerly would have been a general partnership with the unlimited liability of its partners but with a full liability shield. All states now provide for limited liability companies. During the last five years of the twentieth century, another new form of business became recognized. Most states now permit a general partnership to operate under a full liability shield by electing to be organized as a limited liability partnership.[2]

The limited liability company and limited liability partnership are likely to be the entities of choice for many start-up businesses. This is so because the owners will have the protection of limited liability but will not be subject to the burdens of formalities that are necessary to establish and maintain the corporate form.

§ 3.2 SELECTING THE STATE OF INCORPORATION

In selecting the state of incorporation, the attorney makes a decision not only as to the relevant statutory law but also as to the case law that will govern all corporate questions, including the duties of the corporation's officers and directors and the rights of its stockholders. As such, it may be advisable to shop for the jurisdiction that will best suit the organizers' needs. On the other hand, the decision of where to incorporate "should be approached with a strong predisposition to incorporate in the state where the corporation's principal business activity will be located."[3] This local preference is due to several economic considerations. First, incorporating in a state where it would otherwise not have a sufficient presence to subject the corporation to the state's taxing authority visits upon the corporation an unnecessary tax burden. Moreover, businesses not locally domiciled have to qualify to do business in each state where they operate.[4] Under such qualification provisions, the "foreign" corporation will be subject to filing requirements, fees, *and taxes.* The corporation also subjects itself to a state's taxing power by incorporating under that state's laws, even though the corporation does not otherwise "do business" in the incorporating state. Thus, needless multiple taxes are incurred when a corporation is formed in a state that otherwise lacks a sufficient taxing nexus with the corporation. It follows that foreign incorporation fees and expenses may be wasted if one has to pay substantially the same fees for the privilege of qualifying and conducting business as a foreign corporation in the home state where the business is conducted. A second consideration is whether the corporation's counsel, although otherwise knowledgeable in corporate law, can be expected to provide legal advice as efficiently on the sister state's corporate law.

In contrast to the localized business, when faced with a larger business that is likely to cross state lines, forum-shopping becomes a necessary part of the lawyer's role. As noted earlier, some state statutes take a permissive approach, while others adopt "a more 'regulatory' or 'paternalistic' attitude."[5] While Delaware has generally been regarded as a permissive haven, the overall trend in other states has also been toward more and more permissive statutes. The piecemeal revisions to the Model Business Corporation Act have similarly been permissive.

In selecting the most appropriate corporation domicile, there are several factors to be considered. Although the circumstances of a particular situation will frequently narrow the scope of the inquiry, there are a number of general considerations.

1. Does the proposed state of incorporation permit the type of business proposed in corporate form?
2. Does the proposed domicile place restrictions on the residence of incorporators and/or shareholders?
3. Does the proposed domicile have special rules concerning directors and management norms in general?
4. What are the rights and liabilities of shareholders?
5. Do the state's statutes permit the desired capital structure?
6. Does the proposed domicile have an applicable close corporation statute?
7. What are the applicable organizational and annual fees and taxes?

§ 3.3 THE USUAL STEPS IN THE FORMATION AND ORGANIZATION OF A CORPORATION

Incorporation procedure varies somewhat from state to state, but most states follow a general pattern of requirements for formation. Failure to comply with the necessary formalities can result in a failure to obtain corporate status, but more frequently such failure poses no serious problems. In any event, the lawyer should be thoroughly familiar with the requirements of the state of incorporation, as well as the foreign qualification provisions of all states where business activity is contemplated.

The successive steps usually required or advisable for the incorporation and organization of a business corporation under modern corporation statutes are enumerated below:

1. Taking preliminary options and making promotion and financing arrangements by the organizers or promoters with the aid of competent legal advice;
2. Soliciting pre-incorporation subscriptions if desired. In many cases, this activity will be subject to meeting the requirements of the securities act laws in each state in which shares will be offered for sale, as well as to the requirements of the Federal Securities Act of 1933;

3. Reserving the desired corporate name by application to the secretary of state or other designated state office;
4. Selecting a registered office and registered agent;
5. Drafting the articles (certificate) of incorporation;
6. Executing and acknowledging the execution of the articles of incorporation by the incorporators;
7. Filing the articles of incorporation with the secretary of state, along with any required county filings;
8. Paying the filing or organization fees to the secretary of state and any required franchise tax;
9. Holding the first organization meeting of the incorporators, or of the subscribers for shares, to elect directors if the first directors are not named in the articles;
10. Convening the first meeting of the directors (generally called an "organization meeting") to complete the corporation's organization by electing officers, adopting bylaws, issuing shares, and taking subscriptions, accepting pre-incorporation subscriptions and contracts, adopting the form of stock certificate, establishing a principal office, fixing the place for regular meetings of the directors, authorizing a depository for corporate funds as well as identifying who has authority to execute checks against the company's account, adopting contracts made by the promoters on behalf of the proposed corporation, authorizing the application for a permit under state blue sky laws to take subscriptions and issue shares, and appointing a resident agent for the service of process;
11. Obtaining from the secretary of state or other official any permit needed for taking subscriptions and issuing shares, as well as all steps to assure compliance with the Federal Securities Act of 1933;
12. Preparing of minutes of the directors' meeting and opening of corporate books and records;
13. Paying the minimum paid-in capital, if required, and performing other conditions precedent to engaging in business operations;
14. Issuing shares;
15. Qualifying to do business in any state where the corporate business will be conducted.

Some states require a dual filing—one with the secretary of state and another in the office of the county clerk where the corporation has its principal office. In those states, filing copies of the incorporation papers in the offices of the county clerk or recorder is not a condition precedent to corporate existence.

The secretary of state's acceptance or rejection of articles for filing does not create a presumption of the document's validity or invalidity. Generally, the secretary of state should reject the document if it contains illegal or improper provisions. If doubt exists as to the legality of the articles, the secretary of state may submit them to the state's attorney general and his or her staff.[6] Most states allow a direct appeal of the secretary of state's refusal. Under the older view, still found in a few states, review of the secretary of state's refusal occurs through a writ of mandamus.[7]

§ 3.4 DRAFTING THE ARTICLES OF INCORPORATION

The drafting of the incorporation paper, charter, articles of incorporation, certificate of incorporation, or simply "the articles," as the instrument may be called, is usually the first essential step in the incorporation process (in rare cases, the parties may first desire to set forth their understandings in a pre-incorporation agreement). The attorney should carefully review the applicable corporation act, the needs of the business, and the wishes of the organizers. And special emphasis should be given to their plans for controlling, capitalizing, and financing the particular enterprises. For example, it is necessary to examine the statutory requirements for the contents of the articles of incorporation, such as the number, residence, and age of the incorporators (that is, those who are to execute the articles); whether the corporation's initial directors must be set forth in the articles of incorporation; the number of shares that must be subscribed for; and the amount of capital that must be paid in, if any, before commencement of business. Care should also be given to whether, under state statute, the corporation's name as set forth in the articles of incorporation must include an indication that the business is a separate entity, for example, by including "Corporation," "Incorporated," or a suitable abbreviation of corporateness.[8]

The articles of incorporation (or in Delaware, the certificate of incorporation) should set forth all the provisions required by the corporation act, expressing them as nearly as possible in the order and in the exact language found in the statute. The governing corporate statute ordinarily is quite clear in stating what information must be set forth in the articles. Over the years, states have required less and less to be stated in the articles of incorporation so that in most states today the bare minimum contents of the articles can generally be set forth on a single sheet of paper with room to spare. Even though the particular requirements vary from state to state, the typical act usually calls for the following:

1. The corporate name.
2. The purposes, objects, or general nature of the business authorized.[9]
3. Information relevant to the service of process on the corporation, such as identifying a registered agent and perhaps the corporation's principal office.
4. Identification of incorporators and/or initial directors.
5. The types and amount of stock the corporation is authorized to issue.
6. The proper execution of the articles of incorporation by the incorporators.

The articles of incorporation frequently include optional provisions that regulate the business of the corporation, the powers of the directors, and the rights of shareholders. All such provisions are valid as long as they are not inconsistent with the mandates of the statute or the constitution of the state of incorporation.

§ 3.5   SELECTION AND PROTECTION OF A CORPORATE NAME

Choosing a corporate name requires great care. It is advisable to inquire of the names available by contacting the secretary of state or other officer with whom the articles of incorporation must be filed.[10] Most states have procedures that not only allow the availability of names to be learned prior to incorporation but also permit an available name to be reserved for a stated period of time, generally 60 to 90 days, after the payment of a nominal fee.[11] The name must contain words or an abbreviation indicating that the business is an entity.[12]

The question of availability of a proposed corporate name is usually determined in the first instance by personnel in the secretary of state's office or other executive department. Under many statutes, the secretary of state must pass on the question of the similarity of a proposed name to those already in use. Under the influence of earlier versions of the Model Business Corporation Act, nearly a majority of the states require that a name not be "the same or deceptively similar." What is deceptively similar is frequently problematic. Because of this concern and the belief that the real concern of the secretary of state's office was limited to avoiding confusing two or more organizations in the *secretary*'s records, the Revised Model Business Corporation Act requires only that the "name must be distinguishable upon the records of the secretary of state."[13]

The bare fact that articles of incorporation have been accepted and filed by the secretary of state is not an adjudication of the right to the name and does not confer an exclusive right to the name chosen as against previous rights of other corporations or partnerships. There is a vast body of law under the general heading of unfair competition, which, among other things, protects the use of a trademark or trade name.[14]

There is a requirement in most, if not all, states that the name set forth in the articles of incorporation must contain such words as "Company," "Corporation," "Incorporated," "Inc." or "Limited" to indicate its corporate status.[15] Furthermore, there frequently are limitations on filing articles of incorporation setting forth a name including the words "Bank," "Trust," or "Trustee," or related words indicating that the corporation is a bank or trust company, without the certificate of approval of the proper official.[16]

The registered corporate name does not limit the corporation's use of other trade names. Unless there is some express provision to the contrary in a statute, a corporation may assume a name, just as a natural person may, for the purpose of entering into a contract or executing or receiving a conveyance.

§ 3.6 Statement of Purposes and Powers in the Articles

Under the older statutes, it was required that a corporation should be formed for some definite enterprise or line of business; a few states even required specification of a single purpose. This requirement reflects the concession theory of the corporation's existence, as well as a carry over of the pre-nineteenth century practice of jealously granting charters. When the states require an explicit statement of the corporation's purpose, the drafters usually respond with a lengthy multipurpose clause that assures that the corporation may engage in any lawful activity. Such drafting frequently also assures that the document is unreadable. With the death of the concession theory and an ever-increasing quest for flexibility and economy of words, many states in the 1960s authorized the articles to simply state that the corporation's purpose was "to engage in any lawful business" without any further elaboration. The most resolute response to prolix powers and purposes clauses is found in California, where all sets of filed articles are deemed to include an "all purposes" clause, and any other statements are permitted *only* to *limit* the corporation's powers or purposes.[17] A similar approach is taken by the current version of the Model Act.[18]

Generally, there is no need to limit the purposes to the business actually contemplated, and an "all purposes" clause assures flexibility, certainty, and efficiency. However, the occasion can well arise when a narrow purpose clause is a means for fulfilling the desires of the organizers as well as placing a check on management's ability to change the nature of the business.

The statement of the purposes has, as its principal function, the affirmative authorization of the management to enter into those contracts and business transactions that may be considered as incidental to the attainment of the purposes. It also imposes implied limitations on their authority by excluding lines of activity that are not so covered.[19] It does not, however, serve as evidence that the corporation actually engaged in that type of business.[20] The effect of broad purposes or objects is thus to confer wide discretionary authority on the directors and management as to the kinds of business operations in which they may engage. Dealings that are entirely irrelevant to the purposes are unauthorized. Such dealings are referred to as "*ultra vires.*" Statutes do not require repeating in the articles of incorporation the powers that may be enumerated or embodied in the incorporating statute, such as the power to sue, acquire and convey property, make contracts, borrow money, execute bonds and mortgages, sell the entire assets, adopt bylaws, dissolve, merge or consolidate, or amend the articles. Many practitioners, however, for the sake of certainty continue to state in the articles of incorporation many statutory, implied, and incidental powers that might just as well have been left unstated.

§ 3.7 REGISTERED AGENT AND PRINCIPAL PLACE OF BUSINESS

Nearly every state requires the corporation to select and retain a registered agent to serve process within the state. A registered agent may be an individual or a corporation; in either case, the agent must be a resident of the incorporating state. Most states require the articles of incorporation to identify the name and address of the initial registered agent. Thereafter, new agents are added or substituted through a routine filing with the secretary of state.[21] New York's approach is representative of a handful of states that do not require a registered agent; New York designates the secretary of state as the corporation's agent to receive process.[22]

§ 3.8 INCORPORATORS AND INITIAL DIRECTORS

A timing problem arises in the legal mechanics of appointing or electing the first board of directors and adopting bylaws so that the corporation can conduct its business.[23] The link between the inchoate corporation and the completed organization is often the incorporator. Defined functionally, "incorporators" are those who sign the articles of incorporation. They may or may not be subscribers for shares. Most statutes require only a single incorporator.[24] A number of states require that an incorporator be a natural person of at least 18 years of age.[25]

The incorporator's authority under most state statutes transcends executing the articles of incorporation and includes electing the initial directors, if they are not identified in the articles of incorporation, and any other steps to "complete the organization."[26] Because most states do not require the articles to set forth the names of the initial directors, the question frequently arises as to when it is desirable to do so.

If the identities of the members of the first board are known, there are some economies to setting forth their names in the articles of incorporation so as to avoid the empty ritual of the incorporator or incorporators designating the initial directors. But, if the initial directors are not identified in the articles of incorporation, until the directors are elected, the incorporators have the power to complete the organization, which includes steps to obtain subscriptions to stock, to fix the issue price of shares, and to adopt bylaws. Because incorporators are frequently only clerks or "dummies" pressed into service to duly execute the articles, rather than persons with any economic tie to the firm, one must fully consider in each new incorporation the role the incorporators should play in the entity's formation.

Any meeting of the incorporators or directors must be preceded by notice.[27] Generally, three to five days are required under the statutes. However, notice can be waived by all the incorporators or directors either attending the meeting or executing a written waiver of notice. Further flexibility appears in provisions that permit action without a meeting of the incorporators or directors if each incorporator or director, as the case may be, signs a written consent to the action taken.[28]

An incorporators' meeting is usually a cut-and-dried affair. The minutes are prepared in advance by the promoters or their attorney and are adopted at the meeting. If required by statute, the incorporators take just enough stock to qualify, generally with the understanding that they are not bound to pay but will later assign their subscriptions to others, who will be bound to pay for the shares. Such meetings seem a useless and empty form.

§ 3.9 OPTIONAL PROVISIONS IN THE ARTICLES

Under the corporation acts of most states, wide latitude is given to the organizers to include in the articles certain optional provisions and to make certain special variations on the ordinary rules prescribed by statute. Much of what appears in today's broadly enabling corporate statutes are rules for the internal governance that apply in the event the corporation does not specify otherwise. Thus, most of the provisions of the Uniform Partnership Act fill in gaps in a partnership agreement, and corporate statutes increasingly set forth procedural rules that apply unless the articles of incorporation or bylaws provide otherwise. Care must be taken by the attorney to identify not only which state statutory provisions can be varied by an act of the corporation, but also whether the deviation from the statute must appear in a provision in the articles of incorporation or can appear in either the articles or the bylaws. That is, in some instances, the statutes expressly permit variations only in the articles of incorporation. In other instances, the variation may appear in either the articles of incorporation or the bylaws.

The articles of incorporation are not merely a private contract between the incorporators or organizers as to their own individual enterprise. They are much more, viz., the constitution of a continuing statutory business association that consists of a shifting group of associates who are expected to invest their money in the enterprise or take by transfer the places of those who have invested. Future shareholders have no voice in drafting the articles of incorporation that limit and define their rights. Most investors become stockholders without reading the articles of incorporation to ascertain provisions that may deprive shareholders of their customary rights and protections. Special and unusual charter clauses may thus prove traps for unwary investors and give opportunity for abuse and oppression by the management. Grossly unfair or unreasonable provisions will doubtlessly be judicially condemned. There are some limits on the oppressive "contracts" that may have been imposed on a corporation during its infancy by management, who thereby sought to reduce statutory and common law rights and safeguards of future shareholders against fraud.

Under most corporate statutes, certain rules as to corporate organization, meetings, and management are mandatory and cannot be varied by the articles,[29] while other rules apply only in the absence of some variation, which must be stated in the articles (in some cases, the variation may be in either the articles or the bylaws). For example, express permission may be granted to regulate various matters such as voting rights, the quorum of shareholders' and directors' meetings, and the authority to fix the price or consideration at which shares without par value may be issued.

§ 3.10 THE CORPORATE CHARTER AS A CONTRACT

The term "charter" is frequently used in this country in various senses different from its meaning of royal or executive grant in English law. Sometimes "charter" refers to the articles of incorporation, the organic instrument that sets out the corporate structure under the requirements of a general incorporation act. The term is more often used in a broader sense as indicating the entire corporate constitution, including the articles of incorporation document and the relevant laws under which the corporation is created. Sometimes the term "charter" is used in the sense of "franchise," or right granted by law to exist as a corporation.[30]

The charter may be regarded as a formal contract made by the organizers with the state under authorization of statute for the benefit of those who shall become shareholders or members. The future parties to the contract are the corporation and the persons who become, from time to time, shareholders or members of the corporation. The incorporators, as such, drop out of the picture as soon as their formal organization functions are performed. The essence of the contract is the corporation's articles of incorporation and the laws of the state of incorporation. The relationships and their corresponding duties and rights that flow through these documents underscore the view, discussed earlier, that the corporation is a "nexus of contracts." The charter is also sometimes said to be a contract among the shareholders. Organizers and promoters may contract to form a corporation, but it is not perceived how the shareholders have any contract *inter se*. Their contract rights are worked out and established through the medium of the corporate entity; those rights include the right to have the business activities confined to the scope of the authorized purposes or the right to vote but, at least conceptually, not as between majority and minority.

§ 3.11 CORPORATE BYLAWS

The bylaws establish rules for the internal governance of the corporation. Bylaws deal with such matters as how the corporation's internal affairs are to be conducted by its officers, directors, and stockholders. Bylaws also commonly deal with the date of the annual shareholders' meeting, the calling and conducting of shareholders' and directors' meetings, formalities as to proxies and voting, qualifications of directors, executive and other committees of the directors, corporate officers (their duties and spheres of authority), formalities and restrictions as to transfers of shares of stock, execution of papers, reports, and audits, and other internal matters.

Adoption of corporate bylaws is commonly regarded as one of the steps in the organization of the corporation. In broad overview, bylaws must be reasonable, should not conflict with the law of the state of incorporation, and must not limit unduly the rights of shareholders contrary to the policy of the law. Bylaws are subordinate both to the statutes and the charter. Bylaws that conflict with statutes, the articles of incorporation, or public policy are void. Bylaws must be reasonable and must operate equally on all persons of the same class.

The courts exercise a regulating power against provisions deemed contrary to policy. For instance, a bylaws provision that attempts unduly to limit the right of transfer of shares or inspection of the books by shareholders or that requires unanimous voting may be viewed as beyond limits permitted by statute or public policy.[31] In the case of closely held corporations, courts strive to effectuate the intent of the parties and thus may uphold such bylaws as *inter se* contracts between the shareholders. Validation of such restrictions is a reflection of a fundamental change in the way judges and lawyers think about corporations. A board's interpretation of a bylaw is not necessarily conclusive.[32]

The power to approve, amend, or repeal bylaws is primarily vested in the shareholders but may be concurrently delegated to the directors either by statute[33] or charter. The power is sometimes conferred by statute on the incorporators as to the original bylaws. The attorney advising the board of directors that seeks to adopt, amend, or repeal a bylaw provision should carefully consider whether the board can do so without stockholder approval. States vary widely in their approaches to this question. Most states allow board action with respect to the bylaws unless the articles of incorporation provide otherwise.[34]

Frequently, state statutes identify certain areas that can be dealt with by the bylaw provision only if that provision has been approved by the stockholders. The most common areas for such treatment are provisions dealing with the size or composition of the board of directors.[35] Also, in many states a bylaw adopted by the shareholders can be amended or repealed only by the shareholders.[36] Bylaws may be waived or amended informally.

Statutes commonly specify many matters that may be regulated in the bylaws and sometimes give an option to include provisions on certain matters in either the bylaws or the articles of incorporation. Certain matters, such as preferences of different classes of shares, as a rule can be provided for only in the charter, not in the bylaws.[37]

A majority of the states have provisions patterned on the Revised Model Business Corporation Act authorizing the corporation to adopt "emergency bylaws," when, due to a "catastrophic event" a quorum of the directors cannot be readily assembled to act.[38] The corporation's authority extends only to the period of the emergency and includes only the power to adopt bylaws that address legal requirements that otherwise would prevent convening a meeting under the firm's customary procedures. Thus, during an emergency, the corporation may enact bylaw provisions that relax its quorum requirements or that infuse the board of directors with new members.

NOTES

1. *See* WYO. STAT. §§ 17-15-101 to 17-15-136 (1977).
2. *See* ALAN R. BROMBERG & LARRY E. RIBSTEIN, BROMBERG & RIBSTEIN ON LIMITED LIABILITY PARTNERSHIPS AND THE REVISED UNIFORM PARTNERSHIP ACT § 1.02(a), (b) (2001).
3. CHESTER ROHRLICH, ORGANIZING CORPORATE AND OTHER BUSINESS ENTERPRISES at 4.01 (5th ed. 1990).
4. *E.g.*, DEL. CODE ANN. tit. 8, § 371 (2001 & Supp. 2008); MODEL BUSINESS CORP. ACT ch. 15.
5. ALEXANDER H. FREY, JESSE H. CHOPER, NOYES E. LEECH & C. ROBERT MORRIS, JR., CASES AND MATERIALS ON CORPORATIONS 89 (3d ed. 1989).
6. *See, e.g.*, De La Trinidad v. Capitol Indem. Corp., 759 N.W.2d 586, 592 (Wis. 2009) (although secretary of state received a contrary opinion from the state's attorney general regarding the legality of the corporation as a nonprofit, the business was in fact a legal nonprofit corporation since the secretary of state accepted and filed the articles of incorporation).
7. *See* Lloyd v. Ramsay, 183 N.W. 333 (Iowa 1921).
8. DEL. CODE ANN. tit. 8 § 102(a)(1) (2001 & Supp. 2008); MODEL BUSINESS CORP. ACT § 4.01. The name must also not be misleading as to the nature of the business. MODEL BUSINESS CORP. ACT § 4.01(a)(2).
9. Under the Model Act, which is followed in many states, it is no longer necessary to have a purpose clause in the articles of incorporation since it is provided that "Every corporation incorporated under this Act has the purpose of engaging in any lawful business unless a more limited purpose is set forth in the articles of incorporation." MODEL BUSINESS CORP. ACT § 3.01(a).
10. MODEL BUSINESS CORP. ACT § 4.02.
11. *See, e.g.*, N.Y. BUS. CORP. LAW § 303(c) (McKinney 2003).
12. DEL. CODE ANN. tit. 8, § 102(a)(1) (2001 & Supp. 2008) (the corporate name "shall contain 1 of the words 'association,' 'company,' 'corporation,' 'club,' 'foundation,' 'fund,' 'incorporated,' 'institute,' 'society,' 'union,' 'syndicate,' or 'limited' (or abbreviations thereof, with or without punctuation), or words (or abbreviations thereof, with or without punctuation) of like import of foreign countries or jurisdictions (provided they are written in roman characters or letters)"); MODEL BUSINESS CORP. ACT § 4.01(a)(1) (the corporation's name "must contain the word 'corporation' 'incorporated,' 'company,' or 'limited,' or the abbreviation 'corp.,' 'inc.,' 'co.,' or 'ltd.,' or other words or abbreviations of like import in another language").
13. MODEL BUSINESS CORP. ACT § 4.01(d).
14. In addition to federal trademark and trade name protection under the Trademark Act of 1946, which is also referred to as the Lanham Act (15

U.S.C. §§ 1051 *et seq.* (2006)), there is a large body of relevant case law. *See* J. THOMAS MCCARTHY, MCCARTHY ON TRADEMARKS AND UNFAIR COMPETITION (4th ed. 2002).

15. *See* DEL. CODE ANN. tit. 8, § 102(a) (2001 & Supp. 2008); MODEL BUSINESS CORP. ACT § 4.01.

16. DEL. CODE ANN. tit. 8, § 102(a) (2001 & Supp. 2008). *But cf.* Snell v. Engineered Systems & Designs, Inc., 669 A.2d 13 (Del. 1995) (statute prohibiting use of "engineered," by other than licensed engineer, did not impose per se ban).

17. CAL. CORP. CODE § 206 (West 1990).

18. MODEL BUSINESS CORP. ACT §§ 2.02(b)(2)(i) and 3.01(a).

19. For an extreme use of this principle, *see* Cross v. Midtown Club, Inc., 365 A.2d 1227 (Conn. Super. Ct. 1976), where the court construed the purpose of operating a luncheon club as not giving the directors the power to exclude women.

20. WBM, LLC v. Wildwoods Holding Corp., 270 Va. 156, 613 S.E.2d 402 (2005).

21. *See, e.g.,* CAL. CORP. CODE § 1502 (West Supp. 2009).

22. The articles of a New York corporation must designate the secretary of state as an agent to receive service of process on the corporation. N.Y. BUS. CORP. LAW § 402(a) (McKinney 2003).

23. *See* MODEL BUS. CORP. ACT § 2.05.

24. *E.g.,* N.Y. BUS. CORP. LAW § 401 (McKinney 2003).

25. COLO. REV. STAT. § 7–102–101 (2008); D.C. CODE § 29–101.46 (2001); N.Y. BUS. CORP. LAW § 401 (2003); N.D. CENT. CODE § 10-19.1-09 (2005); UTAH CODE ANN. § 16-10a-201 (2005).

26. *See, e.g.,* N.Y. BUS. CORP. LAW § 404(a) (McKinney 2003); MODEL BUSINESS CORP. ACT § 2.05(a)(2).

27. *See, e.g.,* Ray Townsend Farms, Inc. v. Smith, 207 S.W.3d 557, 565 (Ark. Ct. App. 2005).

28. *See, e.g.,* DEL. CODE ANN. tit. 8, § 108(c) (2001).

29. MODEL BUSINESS CORP. ACT § 6.02.

30. Helvering v. Northwest Steel Rolling Mills, Inc., 311 U.S. 46, 50–51 (1940).

31. *E.g.,* Sensabaugh v. Polson Plywood Co., 342 P.2d 1064 (Mont. 1959); E. K. Buck Retail Stores v. Harkert, 62 N.W.2d 288 (Neb. 1954); Clark v. Dodge, 199 N.E. 641 (N.Y. 1936) (agreement by shareholders and directors in close corporation to vote for certain people as officers was permissible despite statutory policy to the contrary).

32. Matanuska Elec. Ass'n, Inc. v. Waterman, 87 P.3d 820 (Alaska 2004).

33. DEL. CODE ANN. tit. 8, § 109 (2001 & Supp. 2008); N.Y. BUS. CORP. LAW § 601(a) (McKinney 2003).

34. *See, e.g.,* MODEL BUSINESS CORP. ACT § 10.20(a).

35. *See, e.g.,* N.Y. BUS. CORP. LAW § 702(b) (increasing/decreasing board's size) and § 704 (McKinney 2003) (classifying board).

36. *See, e.g.,* 805 ILL. COMP. STAT. ANN. § 5/2.25 (West 2004).

37. *See, e.g.,* Judah v. Delaware Trust Co., 378 A.2d 624 (Del. Supr. Ct. 1977).

38. MODEL BUSINESS CORP. ACT § 2.07.

CHAPTER 4

THE SCOPE OF THE AUTHORIZED BUSINESS AND DUTIES TO OTHER CONSTITUENCIES

§ 4.1 Purposes and Powers

At common law, a corporation had the powers enumerated in its purpose clause as well as the implied powers necessary to the accomplishment of its purpose. If a corporation engaged in conduct not authorized by its express or implied powers, the conduct was deemed *ultra vires* and void. With the decline in the concession theory of corporations and the universal recognition of the serious inequities that accompanied sanctioning *ultra vires* acts, courts over time interpreted corporate powers broadly. Legislatures also addressed these concerns by authorizing a corporation's articles to broadly enable the corporation to engage in "any lawful purpose" and by limiting the relief and sanctions available for *ultra vires* acts.

Corporate purposes and corporate powers, although often confused, are fundamentally different. A purpose clause properly refers to a statement describing the business the corporation is to conduct. The stated purpose or object of a corporation, for instance, may be "to manufacture textiles" or "to conduct a retail shoe business and to buy, sell, and deal in all kinds of shoes." The term "corporate powers," on the other hand, refers to methods the corporation may use to achieve its purpose. The retail shoe company, for instance, must have the power to contract and the power to borrow money.

Even though many corporate statutes still require that a "purpose clause" (or, as it is sometimes called, "specific object clause") be included in a corporation's charter, modern corporate statutes introduce a good deal of economy here by permitting the articles of incorporation simply to authorize the corporation to engage "in any lawful purpose." And states following the Revised Model Business Corporation Act do not even require a statement of the corporation's purpose or object.[1]

A statement in a corporation's charter of its objects or purposes or powers has the practical effect of defining the scope of the authorized corporate enterprise or undertaking. Second, the statement both confers and limits the officers' and directors' authority by impliedly excluding activities that are not in furtherance of the stated purposes.

§ 4.2 Sources of Corporate Powers

Because the corporation is a creation of state statutes, it is reasonable to inquire as to the source and extent of its powers. Corporations have express and implied powers. The *express powers* are enumerated in the corporation laws of the state of incorporation as well as in the articles of incorporation. At one time it was standard practice to include in the articles of incorporation an extensive list of general powers the corporation was to possess. Even today, attorneys as a matter of habit, but rarely of necessity, sometimes include in the articles of incorporation a lengthy set of "powers" the corporation will have to carry out its purpose or objectives. These powers may include the power to mortgage the corporation's property, guarantee the debt of another, enter into partnerships, and purchase another corporation's stock. Again, this practice derives from an earlier day, in which corporate status was a privilege jealously guarded by the state and the courts so that the inherent powers of corporations were narrowly authorized and recognized. Today, it is rarely necessary to elaborate the corporation's incidental powers because most modern statutes expressly grant such powers.[2]

The doctrine of implied powers is a general rule that corporate management, in the absence of express restrictions, has discretionary authority to enter into contracts and transactions reasonably incidental to its business purposes. For example, a lumber company with the power to invest in securities cannot operate primarily as an investment trust, but it can invest its excess cash in marketable securities.[3] Courts are usually liberal, however, in finding that corporate acts are within the corporation's incidental or implied powers.

Transactions that are outside the express or implied powers of the corporation are commonly known as "*ultra vires* acts," beyond the powers of the corporation. A more realistic view characterizes such activities as being beyond the actual authority of the directors and other representatives of the corporation under the charter contract. The legal effect of a transaction outside the scope of the actual authority of the management is treated later in this chapter.

§ 4.3 Implied Power—Charitable Contributions and Assistance to Employees

[1] Charitable Contributions

Corporations are regularly solicited to contribute to various charitable enterprises in the communities in which they do business. To refuse such requests entirely would probably excite criticism and injure the goodwill and business of the corporation. Nevertheless, the business of a corporation is primarily to earn a profit for its shareholders. The directors' discretion does not in general extend without limits to humanitarian purposes or to purely philanthropic donations at the expense of the shareholders.[4] A pure gift of funds or property by a corporation not created for charitable purposes is generally unauthorized and in violation of the rights of its shareholders unless authorized by statute.[5] Over the years, however, the courts have become increasingly liberal and have exercised considerable ingenuity in finding a sufficient corporate benefit to sustain contributions for charitable, humanitarian, and educational purposes, though the benefit might be indirect, long-term, or highly conjectural. Today, this power is made explicit in corporate statutes.[6] Corporations routinely make sizable charitable contributions. In 2000, for example, the median for corporate charitable contributions was one percent of the company's pretax income.[7] It is estimated that in 2008 corporations gave a total of $14.5 billion to charitable causes, totaling approximately 5 percent of all charitable donations.

The most eloquent and elucidating opinion on corporate charitable contributions is in *A. P. Smith Manufacturing Company v. Barlow*.[8] At issue was the propriety of a $1,500 gift to the trustees of Princeton University. The plaintiff shareholder challenged the gift as a waste of corporate assets since it resulted in no direct economic benefit to the corporation. The court first traced the history of corporations, concluding that the corporate entity has always had a role to play as a responsible societal member.[9] The court validated the gift not only as a donation to society but also as in furtherance of the free enterprise system on which the corporation's success was dependent.[10]

The *Barlow* case is especially significant because it upheld the gift as a matter of common law. The holding has won legislative confirmation as evidence by the Model Business Corporation Act's express recognition of the corporate power "[t]o make donations for the public welfare or for charitable, scientific or educational purpose."[11] Even under such express statutory authority, however, charitable gifts are subject to challenge if clearly unconnected to the corporation's present or prospective welfare.

The Delaware counterpart[12] of the Model Business Corporation Act's provision was scrutinized in *Theodora Holding Corporation v. Henderson*,[13] wherein a shareholder challenged a corporate charitable contribution in excess of $525,000. The Delaware Court of Chancery upheld the validity of the contribution, relying on both the state corporation statute and the parameters of permissible charitable deductions as established by the federal tax code.[14] In a more recent decision, the Delaware Supreme Court reaffirmed its view that reasonable charitable gifts are proper and that the tax code provides the guide of reasonableness.[15] These guidelines in turn support giving corporate directors great leeway in making charitable contributions.

The Delaware Supreme Court, in *Kelly v. Bell*,[16] reaffirmed the corporation's social responsibility, as the court upheld the corporation's voluntary payments to the county following the repeal of county taxation. The corporation agreed to continue making property tax payments to the county if legislation were passed exempting from taxation all acquisitions of machinery after a specified date. The corporation believed that opposition to the legislation stemmed largely from concerns about the county losing much needed revenues and that its commitment to continue making tax payments would make passage of the exempting legislation more likely. Legislation was enacted that exempted *all* property taxes on machinery, and the corporation continued to make the payments to the county in the amount of its former tax assessments. The court characterized the tax payments as corporate donations. Significantly, the court did not confine its inquiry to the *ultra vires* doctrine but examined the question within the more flexible standards of the business judgment rule. The court upheld the payments because the board of directors had reasonably arrived at a business rationale for continuing to make the payments for a purpose that advanced the corporation's interest.

The court's approach in *Kelly* appears the most sensible and workable approach to questions of *ultra vires* acts because it focuses inquiry on what should be the ultimate question—whether the board of directors acted reasonably in what they believed advanced the corporation's interest.[17]

Today, both by law and by public sentiment, a greatly enlarged social duty and responsibility of businesses exists for the comfort, health, and well-being of their employees. It is not always sufficient merely to pay the actual wage agreed upon.[18] However, if a bonus or other compensation of directors and executives is so large as to have no relation to the value of the services for which it is given, it may be treated as in reality a gift, which even the majority shareholders have no power to make.[19] An important consideration in all cases is whether the compensation arrangement has been approved by outside directors or by the stockholders.

§ 4.4 MODERN STATUTORY TREATMENT OF *ULTRA VIRES* ACTS

The *ultra vires* doctrine is not dead, but its availability today is severely limited. Modern corporation acts severely restrict the relief or sanctions that once accompanied *ultra vires* acts. By doing so, the statutes reject the view that a corporation lacks the *capacity* to act beyond its purposes or powers, and promote stability and certainty in transactions with corporations. In broad overview, the statutes narrowly authorize the relief, if any, available to (1) the corporation, (2) the corporation's stockholders, and (3) the state for *ultra vires* acts. Because most states have adopted the Model Business Corporation Act's treatment of *ultra vires* transactions or their statutes closely parallel the Model Act's provisions in this area, it is useful to examine closely the Model Act's approach to *ultra vires* acts.

First, the Model Act-type provisions prevent either the corporation or the other party to an *ultra vires* transaction from raising the defense of *ultra vires*, even though the contract is completely executory on both sides—that is, neither party can avoid the contract solely because it is *ultra vires*.[20] This changes the common law, which allowed either party to set up the *ultra vires* defense in a suit on a completely executory contract.

Second, the Model Act-type provisions authorize suit for damages by or on behalf of the corporation against the corporate executive responsible for the *ultra vires* act.[21] In such a suit, defendants can be expected to shield the decision by arguing their actions are within the business judgment rule.

Third, in response to a shareholder suit, "the court may, if all the parties to the contract are parties to the proceeding and if it deems the same to be equitable, set aside and enjoin the performance of such contract."[22] Only rarely, however, have such suits met with success. One noteworthy case is *Blue Cross and Blue Shield of Alabama v. Protective Life Insurance Company*,[23] involving a corporation organized for the purpose of providing health care service plans to subscribers. The corporation intended to acquire a subsidiary to provide life insurance. The court reasoned that the acquisition of a subsidiary to provide life insurance was neither necessary nor incidental to the accomplishment of the corporation's stated purpose. The acquisition was therefore *ultra vires*, and the court enjoined the corporation from acquiring the life insurance company. Shareholders who have themselves participated in *ultra vires* acts cannot attack.[24]

As a means of softening the effects of any injunctive relief, the Model Business Corporation Act provides that in such an action the court may allow the corporation or the other party to the contract compensation for the loss or damage sustained by its action "but anticipated profits to be derived from the performance of the contract shall not be awarded."[25] This provision's major thrust is to compensate the parties for any loss suffered as a consequence of the court enjoining the *ultra vires* activity and as such does not seem to have been well thought through. From whom would the corporation recover damages it suffered from the court's action in enjoining performance of a contract? Recovery from the shareholder bringing the proceedings would discourage such suits and does not appear to be contemplated by the statute, and the case will be rare indeed in which the corporation could justly recover from the other party the losses the corporation suffers from a court's injunction in shareholder-instituted litigation of this kind. Furthermore, awarding damages to the other party appears to disserve both the corporation and the third party. To award damages to the third party, the court must believe the corporation is better off without the *ultra vires* contract even after considering the damages it must pay to the third party. This would appear to be such a rare case that it hardly needs to be contemplated in the statute.

Finally, the Model Business Corporation Act authorizes the state to invoke the corporation's *ultra vires* acts as a grounds for its dissolution.[26]

§ 4.5 OTHER-CONSTITUENCIES STATUTES

More than one half of the states have enacted statutes that allow, and in a few cases even require,[27] the board of directors to take into account the interests of persons or groups other than its stockholders—that is, to consider the interest of other constituencies—when making decisions, especially when the decision relates to a potential change in control. In broad overview, "other constituencies" statutes authorize the directors to consider the effect of their actions on nonshareholder groups such as employees, creditors, bondholders, suppliers, and communities. Some go further and provide that the directors' judgments may be guided by state or national economic considerations as well as broader societal interests. The overall focus of such provisions is to alter the traditional orientation that corporate decisions are to be adjudged by their impact on stockholder wealth as contrasted with some greater good, such as happier workers and a more vibrant community. The traditional formulation of the directors' fiduciary obligations was summarized nicely by the Delaware Supreme Court as requiring that before directors may take into account other constituencies in arriving at their decision there must "be some rationally related benefit accruing to the stockholders."[28] It was put more strongly by the Michigan Supreme Court in its review of Henry Ford's decision to forgo special dividends so as to reduce the price of automobiles for the public benefit:

> [I]t is not within the lawful powers of the board of directors to shape and conduct the affairs of a corporation for the merely incidental benefit of shareholders and for the primary purpose of benefiting others, and no one will contend that, if the avowed purpose of the defendant directors was to sacrifice the interests of shareholders, it would not be the duty of the courts to interfere.[29]

More recently, the Delaware Supreme Court stated rather crisply that "[a] board may have regard for various constituencies in discharging its responsibilities, provided there are rationally related benefits accruing to the stockholders."[30] These observations are in stark contrast to other constituencies' statutes' authorization for the board of directors to consider a wider range of interests that may be impacted by the board's decision. For example, Indiana commands that no one corporate constituency shall be a "dominant or controlling factor" in the board of directors' decisions,[31] and Iowa allows other constituencies' interests to guide the decision where they outweigh the financial interests of the corporation or its shareholders when the board is considering an acquisition proposal.[32]

By comparison, consider the breadth of Pennsylvania's statute, which states "directors . . . shall not be required, in considering the best interests of the corporation or the effects of any action, to regard any corporate interest or the interests of any group affected by such action as a dominant or controlling interest or factor."[33] Soon after the statute was enacted, the federal district court held "[i]t was proper for the company to consider the effects the . . . tender offer would have, if successful, on the Company's employees, customers and community."[34] The propriety of the directors' consideration of interests other than the stockholders is nearly unbridled in Pennsylvania because the legislature provided a nearly conclusive presumption of validity for the directors' decision.[35]

The impetus for the states' sudden interest in other-constituencies statutes was the hostile takeovers in the 1980s that frequently led to plant closures, layoffs, and declines in the value of the target corporation's outstanding bonds due to the acquisition being financed by issuing debentures to be paid from the target corporation's future earnings. In essence, other-constituencies statutes are just one of several novel forms of takeover defenses that were developed in the heat of the takeovers that have come to symbolize the "take and break" days of the 1980s. In this context, the state directive or invitation for directors to look beyond the bottom line loses some of its social responsibility zing, especially under most state statutes, where consideration of other constituencies is couched in precatory language.

Minimally, these statutes are vulnerable to the criticism that it removes the bright beacon of wealth maximization as the standard for management's stewardship and replaces it with multiple and sometimes competing standards, thus allowing the directors to choose the constituency by whose interests the directors' action is to be determined.[36] Thus, in the takeover context, the stockholders are benefited by a high takeover premium and disserved if that premium is reduced because the bidder wishes to retain the target company's workforce rather than close inefficient plants.[37] To be sure, these are tragic choices, but ones that are judged by the more objective (and some would say neutral) standard of wealth maximization.

Other-constituencies statutes invite not simply a kinder, gentler standard, but the unbridled discretion of management to choose when to favor stockholders and when to favor workers or bondholders. One can surely expect that workers will not be favored when the issue is abolishing inefficient work rules, but protecting those work rules may well be championed by managers facing a hostile bidder who intends to make reductions not only in the factory workforce but in the target management as well.

Others believe that the courts can fine-tune the other-constituencies statutes, with the effect that the statutes require directors' judgments that are Pareto optimal in that no proscribed constituency is worse off and many are better off because of the board of directors' action. This brings to mind the Achilles' heel of other-constituencies statutes, which is their inherent indeterminacy because they commit complete discretion to the board of directors without any reliable method to adjudge the appropriateness of its exercise. Thus a committee of the American Bar Association concludes:

> [Constituency statutes may be interpreted] to impose new powers and duties on directors. . . . [T]hey may radically alter some of the basic premises upon which corporation law has been constructed in this country without sufficient attention having been given to all the economic, social, and legal ramifications of such a change in the law.[38]

B Corporations

In the twenty-first century, a new corporate form was recognized in a few states that adopted B corporation statutes.[39] A business incorporated under a B corporation act is expressly permitted to have a mission that promotes a public benefit such as going "green" and thereby place wealth maximization as a secondary goal.

§ 4.6 The American Law Institute and Corporate Objectives

Commentators have expressed a good deal of dissatisfaction with the objective of the American corporation. Such commentary provided fuel for the American Law Institute's corporate governance project, particularly section 2.01,[40] which provides:

The Objective and Conduct of the Corporation

(a) Subject to the provisions of Subsection (b) and 6.02 (Action of Directors That Has the Foreseeable Effect of Blocking Unsolicited Tender Offers), a corporation [§ 1.12] should have as its objective the conduct of business activities with a view to enhancing corporate profit and shareholder gain.

(b) Even if corporate profit and shareholder gain are not thereby enhanced, the corporation, in the conduct of its business:
   (1) Is obliged, to the same extent as a natural person, to act within the boundaries set by law;
   (2) May take into account ethical considerations that are reasonably regarded as appropriate to the responsible conduct of business; and
   (3) May devote a reasonable amount of resources to public welfare, humanitarian, educational, and philanthropic purposes.

Section 2.01 is the type of provision that is intended to provide guidance to corporations, their executives, and the courts on permissible objectives of corporate activities. Central to the proscribed objective is the view that the corporation is an economic institution for which the economic objectives embodied in subsection 2.01(a) apply. Nevertheless, subsection (b) also underscores that in today's world corporations are also viewed as social institutions, so that in some instances (i.e., those proscribed in section 2.01(b)(1)) the corporation's economic objective *must* be constrained by certain social imperatives, and in other situations (i.e., those set forth in section 2.01(b)(2) and (3)) its managers *may* qualify its economic objectives by social considerations.

The debate that surrounds section 2.01 focuses on the necessity of adding subsection (b) to the overall economic objectives that are embodied in subsection (a). The critiques of subsection (b) argue that staying within the bounds of the law as well as the appropriateness of corporate activity being undertaken for ethical or social good could easily be handled by continuing the common law approach of examining the activity to determine whether it is reasonably related to the corporation's economic objective. The common law approach does this through the business judgment rule, which accords a high presumption of propriety to board decisions, so that decisions guided by ethical or social considerations are examined for their plausible relationship to the corporation's economic objectives. As seen earlier in this chapter, this approach is reflected in numerous cases where an activity has been challenged as *ultra vires*. It appears that section 2.01 makes two significant modifications in the common law in this regard.

First, section 2.01 mandates that the corporation must abide by the law, as must a natural person. Under the common law's strict obeisance to the economic objective of the corporation, corporations may disobey the law and remain true to their objectives if the benefits of disobeying the law exceed the cost of compliance and/or apprehension. Section 2.01 rejects such cost-benefit determinations; the ALI commentary permits disobeyance only out of necessity or desuetude.[41] A second modification to the common law arises with those actions covered by section 2.01(b)(2) and (3)—deviations from the profit objective supported by ethical or societal considerations. In place of the economic considerations for judging the propriety of such departures, the ALI substitutes a broad standard of "reasonableness," in which the propriety of a corporation's actions motivated by ethical or societal considerations is tested by such varying considerations as the custom among corporations and the relative nexus between the resources the corporation has committed to the activity and the corporation's business.[42]

Section 2.01 purports to operate solely as a constraint on the corporation, with the likely sanction for a violation being injunctive relief. However, lurking in its shadows is the possibility that responsible directors or officers can be held accountable if their conduct falls outside the protection of the business judgment rule. It would appear, therefore, that directors and officers are well advised to proceed cautiously if their actions fall into one of the narrow sets of circumstances that are driven by ethical or societal concerns but cannot independently be premised on serving the corporation's long-term economic objectives.

NOTES

1. MODEL BUS. CORP. ACT ANN. § 3.01 at 3–6 (3d ed. 1994).
2. MODEL BUS. CORP. ACT § 3.02. The Model Act as revised sets out a list of general powers (*id.*) and a list of emergency powers (*id.* § 3.03).
3. Edward Hines W. Pine Co. v. First Nat'l Bank, 61 F.2d 503, 511 (7th Cir. 1932).
4. Dodge v. Ford Motor Co., 170 N.W. 668 (Mich. 1919).
5. Rogers v. Hill, 289 U.S. 582, 591–592 (1933).
6. MODEL BUS. CORP. ACT § 3.02(13) (2007) ("to make donations for the public welfare or for charitable, scientific, or educational purposes").
7. Amy Kao, *Corporate Contributions in 2000*, THE CONFERENCE BOARD (2001).
8. 98 A.2d 581 (N.J. 1953), *appeal dismissed*, 346 U.S. 861 (1953).
9. *Id.* at 583–88.
10. *Id.* at 590.
11. MODEL BUS. CORP. ACT § 3.02(13) (2007).

12. Del. Code Ann. tit. 8, § 122(9) (2009).
13. 257 A.2d 398 (Del. Ch. 1969).
14. I.R.C. §§ 170(b)(2), 545(b)(2) (2002).
15. Kahn v. Sullivan, 594 A.2d 48, 61 (Del. 1991).
16. 266 A.2d 878 (Del. Supr. 1970).
17. *Accord, e.g., Kahn*, 594 A.2d 48, 58.
18. Solimine v. Hollander, 16 A.2d 203, 245–47 (N.J. Ch. 1940).
19. Rogers v. Hill, 289 U.S. 582, 591 (1933); Adams v. Smith, 153 So. 2d 221 (Ala. 1963); Moore v. Keystone Macaroni Mfg. Co., 87 A.2d 295 (Pa. 1952).
20. Cal. Corp. Code § 208 (2009); Conn. Gen. Stat. Ann. § 33-649 (2008); Del. Code Ann. tit. 8, § 124 (2009).
21. *See* Cal. Corp. Code § 208 (2009); 805 Ill. Comp. Stat. 5/3.15 (2009); N.Y. Bus. Corp. Law § 203 (2009).
22. Model Bus. Corp. Act § 3.04(b)(1) (2007); Former Model Bus. Corp. Act § 7(a) (1969).
23. 527 So. 2d 125 (Ala. Civ. App. 1987).
24. *See* Goodman v. Ladd Estate Co., 427 P.2d 102 (Or. 1967).
25. Model Bus. Corp. Act. § 3.04(c) (2007); Del. Code Ann. tit. 8, § 124 (2009).
26. Model Bus. Corp. Act § 3.04 (2007).
27. *See* Conn. Gen. Stat. Ann. § 33-756(d) (West 2009).
28. Revlon, Inc. v. MacAndrews & Forbes Holdings, Inc., 506 A.2d 173, 176 (Del. 1986).
29. Dodge v. Ford Motor Co., 170 N.W. 668, 684 (Mich. 1919).
30. *Revlon, Inc.*, 506 A.2d 173, 182.
31. Ind. Code Ann. § 23-1-35-1(f) (West 2009).
32. Iowa Code Ann. § 491.101B (West 2009).
33. 15 Pa. Cons. Stat. Ann. § 1715(b) (West 2009).
34. Baron v. Strawbridge & Clothier, 646 F. Supp. 690, 697 (E.D. Pa. 1986).
35. *See* 15 Pa. Cons. Stat. Ann. § 1715(d) (2009).
36. *See* ABA Committee on Corporate Laws, *Other Constituencies Statutes: Potential for Confusion*, 45 Bus. Law 2253, 2268–2270 (1990).
37. In this regard, consider § 6.02 of the ALI Principles of Corporate Governance: Analysis and Recommendations (1994), which allows nonshareholder interests to be taken into consideration when there is a hostile bid, provided the shareholder interest is not "significantly" disfavored.
38. ABA Committee on Corporate Laws, *supra* note 36, at 2270–71.
39. Cal. Corp. Code §§ 14600-14631 (West; effective Jan. 1, 2012); N.Y. Bus. Corp. Law. §§ 1701–1709 (McKinney; effective Feb. 10, 2012).
40. ALI 1 Principles of Corporate Governance: Analysis and Recommendations (1994 & Supp. 1998). One of the challenges met by the American Law Institute was to express a view of the role of the corporation as a functioning member of society.
41. *Id.* § 2.01, commentary g.
42. *Id.* § 2.01, commentary i.

CHAPTER 5

THE PROMOTION OF THE CORPORATION

TABLE OF SECTIONS

§ 5.1 FUNCTIONS OF PROMOTERS

Promoters discover business opportunities, prepare plans to take advantage of them, and push those plans to completion. They perform an essential economic function in assembling and coordinating the necessary plan, materials, and personnel for new business enterprises. Although there are many professional promoters, people whose life's work is the conception and organization of business enterprises, most business enterprises are conceived and organized by amateur promoters, people who play the role of promoter only once or twice in a lifetime, usually in connection with a business with which they expect to be permanently identified.

The typical promoter performs many varied services in launching an enterprise, often enlisting the aid of experts, lawyers, bankers, solicitors, and other persons. The various activities of the promoter may be classified as follows: (1) the discovery and investigation of a promising business opportunity; (2) the formulation of business and financial plans; (3) the assembling of the enterprise by negotiating and obtaining some control over the subject matter by options or contracts made on behalf of the proposed corporation or on the promoter's credit; (4) the making of arrangements for financing the enterprise and issuing securities; and (5) the arranging of the promoter's own compensation.

A promoter often is in a position to sell the enterprise to prospective investors, and thus may seek a speculative profit in securities of the new company. Promoters may further attempt to take advantage of their position and seek unreasonable, undisclosed, and excessive compensation. These "secret profits" are often available to promoters because they are usually in complete control of the enterprise in its early stages. Accordingly, courts have ruled that a promoter owes fiduciary duties to the company and cannot profit unduly at its expense.

§ 5.2 PRE-INCORPORATION CONTRACTS: QUESTIONS RAISED

Under modern statutes, formal incorporation is relatively quick, simple, and inexpensive, but promoters may still find it desirable, and in some instances essential, to make arrangements before incorporation of the business to ensure that the corporation will have needed property, funds, patent rights, licenses, services, or key employees. Thus, before a corporation is formed, its promoters may enter into contracts to obtain or "tie down" the needed assets and personnel.[1]

Frequently these contracts are made in the name of the corporation being formed but not yet in existence. Usually the other contracting party is aware that the corporation has not yet come into being but understands that the promoter is contracting on its behalf and for its benefit. In most instances, no problems develop out of promoters' contracts. The corporation is formed; it is adequately financed, at least for the "short run"; those controlling the corporation after its formation do not question that the contract binds the corporation; both the corporation and the other party to the contract perform their respective obligations under the contract; and no need arises for the other party to the contract to try to subject the promoters to liability.

§ 5.3 LIABILITY OF THE CORPORATION ON PRE-INCORPORATION CONTRACTS

It is well established in the law that an agency relationship cannot be recognized without an existing principal.[2] Accordingly, promoters of a corporation are not considered its agents and, apart from statute, they are not recognized as having the power to bind a proposed but not yet formed corporation to contracts made on its behalf. Furthermore, the incorporation of a company will not in itself render that corporation liable on contracts its promoters made on its behalf before incorporation.[3]

§ 5.4 THEORIES OF CORPORATE LIABILITY ON PROMOTERS' CONTRACTS

American courts have professed difficulty in finding a rational explanation of how a corporation can make itself a party to its promoters' pre-incorporation contracts. A corporation may assume the burdens of a contract by agreement with a promoter on sufficient consideration. But such an assumption of the promoter's obligations under the contract does not give the corporation a right to sue on the contract, a right that it could acquire only by assignment from the promoter or as a third-party beneficiary of the contract.

Five theories have been advanced as to how the liability of the corporation on the promoters' contracts can arise: (1) ratification;

(2) adoption; (3) acceptance of a continuing offer; (4) formation of a new contract; and (5) novation.[4]

Adoption. Adoption is a corporation's assent to a contract that was made in contemplation of the corporation's assuming it after organization. In other words, adoption occurs when a corporation takes the contract rights and obligations of the promoter and makes them its own.

Ratification. Ratification is the corporation's acceptance of an act purportedly made on its behalf by an agent. Strictly speaking, a purported principal must have been in existence at the time of a contract in order to have the capacity to ratify it; therefore ratification is only properly applicable to post-incorporation contracts.

Adoption and Ratification Compared. Courts, however, often use the term "ratification" loosely to refer to a corporation's acceptance or adoption of a promoter's contract. Adoption and ratification may be shown by any words or acts of responsible corporate officers showing assent or approval, such as by their knowingly accepting benefits of the contract or proceeding to perform obligations imposed on it.

Some courts have drawn a distinction between the effect of ratification and adoption; a ratified contract relates back to the date the promoter made it,[5] whereas an adopted contract becomes binding on the corporation on the date of adoption.[6] However, nothing seems to prevent a corporation from adopting a promoter's contract as of the date it was originally made if the corporation expressly or impliedly agrees to do so.

Acceptance of a Continuing Offer. On what theory does a person who is not a party to a contract become a party by adoption? One theory is that the original promoter's contract is in the nature of a continuing proposal, which the corporation may accept when it comes into existence.[7]

Formation of a New Contract. Another theory is that a corporation's adoption of a promoter's contract is nothing more than the making of a new contract for new consideration.[8]

Novation. Still another theory is that whenever the parties to a promoter's contract anticipate that the corporation when formed will accept the contract and take over its performance, the contract is to be viewed as contemplating a novation, by which the corporation, when it assents after organization, is substituted for the promoter.[9]

Courts in the past have shown some readiness to take this novation view of a promoter's contract, but more recent decisions have relied on an adoption/ratification theory and have been reluctant to find that such a contract contemplated a novation.[10] Finally, some courts hold corporations liable on promoter's contracts under the principle that one who adopts the benefits of an act that another volunteers to perform in the first person's behalf is bound to take the burdens along with the benefits.[11]

§ 5.5 THE CORPORATION'S RIGHT TO ENFORCE CONTRACTS

Most American courts hold that, if a corporation expressly or impliedly adopts a pre-incorporation contract made for its benefit by its promoters, it makes itself a party to the contract and may sue on it.[12] Some have argued that a corporation cannot claim the benefit of or enforce a promoter's contract made in its name or for its benefit unless it has adopted the contract as its own.[13] The better view is that by bringing an action on the contract, the corporation adopts or ratifies it.[14]

It has been suggested that the corporation might also be allowed to sue as a third-party beneficiary of the promoter's contract. A third-party beneficiary need not be in existence at the time the contract is made.[15] However, a flaw in the third-party beneficiary theory is that the purpose of a promoter's contract is to create mutual obligations after the corporation's formation, with the corporation and the other party becoming bound, rather than merely conferring a naked benefit or right on the corporation. The consideration is usually executory. The better view is that the corporation cannot claim the benefits of the contract without assuming the burden of performance.

§ 5.6 LIABILITY OF PROMOTERS ON PRE-INCORPORATION CONTRACTS

In the absence of an express or implied agreement to the contrary, promoters are generally personally liable on their pre-incorporation contracts even though the contracts are made on behalf of the corporation to be formed. As the Supreme Court of Washington has stated, as a general rule "where a corporation is contemplated but has not yet been organized at the time when a promoter makes a contract for the benefit of the contemplated corporation, the promoter is personally liable on it, even though the contract will also benefit the future corporation."[16] However, cases dealing with a promoter's personal liability on contracts made for the benefit of a proposed corporation present a wide array of factual situations and a number of so-called general rules. The better view is that a promoter's personal liability should depend on the intention of the parties and the form in which the arrangement is cast.[17]

Whenever a promoter entering into a contract on behalf of a projected corporation causes the other contracting party to think that the corporation is already in existence and that the promoter is its agent and contracting for it, the promoter may be held liable (1) on the contract, (2) for deceit, (3) for breach of implied warranty of authority from a principal, or (4) for breach of implied warranty of the existence of a principal.[18]

When a promoter makes a contract in the name of a nonexistent corporation, a court may find that either: (1) the parties intended for the promoter to be a party to the contract; (2) the promoter was only to be a party until the corporation is organized and accepts the contract; or (3) the promoter was simply soliciting an offer that the corporation, after formation, could accept or reject.[19] When contracts are ambiguous as to whether the parties intend the promoter to be bound, some jurisdictions allow the use of parol evidence to show that the personal liability of the promoter was intended or that the third party was to look only to the corporation.[20] Although most decisions passing on whether a promoter is liable on an ambiguous contract have on one theory or another imposed personal liability on the promoter, a number of the more recent decisions show a greater readiness to interpret nonspecific contracts in a way that shields the promoter from liability, thus reaching a result perhaps more in accord with the intention of the parties.[21]

Absent clear intent on the part of the promoter to be liable on a *post-incorporation* contract, the third party is deemed to have relied on the existing corporation, not on the individual promoter, to pay any claim for services or other performance.[22]

NOTES

1. *See, e.g.,* Stanley J. How & Assoc. v. Boss, 222 F. Supp. 936 (S.D. Iowa 1963) (contract with architectural firm to perform services for proposed corporation).
2. WARREN ABNER SEAVEY, AGENCY § 34 (1964).
3. *See, e.g., In re* Vortex Fishing Systems, Inc., 277 F.3d 1057, 1070 (9th Cir. 2002) (applying Montana law).
4. *See* Annot., 41 A.L.R.2d 477 (1955).
5. *See* Rees v. Mosaic Technologies, Inc., 742 F.2d 765 (3d Cir. 1984); Stanton v. N.Y. & E. Ry., 22 A. 300 (Conn. 1890).
6. McArthur v. Times Printing Co., 51 N.W. 216 (Minn. 1892).
7. Kirkup v. Anaconda Amusement Co., 197 P. 1005 (Mont. 1921): "The adoption of such a contract is on the theory that the contract made by the promoters is a continuing offer . . . and that it may be accepted and adopted by the corporation after it is created." *Id.* at 1008.
8. Kridelbaugh v. Aldrehn Theatres Co., 191 N.W. 803 (Iowa 1923); *McArthur,* 51 N.W. 216.
9. Elements of novation are listed in Haggar v. Olfert, 387 N.W.2d 45, 50 (S.D. 1986); B&H Apartments Partnership v. Tharp, 466 N.W.2d 694, 696 (Iowa Ct. App. 1990).
10. Hog Heaven Corp. v. Midland Farm Mgmt. Co., 380 N.W.2d 756, 759 (Iowa Ct. App. 1985). *See also* Moody v. Bogue, 310 N.W.2d 655 (Iowa Ct. App. 1981); Jacobson v. Stern, 605 P.2d 198 (Nev. 1980) (courts using strict standards because finding of novation cuts off promoter's liability); Vodopich v. Collier County Dev., Inc., 319 So. 2d 43 (Fla. Ct. App. 1975).
11. *In re* Vortex Fishing Systems, Inc., 277 F.3d 1057, 1070 (9th Cir. 2002) (applying Montana law).
12. Boatright v. Steinite Radio Corp., 46 F.2d 385, 388 (10th Cir. 1931); Speedway Realty Co. v. Grasshoff Realty Corp., 216 N.E.2d 845 (Ind. 1966).
13. Macy Corp. v. Ramey, 144 N.E.2d 698 (Ohio Com. Pl. 1957) (promoter withdrawing from agreement before ratification by corporation).
14. K&J Clayton Holding Corp. v. Keuffel & Esser Co., 272 A.2d 565 (N.J. Super. 1971) (one way for corporation to adopt promoters' contract is to institute suit thereon); RESTATEMENT (SECOND) OF AGENCY § 97 (1958).
15. Kentucky Tobacco Prods. Co. v. Lucas, 5 F.2d 723, 727 (W.D. Ky. 1925).
16. Goodman v. Darden, Doman & Stafford Assoc., 670 P.2d 648, 651 (Wash. 1983), quoting Harding v. Will, 500 P.2d 91, 97 (Wash. 1972).
17. *See* H. F. Philipsborn & Co. v. Suson, 322 N.E.2d 45 (Ill. 1974) (whether liability will be imposed depends on intent of parties).
18. *See* Annot., 41 A.L.R.2d 477 (1958); 3 AM. JUR. 2d 654–62; AGENCY, *supra* note 2, §§ 293 to 300.
19. *See* White & Bollard, Inc. v. Goodenow, 361 P.2d 571, 573–74 (Wash. 1961).
20. Decker v. Juzwik, 121 N.W.2d 652, 657–58 (Iowa 1963).
21. *See, e.g., In re* Robbins Int'l, Inc., 275 B.R. 456, 468 (S.D.N.Y. 2002); Quaker Hill, Inc. v. Parr, 364 P.2d 1056 (Colo. 1961).
22. Television Events & Mktg. v. AMCON Distrib. Co., 484 F. Supp. 2d 1124, 1138 (D. Hawai'i 2006).

CHAPTER 6

DEFECTIVE FORMATION OF CORPORATIONS AND REVIVAL OF EXISTENCE

TABLE OF SECTIONS

§ 6.1 PROBLEMS ARISING FROM DEFECTS IN FORMATION

There are various degrees of noncompliance with the statutory formalities, some of which are of more and others of less importance in affecting corporate status. The defect, shortcoming, or irregularity complained of may or may not be accidental, may or may not affect the merits of a case being litigated, and may or may not have harmed the person who seeks to raise questions of defective incorporation. In determining the consequences attaching to defective organization, courts typically speak in terms of "de jure corporation," "de facto corporation," and "corporation by estoppel."

Consider the following possibilities: (1) The associates in a business enterprise may brazenly pretend to be incorporated without attempting to take some or any of the required statutory steps or may assume acting as a corporation with knowledge that the steps taken are incomplete. (2) The associates may execute articles of incorporation but, by some inadvertent mischance, may fail to get them filed in any public office.[1] (3) The associates may file the articles of incorporation with a state official, who may reject them.[2] (4) In one of the few states that still require the articles to be filed in two different government offices, they may file the articles in only one of the two prescribed offices. (5) The articles as filed may not be in proper form, may omit required provisions, or may be incorrectly executed or acknowledged by the incorporators. (6) The associates may fail to pay in the minimum required capital in a state in which that is still prescribed as a condition precedent to doing business. (7) The associates may fail to hold an organizational meeting of incorporators, shareholders, or directors, or fail to adopt bylaws or to elect directors and officers.[3] (8) The statute under which the associates attempt to incorporate may be unconstitutional or may not authorize formation of corporations to do the kinds of business the corporation is being organized to conduct. (9) The associates may purport to continue to do business as a corporation after its prescribed term of existence has expired, after revocation of its charter, or after it has been dissolved.[4]

If business associates purport to conduct their enterprise as a corporation but have not complied with statutory requirements for the organization of a corporation, or if the organization is otherwise defective in one or more of the respects just enumerated, will their association be treated as a corporation? Or perhaps the more accurate question is, which of the normal corporate attributes and incidents will the association be recognized as having, under what circumstances, and for what purposes?

Among the diverse problems arising from defects in organization, the following are perhaps the most important:

1. May the association sue as a corporation to enforce a contract if the other party to the contract challenges its capacity to sue or to contract?

2. May the association's creditors and other persons dealing with it sue it as a corporation? And may the association deny its existence as a corporation to defeat litigation brought against it?

3. May the purported corporation receive or make conveyances of property?

4. May the incorporators, subscribers, shareholders, directors, or officers in a seriously defective corporation be held to unlimited personal liability as partners or otherwise? For a debt claim against the business? For a tort committed by an employee of the enterprise? In answering these questions, important considerations may be whether the particular persons charged with liability had knowledge of the defects or actively participated in doing or authorizing the transaction giving rise to the liability.[5]

5. May the association, although defectively formed, enforce pre-incorporation subscriptions?

6. May the association exercise the right of eminent domain?

7. May the purported corporation be dissolved for defective incorporation in an action by the shareholders? In a quo warranto proceeding brought by the attorney general to oust it from the exercise of corporate power and the usurpation of a corporate franchise?

8. May a corporation doing business in a state other than its state of incorporation without qualifying to do business in that state nevertheless obtain de facto status in that state?

The answers given in the mass of judicial decisions that have dealt with these questions present a discouraging and baffling maze. To generalize the results of the decisions is indeed a difficult task. Satisfactory formulae or mechanical rules simply do not exist. Perhaps the most important question is under what circumstances the associates, active or passive, with or without knowledge of the defects, will be held personally liable for the debts of the supposed corporation.

§ 6.2 Corporation De Jure

A de jure corporation is recognized as having a corporate existence for all purposes, even as against a direct attack by the state of incorporation. No one, not even the state, can successfully challenge its existence as a corporation. To prove that it is a de jure corporation, it must show not only a valid law under which it might be created, and an attempt to organize under that law, but also compliance with all the mandatory requirements of the law that are conditions precedent to corporate existence.[6]

§ 6.3 The De Facto Doctrine

In the absence of substantial compliance with incorporation require-ments, a court may nevertheless treat a defectively organized corpo-ration as a "de facto corporation" and recognize it as having continuity of life, limited liability, and the other corporate attributes. Except in a direct action by the state and perhaps in a few other minor instances, a de facto corporation is treated as though it were de jure. The state in quo warranto proceedings can terminate its life, but no one else can successfully challenge its existence.[7]

Under the de facto doctrine as usually stated, a de facto corporation results if the following essentials are met:

1. A valid statute under which the corporation could have been formed (or, according to some, an apparently valid statute).
2. A good faith attempt to comply with the requirements of the statute.
3. A "colorable compliance" with the statutory requirements— that is, a sufficient compliance to give an appearance of validity to the incorporation.
4. A use of corporate powers—that is, the transaction of busi-ness by the organization as if it were a corporation. This ele-ment seems to be of only minor importance. Occasionally, in stating the essentials of the doctrine, a court has omitted the

requirement of colorable compliance with the statute, but it is not clear whether this omission is deliberate or inadvertent.[8]

On the other hand, courts have sometimes added a fifth requirement—namely:

> 5.   Good faith in claiming to be a corporation and in doing business as a corporation. Initial good faith may not be sufficient. Later discovery of defects by the associates may thereafter preclude application of the de facto doctrine to their organization.

As discussed in a later section, there is some authority supporting the abolition of the de facto doctrine in states adopting the Revised Model Act; but not all courts agree.

§ 6.4 Basis of the De Facto Doctrine

The incorporation statutes of various states set forth certain conditions precedent to corporate existence. It may well be asked: Why do courts recognize an organization as being a corporation de facto when it has failed to comply with the legislative conditions precedent?

The recognition of de facto existence promotes the security of business transactions and tends to eliminate quibbling over irregularities. Persons dealing with a corporation will rarely be prejudiced if the company is recognized as a corporation in spite of minor omissions or defects in its formation. A wrongdoer should not be allowed to quibble over incorporation defects to escape liability to the corporation. Similarly, a creditor of a supposed company usually should not be allowed to assert the individual liability of innocent, passive investors on the basis of flaws in the formal steps of incorporation when to do so would be contrary to the investors' expectations and the bargained-for agreement. This would simply give the creditor a windfall.

§ 6.5 Corporation by Estoppel

Persons may presume to do business as a corporation without having gone far enough in their incorporation attempt to acquire a de facto standing. Nevertheless, under some circumstances and for some purposes, courts sometimes hold either the purported corporation or persons contracting with it estopped to deny its corporate status. The corporation then is often referred to as a "corporation by estoppel."[9] The use of the term "estoppel" in this type of case may be misleading. When a court says that the other parties to a contract are "estopped," this may mean nothing more than that it or they are precluded for some reason from denying the corporate capacity. The word "estopped" does not reveal the reason for the conclusion, as the elements of a true estoppel are lacking in many of the decisions in which the term is used. It might be preferable in some of these decisions to say that the person contracting or dealing with the defective organization is considered to have "admitted" its corporate existence, rather than as being estopped to deny it.

The application of the so-called estoppel doctrine does not mean that the irregular corporation has acquired a corporate status generally and for all purposes. Rather, on the appropriate facts, corporation by estoppel may be used to bar collateral attacks on corporateness in a particular setting even though the de facto doctrine has been abrogated by statute in the state or is inappropriate given the factual setting. The doctrine is limited in its application to the consequences of a particular transaction done in the corporate name by associates assuming to be a corporation. Estoppel requires a reasonable consideration of the equities of each case and whether the defects or irregularities should be open to inquiry in that particular situation. Just as in the de facto corporation doctrine, procedural convenience, the avoidance of inquiry into irrelevant formalities, and fairness to all parties may favor treating a defective association purporting to be a corporation as though it has certain corporate incidents.

In one situation, all the elements of a true estoppel exist. Associates who hold out their association as a corporate body, and thereby induce persons to deal with it as such, are properly said to be estopped from denying their representation where to do so would prejudice those persons.[10] Thus it has long been established that a person contracting with an association that pretends to be a corporation may sue the associates as a corporation, and the principle of estoppel will prevent the associates from setting up as a defense the falsity of their own representation of corporateness.[11] The representation of corporateness can be to the general public, rather than to a specific party, and still give rise to estoppel.[12] Also, an associate who transacts business in the corporate name is estopped to deny the validity of the corporation for the purpose of holding other associates personally liable on contracts entered into between them in carrying on the firm's business.[13]

In a different type of case—where a defective corporation brings suit against the other party to a contract to enforce the contract—courts often say that the party who has contracted with the supposed corporation is estopped from denying its existence. For example, in the leading case, *Cranson v. International Business Machines Corporation*,[14] a contract creditor was estopped to deny the corporation's existence solely by having carried on all dealings with the defectively formed corporation in that corporation's name. The certificate of incorporation had not been filed with the secretary of state until after the plaintiff had delivered several office machines on account to the business. The business's president, and substantial shareholder, was unaware of the attorney's oversight in making the tardy filing. In contrast with *Don Swann Sales Corporation v. Echols*,[15] on facts identical to those in *Cranson*, the court, although recognizing that the legislature had intended to preserve the corporation by the estoppel doctrine, refused to recognize the doctrine's application to protect an *individual* purporting to act for a nonexistent corporation. The court relied on a state statute imposing liability on anyone who acts on behalf of a corporation before the secretary of state has issued a certificate of incorporation.

§ 6.6 LIABILITY OF PARTICIPANTS: ACTIVE VERSUS PASSIVE PARTICIPATION

Should persons having dealt with a defectively organized corporation on a corporate basis be allowed to assert full individual liability against the associates in the business? Numerous decisions hold that associates who deliberately engage in business under the name and pretense of a corporation should be held individually liable if they have not achieved at least a de facto corporate status.[16] The fact that by their pretense they lead outsiders to contract with them as a corporation is said to be no ground of estoppel in their favor. The associates are the principals and co-owners of a business that is carried on by their authorization and for their benefit.

Under this view, if the attempt to comply with the incorporation law does not go far enough to create a corporation de facto, associates who actively participate in the business are held to full liability on contracts authorized or ratified by them, either as partners or as principals.[17] There is said to be no estoppel of one who deals with business associates masquerading under a name that fails to represent a corporation de facto, because the elements of estoppel, viz., action induced by misrepresentation of the party against whom the estoppel is asserted, do not exist.[18]

§ 6.7 STATUTES PERTAINING TO DEFECTIVE CORPORATIONS

By simplifying the mechanics of incorporation, modern corporation statutes have reduced the number of defective incorporations and thereby the amount of litigation. Furthermore, most modern corporation acts contain provisions designed to clear up some of the problems of defective organization. Such provisions either dictate the moment in the incorporation process that a corporation comes into existence by providing that the filing of the articles of incorporation or the issuance of a certificate of incorporation by the secretary of state is either presumptive evidence or "conclusive evidence" or "conclusive proof" that all conditions precedent to incorporation have been met, or they specify the consequences of particular defects in the organization process, as well as forbidding collateral attack on incorporation in certain types of cases. The effect of some of these provisions on traditional doctrines, such as de facto incorporation and corporation by estoppel, is far from clear.

In many jurisdictions, the corporation statute states that a corporation comes into existence either when its articles of incorporation are filed or when the secretary of state issues a certificate of incorporation, and in addition provides that either acceptance and filing of articles of incorporation by the secretary of state or the secretary's issuance of a certificate of incorporation shall be "conclusive evidence," except against the state, that all conditions precedent to incorporation have been performed.

Statutes containing "conclusive evidence" or "conclusive proof" language seemingly do away with the necessity of litigating some of the questions that might arise under the de facto doctrine, such as what effect defects in the incorporation papers or their execution have and what amounts to sufficient use of corporate powers. In a "conclusive evidence" or "conclusive proof" jurisdiction, de facto questions can arise only if the articles are not filed or the certificate is not issued, or if a corporation of some other state is involved. On the other hand, in states with statutes providing that a certified copy of the articles is only "prima facie evidence" or "evidence" of corporate existence, presumably only the burden of proof or the amount of proof is changed, and the traditional questions as to colorable compliance, use of the franchise, and the need of dealings on a corporate basis may still be raised.

In addition to adopting the Model Act provision on when corporate existence commences, some states have enacted a provision from the 1950 and 1969 versions of the Model Act, which stated: "All persons who assume to act as a corporation without authority so to do shall be jointly and severally liable for all debts and liabilities incurred or arising as a result thereof." The District of Columbia Court of Appeals held that the impact of this provision and the corporate commencement section, taken together, is "to eliminate the concepts of estoppel and de facto corporateness."[19] The court reasoned that one purpose of modern corporation statutes is to eliminate problems and confusion inherent in the de jure, de facto, and estoppel concepts. It concluded that under the District of Columbia equivalent of the Model Act there is no corporation de jure, de facto, or by estoppel before a certificate of incorporation is issued[20] and, further, that individuals assuming to act as a corporation before a certificate of incorporation has been issued will be held jointly and severally liable.[21]

In the Maryland case of *Cranson v. International Business Machines*,[22] because of an attorney's oversight the articles of incorporation had not been filed. A creditor of the company sought to hold its president personally liable on the ground that failure to file the articles precluded corporate existence. Although the court did not find it necessary to decide whether the failure to file absolutely ruled out a de facto corporation, the court held that the plaintiff was "estopped" from denying the corporation's existence. At the time of this decision, Maryland had a statutory section similar to the Model Act provision on when corporate existence commences.[23] The approach of the Maryland court seems highly preferable to the mechanistic, nothing-or-all (nothing before certificate issues; unassailable de jure corporation afterward) rule adopted in the District of Columbia.[24]

Statutes in a number of states forbid collateral attack on incorporation. The Delaware statute, for example, provides that "no corporation of this State and no person sued by any such corporation shall be permitted to assert the want of legal organization as a defense to any claim."[25] A provision of this kind seems to be merely declaratory of the common law and does not supersede the usual rules as to de facto corporations and corporations by estoppel.[26]

Notes

1. *See, e.g.*, Cranson v. International Bus. Machines Corp., 200 A.2d 33 (Md. 1964) (defendant shown articles of incorporation, which corporation's attorney failed to file).
2. *See, e.g.*, Cantor v. Sunshine Greenery, Inc., 398 A.2d 571 (1979).
3. *See* Beck v. Stimmel, 177 N.E. 920 (Ohio Ct. App. 1931).
4. *See* Adam v. Mt. Pleasant Bank & Trust Co., 355 N.W.2d 868 (Iowa 1984).
5. *See, e.g.*, Edward Shoes, Inc. v. Orenstein, 333 F. Supp. 39, 42 (N.D. Ind. 1971) (shareholders purporting to be doing business as corporation under Indiana law will be held personally liable to creditors only if they acted fraudulently or in bad faith).
6. *See, e.g.*, People v. Larsen, 106 N.E. 947 (Ill. 1914); Attorney General, *ex rel.* Joseph L. Miner v. Belle Isle Ice Co., 26 N.W. 311 (Mich. 1886).
7. *See, e.g.*, Thies v. Weible, 254 N.W. 420, 423 (Neb. 1934).
8. *See, e.g.*, Mun. Bond & Mortgage Corp. v. Bishop's Harbor Drainage Dist., 182 So. 794 (Fla. 1938); Cranson v. International Bus. Mach. Corp., 200 A.2d 33 (Md. 1964); Paper Prods. Co. v. Doggrell, 261 S.W.2d 127 (Tenn. 1953).
9. *See* Zoning Comm'n v. Lescynski, 453 A.2d 1144 (Conn. 1982); Harry Rich Corp. v. Feinberg, 518 So. 2d 377 (Fla. Dist. Ct. App. 1987). *Cf.* Sullivan v. Buckhorn Ranch P'ship, 119 P.3d 192 (Okla. 2005) (estoppel to deny corporate existence may not be invoked unless corporation had at least de facto existence).
10. *See* United States v. Harrison, 653 F.2d 359 (8th Cir. 1981) (trustees estopped to deny corporate existence to prevent disclosure to IRS of business records pertaining to family trust where separate tax returns had been filed on behalf of trust entity).
11. Empire Mfg. Co. v. Stuart, 9 N.W. 527 (Mich. 1881).
12. United States v. Theodore, 347 F. Supp. 1070 (D. S.C. 1972) (claim company records were personal records so privilege against self-incrimination applied denied because business had represented itself to public as corporation).
13. Kingsley v. English, 278 N.W. 154 (Minn. 1938); Dargan v. Graves, 168 S.E.2d 306 (S.C. 1969).
14. 200 A.2d 33 (Md. 1964). *Cranson* has been followed in a number of cases. *See, e.g.*, Turner v. Turner, 809 A.2d 18, 63 (Md. App. 2002).

15. 287 S.E.2d 577 (Ga. Ct. App. 1981). *But see* Gardner v. Marcum, 665 S.E.2d 336 (Ga. Ct. App. 2008) (third party who deals with business as corporation cannot deny its corporate existence and hold principal individually liable).

16. *See, e.g.*, Puro Filter Corp. v. Trembley, 41 N.Y.S.2d 472 (App. Div. 1943); Conway v. Samet, 300 N.Y.S.2d 243 (Sup. Ct. 1969).

17. *See, e.g.*, Harrill v. Davis, 168 F. 187 (8th Cir. 1909); Clinton Inv. Co. v. Watkins, 536 N.Y.S.2d 270 (App. Div. 1989); Minich v. Gem State Dev., Inc., 591 P.2d 1078 (Idaho 1979); *cf.* Chatman v. Day, 455 N.E.2d 672 (Ohio Ct. App. 1982). *See* E. Merrick, Dodd, Jr., *Partnership Liability of Stockholders in Defective Corporations*, 40 Harv. L. Rev. 521, 558–60 (1927); Edward H. Warren, Corporate Advantages Without Incorporation 814–25 (1929).

18. One of the strongest cases on this point is *Harrill v. Davis*, 168 F. 187 (8th Cir. 1909), holding that four associates who had actively engaged in the lumber business under a corporate name before filing the articles of incorporation in any public office and who never issued any shares of stock could not escape individual liability.

19. Robertson v. Levy, 197 A.2d 443, 447 (D.C. 1964).

20. *Id.* at 446.

21. *Id.* at 447.

22. 200 A.2d 33 (Md. 1964).

23. Md. Corp. & Ass'ns Code Ann. § 2-102(b) (2009), formerly Md. Code Ann. art. 23, § 131(b) (1966).

24. *See, e.g.*, Dargan v. Graves, 168 S.E.2d 306 (S.C. 1969) (recognizing estoppel).

25. Del. Code Ann. tit. 8, §§ 329(a) (2009), 7104(a) (2008).

26. Davis v. Stevens, 104 F. 235, 238 (D. S.D. 1900). In fact, the Delaware statute itself states that. Del. Code Ann. tit. 8, § 329(b) (2009).

CHAPTER 7

THE SEPARATE CORPORATE ENTITY: PRIVILEGE AND ITS LIMITATIONS; PIERCING THE CORPORATE VEIL

TABLE OF SECTIONS

§ 7.1   THE CORPORATE ENTITY

Recognition of a corporate personality generally is considered to be the most distinct attribute of the corporation.[1] To speak of a corporation as "a legal person" is a convenient figure of speech used to describe the corporation as a legal unit, a separate concern with a capacity, like a person's, to hold property and make contracts, to sue and be sued, and to continue to exist notwithstanding changes of its shareholders or members.

If *A*, *B*, and *C* are incorporated into the *A*, *B* & *C Co.*, the entity in its corporate capacity is the holder of the rights and liabilities arising from the transactions of the company. The property or rights acquired, or the liabilities incurred on behalf of the corporation, are treated as the property rights and liabilities of the corporate legal person distinct from those of the shareholders who comprise it.[2] A contract entered into by the shareholders of a corporation is not the contract of the corporation unless adopted by authority of its directors. Thus, if a sole shareholder borrows money on a personal note secured by shares of stock for the company's use and benefit even though the money is used to pay off corporate bills, the corporation is not liable on the note when credit was extended to the sole shareholder.[3] A corporation and its shareholders are not liable on each other's contracts. Shareholders' immunity from corporate obligations is one of the most important incidents and advantages of the separate legal entity and serves a useful purpose in business life. Under some circumstances, however, sufficient equity may be shown to disregard the distinct legal personality and thereby pierce the corporate veil.

§ 7.2   PIERCING THE CORPORATE VEIL—APPROACHES USED TO DISREGARD THE CORPORATE ENTITY

In general, a corporation may exist and act as an entity or legal unit separate and apart from its shareholders. In many cases, however, the courts place limitations on this privilege. These limitations usually are expressed in terms of "disregarding the corporate fiction," "piercing the corporate veil," or "looking at the substance of the business operation rather than at its form."[4]

The disregard of the corporate entity occurs in a variety of settings, the most common being to impose personal liability on the corporation's stockholders. If the corporation is insolvent, its unsatisfied creditors, including any tort claimants, can be expected to pursue all reasonable avenues to reach the personal assets of its shareholders by arguing that the corporation is not truly a separate entity. Sometimes it is important to determine whether the real party in interest is the corporation or an individual. For example, state usury laws frequently apply if the borrower is an individual but not if the borrower is a corporation. Cases have therefore posed the question whether the corporate entity should be disregarded for the purpose of applying the state usury law.

If the separate corporate capacity is used dishonestly, such as to evade obligations or statutory restrictions, the courts will intervene to prevent the abuse.[5] The figurative terminology and formulae invoked by the judges to disregard legal fictions often obscure the real issues presented.[6] Concepts such as "alter ego" and "instrumentality" do not provide general formulae applicable in all cases; the court must consider each set of circumstances on its merits.[7] The facts presented must demonstrate some misuse of the corporate privilege or establish a need to limit it in order to do justice.[8] Disregard of the separate corporate entity privilege for one purpose does not mean necessarily that it will be disregarded for other purposes.[9] The absence of clear-cut rules and the reliance on the equities of each fact situation make it difficult to generalize as to the factors that will lead a court to find individual shareholder liability. Thus, drawing the line between a proper use of corporate form in order to avoid personal liability and an abuse of corporate form to defraud a corporation's creditor is sometimes quite difficult.[10]

There are three primary variants within the "piercing the corporate veil" jurisprudence—(1) the "instrumentality" doctrine, (2) the "alter ego" doctrine, and (3) the "identity" doctrine. The instrumentality doctrine's overall approach focuses on the presence of three factors, as reflected in the frequently cited language of its leading case, *Lowendahl v. Baltimore & Ohio Railroad*:[11]

1. Control, not merely majority or complete stock control, but complete domination, not only of finances, but of policy and business practices in respect to the transaction attacked so that the corporate entity had at the time no separate mind, will, or existence of its own; and
2. Such control must have been used by the defendant to commit fraud or wrong, to perpetuate the violation of a statutory or

other positive legal duty, or a dishonest and unjust act in con-
travention of the plaintiff's legal rights; and

3. The aforesaid control and breach of duty must proximately
    cause the injury or unjust loss complained of.[12]

The "alter ego" doctrine is stated with a far greater economy of
words but with much less precision than the statement of instrumentality doctrine. The alter ego doctrine holds that it is appropriate to pierce
the veil when (1) a unity of ownership and interests exists between the
corporation and its controlling stockholder such that the corporation
has ceased to exist as a separate entity and the corporation has been
relegated to the status of the controlling stockholder's alter ego and
(2) to recognize the corporation and its controlling stockholder as separate entities would be sanctioning fraud or would lead to an inequitable result.[13] Although stock ownership is a significant factor under the
"identity" approach, a court may impose personal liability on a controlling person even if he or she is not a shareholder.[14]

On close scrutiny, none of the three above variants of "piercing the
veil" offers precision or a characteristic that distinguishes it from the
other two variants. In practice, they are virtually indistinguishable from
one another, and the outcome of the cases does not appear to depend on
which standard is applied. As commentators have frequently noted, the
results in cases appear guided not so much by the doctrine invoked as by
a mist of metaphors.

§ 7.3 LACK OF FORMALITY AND CONFUSION OF AFFAIRS AS BASES FOR PIERCING THE CORPORATE VEIL

When the dominant shareholders treat the corporate business and
property as their own and the affairs of the corporation and the shareholders are confused or intermingled, the separate corporate entity no
longer can be respected. If the shareholders themselves disregard the
separateness of the corporation, the courts also will disregard it so far as
necessary to protect individual and corporate creditors.[15]

When the same facts arise in the parent-subsidiary context, courts
frequently characterize the parent's control as that of treating the subsidiary as though it is merely a department of the parent company.[16]

Similarly, a court may disregard separate entities when related corporations under common control fail to observe the formal barriers between them.[17]

A frequent factor supporting a finding of confusion is the failure to comply with corporate formalities in the conduct of the corporation's business.[18] Lapses in corporate formalities that are emphasized in veil-piercing cases are: failing to hold stockholders' or directors' meetings;[19] directing receipts to the controlling stockholder's bank account and using a single endorsement stamp for all affiliated companies;[20] the parent company's board of directors establishing salaries, appointing auditors, and declaring dividends of its subsidiary;[21] and the parent company's providing interest-free loans to its subsidiary without documenting those loans with promissory notes.[22]

Disregard of corporate formalities, however, does not appear sufficient by itself to pierce the corporate veil.[23] Some have even sought to restrict this factor further by requiring a causal relationship between the failure to observe corporate formalities and the fraud or inequitable result that would follow if the veil were not pierced.[24] The mere fact that the business's affairs have been carried out with strict obeisance to corporate formalities, however, does not immunize the corporation from having its separate entity disregarded if other factors justify piercing the corporate veil.[25] The want of corporate formalities is but one consideration, and courts customarily require some suggestion of fraud, illegality, or unfairness that will result if the veil is not disregarded.[26] A disregard of form standing by itself, thus, will not be enough to pierce the corporate veil.[27]

A related consideration is whether there has been mingling of business or assets of the controlling stockholder and the corporation or among affiliated corporations. For example, one court found sufficient justification to pierce the corporate veil where the controlling stockholder had included his personal assets among those that were depreciated on the corporation's tax return, had executed the company leases and had filed other company reports in his own name, and had endorsed company checks by signing his own name.[28] Cases that have pierced the veil because of mingling of assets and affairs customarily involve facts suggesting there has been such control exercised over the corporation's assets by its dominant stockholder that the stockholder has essentially ignored the corporation as a distinct entity.[29]

There are several rationales that can be suggested as to why mingling or a lack of obeisance to corporate formalities should lead to the corporation's separate entity being disregarded. One theory is that logic compels treating the dominated corporation and its controlling stockholder as inseparable because the dominant stockholder has chosen to ignore the corporation as a distinct entity. This reasoning does not itself answer why such draconian results should follow from the fact that the dominant shareholder has caused the corporation to conduct its business informally. One would expect some greater purpose should underlie the imposition of personal liability on the dominant stockholder than the rather hollow purpose of assuring the corporation's separate personality is preserved through a respect for formal operations.

Veil piercing for lack of corporate formalities and the mingling of affairs and assets are most appropriate where the facts are sufficiently strong to create a serious doubt whether creditors have been prejudiced by the transfer of corporate assets without sufficient consideration. This is most easily established in cases where there has been mingling of affairs or assets. A breach of corporate formalities should also be sufficient where the breach is so pervasive as to raise grave concerns that it is not possible to determine whether the corporate assets had ever been transferred to its stockholders without fair consideration or the lack of formalities may have caused a sufficient misimpression of personal rather than corporate responsibility for the debts contracted.

§ 7.4 DOMINATING THE CORPORATION'S AFFAIRS AS THE BASIS FOR PIERCING THE CORPORATE VEIL

A frequent consideration in veil-piercing cases is whether the controlling stockholder has so dominated the affairs of the corporation that the corporation has no existence of its own. Usually there is the additional requirement that fraud, illegality, or gross unfairness will result if the corporate existence is not disregarded.[30]

Domination can be the basis of piercing to an individual shareholder[31] as well as to a parent corporation. Domination is far more frequently a consideration in the parent-subsidiary context than in cases in which the veil is being pierced to reach an individual stockholder.[32] The lesser role of domination in veil-piercing cases involving individual-close corporations is a sensible recognition that it defies even metaphysics to expect such a corporate entity to have a mind or soul distinct from its controlling stockholder. In contrast, even though it is equally unrealistic to expect a subsidiary to act independently of its parent corporation's strategies and wishes, both parent and subsidiary corporations can be expected to at least formalistically separate their decision-making so as to avoid creating the false impression that the subsidiary is but a branch or division of the parent corporation. Such an impression assumes significance because it misrepresents the status of the subsidiary to third parties, and also suggests a mingling of assets and affairs of the two entities such that there may be fraud on creditors lurking in the background. There also may be facts supporting the conclusion that the subsidiary has no independent profit objective such that creditors are presented with a corporate debtor that has only down-side risks.[33]

Professor Blumberg identifies four factors that are frequently emphasized in parent-subsidiary veil-piercing cases finding undue domination of the subsidiary's affairs:

1. the parent's participation in day-to-day operations;
2. the parent's determination of important policy decisions;
3. the parent's determination of the subsidiary's business decisions, bypassing the subsidiary's directors and officers; and
4. the parent's issuance of instructions to the subsidiary's personnel or use of its own personnel in the conduct of the subsidiary's affairs.

§ 7.5 INADEQUATE CAPITALIZATION AS A FACTOR FOR PIERCING THE VEIL

Inadequate capitalization is frequently a factor considered by courts in veil-piercing cases.[34] This consideration most frequently appears in tort cases involving close corporations and in the parent-subsidiary context.[35] *Minton v. Cavney*[36] is the leading case for a seemingly aggressive use of inadequate capitalization as grounds to pierce the corporate veil. Plaintiff had secured a $10,000 tort judgment against the corporation for the death of her daughter, who had drowned in the corporation's swimming pool. The corporation operated a public swimming pool in a facility it leased and had received no consideration for its stock. Justice

Roger Traynor reasoned that there had been "no attempt to provide adequate capitalization," reasoning the corporation's "capital was 'trifling compared with the business to be done and the risks of loss.'"[37] The court therefore upheld the complaint against a shareholder with a one-third interest who was also an officer and director of the corporation.

Minton stands alone as a case that pierced the veil solely for inadequate capitalization. Subsequent cases have relegated inadequate capitalization to one of many factors courts can consider to determine whether to disregard the corporate entity.[38] *Minton* can therefore be seen as a case where it was not simply a matter of capital inadequacy but where there was no attempt to provide any capitalization. This view brings it closer to the cases that have pierced the veil when the facts suggest the corporation is a sham.[39]

In a leading case, the New York Court of Appeals in *Walkovszky v. Carlton*[40] refused to apply the "thin capitalization" theory of piercing the corporate veil. The individual defendant was the sole shareholder of 10 corporations, each of which owned two taxicabs and carried only the minimum amount of automobile insurance allowed by the law. The plaintiff was injured due to the negligence of one of defendant's drivers. The court, despite a vigorous dissent, deferred to the legislature in holding that by maintaining the statutory minimum insurance the corporation was not too thinly capitalized. The only basis for piercing the corporate veil would be on a showing that there was such an intermingling of assets as to constitute an abuse of the corporate privilege.[41]

On close inspection, the role of inadequate capitalization is best left as a surrogate for the promoter's possible bad faith as that factor may relate on the overall equities of disregarding the corporate entity.[42] Consider in this regard that the inadequacy of the firm's capital is to be measured at the time of the corporation's inception.[43] Capital must then have been sufficient to meet the prospective risks of the business in which the corporation is to engage.[44]

§ 7.6 DEFINITIONS: "PARENT COMPANY," "HOLDING COMPANY," "SUBSIDIARY," AND "AFFILIATE"

Subsidiary and affiliated corporations have become important instruments of large-scale business. The same shareholder or group of shareholders may form or acquire various affiliated corporations for use as related branches of an enterprise under the unified management of common directors and officers. Much the same result is accomplished by subincorporation, when a parent or holding company reincorporates itself and splits its personality into several branches of the business.

A corporation with the power to elect a majority of the directors of another corporation and thus exercise working control is a parent company with reference to the corporation so controlled.[45] The parent company may have this power directly by virtue of its controlling equity interest or indirectly through another corporation or series of corporations. The term "holding company"[46] is used most frequently to refer to a corporation created specifically to acquire and hold shares in other corporations for investment purposes, with or without actual control. However, the term sometimes is used interchangeably with "parent company" when the corporation has sufficient equity interest in, or power of control over, another corporation to elect its directors and influence its management.[47]

A corporation subject to control by a parent or holding company is a "subsidiary" of the controlling company, even when it may in turn be the parent or holding company of a third corporation. Corporations related to each other by common control of voting stock and operated as parts of a system or enterprise are "affiliates."

§ 7.7 DISREGARDING THE SEPARATE ENTITY IN THE PARENT–SUBSIDIARY CONTEXT

Problems regarding the corporate entity frequently arise within the context of parent and subsidiary or between affiliated corporations. The same principles apply here as to individual shareholders and their corporations. There is no general formula that furnishes an objective test to determine shareholder liability for the torts or contracts of controlled corporations. Courts exercise their discretion to prevent abuses and regulate the privilege of separate corporate capacities, and in doing so they weigh various factors in deciding the question.[48] At the same time courts will not ordinarily disregard the separation of corporate entities in the absence of a showing that injustice or unfairness would otherwise result.[49]

§ 7.8 THE CORPORATION'S SEPARATE ENTITY UNDER STATE AND FEDERAL STATUTES

A significant number of cases regarding the piercing of the corporate veil are those arising in disputes involving the application of a state or federal statute. The greater frequency of veil-piercing in statutory contexts rather than in the contract claim contexts is due to the different objectives served in the statutory contexts—invariably the objective and policy of state and federal statutes invite a more liberal application of veil-piercing considerations.[50] Furthermore, federal courts are more likely to pierce the veil in order to effectuate federal policy and thereby prevent state corporate laws from being used to frustrate the federal objectives.[51] Courts do not purport to invoke different standards for piercing the veil in the context of interpreting state or federal statutes than they use in cases involving creditors who seek payment. The greater willingness to pierce the veil in the statutory context reflects in part that the consequences are not nearly as severe as in veil-piercing cases where the object is to impose liability on the dominant stockholder for all the insolvent corporation's debts. Also, there are numerous related questions in the statutory context that call for expanding responsibility beyond a single corporate actor so as to include perhaps its sister corporations, its parent corporation, or even an individual controlling stockholder. Such expansion can occur by either piercing the corporate veil or by holding that the act's language reaches controlling stockholders or controlled companies regardless of whether the facts support piercing the veil.

In broad overview, the question that drives veil-piercing in the statutory context is whether the statutory purpose would be furthered or frustrated if the individual controlling stockholder or parent corporation is not swept within the scope of the statute. This question can sometimes be answered in a straightforward fashion by relying on statutory intent; in other instances, however, courts invoke the equitable principles embodied in the traditional standards of the "piercing the corporate veil" doctrine.

NOTES

1. *See* Anderson v. Abbott, 321 U.S. 349, 361 (1944); *supra* § 1.3 Chapter 1, § 1. The Concept of Corporate Entity or Personality.

2. In *Donnell v. Herring-Hall-Marvin Safe Co.*, 208 U.S. 267, 273 (1908), Justice Holmes observed: "A leading purpose of [corporation] statutes and of those who act under them is to interpose a non-conductor, through which, in matters of contract, it is impossible to see the men behind."

3. *E.g., In re* John Koke Co., 38 F.2d 232 (9th Cir. 1930), *cert. denied*, 282 U.S. 840 (1930).

4. *See, e.g.*, Establissement Tomis v. Shearson Hayden Stone, Inc., 459 F. Supp. 1355, 1365 (S.D.N.Y. 1978); Minton v. Cayaney, 364 P.2d 473 (Cal. 1961).

5. *See, e.g.*, Toshiba Am. Med. Sys., Inc. v. Mobile Med. Sys., Inc., 730 A.2d 1219, 1223 (Conn. App. Ct. 1999) (defendant held personally liable after conveying funds from one corporation to another so as to avoid payment on contracts made by first corporation).

6. *See* Robert W. Hamilton, *The Corporate Entity*, 49 TEX. L. REV. 979, 983 (1971).

7. *E.g.*, DeWitt Truck Brokers, Inc. v. W. Ray Flemming Fruit Co., 540 F.2d 681 (4th Cir. 1976) (South Carolina law).

8. Pepper v. Litton, 308 U.S. 295, 310 (1939).

9. Cooperman v. Unemployment Ins. Appeals Bd., 122 Cal. Rptr. 127, 132 (Ct. App. 1975).

10. *Compare* Yacker v. Weiner, 263 A.2d 188 (N.J. Super. Ct. Ch. 1970) (corporate entity disregarded when used as subterfuge) *with* Bartle v. Home Owners Co-op., Inc., 127 N.E.2d 832 (N.Y. 1955) (law permits use of corporate entity to limit liability).

11. 287 N.Y.S. 62 (App. Div.), *aff'd*, 6 N.E.2d 56 (N.Y. 1936).

12. *Id.*

13. *See* Southern Cal. Fed. Sav. & Loan Assoc. v. United States, 422 F.3d 1319 (Fed. Cir. 2005) (applying California law) (court may disregard corporate entity to prevent grave injustice, including injustice to shareholders).

14. McCormick v. City of Dillingham, 16 P.3d 735, 744 (Alaska 2001); LFC Marketing Group, Inc. v. Loomis, 8 P.3d 841, 847 (Nev. 2000).

15. Gardemal v. Westin Hotel Co., 186 F.3d 588, 593 (5th Cir. 1999) (citing Castleberry v. Branscum, 721 S.W.2d 270, 272 (Tex. 1986)).

16. Consolidated Rock Prods. Co. v. Du Bois, 312 U.S. 510 (1941).

17. *See* NLRB v. G&T Terminal Packaging Co., 246 F.3d 103, 118–19 (2d Cir. 2001).

18. *See, e.g.*, Walter E. Heller & Co. v. Video Innovations, Inc., 730 F.2d 50, 53 (2d Cir. 1984).

19. *See, e.g.*, Iron City Sand & Gravel v. West Fork Towing Corp., 298 F. Supp. 1091, 1098 (N.D. W. Va. 1969); Fiumetto v. Garrett Enters., 749 N.E.2d 992, 1006 (Ill. App. Ct. 2001).

20. *See* Brown v. Benton Creosoting Co., 147 So. 2d 89, 93 (La. Ct. App. 1962).

21. *See, e.g.*, Gentry v. Credit Plan Corp., 528 S.W.2d 571 (Tex. 1975).

22. *See* Doe v. Unocal Corp., 248 F.3d 915, 927 (9th Cir. 2001).

23. Soloman v. Western Hills Dev. Co., 312 N.W.2d 428, 434 (Mich. Ct. App. 1981).

24. *See* Transamerica Cash Reserve, Inc. v. Dixie Power & Water, 789 P.2d 24 (Utah 1990).

25. *See, e.g.,* Bridas S.A.P.I.C. v. Government of Turkm., 447 F.3d 411, 419–20 (5th Cir. 2006).

26. *See, e.g.,* Pepsi-Cola Metro. Bottling Co. v. Checkers, Inc., 754 F.2d 10 (1st Cir. 1985).

27. *See, e.g.,* Rogerson Hiller Corp. v. Port of Port Angeles, 982 P.2d 131, 134 (Wash. App. 1999) ("Corporate disregard requires proof of two elements: 'first, the corporate form must be intentionally used to violate or evade a duty; second, disregard must be "necessary and required to prevent unjustified loss to the injured party"'"), quoting from and relying on Meisel v. M&N Modern Hydraulic Press Co., 645 P.2d 689 (Wash. 1982).

28. Kramer v. Keys, 643 F.2d 382, 385–86 n.4 (5th Cir. 1981).

29. *See, e.g.,* NLRB v. Bolivar-Tees, Inc., 551 F.3d 722, 729 (8th Cir. 2008).

30. *See, e.g., Bridas S.A.P.I.C.,* 447 F.3d 411, 417.

31. *See, e.g.,* Carter Jones Lumber Co. v. LTV Steel Co., 237 F.3d 745 (6th Cir. 2001).

32. *See, e.g.,* William J. Rands, *Domination of a Subsidiary by a Parent,* 32 IND. L. REV. 421 (1999).

33. *See* Clinical Components, Inc. v. Leffler Indus., Inc., 1997 WL 28246, at *6 (Ohio Ct. App. 1997) (creditors efforts to pierce corporate veil withstood summary judgment where alleged that wholly owned subsidiary paid significant fees for consulting services to parent when subsidiary's substantial debts remained outstanding).

34. *See, e.g.,* HOK Sport, Inc. v. FC Des Moines, L.C., 495 F.3d 927, 936 (8th Cir. 2007).

35. *See* PHILLIP I. BLUMBERG, THE LAW OF CORPORATE GROUPS: PROBLEMS OF PARENT AND SUBSIDIARY CORPORATIONS UNDER STATUTORY LAW OF GENERAL APPLICATION 202 (1989).

36. 364 P.2d 473 (Cal. 1961).

37. *Id.* at 475, quoting Automotriz Del Golfo De Cal. v. Resnick, 306 P.2d 1, 4 (Cal. 1957).

38. *See, e.g.,* Hambleton Bros. Lumber Co. v. Balkin Enters., 397 F.3d 1217, 1229 (9th Cir. 2005) ("The mere fact that the two entrepreneurs began their corporation with a small amount of capital is, without more, insufficient to justify the 'extraordinary remedy' of piercing the veil.").

39. *See, e.g.,* Wesco Mfg. v. Tropical Attractions of Palm Beach, Inc., 833 F.2d 1484 (11th Cir. 1987); Hart v. Steel Products, Inc., 666 N.E.2d 1270 (Ind. Ct. App. 1996) (undercapitalization and fraud justified piercing the veil).

40. 223 N.E.2d 6 (N.Y. 1966).

41. The plaintiff subsequently amended her complaint to comport with this alter-ego rationale, and the cause of action was sustained. Walkovszky v. Carlton, 287 N.Y.S.2d 546 (App. Div.), *aff'd,* 244 N.E.2d 55 (N.Y. 1968).

42. *See, e.g.,* Haynes v. Edgerson, 240 S.W.3d 189, 197 (Mo. Ct. App. 2007) ("Such undercapitalization is circumstantial evidence of an improper or reckless disregard for the rights of others.").

43. *See, e.g.,* Trustees of the Nat'l Elevator Indus. Pension, Health Benefit & Educ. Funds v. Lutyk, 332 F.3d 188, 196 (3d Cir. 2003).

44. *See* Pfohl Bros. Landfill Site Steering Comm. v. Allied Waste Sys., 255 F. Supp. 2d 134, 181 (W.D.N.Y. 2003) (when piercing the corporate veil in a CERCLA action "the inadequate capitalization factor pertains only

to capitalization 'in light of the purposes for which the corporation was organized.'").

45. A "parent corporation" is one that has working control through stock ownership of its subsidiary corporations. Culcal Stylco, Inc. v. Vornado, Inc., 103 Cal. Rptr. 419, 421 (Ct. App. 1972).

46. *See, e.g.,* 12 U.S.C.A. § 1841(a)(1) (2001) ("'bank holding company' means any company which has control over any bank").

47. *E.g.,* Kelley, Glover & Vale, Inc. v. Heitman, 44 N.E.2d 981 (Ind. 1942), *cert. denied,* 319 U.S. 762 (1943).

48. *See* Corrigan v. United States Steel Corp., 478 F.3d 718, 724 (6th Cir. 2007).

49. *E.g., id.* at 724–25 (noting courts should focus on "whether the relationship is so dominating that respecting it would be unjust").

50. An exhaustive study of this subject appears in PHILLIP I. BLUMBERG, THE LAW OF CORPORATE GROUPS: PROBLEMS OF PARENT AND SUBSIDIARY CORPORATIONS UNDER STATUTORY LAW OF GENERAL APPLICATION (1989).

51. Illinois Bell Tel. Co. v. Global NAPS Illinois, Inc., 551 F.3d 587, 598 (7th Cir. 2008).

CHAPTER 8

POWERS OF OFFICERS AND AGENTS; TORTS AND CRIMINAL LIABILITY OF CORPORATIONS; CRIMINAL LIABILITY OF OFFICERS AND DIRECTORS

TABLE OF SECTIONS

§ 8.1 CORPORATE OFFICERS AND THEIR SOURCES OF POWER

The chief executive officer, president, vice president, treasurer, and secretary are the traditional officers of the corporation, and these are the officers that were most often mentioned in the corporation statutes.[1] The modern trend is not to be wed to specific statutory nomenclature.[2]

Although most officer functions have remained relatively constant over time, the roles, duties, and titles in corporate management are constantly changing. Many corporations, especially the large publicly held corporations, now have other executives and agents who are denominated "officers." For example, the title of "chief executive officer" (CEO) was rarely used 50 years ago, and the title of "president" was reserved for the head corporate officer. Today, presidents are frequently subordinate to the CEO. Many of the older cases use "president" to describe today's CEO, but what is said in those cases for the president applies with equal force to the CEO position. However, it must be borne in mind that when both positions exist within a single corporation, the CEO's power is superior and broader than that of the president. The president in such a situation is likely to be more of a chief operating officer (COO). In many respects, the COO resembles the position of general manager[3] that may exist in small business or within corporate divisions.

A large corporation may have a number of vice presidents, assistant vice presidents, assistant secretaries, assistant treasurers, and so on. A number of modern corporation statutes provide flexibility by permitting officer titles and duties to be stated in the bylaws or determined by the board of directors.[4] As the number of vice presidents in corporations has proliferated, super vice presidencies under such titles as "executive vice president" or "senior vice president" have been created in an effort to retain distinctive titles. Most large corporations have a "chairman of the board," and in fact, in a considerable number of companies, that is the title given the chief executive officer. In some companies, however, where there is a desire to provide a system of checks and balances, different individuals hold the offices of CEO and chairman of the board.

An officer's authority to act is most often derived from the corporation's bylaws, a resolution of the board of directors, or a job description of that particular officer's or agent's duties approved by the board or some superior corporate agent. Much of a large corporation's work is conducted by agents selected and given authority by other corporate agents, who may be a number of levels removed from the corporation's board of directors. An agent so selected often has power to affect the legal relations of the corporation but usually does not have the power to act for or to bind the appointing agent.[5]

§ 8.2 SELECTION OF OFFICERS

The board of directors usually selects a corporation's principal officers. Applicable statutes, however, vary considerably. In some states, the corporation statute expressly designates the board of directors as the body to elect or appoint officers. In other states, the statutes are more flexible because they provide that the officers will be selected in the manner provided in the bylaws,[6] or that the board shall elect the officers unless the bylaws provide otherwise.

Corporation statutes commonly state that the same person may hold more than one corporate office. The 1969 Model Business Corporation Act, for instance, provided that "any two or more offices may be held by the same person, except the offices of president and secretary."[7] A few state statutes provide that the same person may not hold the offices of president and vice president.[8] The rationale underlying the foregoing limitations is that under certain circumstances the presence of two separate individuals is designed to establish a system of checks and balances. The modern trend, however, is to be more permissive and to permit corporations to fashion their own rules. Thus, for example, the California and Delaware statutes state that the same person may hold any two offices unless otherwise provided in the corporation's charter or bylaws.[9] The current version of the Model Act is similar.[10]

§ 8.3   REMOVAL OR RESIGNATION
OF OFFICERS OR AGENTS

The board of directors can remove an officer, with or without cause, even though the corporation has entered into an employment contract and the term has not expired.[11] The corporation, however, may be liable to the officer for damages for breach of an employment contract if the officer is removed without cause before his contract term expires.[12] In many states, the corporation statute provides that the board's power of removal does not destroy any rights the removed officer may have under an employment contract, shareholders agreement, or other contract.[13] In general, courts have not challenged the removal of officers by boards of directors unless the directors have clearly abused their discretion as to what is in the corporation's best interest.[14]

§ 8.4   THE CHIEF EXECUTIVE OFFICER'S
AND PRESIDENT'S AUTHORITY

For most of the history of American corporations, the corporation's chief executive officer was its president, who simply carried the title of president. Over time, corporations, especially publicly held corporations, changed the titles of their officers. The chief executive officer (CEO) became the official title. Many CEOs have both titles of president and chief executive officer. Other companies have reserved the title of president for the general manager or chief operating officer ("COO"). Smaller corporations are more likely to retain the traditional nomenclature of president.

Under the traditional governance norms, a corporation's CEO or president may be given the authority by the corporation's charter, bylaws,[15] resolutions of the directors, or the board's acquiescence to make particular contracts, including the power to hire employees,[16] to borrow money, or to execute conveyances and mortgages and do other acts. The CEO or president may be expressly given general authority to supervise and manage the business of the corporation, or a particular part of it. In such a case, the president's authority extends impliedly to any contract or other act that is incident to the ordinary business of the corporation, or to that part with which he or she is entrusted; thus, there is no need for special authority for the particular acts within the ordinary business of the corporation or that part of its operations to be expressly granted. Furthermore, in the absence of express authority, a corporation may be estopped to deny the authority of its president where it has created apparent authority in the president to make contracts or do other acts, as when a corporation allows its managing officers generally or habitually to make contracts or perform acts of that type.[17] The president's implied, apparent, or inherent authority is limited to carrying on the corporation's ordinary business and does not extend to extraordinary transactions. In any particular case, the scope of the CEO's authority necessarily boils down to a question of fact.

The decisions of the courts are in conflict regarding a corporate president's power, in the absence of any express or implied conferring of authority, to act on behalf of the corporation.[18] The president of a corporation, as its executive head, is often expressly or impliedly given supervision and control of its business. In view of this general practice, some courts have adopted a doctrine of "inherent authority"—namely, that the president of a business corporation, solely by virtue of the office, may bind the corporation by contract and by other acts in the usual course of its business.[19] Other courts recognize a "presumptive authority," taking the position that contracts entered into or acts performed by the president of a corporation in the ordinary course of the corporation's business are presumed to be within his or her authority until the contrary is proven.[20] The presumption is limited, however, to acts in the ordinary course of business and does not extend to all matters that can be authorized by the board of directors.[21]

According to a third group of courts,[22] the president's power to act for the corporation is limited to authority conferred by the corporation's charter or bylaws or by action of its board of directors. Nevertheless, even where the strict rule prevails, the president or other officer may of course be given authority to represent the corporation and to contract for it (1) by the corporation's articles or bylaws; (2) by a resolution of the board of directors; or (3) by acquiescence of the directors or shareholders in the known exercise or assumption of power.[23]

§ 8.5 AUTHORITY OF THE CHAIRMAN OF THE BOARD

Many corporations have an office titled "chairman of the board." The functions of the chairman of the board vary widely from company to company. In some companies, the chairman of the board has no other duty than presiding at meetings of the board, a responsibility that of course is not executive in nature. In other companies, the chairman of the board provides advice and counsel to the president or the board of directors.[24] In all other companies, the chairman is the chief executive officer or general manager, with vast responsibility and power. Whenever a company's chief executive officer is titled "chairman of the board," the title of "president" is often conferred on the company's chief executive officer. The same person may be both chairman of the board and president. Such appointments create the apparent authority to bind the corporation on transactions within the ordinary course of its business.[25] The same authority applies to one appointed as a managing director.[26]

The title of chairman of the board and chief executive officer, when held by a single person, identifies the center of actual power within the organization. Recently there has been much discussion whether the governance of the public corporation would be improved by separating the two positions and assigning to an outside director the role of chairmanship of the board of directors so as to provide something of a counterweight to the inertial flow of power to the chief executive officer.

Most corporation statutes do not define the responsibilities and powers of the chairman of the board, and the judicial decisions on that subject are few in number and are not very helpful. As many people dealing with a corporation are likely to consider a person with the title of "chairman of the board" to be a principal corporate officer, with authority to enter into important transactions, the courts should hold that a board chairman, even in the absence of an additional title such as "president" or "general manager," has by virtue of the position and title very broad power (whether classified as implied, inherent, or apparent authority) to act for the corporation.[27] The courts nevertheless are hesitant to accord autonomous power to the chairman of the board. Therefore, even though a corporation's bylaws provide that the president is to exercise general management responsibilities "subject to the direction of the chairman and the board," a court has held that the chairman lacked the authority to strip the president of his authority.[28] Such a result is consistent with the well-established principle that only as a deliberative body, not as individuals, does the board have corporate power.[29]

§ 8.6 The Vice President's Authority

A corporation's vice president is generally held to have no authority merely by virtue of the office to dispose of the corporation's property or to bind the corporation by notes or other contracts.[30] A vice president, however, is sometimes entrusted with management of the business or a particular part of it, and, in such a case, he or she may bind the corporation by a contract within the scope of express or apparent authority.[31] Even the more liberal courts, however, have held that a vice president does not have power to act on behalf of the corporation in highly important and unusual transactions in the absence of specific authorization in the bylaws or a resolution of the board of directors.[32]

§ 8.7 The Secretary's Authority

The principal duties of a corporation's secretary are to make and keep the corporate records and to properly record votes, resolutions, and proceedings of the shareholders and directors as well as other matters that should be entered on corporate records.[33] The secretary's certification of a corporate resolution or the content of a corporate record is conclusive in favor of a person reasonably relying thereon.[34]

The secretary traditionally has been thought of as "merely a ministerial officer who keeps the books and minutes of the stockholders' and directors' meetings and has charge of the seal of the company."[35] Accordingly, the secretary has no authority merely by virtue of the office to make contracts on behalf of the corporation or to bind it by other acts.[36]

In a modern publically held corporation, however, the secretary is generally more than a functionary with purely ministerial duties. The secretary is often a lawyer by profession and, not uncommonly, is also a director.

§ 8.8 The Treasurer's Authority; The CFO's or Comptroller's Duties

The treasurer of a corporation is the proper officer to receive and keep the moneys of the corporation, and to disburse them as he or she may be authorized.[37] As is the case with the corporate secretary, the treasurer is frequently referred to as a "ministerial" position.[38] As a general rule, a corporation's treasurer has no implied authority, merely by virtue of the office, to bind the corporation by contracts or other acts made or done in its name, or to dispose of its assets except as authorized by the directors or other managing officers.[39]

Just like any other corporate officer, the treasurer may be entrusted with the general management of the corporation's business or a particular part of it; in such a case, he or she has the same authority, in the absence of restrictions, as any other manager.[40] Even if the treasurer is not given broad general management powers, the directors or corporate executive officers, by acquiescence in the treasurer's actions or by otherwise leading other persons reasonably to believe that he or she has authority to act for the corporation in particular kinds of transactions, may create an apparent authority to enter into such transactions on the corporation's behalf.[41]

The Chief Financial Officer (CFO), comptroller or, as this officer is sometimes called, the "controller," is the chief accounting officer.[42] The comptroller's duties are to keep, or cause to be kept, all the corporation's books of accounts and accounting records and to prepare, or have prepared, appropriate financial statements for submission to the board of directors, the board's executive committee, appropriate corporate officers, and the shareholders.[43]

§ 8.9 FORMAL EVIDENCE OF AN OFFICER'S AUTHORITY

In highly important matters, such as the execution of conveyances, mortgages, and long-term contracts, a person dealing with a corporation should insist on evidence of the agent's authority in the form of a certified copy under the corporate seal of a resolution of the board of directors. A certified copy of a duly adopted bylaw is also satisfactory evidence of authority.

In the absence of a contrary charter or bylaw provision, the secretary is the custodian of the corporate seal,[44] and the proper person to affix the seal to an instrument is the secretary or assistant secretary.[45] The affixing of the corporate seal to an instrument is generally held to be prima facie evidence of the corporation's approval of the transaction and of the authority of the officer or officers who signed the instrument. The burden of showing lack of authority is then on the party attacking the instrument.[46]

§ 8.10 RATIFICATION OF UNAUTHORIZED CONTRACTS OR TRANSACTIONS

A corporation can ratify a contract or other act of a corporate officer or agent that was unauthorized if the act is legal and the corporation has the legal capacity to perform it.[47] In general, whoever could have originally authorized a transaction on behalf of a corporation can ratify it. Thus, an unauthorized act of a corporate officer or agent can be ratified for the corporation by its board of directors, its shareholders, or one or more of its officers, depending on which of these has the power to authorize the kind of act in question.[48]

Ratification need not be by formal vote or even by parol assent; as in the case of ratification by a natural person, it may be implied from the acts of the shareholders or officers having authority to ratify, in accepting the benefits with knowledge of the facts or otherwise treating or recognizing the contract or act as binding. Under some circumstances, ratification may be implied from a mere failure to repudiate or disaffirm.[49] Where the board of directors has the power to ratify, some courts say that knowledgeable acquiescence by the entire board is necessary to constitute ratification, while other courts say knowledgeable acquiescence by a majority of the directors is sufficient.[50]

The party alleging ratification has the burden of proving it.[51] When ratification is established, it relates back to the time the unauthorized act occurred and is legally equivalent to original authority.[52]

§ 8.11 CORPORATION'S CONSTRUCTIVE KNOWLEDGE

"A corporation cannot see or know anything except by the eyes or intelligence of its officers."[53] It is well settled that if an officer or agent of a corporation acquires or possesses knowledge in the course of her employment as to matters that are within the scope of her authority, this knowledge is imputed to the corporation.[54] As one court has put it, "[t]he knowledge possessed by a corporation about a particular thing is the sum total of all the knowledge which its officers and agents, who are authorized and charged with the doing of the particular thing acquired, while acting under and within the scope of their authority."[55] Conversely, knowledge acquired by a corporate officer or agent in relation to a matter that is not within the scope of her authority is usually not imputed to the corporation.[56] If duties do not require transmittal of knowledge to other corporate representatives acting in transactions in which the agent is not involved, the corporation's rights and liabilities arising out of those transactions are not affected by the agent's knowledge.

Courts generally base the doctrine that a principal is chargeable with knowledge of facts known to an agent on the agent's duty to communicate his knowledge to the principal and the presumption that this duty has been performed;[57] the presumption is usually treated as conclusive. According to many courts, such a presumption does not arise if the agent is acting out of self-interest or his interest is adverse to that of the principal. Therefore, whenever a director or officer has an interest adverse to the corporation, his knowledge relevant to the transaction is generally not imputed to the corporation.[58]

§ 8.12 CORPORATE CRIMINAL LIABILITY

The extent of corporate criminal liability has been in dispute since early days. It was formerly doubted whether a corporation could be prosecuted for any crime. The early cases declared that a corporation could not commit a crime for want of the requisite mens rea or intent.[59] Today, it is generally accepted that a corporation may be criminally liable for actions or omissions of its agents in its behalf. While a corporation cannot be imprisoned, it may be fined, and the fine may be enforced against its property, its charter may be forfeited because of its misuse or abuse, or other sanctions may be imposed as a condition of probation.

Over a century ago, the criticism emerged that that punishments levied on the corporate entity are in reality inflicted on the shareholders for the acts of others out of corporate assets by the prosecution and fining of the corporation.[60] These criticisms reemerged in the twenty-first century.[61] For example, criminal accountability of a large corporation can result in significant losses by innocent employees and retirees, as was the case with the demise of Arthur Andersen in the wake of the Enron scandal.[62]

A large number of regulatory statutes—both federal and state—now expressly subject corporations to criminal liability for offenses defined in the statutes,[63] and corporations have often been convicted of violating this kind of regulatory legislation. Instances include violation of a statute punishing usury,[64] violation of statute punishing contractors for exacting from laborers more than a stated maximum number of hours per day,[65] violation of a law regulating child labor,[66] violation of a labor-management relations act,[67] peddling by an agent without a license,[68] violation of the weights and measures law by giving short weight on a sale of ice,[69] violating a price regulation,[70] violation of the antitrust laws,[71] violation of federal campaign contribution statutes,[72] as well as violation of the securities laws. There is a lively debate whether such regulatory matters are appropriate for, and effectively addressed within, the criminal arena rather than the procedurally more flexible civil prosecution.[73]

In some of the legislatively defined offenses, the employer is subjected to criminal sanctions for acts of employees without regard to any fault or culpability on his part, even though he may have given his employees instructions to comply with the law.[74] By definition, mens rea on the part of the corporation or its agents is not an element of the offense proscribed by a strict liability statute. The criminal penalties often form an integral part of regulatory practice and may be based on pragmatic experience indicating their usefulness. In many cases, however, criminal penalties seem to have been added to legislation hastily and without adequate consideration of their necessity or usefulness.

§ 8.13 CRIMINAL LIABILITY OF OFFICERS AND DIRECTORS

Corporate officers and directors are individually liable for the crimes they commit as well as the crimes the corporation commits in which it has participated and meets the requisite mens rea for the offense.[75] The individual does not have a defense that she committed the crime to further the corporation's interests.[76] Conscious avoidance can be the equivalent to the officer acting with knowledge.[77] Because mens rea has been a staple of English common law,[78] officers and directors in most instances are not vicariously responsible under the criminal law for the violations of their subordinates. However, with the enactment of strict liability criminal provisions in public welfare and regulatory statutes, the traditional bases for criminalizing conduct shifted from punishment of misbehavior to protection of the public from harm. This shift in emphasis has given rise to the "responsible corporate officer" doctrine whereby a corporate official can be criminally responsible without proof of his knowledge of a violation. The doctrine, however, is limited to violation of certain "public welfare" or "regulatory" statutes encompassing a strict liability standard.

The responsible corporate officer doctrine traces its genesis to two Supreme Court decisions, the most significant being *United States v. Park.*[79] Park was president and CEO of a national food chain whose warehouse was found to have evidence of rodents. He was prosecuted under the Food, Drug and Cosmetic Act's provision that imposed strict liability for adulterated products. The Supreme Court affirmed a jury instruction that he violated the act if the jury found he "had a responsible relation" to the violation.[80]

The most important limitation on the scope of the responsible corporate officer doctrine is found in *Parks'* facts. A predicate to the Court's holding was its emphasis that the violation was of a "public welfare" statute. Moreover, the offense was a misdemeanor punishable by a very small fine.[81] These factors should have a significant influence in restricting application of the doctrine beyond the food, health, and safety area.[82] The doctrine has been invoked in tax matters,[83] and has been followed in many state court decisions.[84]

In 2002, there was a flurry of criminal indictments in the wake of the Enron, Worldcom, and Tyco calamities. Excluding insider trading prosecutions, there has been an absence of high profile criminal charges arising out of the 2008 financial crisis.

NOTES

1. *E.g.,* FORMER MODEL BUS. CORP. ACT § 50 (1969). *Cf.* MODEL BUS. CORP. ACT § 8.40(a) (1984) ("the offices described in its bylaws or designated by the board of directors in accordance with the bylaws").
2. *E.g.,* MODEL BUSINESS CORP. ACT § 8.40(a).
3. *See* MODEL BUSINESS CORP. ACT § 8.11.
4. *See, e.g.,* 805 ILCS 5/8.50 (Smith-Hurd 1993); MODEL BUSINESS CORP. ACT §§ 8.40, 8.41.
5. *See* DETLEV F. VAGTS, BASIC CORPORATION LAW: MATERIALS-CASES-TEXT 323 (2d ed. 1979).
6. *E.g.,* DEL. CODE ANN. tit. 8, § 142 (2001). *See also* MODEL BUS. CORP. ACT § 8.40(b) (1984) ("[t]he board of directors may elect individuals to fill one or more offices of the corporation").
7. FORMER MODEL BUSINESS CORP. ACT § 50 (1969).
8. MD. CODE ANN., CORPS. & ASSNS. § 2-415(a) (1999).
9. CAL. CORP. CODE ANN. § 312 (West 1990); DEL. CODE ANN. tit. 8, § 142(a) (2001).

10. MODEL BUSINESS CORP. ACT § 8.40(d) (1984) ("The same individual may hold more than one office in a corporation").

11. United Prod. & Consumers Co-op. v. Held, 225 F.2d 615 (9th Cir. 1955) (bylaw stated officers hold office at pleasure of board).

12. *In re* Paramount Publix Corp., 90 F.2d 441 (2d Cir. 1937); Pioneer Specialties, Inc. v. Nelson, 339 S.W.2d 199 (Tex. 1960).

13. Statutes frequently clearly state that election or appointment of an officer does not itself create contract rights. MODEL BUSINESS CORP. ACT § 8.44(b) (1984).

14. Franklin v. Texas Int'l Petroleum Corp., 324 F. Supp. 808 (W.D. La. 1971).

15. *See* Squaw Mountain Cattle Co. v. Bowen, 804 P.2d 1292, 1295 (Wyo. 1991).

16. Diston v. EnviroPak Medical Products, 893 P.2d 1071 (Utah App. 1995) (president had apparent authority to hire employees); Lee v. Jenkins Bros., 268 F.2d 357, 365 (2d Cir.), *cert. denied*, 361 U.S. 913 (1959) (apparent authority of corporate president was question of fact).

17. Schmidt v. Farm Credit Servs., Inc., 977 F.2d 511 (10th Cir. 1992); Lettiori v. American Sav. Bank, 437 A.2d 822 (Conn. 1980).

18. Note, *Inherent Power as a Basis of a Corporate Officer's Authority to Contract*, 57 COLUM. L. REV. 868 (1957).

19. *In re* Lee Ready Mix & Supply Co., 437 F.2d 497 (6th Cir. 1971); DuSesoi v. United Refining Co., 540 F. Supp. 1260 (1982).

20. Adams v. Barron G. Collier, Inc., 73 F.2d 975 (8th Cir. 1934) (president has prima facie the power "to do any act which the directors could authorize or ratify").

21. Southwest Forest Indus. v. Sharfstein, 482 F.2d 915 (7th Cir. 1972).

22. *See, e.g.,* Buxton v. Diversified Resources Corp., 634 F.2d 1313 (10th Cir. 1980), *cert. denied*, 454 U.S. 821 (1981).

23. *See* Juergens v. Venture Capital Corp., 295 N.E.2d 398 (Mass. App. Ct. 1973) (finding a combination of apparent authority and ratification).

24. *See* Whitley v. Whitley Constr. Co., 175 S.E.2d 128 (Ga. App. 1970).

25. *See, e.g.,* American Express Co. v. Lopez, 340 N.Y.S.2d 82, 84 (Civ. Ct. 1973); FDIC v. Texas Bank of Garland, 783 S.W.2d 604 (Tex. App. 1989).

26. *See* Covington Hous. Dev. v. City of Covington, 381 F. Supp. 427 (E.D. Ky. 1974).

27. *See* City Nat'l Bank v. Basic Food Indus., 520 F.2d 336 (5th Cir. 1975); American Express Co. v. Lopez, 340 N.Y.S.2d 82 (Civ. Ct. 1973).

28. *See* Delaney v. Georgia-Pacific Corp., 564 P.2d 277, 288 (Or. 1977).

29. *See* Star Corp. v. General Screw Prod. Co., 501 S.W.2d 374, 380 (Tex. Civ. App. 1973).

30. Clements v. Coppin, 61 F.2d 552, 557 (9th Cir. 1932).

31. Townsend v. Daniel, Mann, Johnson & Mendenhall, 196 F.3d 1140 (10th Cir. 1999) (discussion concerning the apparent authority of a corporate vice president).

32. Colish v. Brandywine Raceway Ass'n, 119 A.2d 887 (Del. Supr. 1955) (no implied authority to consummate such extraordinary transaction as employing architect to design new plant); Jennings v. Pittsburgh Mercantile Co., 202 A.2d 51 (Pa. 1964) (officer, who was both vice

president and treasurer-comptroller, did not have apparent authority to accept offer of sale-and-leaseback of all corporation's real estate).

33. *See* Field v. Oberwortmann, 148 N.E.2d 600 (Ill. App. Ct. 1958), *cert. denied*, 358 U.S. 833 (1958) (discussing secretary's obligations in keeping minutes); DEL. CODE ANN. tit. 8, § 142(a) (2001) (one officer shall record proceedings of shareholders' and directors' meetings in books kept for that purpose).

34. *See, e.g.*, McMan Oil & Gas Co. v. Hurley, 24 F.2d 776 (5th Cir. 1928).

35. *See* Meyer v. Glenmoor Homes, Inc., 54 Cal. Rptr. 786, 801 (Ct. App. 1966), *reh'g denied*, 55 Cal. Rptr. 502 (Ct. App. 1966).

36. Emmerglick v. Philip Wolf, Inc., 138 F.2d 661 (2d Cir. 1943) (secretary "is merely a ministerial officer" and therefore execution of affidavit by corporation's secretary cannot be deemed execution by corporation).

37. Clark v. Minge, 65 So. 832 (Ala. 1914).

38. *E.g.*, Ideal Foods, Inc. v. Action Leasing Corp., 413 So. 2d 416 (Fla. Dist. Ct. App. 1982).

39. Ideal Foods, Inc. v. Action Leasing Corp., 413 So. 2d 416 (Fla. App. 1982) (no authority to bind corporation to third party unless expressly or impliedly authorized).

40. Vaught v. Charleston Nat'l Bank, 62 F.2d 817 (10th Cir. 1933).

41. Kilpatrick Bros. v. International Bus. Mach. Corp., 464 F.2d 1080 (10th Cir. 1972).

42. This is the general understanding even though the corporation statutes do not mention the comptroller. *See, e.g.*, MODEL BUSINESS CORP. ACT § 8.40 (1984); FORMER MODEL BUSINESS CORP. ACT § 50 (1969).

43. *See* Jennings v. Ruidoso Racing Ass'n, 441 P.2d 42 (N.M. 1968).

44. Stovell v. Alert Gold Mining Co., 87 P. 1071 (Colo. 1906).

45. Meyer v. Glenmoor Homes, Inc., 54 Cal. Rptr. 786 (Ct. App. 1966), *reh'g denied*, 55 Cal. Rptr. 502 (Ct. App. 1966).

46. *Id.* at 792–93.

47. E. Edelmann & Co. v. Amos, 277 F. Supp. 105 (N.D. Ga. 1967), *aff'd per curiam*, Transonic Corp. v. E. Edelmann & Co., 386 F.2d 996 (5th Cir. 1967) (express ratification of all officers' acts for previous year).

48. Lewis v. Dansker, 357 F. Supp. 636, 644 (S.D.N.Y. 1973) (shareholders may only ratify corporate agent's unauthorized actions if shareholders could have originally authorized such acts).

49. *See, e.g.*, 3 A's Towing Co. v. P&A Well Serv., Inc., 642 F.2d 756 (5th Cir. 1981).

50. *Compare, e.g.*, Hurley v. Ornsteen, 42 N.E.2d 273 (Mass. 1942) (except in rare circumstances, knowledge and acquiescence by all the directors is necessary) *with* Mickshaw v. Coca Cola Bottling Co., 70 A.2d 467 (Pa. Super. Ct. 1950) (majority of directors was sufficient).

51. Home Tel. Co. v. Darley, 355 F. Supp. 992, 1000–01 (N.D. Miss. 1973), *aff'd*, 489 F.2d 1403 (5th Cir. 1974).

52. *3 A's Towing Co.*, 642 F.2d 756.

53. Factors' & Traders' Ins. Co. v. Marine Dry-Dock & Shipyard Co., 31 La. Ann. 149, 151 (1879). *Accord*, Schoenbaum v. Firstbrook, 405 F.2d 200, 211 (2d Cir. 1968).

54. Volkswagen of Am., Inc. v. Robertson, 713 F.2d 1151, 1163 (5th Cir. 1983).
55. Copeman Labs. Co. v. General Motors Corp., 36 F. Supp. 755, 762 (E.D. Mich. 1941).
56. England v. American Southern Ins. Co., 380 F.2d 137, 140 (4th Cir. 1967) (notice to agent not ascribable to principal unless "'in regard to matter coming within the sphere of the agent's duty'").
57. *E.g., In re* Parmalat Securities Litig., 659 F. Supp. 2d 504, 519–521 (S.D.N.Y. 2009).
58. American Nat'l Bank v. Miller, 229 U.S. 517 (1913); First Nat'l Bank v. Transamerica Ins. Co., 514 F.2d 981, 986 (8th Cir. 1975).
59. 1 W. Blackstone, Commentaries 476. *See Anonymous*, 88 Eng. Rep. 1518 (K.B. 1701).
60. Frederic P. Lee, *Corporate Criminal Liability*, 28 Colum. L. Rev. L. 4 (1928).
61. Richard A. Bierschbach & Alex Stein, *Overenforcement*, 93 Geo. L.J. 1743, 1771–72 (2005).
62. *See, e.g.,* Wilson Meeks, *Corporate and White-Collar Crime Enforcement: Should Regulation and Rehabilitation Spell an End to Corporate Criminal Liability?*, 40 Colum. J.L. & Soc. Probs. 77, 84 (2006).
63. *See, e.g.,* Federal Food, Drug and Cosmetic Act, 52 Stat. 1040, 21 U.S.C. 321(e) (1970); N.Y. Evntl. Conserv. Law § 3302 (24) (Supp. 1976 to 77).
64. State v. Security Bank, 2 S.D. 538, 51 N.W. 337 (1892).
65. United States v. John Kelso Co., 86 F. 304 (N.D. Cal. 1898).
66. People v. Sheffield Farms-Slawson-Decker Co., 225 N.Y. 25, 121 N.E. 474 (1918).
67. Korholz v. United States, 269 F.2d 897 (10th Cir. 1959), *cert. denied*, 361 U.S. 929 (1960) (the corporation, its president, and a union official were all convicted).
68. New Jersey Good Humor, Inc. v. Board of Comm'rs, 123 N.J.L. 21, 7 A.2d 824 (1939).
69. State v. People's Ice Co., 124 Minn. 307, 144 N.W. 962 (1914).
70. United States v. Armour & Co., 168 F.2d 342 (3d Cir. 1948).
71. United States v. General Motors Corp., 121 F.2d 376, 411 (7th Cir.), *cert. denied*, 314 U.S. 618 (1941).
72. 2 U.S.C. § 441b (1982).
73. *See* V.S. Khanna, *Corporate Criminal Liability: What Purpose Does It Serve?*, 109 Harv. L. Rev. 1477 (1996).
74. *E.g.,* State v. Zeta Chi Fraternity, 696 A.2d 530, 535 (N.H. 1997) (corporation held responsible even though it had expressly instructed agents not to engage in the prohibited acts).
75. *See, e.g.,* United States v. Sherpix, Inc., 512 F.2d 1361 (D.C. Cir. 1975).
76. *See, e.g.,* Pugh v. State, 536 So. 2d 99 (Ala. Crim. App. 1986).
77. *See, e.g.,* United States v. Gold, 743 F.2d 800 (11th Cir. 1984).
78. For an elegant and thorough review of the history of mens rea, *see* United States v. Cordoba-Hincapie, 825 F. Supp. 485, 489–96 (E.D.N.Y. 1993) (J. Weinstein).
79. 421 U.S. 658 (1975). The other Supreme Court decision, *United States v. Dotterweich*, 320 U.S. 277 (1943), is less important because its actual

holding was limited to whether individuals were included within the statutory proscription of "persons." Its contribution to the subject is that in reaching its conclusion that they are, the court held that defendants include those who had a "responsible share in the furtherance of the activity." *Dotterweich*, 320 U.S. at 284.

80. 421 U.S. at 666 n.9.

81. The fine for each violation (there were five in *Parks*) was $50. 421 U.S. at 666.

82. *See, e.g.,* United States v. MacDonald & Watson Waste Oil Co., 933 F.2d 35 (1st Cir. 1991) (responsible officer doctrine does not apply to felony prosecution involving specific intent). The environmental area is an area of intense efforts to apply the doctrine, with only limited success.

83. *See* Purcell v. United States, 1 F.3d 932, 936 (9th Cir. 1993).

84. *See e.g.,* State v. Kailua Auto Wreckers, 615 P.2d 730 (Hawai'i 1980) (spouse who was figurehead president deemed a responsible party for environmental violations).

CHAPTER 9

FUNCTIONS AND POWERS OF DIRECTORS

§ 9.1 THE TRADITIONAL PATTERN OF CORPORATE GOVERNANCE

The traditional corporate pattern is triangular, with the shareholders at the base. The shareholders, who are generally viewed as the ultimate or residual owners of the business, select the personnel at the next level—namely, the board of directors. According to accepted wisdom, the board of directors appoints the chief executive officer and other corporate officers, determines corporate policies, oversees the officers' work, and in general manages the corporation or supervises the management of its affairs. The directors' control of a corporation is limited by statutory requirements that shareholder approval be obtained for fundamental corporate acts such as charter amendments, consolidations, mergers, voluntary dissolution, and sale or lease of all or substantially all corporate assets.

The principal corporate officers, or executives, are at the top of the corporate triangle. These officers execute policies that supposedly have been fixed by the board of directors. The corporation's executives and operating management are said to derive their authority and legitimacy from the board.[1]

Directors are elected by shareholders. Election of directors traditionally has been by a plurality vote. However, in recent years, an increasing number of corporations are requiring a majority of affirmative votes to elect a director.[2] In 2006, Delaware amended its corporate law to allow a shareholder-adopted bylaw (not subject to repeal or amendment by the board) to proscribe the method of director selection.[3] Other states also permit majority election requirements. Directors customarily serve annual terms, though modern statutes permit staggered three-year terms.

In legal theory, the directors are supreme during their term of office. As will be examined later in this chapter, many modern statutes empower shareholders to remove directors at any time with or without cause[4] and, even in the absence of such a statute, removal power may be conferred on the shareholders by the corporation's charter or bylaws. The power of the removal is not the only mechanism for assuring accountability to the company's owners. Other forces at play here are the demands of product markets, reputational considerations, and changes in control either through a tender offer or proxy solicitation.

Majority rule is the traditional governing principle, and the holders of a majority of the voting shares certainly have the ultimate power to control the corporation.[5] The holders of a majority of the voting shares elect the directors, or most of them.[6] And as can be expected, the board of directors usually acts by majority vote of directors present and voting.

§ 9.2 CONTINUING EFFORTS TO STRENGTHEN THE MONITORING ROLE OF THE BOARD OF DIRECTORS

How and why corporate governance has evolved for the public corporation in the United States are best illustrated by the contrasting approaches in two leading decisions in Delaware. In a 1963 decision, the Delaware Supreme Court in *Graham v. Allis-Chalmers Manufacturing Co.*,[7] dismissed a derivative action against the directors of a large publicly held corporation that sought to recover from the directors losses the corporation suffered as a consequence of illegal price fixing by subordinates in one of the numerous divisions within the highly decentralized management structure of the large public corporation. The plaintiff argued the directors were remiss in not installing surveillance and compliance programs that would have prevented the antitrust violation. The court dismissed the action, reasoning that "absent cause for suspicion there is no duty upon the directors to install and operate a corporate system of espionage to ferret out wrongdoing which they have no reason to suspect exists."[8]

Ten years later, in *Stone v. Ritter*, the Delaware Supreme Court expressly approved the standard articulated by the Court of Chancery in an earlier decision.[9] Under Delaware law, directors incur personal liability for failing to discharge their oversight responsibilities if they utterly failed to implement any reporting information system or controls, or if they implemented a system but consciously failed to monitor or oversee its operations.

The contrasting approaches illustrate the movement from the view that the board of directors is a "super management" body that reviews and approves corporate strategies to today's widely held view that the board's essential function is to monitor the officer's stewardship. That movement did not occur without intense debate. It is a debate that continues to inform the expectations, and hence, demands placed upon the modern board of directors.

The heyday for calls for reform was the 1970s. Studies of the composition of boards and how directors discharged their tasks documented serious weaknesses in the operation of the board. Studies revealed that in most public corporations the executive officers carried out most of the functions that were commonly thought to be initiated by the board. Officers set the corporation's goals, develop plans for their achievement, allocate the company's resources, and make important policy decisions, including the selection of their successors and nominees to the board.

Between the 1960s and the mid-1980s, a tremendous change in the composition of the American boardroom occurred. Where in 1960 approximately 63 percent of the corporations could report that a majority of their directors were outsiders, by 1989 the percentage had climbed to 86 percent. More generally, the trend that began three decades ago has resulted in (1) boards of directors of publicly held corporations having a higher percentage of independent outside directors; (2) independent outside directors now serve on key committees and on some committees, for example audit and compensation committees, are a majority; (3) director fees have generally increased over time; (4) outside directors are devoting more time to corporate affairs; (5) there is evidence that outside directors are developing greater expertise in the work of the committees on which they serve; and (6) independent outside directors are more engaged in determining policy and monitoring the performance of executives.

Through most of the 1980s, the major forum, and even focal point, of debate on corporate governance was not the epic tales that were to be told in the heyday of takeover contests, but rather the American Law Institute's Corporate Governance Project. Historically, the ALI produced thoughtful restatements of the law whose black letter law and supporting commentary nurtured efforts for greater uniformity among the states, frequently recognizing that the better approaches were not those followed by a minority of the states. The project's reporters, led by Professor Mel Eisenberg, professed (1) to restate the law where judicial authority was deemed satisfactory under modern standards and (2) proffer recommendations where no judicial authority existed or where judicial decisions were unsatisfactory by modern standards.[10] This said, the project's critics believed there was too much reform, certainly in the early drafts of the Corporate Governance Project, so that throughout, the project was never seen as the more traditional restatement of the law. This caused it to become the most controversial of all ALI projects and, equally visible, to drop any reference to "restatement" from its title. But the primary theme that public corporations are to have independent directors who are to adhere to an active, monitoring model survived the more than decade-long assaults on the project. The membership of the American Law Institute approved the final draft in May 1992.

The overarching principle of the ALI is its recognition of the board of directors as a corporate organ that can and should perform a monitoring function, and among other things, to address potential overreaching by management, to replace management if it is not meeting established corporate goals, and to prevent the commission of illegal acts.[11] Significantly, the ALI project, in addition to calling for an independent audit committee, recommends that large public corporations also have nominating and compensation committees. The project also strengthens the role that independent directors are to play in policing conflicts of interest, usurpation of corporate opportunities, and the conduct of derivative suits.

Among the most recent trends among American boardrooms is the movement toward encouraging, and in some instances requiring, the outside director to have a substantial equity position in the corporation on whose board the director serves. The call is to reduce the customary perquisites enjoyed by the outside director, and particularly providing health and retirement benefits, and providing for the director to devote some of his director's fees to the purchase of shares in the company. The obvious objective is to more closely align the outside director with the firm's owners.[12] Another trend has been reexamining certain matters bearing directly on the commitment of outside directors to monitor management, as well as internal procedures that nurture a viable monitoring role. In 1996, a Blue Ribbon Commission suggested a number of practices for public corporations that would enhance the effectiveness of their outside directors.[13] Among the commission's recommendations were the call that directors not serve on more than six boards, that there be procedures for independent review of the CEO's and directors' effectiveness, that there be created a board governance committee, that an outside director be designated to chair the board, and that there be periodic executive sessions for outside directors.

Prior to 1992, the SEC's regulations for proxies stilled the voice of financial institutions.[14] By broadly defining proxies to include any communication that would encourage or discourage a holder in how to vote, and subjecting each such solicitation to nontrivial regulation, institutions faced excessive coordination costs with respect to not only pursuing common objectives, but also simply learning whether they indeed had common objectives or concerns with respect to their portfolio companies. Important steps were taken in 1992 by the SEC to facilitate the institutions in exercising their collective voice within the boardroom.[15] The SEC amended its rules, with the overall effect of reducing the restrictions on stockholder communication among themselves. For example, new Rule 14a-2(b)(1) exempts from the filing and format requirements communications by a person who is not seeking proxies and does not have certain specified types of "substantial interest" in the subject matter. Further, new Rule 14a-1(l)(2)(iv) permits holders to announce how they will vote on any matter. Under these rules, holders, and particularly financial institutions, can more easily coordinate their actions to maximize their influence at stockholders' meetings, because they no longer face costly and burdensome prefiling and format requirements.[16] In recent years, there has been a new push for shareholder access to the director nomination process.[17] In addition to permissive amendments to the Delaware statute, the SEC adopted rules permitting shareholder access to management's proxy statement for director nominations, but those rules have been put on hold pending litigation challenging the SEC's rulemaking.[18]

In the wake of growing concern about the prevalence of "earnings management," restatements of reported income, and massive accounting frauds by public companies, then-chairman of the SEC Arthur Levitt in 1998 called for "nothing less than a fundamental cultural change on the part of corporate management as well as the whole financial community."[19] Front and center in this reform initiative were changes that the SEC, with the aid of a Blue Ribbon Committee, brought about for audit committees of corporations listed on the NYSE, AMEX, and Nasdaq.

Informing the thrust of the changes for the audit committee was a 1999 study of companies charged by the SEC with financial fraud from 1987 to 1997, which found, among other factors, that 25 percent of the surveyed companies did not have an audit committee, that of those that did have audit committees nearly one-third of the committee members' independence was compromised by close relationship with, or actual participation in, the firm's management, and that 65 percent of the committee members lacked accounting or financial expertise. Though some of the recommendations of the Blue Ribbon Committee[20] were ultimately modified, most of its proposals were embraced by the financial community and are now part of the listing requirements of the NYSE, AMEX, and Nasdaq.[21]

The core considerations of each organization's listing requirements pertaining to audit committees are substantially identical: listed firms are to have an audit committee of three "independent" directors (in exceptional circumstances, one member may be non-independent); independence requires, among other features, that the member have not been an employee within three years or received (excluding board fees) compensation greater than $60,000 (the NYSE expresses this more generally in terms of a relationship that will impede independence); each member must be financially literate; one member must have financial sophistication, such as employment experience in finance or accounting; and the committee must have a written charter.[22]

The SEC's disclosure requirements reinforced the listing requirements for audit committees. The audit committee must disclose whether it has recommended to the board that the audited financial statements be included in the company's annual report on Form 10–K.[23] Moreover, the audit committee must acknowledge whether it has had discussions with management and the independent accountants, and whether those discussions were the basis for its recommendations regarding the inclusion of the financial reports.[24] The significance of this is it draws the audit committee members closer to the information contained in any included financial report, thus making it easier to establish they are primary participants with respect to any misrepresentation that may be committed in the financial statements. This may not be that significant a development since all directors must sign the Form 10–Q that is filed with the SEC, and at least one circuit has held this is sufficient to make each director a primary participant in any resulting suit under the antifraud provision.[25] A further disclosure requirement is that each proxy statement must disclose whether the company has an audit committee, and once every three years the proxy statement must disclose the responsibilities and duties of the audit committee as embodied in its charter.[26]

The most recent developments for corporate governance began with the collapse in the fall of 2001 of Enron Corporation, a company that was the sixth largest American corporation and that had been ranked the most innovative for five straight years by *Fortune 500* executives. Within a few weeks, its stock plummeted from a trading in the high $40s to being nearly worthless when it filed for bankruptcy in early November 2001. Enron's final achievement was its becoming the largest bankruptcy every filed; an honor it held only briefly, being dwarfed by the bankruptcy of WorldCom in 2002, another failure that was linked to serious financial fraud by senior executives.[27] Enron, WorldCom, and no fewer than a dozen other large public companies shocked the public conscience, not because they failed, but because of the revelations of extensive reporting frauds, overreaching, and wasteful misbehavior by their most senior executives. Certainly, there were multiple failures in the role of each company's outside directors, their certified public accountants, and others. The collapse of Enron et al. came when investors were witnessing a meltdown in market capitalization on Wall Street of approximately $4 trillion. The national mood was not to turn a blind eye to the problems of the American corporation.

The first wave of regulatory responses came from the New York Stock Exchange and Nasdaq, both of which strengthened their corporate governance requirements for listed companies by mandating at least a majority of the board be independent (this requirement does not apply to so-called controlled companies where there is a definite controlling stockholder). Not surprisingly, a central focus of their efforts was the audit committee. Both bodies require listed companies to have a majority of their board of directors to meet the new tightened standard for independence and that the audit committee must be comprised solely of independent directors. The nominating and compensation committees of NYSE listed companies must also be comprised only of independent directors. Nasdaq instead permits nominating committees to have one non-independent member (if disclosed) or nominations can instead be approved by a majority of the independent directors. The NYSE's new requirements provide that the board is to determine whether a director has a "material relationship" that would prevent a director from being independent; the NYSE does not further define specifically what such a relationship would be but asks that the board consider "all relevant facts and circumstances."[28] In 2008, the NYSE further amended its rules to allow for a director to qualify as independent so long as the director has not received compensation, excluding director fees, in excess of $120,000 during any 12-month period within the previous three years. These new independence rules also look to immediate family members of directors, who may not be involved with the company's auditing procedures or likewise have received compensation in excess of $120,000 during any 12-month period within the previous three years. Nasdaq also specifies that a director would not be independent if he or she, or a family member, received payments in excess of $120,000. Both the NYSE and Nasdaq further require that all non-management directors meet regularly in executive sessions. And, subject to certain limitations, shareholders must be allowed to vote on all equity-based compensation plans. Finally, the NYSE mandates that companies adopt corporate governance guidelines, and both the NYSE and Nasdaq require codes of conduct with prompt publication of any waiver of their requirements for senior executive officers. The NYSE requires the CEO to annually certify to the Exchange that the company complies with the governance provisions for listing. Nasdaq enters the field of conflict-of-interest transactions by requiring the audit committee to approve all related party transactions.

Congress too entered the fray, passing in July 2002 the far-reaching Sarbanes-Oxley Act, which, among other features, amended the Securities Act of 1933 and the Securities Exchange Act of 1934. In response to the common practice of auditors to provide substantial non-audit services to their audit clients, Section 10A of the Exchange Act was amended to bar auditors from providing certain non-audit services.[29] The amendments also seek to centralize the company-auditor relationship with the audit committee by requiring that all services provided by the auditor be approved by the audit committee, subject to a 5 percent de minimus exemption.[30] And, the auditor is required to make timely reports to the audit committee of all critical accounting policies, alternative treatments that have been discussed, and other material communications with management.[31] Issuers must disclose whether its audit committee has a "financial expert," thus putting pressure on companies to assure that at least one member of the audit committee meets this indirect requirement. Finally, audit partners are to rotate every five years,[32] thereby hopefully avoiding too cozy a relationship from forming between the issuer and the engagement partner. Sarbanes-Oxley also has extensive provisions for the audit committee, calling for the committee to be comprised totally of independent directors (meaning at least one can receive fees other than director fees from the corporation or otherwise be deemed an "affiliate") and the audit committee must establish a process for addressing complaints or reports of accounting irregularities.[33]

Perhaps the most radical step for Sarbanes-Oxley was its entering into an area that heretofore was exclusively the domain of the states. The Act amends section 13 of the Securities Exchange Act to bar reporting companies from making personal loans to directors or officers.[34] The initial issue posed by this bar is what impact it would have on a wide range of standard practices such as advancing relocation expenses, litigation expenses per state indemnification statutes, and stock option plans that envision cashless exercise by their holder.

The Act duplicated efforts already under way at the SEC by mandating the chief executive officer and the chief financial officer to certify that the periodic reports filed with the SEC (1) have been reviewed, (2) to the certifying officer's knowledge the report "does not contain any untrue statement of material fact," and (3) to the certifying officer's knowledge "the report fairly presents in all material respects the financial condition and results of operations of the issuer."[35] The sobering experience of periodically having to so attest may well introduce a bit of conservatism into the dynamics between senior management and the outside auditor that heretofore has been missing.

§ 9.3 CHANGES IN THE STATUTORY DESCRIPTION OF FUNCTIONS OF THE BOARD OF DIRECTORS

Representative of early statutory expressions of the board's power are the early versions of the Model Business Corporation Act that provided simply that "the business and affairs of a corporation shall be *managed* by a board of directors."[36] As discussed in the preceding section, boards as a practical matter do not manage the company's affairs; this is a task commended to its officers, even within the closely held corporation. To reflect this reality, in 1974 the Model Act's language was amended to provide that corporate power was exercised "by or under the authority" of the board and that the corporation's affairs would be managed "under the direction" of the board.[37] This is the pattern of most modern statutes. Hopefully, among the effects of the modern expression of the board's role is to dissuade courts from otherwise harboring the view that the board of directors is to involve itself in the day-to-day management of the corporation or imposing liability for failure to exercise close supervision over the firm's executives.

Another change in the expression of the board's power is the invitation for corporation's to deviate from the statutory norm of a centralized management. This invitation appears in conjunction with language that provides that corporate powers and management occur pursuant to the authority or direction of the board, "except as otherwise provided in the articles of incorporation."[38] The statute's broad invitation recognizes the validity of transferring to the shareholders (and likely a third party, such as a creditor) powers or authority customarily exercised by the board of directors. Because the exact scope of such a transfer has not been litigated, it remains to be seen whether a court might nonetheless impose important limits on the ability of the shareholders to transfer to themselves fundamental board powers. One potential area of conflict arises from the consistent practice of corporate statutes to require board approval as a condition to the stockholders considering certain transactions, such as the amendment of the articles, a merger, or a sale of substantially all the firm's assets.[39] Because the clear reading of the statute calls for board approval, not the approval of someone who has the authority to act for the board, there is a reasonable basis to doubt that a special provision in the articles of incorporation can change this part of the normative structure of the corporation.[40]

§ 9.4 AUTHORITY AND POWERS OF THE DIRECTORS

A corporation's board of directors is legally the supreme authority in matters of the corporation's regular business management. Most corporate statutes provide that the corporate business is managed by or under the direction of the board of directors.[41] The basic management function of directors, as traditionally defined, can be summarized as including: (1) setting the course of the enterprise by determining the company's general objectives, goals, and philosophies; (2) selecting the chief executive and senior officers and seeing that able young executives are developed; (3) determining executive compensation, pension, and retirement policies; (4) delegating to the chief executive and subordinate executives authority for administrative action; (5) providing advice, counsel, and assistance to corporate officers, (6) fixing policies relating to such matters as pricing, labor relations, expansion, and new products; (7) determining the dividend payments, financing, and capital changes; (8) monitoring the company's progress, exercising vigilance for its welfare, and taking appropriate action in light of its progress; (9) submitting for shareholder action proposals requiring their approval; and (10) creating adequate machinery for conducting the board's business.[42]

The board of directors has the power to select corporate officers and to determine their compensation.[43] Perhaps the single most important board function is choosing the company's chief executive officer. The board has authority to direct the use of the corporation's property in the operation of its business.[44] It can sell or otherwise dispose of corporate assets,[45] including real estate,[46] in the normal course of business.[47] The board has the power and responsibility to determine whether the financial condition of the company is such as to warrant the declaration and payment of dividends.[48] It can create and control a corporate pension plan;[49] apply the funds of the corporation to the payment of its debts and agree with creditors on an extension of debts;[50] authorize an assignment of all the corporation's property for the benefit of its creditors or the filing of a voluntary petition in bankruptcy;[51] determine whether the corporation will sue to rectify corporate injuries;[52] and waive the corporation's rights to attorney's fees.[53]

The board of directors, not the shareholders, has the original and supreme authority to make corporate contracts. Thus, the board can borrow money needed for corporate business, execute or authorize the execution of negotiable notes or bonds to secure borrowing, pledge or mortgage real or personal corporate property, secure debts lawfully contracted, enter a guaranty contract, enter leases, and execute compromise agreements.

The directors' authority generally is restricted to the management of the corporation's business affairs. Without shareholder approval, they cannot effect fundamental changes in the corporation's charter or organization or dissolve the corporation, since such actions do not relate to ordinary business.

There is one area—the making and amending of bylaws—where the board's power as directors, vis-à-vis the power of the shareholders, has increased in recent years. The power to make bylaws was traditionally with the shareholders as an incident of their ownership of the business.[54] On the other hand, virtually all current statutes grant the directors the power to adopt, amend, and repeal bylaws or provide a method by which they can be given such power, such as by appropriate provision in the articles of incorporation.[55]

Directors, as a practical matter, often have almost exclusive control over the corporation's issuance of additional stock. Shareholder approval is required to amend the corporation's charter to increase the kind or amount of stock authorized to be issued. Modern statutes do not require that all authorized stock be issued at once, and the widespread practice is to authorize in the original charter or by charter amendments large amounts of stock in excess of that expected to be issued in the near future.

§ 9.5　NECESSITY FOR BOARD ACTION IN A LAWFULLY CONVENED MEETING

The authority to manage the affairs of the corporation is vested in the directors not individually but as a board.[56] The traditional rule, as usually stated, is that directors cannot act individually to bind the corporation but must act as a board at a legally convened meeting. Directors who act collectively at an informal meeting are not considered to have acted at a duly convened meeting. As such, the action is not valid and must await a formal meeting of the board.[57] As will be seen, statutes frequently authorize important exceptions to this rule, and courts have upheld informal director approval where it is equitable to bend the requirements that the board act as a deliberative body.

Many cases have held that if directors act or give their consent separately or if they act at anything other than a legal meeting, their action is not that of the corporation, even though all may consent, and, in the absence of statute, ratification, or estoppel, the corporation is not bound.[58] These holdings proceed on the theory that the directors must meet and counsel with each other, and that any determination affecting the corporation shall only be arrived at after a consultation at a meeting of the board on notice to all and attended by at least a quorum of its members.[59] The shareholders are entitled to the directors' combined wisdom, knowledge, and business foresight, which give efficiency and safety to corporate management.

Modern technology has modified the concept of a board meeting. A number of corporation statutes now specifically provide that meetings of directors can be validly held by conference telephone or similar communications methods.[60] Even in the absence of statutory authorization, a meeting of this kind should be held to be a valid formal meeting, as the directors have full opportunity to consult and counsel with each other.

Courts in many instances have upheld the directors' approval, even though the directors' approval was not the product of a meeting convened in accordance with the statutes or bylaws. Considerable judicial support exists for the proposition that even in the absence of a statute, the separate consent of all the directors is sufficient to bind the corporation without a formal meeting as a board,[61] and some support exists for the proposition that consent of a majority of the board, although acting separately, will suffice.[62]

If the directors own all of a corporation's shares, a conveyance, mortgage, or contract authorized by them, although not assembled at a meeting, is valid.[63] Courts have repeatedly departed from the traditional rule in order to sustain action taken by owner-directors in family and close corporations.[64]

Waiver by Shareholders. The shareholders may waive the necessity of a board meeting and thereby authorize acts to be done by agents of the corporation or ratify acts already done and thus bind the corporation. Where, by acquiescence, the shareholders vest the executive officers with the powers of the directors as the usual method of doing business and the board is inactive, the acts of such officers, although not authorized by a vote of either shareholders or directors, generally will bind the corporation.[65]

Estoppel. A corporation may be estopped, as against an innocent third person, to deny the validity of a mortgage or other act done or authorized by the directors separately, or otherwise than at a legal meeting, by long acquiescence or voluntary receipt or retention of benefits with either actual or presumed knowledge.[66]

Ratification. Ratification by vote or acquiescence of the shareholders, on full disclosure of the circumstances, is generally held effective to validate irregular or voidable acts of the directors;[67] but not as to action that is void *ab initio*.[68] A few cases hold that the shareholders cannot ratify any irregular or invalid act of the board that they, as shareholders, could not authorize.[69] But even when an effective ratification does not take place, the corporation may be "estopped" by the receipt or retention of benefits to deny its liability.[70]

Single Shareholder Corporations. Many cases hold that where a single shareholder owns substantially all the shares of stock, she may bind the corporation by her acts without a resolution of the board of directors.[71] This is usually based on the ground of disregarding the separate corporate entity but may better be explained as a liberalized agency doctrine and a dispensing with the formalities of usual corporate procedure where they can serve no useful purpose.

§ 9.6 STATUTES AUTHORIZING INFORMAL BOARD ACTION

In many states, the corporation statutes now depart from the traditional requirement of formal board meetings and permit directors to act informally and without a meeting by signing a written consent.[72]

Under these statutes, *all* the directors must sign for the written consent to be effective. To some extent, the unanimity requirement "precludes the stifling of opposing argument"[73] in that a single director can force a meeting at which she will have an opportunity to reason with her colleagues. The written consent is effective when the last director executes her consent, unless a different date is specified.[74]

§ 9.7 THE NOTICE REQUIREMENT FOR BOARD MEETINGS

Subject to the exceptions noted in the preceding sections, directors must act as a board at a legal meeting, regular or special, at which a quorum is present. As a general proposition, all directors must be properly notified of board meetings.[75]

A distinction is made between regular and special meetings. Unless otherwise provided by statute, the charter, or bylaws, if the time and place of regular meetings of the board of directors are fixed in the corporation's charter or bylaws, by resolution of the board or by usage, such meetings may be held without additional notice.[76] It is common practice, however, to send a courtesy notice or reminder to the directors. The great weight of authority is that every director must be given notice of a special meeting of the board.[77] A special meeting held without due notice to all directors is illegal and, though a quorum may be present, action taken at such a meeting is invalid.[78]

Most current statutes provide that the bylaws may prescribe what shall constitute notice of a meeting of the board of directors.[79] Some jurisdictions specify what notice must be given in the absence of a bylaw provision. The bylaws customarily specify how many days in advance of a meeting notice must be given. In the absence of a bylaw authorizing other means of giving notice,[80] the notice of a directors' meeting must be a personal notice,[81] unless, by custom, notice by mail or otherwise is authorized[82] or unless some of the directors are absent and notice cannot be given to them except by mail or telegram.[83] The notice must be given a reasonable length of time before the hour or day fixed for the meeting.[84] Bylaws may also call for specificity regarding the nature of the business to be conducted.

In the absence of a contrary provision in the charter or bylaws, general notice of the time and place of a directors' meeting, even though it does not specify the business to be transacted, is sufficient, at least to authorize the transaction of the corporation's ordinary business affairs.[85] Many corporation statutes broadly state that neither the business to be transacted at a meeting of the board, whether regular or special, nor the purpose of the meeting need be specified in the notice unless required by the bylaws, thus apparently eliminating any necessity of reference even to extraordinary business to be transacted at a meeting.[86] In the absence of such broad statutory permission, it is doubtful that extraordinary business may be transacted if not specified in the notice.[87]

If a director has notice of a meeting and fails to attend, he waives his rights.[88] A director has constructive notice when he purposely refuses to accept a registered letter giving notice of the meeting.[89] Similarly, a director may waive notice by signing a written waiver of notice before the meeting. A waiver of notice by an absent director, subsequent to a meeting, has been held invalid by some courts[90] and valid by others.[91]

§ 9.8 DIRECTORS' MEETINGS: PLACE, CALL, QUORUM, VOTES, DISQUALIFICATION BY INTEREST

The time and place of board meetings are usually fixed by the bylaws or by procedures set up therein; however, if no provision on these matters is included in the bylaws, the board of directors may determine the time and place.[92] Most current corporation statutes provide that directors may hold both regular and special board meetings outside the state of incorporation.[93]

A majority of the entire board of directors constitutes a quorum[94] for the purpose of transacting business, unless a greater or lesser number is required by statute, the corporation's charter, or its bylaws.[95] The quorum remains the same even though vacancies occur on the board.[96]

Unless authorized by statute, charter, or bylaw, less than a majority of the full number of directors cannot meet and bind the corporation by any act or resolution.[97] All they can do is adjourn.[98] Action at a meeting of directors that was invalid because of the absence of a quorum may be subsequently ratified at a legal directors' meeting or by the shareholders, at least if they could have authorized the action in the first instance.[99]

The attending directors must be personally present and act for themselves. Votes at a directors' meeting cannot be by proxy unless that privilege is conferred by charter or bylaw provision.[100] Although the rule is not settled in most jurisdictions, a meeting at which a quorum is initially present should be able to continue to transact business, notwithstanding the withdrawal of directors, at least if any action taken is approved by a majority of the required quorum for the meeting.

Modern corporation statutes typically provide that a majority of the number of directors fixed in the bylaws or otherwise will constitute a quorum and that the act of a majority of the directors present at a meeting at which a quorum is present shall be the act of the board. Nevertheless, the statutes permit charter provisions requiring a higher quorum or a greater vote or, more liberally, permit such provisions in either charter or bylaws[101] or, even more liberally, in the charter, bylaws, or a shareholder's agreement.[102] Some statutes permit the quorum to be fixed by charter or bylaw provision at *less* than a majority of the entire board but not less than one-third.[103]

§ 9.9   THE VIRTUAL BOARD: MELDING ELECTRONIC MEDIA TO THE CONDUCT OF BOARD MEETINGS

As seen earlier, all states permit a director to participate telephonically in a meeting of the board; this permission is generally conditioned upon prior consent on the part of the corporation, such as authorization in its bylaws, and, furthermore, that each director present, physically or telephonically, be able to hear and speak with each of the other participating directors. As breathtaking as this development was many years ago, it now appears primitive compared with the steps a majority of the states have recently taken to incorporate new communication technologies into their corporate governance procedures. Not surprisingly, the trend to expressly embrace new electronic media began with California's 1995 amendment of its Corporations Code to permit notice of board meetings to be given via "electronic mail or other electronic means"[104] and further provided that members of the board could participate in meetings through "electronic video screen communication, or other communications equipment" so long as each member is able to communicate with all others "concurrently." Without such technical reference, the more general, traditional statutory authorization for remote participation so long as each participating director can "hear each other during the meeting"[105] certainly reaches all imaginable media that transmits the directors' voices. The California-like statute broadens the range of permissible communications to written, not voice, transmissions, provided the technology used meets the requirement that they occur concurrently. Nevertheless, a minority of statutes authorize director participation via "a conference telephone or *similar* communications equipment."[106] These jurisdictions risk an unduly narrow and rigid construction of state statutes that incorporate the language when the medium used is not telephone based, such as a webcast. It was this concern that prompted Delaware in 2000 to amend its statute to substitute "other" for "similar" when referencing the range of "communications equipment" that could be used.[107]

§ 9.10 THE POWER OF SHAREHOLDERS TO CONTROL THE ACTS OF DIRECTORS

Directors are not the servants of a majority of the shareholders. One of the basic advantages of the corporate form of doing business, found also in unincorporated joint stock companies and business trusts, is that the collective interests of the owners (shareholders) are represented by the centralized management of a board of directors. The directors control and supervise the conduct of the business. Individual shareholders generally have little direct voice in determining the corporation's business policies.

Each shareholder has a right to have the corporation's affairs managed by its board of directors. This right is derived from the statute under which the corporation is organized and from the corporation's charter and bylaws. Statutory, charter, and bylaw provisions for management by the directors are viewed as part of a control among the shareholders. Consequently, a majority of the shareholders cannot deprive the minority of their right to the directors' judgment and discretion.

The shareholders' participation in a corporate decision is usually "in the form of an assent, request, or recommendation."[108] Traditionally, they have only limited powers of initiative. Even fundamental corporate action that requires a favorable shareholder vote, such as a charter amendment, merger, consolidation, voluntary dissolution, or sale of substantially all corporate assets other than in the usual course of business is, in practice, usually initiated by the directors, and, in any case, reaches the stockholders *only after* approval by the board of directors. Indeed, most statutes expressly require board approval of such action before submission to the shareholders.[109] The shareholders may act as a ratifying or approving body and thereby validate an unauthorized act or voidable corporate contract.[110] It thus would be wrong to conclude that shareholders have no capacity to act affirmatively to change corporate policies or practices. Shareholders may also be able to voice their views on matters that cannot act on directly. For example, Although the shareholders, by endorsing the administration of the old president, would not be able directly to effect a change in officers, they were entitled to express themselves and thus alert the directors who would stand for election at the next annual meeting.[111]

Though the primacy of the board of directors is well recognized, there continues to be uncertainty regarding the ability of the stockholders to tailor governance procedures for the corporation to enhance their voice or participation, or even to qualify the otherwise unconditional authority of the board. The source of this uncertainty is the uneasy fit of two standard provisions of corporate statutes. First is the broad grant of authority to the board of directors to manage or direct the corporation's affairs, except as may be otherwise provided in the statute or the articles of incorporation.[112] Second, statutes authorize bylaws not inconsistent with law or the articles of incorporation, and empower the stockholders to adopt, amend and repeal the bylaws.[113]

Just how much restraint can a shareholder-adopted bylaw impose on the broad command that the affairs of the corporation are to be managed by or under the direction of the board of directors? Should the qualification on the board's authority found in the statutory reference to "except as otherwise provided in this statute" incorporate limitations that can be imposed by the bylaws? Professor Lawrence Hamermesh argues that the exception refers only to statutory provisions that deal specifically with the allocation of power between stockholders and the board of directors, such as provisions requiring stockholder approval of mergers or the authority of court appointed trustees or custodians; more generally, he advises the corporate statute must be interpreted in light of the contemporary view of the strong board with limited involvement by the stockholders in the conduct of company affairs.[114] On the other hand, Professor John Coffee argues that stockholders can through their amendment of the bylaws introduce significant, albeit reasonable, departures from the traditional model of the board primacy.[115]

Not surprisingly, this issue has surfaced in the context of management's steps to prevent a takeover, a subject in which managers frequently are not of the same mind as the company's stockholders. In one case, *International Brotherhood of Teamsters General Fund v. Fleming Companies*,[116] the shareholders proposed a bylaw which would restrict the board of directors from implementing a rights plan (poison pill) that would impede a hostile takeover of the firm. The Oklahoma Supreme Court upheld the shareholders' power to propose the restriction on the directors, reasoning that a rights plan is similar to stock option plans whose approval or content are appropriate for shareholder action. If the court's analogy to the stockholders' power with respect to stock options is not central to its decision, then *Fleming*'s holding is even more profound. *Sans* the analogy to options, there would appear to be few limits upon the stockholders' power to adopt bylaws that either limit the discretionary authority of the board of directors or, as was part of the proposed bylaw in *Fleming*, mandate that the board pursue a specific course of action (in *Fleming*, to redeem the outstanding rights).

A court favoring a strong board can easily and quite reasonably reach a result different from that arrived at in the Oklahoma decision, as was the case in a more recent Delaware case, *CA, Inc. v. AFSCME Employees Pension Plan*.[117] The Delaware Supreme Court addressed the distinction between shareholder proposed bylaws that mandate specific board action and those that are process oriented. Nevertheless, the Court struck down the bylaw because, as drafted, it would cause the board to violate its fiduciary duties under Delaware law.[118]

Effective as of August 2009, the Delaware codified the court's holding in *CA, Inc.* allowing shareholder bylaws for reimbursement for proxy expenses in connection with electing directors.[119] However, to avoid the problems of the shareholders' in *CA, Inc.*, the statute lists appropriate situations where reimbursement may be required, though the list is not inclusive.

A further question is whether the stockholders can provide that the bylaw they have adopted cannot be amended or repealed by the board. This is directly answered in the Model Act, which allows the adopting shareholder to place a bylaw beyond the reach of the board of directors.[120] The cases suggest that such a limitation would not be valid when a provision of the articles of incorporation confers broad authority on the board with respect to the bylaws.[121]

An equally uncharted area in which stockholders may presume to act arises when the articles of incorporation expressly authorize action by the stockholders in areas that historically were the exclusive domain of the board of directors. Most corporate statutes provide that "subject to any provision in the articles of incorporation" to the contrary, corporate powers are to be exercised exclusively by or under the authority of the board of directors.[122] It would appear that such statutes expressly authorize the corporate charter to carve out areas in which the board's powers would be shared or assumed by the stockholders. Certainly, on the reasoning that a corporation is a nexus of contractual relationships, such an extraordinary provision in the corporation's charter should be enforced in a manner consistent with the intentions of its drafters; doubly so if the provision is being enforced against conspiring third parties.

§ 9.11 BOARD VACANCIES

A vacancy on the board can arise through the resignation, death, or removal of a director. Newly authorized directorships not yet filled are customarily considered creating a "vacancy" on the board. A few corporate statutes specify what constitutes a vacancy, and all states have provisions dealing with how any vacancy is to be filled.[123]

In broad overview, all states variously authorize either the shareholders or the board to fill vacancies on the board.[124] Obviously, once either of these bodies has acted to fill a vacancy the vacancy no longer exists and, hence, there no longer is authority for the other body to appoint someone to fill the formerly vacant seat. When a vacancy arises, there can be a question regarding what constitutes a quorum for the board. The first step in addressing this question is the language of the quorum requirement; if it does not set a specific number for a quorum, does it specify a certain percentage of the "authorized" or the number "in office"? The Utah court provided an expedient answer to the quorum issue in resolving the validity of board action taken by a vote of three to one after the articles had been amended expanding the board from four to seven, but before the three new directorships had been filled. The quorum requirement was a majority of the directors. The court held that the unfilled directorships were not to be counted in determining a quorum.[125] This question is directly dealt with in the great majority of the state statutes because they expressly authorize the majority of the directors to fill a vacancy, even though they are less than a quorum.[126] Those states following the Model Business Corporation Act restrict the board's authority to act by a vote of a majority of its remaining members to instances in which "the directors remaining in office constitute fewer than a quorum."[127] The Model Act's provision is consistent with the holding in *Tomlinson v. Loew's Inc.*[128] arising from a proxy contest for control of MGM. One provision of the company's bylaws provided that the board could act only through a majority vote at a meeting with a quorum present; another bylaw provision provided directors in office could fill a vacancy "although less than a quorum." The court held the latter provision applied only when it was not possible to convene a quorum; it accordingly held that the new directors appointed at a meeting without a quorum were not validly selected since it was under the circumstances possible to convene a quorum.[129] Thus, two of three remaining directors acted properly to fill a vacancy on the five-person board pursuant to a bylaw provision authoring "directors in office" to appoint a "successor or successors," even though the articles of incorporation and bylaws had a general provision requiring 75 percent of the directors to be present for a quorum.[130]

§ 9.12 REMOVAL OF DIRECTORS BY SHAREHOLDERS

Shareholders have the inherent power to remove a director for cause, even in the absence of a statute or a clause in the corporation's charter or bylaws providing for such a removal.[131] Even though a shareholders' agreement provides that a particular director shall be maintained in office, the shareholders usually may remove the director for cause, because the agreement is subject to an implied condition that the director faithfully perform the duties of the office.[132] The inherent right of the shareholders to remove a director for cause, however, can only be exercised by shareholders controlling a majority of the votes or, if the corporation's charter requires a higher vote for shareholder action, such number greater than a majority as is provided in the charter.[133]

A proceeding to remove a director for cause need not be conducted with the same formality as a judicial proceeding, but the accused director must be served with the specific charges, be given adequate notice, and be afforded full opportunity to meet the accusations.[134] In a publicly held corporation, where only a fraction of the shareholders attend meetings in person, an accused director must be afforded an opportunity to communicate with the shareholders. In a leading Delaware case,[135] the chancellor provided a fair hearing by requiring that the accused directors be given an opportunity, at the corporation's expense, to present their defense to the shareholders in the form of a statement that would "accompany or precede the initial solicitation of the proxies seeking authority to vote for the removal of such director for cause."

Whether cause exists for the removal of a director or directors is subject to judicial review.[136] As a general proposition, a director must be guilty of some abuse of trust or malfeasance or nonfeasance in office to justify dismissal. Thus, a director's disagreement with shareholders on corporate policy or a mistake by a director is not grounds for dismissal.[137] A desire to take over control of the corporation or failure to cooperate with the president has been held insufficient cause for director removal.[138] On the other hand, improper withdrawal of funds and payment of salaries, commissions, and management fees have been held to constitute an abuse of trust and thus cause for dismissal.[139] Other improprieties that have been held to constitute sufficient cause include a director's allowing the payment of rebates contrary to the board's orders[140] and a director organizing a competing company or accepting employment with a competing company.[141]

In the absence of a controlling statute or valid charter or bylaw provision, courts have generally held that the shareholders do not have the power to remove a director without cause; consequently, a director who is serving the corporation faithfully is privileged to continue in office until the end of the term despite the opposition of a majority of the shareholders.[142] In some states, until recently, the corporation's statute's silence had left this common law rule unchanged.[143] In most states, clear statutory or judicial support exists for the use of a charter or bylaw provision for removal without cause, and such provisions are common.

A large number of corporation statutes now specifically grant power to a majority of the shareholders to remove directors without cause or specifically authorize charter or bylaw provisions granting such power.[144] The Model Business Corporation Act, for example, states in part that "[t]he shareholders may remove one or more directors with or without cause unless the articles of incorporation provide that directors may be removed only for cause."[145] Under a statute of this kind, "the right of removal hinges not upon the propriety of a director's conduct but upon the bare question of whether the shareholders desire to retain him as a representative on the board for whatever reason."[146]

In a corporation with a number of classes of shares, with each class electing a specified number of directors, the issue may arise as to whether directors elected by a particular class of stock can be removed by a vote of the shareholders generally or only by a vote of holders of the class of shares that elected the directors. The better view is that shareholders of a specific class should have exclusive power to remove the directors whom they elect,1 although the case law bearing on this point is sparse.[147] Many corporation statutes now specifically protect directors elected by a particular class of shares under a system of class voting against removal by the votes of holders of other classes of shares.[148]

Cumulative voting rights also need protection against shareholder removal of directors elected by minority shareholders. To permit majority shareholders to remove, without cause, the directors elected by minority shareholders under cumulative voting would obviously be unfair to the minority. Most modern statutes empowering shareholders to remove directors contain a clause designed to protect cumulative voting rights.[149] A surprising decision held that the articles of incorporation and bylaws could not provide a greater vote to remove a director than the two-thirds vote set forth in the state statute.[150]

A novel question is whether removal without cause is inconsistent with a provision of the articles of incorporation that calls for directors to serve staggered three-year terms. The Delaware Chancery Court held that a bylaw provision providing for removal without cause was invalid in the face of the articles mandating staggered director terms, reasoning that otherwise the bylaws would frustrate the purpose sought by having the directors serve three-year terms.[151] The decision quite likely would have gone the other way if the authority to remove the directors without cause had been included in the articles of incorporation rather than in the bylaws.

§ 9.13 REMOVAL OF DIRECTORS BY ACTION OF THE BOARD OF DIRECTORS

In the absence of authorization by statute or charter or bylaw, the directors do not have the power to remove one of their members even for cause.[152] Charter and bylaw provisions empowering a board of directors to remove a director for cause probably are valid in most states under statutes broadly authorizing optional charter and special bylaw provisions. A few statutes specify that a charter or bylaw provision adopted by the shareholders may empower the board of directors to remove a director for cause.[153]

§ 9.14 JUDICIAL REMOVAL OF DIRECTORS

Modern court decisions are fairly consistent in holding that, absent statutory authorization, there is no judicial power to remove legally elected directors, even on a showing of directors' dishonesty or inability to perform their duties.[154] These holdings are in stark contrast to the result reached during the early formative period of corporate law, when courts were willing to invoke their well-established equity powers to remove trustees for substantial cause, such as misappropriation, long continued absence, and antagonism of interest.

The language of Section 8.09 of the Model Act illustrates the high threshold for misbehavior required for a director's removal by the court:

> (a) The [name of the court] . . . may remove a director . . . if the court finds that (1) the director engaged in fraudulent or dishonest conduct, or gross abuse of authority or discretion, with respect to the corporation and (2) removal is in the best interest of the corporation.

In 2009, Delaware amended its corporate laws to permit judicial removal of directors, but the process is even more restrictive than the approach proffered in the Model Act.[155] If a director is convicted of a felony or is

shown to have breached the duty of loyalty, either the corporation or the
shareholders via a derivative suit may apply to the Chancery Court for
removal. Upon review, the court may only order removal "if the Court
determines that the director or directors did not act in good faith in performing the acts resulting in the prior conviction or judgment and judicial removal is necessary to avoid irreparable harm to the corporation."[156]

The showing required in either circumstance is set high in recognition of the primacy of stockholder suffrage rights that elected the director
to office. The exercise of stockholders' voting power should not easily be
undone by a court.[157] At the same time, access to a court is an important
safety valve in those instances in which traditional internal governance
procedures cannot reasonably be expected to protect the corporation or
its stockholders from the ongoing misbehavior by a director.

§ 9.15 Committees of the Board of Directors

Boards of directors of publicly held corporations have long used committees to structure their control and supervision of corporate operations.
The committee system permits a board to operate more effectively and
expeditiously. Committees can study assigned problems in much greater
depth than is possible for the full board;[158] they can develop and utilize
specialized knowledge and experience; and they can provide a sharper
and more intensive focus on particular business issues and activities.[159]
Indeed, the boards of the large, publicly held corporations could not
function effectively without committees.

Committees also permit governance of the firm to be improved by
parceling out responsibilities among directors in ways that more closely
address concerns for good corporate practices.[160] The ALI's Principles
of Corporate Governance strongest recommendation in this area is that
state statutes should include a provision requiring that "large publicly
held corporations"[161] should have an audit committee of at least three
disinterested members.[162] All the other ALI provisions concerned with
the board's structure and its committees are mild suggestions directed
exclusively to corporations and their counselors, not to courts and
legislatures. The recommendations in this regard are not normative,
so non-compliance is not the basis of liability. For example, the ALI
recommends that a majority of the board of directors of large publicly
held corporations not have a significant financial relationship to the

company's senior executives,[163] and other publicly held corporations should have at least three disinterested directors.[164] An audit committee[165] and a nominating committee[166] are each recommended for all public corporations, and a compensation committee is recommended for large publicly held corporations.[167]

Executive Committee. Historically, the "executive committee"[168] has been the most important and the most widely prevalent committee. The bylaws of most publicly held corporations provide for an executive committee and define its powers, usually in broad and general terms. The bylaws or board resolution setting up an executive committee typically vests the committee with "the powers of the board" or "the full powers of the board." The Model Business Corporation Act limits the authority executive committees can exercise, for example, executive committees cannot fill vacancies in the board and cannot amend either the articles of incorporation or bylaws.[169]

Executive committees once were expected to act only between meetings of the board. The present practice in many corporations is for the executive committee not only to act between meetings of the full board but also to review, before presentation to the full board, virtually all matters going before the board for action, including major policy decisions and long-range planning.

Almost invariably, executive committees are controlled by a small number of key "inside" (management) directors. A typical executive committee, for example, might be composed of the chief executive officer, one or two inside directors, and an outside director.[170] There is little doubt that the use of an executive committee composed entirely or largely of management directors raises a serious question regarding the role of the full board of directors. However, a broadly empowered executive committee composed of entirely inside directors is not necessarily inconsistent with the outside directors serving an aggressive monitoring role of management's stewardship. In such a context, one needs to bear in mind that there is a difference between management and monitoring, and in the public corporation it is the latter role that is commended to outside directors. That role does not require that outside directors be involved in the formulation and execution of corporate decisions. One must, however, be concerned that an executive committee not be the tool to exclude directors representing minority interests from real participation in board decisions.[171]

Executive committees have often been aggressive in exercising powers allegedly granted them. Occasionally, they have even tried to usurp the powers of the full board. Courts have usually condemned such attempts to seize complete control of a corporation and exclude the other directors from their management powers.[172]

Audit Committee. The role of the audit committee has long been an evolving one. There has long been considerable divergence of opinion on what the duties and objectives of such a committee are or should be; these differences continue today.[173] It has been observed that "[t]he primary purpose and function of the Audit Committee, as originally conceived and, in most cases, as currently intended, is limited to providing an opportunity for direct communication with the Board of Directors by the corporation's independent auditors, thereby tending to strengthen their independence and objectivity."[174]

Compensation Committee. The compensation committee is becoming increasingly common. It approves or recommends to the full board compensation arrangements for the company's senior management and any compensation plans in which the directors or officers are eligible to participate.[175] The compensation committee should be composed exclusively of non-management directors to assure an impartial and independent judgment on the fairness of management compensation.[176] In 1992, the SEC amended the reporting requirements for public corporations so that today a graphic representation of the senior executives' total compensation must be matched against data tracking the company's overall financial performance. The obvious impact of the disclosure rules is to heighten the directors' sense of obligation when establishing executive compensation. An unintended consequence of the new disclosure is to introduce to executive compensation a phenomenon previously enjoyed only in Lake Wobegon, a mythical community where everyone is above average. An observed consequence of the 1992 disclosures is more-rapid ratcheting upward of the executives' compensation, lest they be below the median for their industry.[177] Nevertheless, in the years that followed, the SEC has continued to focus on increased and more detailed disclosure concerning executive compensation.[178] The Dodd-Frank Wall Street Reform Act of 2010 addressed shareholders' say on pay by including a requirement that management solicit proxies for non-binding shareholder vote on a resolution seeking shareholder approval of Named Executive Officer (NEO) compensation.[179] These "say-on-pay" shareholder votes must take place on a regular basis—every one, two or three years as determined by a shareholder vote.[180]

Nominating Committee. The nominating committee or, more rarely, the "committee on succession," has greater potential for improving corporate governance. This committee selects, or recommends to the full board, candidates for election to the board. The committee's responsibility should include passing on the performance of incumbent directors and determining whether they should be retained. In some corporations, the nominating committee recommends to the full board the membership of board committees and, even more importantly, the choice of successor to top management posts. The nominating committee might also develop and submit to the full board for approval the criteria for board membership. While a minority view holds that a corporation's chief executive officer should be a member of the nominating committee, the better view, and the one gaining increasing acceptance, is that the committee should be composed exclusively of independent, non-management directors. The benefits of assuring the nominating committee's independence from its CEO has strong empirical support.

§ 9.16 LIMITATIONS ON DELEGATION OF BOARD POWERS TO COMMITTEES

Under both common law and statutes, as well as under charter or bylaw provisions, questions arise as to the extent to which the board of directors can delegate its powers to a committee. Does the power to delegate extend to delegation of acts requiring the exercise of judgment and discretion? Is this power limited to delegating authority to act in ordinary business transactions? Or does it extend to important decisions, such as approving a merger and recommending it to the shareholders, adopting a pension or profit-sharing plan, declaring dividends, selecting the company's principal executive officers, fixing the officers' compensation, removing officers, and amending the bylaws?[181]

Some of the earlier cases held that the board could delegate "ministerial" duties to a committee but could not grant authority to a committee to determine matters involving high judgment or discretion or to inaugurate reversals of or departures from fundamental corporate policies.[182] Most modern statutes first state that a committee of the board "shall have and may exercise all the authority of the board" to the extent provided in a resolution of the board or in the corporation's charter or bylaws, but then carve out exceptions by specifying extraordinary acts that cannot be delegated.[183] Many statutes do not permit delegation to a committee of the power to act on fundamental corporate changes, such as approving a charter amendment, adopting a plan of merger or consolidation, recommending to the shareholders the sale, lease, or other disposition of all or substantially all of the corporation's assets, or recommending a voluntary dissolution. Other nondelegable duties in a substantial number of states include filling vacancies on the board or board committees, electing or removing officers, altering resolutions of the full board, declaring dividends or distributing corporate assets, and issuing or retiring shares of stock.[184]

§ 9.17 RESPONSIBILITY OF NONCOMMITTEE DIRECTORS FOR COMMITTEE ACTIONS

Directors can delegate power to act, but they cannot shed responsibility for oversight and supervision.[185] They cannot abdicate their responsibilities by delegation of authority and thereby immunize themselves from liability. Delegation of the entire supervision and control of a corporation to an executive committee has been held to be inconsistent with the duty imposed on directors by statute or corporate charter to manage the corporation's business and affairs or to supervise that management.[186] As a matter of good corporate practice, there should be formal action by the full board on all matters of major or fundamental corporate policy.[187]

Most corporation statutes contain provisions designed to emphasize the board's continuing duty of supervision and consequent responsibility in the important areas of corporate activity. Some statutes specify that the board may designate authority to committees, but only to the extent that such delegation is consistent with the duties of the board generally.[188] Nevertheless, when action by the full board of directors is taken in a matter after a report or recommendation by a committee, the directors may rely on the committee unless there is reason to believe such reliance would be misplaced.[189] Similarly, directors are not under an affirmative duty to investigate the activities or decisions of a committee unless the circumstances are such that a reasonable person would believe investigation was warranted.

§ 9.18 MANAGEMENT AGREEMENTS AND OTHER CORPORATE CONTRACTS DELEGATING CONTROL

Corporations sometimes execute agreements entrusting management or control over certain aspects of corporate operation to a creditor or to some other individual or corporation. In a management agreement,[190] the corporation is one of the principal contracting parties, and by agreement the corporation *itself* undertakes to vest its management in the other contracting party. The difference between an internal arrangement delegating authority to a committee, or some of the corporation's officers,[191] and a management agreement is that the former is always subject to the supervision and overriding power of the board of directors, which usually can modify or terminate the authority of a committee or an officer at any time, while a management agreement does not leave ultimate power in the board.

The decisions indicate that in general a management contract may be subject to attack on two grounds: (1) violation of a statute providing that the affairs of a corporation shall be managed by its board of directors;[192] and (2) the directors, in view of their limited term of office, do not have the capacity to enter into long-term contracts on basic policy or management matters binding future boards for long or indefinite periods.[193] Insofar as a challenge to a management contract is based on the first ground, the authorities dealing with the supposed conflict between shareholders' agreements and the statutory norm conferring management powers on directors appear to be equally applicable to management contracts.[194]

The validity of a contract by which a corporation vests control of its affairs in another person or entity seems to depend on the relative quantity of the powers that are delegated, on the length of time for which the powers are to be held,[195] and perhaps on the purpose of the contract or the situation out of which it arises. Simply stated, when the board's authority is relatively unfettered to withdraw from the arrangement and substitute its judgment for that of the third party, the delegation it can validly make is much greater than the powers it can cede to another when its ability to withdraw from the arrangement is significantly restricted.[196] To illustrate this, consider *Grimes v. Donald*,[197] which provided that the chief executive officer would, among other benefits, be paid $20 million and receive handsome retirement benefits, if he should conclude there was "unreasonable interference" by the board of his management of the company. The Delaware Supreme Court held as a matter of law the contract was not void on the ground it constituted an impermissible abdication of the board's power over the company's affairs. The court reasoned that the sum payable to the executive was not so significant, given the size of the company, that its payment would preclude the board from exercising its responsibilities for overseeing the firm's affairs. The court further reasoned that judgments regarding the extent the board can restrict its future freedom are ones best commended to the business judgment of the board. In contrast, contracts delegating substantially all management powers to outsiders for indefinite or extended periods of time are usually held invalid. Thus, a contract between two insurance companies that gave one the "underwriting and executive management" of the other for a period of 20 years was struck down.[198] From the terms of the agreement and the length of time it was to remain in effect, the court concluded that "not only managerial powers were delegated, but the entire policy" of one company was to be fixed and determined by the other.[199] Similarly, an agreement by a corporation giving the purchaser of some of its five-year convertible bonds the power to designate a comptroller for the corporation and providing that the comptroller would have complete charge of all finances of the company and that no expenditures should be made or authorized without his prior approval was declared against public policy and unenforceable.[200] On the other hand, corporations have been permitted to delegate to outsiders at least for a limited period some of the functions usually performed by its directors and officers. For instance, an agreement employing an executive for a period of five years and giving him the position of editor and manager of a large daily newspaper, with power to determine editorial policy, has been held to be permissible.[201] A management contract will be upheld where authorized by a separate provision of the state's general corporation law.[202]

NOTES

1. The powers of officers and agents are discussed in Chapter 8.
2. CAL. CORP. CODE § 708.5 (permitting public companies to adopt a bylaw provision requiring majority election of directors); 8 DEL. C. § 216 (same).
3. 8 DEL. C. § 216.
4. *See, e.g.*, MODEL BUS. CORP. ACT. § 8.08 (1984) [hereinafter MBCA].
   Accord, MODEL BUS. CORP. ACT § 39 (1969) [hereinafter Former MBCA].

5. In many publicly held corporations, however, shares are so widely distributed, perhaps with no person holding or controlling over a fraction of 1 percent of shares outstanding, that the shareholders cannot organize into effective political or decision-making units. The consequence is that real control is severed from ownership, and the chief executive officer or a group of the corporation's principal executives actually control the corporation.

6. *See* MBCA §§ 7.21, 8.03 (1984).

7. 188 A.2d 125 (Del. 1963).

8. *Id.* at 130. *See In re* Caremark International Inc. Derivative Litigation, 698 A.2d 959 (Del. Ch. 1996).

9. 911 A.2d 362 (Del. 2006). In that derivative action, the court found that the directors were not personally liability for the failure of bank employees to file suspicious activity reports. The court observed that it is very difficult to establish director liability premised on employee failures in the absence of "red flags."

10. *See* James S. Mofsky & Robert D. Rubin, *Introduction: A Symposium on the ALI Corporate Governance Project*, 37 U. MIAMI L. REV. 169, 170 (1983).

11. ALI, CORPORATE GOVERNANCE PROJECT, § 3.02 dictates the following:

> (a) The board of directors of a publicly held corporation [§ 1.31] should perform the following functions:
>
> (1) Select, regularly evaluate, fix the compensation of, and, where appropriate, replace the principal senior executives [§ 1.30];
>
> (2) Oversee the conduct of the corporation's business to evaluate whether the business is being properly managed;
>
> (3) Review and, where appropriate, approve the corporation's financial objectives and major corporate plans and actions;
>
> (4) Review and, where appropriate, approve major changes in, and determinations of other major questions of choice respecting, the appropriate auditing and accounting principles and practices to be used in the preparation of the corporation's financial statements;
>
> (5) Perform such other functions as are prescribed by law, or assigned to the board under a standard of the corporation [§ 1.36].

Comparable specifications for the board of directors are embraced in ABA COMMITTEE ON CORPORATE LAWS, CORPORATE DIRECTOR'S GUIDEBOOK 3–5 (3d ed. 2001), reprinted in 56 BUS. LAW. 1571, 1578–80 (2001).

12. *See* REPORT OF THE NATIONAL ASSOCIATION OF CORPORATE DIRECTORS BLUE RIBBON COMMISSION ON DIRECTOR COMPENSATION 12 (1995).

13. *See* REPORT OF THE NACD BLUE RIBBON COMMISSION ON DIRECTOR PROFESSIONALISM (1996).

14. *See* Bernard Black, *Shareholder Passivity Reexamined*, 89 MICH. L. REV. 520 (1990).

15. *See* SECURITIES EXCHANGE ACT Release No. 34-31326 (Oct. 16, 1992).

16. However, their communication remains a "proxy solicitation" that is subject to Rule 14a-9's prohibition against material omissions or misstatements in a proxy solicitation.

17. *See, e.g.,* CA, Inc. v. AFSCME Employees Pension Plan, 953 A.2d 227 (Del. 2008) (a shareholder proposal relating to procedures regarding director elections was a proper matter for shareholder consideration but not mandating reimbursement of proxy expenses was not proper). As of 2009, the Delaware statute expressly permits bylaws giving shareholders access and also bylaws to provide for reimbursement of expenses incurred by shareholders (when soliciting proxies to in an election of directors). DEL. CODE ANN. tit. 8, §§ 112, 113.

18. *See Facilitating Shareholder Director Nominations,* SEC. ACT Rel. No. 33-9136, SEC. EXCH. ACT Rel. No. 34-62764, INV. Co. ACT Rel. No. IC-29384, 2010 WL 3343532 (SEC Aug. 25, 2010), SEC. ACT Rel. No. 33-9149, SEC. EXCH. ACT Rel. No. 34-63031, INV. Co. ACT Rel. No. IC-29456 (SEC Oct. 4, 2010) (order granting stay).

19. Arthur Levitt, Chairman, SEC, *Address to the NYU Center for Law and Business* (Sept. 28, 1998), quoted in Edward Brodsky, *New Rules for Audit Committees and Quarterly Statements,* 223 N.Y. L.J. 3 (April 12, 2000).

20. *See Report and Recommendations of the Blue Ribbon Committee on Improving the Effectiveness of Corporate Audit Committees,* reprinted in 54 BUS. LAW. 1067 (1999).

21. The SEC's actions occurred on two fronts. First, it approved amendments to the listing requirements adopted by the NYSE, AMEX, and Nasdaq to embrace the reforms for audit committees. *See* SEC Release No. 34-42231 (Dec. 1, 1999). Second, it amended its own disclosure requirements for Regulation S-K. *See* SEC Release No. 34-422266 (Dec. 14, 1999).

22. The charter must, among other matters, specify the scope of the committee's responsibilities, the outside auditor's responsibilities to the board and the audit committee, and the audit committee's responsibility in the selection and oversight of the auditor.

23. *See* Item 306(a)(4) of Regulation S-K, 17 C.F.R. § 228.306(a)(4) (2009).

24. 17 C.F.R. § 228.306(a)(4) (2009). This acknowledgment and recommendation are to include the printed names of each member of the audit committee.

25. *See* Howard v. Everex Sys. Inc., 228 F.3d 1057 (9th Cir. 2000).

26. *See* Regulation Rule 14a-101(e)(ii) & (iii), 17 C.F.R. § 240.14a-101(e)(ii) & (iii) (2002).

27. For discussions of Enron and the causes of its collapse, *see, e.g.,* William Bratton, *Enron and the Dark Side of Shareholder Value,* 76 TULANE L. REV. 1275 (2002); John C. Coffee, Jr., *Understanding Enron: "It's About Gatekeepers, Stupid,"* 57 BUS. LAW. 1403 (2002).

28. The NYSE does provide for a five-year cooling-off period, and Nasdaq has a three-year period in the case of former employees before they can be deemed independent.

29. 15 U.S.C. § 78j-1(g) (2009).

30. *Id.* § 78j-1(i).

31. *Id.* § 78j-1(k).
32. *Id.* § 78j-1(j).
33. *Id.* § 78j-1(m).
34. *Id.* § 78m(k).
35. *Id.* §§ 78n & 78(d).
36. *See* Former MBCA § 33 (1950) & (1960) (emphasis added).
37. *See* MODEL BUSINESS CORPORATION ACT ANN. § 8.01 (3d ed. 1994).
38. *See, e.g.*, MICH. COMP. STAT. ANN. § 450.1501 (West 1990); DEL. CODE ANN. tit. 8, § 141(a) (2001) ("except as may be otherwise provide in this chapter or in its certificate of incorporation").
39. *See, e.g.*, DEL. CODE ANN. tit. 8, § 271 (2001); MBCA § 12.02 (1984).
40. In *Jackson v. Turnbull*, 1994 WL 693503, *aff'd*, 653 A.2d 306, the court held the board of directors violated section 251(b) of the Delaware General Corporation Law by delegating to a third party the responsibility for determining the price at which a merger was to occur.
41. Many states have varied this formula by permitting restrictions on board authority in the articles or elsewhere. *E.g.*, Former MBCA § 35 (1969, as amended). *Accord*, MBCA § 8.01 (1984).
42. Express authorization for the board of directors to take designated action of various kinds can be found in scattered sections of the Model Business Corporation Act and other corporation statutes.
43. MBCA §§ 8.40, 8.44 (1984).
44. Continental Sec. Co. v. Belmont, 99 N.E. 138 (N.Y. 1912).
45. Hayes v. Johnson, 299 So. 2d 566 (La. Ct. App. 1974) (articles of incorporation granted power to board).
46. Jeppi v. Brockman Holding Co., 206 P.2d 847 (Cal. 1949).
47. Most jurisdictions have statutes requiring shareholder approval for a sale or other disposition of all or substantially all of a corporation's assets other than in the regular course of business. *E.g.*, N.Y. BUS. CORP. LAW § 909 (McKinney 1986); MBCA § 12.01 (1984).
48. Liebman v. Auto Strop Co., 150 N.E. 505 (N.Y. 1926).
49. Delany v. St. Louis Union Trust Co., 518 S.W.2d 704, 708 (Mo. Ct. App. 1974).
50. Puma v. Marriott, 283 A.2d 693 (Del. Ch. 1971).
51. Royal Indem. Co. v. American Bond & Mortg. Co., 289 U.S. 165 (1933).
52. Burks v. Lasker, 441 U.S. 471 (1979).
53. Tasby v. Estes, 416 F. Supp. 644 (N.D. Tex. 1976).
54. Rogers v. Hill, 289 U.S. 582, 588–89 (1933); North Milwaukee Town-Site Co., No. 2 v. Bishop, 79 N.W. 785 (Wis. 1899).
55. *See, e.g.*, Former MBCA § 25 (2001). *But see* MBCA §§ 22.06, 10.20 (1984) (shareholder may freely amend bylaws even if adopted by board).
56. *See, e.g.*, American Bank & Trust Co. v. Freeman, 560 S.W.2d 444 (Tex. Civ. App. 1977) (individual director without authorization from the board cannot bind corporation on a promise to secure plaintiff's election to the board). However, liability for misfeasance falls on the directors individually and not on the board as a separate entity. *See, e.g.*, Flarey v. Youngstown Osteopathic Hosp., 783 N.E.2d 582 (Ohio Ct. App. 2002) (holding that

the board of directors is not a separate entity capable of suing or being sued and "members of the board are liable in their individual, but not their collective, capacity").

57. *See* Fogel v. United States Energy Systems, 2008 WL 151857 (Del. Ch. 2008) ("When a corporate action is void, it is invalid *ab initio* and cannot be ratified later").

58. *See, e.g.,* Hotaling v. Hotaling, 224 P. 455 (Cal. 1924).

59. *In re* Rye Psychiatric Hosp. Ctr. v. Schoenholtz, 476 N.Y.S.2d 339 (App. Div. 1984).

60. *See, e.g.,* Cal. Corp. Code § 307(a), (b) (West Supp. 2001); MBCA § 8.20 (1984).

61. National State Bank v. Sandford Fork & Tool Co., 60 N.E. 699 (Ind. 1901).

62. Forrest City Box Co. v. Barney, 14 F.2d 590 (8th Cir. 1926); Holy Cross Gold Mining & Milling Co. v. Goodwin, 223 P. 58 (Colo. 1924).

63. Jordan v. Collins, 18 So. 137 (Ala. 1895).

64. *See, e.g.,* Haff v. Long Island Fuel Corp., 251 N.Y.S. 67, 71 (App. Div. 1931).

65. Galbraith v. First Nat'l Bank, 221 F. 386 (8th Cir. 1915); Cunningham v. German Ins. Bank, 101 F. 977 (6th Cir. 1900); Lahnston v. Second Chance Ranch Co., 968 P.2d 32 (Wyo. 1998).

66. Wood Estate Co. v. Chanslor, 286 P. 1001 (Cal. 1930).

67. Morisette v. Howard, 63 P. 756 (Kan. 1901); Myhre v. Myhre, 554 P.2d 276, 282 (Mont. 1976).

68. *See* Fogel v. United States Energy Systems, 2008 WL 151857 (Del. Ch. 2008).

69. Curtin v. Salmon River Hydraulic Gold-Mining & Ditch Co., 62 P. 552, 555 (Cal. 1900).

70. New Blue Point Mining Co. v. Weissbein, 244 P. 325 (Cal. 1926).

71. Wenban Estate, Inc. v. Hewlett, 227 P. 723 (Cal. 1924), noted in 13 Cal. L. Rev. 235 (1925).

72. *See, e.g.,* Del. Code Ann. tit. 8, § 141(f) (2001).

73. 1 Former MBCA Ann. § 44, Comment ¶ 2 (2d ed. 1971).

74. Herskowitz v. Pilot House Motor Inns, Inc., 806 S.W.2d 531 (Tenn. Ct. App. 1990).

75. *See* Rare Earth, Inc. v. Hoorelbeke, 401 F. Supp. 26 (S.D.N.Y. 1975).

76. White v. Penelas Mining Co., 105 F.2d 726 (9th Cir. 1939). Many statutes expressly authorize regular meetings of the board to be held without notice if the bylaws or the board of directors fix the time and place of such meetings. *See, e.g.,* Cal. Corp. Code § 307(a)(2) (West Supp. 2001).

77. Rare Earth, Inc. v. Hoorelbeke, 401 F. Supp. 26, 32 (S.D.N.Y. 1975) (Michigan law); Schroder v. Scotten, Dillon Co., 299 A.2d 431 (Del. Ch. 1972); MBCA § 8.22 (1984).

78. *See* Whitman v. Fuqua, 549 F. Supp. 315 (W.D. Pa. 1982) (meeting called without notice and purpose given was without authority in law and any action taken was invalid or *ultra vires*).

79. *E.g.,* N.Y. Bus. Corp. Law § 711(b) (McKinney 1986); MBCA § 8.22 (1984).

80. *See, e.g.,* Johnson v. Busby, 278 F. Supp. 235 (N.D. Ga. 1967) (by telephone).

81. Harding v. Vandewater, 40 Cal. 77 (1870).

82. Stockton Combined Harvester & Agric. Works v. Houser, 41 P. 809 (Cal. 1895).
83. Chase v. Tuttle, 12 A. 874 (Conn. 1888).
84. Hayes v. Canada, Atlantic & Plant S.S. Co., 181 F. 289 (1st Cir. 1910).
85. *In re* Argus Co., 34 N.E. 388 (N.Y. 1893).
86. *E.g.*, N.Y. Bus. Corp. Law § 711(b) (McKinney 1986); 2 MBCA Ann. § 8.22 (3d ed. 1994).
87. *See* Mercantile Library Hall Co. v. Pittsburgh Library Ass'n, 33 A. 744 (Pa. 1896). Especially where a notice states that the meeting is called for a particular purpose or for ordinary business, extraordinary business outside of such purpose cannot be transacted unless all the directors are present. Fay v. Charles Michel & Sons, 147 N.Y.L.J. 15 (Sup. Ct. 1962).
88. Potter v. Patee, 493 S.W.2d 58, 64 (Mo. Ct. App. 1973); Avien, Inc. v. Weiss, 269 N.Y.S.2d 836 (Sup. Ct. 1966). *See* Holcombe v. Trenton White City Co., 82 A. 618, 624 (N.J. Ch. 1912), *aff'd mem.*, 91 A. 1069 (N.J. 1913).
89. Schroder v. Scotten, Dillon Co., 299 A.2d 431 (Del. Ch. 1972).
90. United States v. Interstate R.R., 14 F.2d 328 (W.D. Va. 1926).
91. Stafford Springs St. Ry. v. Middle River Mfg. Co., 66 A. 775 (Conn. 1907).
92. Bylaws typically specify that regular board meetings be held on a specified day each month. *See, e.g.*, MBCA § 8.20 (1984).
93. *Id.*
94. The term "quorum" refers to the number of members of a body that, when properly assembled, is legally competent to transact business. *See* Model Bus. Corp. Act § 8.24.
95. *In re* Webster Loose Leaf Filing Co., 240 F. 779, 784 (D.N.J. 1916).
96. Currie v. Matson, 33 F. Supp. 454, 456–57 (W.D. La. 1940).
97. *In re* Rye Psychiatric Hosp. Ctr. v. Schoenholtz, 476 N.Y.S.2d 339 (App. Div.), *appeal dismissed*, 480 N.Y.S.2d 206, 469 N.E.2d 527 (Ct. App. 1984).
98. A meeting without notice or a quorum is invalid. Rare Earth, Inc. v. Hoorelbeke, 401 F. Supp. 26, 31–32 (S.D.N.Y. 1975).
99. Michelson v. Duncan, 407 A.2d 211, 219 (Del. 1979).
100. Perry v. Tuscaloosa Cotton-Seed Oil-Mill Co., 9 So. 217, 219 (Ala. 1891).
101. *E.g.*, MBCA § 8.24 (1984).
102. *See* 1 O'Neal & Thompson, O'Neal's Close Corporations Law and Practice § 1.14.
103. *E.g.*, Del. Code Ann. tit. 8, § 141(b) (2001).
104. Cal. Corp. Code § 307(a)(2) (West Supp. 2001). California further amended the statute in 2004, replacing the 1995 language and permitting notice "by electronic transmission by the corporation." Cal. Corp. Code § 307(2) (West Supp. 2009).
105. *See, e.g.*, Colo. Rev. Stat. § 7-108-201(2) (2000).
106. *See, e.g.*, Alaska Stat. § 10.06.475 (Michie 2009).
107. *See* Del. Code Ann. tit. 8 § 141(i) (2001).
108. Continental Sec. Co. v. Belmont, 99 N.E. 138, 141 (N.Y. 1912).
109. *See, e.g.*, MBCA § 10.03 (1984).
110. *See, e.g.*, Goldboss v. Reimann, 55 F. Supp. 811, 819 (S.D.N.Y. 1943), *aff'd mem.*, 143 F.2d 594 (2d Cir. 1944).

111. *See* Auer v. Dressel, 118 N.E.2d 590 (N.Y. 1954). The corporation's charter provided for 11 directors; the class A shareholders elected nine, and the common shareholders elected two. The directors removed and replaced the corporation's president. A majority of the class A shareholders were displeased with that action and duly invoked a bylaw that imposed a duty on the president to call a meeting when requested in writing by holders of a majority of shares entitled to vote. Among the objectives for the meeting were: (1) to adopt a resolution endorsing the administration of the old president and demanding that he be reinstated; (2) to consider a proposal to amend the charter and bylaws to provide that vacancies in the board of directors caused by shareholder removal of a director or by resignation of a director against whom charges had been proffered, could be filled with the unexpired term only by the shareholders of the class represented by the director; and (3) to hear charges proffered against four of the directors, vote on their removal, and select successors if needed. The court held that all of the reasons advanced were proper purposes for holding a shareholder meeting.

112. *See, e.g.,* DEL. CODE ANN. tit. 8, § 141(a) (2009); N.Y. BUS. CORP. LAW § 701 (McKinney 2009); MBCA § 8.02(b) (1984).

113. *See, e.g.,* DEL. CODE ANN. tit. 8, § 109(a), (b) (2009); N.Y. BUS. CORP. LAW § 601 (McKinney 1986); MBCA § 10.20 (1984).

114. Lawrence A. Hamermesh, *Corporate Democracy and Stockholder-Adopted By-Laws: Taking Back the Street?*, 73 TULANE L. REV. 409, 431 & 452 (1998).

115. John C. Coffee, Jr., *The Bylaw Battlefield: Can Institutions Change the Outcome of Corporate Control Contests?*, 51 U. MIAMI L. REV. 605, 608 (1997). Professor Coffee believes bright-line tests for legitimacy could be based on consideration whether the bylaw involved ordinary versus fundamental issues, constituted affirmative or negative instructions to the board, deals with procedural or substantive matters, and can be seen as related to corporate governance or business decisions. *Id.* at 613–14. For a reply to these categories, *see* Hamermesh, *supra* note 114, at 433–42.

116. 975 P.2d 907 (Okla. 1999).

117. 953 A.2d 227 (Del. 2008).

118. *Id.*

119. DEL. CODE ANN. tit. 8 § 113 (2009).

120. *See* MBCA § 10.20(a) (1984).

121. *See, e.g.,* Centaur Partners, IV v. National Intergroup, Inc., 582 A.2d 923, 929 (Del. 1990).

122. *See, e.g.,* DEL. GEN. CORP. L. tit. 8 § 141(a) (2009).

123. *See, e.g.,* Grossman v. Liberty Leasing Co., 295 A.2d 749 (Del. Ch. 1972) (relying in part on the legislature having eliminated any statutory distinctions among types of vacancies, the court upheld the power of the board to fill a seat that had not, in response to a recommendation by the board of directors, been filled for two years by the shareholders).

124. *See, e.g.,* CONN. BUS. CORP. ACT § 33-744 (West 1997); IDAHO CODE § 30-1-810 (1999); OR. REV. STAT. § 60-331 (2001); & VA. CODE § 13.1-682 (2009).

125. *See* Rocket Mining Corp. v. Gill, 483 P.2d 897 (Utah 1971).

126. *See, e.g.,* DEL. CODE ANN. tit. 8, § 223 (2009).

127. *See* MBCA § 8.10(a)(3) (1984).
128. 134 A.2d 518 (1957).
129. But, when a statute expressly authorizes a majority of the remaining directors to fill a vacancy, then action to fill vacancies by two of three remaining directors of a board of five under statutes such as the Model Act provisions that expressly provide for a vacancy to be filled by a majority of the directors even though less than a quorum. *See* Avien, Inc. v. Weiss, 269 N.Y.S.2d 836 (Sup. Ct. 1966).
130. *See* Jacobson v. Moskowitz, 261 N.E.2d 613 (N.Y. 1970).
131. Pardue v. Citizens Bank & Trust Co., 247 So. 2d 368 (Ala. 1971).
132. *See* Springut v. Don & Bob Restaurants of Am., Inc., 394 N.Y.S.2d 971 (App. Div. 1977). The question of whether a corporation's shareholders can by appropriate charter or bylaw provision deprive themselves of their inherent power to remove directors for cause was left open in *Campbell v. Loew's, Inc.*, 134 A.2d 852, 858 (Del. Ch. 1957).
133. *See Springut*, 394 N.Y.S.2d 971.
134. Schirmer v. Bear, 672 N.E.2d 1171 (Ill. 1996).
135. *Campbell*, 134 A.2d at 861–62, noted in 71 Harv. L. Rev. 1154 (1958).
136. *See, e.g.,* Grace v. Grace Inst., 226 N.E.2d 531 (N.Y. 1967) (court reluctant to interfere with judgment for or against removal of those running charitable corporation when evidence exists to support each judgment).
137. *See* Abreu v. Unica Ind. Sales, Inc., 586 N.E.2d 661 (Ill. App. Ct. 1991) (dealing with cause for removal by a court).
138. *Campbell*, 134 A.2d at 860–61.
139. People v. Singer, 85 N.Y.S.2d 727 (Sup. Ct. 1949) (action by attorney general).
140. Koppitz-Melchers, Inc. v. Koppitz, 24 N.W.2d 220 (Mich. 1946).
141. Eckhaus v. Ma, 635 F. Supp. 873 (S.D.N.Y. 1986).
142. *E.g.,* Toledo Traction, Light & Power Co. v. Smith, 205 F. 643 (N.D. Ohio 1913).
143. An earlier Illinois corporation statute, for example, did not contain a provision for removing directors without cause. *But see* 805 Ill. Comp. Stat. Ann. § 5/8.35 (1993).
144. *See, e.g.,* Del. Code Ann. tit. 8, § 141(k) (2009) (permitting removal with or without cause unless provided otherwise in the articles of incorporation).
145. MBCA § 8.08(a) (1984). *Accord,* Former MBCA § 39 (1969).
146. Former MBCA Ann. § 39, Comment ¶ 2 (2d ed. 1971).
147. *See* Murray v. Conseco, Inc., 795 N.E.2d 454 (Ind. 2003) (a director elected by a specific "voting group" may only removed by that group).
148. Cal. Corp. Code § 303(a)(2) (West 1990) (removal without cause); Del. Code Ann. tit. 8, § 141(k) (2009) (removal without cause); Mont. Code Ann. § 35-1-424(2) (1993); N.Y. Bus. Corp. Law § 706(c)(2) (McKinney 1986) (removal with or without cause); N.D. Cent. Code § 10-19.1-41(3) (2009) (with or without cause); Ohio Rev. Code Ann. § 1701.58 (West 2009); Former MBCA § 39 (1969) (query whether statute covers removal with cause); MBCA § 8.08 (1984) (with or without cause). The Delaware statute, which seemingly shields directors only against removal without

cause, leaves directors elected by a particular class vulnerable to being charged with misconduct and tried by a different and perhaps less friendly forum than the shareholders who elected them. *See* DEL. CODE ANN. tit. 8, § 141(k) (2009).

149. *See, e.g.*, CAL. CORP. CODE § 303(a)(1) (West 1990); DEL. CODE ANN. tit. 8, § 141(k)(2) (2009); N.Y. BUS. CORP. LAW § 706(c)(1) (McKinney 1986).

150. *See* Georgia-Pacific Corp. v. Great Northern Nekoosa Corp., 731 F. Supp. 38 (D. Me. 1990) (citing commentary to Maine statute that "if shareholders have acquired sufficient votes to command a two-thirds majority, they should be able to put in their own board of directors, as a matter of right."). The decision may well be understood as guided by its circumstances, a battle for control, and the court wishing to preserve as best it could a level playing field among the combatants. In *Smith v. Orange & Rockland Utilities, Inc.*, 617 N.Y.S.2d 278 (Sup. Ct. 1994), the court, though critical of the bylaws' imposition of an 80 percent vote requirement to remove a director, nevertheless permitted the polls to remain open (even after closing the voting on two other agenda items) until the next meeting of the stockholders so that additional votes could be obtain to remove the director.

151. Essential Enter. Corp. v. Automatic Steel Prods., Inc., 159 A.2d 288 (Del. Ch. 1960).

152. Dillon v. Berg, 326 F. Supp. 1214, 1225 (D. Del.), *aff'd per curiam on other grounds*, 453 F.2d 876 (3d Cir. 1971).

153. *See, e.g.*, N.J. STAT. ANN. § 14A:6-6(3) (Supp. 2000); N.Y. BUS. CORP. LAW § 706(a) (McKinney 1986) (except when there is cumulative voting).

154. Ross Sys. Corp. v. Ross, No. Civ. A. 10378, 1993 WL 49778 (Del. Ch. 1993); Harkey v. Mobley, 552 S.W.2d 79 (Mo. Ct. App. 1977).

155. DEL. CODE ANN. tit. 8, § 225(c) (2009).

156. *Id.*

157. *See, e.g.*, Tarin v. Pellonari, 625 N.E.2d 739 (Ill. App. Ct. 1993) (among the statutory conditions is proof of "fraudulent conduct" which requires more than proof of self dealing and must be established by clear and convincing evidence).

158. *See, e.g.*, Gaillard v. Natomas Co., 256 Cal. Rptr. 702 (Cal. Ct. App. 1989) (use of committees is intended to enhance level of scrutiny).

159. *See The Role and Composition of the Board of Directors of the Large Publicly Owned Corporation: Statement of the Business Roundtable*, reprinted in 33 BUS. LAW. 2083, 2109 (1978).

160. The Securities and Exchange Commission, the national stock exchanges, and various persons and organizations concerned with improving corporate governance have tried to enhance the ability and inclination of corporate boards to monitor management performance. One recommendation that has gained wide support is that boards of publicly held corporations appoint a committee composed entirely or largely of independent outside directors to deal with issues in which disinterested oversight is especially important.

161. The ALI defines this term to mean a corporation having 2000 shareholders and $100 million in assets. ALI, PRINCIPLES OF CORPORATE GOVERNANCE ANALYSIS AND RECOMMENDATIONS 1.24 (1992).

162. *Id.* § 3.05. A director is disinterested if the director has not been employed by the company during the preceding two years and has no significant relationship with the company's senior executives.
163. *Id.* § 3A.01(a).
164. *Id.* § 3A.01(b).
165. *Id.* § 3A.02.
166. *Id.* § 3A.04.
167. *Id.* § 3A.05.
168. *See generally* Nancy F. Halliday, Note, *Corporation Executive Committees*, 16 CLEV.–MAR. L. REV. 167 (1967).
169. MBCA § 8.25(e).
170. *See* Avery S. Cohen, *The Outside Director—Selection, Responsibilities, and Contributions to the Public Corporation*, 34 WASH. & LEE L. REV. 837, 854 (1997) (recommending that "executive committees draw a majority of their membership from among the outside directors, to serve the same function, in essence, as is served by those directors on the board as a whole.").
171. This is achieved by reaching decisions at the committee level and then formally convening the full board to summarily approve the committee's recommendations.
172. *E.g.*, Robinson v. Benbow, 298 F. 561, 570 (4th Cir. 1924).
173. Functions often performed by an audit committee include:

    1. employing the company's independent auditors or making recommendations to the full board on such employment;
    2. reviewing the engagement of the independent auditors, including the scope and timing of the audit and the auditors fee;
    3. consulting with the company's independent auditors on the plan of audit;
    4. reviewing with the independent auditors the results of the audit;
    5. inquiring into the corporation's financial practices and the adequacy of internal controls; and
    6. consulting with the independent auditors, out of the presence of the management, on the adequacy of internal controls and, if need be, consulting with internal auditors.

    Sound advice appears in the calls for the audit committee to be more proactive with respect to the firm's financial reporting. For example, the leading authority on the liability of accountants, envisions an important protective function by the audit committee that includes (1) establishing the right kind of financial reporting environment, (2) assuring that the financial reporting system is physically capable of delivering accurate reports on a timely basis, and (3) assure a system of information flows so that the committee is abreast of financial developments within the firm. *See* Michael R. Young, *What Is an Audit Committee to Do*, 222 N.Y. L.J. 1 (Dec. 16, 1999). *See generally* ACCOUNTING IRREGULARITIES AND FINANCIAL FRAUD (M.R. Young ed. 1999).

174. *The Overview Committee of the Board of Directors: A Report by the Committee on Corporate Laws*, 34 BUS. LAW. 1837, 1861 (1979).

175. "Its chief function is to monitor compensation arrangements with a view to insuring that the corporation is attracting and retaining highly qualified management through competitive salary and benefit programs and by encouraging extraordinary effort through incentive rewards." The Overview Committee of the Board of Directors, *A Report by the Committee on Corporate Laws*, 34 Bus. Law. 1837, 1848 (1979). *See, e.g., In re* Walt Disney Co. Derivative Litig., 906 A.2d 27 (Del. 2006) (rejecting shareholders' claim that committee breached fiduciary duty of care in approving compensation and severance package for corporate president without informing themselves of full magnitude of potential payout).

176. One court has held that it is inappropriate to grant the committee members' motion for summary judgment to a challenge to golden parachutes approved by the committee's independent members. Gaillard v. Natomas Co., 256 Cal. Rptr. 702 (Cal. Ct. App. 1989) (the possibility of facts removing the committee's decision from the business judgment rule's protection was present because the golden parachutes were initiated and approved after management had approved the merger).

177. *See* Randall S. Thomas & Kenneth J. Martin, *The Effect of Shareholder Proposals on Executive Compensation*, 67 CINN. L. REV. 1021 (1999).

178. *See, e.g.*, Regulation S-K Item 402, 17 C.F.R. § 229.402 (2009).

179. DODD-FRANK WALL STREET REFORM AND CONSUMER PROTECTION ACT § 951, Pub. Law 111-203, H.R. 4173 (111th Cong. 2d sess. 2010), adding 1934 Act § 14A(a), 15 U.S.C.A. § 78n-1(a).

180. *Id.* At least every six years, the company's annual proxy statement must include a separate shareholder resolution to determine how frequently the "say-on-pay" votes will occur. In addition, if a company solicits a shareholder vote or consent on a business combination, the company must disclose (1) any agreements or understandings that the soliciting person has with any NEO of the issuer concerning any compensation that is based on or otherwise relates to the transaction being voted on, (2) the aggregate total of all compensation that may be paid or payable to that officer and the conditions under which it may be paid or payable, and (3) a separate nonbinding shareholder vote to approve any such agreements, understandings and compensation, unless the agreements or understandings were subject to an earlier nonbinding say-on-pay vote.

181. *See In re* Walt Disney Co. Derivative Litig., 906 A.2d 27 (Del. 2006) (committee may set executive compensation, since nothing in Delaware law mandates that entire board must make compensation decisions).

182. *E.g.*, Fensterer v. Pressure Lighting Co., 149 N.Y.S. 49, 53 (City Ct. 1914).

183. *E.g.*, MBCA § 8.25 (1984); DEL. CODE ANN. tit. 8, § 141(c) (2009); N.Y. BUS. CORP. LAW § 712(a) (McKinney 2009).

184. For example, the MBCA provides that board committees do *not* have the authority to:

  (1) authorize or approve distributions, except according to a formula or method, or within limits, prescribed by the board of directors;

  (2) approve or propose to shareholders action that the act requires to be approved by shareholders;

(3) fill vacancies on the board of directors or on any of its committees; or (4) adopt, amend, or repeal bylaws.

MBCA § 8.25(e). *Compare, e.g.,* Del. Code Ann. tit. 8 § 141(c)(2) (2009):

> [N]o such committee shall have the power or authority in reference to the following matters: (i) approving or adopting or recommending to the stockholders, any action or matter expressly required by this chapter to be submitted to stockholders for approval or (ii) adopting, amending or repealing any bylaw of the corporation

185. *See* De Met's Inc. v. Insull, 122 F.2d 755 (7th Cir. 1941), *cert. denied,* 315 U.S. 806 (1942).
186. *See* Williams v. McKay, 18 A. 824 (N.J. Ch. 1889).
187. The Securities and Exchange Commission has indicated that the board of directors should not leave the major corporate decisions solely to an executive committee. *See Report of Sterling Homex Corp. Investigation,* [1975–1976 Transfer Binder] Fed. Sec. L. Rep. (CCH) ¶ 80,219 (1975).
188. *See, e.g.,* Ga. Code Ann. § 14-2-825(e) (West 2009); N.Y. Bus. Corp. Law § 712(c) (McKinney 2009).
189. *See* MBCA § 8.30; 1 ALI, Principles of Corporate Governance: Analysis and Recommendations § 4.03 (1994).
190. If a contract attempts to vest the entire management of the corporation or even substantial management powers in another corporation or an individual, especially if a substantial fee is to be paid for these management services, the contract is usually referred to as a "management agreement." A common example of this relationship is found in investment companies (e.g., mutual funds), where the investment management is contracted out to investment advisors.
191. *See, e.g.,* Schoonejongen v. Curtiss-Wright Corp., 143 F.3d 120 (3d Cir. 1998) (upholding delegation to an officer of retirement plan matters, including amendments thereto).
192. Marvin v. Solventol Chem. Prods., Inc., 298 N.W. 782 (Mich. 1941); Long Park, Inc. v. Trenton–New Brunswick Theatres Co., 77 N.E.2d 633 (N.Y. 1948).
193. *See* General Paint Corp. v. Kramer, 57 F.2d 698 (10th Cir. 1932).
194. *See, e.g.,* Walton Motor Sales, Inc. v. Ross, 736 F.2d 1449 (11th Cir. 1984) (upholding shareholders agreement conferring significant management powers upon a creditor).
195. *See* McKinney v. Gannett Co., 817 F.2d 659 (10th Cir. 1987).
196. Thus, the delegation to a management company of complete authority over the company's investments was valid because the company reserved the right to cancel the arrangement upon notice. *See* Canal Capital Corp. v. French, 1992 WL 159008 (1992).
197. Grimes v. Donald, 673 A.2d 1207 (Del. 1996), *overruled in part by* Brehm v. Eisner, 746 A.2d 244 (De. 2000).
198. Sherman & Ellis, Inc. v. Indiana Mut. Cas. Co., 41 F.2d 588 (7th Cir.), *cert. denied,* 282 U.S. 893 (1930).

199. *Id.*
200. Marvin v. Solventol Chem. Prods., Inc., 298 N.W. 782 (Mich. 1941).
201. Jones v. Williams, 39 S.W. 486, 40 S.W. 353 (Mo. 1897).
202. *See, e.g.,* Cal. Corp. Code § 300(a) (West 1990) ("The board may delegate the management of day-to-day operations of the business of the corporation to a management company. . . .").

CHAPTER 10

DIRECTORS' AND OFFICERS' DUTIES OF CARE AND LOYALTY

PART A. DILIGENCE, SKILL, AND CARE; LIABILITY FOR NEGLIGENCE IN MANAGEMENT

§ 10.1 LIABILITY FOR IMPRUDENCE AND HONEST ERRORS OF JUDGMENT: THE "BUSINESS JUDGMENT RULE"

What is the liability of directors for incompetence? Although directors are commonly said to be responsible both for reasonable care and for prudence, the formula is continually repeated that directors are not liable for losses due to imprudence or honest errors of judgment.[1] This formula is frequently referred to as the "business judgment rule."[2] Taken in its most cynical light, the business judgment rule means that management's position is vindicated.[3]

> Courts do not measure, weigh, or quantify directors' judgments. We do not even decide if they are reasonable in this context. Due care in the decision-making context is *process* due care only. Irrationality is the outer limit of the business judgment rule. Irrationality may be the functional equivalent of the waste test or it may tend to show that the decision is not made in good faith, which is a key ingredient of the business judgment rule.[4]

The above description of the business judgment rule is best understood by distinguishing between the duty of care and the business judgment rule. The former can be seen as embracing a standard for officer and director conduct, whereas the latter embodies a standard of judicial review.[5] The twin features of the business judgment rule's application to a decision of the directors are that the directors will not be liable for any losses proximately caused by that decision and that the court will not substitute its judgment or that of the plaintiff for the decision made by the directors. We can therefore understand judicial incantations regarding the care obligations of directors and officers as aspirational, even normative. However, whether the officer's or director's departure from an understood norm results in liability (or the court substituting its judgment for that of the corporate decision-maker) depends on how her conduct is assessed under the review standard embraced in the business judgment rule.[6]

In general, courts will not undertake to review the expediency of contracts or other business transactions authorized by the directors. Directors have a large degree of discretion. Questions of value and policy have been said to be part of the directors' business judgment, although their errors may be so gross as to show their unfitness to manage corporate affairs.[7] According to the better view, the business judgment rule presupposes that reasonable diligence and care have been exercised.[8] But are there not, in addition, some limits on the immunity for losses due to honest errors resulting from a director's lack of intelligence, foresight, and business sense? Hasty action by an ill-informed board will not be insulated by the business judgment rule.[9] However, directors and officers do not operate in a world that permits them to have all the information they would prefer to have before they act. "The need to make judgments with only imperfect information available, and other elements of risk taking, are often inherent in business decision-making."[10] When the board has not acted in breach of a fiduciary duty, its members will be entitled to the protection of the business judgment rule.[11]

Courts developed the business judgment rule long before statements on directors' duties were included in the corporation statutes. Even though corporation statutes in most states now contain an express statement defining directors' duties and omit any reference to a business judgment rule, courts continue to apply the rule.[12]

§ 10.2 STANDARD OF CARE AND DILIGENCE

There has been some difference in the language used by the legislatures and the courts to designate the standard of care and diligence required of the directors of a corporation in the management or supervision of its affairs. It is difficult, however, to tell whether the differing standards, which have been referred to as "semantic,"[13] make much difference in practical application. The particular statute's precise formulation of the director's duty of care does not assume great importance in the court's judgment whether the director has breached her duty.[14]

In New York, an early theoretical standard was declared to be the care and diligence that an ordinarily prudent man would exercise in the management of his own affairs.[15] The fairer and more satisfactory rule is that degree of care and diligence that an ordinarily prudent director can reasonably be expected to exercise in a like position under similar circumstances.[16] This standard was adopted by the Model Act, and a great number of states have followed suit.[17] However, in 1997, the Revised Model Act provision was changed so as to eliminate reference to this negligence-type standard. Instead, the 1997 version merely provides that "Each member of the board of directors, when discharging the duties of a director, shall act (1) in good faith, and (2) in a manner the director reasonably believes to be in the best interests of the corporation."[18] The conflict of standards, however, may be more apparent than real; in practical application such vague abstractions are meaningless, and a judge and jury will necessarily formulate their own measuring rods according to their own standards. For example, the changes to the Model Act still refer to "director reasonably believes to be in the best interests of the corporation,"[19] which still captures the negligence concept of how a reasonable director would act under like circumstances. It would be most unfortunate should this change in wording result in lowering director accountability for breaches of the duty of care. The 1997 revisions to the Model Act also brought in a new section dealing with the standards of liability for directors.[20]

Directors are to use such care and diligence and give such time and attention as ordinarily careful and prudent persons can reasonably be expected to exercise on behalf of such a corporation under similar circumstances.[21] What is a failure to exercise reasonable care and diligence is always to be determined with reference to the circumstances of the particular corporation and, to some extent, of the particular director. Whether the breach of that duty gives rise to liability depends upon both a more extreme departure from the objective standard so that the business judgment rule does not apply, and a finding that losses were proximately caused because of the breach.

The duty of care can be divided into three distinct segments. First, there is the obligation of directors and officers to be attentive to the corporation's affairs. Second, the duty of care also requires that the directors reasonably inform themselves on all matters coming before the board and that their decision be duly deliberated. Finally, the duty of care has a substantive component—namely, that directors and officers have a rational basis for their decisions. These components are discussed in the next three sections.

§ 10.3 THE DIRECTORS' OBLIGATION TO BE ATTENTIVE

A directorship, although conferring prestige and power, comes with the heavy demand that the director regularly attend board meetings and otherwise be attentive to the corporation's affairs.[22] The precise commands of these obligations are gleaned from the few cases that have considered the fate of directors held to have shirked their responsibility. The obligation to attend meetings on a regular basis is breached by the director who is habitually absent.[23] Moreover, there is not one standard for a nonresident director who is retired and another for active resident directors.[24] But the duty of attentiveness commands more than regular attendance at meetings. In an early New York case,[25] the court held that an outside director whose tenure was less than nine months, breached his duty to inform himself adequately about the newly created company's operations. Even though the firm had raised a substantial amount of capital through a public offering, possessed a well-equipped and staffed factory, and produced enough parts for starter motors, the firm was experiencing dramatic delays in assembling starter motors. The company ultimately failed. The court held the outside director breached his duty by failing to inform himself adequately about the firm's performance and position.[26]

There is a collective view in business, government, and academia that we must discard the predominance of the inside board of directors and replace them with substantial monitoring obligations for outside directors.[27] This view is reflected in the reasoning of cases such as *Francis v. United Jersey Bank*,[28] where a director who was unfamiliar with the rudiments of the corporation's business, never read annual reports, and visited the corporation's offices only once during her five-year tenure on the board (during most of which she was in poor physical health), was held liable for the embezzlements committed by her two sons, who were the corporation's officers and remaining directors. *Francis* expresses the prevailing view regarding the director's duty of attentiveness:

Directors are under a continuing obligation to keep informed about the activities of the corporation. . . . [D]irectors may not shut their eyes to corporate misconduct and then claim that because they did not see the misconduct, they did not have a duty to look. The sentinel asleep at his post contributes nothing to the enterprise he is charged to protect.

Directorial management does not require a detailed inspection of day-to-day activities, but rather a general monitoring of corporate affairs and policies.[29]

Francis also reflects the prevailing view that directors are not excused because of intellectual or physical incapacity from their obligation to inform themselves on a regular basis on the financial and operational status of the business.[30] But does the obligation to be attentive command more than regular attendance of meetings? The cases do not emphasize the number of meetings missed, but instead focuses on the necessity for the director to stay abreast of the corporation's financial position, progress, and performance.[31]

There indeed are a good many cases imposing the responsibility on directors to investigate and check the possible wrongdoing of co-directors, officers, and subordinates.[32] Where suspicions are aroused, or should be aroused, it is the director's duty to make the necessary inquiries; ignorance is no basis for escaping liability.[33] And the director's obligation does not end with a reasonable investigation but carries forward the duty to act reasonably in light of the information gained thereby.[34] However, absent such reasonable suspicion, the director or officer acts reasonably in relying upon others, whether they be officers, employees or outside consultants.[35]

A somewhat different question is whether directors are under an obligation to install systems designed to discourage and detect the fraudulent, illegal, or criminal activities of subordinates. An early Delaware decision on the obligation of directors to monitor the activities of subordinates for the purpose of discouraging or detecting illegal activities is *Graham v. Allis-Chalmers Manufacturing Company*.[36] In *Allis-Chalmers*, a derivative suit was brought against the company's directors to recover damages the company suffered because its employees engaged in massive bid-rigging with competitors, a flagrant violation of the antitrust laws. One theory of the plaintiff's action was that the directors had acted unreasonably in failing to establish a system to detect and prevent the bid-rigging. The Delaware Supreme Court dismissed the suit, reasoning that within a large multinational firm such as Allis-Chalmers, with over 30,000 employees, it is unreasonable to require the directors to undertake an active investigation of each division of the firm absent their being on adequate notice of any wrongdoing.[37] The court held the directors acted reasonably in relying on the reports and summaries of operations, which they had no reason to believe were untrustworthy.[38] More important, the court held the Allis-Chalmers directors had no responsibility to establish and maintain a system of surveillance unless there was suspicion of wrongdoing.[39]

One finds a good deal of dissonance between the *Allis-Chalmers* holding and the reasoning quoted above from *Francis v. United Jersey Bank.* The difference may likely be explained by their placement in time. *Francis* is far more consistent with the perceived role of today's outside directors as monitors. Moreover, since *Allis-Chalmers* was decided, there is a solid perception that it is good corporate practice for public corporations to design and implement legal compliance systems such as those argued for in *Allis-Chalmers.*[40] In the widely celebrated decision *In re Caremark International Derivative Litigation,*[41] involving approval of a settlement of a derivative suit alleging directors failed to properly oversee employees who engaged in felonious payments for patient referrals, Chancellor Allen opined that:

> [I]t would be . . . mistake to conclude that . . . corporate boards may satisfy their obligation to be reasonably informed concerning the corporation, without assuring themselves that information and reporting systems exist in the organization that are reasonably designed to provide to senior management and to the board itself timely, accurate information sufficient to allow management and the board, each within its scope, to reach informed judgments, concerning both the corporation's compliance with law and its business performance. . . .

> Thus, I am of the view that a director's obligation includes a duty to attempt in good faith to assure that a corporate information and reporting system, which the board concludes is adequate, exists, and that failure to do so under some circumstances may, in theory at least, render a director liable for losses caused by non-compliance with applicable legal standards.[42]

Though dicta in the matter—the approval of a settlement of a derivative suit—Chancellor Allen appears to accurately reflect the likely result that should be reached today with the monitoring role of the board of directors so widely entrenched in corporate governance practices. If seen as a component of the duty of care, the case would be stronger than the oversight called for by *Caremark* is an objective one, so that the practices prevalent within an industry and across types of corporations would be normative in assessing whether a board of directors has acted properly under the circumstances. We could then more easily marry perceived and practiced good corporate governance to the demands of good faith. The prevalence of compliance programs across all types of companies and industries make the absence of such a program in a particular company appear to be an dangerous departure from custom. Accordingly, there is ample reason to doubt the continuing force of *Allis-Chalmers*'s sweeping rejection of the responsibility of directors to install a compliance system.[43]

Even though the directors may be held to have breached their duty of care by failing to install a certain type of compliance system, their breach does not necessarily mean they are liable for any losses associated with the subordinate's violations. It is a well-established principle of corporate law that the plaintiff has the burden of proving not only the breach but also what damages were proximately caused thereby. Even a reasonably designed and superintended compliance program will not detect or deter all misbehavior. Some violators will invariably slide through the screening process, so that the directors' technical breach in failing to install a compliance system may ultimately bear no causal relationship with the harm caused by the subordinates' wrongdoing.

Caremark is qualified by *Stone v. Ritter*[44] where the Delaware Supreme Court rejected the view held by some that *Caremark*'s invocation of the director's duty of good faith introduced a distinct, third, fiduciary duty. *Stone v. Ritter* holds there are only two fiduciary duties: the duty of loyalty and the duty of care, so that good faith is subsumed within the director's duty of loyalty. Earlier the Delaware Chancery Court identified three (nonexclusive) illustrations of conduct not in "good faith:"

> A failure to act in good faith may be shown, for instance, where the fiduciary intentionally acts for the purpose other than that of advancing the best interests of the corporation, where the fiduciary acts with the intent to violate applicable positive law, or where the fiduciary intentionally fails to act in the face of a known duty to act, demonstrating a conscious disregard for his duties.[45]

Thus, good faith entails a consciousness of wrongdoing on the part of the actor; it is this feature that distinguishes the absence of good faith from an extreme departure from the objective standard of care, such as the multiple missteps that occurred on the part of the TransUnion directors in *Smith v. Van Gorkom*, discussed in the next section.

In re Abbott Laboratories Derivative Shareholders Litigation,[46] although addressing the question whether a demand upon the board was excused because the allegations created a reasonable doubt the actions of the board of directors were protected by the business judgment rule, illustrates not only the obligation of the board of directors to reasonably pursue facts that put them on notice of conduct that if not addressed would lead to substantial corporate losses, but also illustrates the consciousness element for a good faith violation.

A novel approach to allocating the burden of proof was taken in *Cede & Co. v. Technicolor, Inc.*,[47] where the Delaware Supreme Court held that once the presumptions of the business judgment rule are removed because of the absence of good faith or care on the part of the directors, the directors have the burden of proving the transaction's "entire fairness." Failing this burden, the directors are subject to a full panoply of remedies.[48] *Cede & Co.* does not accord the directors the protection of a presumption of propriety on the part of directors. Nor are they provided the protection of the plaintiff having the burden of proving what damages were proximately caused by the directors' breach of their duty of care.[49] Delaware thus treats causation similarly in cases of directors who breach their duty of loyalty and those who breach their duty of care. It remains to be seen whether Delaware's approach in *Cede & Co.* will be followed in other jurisdictions or will remain, as it was when the case was decided, a unique approach. Even in Delaware, it is uncertain just what range of factors the breaching-directors can invoke to meet the "entire fairness" defense. In *Cede & Co.*, the court reviewed a variety of factors in concluding that the board had met the entire fairness test. Among the factors it considered were many that bore directly upon whether the board had acted negligently, so that its inquiry appears to be more focused on the defendant's rebutting the substantive charge they acted with gross negligence and less on an inquiry to whether their actions caused financial harm to the corporation or its stockholders. Upon the directors' breach of the duty of care being established, *Cede & Co.* clearly invites a review of the substantive merits of the decision for which the directors acted negligently.[50] Consequently, though procedural due care may be lacking, even bumblers can make good decisions. Under the formulation in *Barnes*, once a breach of care is established the inquiry was just what harm flowed proximately from the breach.

§ 10.4 DIRECTORS' ACTIONS SHOULD BE THE PRODUCT OF REASONABLE INVESTIGATION AND CONSIDERATION

Lawyers are well acquainted with the connection between reasonable processes and the quality of decision-making. Not only does procedural due process enhance the validity of a decision but also the discipline yields a better decision. These benefits are the object of the courts' preoccupation with whether directors' decisions are the product of a reasonable investigation and consideration of facts and issues surrounding any matter before the board. A director is reasonably informed if the director considers the *material* facts that are *reasonably available;* there is no need to pursue immaterial facts or information that could not be acquired reasonably under the circumstances.[51]

Any doubt about the force of this judicial preoccupation is removed by the Delaware Supreme Court's landmark decision in *Smith v. Van Gorkom*,[52] where the court held the directors breached their duty of care in approving the sale of Trans Union Corporation. The board of directors approved the sale at a meeting that lasted only two hours. The presentation was completely oral, no written drafts of the acquisition agreement were circulated, and Van Gorkom (Trans Union's president) did not disclose that the sales price was proposed not by the buyer but rather by Van Gorkom. The board was not told that the selling price of $55 per share reflected the price Trans Union's own cash flow would justify if the purchase were a management buyout. Thus, the selling price did not indicate in any way the significant synergies of any profitable firm acquiring Trans Union. Furthermore, there was no evidence in the record of the directors questioning Van Gorkom on the sale. Indeed, the case reflects the board's uncritical acceptance of the senior management's recommendation. Several facts were in evidence that supported the directors' quick approval of the sale. For example, the selling price represented nearly a 50 percent premium over the prevailing market price for Trans Union stock; furthermore, the buyer's offer was open for only

48 hours. These factors appear to explain why the directors so quickly approved the sale and in doing so they did not consult any outside financial consultants regarding the sale. Despite these factors that appeared to call for the board to act quickly, the Delaware Supreme Court held that the directors failed to inform themselves adequately and therefore acted with "gross negligence" in approving Trans Union's sale.[53] The court chastised the directors for failing to inquire how the sales price was determined and for failing to inform themselves of the intrinsic value of the firm.[54] *Smith v. Van Gorkom* does not hold that the directors approved the sale of their firm at too low a price; its holding is that the corporation was deprived of a reasonable determination of the sales price by its directors. The case was therefore remanded for determination of whether any damages in fact befell the stockholders because of the faulty deliberations by the board of directors.[55]

Smith v. Van Gorkom illustrates the *process* component of the duty of care, as contrasted with the substantive component that is discussed later in connection with the rational basis requirement of the duty of care. To meet the duty of care's concern for process, whenever practicable, it is good corporate practice to circulate in advance of the board meeting an agenda of such information as is useful to the board to understand the items to be discussed at the upcoming meeting. Such advance circulation, however, is not a prerequisite for the directors to be deemed to have acted reasonably. Director decisions are within the protection of the business judgment rule, even when made at meetings convened without an agenda or when material has not been circulated earlier, provided the facts otherwise reflect that the board was informed and adequately deliberated the matter.[56]

Just what is required for the board to act reasonably to inform itself varies with the facts. Some decisions and some circumstances may call for less information, and less consideration, than others.

In addition to sparking a good deal of commentary[57] and adding to the demand for consultants such as investment bankers, *Smith v. Van Gorkom* reinforces the importance of the board's counselor to assure that the directors act in as deliberate and thorough manner as is possible under the circumstances. Courts repeatedly accord greater weight to the actions of directors who are informed by outside experts and consultants.[58] Similarly, a board's delegation to or reliance upon a committee of directors charged with responsibility to handle a matter is a reasonable practice.[59] The consultants need not be from outside the organization; reliance on officers and employees within the organization is appropriate, provided the directors are not on notice of any facts suggesting such reliance is unjustified.[60] Many corporate statutes expressly provide that directors in discharging their duties may rely on information, opinions, and reports of consultants, experts, subordinates, and committees.[61]

The ability of directors to rely on information, opinions, and reports prepared by others is not an open invitation to shirk their responsibilities. Minimally, their duty to act in good faith requires the directors to have read the report or attended the meeting at which the information or opinion was orally presented, or to have otherwise taken reasonable steps to familiarize themselves with its contents.[62] There is also the qualification that the directors have some reason to believe the matter is within the competence or expertise of the consultant, subordinate, or committee on whom they are relying.[63] Thus the directors are not entitled to rely on an attorney's advice that pertains mainly to factual questions for which the attorney is no better equipped to opine than the directors. On the other hand, directors act reasonably in relying on their attorney's advice on either purely legal, as well as a matter that involves a mixture of law and facts, unless the advice is patently incorrect. There is always the substantial qualification that a director may not rely on a consultant's, subordinate's, or committee's report if a director is on notice that such reliance is not warranted.[64] Directors breach their duty of care if they fail to question facts or opinions expressed in a report where the circumstances call for further elucidation or challenge.[65]

Directors' knowledge of the facts raising their suspicions can occur as a result of information gained through their non-director status.[66] Thus, the Second Circuit held in *Hanson Trust PLC v. ML SCM Acquisition, Inc.*[67] that the directors breached their duty of care by uncritically accepting their investment banker's opinion respecting the fair value of a product line without probing how such value was determined; had they made such an inquiry the board would have learned that the advisor had failed to calculate a range of values in determining the fairness of the price.[68] Also, reliance is not reasonable when the expert's advice is clearly inconsistent with all other facts before the directors.[69] Directors do not act reasonably in informing themselves as to a transaction's benefits by relying solely on the representations of a person known to have a financial interest in the transaction.[70]

An important qualification on the directors' ability to rely with impunity on the reports of others appears in a critical passage of *Smith v. Van Gorkom*:

> Under 8 Del. C. 141(e), directors are fully protected in relying in good faith on reports made by officers. . . . However, there is no evidence that any "report" . . . was presented to the Board. . . . Van Gorkom's oral presentation of his understanding of the terms of the proposed Merger Agreement, which he had not seen, and Roman's brief oral statement of his preliminary study regarding the feasibility of a lever- aged buy-out of Trans Union do not qualify as 141(e) "reports" for these reasons: The former lacked substance because Van Gorkom was basi- cally uninformed as to the essential provisions of the very document about which he was talking. Roman's statement was irrelevant to the issues before the Board since it did not purport to be a valuation study.[71]

Smith therefore adds to the qualification that the directors not be aware of cause for believing reliance on an officer is unjustified. What *Smith* thus provides is the further requirement that the subordinate's pre- sentation pertain to the very issue before the board (Roman's fairness opinion did not), and the officer must herself be adequately informed regarding the matter addressed. Certainly the latter is far more trou- bling, because, if *Smith* is taken literally, it would deny the protections of the business judgment rule to directors who were otherwise unaware that the officer was not adequately informed on the topic. This clearly is a major departure from established principles[72] and appears inconsistent with provisions that permit directors to rely unless they are on notice of circumstances that make such reliance unjustified. It would appear a far better approach in *Smith* if the court had instead denied the directors' the ability to raise as a defense for failing to be adequately informed that they had relied upon Van Gorkom's and Roman's presentation by the court, holding instead that his report did not deal with the substantive fairness of the price. Viewed in this way, it could fairly be said that the board had received no information on which to base its decision.[73]

§ 10.5 DIRECTORS' DECISIONS SHOULD EMBODY A RATIONAL BASIS FOR ACTION

The duty of care has both procedural and substantive requirements. The requirements that the directors be attentive and reasonably informed are procedural in nature; the substantive requirement is that their decisions have a "rational basis" or, as it is sometimes expressed, be "reasonable."[74] At first glance, this requirement would appear to invite a good deal of second-guessing and intrusion by the courts and disappointed stockholders. But public policy considerations, discussed earlier, have caused the courts not to apply these standards rigorously but instead to afford directors and officers great latitude in their actions and decision-making.[75] In its most rigorous form, the duty of care requires only that managers have a reasonable basis for their decisions, despite the availability of more compelling alternative choices available to them. One court has held for the standard to be violated, the directors' decision must be "so unwise or unreasonable as to fall outside the permissible bounds of the directors' sound discretion."[76]

To illustrate the wide latitude accorded directors under the rational basis standard, consider the leading case of *Kamin v. American Express Company*.[77] A derivative suit was brought against the directors of American Express Company, questioning their decision to distribute as a dividend in kind nearly 2 million shares of Donaldson, Lufken, and Jenrette (DL&J) stock that American Express had acquired for investment at a cost of $29.9 million. The directors decided to distribute the shares as a dividend rather than to realize a $25 million loss by selling the DL&J shares in the market. The derivative suit plaintiff asserted this was a waste of the nearly $8 million American Express would have realized in tax savings had the shares been sold and the loss reported on its tax return. By distributing the DL&J shares to its stockholders, American Express avoided recognizing the loss on either its tax return or income statement.[78] The board of directors rationalized its decision as an attempt to avoid depressing American Express' stock price by reporting a $25 million loss on its income statement, which would have been required if the shares had been sold. As it was, the loss on the DL&J shares was merely reported as a deduction to stockholders' equity on the company's balance sheet. Certainly those who believe capital markets are efficient have good cause to question whether astute investors would overlook the true economic significance of the board's decision. Indeed, a compelling case can be made that the *wiser* course was that advocated in the derivative suit, especially since American Express did not deny that its financial statements would have to give some prominence to removing the DL&J shares from among its assets. Nevertheless, the court held that the directors acted reasonably under the circumstances, and dismissed the case.

Kamin clearly underscores that the "rational basis" or "reasonableness" standard does not require directors to reach the best or even optimal result. It is sufficient that the decision have the appearance of being a reasoned response to a situation. Thus, entering into a multi-million dollar settlement with a terminated executive is not waste where the alternative was to incur uncertainty as to whether the executive could be fired and paid less.[79] To be sure, the result is a standard unlikely to command much respect in business schools and executive education programs, where the emphasis is on the optimal or even right response. On the other hand, a more demanding standard would most clearly result in less risk-taking by directors.

§ 10.6 Knowing Violations of a Criminal Statute

As has been seen, the commentators have offered many suggested approaches to conform the corporation's behavior to desirable social goals. The cry that corporations must act in a socially responsible manner is in fact an invitation to corporations to act beyond the commands of the law. That is, the call to act in a socially responsible manner seeks more than staying within the bounds of the law by, for example, assuring that their effluents into the air and rivers not violate state or local directives. Corporations are socially responsible when their internal goal is to surpass the minimum standard of acceptable behavior embodied in state and federal directives. A socially responsible corporation thus is one that avoids walking close to the line.

But what corporate-law-based punishment awaits the corporation directors or officers who cross the line by knowingly engaging in a criminal act? For example, what is the liability of directors who knowingly flout pollution requirements by failing to install in their plant's chimneys the expensive scrubbers that are mandated by federal law, if the corporation is ultimately fined $75,000? Assume, however, that the delay in complying with the law allows the corporation to operate more efficiently, so that over the course of its noncompliance the violation yielded a net savings of $1 million—does corporate law provide its own disciplining force to discourage such conduct, or does crime pay?

Two early decisions appear to remove the protections of the business judgment rule entirely on proof of a knowing violation of a criminal statute. In *Roth v. Robertson*,[80] the manager of an amusement park paid hush money to individuals who threatened to prevent the park from operating in violation of the state's Sunday closing laws. Even though the corporation received a large percentage of its total revenues from Sunday operations, the court upheld a jury award of $800, the amount of the hush money payments. The court partially based its holding on the payments being a violation of the state's criminal statutes. Another early leading case is *Abrams v. Allen*,[81] where the criminal violation was the corporation's board of directors' approval of the dismantling of plants for the purpose of intimidating union organizing efforts. One of four possible theories of recovery embraced by the court was the illegality of the board's actions.

The contemporary view of the impact a knowing violation of a criminal statute has on the availability of the business judgment rule is reflected in *Miller v. American Telephone & Telegraph Company*,[82] a derivative suit seeking to recover a $1.5 million phone bill of the Democratic National Committee, which the AT&T directors forgave. The plaintiff attacked the directors' decision as an unlawful political contribution. Reasoning that "directors must be restrained from engaging in activities which are against public policy,"[83] the *Miller* court, relying on *Roth* and *Abrams*, concludes that the business judgment rule's presumption of propriety does not extend to directors who knowingly violate a criminal statute.[84] However, finding a knowing violation did not record an automatic award for the derivative suit plaintiff. Miller, a diversity action, was bound by New York law, which since Roth and Abrams has evolved to require the plaintiff to prove not only that the directors have knowingly violated a criminal statute but also that the corporation has suffered a *net loss* through the acts challenged.[85] Thus, if the overall gains of the violation exceed the losses directly associated with the violation, such as fines and attorneys' fees, there is no liability on the part of the responsible directors or officers. Stated more bluntly, purely from the perspective of corporate law, crime may well pay. As one of the authors has written:

> This limitation prevents the derivative suit from serving as a vehicle for redressing social harms committed by the corporation's managers. However offensive the conclusion that within the derivative suit context "crime pays," the net loss requirement may signal no more than the fact the derivative suit is otherwise a poor medium for enforcing societal directives not devoted exclusively to the corporation's efficient performance. The state's concern for pure air and water, safe consumer products, and fair employment practices implicates protections

for a more diverse group than the class of shareholders with standing to maintain a derivative suit. When the deterrence question is instead focused upon a threatened harm to the shareholders themselves, there is a stronger basis to permit some recovery out of prophylactic considerations to remind the directors and officers that their ultimate responsibilities are to the shareholders.[86]

The American Law Institute's Principles of Corporate Governance is resolute in dealing with directors and officers who knowingly participate in illegal conduct. Their violations are outside the protections of the business judgment rule[87] and are not within the permissible bounds of a charter provision that otherwise can immunize directors from liability for damages.[88] And when the conduct is the subject of a derivative suit, the recommendation of the board or committee that the suit be dismissed is subject to a higher level of review by the court than are care violations and most categories of overreaching behavior.[89] More generally, the ALI incorporates into its broad duty of care the obligation that directors and officers act within the bounds of the law.[90]

The great hurdle in any suit not premised on the directors' knowing violation of a criminal statute but rather on their negligence in failing to detect the violations of subordinates is the problem of causation. No law compliance program is foolproof, and many violations by subordinates are likely to go undetected even under the most aggressive compliance systems. This poses a serious problem to the plaintiff who seeks to impose liability on the directors on the theory that the directors' failure to install *any* compliance program is a breach of the directors' duty of care. Because the plaintiff has the burden of proving not only that the directors breached their duty of care but also that their breach proximately harmed the corporation, the plaintiff generally will have great difficulty establishing a causal relationship between the absence of a compliance system and the injury to the corporation flowing from the violation.[91] The court may well conclude that the directors' failure to install any law compliance system constitutes only a technical breach, much as Andrew's failure to inform himself was so held in *Barnes v. Andrews*, discussed earlier. Thus the causation requirement lifts some of the pressure of personal liability from the directors' shoulders to aggressively pursue law compliance systems. Because the ALI does not have its own provision on causality, its various provisions dealing with directors' obligations to assure compliance with the law are accordingly weakened.

§ 10.7 STATUTORY DEVELOPMENTS LIMITING DIRECTORS' LIABILITY FOR DUTY-OF-CARE VIOLATIONS

In 1986, the Delaware legislature amended its general corporation law to allow the charters of Delaware corporations to include provisions that limit the liability of directors for damages arising from breaches of their duty of care.[92] Following Delaware's lead, numerous states have since enacted similar statutory provisions. The standard format of such exoneration statutes is that they authorize the articles of incorporation to include a provision eliminating or limiting the liability of a director, except for certain types of breaches. For example, section 102(b)(7) of the Delaware general corporation statute provides:

> A provision eliminating or limiting the personal liability of a director to the corporation or its stockholders for monetary damages for breach of fiduciary duty as a director . . . [except] (i) for any breach of the director's duty of loyalty to the corporation or its stockholders; (ii) for acts or omissions not in good faith or which involve intentional misconduct or knowing violation of law; (iii) . . . [for unlawful distributions]; (iv) for any transaction from which the director derived an improper personal benefit.

The above excepted categories are typical of those found in other state statutes.[93] Three important facets of the exoneration statutes narrow their impact. First, its protection is limited only to breaches committed as a director. Thus, if a person serves as both a director and an officer and breaches duties in both capacities,[94] he would not be protected by such a provision for any violations of care committed as an officer.[95] Second, the provision's protections are limited to actions for damages. Equitable actions, such as for injunctive relief or rescission, are unaffected by the charter limitation on damages. Finally, the directors remain responsible for damages they cause to third parties; the charter provision protects the directors only from liability to the corporation or its shareholders. The typical exoneration statute is in the nature of an affirmative defense so that the burden is upon the person seeking the protection of the exculpatory provision to demonstrate the conduct fell within that provision.[96]

Other states have taken a different approach by stating affirmatively the types of actions for which directors can be held personally liable.[97]

Thus, Florida provides that directors are personally liable only for certain violations of criminal statutes, receiving an improper personal benefit, unlawful distributions, consciously disregarding the corporation's interest, and willful misconduct.[98]

There is an interesting interplay between the exoneration statute and the court's review of a transaction alleged to pose a conflict of interest. In *Emerald Partners v. Berlin*,[99] the Delaware Chancery court dismissed the plaintiff's suit against the three directors based upon allegations that a merger of the corporation with 13 companies owned by the controlling stockholder was unfair to the minority stockholders. The Chancery Court justified the dismissal upon its belief the defendant directors had established their defense under the company's exoneration provision by showing they had received no benefit from the transaction not enjoyed by other stockholders and had acted independently of the controlling stockholder. The Delaware Supreme Court reversed the dismissal, holding that the lower court had proceeded improperly by considering the exoneration provision before first determining whether the merger met the "entire fairness" standard.[100] Thus, *Emerald Partners* requires that in cases where the complaint properly pleads a conflict-of-interest transaction, breach of duty of loyalty, or otherwise a failure to act in good faith that the court must first determine whether the transaction meets the entire fairness standard. If it does not, the court then is to assess the role the directors played in this failure and more particularly whether their lapse was a result of conduct exonerated by the charter provision. This approach is likely to lead not only to closer scrutiny of the transaction but also to the individual director's engagement with the challenged transaction. Under the Delaware entire fairness standard, the court evaluates not just the price but the manner in which the transaction was considered. This would appear to result in closer attention to the director's involvement at each stage of the approval process than if the review focused only upon the grounds set forth in the state exoneration statute that removed its protection for the director.

A final variation on statutory responses to director liability is that embraced in Virginia, which in 1987 amended its general corporation law to impose a specific cap on damages that are recoverable from officers and directors in any action brought by or on behalf of the corporation. The specific cap is the *lesser* of (1) the monetary amount stated, if any, in the corporation's articles or bylaws (which must have been adopted by the stockholders) or (2) the greater of $100,000 or the cash compensation received by the officer or director in the 12 months preceding the action or omission charged.[101] A similar cap is suggested by the American Law Institute, except the American Law Institute's approach allows the corporation to opt into the cap, whereas the Virginia statute mandates the cap for all corporations and permits the charter or bylaw merely to prescribe a *lower* cap than would otherwise apply.

The overall effect of such charter provisions is to focus attention on the transaction itself through a prayer for injunctive relief, rather than focusing on the personal liability of the directors. While appearing to be a major retreat from directors' responsibilities, the irony of charter provisions such as Delaware's is that they may actually stimulate an increase in the amount of litigation that questions director judgment. When the object of a suit is damages for the losses related to the directors' breaching their duty of care, there is the ever-present disquiet that the sanction for the breach is disproportionate to the directors' fault. The draconian nature of the suit therefore has caused the courts to insulate the directors through heightened procedural and substantive rules. A charter provision shielding directors from liability for breaches of care may well encourage the courts to scrutinize directors' decisions more closely without fear that substituting the court's judgment for that of the directors will also visit a draconian remedy on the individual director. The object of such a suit is an injunction or rescission.

Moreover, the elimination of a damage recovery does not reduce the incentive for care-based suits, because plaintiffs' attorneys' fees still are awarded on proof that the directors breached their duty of care so that equitable relief is appropriate.[102] Thus, the overall impact of the very popular exoneration provisions may well be that of encouraging plaintiffs to sue earlier and more frequently for protective equitable relief as well as lessening modestly the historical reluctance of courts to closely scrutinize director decisions.

§ 10.8 EXECUTIVE OFFICERS; SUPERVISION OF SUBORDINATES

The president, cashier, or general manager may come under even greater responsibility for the fraud or neglect of subordinates than do directors.[103] Thus, where it is the duty of the president of a corporation to supervise its affairs and to take and keep bonds from subordinate officers, and the president negligently fails to take the required bond from an officer who is entrusted with funds and becomes a defaulter, it is the president who is liable to the corporation for the loss.[104]

In a leading Supreme Court case,[105] a bookkeeper of a small national bank on a salary of $12 per week defrauded the bank during a series of years of over $300,000, aggregating more than the bank's capital and more than the normal average of its deposits. This was accomplished in a novel and ingenious way by falsifying the deposit ledger and making false charges against deposits, thereby diminishing the apparent liability to depositors. The fraud could have been discovered by the cashier had he examined checks as they came from the clearinghouse, or had he compared the deposit ledger with the depositors' pass books. But he negligently placed too much trust in the bookkeeper. The directors, serving gratuitously, were held not to be negligent in accepting the cashier's statements of liabilities and were not bound to inspect the depositors' ledger or call in the pass books and compare them with it. The president, who had received certain warnings that the bookkeeper was living fast and dealing in stocks, was held to have been negligent in failing to make an examination, especially as he was in control of the bank's affairs, with immediate access to the depositors' ledger.[106] More recently, the Supreme Court upheld the criminal conviction of the president of a 36,000-employee concern with 870 retail outlets, where the president's failure to supervise resulted in one of the company's 12 warehouses being in violation of federal sanitary standards.[107]

PART B. DEALINGS BETWEEN DIRECTORS AND THEIR CORPORATIONS— CONFLICTS OF INTEREST

§ 10.9 THE SCOPE OF THE OFFICERS' AND DIRECTORS' DUTY OF LOYALTY

Mapping the scope of the directors' or officers' fiduciary obligations is not easy. The nature of the challenge is concisely stated in the now classic observation by Supreme Court Justice Felix Frankfurter in *Securities and Exchange Commission v. Chenery Corp.*: "[T]o say that a man is a fiduciary only begins the analysis; it gives direction to further inquiry. To whom is he a fiduciary? What obligations does he owe as a fiduciary? In what respect has he failed to discharge these obligations?"[108] In the early formative years of corporate law, it was assumed that the rules governing directors and officers should conform to the strict rules governing trustees and agents. Hence, courts frequently referred to directors as both trustees and agents with the effect of holding directors to the same strict rules of disqualification to contract with their principal the corporation.[109] However, the functions performed, and hence the obligations implicit to fulfill the fiduciary's undertakings, are not the same for trustees, guardians, executors, administrators, agents, partners, promoters, directors and officers.[110] The differences in the expressed tasks, and the undertakings implicit for their accomplishment, necessarily weaken the analogy between, on the one hand, trustees and, on the other hand, corporate directors or officers.[111] Nevertheless, an aspect of the relationship of directors and officers to the corporation is a fiduciary relationship, and the corporation's owners are the beneficiaries of the duties owed by the officers and directors. The rhetoric of the director or officers as a trustee, therefore, continues to appear in today's decisions, although the guidance that courts invoke to determine the content of the officer's or director's fiduciary obligation is gleaned not by reference to the law of trusts but to the extensive body of corporate fiduciary case law.

The preceding sections of this chapter have closely examined the many facets of the duty of care. Directors and officers must also comply with their duty of loyalty[112] if they are to enjoy the protective benefits of the business judgment rule. The divide between the duty of care and loyalty is not a sharp one, and the courts frequently blur the distinction between these twin obligations.[113] As seen in the preceding material of this chapter, there are many dimensions to the duty of care. In broad overview, the duty of care is about process by which officers and directors are to reach decisions and, more generally, fulfill their monitoring obligations. Hence the material earlier in this chapter focused upon the obligations to be attentive, make reasonable inquiry and have a rational basis for decision-making. In contrast, loyalty is not about the decision-making process or, for that matter, monitoring. The duty of loyalty is about the director's or officer's motives and purposes, and the goals that are necessary if his action is to enjoy the protective benefits of the business judgment rule.

The duty of loyalty most certainly includes officer or director self-dealing contracts and transactions that more generally are referred to as conflict-of-interest transactions. But an officer or director can be disloyal to her corporation in many more ways than merely transacting business with the corporation. Material elsewhere in this treatise reviews many instances in which special doctrines have evolved in situations that raise concern for the director's or officer's loyalty. A prime example of such a situation is the directors' defense of control where the courts uniformly remove the actions of the board of directors from the protective presumption of the business judgment rule for fear that the directors may be acting to protect their personal self-interest and not serving the interests of the corporation or its stockholders. An even more blatant form of loyalty breach arises when the officer or director has usurped a corporate opportunity. The duty of loyalty places directors under a duty of confidentiality. Breaches of the duty of confidentiality can, for example, form the basis of insider trading liability. There also have been highly celebrated instances of board members inappropriately leaking information to the press. Interestingly, in special instances, loyalty violations can even arise when the directors or officers are acting in their good faith belief they are advancing the corporation's interest.[114] Thus, most certainly the duty of loyalty includes more than either self-dealing or usurping corporate opportunities.

An important question regarding the scope of the duty of loyalty is whether it requires more than the absence of self-interest, personal gain, and the like on the part of a director or officer. Or, does the duty of loyalty move beyond such minimalist considerations to require the fiduciary to act positively to advance the corporation's interests? That is, does the duty of loyalty have both negative and positive descriptions for how officers and directors are to behave?[115] For example, the American Law Institute's Corporate Governance Project sweeps the duty of loyalty into its obligation for "fair dealing," which prescribes a course of behavior when an officer, director, or controlling stockholder is financially interested in a matter. Pronouncements of the Delaware Supreme Court can be seen as embodying a more expansive view of the duty of loyalty. For example, in a leading case on the disclosure obligations of officers and directors, the court analogized the duty to a "compass" that is to serve as constant guide for the fiduciary when acting for the corporation.[116] And, in a leading corporate opportunity case, *Guth v. Loft, Inc.*,[117] the court observed that the directors have a duty "affirmatively to protect the interests of the corporation committed to his charge."[118]

To so view the duty of loyalty places the obligations of directors and officers on a footing equal to that of contemporary standards for fiduciaries generally where the obligation is not simply to subordinate self-interested behavior, but also to "act exclusively for the benefit of the other party."[119] So viewed, the duty of loyalty is not merely regulatory, but has a strong moral element.

An example of a breach of the director's duty of loyalty arises when the director, even though financially disinterested, knowingly fails to warn his fellow directors of material facts relevant to a transaction before the board.[120]

§ 10.10 INTERESTED OFFICER AND DIRECTOR TRANSACTIONS: DEFINED AND HISTORICAL TREATMENT

A few early American decisions adopted the inflexible English rule of disqualification whereby directors were forbidden to enter into contracts in which they have a personal interest that conflicts with their fiduciary duty of loyalty to the corporation. Under this view, unless there had been shareholder ratification, any contract with a director is voidable at the election of the corporation, regardless of whether it is fair and honest.[121] The theory of disqualification was that the corporation is entitled to the advice of each of its directors, and that directors may not abdicate their duty to the corporation and bargain with it in their own interest as a stranger, even if the corporation is represented by an independent majority of its directors.[122] It is argued that there cannot be real bargaining where the same person is acting on both sides of the transaction.[123]

Today, all American jurisdictions have found it impractical to disqualify directors or officers from contracting with their corporation. The earlier fear that a corporate fiduciary's dealings with the corporation was rife with the possibility of dishonesty or unfairness has given way to the belief that there are commercial advantages to such transactions and that regulation, rather than strict prohibition, is the approach with the greatest social welfare. In most jurisdictions, interested directors may be counted toward the quorum necessary for the board to take action on the transaction in which the directors have an interest.[124] An in broad overview, the approach in all states is that a corporation's contract with its director or officer is not voidable if approved by a disinterested body of directors or stockholders, or if the contracting director or officer successfully bears the burden of showing the fairness of the transaction.[125] As discussed below, this rule is now declared by most corporation statutes.[126]

§ 10.11 Burden of Proof of Fairness in Fiduciary Contracts

It has long been the prevailing rule that directors or officers seeking the benefits of a contract or transaction with their corporation have the burden of showing that the transaction meets the requirements of state conflict-of-interest provision. This is the case whether the suit is by the corporation to rescind or by the director or officer to enforce the contract.[127] However, proof that the transaction was approved by disinterested directors after full disclosure shifts the burden back to the complaining stockholder.[128] Similarly, approval of the transaction by the shareholders[129] or an independent committee will shift the burden back to the person challenging the transaction. However, when the committee lacks independence, the defendants retain the burden of proving the transaction's fairness.[130]

§ 10.12 Statutory Treatment of Transactions With Interested Officers and Directors

A provision of the California general corporation law, adopted in 1931, changed the former rule as to the disqualification of directors or officers to represent their corporation. Under that statute, if financially interested directors have to be counted to make up a quorum or majority to authorize a transaction, such transactions would no longer be voidable at the option of the corporation solely because of such director's participation, provided one of three alternative safeguards or conditions is met: (1) ratification by an independent majority of directors, (2) approval or ratification by the shareholders, or (3) a showing that the contract is just and reasonable as to the corporation. The statute thus set forth procedures for contracts between a corporation and its officers or directors, as well as between corporations that have some overlap of directors or officers.

Following the lead of the California statute, the 1950, 1969, and 1984 versions of the Model Business Corporation Act embraced the same three alternative safe harbors as were adopted in the path-breaking

California provision.[131] Thus, under Section 8.31 of the 1984 Model Act, an interested director may be counted in the quorum, and a particular contract or transaction is not void or voidable "because of such relationship or interest." The statute does not provide per se validation of all contracts where the statutory procedure has been followed and thus does not preclude further scrutiny.[132] The Model Act deals only with director conflict-of-interest transactions. Conflict-of-interest transactions involving non-director officers or employees are dealt with under the general principles of fiduciary obligations and the law of agency. All states except Massachusetts and South Dakota have conflict-of-interest statutes that mirror the approach first taken in California; most of the states have patterned their statutes after the pre-1988 versions of the Model Act.[133] Section 8.31 provides somewhat detailed descriptions of what constitutes an "indirect" conflict-of-interest as well as the voting requirements for *impartial* director or shareholder approval; this section, like earlier vintages of the Model Act, is general, even sometimes vague, in its requirements and scope. Because generality and vagueness necessarily robs transactions of predictability, the 1988 revision of the Model Business Corporations Act substitutes new sections 8:60 to 8:62. The overall philosophy of the 1988 amendments is to adopt a bright-line test and to make the provisions' proscription exclusive (circumstances falling outside the statutory definition of conflicting interests cannot be challenged on the basis of the transaction involves a conflict of interest, although challenges on other grounds are not foreclosed). The most distinguishing characteristics of the 1988 amendments are the level of detail with which they define "conflicting interests" and specify when judicial intervention is appropriate.

Scope of Conflict-of-Interest Statutes. In broad overview, conflict-of-interest statutes pose three distinct questions to the practitioner. The first is whether a given transaction falls within the statute's coverage. For example, is a subsidiary's declaration of a dividend in response to the influence of its parent a conflict-of-interest transaction? One may consider that declaring a dividend entails creating a "contract or transaction" between the subsidiary and its parent, on whose board many of the subsidiary's directors are also directors, especially since the declaration of a dividend establishes a distinct contractual relationship between the corporation and the stockholders entitled to the dividend. The Delaware Supreme Court, however, has held that, because a dividend is proportional to all the company's stockholders, it is not a conflict-of-interest transaction.[134] The 1989 amendments to the Model Business Corporation Act strive to provide greater specificity to the questions of what is a conflict of interest transaction, the means for its approval, and the consequences of the transaction being approved as set forth by the statute.[135]

However, even the Model Business Corporation Act does not deal with the more problematic inquiry as to the meaning of a "contract or transaction."[136] Thus, a finder's fee that an officer can earn upon a sale of the company to a third party was held within a conflict-of-interest transaction.[137] The question whether a given contract or transaction falls within a state's conflict-of-interest statute is not purely an academic question. As will be seen below, two distinct philosophies can be attributed to the purpose of conflict-of-interest statutes, one being that compliance with the statute immunizes the transaction from attack on any grounds. Under this view, the conflict-of-interest statute has a broad regulatory purpose. So viewed, one seeking to assure no successful attack can be brought against the transaction on grounds that it is unfair or unreasonable can approach the conflict-of-interest statute's alternative validating mechanisms as desirable and useful safe harbors to shield the transaction from further challenge or scrutiny. On the other hand, a second view of conflict-of-interest statutes is that they serve only as a procedural mechanism to overcoming the automatic voidability that existed at common law. Under this approach, satisfaction of one of the conflict-of-interest provisions merely removes any adverse inference that otherwise would be drawn from the director's interest in the transaction. This narrower construction of the statute's scope means the transaction may still be examined under the broader and less predictable standards of the director's or officer's fiduciary obligations; this approach is thus less attractive to the lawyer who wishes certainty and predictability when planning a transaction.

Methods of Satisfying the Statute. The second practical question posed by state conflict-of-interest statutes is how to comply with the statute's requirements. The typical conflict-of-interest statute sets forth three *alternative* mechanisms for validating a conflict-of-interest transaction: impartial director approval, impartial shareholder approval, or proof of the transaction's fairness. From the view of counseling a client, the least attractive of the three options is relying on proof of the transaction's fairness or reasonableness to the corporation. Courts uniformly place the burden of establishing fairness on the interested director or officer.[138] Fairness typically requires that the transaction reflect terms one would expect in an arm's-length transaction, which means generally that a self-dealing fiduciary must treat his corporation's interest as his own.[139] The fiduciary should neither take any advantage from his position on both sides of the transaction nor act in conflict with the corporation's interest to even the slightest extent.[140] Moreover, fairness is more encompassing than the adequacy of consideration; it includes the entirety of the transaction.[141] An important factor in any such fairness inquiry is the actual consideration paid compared with an independent appraisal of the property's fair market value.[142] Thus, the fairness of a lease transaction was considered in light of evidence of the market price of similar leases, the corporation's need for the property, the absence of any evidence that a better deal was possible with a noninterested party, the possibility that the interested party was diverting gain to himself, and whether full disclosure to the disinterested directors and shareholders was made.[143] The provision of the same benefits to noninterested parties is also relevant in concluding the transaction is fair.[144]

As between the two other validating mechanisms—impartial approval by the shareholders and impartial approval by the directors—the latter is certainly the more efficient. One needs to take care when seeking ratification of a completed conflict-of-interest transaction as to whether the applicable statute permits the disinterested directors to *ratify* a consummated conflict-of-interest transaction or merely to *approve* a yet to be consummated conflict-of-interest transaction. It is generally recognized and so expressed in most conflict-of-interest statutes that the shareholders have the inherent power to both approve and ratify conflict-of-interest transactions. Central to the power of the disinterested directors or stockholders to approve or ratify a conflict-of-interest transaction is that their approval be impartial, in good faith, and follow full disclosure of the material facts as to the director's or officer's interest as well as to the transaction itself. Each of these requirements is examined in the following paragraphs.

Many state statutes adhere to the 1984 Model Business Corporation Act's scheme of providing detailed rules for ascertaining whether the approving or ratifying body, whether stockholders or directors, is impartial—that is, disinterested. For example, the Model Business

Corporation Act requires that approval be by a majority of the voting shares not owned or under the control of the interested party. In states whose statutes do not so limit the shares that can approve or ratify a conflict-of-interest transaction, the result similar to that achieved in the Model Business Corporation Act can be achieved by a reasonable construction of the "good faith" approval requirement so that good faith minimally requires impartiality on the part of the decision-maker.[145]

Special care must be taken with respect to the type of vote required to satisfy a state's conflict-of-interest statute via impartial director approval. Different patterns exist among the states. Delaware, for example, requires that the approval be "by a majority of the disinterested directors."[146] On the other hand, some states merely condition approval being by votes normally sufficient after disregarding the votes of the interested directors.[147] Thus, consider the vote necessary at a meeting attended by a corporation's seven authorized directors and approval is sought for a transaction in which four of the directors are interested. The Delaware conflict-of-interest provision would be satisfied if at least two of the disinterested directors vote favorably.[148] But, in a state that merely disregards the votes, but not the physical presence of the interested directors, the transaction would not be approved. A common mechanism for overcoming any problems in securing a proper vote at the board of directors is for the board to exercise its powers under the charter or bylaws to create a committee of disinterested directors and to assign to that committee the responsibility to approve or ratify the conflict-of-interest transaction. A further point is that statutes customarily permit the interested director to count toward a quorum; this feature reflects the somewhat narrow feature of conflict of interest statutes, namely to address self-dealing by officers and directors. Hence, if directors who vote in approval of a transaction are interested, this does not prevent there being board approval of that transaction such that the transaction is vulnerable to attack for never being authorized.[149] The transaction should be viewed as being approved; nonetheless, there are separate questions whether it is voidable or otherwise protected by the business judgment rule because of the lack of disinterested director approval.

Whether authorization or ratification is by the board of directors or by the stockholders, it is subject to the statute's requirement that the decision-maker have acted in "good faith." As seen earlier in this chapter, good faith implicates the motives or intentions of the approving or ratifying body. As is true in any area of the law that turns on a person's intentions or motives, good faith is established circumstantially. In this regard, impartiality in terms of the voting directors or shareholders not having a financial interest served by the contract or transaction (except to the extent it is beneficial to the corporation itself) is the best measure of whether their approval or ratification is in good faith. Minimally, therefore, good faith requires impartiality. Thus a shareholder who controlled 99 percent of the corporation's stock and was himself an interested party in the transaction was held not to have acted in good faith in approving that transaction.[150] Lack of good faith was established by the self-interested dominating director convening a special board meeting without notice to ratify the conflict-of-interest transaction.[151] Substantial prior business relations with the interested party or apathy, such as rarely attending meetings at which the transaction was discussed, are each inconsistent with the good faith requirement.[152] Evidence of an ulterior motive hostile to the corporation's best interest also established a lack of good faith.[153] Furthermore, neither the directors nor the stockholders can by a majority vote ratify a fraudulent or wasteful transaction.[154] When the approving body is the board of directors, the inquiry into whether they did so in "good faith" focuses on challenges to their independence.[155]

Disclosure can well be viewed as the sine qua non of conflict-of-interest statutes. Not only have courts equated the absence of disclosure with inherent unfairness,[156] but also the efficacy of impartial director or shareholder approval is necessarily dependent on the reviewing body's knowledge of all material facts.[157] It is that body's independent and thoughtful approval after deliberating on all the facts that is intended by the conflict-of-interest statute to protect the corporation from the director's or officer's conflict of interest. Disclosure requires that the interested director or officer bring to the approving or ratifying body of directors or shareholders all facts material bearing on the transaction, not merely disclosing that the transaction involves self-dealing by the director or officer. Nonetheless, the 1989 Amendments to the Model Business Corporation Act provide an exception to the conflicted director making full disclosure. Under the Model Act, the full disclosure by the conflicted director that is normally required is excused when the director reasonably believes she has an extrinsic duty of confidentiality that justifies no disclosure.[158] The Official Comment states this provision "will apply to the frequently recurring situation where transacting corporations have common directors (or where a director of one party is an officer of the other)."[159] In this instance, the director must still inform the approving body of directors that there exists on her part a conflict of interest, disclose all information bearing on the transactions that the director can disclose without violating the independent duty of confidentiality, and finally must disclose the nature of the director's confidential duty.[160] This exception, however, applies only when there is an indirect conflict of interest transaction: a transaction between the corporation and an entity in which the director is a director, member, trustee or the like as well as a transaction with an entity that is controlled by the director's employer.[161]

The central consideration for effective approval by the stockholders is the fullness of disclosure of the director's or officer's interest as well as the material facts of the transaction and the independence of the approval. Impartial approval is absent if a majority of the votes favoring the transaction are held or controlled by the interested director or officer.[162] It is possible that the stockholder approval can occur informally, by open acquiescence or accepting the benefits of the transaction, provided there is strong evidence that the holders of a majority of the shares were aware of the material facts bearing on the transaction.[163]

Effect of Compliance with Statute. The final question posed by conflict-of-interest statutes is the effect of complying with one of its alternative validation provisions. The preamble to most conflict-of-interest statutes provides that the contract or transaction will not be voidable solely because of the director's or officer's interest if one of the three validating alternatives is satisfied.[164] Some courts interpret this language literally so that the effect of, for example, good faith independent stockholder approval is that such approval shields the transaction from being rescinded *solely* because it involves a conflict of interest.[165] Thus, under this approach, the effect of a transaction having satisfied one of the conflict-of-interest statute's three authorizing provisions is that such satisfaction removes any adverse inference that otherwise would be drawn because of the director's interest. As a correlative proposition, satisfaction of the statute's authorizing provisions shifts the burden of proof back to the objecting stockholder.[166] The result of such an interpretation is to allow the transaction to be questioned as beyond the protection of the business judgment rule because it was wasteful or not in the corporation's best interests. In such a suit, the plaintiff would bear the burden of proof.[167] Thus, under this view of compliance with the conflict-of-interest statute, the impact of the statute is primarily returning the burden of proof to the one challenging the transaction. If there had not been impartial director or stockholder approval, the burden of proving fairness to the corporation would have been on the director or officer with the conflict of interest.[168]

A different and more sweeping view of satisfying any of the conflict-of-interest statute's validating mechanisms is that it removes the transaction from any further scrutiny. That is, the requirements within the validating mechanisms of the statute that are relied on become the exclusive focus of any judicial attack. Thus, once the court is satisfied that the shareholders have independently and in good faith approved a self-dealing transaction after full disclosure of all material facts, the inquiry is closed.[169] Under this view, proof of the transaction's overall unfairness is pushed aside by deference to the will of the independent approving body acting in good faith. Such a perspective appears to comport with a sound view of the role of the reviewing court. A court should avoid second-guessing the diligent and fair deliberations of the independent stockholders or directors. However, there is ample authority to the contrary. Courts have been much influenced in this area by a leading conflict-of-interest case, *Remillard Brick Co. v. Remillard-Dandini Company*,[170] which held that bare technical compliance with the validating provisions of the California conflict-of-interest statute did not remove the transaction from having to be inherently fair to the corporation. *Remillard Brick Co.* has been consistently relied on as standing for the proposition that good faith impartial approval after full disclosure does not obviate the need for the transaction to also be fair to the corporation. While this view is consistent with the *language* used by *Remillard Brick Co.*, the facts of the case are considerably narrower: the defendants held proxies for most of the voting shares of the company and voted those shares in approval of an arrangement that would allow the defendants to divert much of the company's sales to themselves. The court could easily have found that the approval expressed by the defendants was not granted in "good faith," as expressly required by the statute. Instead, the court assumed the statute was complied with, albeit technically, and proceeded to add its own veneer by requiring that the transaction be fair. Ever since *Remillard Brick Co.*, there has been a good deal of confusion as to the substantive effects of satisfying a conflict-of-interest statute's provisions pertaining to impartial director or shareholder approval.

Loans to Officers and Directors: Sarbanes-Oxley Act of 2002. In 2002, Congress made a historic and significant entry into the historically exclusive state domain of corporate law by enacting section 402 of the Sarbanes-Oxley Act. This provision proscribes the extension of credit "in the form of personal loans" by reporting companies making loans to their executive officers or directors.[171] Generally, personal loans do not reach advances made to further the company's business. And overall "personal loans" can be understood to be a narrower class of transactions than the extension of credit so that many items that are advancements are likely not reached, such as travel advances for reimbursable expenses, since such expenses were incurred in furtherance of the firm's business. We might also see that advances of litigation costs are not prohibited since they reflect costs incurred in connection with company service.[172]

§ 10.13 THE POWER OF THE SHAREHOLDERS TO RATIFY

A fundamental principle of corporate law is that waste, gifts, fraud, and ultra vires acts cannot be approved by a mere majority vote; unanimity is the only means to ratify waste.[173] The presence of waste thus is a major qualification of the fundamental principle of majority rule within the corporation. The analogy to constitutional law is apt in such a case. Just as the Bill of Rights protects the minority from the tyranny or misdirection of the mob, so it is that a requirement of unanimity protects the minority from opportunism or improvidence sought by the majority.[174] It is just such thinking that qualifies the operation of conflict-of-interest statutes, discussed in the preceding section, where the statute's bare language would appear to authorize informed stockholder ratification as a means for validating self-dealing transactions. As seen there, the effect of such approval is merely to restore the presumption of the business judgment rule so that the transaction can still be subject for challenge on the grounds of waste. Placing the burden on the minority in such a case overcomes concern for the tyranny of the minority.[175]

A heuristic the courts sometimes use in determining what conduct may not be ratified by the majority is whether the complaint implicates the directors' or officers' duty of care or does it raise the specter of a duty of loyalty violation. The approval of an informed majority extinguishes the shareholder's duty of care claim.[176] This result would appear best understood if limited to questions of the process the directors or officers pursued in their consideration and approval of the transaction. Majority approval should not, however, prevent the plaintiff from the option of his bearing the substantial burden of proof that the transaction is so one-sided as to constitute waste.[177] When the wasteful transaction is approved by all the stockholders and accompanied by full disclosure, any claim the corporation may have had for the misconduct is released.[178]

To be valid, ratification must be after full disclosure of all material facts.[179] If shares owned or controlled by the interested party are needed to satisfy the majority approval, the better view is that the transaction should be proven to be fair to the corporation.[180] However, absent a fraud on creditors the sole stockholder's approval of her one-sided self-dealing transactions prevented the company's bankruptcy trustee from later seeking to recover for the damages the corporation suffered on the earlier transactions.[181] A purported ratification should not take the form of a blanket or whitewash resolution of approval of everything done by the directors for the past year or more, given by proxies solicited by the management of the corporation for the occasion.

An important distinction exists between the power of a majority of the shareholders to ratify a transaction between the corporation and its director and their power to ratify breaches of the directors' duty of loyalty. Approval by a majority of the shareholders after full disclosure of all the facts of the transaction should not also be viewed as their ratification of any misconduct that occurred in connection with that transaction unless the resolution and accompanying disclosures clearly call for the shareholders to ratify any director's misconduct.[182] When shareholder approval is so expressly sought, and there has been full disclosure of the self-dealing and the surrounding facts, the ratification of the majority can easily be seen as their determination that the corporate interest is not advanced by pursuing an action against the officers or directors.[183]

§ 10.14 ACTIONS AGAINST DIRECTORS AND OFFICERS FOR MISMANAGEMENT: CORPORATE, INDIVIDUAL, AND CREDITOR GROUNDS TO COMPLAIN

When directors or officers are guilty of mismanagement or negligence in conducting corporate affairs, the right of action is primarily in the corporation or, in the case of insolvency, in the corporation's receiver or trustee in bankruptcy. It is generally held that the corporation or its receiver may sue the delinquent officers to avoid multiplicity of suits against several officers and to do complete justice in one proceeding.[184] Creditors cannot sue individually for any loss suffered as a consequence of a director's or officer's breach of a duty to the corporation.[185] Individual shareholders cannot sue in their own right for impairment of the value of their shares by mismanagement of directors, but under certain conditions they may sue in a derivative or shareholders' suit for the benefit of the corporation, making the corporation and the guilty officers parties-defendants.[186]

To permit shareholders to sue separately for impairment of the value of their shares by wrongs done to the corporation would ordinarily result in confusion and wasteful multiplicity of actions and, further, would not protect the prior rights of creditors to corporate assets. Directors are liable to those who are injured by the directors' own tortious conduct regardless of whether the corporation is also liable.[187]

It is broadly recognized that the directors of a financially healthy corporation owe their fiduciary obligations to the corporation and its shareholders;[188] creditors' rights are accordingly limited to the fair construction of a creditor's contract with the corporation.

The suggestion has been made that directors do owe a fiduciary duty to creditors when the corporation is insolvent or is approaching insolvency.[189] In 1991, this suggestion was given greater attention by Chancellor Allen in *Credit Lyonnais Bank Nederland, N.V. v. Pathe Communications Corporation*,[190] involving a question of whether the board of directors of a corporation in financial distress acted properly in rejecting pressure from its controlling shareholder to engage in certain asset sales but he upheld the directors' actions. Deleware has since expressly rejected that the approach taken in *Credit Lyonnais* by holding that fiduciary duties are not owed directly to creditors, even when the firm is in the zone of insolvency.[191] The cases in which creditors have successfully invoked fiduciary obligations owed to them arise in decisions involving closely held corporations and the directors or those in control of the corporation that have been engaged in self-dealing.[192]

The major advantage to creditors of pursuing the directors on the theory that they have breached a fiduciary obligation owed to creditors is that the creditors can potentially recover a greater amount than can be recovered under the more traditional fraudulent-conveyance or preferential-transfer claim, where only the amount of the transfer can be recovered.

§ 10.15 DISCLOSURE OBLIGATIONS BASED UPON FIDUCIARY PRINCIPLES

A rapidly developing area of fiduciary responsibility is the disclosure duty owed shareholders by directors, officers, and controlling shareholders. Though there has long been a developed body of state law pertaining to directors' and officers' disclosure obligations when trading in their company's shares on the basis of material non-public confidential corporate information, only recently has there been the recognition of broader disclosure obligations for company fiduciaries. In the seminal case,[193] the Delaware Supreme Court held that directors owe shareholders a duty of "complete candor," so that the objective was "completeness and not adequacy."[194] From this broad language, Delaware courts have imposed a duty of full disclosure on directors[195] and controlling shareholders.[196] Courts outside of Delaware also impose a duty of candor in a variety of settings.[197]

Materiality of any alleged misrepresentation is judged by the same standards as apply under the federal securities laws.[198] Materiality is sometimes confused with duty in these cases. There are many items that the reasonable stockholder would consider important; but whether such an item must be disclosed turns on the context. Thus, the relative certainty of a third-party bid to acquire a firm can justify imposing a disclosure obligation to stockholders considering a buyback offer.[199] The duty is most readily applied when shareholder approval has been sought through proxy materials that omit or misstate material facts.[200] The duty to disclose applies to information within the fiduciary's control or possession; it does not require, even in transactions requiring stockholder approval, to disclose either information that does not exist or which could have been created.[201]

Directors who breach the duty are liable for damages that the shareholders suffer as a consequence of their breach, even though they did not benefit personally because of their omission or misstatement.[202] However, a breach of a disclosure duty does not automatically result in damages or for that matter even nominal damages; according to the Delaware Supreme Court damages to be recovered must be "logically and reasonably related to the harm or injury for which compensation is being awarded."[203] Because so often material disclosure violations pose irreparable harm to the shareholders, the much preferred remedy is remediation through an appropriate equitable remedy such as a preliminary injunction.[204] By far the most significant expansion of *Lynch* was made in *Malone v. Brincat*,[205] which held that directors and officers breached their duty of candor by knowingly releasing false financial information regarding the company's performance and financial position. The significance of *Malone* is that the court expressly held that *Lynch*'s duty of candor applied even when shareholders were not being asked to vote or otherwise approve a matter.

Since the duty of candor is a component of the officers', directors', and dominant stockholders' fiduciary obligation its scope is limited to those to whom there is a fiduciary relationship.[206] Another possible restriction may arise where the unlawful conduct is a matter that historically was regulated by federal securities laws, and not state fiduciary law. Thus, complaints alleging manipulation of securities prices via short selling were dismissed on the ground that market manipulation is beyond the purview of state fiduciary law.[207]

NOTES

1. *In re* Reading Co., 711 F.2d 509 (3d Cir. 1983); Lewis v. Curtis, 671 F.2d 779 (3d Cir. 1982).
2. *E.g.*, Burks v. Lasker, 441 U.S. 471 (1979); Abbey v. Control Data Corp., 603 F.2d 724 (8th Cir. 1979), *cert. denied*, 444 U.S. 1017 (1980); Auerbach v. Bennett, 393 N.E.2d 994 (N.Y. 1979). *See generally* Myron T. Steele, *Judicial Scrutiny of Fiduciary Duties in Delaware Limited Partnerships and Limited Liability Companies*, 32 DEL. J. CORP. L. 1 (2007).
3. As one commentator has put it, when the court finds no breach of a duty of care "[t]he court in effect [is] applying the business judgment rule." *See* HARRY G. HENN, CORPORATIONS: CASES AND MATERIALS 587 (1974).
4. Brehm v. Eisner, 746 A.2d 244, 264 (Del. 2000) (emphasis original).
5. *See* Melvin Aron Eisenberg, *The Divergence of Standards of Conduct and Standards of Review in Corporate Law*, 62 FORDHAM L. REV. 437 (1993). Thus, section 8.30(b) of the Model Business Corporation Act sets forth a standard of care for directors, but a breach of that standard assumes legal significance only if the director's decision is not protected pursuant to the review standards set forth in section 8.31. *See* MODEL BUSINESS CORPORATION ACT § 8.31 Official Comment (2008) [hereinafter MBCA]. For an example of a court distinguishing between the business judgment "rule" and the business judgment "doctrine," with the effect that the former was viewed to shield the directors from liability for their decisions

and the latter protects the transaction from further scrutiny, *see* Gries Sports Enterprises, Inc. v. Cleveland Browns Football Co., 496 N.E.2d 959, 964 (Ohio 1986).

6. *See generally* Joy v. North, 692 F.2d 880, 885 (2d Cir. 1982) (in contrast to actors in common tort cases, corporate officers or directors are rarely responsible for their mistakes in judgment).

7. Everett v. Phillips, 43 N.E.2d 18, 20 (N.Y. 1942).

8. FDIC v. Stahl, 89 F.3d 1510 (11th Cir. 1996) (business judgment rule assumes that the directors have been diligent and careful; plaintiffs need not establish gross negligence, ordinary negligence is sufficient).

9. Smith v. Van Gorkom, 488 A.2d 858 (Del. 1985).

10. ALI, 1 PRINCIPLES OF CORPORATE GOVERNANCE: ANALYSIS AND RECOMMENDATIONS § 4.01(c), Comment f at 182.

11. *See, e.g.,* Williams v. Geier, 671 A.2d 1368 (Del. 1996) (business judgment rule applied to independent majority's recommendation of articles amendment relating to voting rights).

12. *See, e.g.,* Smith v. Brown-Borhek Co., 200 A.2d 398, 398–402 (Pa. 1964).

13. RICHARD W. JENNINGS & RICHARD M. BUXBAUM, CORPORATIONS; CASES AND MATERIALS 178 (5th ed. 1979).

14. *See* EDWARD BRODSKY & M. PATRICIA ADAMSKI, THE LAW OF CORPORATE OFFICERS AND DIRECTORS: RIGHTS, DUTIES AND LIABILITIES § 2.04 (1984).

15. Hun v. Cary, 82 N.Y. 65 (1880).

16. Briggs v. Spaulding, 141 U.S. 132 (1891); DePinto v. Provident Sec. Life Ins. Co., 374 F.2d 37, 43–44 (9th Cir. 1967), *cert. denied*, 389 U.S. 822 (1967).

17. MODEL BUS. CORP. ACT § 35 (1980) [hereinafter Former MBCA] provides in relevant part:

> A director shall perform his duties as a director, including his duties as a member of any committee . . . in good faith, in a manner he reasonably believes to be in the best interests of the corporation, and with such care as an ordinarily prudent person in a like position would use under similar circumstances.

Accord, MBCA § 8.30 (2008).

18. MBCA § 8.30(a) (2008). *See* Committee on Corporate Laws, *Changes in the Model Business Corporation Act—Amendments Pertaining to Electronic Filings/Standards of Conduct and Standards of Liability for Directors,* 53 Bus. Law. 157 (1997).

19. MBCA § 8.30(a) (2008).

20. *Id.* § 8.31.

21. *In re* Illinois Valley Acceptance Corp. v. Martin, 531 F. Supp. 737 (C.D. Ill. 1982).

22. For rejection of the notion that the directors' oversight should extend to the personal affairs of its controlling stockholder, *see* Beam v. Stewart, 833 A.2d 961, 971–72 (Del. Ch. 2003).

23. *See, e.g.,* Hoye v. Meek, 795 F.2d 893, 896 (10th Cir. 1986).

24. Bowerman v. Hamner, 250 U.S. 504, 513 (1919).

25. Barnes v. Andrews, 298 F. 614 (S.D.N.Y. 1924).

26. *Barnes*'s holding is in sharp contrast with *Briggs v. Spaulding*, 141 U.S. 132 (1891), where the bank's board of directors allowed its president nearly absolute control without any close supervision. In a few months the bank was wrecked because of loans to the president and his relatives on worthless collateral, and no directors' meetings were held during a nearly six-month period. In a five-to-four decision, the Court excused the directors from liability on such questionable grounds as newness to office, ill health, and old age. *Briggs*'s bases for excusing the directors' failure to supervise are very much out of step with contemporary decisions.

27. *See* James D. Cox & Nis Jul Clausen, *The Monitoring Duties of Directors Under the EC Directives: A View from the United States Experience*, 2 DUKE J. COMP. & INT'L L. 29, 31–44 (1992).

28. 432 A.2d 814 (N.J. 1981).

29. *Id.* at 822. *See also Hoye*, 795 F.2d 893, 895(liability imposed on chairman whose attendance at board meetings was irregular).

30. *Contra*, Berman v. Le Beau Inter-Am., Inc., 509 F. Supp. 156, 161 (S.D.N.Y.), *aff'd mem.*, 679 F.2d 872 (2d Cir. 1981) (director who was "virtual figurehead" not liable).

31. *See also* Brane v. Roth, 590 N.E.2d 587 (Ind. Ct. App. 1992) (directors of cooperative breached duty by retaining inexperienced manager and failing to reasonably supervise manager to assure adequate hedging against possible declines in price of grain).

32. *See, e.g.*, Michelsen v. Penney, 135 F.2d 409, 419 (2d Cir. 1943).

33. *Hoye*, 795 F.2d 893, 896.

34. *In re* Tri-Star Pictures, Inc., Litig., 1995 WL 106520 (Del. Ch. 1995) (interested directors did not breach their fiduciary obligations by recusing themselves while other directors considered the transaction); Berkman v. Rust Craft Greeting Cards, Inc., 454 F. Supp. 787 (S.D.N.Y. 1978) (failure to warn fellow directors that investment banker had a material financial interest in the transaction on which opinion was being expressed constituted material fact regarding non-disclosing directors' fitness to serve as a director and should have been disclosed in the proxy statement seeking the directors' election).

35. *See, e.g.*, Dellastatious v. Williams, 242 F.3d 191 (4th Cir. 2001).

36. 188 A.2d 125 (Del. 1963).

37. The court rejected the plaintiff's argument that antitrust consent decrees 19 years earlier imparted such notice, reasoning in part that the current board of directors was not aware of those decrees. 188 A.2d at 129–30.

38. *Id.* 130.

39. *Id. Cf.* the internal controls reporting obligation of public companies under federal law. *See* 15 U.S.C. § 78m(b)(2) (1988).

40. *See* CORPORATE DIRECTOR'S GUIDEBOOK at 27–36; ABA, Section of Corporation, Banking and Business Law, *The Role and Composition of the Board of Directors of the Large Publicly Owned Corporation*, 33 BUS. LAW. 2083, 2101 (1978).

41. 698 A.2d 959 (Del. Ch. 1996).

42. *Id.* at 970.

43. Two leading Delaware practitioners (one to become Chief Justice of the Delaware Superior Court) conclude that *Allis-Chalmers* would likely be decided differently today because of the changed perception of the role of outside directors.
44. 911 A.2d 362 (Del. 2006).
45. *In re* Walt Disney Co. Deriv. Litig., 906 A.2d 27, 67 (Del. 2006). *Stone v. Ritter*, 911 A.2d 362 (Del. 2006), elaborates on the oversight liability.
46. 325 F.3d 795 (7th Cir. 2003).
47. 634 A.2d 345 (Del. 1993).
48. *Id.* at 371.
49. However, not every breach of duty will result in actionable damages. Thus, for example, breaches of disclosure duties that did not result in harm could not support damage recovery. Loudon v. Archer-Daniels-Midland Co., 700 A.2d 135 (Del. 1997).
50. For a highly critical review of *Cede & Co.* for departing from precedent by inviting the court to undertake a review of the substantive merits of the directors' decision so that, because of the substantive quality of the decision, the directors are not accountable for their carelessly rendered decision, *see* Lyman Johnson, *The Modest Business Judgment Rule*, 55 Bus. Law. 625 (2000).
51. Brehm v. Eisner, 746 A.2d 244, 259 (Del. 2000).
52. 488 A.2d 858 (Del. 1985).
53. *Id.* at 874.
54. *Id.*
55. The case was settled for $23.5 million, with $10 million coming from the corporation's directors' and officers' liability policy and most of the remainder from the buyer. Bayless Manning, *Reflections and Practical Tips on Life in the Boardroom After* Van Gorkom, 41 Bus. Law. 1 (1985).
56. Unocal Corp. v. Mesa Petroleum Co., 493 A.2d 946 (Del. 1985) (consultations over 11 hours with legal and financial advisors).
57. *See, e.g.,* Daniel R. Fischel, *The Business Judgment Rule and the Trans Union Case*, 40 Bus. Law. 1437 (1984).
58. *See, e.g.,* Pirelli Armstrong Tire Corp. Retiree Med. Benefits Trust v. Raines, 534 F.3d 779, 790 (D.C. Cir. 2008) (reliance on accountant to explain $200 million discrepancy "turned this allegedly red flag into a green flag").
59. Pogostin v. Rice, 480 A.2d 619 (Del. 1984).
60. It is on this point that the circumstances that separate the inside from the outside director are significant. For example, in the leading case, *Bates v. Dresser*, 251 U.S. 524 (1920), Justice Holmes held that a teller's flashy lifestyle should have prompted the bank's president to inquire whether shrinkages in the bank's deposits were the result of the teller's embezzlements. *Id.* at 530. The bank's outside directors, however, not being similarly on notice, were entitled to rely on the reassurances of the president and the government examiner that nothing was amiss. *Id.* at 529.
61. *See, e.g.,* Cal. Corp. Code § 309(b) (West 1990); Del. Code Ann. tit. 8, § 141(c) (2001); N.Y. Bus. Corp. Law § 717 (McKinney 1986); MBCA § 8.30(b) (2008).

62. MBCA § 8.30(b), Official Comment (2008).
63. *See, e.g.,* MBCA § 8.30(b) (2008).
64. Gould v. American Hawaiian S.S. Co., 351 F. Supp. 853, 865 (D. Del. 1972), *rev'd and remanded on other grounds,* 535 F.2d 761 (3d Cir. 1976).
65. Spirt v. Bechtel, 232 F.2d 241 (2d Cir. 1956).
66. *See* Rowen v. Le Mars Mut. Ins. Co., 282 N.W.2d 639, 655 (Iowa 1979).
67. 781 F.2d 264 (2d Cir. 1986).
68. *Id.* at 275.
69. Harris v. Pearsall, 190 N.Y.S. 61 (Sup. Ct. 1921).
70. *See* Fitzpatrick v. Federal Deposit Ins. Corp., 765 F.2d 569, 577 (6th Cir. 1985).
71. *Smith,* 488 A.2d 858, 874–75.
72. *See* Fitzpatrick v. Federal Deposit Ins. Corp., 765 F.2d 569, 577 (6th Cir. 1985) (duty to inquire into reasonableness of subordinate's investigation does not arise until directors are already on inquiry notice).
73. Panter v. Marshall Field & Co., 486 F. Supp. 1168, 1180, 1194 (N.D. Ill. 1980), *aff'd,* 646 F.2d 271 (7th Cir.), *cert. denied,* 454 U.S. 1092 (1981).
74. Meyers v. Moody, 693 F.2d 1196, 1211 (5th Cir. 1982).
75. *See, e.g.,* Hills Stores Co. v. Bozic, 769 A.2d 88 (Del. Ch. 2000) (directors' decision to reject bid for control upheld, even though as a consequence it triggered contractual rights of officers for substantial severance award).
76. Cramer v. General Tel. & Elecs. Corp., 582 F.2d 259, 275 (3d Cir. 1978), *cert. denied,* 439 U.S. 1129 (1979).
77. 383 N.Y.S.2d 807 (Sup. Ct.), *aff'd,* 387 N.Y.S.2d 993 (App. Div. 1976).
78. Moreover, the American Express stockholders would not be able to recognize the loss because their basis in the shares they received was the fair market value of the shares on the date the DL&J were distributed. Thus the real gainer in the transaction was the U.S. government.
79. *See* Brehm v. Eisner, 746 A.2d 244, 266 (Del. 2000).
80. 118 N.Y.S. 351 (Sup. Ct. 1909).
81. 74 N.E.2d 305 (N.Y. 1947).
82. 507 F.2d 759, 762–63 (3d Cir. 1974).
83. *Id.*
84. *Id.* at 762.
85. *See, e.g.,* Smiles v. Elfred, 149 N.Y.L.J., Feb. 20, 1963, at 14, col. 6 (N.Y. Sup. Ct. 1963); Borden v. Cohen, 231 N.Y.S.2d 902 (Sup. Ct. 1962); Clayton v. Farish, 73 N.Y.S.2d 727 (Sup. Ct. 1947).
86. James D. Cox, *Compensation, Deterrence, and the Market as Boundaries for Derivative Suit Procedures,* 52 Geo. Wash. L. Rev. 745, 765 (1984).
87. ALI, Principles of Corporate Governance: Analysis and Recommendations § 4.01 (1994).
88. *Id.* § 7.19(1) (1994).
89. *Id.* § 7.10(a)(2) (1994).
90. *Id.* §§ 2.01(b)(1) and 4.01(a) (1994) and commentary at pp. 195–97.
91. See § 10.4.
92. *See* Del. Code Ann. tit. 8, § 102(b)(7) (2001).
93. Notable differences include California's statute, whose section affects actions "brought by or in the right of the corporation," so that they are

not applicable to actions brought directly by shareholders. *See* Cal. Corp. Code § 204(a)(10) (West 1990).

94. *See* Smith v. Van Gorkom, 488 A.2d 858 (Del. 1985) (misconduct by Van Gorkom, who was both director and CEO).

95. Section 102(b)(7) shields the directors from damages whether they arrive in law or equity for rescission.

96. *See* Emerald Partners v. Berlin, 726 A.2d 1215, 1224 (Del. 1999) (*dicta* because complaint only alleged a violation of the duty of care).

97. *See, e.g.,* Ohio Rev. Code Ann. § 1701.59(D) (West Supp. 2001); Wis. Stat. Ann. § 180.0828 (West 2002).

98. Fla. Stat. Ann. § 607.0831(1) (West 2001). The last offense gives rise to liability only if the action is by the corporation or shareholder. A fifth category of director personal liability arises for reckless or wanton misconduct, omissions committed in bad faith, or wanton and willful disregard of human rights, safety, or property when the action is brought by a plaintiff other than the corporation or its stockholders.

99. 787 A.2d 85 (Del. 2001).

100. *Id.*

101. Va. Code § 13.1-692.1 (LexisNexis 2006).

102. Tandycrafts, Inc. v. Initio Partners, 562 A.2d 1162, 1164 (Del. 1989).

103. *Cf.* United States v. Park, 421 U.S. 658 (1975) (upholding conviction of president where unsanitary conditions existed at one of 12 warehouses; corporation had 36,000 employees and 874 retail outlets).

104. Pontchartrain R.R. v. Paulding, 11 La. 41 (1837).

105. Bates v. Dresser, 251 U.S. 524 (1920).

106. *Cf.* Bates v. Seeds, 272 N.W. 515 (Iowa 1937).

107. United States v. Park, 421 U.S. 658 (1975).

108. 318 U.S. 80, 85–86 (1943).

109. *See, e.g.,* North Confidence Mining & Dev. Co. v. Fitch, 208 P. 328 (Cal. Ct. App. 1922).

110. *See* Austin Wakeman Scott, *The Trustee's Duty of Loyalty,* 49 Harv. L. Rev. 521 (1936). *But see* Bovay v. H.M. Byllesby & Co., 38 A.2d 808 (Del. 1944).

111. For early recognition of the problems of extrapolating from the law of trusts obligations for directors and officers, *see* York v. Guaranty Trust Co., 143 F.2d 503, 514 (2d Cir. 1944), *rev'd on other grounds,* 326 U.S. 99 (1945).

112. The duty of loyalty is equated to the "good faith" requirement that appears in statutes and in court opinions dealing with the obligations of directors and officers. *See, e.g., In re* Gaylord Container Corp. Shareholders Litigation, 753 A.2d 462, 475–76 n.41 (Del. Ch. 2000).

113. *See* Mills Acquisition Co. v. MacMillan, Inc., 559 A.2d 1261, 1284 n.32 (Del. 1989) (disinterested directors who abandon their oversight responsibilities in context of takeover breach their duties of care and loyalty).

114. *See* Blasius Indus. v. Atlas Corp., 564 A.2d 651, 663 (Del. Ch. 1988) (even though acting in the good faith belief they are serving the corporation's interest, management must demonstrate a compelling justification for action taken for purpose of thwarting the ongoing efforts of a stockholder to exercise its rights of corporate suffrage).

115. *See* Lyman Johnson, *Enron: Loyalty Discourse in Corporate Law*, 28 DEL. J. CORP. LAW 27 (2003).

116. *See* Malone v. Brincat, 722 A.2d 5, 10 (Del. 1998).

117. 5 A.2d 503 (Del. 1939).

118. *Id.* at 510.

119. *See* Gregory S. Alexander, *A Cognitive Theory of Fiduciary Relationships*, 85 CORNELL L. REV. 767, 776 (2000).

120. *See, e.g.*, Berkman v. Rust Craft Greeting Cards, Inc., 454 F. Supp. 787 (S.D.N.Y. 1978) (some of the directors failed to disclose to their fellow directors their knowledge that the investment banker whose fairness opinion the board would rely upon had a material financial interest in the outcome of the transaction).

121. Morgan v. King, 63 P. 416 (Colo. 1900); Pearson v. Concord R. Corp., 62 N.H. 537 (1883).

122. Rothenberg v. Franklin Washington Trust Co., 13 A.2d 667, 672 (N.J. Ch. 1940).

123. *See generally* Snead v. United States Trucking Corp., 380 So. 2d 1075 (Fla. Dist. Ct. App. 1980) (deal not at arm's length when officer-director-stockholder of one corporation contracted with second corporation of which he was salaried employee).

124. *See, e.g.*, Karris v. Water Tower Trust & Sav. Bank, 389 N.E.2d 1359 (Ill. App. Ct. 1979).

125. Pepper v. Litton, 308 U.S. 295 (1939); Norlin Corp. v. Rooney, Pace, Inc., 744 F.2d 255 (2d Cir. 1984).

126. *See* Former MBCA § 41 (1969); *accord*, MBCA § 8.31 (2008).

127. *See, e.g., Pepper* 308 U.S. at 306; Ohio Drill & Tool Co v. Johnson, 498 F.2d 186 (6th Cir. 1974); Pappas v. Moss, 393 F.2d 865 (3d Cir. 1968); *In re* Wheelabrator Technologies Shareholder Litigation, 663 A.2d 1194 (Del. Ch. 1995).

128. Weiss v. Kay Jewelry Stores, 470 F.2d 1259 (D.C. Cir. 1972).

129. Solomon v. Armstrong, 747 A.2d 1098, 1117 (Del. Ch. 1999), *aff'd*, 746 A.2d 277 (Del. 2000).

130. Kahn v. Tremont Corp., 694 A.2d 422 (Del. 1997) (lower court erred in shifting the burden of proof to plaintiffs challenging corporation's stock purchase from a related company).

131. Former MBCA § 41 (1969); *accord*, MBCA § 8.31 (2008).

132. *See* Remillard Brick Co. v. Remillard-Dandini Co., 241 P.2d 66, 72 (Cal. Ct. App. 1952), where the court held that notwithstanding compliance with statutory formalities, the contract if "unfair and unreasonable to the corporation may be avoided."

133. MODEL BUS. CORP. ACT ANN. § 8.61 at 8.43 (3d ed. 1994).

134. Sinclair Oil Corp. v. Levien, 280 A.2d 717 (Del. 1971).

135. MBCA §§ 8.60 to 8.63 (2008).

136. The 1989 Model Act "conflicting interest transaction" reaches "transactions" which the commentary describes as "negotiations or a consensual bilateral arrangement between the corporation and another party or parties that concern their respective and differing economic rights or interests—not simply a unilateral action by the corporation, but

rather a 'deal.' " MBCA Subchapter F. Directors' Conflicting Interest Transactions, Comment 2 (2008).

137. *See* Ryan v. Tad's Enterprises, Inc., 709 A.2d 682 (Del. Ch. 1996) (consulting agreement secured by dominant stockholders in their sale of restaurant business was linked to their purchase of the two remaining divisions).

138. *See, e.g.,* Cascades West Assocs. Ltd. P'ship v. PRC, Inc., 36 Va. Cir. 324 (1995) (because directors are akin to trustees, they must meet burden of proof pursuant to the clear and convincing evidence standard).

139. Noe v. Roussel, 310 So. 2d 806 (La. 1975); Harris Trust & Sav. Bank v. Joanna-Western Mills Co., 368 N.E.2d 629 (Ill. App. Ct. 1977) (transaction should be one that commended itself to a wholly independent board).

140. *In re* Brokers, Inc., 363 B.R. 458, 473 (Bankr. M.D.N.C. 2007).

141. Johnson v. Witkowski, 573 N.E.2d 513, 521 (Mass. App. Ct. 1991).

142. Straight v. Goss, 678 S.E.2d 443, 453 (S.C. Ct. App. 2009).

143. *See, e.g.,* Pittsburgh Terminal Corp. v. Baltimore and Ohio R.R., 875 F.2d 549 (6th Cir. 1989) (dominant consideration is fairness of the price and that there is no further requirement of "fair dealing" as occurs under the Delaware jurisprudence); Oberly v. Kirby, 592 A.2d 445 (Del. 1991) (fairness satisfied by evidence of lengthy bargaining, value approached midpoint of both sides, and absence of viable alternatives).

144. Nalty v. D.H. Holmes Co., Ltd., 882 So. 2d 1, 10 (La. Ct. App. 2004).

145. Even upon approval of a majority of the disinterested shares, the transaction can still be reviewed under a waste standard meaning "an exchange to which no reasonable person not acting under compulsion and in good faith could agree" that the transaction is fair. *See* Lewis v. Vogelstein, 699 A.2d 327 (Del. Ch. 1997).

146. DEL. CODE ANN. tit. 8, § 144 (2001).

147. *See* Weiss Med. Complex v. Kim, 408 N.E.2d 959 (Ill. App. Ct. 1980) (quorum not present when four of seven directors had a personal interest in a matter).

148. *See* Rapoport v. Schneider, 278 N.E.2d 642 (N.Y. 1972) (five-to-one vote deemed approval of transaction when three of yes votes were interested).

149. *See, e.g.,* Nalty v. D.H. Holmes Co., Ltd., 882 So. 2d 1, 8–9 (La. Ct. App. 2004).

150. Rivercity v. American Can Co., 600 F. Supp. 908, 921 (E.D. La. 1984).

151. Groves v. Rosemound Improvement Ass'n, 490 So. 2d 348, 350–51 (La. Ct. App. 1986).

152. *See* Kahn v. Tremont Corp., 694 A.2d 422 (Del. 1997).

153. *See* Nord v. Eastside Ass'n, 664 P.2d 4, 6 (Wash. Ct. App. 1983).

154. *See, e.g.,* Wolf v. Frank, 477 F.2d 467 (5th Cir. 1973) (all disinterested directors cannot ratify fraud on part of other directors); Lewis v. Vogelstein, 699 A.2d 327 (Del. Ch. 1997) (wasteful options granted directors cannot be ratified by mere majority vote of stockholders).

155. *See* Benihana of Tokyo, Inc. v. Benihana, Inc., 891 A.2d 150, 175–77 (Del. Ch. 2005), *aff'd*, 906 A.2d 114 (Del. 2006) (finding the following did not render approving directors not independent: director's interest

in retaining office and accompanying directors' fees or having a close friendship to the interested party).

156. *See, e.g.,* Kim v. Grover C. Coors Trust, 179 P.3d 86, 93–94 (Colo. Ct. App. 2007) (in assessing the transaction's overall fairness, it is relevant that the interested directors made full disclosure but irrelevant to the fairness inquiry that the independent directors did not review all the material information so disclosed).

157. *See, e.g., In re* Brokers, 363 B.R. 458 (Bankr. M.D.N.C. 2007).

158. MBCA § 8.62(b) (2008).

159. MBCA § 8.62(b) (2008) Comment 2 (2008).

160. MBCA § 8.62(b) (2008). *See, e.g.,* Fisher v. State Mutual Ins. Co., 290 F.3d 1256 (11th Cir. 2002) (duty of confidentiality supporting use of procedure in Georgia's version of this section found where defendant was a member of each company's board, even though one of the company allegedly was a shell company).

161. MBCA §§ 8.62(b) & 8.60(5)(v) & (vi) (2008).

162. *See, e.g.,* Pappas v. Moss, 393 F.2d 865 (3d Cir. 1968) (burden not shifted by shareholder approval when interested party held a majority of the shares).

163. *See* Robert A. Wachsler, Inc. v. Florafax Int'l, Inc., 778 F.2d 547 (10th Cir. 1985).

164. Being phrased in terms of a transaction being possibly "void" or "voidable," the statute lends itself naturally to both offensive and defensive applications. Hicks v. Midwest Transit, Inc., 500 F.3d 647 (7th Cir. 2007).

165. *See, e.g.,* Fliegler v. Lawrence, 361 A.2d 218 (Del. 1976).

166. *See, e.g.,* Palumbo v. Deposit Bank, 758 F.2d 113 (3d Cir. 1985); Cohen v. Ayers, 596 F.2d 733 (7th Cir. 1979); Rosenfield v. Metals Selling Corp., 643 A.2d 1253 (Conn. 1994).

167. *See, e.g.,* Melrose v. Capitol City Motor Lodge, Inc., 705 N.E.2d 985 (Ind. 1998).

168. *See, e.g.,* Pittsburgh Terminal Corp. v. Baltimore and Ohio R.R., 875 F.2d 549 (6th Cir. 1989); Byelick v. Vivadelli, 79 F. Supp. 2d 610 (E.D. Va. 1999).

169. *See* Camden v. Kaufman, 613 N.W.2d 335 (Mich. Ct. App. 2000).

170. 241 P.2d 66 (Cal. Ct. App. 1952).

171. 15 U.S.C. §§ 7291, *et seq.,* amending Securities Exchange Act, section 13(k), 15 U.S.C. § 78m(k) (operative language focuses on "to extend or maintain credit, to arrange for the extension of credit, or to renew an extension of credit, in the form of a personal loan to or for any director or executive officer . . ." subject to certain enumerated exceptions for banking institutions as part of their normal business).

172. *See Sarbanes-Oxley § 402—Interpretation Issued by 25 Law Firms* (Oct. 15, 2002) *available at* http://content.lawyerlinks.com/sec/directors_officers/pdfs/soxact_402___25_firm_mailing.pdf

173. *See* Michelson v. Duncan, 407 A.2d 211, 219 (Del. 1979).

174. *See* MELVIN A. EISENBERG, THE STRUCTURE OF THE CORPORATION: A LEGAL ANALYSIS 392–95 (1976).

175. For the contrary view, namely, that informed majority ratification should remove the transaction from any further scrutiny, *see* Mary A. Jacobson,

Interested Director Transactions and the (Equivocal) Effects of Shareholder Ratification, 21 Del. J. Corp. L. 981, 1021 (1996).

176. *See, e.g., In re* Wheelabrator Technologies, Inc. Shareholder Litigation, 663 A.2d 1194 (Del. Ch. 1995) (plaintiff can continue to pursue duty of loyalty claim).

177. The one instance where stockholder ratification should itself immunize the challenged conduct is in the instance of a claim the directors lacked authority to take action that was later ratified. *See* Gantler v. Stephens, 965 A.2d 695, 713 n. 54 (Del. 2009).

178. *In re* Mi-Lor Corp., 348 F.3d 294 (1st Cir. 2003).

179. Robert A. Wachsler, Inc. v. Florafax Int'l, Inc., 778 F.2d 547 (10th Cir. 1985) (Delaware conflict-of-interest statute requires vote or acquiescence by majority shareholders after full disclosure); *Gantler*, 965 A.2d at 712 (failure to disclose material facts robs vote of essential predicate to apply doctrine of ratification).

180. *See* Stevens *ex rel.* Park View Corp. v. Richardson, 755 P.2d 389, 395 (Alaska 1988); Fliegler v. Lawrence, 361 A.2d 218 (Del. 1976).

181. *See* Dannen v. Scafidi, 393 N.E.2d 1246 (Ill. Ct. App. 1979).

182. *See Gantler*, 965 A.2d at 713 (holding that the doctrine of shareholder ratification "must be limited to its 'classic' form; that is, to circumstances where a fully informed shareholder vote approves director action that does *not* legally require shareholder approval in order to become effective. Moreover, the only director action or conduct that can be ratified is that which the shareholders are specifically asked to approve.") (emphasis original).

183. *See* Berkwitz v. Humphrey, 163 F. Supp. 78 (N.D. Ohio 1958).

184. Meyers v. Moody, 693 F.2d 1196 (5th Cir. 1982); Baker v. Allen, 197 N.E. 521, 524 (Mass. 1935).

185. Speer v. Dighton Grain, Inc., 624 P.2d 952 (Kan. 1981).

186. Shareholder litigation is discussed in Chapter 15. For the distinction between direct or class and derivative suits.

187. *See* Frances T. v. Village Green Owners Ass'n, 229 Cal. Rptr. 456, 723 P.2d 573 (1986) (directors of nonprofit corporation who have met minimum standard of care owed to corporation are not protected by business judgment rule from liability to third parties if directors have engaged in tortious conduct).

188. *See, e.g.,* Simons v. Cogan, 549 A.2d 300 (Del. 1988).

189. *See, e.g.,* Rapids Constr. Co. v. Malone, 139 F.3d 892 (4th Cir. 1998) (shareholders of financially shaky corporation breached fiduciary duty to creditors when they caused corporation to engage in stock repurchase; applying Virginia law).

190. Credit Lyonnais Bank Nederland, N.V. v. Pathe Communications Corporation, 1991 WL 277613 (Del. Ch. 1991).

191. North American Catholic Educational Programming Fdn. Inc. v. Gheewalla, 930 A.2d 92 (Del. 2007) (dismissing creditor's direct breach of fiduciary suit against directors).

192. Rapids Constr. Co. v. Malone, 139 F.3d 892 (4th Cir. 1998) (repurchase of shares breached fiduciary duty to creditors; applying Virginia law).

193. Lynch v. Vickers Energy Corp., 383 A.2d 278 (Del. 1977).
194. *Id.* at 281.
195. *See, e.g.,* Arnold v. Society for Savings Bancorp, 650 A.2d 1270 (Del. 1994).
196. *See, e.g.,* Weinberger v. UOP, Inc., 457 A.2d 701, 711–12 (Del. 1983).
197. *See, e.g.,* Kennedy v. VenRock Associates, 348 F.3d 584 (7th Cir. 2003) (applying Maryland law to conclude reincorporation for which there was full disclosure of material differences in laws of Maryland and new domicile, Delaware).
198. *See, e.g.,* Zirn v. VLI Corp., 621 A.2d 773, 779 (Del. 1993).
199. *Compare* Bershad v. Curtiss-Wright Corp., 535 A.2d 840 (Del. 1987) (no disclosure breach where firm not for sale and no third-party offer was ever made); *with* Alessi v. Beracha, 849 A.2d 939 (Del. Ch. 2004) (duty breached where firm for sale and discussions with third party were ongoing when shareholders accepted offer of their company to repurchase their shares).
200. Lacos Land Co. v. Arden Group, Inc., 517 A.2d 271 (Del. Ch. 1986).
201. *In re* JCC Holding Co., Inc. Shareholder Litig., 843 A.2d 713 (Del. Ch. 2003) (rejecting argument that directors should have performed a discounted cash flow analysis and made that information available when seeking stockholder approval for a merger).
202. Zirn v. VLI Corp., 621 A.2d 773 (Del. 1993), *aff'd*, 681 A.2d 1050 (Del. 1996).
203. *In re* J.P. Morgan Chase & Co. Shareholder Litig., 906 A.2d 766, 773 (Del. 2006).
204. *See, e.g., In re* Transkaryotic Therapies, Inc., 954 A.2d 346, 362 (Del. Ch. 2008).
205. 722 A.2d 5 (Del. 1998).
206. Alexandra Global Master Fund, Ltd. v. Ikon Office Solutions, Inc., 2007 WL 2077153 (S.D.N.Y. 2007) (no duty owed to holder of convertible notes to disclose secret intent to redeem the notes shortly after their issuance).
207. *See* RGC International Investors, LDC v. Greka Energy Corp., 2001 WL 984689 (Del. Ch. 2001).

CHAPTER 11

FIDUCIARY DUTIES FOR EXECUTIVE COMPENSATION, CORPORATE OPPORTUNITIES, AND CONTROLLING STOCKHOLDERS

PART A. EXECUTIVE COMPENSATION

§ 11.1 Contracts for Compensation of Directors and Officers

No matter is more delicate or important in a corporation, whether it be closely held or publicly held, than the compensation arrangement between the corporation and its executives. A well-designed and thoughtful compensation arrangement provides incentives for managers to reduce the agency costs that are inherent in a public corporation, and in a close corporation it serves as a significant component of how the stockholders will divide the company's cash flows among themselves. Just as there are perplexing planning problems concerning how best to provide rewards and incentives to managers,[1] there are equally challenging jurisprudential questions of the proper role of the courts when asked to judge the propriety of a particular compensation arrangement.[2]

Courts traditionally have been reluctant to imply contracts for director compensation. It has long been a presumption at common law that directors serve without pay. They cannot recover on an implied contract for the reasonable value of their services, because both custom and their fiduciary relationship repel any implication that official services are to be paid for.[3] This presumption also applies to executive officers such as president, vice president, secretary, and treasurer, who are not entitled to recover compensation for performing the ordinary duties of their office as directors in the absence of an express agreement.[4] Similarly, no claim will lie in an action for quantum meruit.[5]

In the absence of a statute[6] or a delegation of authority, the fees for compensation of the directors for their ordinary duties must be fixed by the shareholders or by a provision in the bylaws.[7] However, the clear statutory trend is to authorize the board of directors to set the compensation for directors.[8] Even where no statutory authority exists, the charter or the shareholders frequently authorize directors to fix their own fees or salaries[9] and, as such, the presumptions of the business judgment rule apply to even sizable awards to the directors.[10] Substantial fees are frequently provided for attendance at directors' meetings or at meetings of committees of the board of large corporations.

Typically, the compensation of officers is established yearly by a resolution of the board of directors, although it is not uncommon for executive compensation to be set forth in the bylaws[11] or approved by the stockholders. When a person is selected to be an officer or employee under circumstances indicating an expectation of payment but without any express contract, the law will imply a promise on the part of the corporation to pay a reasonable compensation.[12] It has long been recognized that officers involved in the active management of the company are entitled to reasonable compensation for services as managers even if no compensation had been previously fixed, because the company could not expect such onerous managerial services to be performed for nothing.[13]

By the great weight of authority, the presumption against an implied contract of compensation for the directors and officers of a corporation does not apply to unusual or extraordinary services—that is, services that are not properly incidental to their office and are rendered outside of their regular duties. If directors or other officers perform such services at the request of the board of directors with the understanding that they are to be paid for, the law will, in the absence of any special agreement, imply a promise to pay what they are reasonably worth.[14] Thus, the president of a company who acted as the general contractor for the construction of an office building was not entitled to be compensated additionally for the services he rendered as the general contractor, where the costs of constructing the building exceeded the funds available and he took on the additional responsibilities to cut costs. Furthermore, the president had not been asked by the stockholders to assume the role of general contractor.[15]

§ 11.2 Methods of Paying Executive Compensation

Traditionally, there have been three basic ways of compensating the corporate executive: (1) salary, (2) bonuses, and (3) a pension or other deferred compensation. As a result of increased sophistication in planning, the variations of the three basic forms of compensation defy exhaustive categorization. The growing use of compensation "packages" arises out of a desire to attract and hold top-flight personnel, provide them with incentives for greater effort and dedication, and fully utilize tax advantages offered by some forms of compensation. Tailoring the most advantageous compensation plan requires careful consideration of the securities law, tax consequences, and the Federal Employment Retirement Income Security Act (ERISA).[16] There is a widespread use in publicly held corporations, and in the large close corporations for that matter, of various kinds of contingent or deferred compensation—cash bonuses, stock bonuses, stock options, stock purchase plans, profit-sharing plans, pension programs, allowances to surviving spouses and dependents, medical and dental payment plans, and other kinds of employee benefits.

Stock options are a highly popular form of executive compensation in the United States. The granting of stock options does not require a present expenditure of corporate funds, which may be badly needed for business operations or for expansion. Executives find stock options attractive because of their speculative appeal in offering a chance for really large financial gain. Further, under some circumstances, stock options carry substantial tax advantages for executives. When the options are exercised, the proportionate interests of existing shareholders in the company will be diluted, but presumably by that time the employees exercising the options will have proved their worth and have benefited the shareholders by contributing to an increase in the value of the corporation's shares.

A deferred compensation unit plan ("phantom stock" plan) is sometimes used as an alternative to or in addition to traditional pension arrangements for executive employees. Under a phantom stock plan, the company, instead of requiring the employee to buy stock or giving the employee stock in the company, pays the employee additional annual compensation or gives credit toward retirement benefits equal to dividends paid on a share of the company's stock multiplied by the number of units the employee holds in the plan, and on retirement the employee gets deferred compensation based on the increase, if any, in the market value of the company's stock during the time the employee has held units in the plan.

Restricted stock plans have become more common in recent years. Under this arrangement, stock or units are actually issued to the employee, but subject to conditions related to vesting, transferability and even forfeiture conditions. Lifting of the conditions is service based but frequently is dependent on certain performance requirements. The shares may even be subject to repurchase requirements at a predetermined price. Restricted stocks confer ownership immediately to their holders, such as dividends and voting rights, and the corporation's tax deduction equals the value of the shares when the restrictions lapse. Hence, if the stock appreciates in value between the grant date and the date the restriction lapses, the corporation is able to deduct the value of the shares as of the latter date, not the grant date, as is the case with qualified stock options, whereas the accounting charge to earnings is based on the value of the granted shares less any payment by the recipient. Hence, subsequent price increases do not penalize the company's reported net income by increasing the compensation costs related to the earlier grant.

§ 11.3 COMPENSATION FOR PAST SERVICES

Formerly, paying a bonus or to increasing an officer's or employee's compensation for services already rendered was invalid. Such a payment was regarded as a gift and thus a misapplication of corporate funds.[17] The rule against compensation for past services does not apply, however, where the services were rendered with a formal or informal understanding that the fixed salary was only a minimum compensation and that additional allowances or compensation, although indefinite, would be paid.[18] The compensation in such a case can be seen as not in fact being for past services, and the courts accordingly permit the directors to pay additional compensation in the exercise of reasonable discretion after the services have been performed or the contract for fixed compensation has been entered into.[19]

In recent years, with respect to payments based on past services, there has been a significant retreat from formalistic attitudes and movement toward a rule of reasonableness.[20] In some states, statutes expressly grant authority to provide bonuses and retroactive pension plans.[21]

§ 11.4 JUDICIAL REVIEW OF FAIRNESS OF EXECUTIVE COMPENSATION: SELF-DEALING AND GOOD FAITH

Most states have enacted conflict-of-interest statutes[22] that are sufficiently broad to include board-of-director action establishing the compensation of one of its members. Close judicial scrutiny customarily occurs when those receiving the compensation are the same individuals approving the compensation.[23] Conflict-of-interest statutes set forth steps that, if satisfied, invoke the protection of the business judgment rule for executive compensation. In broad overview, the steps require good faith, impartial approval by the directors or shareholders after full disclosure of all material facts. Where such a statute does not exist, the courts similarly consider the circumstances of the directors' or stockholders' approval of the interested director's executive compensation.[24]

Sometimes an attempt is made to give the illusion of a disinterested quorum and majority by having the directors vote on compensation for each office separately, with each director abstaining from voting on her own compensation but voting on the compensation of her co-directors. It has generally been held that where the directors have the common object of procuring a salary or a salary increase for each of them as officers, the device of passing a separate resolution for each instead of one joint resolution for all will not be effective to validate the salary increases. The mutual back-scratching or reciprocal voting voids the action as to each.[25]

Many companies provide "golden parachutes" for their most senior executives. The large payment, in the event of a change in control, that the arrangement provides is designed to assure greater neutrality on the part of managers when assessing the merits of an offer from the firm's suitor and to secure their services through the uncertainty created by the bid for control. Because the objective of the golden parachute is upon the officers' conduct before the change in control occurs, it is understandable that the courts have not conditioned the validity of a golden parachute upon any requirement that the manager exercise reasonable efforts to find comparable compensated employment.[26]

§ 11.5 JUDICIAL REVIEW OF EXECUTIVE COMPENSATION: EQUITABLE LIMITS

Directors have wide business discretion in fixing executive compensation.[27] However, in appropriate cases at the suit of a shareholder attacking executive compensation as excessive, courts will review the fairness and reasonableness of compensation of executives and shareholder-employees.[28] A majority shareholder cannot give away the corporate funds in the guise of compensation as against the interest of a dissenting minority or in fraud of creditors.[29] Similarly, even if there are no injured shareholders or creditors, exorbitant compensation withdrawals by corporate officers may be classified in part as dividends and as an attempt to evade taxes. However, judicial reversal of executive compensation decisions in public corporations is rare.

A striking factor among the reported decisions holding that a particular executive compensation arrangement is wasteful or excessive is that they universally involve close corporations. There are several reasons why public corporations are not represented among the decisions upsetting executive compensation arrangements. The first explanation is procedural. As will be seen later in Chapter 15, a precondition to any successful derivative suit is convincing the court that the plaintiff need not make a demand on the board of directors. It is far more likely that there will be outside directors in the public corporation and that their presence will erect an unsurpassable barrier in the plaintiff's quest to challenge executive compensation.[30] The Delaware Supreme Court strongly embraced the view that the size and structure of executive compensation are inherently matters of the directors' judgment, unless they act "irrationally."[31] Thus, the demand requirement for maintaining a derivative suit poses a significant obstacle to challenge compensation in the public corporation.

A second consideration that reduces the viability of a challenge to executive compensation in public corporations is also related to the presence of outside directors. A major concern is whether the arrangement is protected by the business judgment rule. Courts are loath to substitute their judgment for that of the directors in such matters, particularly if the decision carries the imprimatur of a critical mass of independent directors. To this end, compensation decisions are routinely submitted to the outside directors for their separate approval, and compensation plans involving stock options and special bonus arrangements are more frequently approved by the stockholders. Such independent approvals dampen the derivative suit attorney's interest in trying to convince the court that it should substitute its judgment for that of the outside directors, or perhaps that of the stockholders. As a result, the modern cases setting aside executive compensation arrangements arise in the close corporation setting, where such impartial approval is absent.

The courts have had great difficulty in formulating definitive standards to determine the propriety of the amount of compensation paid corporate executives. Indeed, this is an area where the role of the business judgment rule is viewed as essentially a rule of abstention and not a legal standard for determining the appropriate level of form of compensation. One court or another has said that controlling shareholders may not take advantage of their control to vote themselves excessive salaries or to cause excessive salaries to be voted to them by directors they control;[32] that directors must act honestly and reasonably in fixing executive compensation;[33] that directors may not "waste" the corporation's assets by granting excessive compensation;[34] that compensation must bear a reasonable relation to the value of the services rendered[35] and to the ability of the corporation to pay;[36] and that courts of equity will review the fairness and reasonableness of compensation.[37]

Whether executive compensation is excessive is a fact question.[38] Courts proffer a variety of tests for judging whether the challenged compensation arrangement should be struck down, using such expressions as "fraud," "bad faith," "oppression," "excessive and unreasonable," or "a waste of corporate assets."[39] Such labels, at best, communicate a sense that when viewed in its totality, the compensation arrangement departs substantially from what one can view as normative. A wide range of factors[40] are weighed by courts reviewing executive compensation: the executive's qualifications,[41] the nature, extent, and scope of the executive's work, the size and complexities of the business, economic conditions of the company, industry, and country, comparison of salaries to those of similarly situated executives,[42] as well as to the company's dividends, past compensation of the executive,[43] the time devoted to the job, the success of the company, if any, during the executive's tenure,[44] and whether the Internal Revenue Service has disallowed the salary.

Particularly important in weighing these factors is whether the executive compensation has received the impartial approval of the directors or the stockholders. In an attack on allegedly exorbitant compensation, the scope of review depends on whether the recipient officers or directors have participated in fixing the compensation. Where the person compensated does not fix the compensation and the amount is set by directors without any adverse interest or influence that would prevent the exercise of a fair judgment, judicial review is very limited.[45] It is considered outside the proper judicial function to go into the business question of the fairness or reasonableness of the compensation as determined by the board of directors. In contrast, if there is self-dealing because the directors stand to gain from their actions, the business judgment rule is not available, and the burden shifts to those receiving the compensation to show good faith and overall fairness to the corporation.[46]

A major portion of an executive compensation package frequently takes the form of a bonus or profit-sharing arrangement, and today more typically pursuant to stock options. Bonus and profit-sharing arrangements are of various types, such as an individual cash or stock bonus based on a percentage of the company's annual earnings, an employees' stock purchase plan, or an interest in a bonus or management fund in which a number of important executives may share. To afford the managers of large companies, as well as other key employees, some share of the profits, is generally considered a good business policy.[47] Certainly, linking the employee's pay, or at least an important component of it, to future increases in the value of the firm, addresses directly the separation of ownership from management problem. However, equity-based compensation, while portending significant rewards to the manager, also carries with it great costs to the firm. In some smaller companies, however, an undue share of the income is sometimes paid to the principal owners by way of compensation, and little or nothing is paid in dividends. Even in publicly held companies, a substantial percentage of the earnings is frequently paid to the executive group. A fundamental issue is raised as to the real relationship between management and the shareholders of publicly held corporations. Should directors be regarded as fiduciaries, representatives of the owners, or managers of the enterprise for the sole benefit of the shareholders? Or should they be viewed as managing partners, conducting the business partly for themselves, as well as for the benefit of the passive and silent partners, the shareholders, who contribute the capital for an uncertain return, a contingent share of the profits, when and as fixed by management?

The most famous compensation litigation came before the United States Supreme Court in *Rogers v. Hill*.[48] The case challenged the emoluments of the American Tobacco Company's president and executives, who received large fixed salaries and in addition participated in company profits through a huge annual bonus and certain profitable stock subscription plans.[49]

Rogers v. Hill represents one of the few successful challenges to executive compensation arrangements within a publicly held corporation based exclusively on its excessiveness. The case provides, however, little guidance as to how excessiveness is to be determined. Cases involving public corporations decided after *Rogers v. Hill* emphasize the process by which the bonus or profit-sharing arrangement was approved over the more indefinite question of whether the amounts actually awarded are excessive.

Over the years, the Delaware Supreme Court has been an important influence on the standards to be used in assessing bonus and profit-sharing arrangements. In the leading case concerning stock options, *Beard v. Elster*,[50] the court upheld lucrative stock options granted to officers and supervisory personnel, emphasizing that the option plan had been approved by the disinterested directors, that the terms of the plan required that the optionee must be an employee when the option is exercised, and that most of the beneficiaries of the option plan had remained in the company's employ after the plan had been adopted.

On closer analysis, the above tests provide very little specificity. *Beard* reveals that the truly significant test for stock options and profit-sharing arrangements, and executive compensation generally, is not the content that the courts give to the tests or standards they articulate; the dominant consideration is the *process* by which the corporate decision-maker arrives at the executive compensation package that is awarded. The most important consideration, indeed the sole consideration in the public corporation, is good faith impartial approval by the directors and/or the stockholders.

Good faith ratification by the stockholders after full disclosure also invokes the same presumptions, even if the approving directors lack authority to approve or modify a stock option plan.[51] When a plan receives the impartial approval of the directors or stockholders, the burden of proof is on the challenging party to prove the stock option or profit-sharing plan constitutes waste.[52] Not since *Rogers v. Hill* has there been a reported case involving a public corporation where executive compensation in a public corporation was struck down solely on the basis of being excessive.[53]

§ 11.6 Executive Compensation and the Internal Revenue Code

An important limitation on senior executive compensation was the addition in 1993 of section 162(m) of the Internal Revenue Code, which denies a federal income tax deduction for all taxable years commencing after January 1, 1994, to publicly held corporations for compensation in excess of $1 million per year to any of the corporation's top five officers.[54] An important exemption to this provision applies to "performance-based compensation" arrangements.[55] This exemption applies when compensation is awarded pursuant to a predetermined compensation arrangement that contains objective performance goals established by a committee of outside directors and approved by the shareholders after full disclosure of the arrangement's material terms. Also beyond the scope of section 162(m) is deferred compensation that is paid to a person who is no longer one of the five top officers of the corporation. In applying this provision to stock options and other contingent compensation arrangements, the tax consequences are determined on the date of exercise, not on the date the option is granted. There is no evidence that section 162(m) has retarded the rate of increase in executive compensation.[56]

A further attempt to restrict excessive awards appears in sections 280G and 4999 of the Internal Revenue Code.[57] These provisions, respectively, disallow the tax deduction for a company's "excess parachute payments" and impose a 20 percent excise tax on the recipient. Non-public companies are exempt from the provisions, provided the payments are approved by holders of 75 percent of the stock (but only after disclosure of the *actual* event that will trigger the parachute). The provision defines excessive compensation as being three times the executive's annual compensation. If the provision applies, not only is the corporation denied a deduction, but also the recipient incurs a 20 percent excise tax. The clear intent of Section 280G is to reach "excessive" golden parachute arrangements; however, a strategy that is sometimes followed is merely to "gross up" the recipient's award to cover the anticipated tax effects and to forgo the deduction.

Because a corporation can deduct salary payments, whereas dividends are paid out of after-tax dollars,[58] there is a powerful tax incentive to pay as much as possible in salary. This is an especially critical factor when dealing with closely held enterprises because of the close identity of ownership and management. Accordingly, there are a good many cases in which the Internal Revenue Service challenges compensation in a closely held corporation as a disguised dividend.[59] In such cases, excessive compensation, if found, results in the excess payment being treated as a dividend so that the corporation is denied a deduction for that disallowed amount. The traditional approach to determining under the IRC whether compensation is excessive is the multifactor test. Under this approach, the court weighs a number of considerations, with no single factor being dispositive. Factors include (1) the employee's role, position and qualifications in the corporation, (2) duties of, and hours devoted to company, by the employee, (3) comparison of challenged compensation with that of similar companies, (4) character and financial condition of the company including return on investment and changes in market value of firm, (5) dividend record of the company, and (6) the consistency with which the compensation has been paid.[60] An emerging approach is the so-called "independent investor test," whereby a salary is presumptively reasonable when it is paid by a company whose owners are enjoying a desirable rate of return.[61] Applying this test, a court upheld compensation of $1.3 million in the face of expert evidence that investors would expect a 13 percent return on their investment and were in fact enjoying a 50 percent return.[62]

§ 11.7 REGULATING EXECUTIVE COMPENSATION THROUGH IMPROVED GOVERNANCE AND DISCLOSURE

In recent years, the amount of compensation garnered by executives of publicly held corporations has become a public issue eliciting cries within the Congress, demanding either capping of executive compensation or subjecting the compensation to severe tax consequences. Two important corporate responses to this national malaise are the increasing use of compensation committees and enhanced mandatory disclosure rules for public corporations.

Nearly all sizable public corporations today have compensation committees.[63] The composition, powers, and practices of compensation committees vary widely across corporations, although increasingly compensation committees are composed exclusively of outside directors and are given the authority to establish compensation policies and particular packages for senior executives. The provisions of the American Law Institute embody a prevalent sphere of authority for the compensation committee:

(b) The compensation committee should:
  (1) Review and recommend to the board, or determine, the annual salary, bonus, stock options, and other benefits, direct and indirect, of the senior executives.
  (2) Review new executive compensation programs; review on a periodic basis the operation of the corporation's execu-

tive compensation programs to determine whether they are properly coordinated; establish and periodically review policies for the administration of executive compensation programs; and take steps to modify any executive compensation programs that yield payments and benefits that are not reasonably related to executive performance.[64]

The great virtue of a compensation committee is the independence of judgment its members can bring to compensation questions. This approach, of course, demands that its membership be composed of outside directors and that the committee has broad authority to establish, review, and modify the compensation of senior executives. Nevertheless, there is a distinct disquiet that executive compensation could have soared to such prominence in the national consciousness during a time when most public corporations have had compensation committees. Until studies are made of the actual operation of compensation committees, there will continue to be some doubt as to whether they are an effective fulcrum for balancing the interests of the stockholders against the managers' quest for ever-increasing compensation.

Over the years, the SEC has confronted the issue of executive compensation by adopting successively expanded disclosure requirements for the express purpose of providing a clearer presentation of senior executive compensation.[65] There is also the important collateral and moderating influence that arises with any revealing disclosure requirements such as are now required by the SEC. In this respect, recall Brandeis's wise observation: "Sunlight is said to be the best of disinfectants; electric light the most efficient policeman."[66] Among the executive compensation disclosures required is that the board of directors or compensation committee discuss the relationship of corporate performance to executive compensation with respect to the compensation awarded for the last fiscal year.[67] Even more detailed discussion is required with respect to the relationship of the chief executive officer's compensation to the company's financial performance.[68] The SEC requires a line-graph plotting for five years the relationship of executive compensation to overall corporate performance as embodied in a measure of cumulative total shareholder return, which itself is contrasted with an acceptable stock index. Matters that may compromise the directors' independence must also be disclosed.[69] The disclosures are required to identify the directors or committee members who had responsibility for making the disclosures mandated by the executive compensation disclosure rules.[70] While disclosure has multiple virtues, there is scant evidence that disclosure retards compensation levels for executives.

In 2006, the SEC amended Item 402 of Regulation S-K[71] to significantly expand the disclosure requirements for executive compensation. In broad overview, the 2006 additional disclosure requirements focus on five primary areas:

1. Addition of a "Compensation Discussion and Analysis" (CD&A) section to SEC filings and a new Compensation Committee Report.
2. Detailed disclosure of compensation for "named executive officers" (NEOs) for the last fiscal year and the two preceding fiscal years.
3. Extensive disclosure of grants, holdings, and realization of equity-related interests (e.g., stock options, stock appreciation rights) to NEOs.
4. Retirement plans, deferred compensation, and other post-employment payments and benefits for NEOs.
5. Director compensation.

CD&A is a central component of the new disclosure requirements. The rules for this new part of SEC filings are principles based, meaning Item 402 broadly calls for registrants to set forth in a comprehensive way the material factors underlying the company's executive compensation policies and practices (instead of setting forth narrow categories of information that is to be provided). Areas of policy to be addressed include what are the objectives of the company's compensation program, what is sought to be rewarded by the compensation, the elements of the executive's compensation, how did the company determine the amount for each such element, and how does each element fit with the company's overall compensation objectives. The CD&A is also part of the CEO's and CFO's certification requirements.

The Compensation Committee Report must address two items: first, whether the committee has reviewed and discussed the CD&A; and, second, based on any review and discussion, the committee has recommended to the board that the CD&A be included in the company's SEC Filing.

NEOs are the firm's principal executive officer (e.g., CEO) and principal financial officer (e.g., CFO), plus the other three most highly compensated officers (provided the person's compensation exceeds $100,000).

In July 2010, Congress enacted the Dodd-Frank Wall Street Reform and Consumer Protection Act, which adds section 14A to the Securities Exchange Act to require, at least once every three years, a non-binding shareholder vote on executive compensation in public companies. The "say on pay"[72] provision is modeled after one that became mandatory in the United Kingdom in 2002.[73] Studies of U.K. say-on-pay practices have found they tend to improve the link between compensation and performance.[74]

PART B. CORPORATE OPPORTUNITIES

§ 11.8 MISAPPROPRIATION OF CORPORATE OPPORTUNITIES: DISLOYAL DIVERSION OF BUSINESS

Directors and officers as insiders cannot utilize their strategic position for their own preferment or use their powers and opportunities for their own advantage to the exclusion or detriment of the interests they are to represent. Thus, directors and officers as corporate insiders cannot utilize their strategic position, or their powers and opportunities, for their personal advantage to the detriment of other corporate constituencies.[75] They cannot sell their votes or their influence in the management of the corporation. A few cases have employed the corporate opportunity doctrine-type analysis to shareholders.[76] There appears little reason why the test should be limited to fiduciaries who are directors or officers; the policy considerations underlying proscribing some opportunities as belonging to the firm are applicable to all who have a fiduciary relationship to the firm.[77] Fiducaries cannot profit personally from information and knowledge that they have acquired in confidence in their corporate capacity, even though the corporation suffers no injury.[78] For similar reasons, partners may be held accountable for taking of partnership opportunities.[79]

Of special concern, and the focus of this section, is that directors and officers not acquire for themselves property or business opportunities that are an opportunity or advantage that belongs to the corporation. In broad overview, corporations have a prior claim vis-à-vis their directors, officers, and agents to opportunities for business and profit that may be regarded as sufficiently incident or connected to the corporation's business, or the director's and officer's acquisition of the opportunity is otherwise accomplished through disloyalty and unfairness to the corporation. What opportunities are so related to the corporation's business, or the behavior that is disloyal or unfair to the corporation, is answered only in the context of the circumstances of the particular case and sometimes depends on the particular test followed by the jurisdiction. In making this determination, the facts and circumstances when the fiduciary acquired the opportunity are considered and not those that exist thereafter.

There are several widely differing tests applied by the courts. While the discussion that follows examines each of the prevalent tests, a word of caution is in order. Courts rarely articulate a specific test[80] and apply it strictly. Instead, courts examine a number of factors common to two or more of the tests described below. And, even when purporting to apply a specific test, the factors of each test are so general that the outcome is more sensitive to the egregiousness of the director's or officer's behavior than to the particular test the court applies. Overall, this area of the law is very fact-specific, and a good deal of uncertainty exists as to what constitutes a usurpation of a corporate opportunity (sometimes also referred to as the taking of a corporate advantage).

Interest or Expectancy Approach. A few cases impose the "interest or expectancy" test first announced in a Delaware case.[81] The court said: "Good faith to the corporation does not require of its officers that they steer from their own to the corporation's benefit enterprises or investments which, though capable of profit to the corporation, have in no way become subjects of their trust or duty."[82] In another case, a corporation was deemed to have an interest or expectancy in a contract with a customer with whom it had an ongoing relationship such that when its former officer contracted with that customer to provide the same services, it was deemed a usurpation of the corporation's opportunity.[83] And, the corporation had an interest in land adjacent to the corporation's existing property, which the stockholders had frequently discussed acquiring at their meetings.[84] A consideration frequently invoked in connection with the "interest or expectancy" inquiry is whether the opportunity is "essential" to the corporation's operation or existence.[85]

Line of Business. In contrast to the narrowness of the "interest or expectancy" test is the "line of business" test, which treats as belonging to the corporation an opportunity that is related to or is in the company's line of activities and is an activity that the company could reasonably be expected to enter.[86] In the leading line-of-business case, *Guth v. Loft, Inc.*,[87] Guth was the president of Loft Inc., which was engaged in the manufacture and sale of beverages and candy. Guth bought the Pepsi-Cola secret formula and trademark from a bankrupt corporation and, with *M*, organized a new corporation with the aid of money from Loft. Guth used Loft's capital, plant facilities, materials, credit, and employees to perfect the mixture, and the product was sold to Loft for distribution at cost plus 10 percent. The Delaware court held that Guth had appropriated a business opportunity that belonged in equity to Loft Inc., and had made profits to which Loft was entitled.[88] The opportunity was so closely associated with the existing business activities of Loft and so important to those activities as to bring it within the scope of Guth's fiduciary duty, even if Guth had not used Loft's facilities and resources to engage in a competing business.

What is within a corporation's line of business is not always easy to identify *ex ante*. Though the test is broader than the interest or expectancy test, courts can still have a very narrow view of what is within a firm's line of business.[89] Furthermore, fine factual distinctions abound even under the broader line of business test. Thus, an opportunity to earn a large profit quickly by purchasing a parcel of land should be considered within the line of business of a company that generally develops land but rarely itself speculates in land.[90] The question would be much closer, however, if the company only developed land and never speculated in land. Of course, the corporation may have in its articles, bylaws, or a resolution of its board of directors a provision that unequivocally identifies the types of business or activity in which the company does not have an interest and that are fair game for its directors or even officers.[91] Such an approach is expressly authorized by the American Law Institute's Corporate Governance Project, which otherwise applies a line-of-business approach to opportunities acquired by senior executive officers. There is another route, built on the view that the corporation is but a web of contracts. This school has provided the impetus for statutes authorizing provisions, to be included in the corporation's articles of incorporation, that prescribe what will not be deemed corporate opportunities.[92]

Multiple Factors. A majority of the cases determine whether the director or officer has usurped a corporate opportunity by weighing a range of factors. Even Delaware, which purports to apply a combined line of business and interest or expectancy test, acknowledges that *Guth* enunciates factors that need to be taken into account by the reviewing court in balancing the equities of the individual case.[93] Among the factors or circumstances having significance in distinguishing between corporate opportunities that impose a "mandate" or duty to act for the corporation and those opportunities that are open to appropriation by corporate officers are: (1) Is the opportunity to acquire real estate, patents, etc., of special and unique value, or needed for the corporate business and its expansion?[94] (2) Did the discovery or information come to the officer by reason of his official position?[95] (3) Was the company in the market, negotiating for, or seeking such opportunity or advantage, and, if so, has it abandoned its efforts in this regard?[96] (4) Was the officer especially charged with the duty of acquiring such opportunities for his enterprise?[97] (5) Did the officer use corporate funds or facilities in acquiring or developing it?[98] (6) Does taking the opportunity place the director in an adverse and hostile position to his corporation?[99] (7) Did the officer intend to resell the opportunity to the corporation?[100] (8) Was the corporation in a favorable position to take advantage of the opportunity, or was it financially or otherwise unable to do so?[101] Such factors are among those that must be weighed and balanced, but it is not possible for the most part to lay down any hard-and-fast rules as to their effect in imposing a mandate, and variable results have been reached. The multifactor approach is the least rigorous of the tests and therefore provides the least certainty to the director or officer considering *ex ante* whether she can acquire a business opportunity or whether it must first be offered to the corporation.[102]

The American Law Institute Approach. The American Law Institute's Corporate Governance Project may have a considerable impact on future judicial decisions on corporate opportunity. The Supreme Courts of Maine, Massachusetts, and Oregon have already adopted the definition of "corporate opportunity" as it appeared in a tentative draft of the Governance Project, even though that definition was subject to being revised by the American Law Institute.[103] The American Law Institute defines "corporate opportunity" as follows:

> (1) Any opportunity to engage in a business activity of which a director or senior executive becomes aware, either
> > (A) in connection with the performance of functions as a director or senior executive, or under circumstances that

should reasonably lead the director or senior executive to believe that the person offering the opportunity expects it to be offered to the corporation;[104] or

(B) through the use of corporate information or property, if the resulting opportunity is one that the director or senior executive should reasonably be expected to believe would be of interest to the corporation; or

(2) Any opportunity to engage in a business activity of which a senior executive becomes aware and knows is closely related to a business in which the corporation is engaged or expects to engage.[105]

The American Law Institute provides a much broader proscription of business opportunities for senior executive officers than for outside directors, essentially applying a line-of-business test to opportunities before the senior executive officer. The American Law Institute also casts aside the multifactor approach, opting for the more certain inquiries of the circumstances surrounding the fiduciary learning of the opportunity or its acquisition as well as, in the case of senior executive officers, its relationship to a present or contemplated business of the corporation. Although there is not much precedent to support its position, the American Law Institute separately proscribes the fiduciary obligation of controlling stockholders.[106] Finally, the American Law Institute eliminates the possible defenses of incapacity or inability, financial or otherwise, of the corporation to embrace the opportunity.[107] If the activity falls within the ALI's proscription of a corporate opportunity, the sole defense is that the board or stockholders have rejected the opportunity. The truly significant contribution of the Corporate Governance Project's section 5.05 is that it causes the director or senior executive officer to *first* obtain disinterested approval of the board of directors. More significantly, the directors are allowed to approve the director's or senior executive officer's acquisition of the business opportunity only in advance of its acquisition; their approval after the acquisition is given no operative effect under the provision.[108] Absent such approval, the only option is the more cumbersome and expensive process of obtaining shareholder approval or the less predictable burden of proving no unfairness to the corporation.[109]

The Close Corporation Setting. In the close corporation context, there is growing support for greater flexibility in resolving whether a director or officer has usurped a corporate opportunity:

A more flexible approach, however, is dictated when dealing with a small corporation which is generally contractual in nature. . . . [T]he small number of players in a private venture result in better communication between the members. Additionally, agreements are entered into which are tailored to particular situations and objectives.[110]

Factors in a close corporation setting that shape the conclusion that no corporate opportunity was usurped are the co-owners' awareness when the corporation was formed that their defendant-fiduciary actively engaged in similar outside activities[111] and whether the opportunity appeared within the parties' reasonable expectation.[112] Absent strong evidence of prejudice to creditors, there is little reason to hold that the sole shareholder can usurp a corporate opportunity.[113]

The Inability or Incapacity Defense. Directors and officers commonly defend their acquisition of a business opportunity on the grounds that, because of financial distress, or legal restrictions, or otherwise, the corporation was unable itself to acquire the opportunity.[114] In a leading case,[115] the United States Court of Appeals, Second Circuit, invalidated the directors' formation of a syndicate to purchase controlling interests in certain radio patents that the corporation had an option to purchase. The defense was that the corporation was financially unable to take advantage of the opportunity, but it was not clearly shown that greater efforts on their part would not have enabled the corporation to obtain the necessary funds. Not all courts would feel impelled to adopt such a rule of "uncompromising rigidity" as to inability.[116] In a later Delaware case,[117] for example, the court rejected a rigid rule but held that the burden of proving financial inability rested with the defendant officers and directors. The better choice is to place the burden of proving financial inability or legal incapacity and the like on the defendant.[118] Recall that the fiduciary has had the chance to present the opportunity to his corporation before taking it for himself. Having not taken that course because the fiduciary believed it would have been a useless exercise, it is only appropriate that the fiduciary should later have the burden of proving such futility.

Courts are divided whether a third party's purported refusal to contract or deal with the corporation relieves the director or officer of presenting the opportunity to the corporation.[119] Unless the third party's refusal has at least first been disclosed to the corporation, there is no adequate means to test the assertion the corporation could not have acquired the opportunity had its directors or stockholders desired to take the plunge.[120]

Other Considerations. The overall thrust of proscribing the fiduciary's usurpation of a corporate opportunity is to avoid self-seeking behavior to prevail over the fiduciary's loyalty to the corporation.[121] Some business opportunities, however, may be regarded as coming to the officer in his individual capacity or under circumstances free from any prior corporate claim. If the opportunity genuinely came to the director or officer in her individual, nonfiduciary capacity, she will not be under a duty to act or contract as a representative of the corporation. This is an important consideration in defending against the charge that her acquisition of the opportunity was a breach of fiduciary duty. Indeed, this is one of two grounds under the ALI approach for proscribing corporate opportunities by non-senior management personnel.[122] For this defense to be successful, there should not be countervailing considerations, such as the wrongful use of the corporation's assets or personnel to acquire or nurture the opportunity or that the business opportunity was necessary to the corporation.[123] It should not be a defense that the director or officer was not such when the opportunity was acquired, if he learned of the opportunity while an officer or director. Resigning from the position does not rid a person of a fiduciary obligation to turn over opportunities discovered while a director or officer.[124]

The ultimate defense is that the board of directors or stockholders have rejected the business opportunity or otherwise have approved or ratified the director's or officer's acquisition of the opportunity.[125] Mere hesitation in response to the third party's terms does not alone amount to a rejection such that the fiduciary may then acquire the opportunity.[126] The approval or ratification need not be formal; it can occur informally by the disinterested directors or stockholders acquiescing in the director's or officer's acquisition of the opportunity.[127] However, the defense of rejection, approval, or ratification is conditioned on *full disclosure* of all material facts to the rejecting, approving, or ratifying body.[128] Disclosure to a lower-level employee does not satisfy the fiduciary's obligation to disclose relevant information to the corporation.[129] Absent such disclosure, the fiduciary has the burden of proving that acquiring the opportunity has not harmed the corporation.[130]

Where there has been a usurpation of a corporate opportunity, the corporation may elect to claim the benefits of the transaction.[131] The property the officer or director has acquired in violation of his fiduciary duty is held in constructive trust for the corporation.[132] Even if the defendant lost money on the usurped opportunity, the corporation is entitled to recover damages from the defendant for the profits it would have made.[133]

§ 11.9 FORBIDDEN PROFITS: GAINS BY ABUSE OF OFFICIAL POSITION

Directors and officers are fiduciary representatives and as such are not allowed to obtain or retain a commission, bonus, gift, or personal profit or advantage "on the side" for their official action, as in connection with a purchase, sale, lease, loan, or contract by the corporation.[134] Accordingly, they may not keep such rewards without the knowledge and consent of the corporation.[135] A director or officer who has used corporate property or her position to profit personally cannot avoid disgorgement of the ill-gotten gains by invoking that she acted in good faith.[136] Similarly, the officers and directors may not permit any secret profit to be obtained by others.[137]

The rule against insider secret profits by directors and officers is similar to that which applies to agents generally. If an agent receives anything for his acts as such without the knowledge and consent of his principal, he is subject to liability to deliver it or its value or proceeds to the principal.[138] Compensation paid by third persons to a corporate officer for a loan made by the corporation is properly regarded as part of the consideration for the loan or as a commission given for the officer's supposed influence in obtaining the loan.[139]

A director of a corporation cannot remain silent when she knows that a fraud is being attempted against her corporation (and ultimately against its shareholders). It is her duty to acquaint the other officers of the corporation with the facts and to use every effort to prevent the consummation of the fraud. If, by passive acquiescence, she permits any part of the assets of the corporation to be fraudulently diverted or secret profits to be obtained, she is guilty of neglect of duty to the corporation, for which she is liable in damages notwithstanding the fact that she did not herself profit financially thereby.[140]

Section 504 of the American Law Institute comprehensively addresses the use of corporation property and information by directors and senior executives.[141] In broad overview, the ALI proscribes the use of corporate position, property, or information without proof of harm to the corporation, except when non-proprietary information is used (for other than a transaction in securities), in which case proof of harm to the corporation is required.[142] Under the ALI's formulation, the officer or director can defend the charges by proving authorization or ratification by disinterested directors or shareholders after full disclosure.[143]

§ 11.10 THE DUTY OF EMPLOYEES NOT TO COMPETE

Employees (including officers) are precluded from actively competing with their employer during the course of their employment, even though they are not subject to a covenant not to compete.[144] The application of this universal principle occurs within the conflicting tugs of two important commercial considerations. On the one hand, our society prizes entrepreneurial activity and generally nurtures free and vigorous competition. It is with this spirit that fiduciaries are allowed to make important preparations to compete while still in their company's employ and also are allowed, within broad limits, to leave with skills and knowledge acquired from the company.[145] On the other hand, there is the strong view that it is unfair for the employing company to compete with the very individuals in whom it then places trust and responsibility for serving its best interests.

To what extent may an employee prepare to compete with his employer? Within the broad principles discussed below, the answer to this question is heavily dependent on the facts of the individual case.[146] Most courts recognize the right of an employee, while still an employee, to incorporate a rival corporation and procure land, buildings, and equipment for its future operation.[147] Obviously, there is a concern that the employee not usurp any opportunity belonging to the employer company when acquiring assets for the employee's own business.[148] Indeed, many cases that appear to raise questions of an employee competing with her employer are instead examined through the usurpation of the corporate opportunity window examined in the preceding section.[149] The employee is not allowed to venture beyond the formation and outfitting while an employee; once the employee terminates his relationship with the employer, however, he may actively compete.[150]

Setting up any prospective business involves recruiting employees, and there has been a good deal of litigation whether a departing officer has breached his fiduciary duty by recruiting his employer's employees to work for him in the business to be established. Absent evidence of an intent to cripple the current employer by raiding its key employees, some jurisdictions permit informing fellow workers of an intent to start a competing firm and even permit mild forms of solicitation of co-workers.[151] There are, however, more restrictive jurisdictions that proscribe an employee soliciting co-workers to join him in a competing enterprise before he has severed his own employment relationship with the employer.[152]

Even though employees cannot solicit their employer's customers as long as they are employees, they can advise the customers of their intent to leave and start a competing business.[153] Regardless of whether customers are permanent or continuous or that their business can be obtained only by competitive bidding, solicitation is still a violation of the employee's fiduciary obligation.[154] The corporation has a right to be free from interference with its customers from those employed by the corporation.[155] The line between solicitation and advising is not always a bright one. The question turns upon just how specific the communication is so that the more general the communication the more it appears to be mere preparation to leave and not to compete as such. Merely informing customers of an intent to leave and of a desire for their business in the future does not constitute solicitation.[156] However, pressing the customer for business[157] and *a fortiorari* filling customer orders while still an employee[158] are impermissible solicitations.

Normally, once the employee leaves the corporation, she can solicit its customers.[159] However, if the customer list is confidential or amounts to a trade secret, the former employee cannot use the information to approach customers.[160] Customer lists may become a trade secret when they are unusually sensitive, are not generally known in the trade, or were built after great effort and expense by the plaintiff. The Ninth Circuit provides a very clear expression of a rule of thumb for whether information is a trade secret: "the most important consideration [in determining whether something is a trade secret] is whether the information is readily accessible to a reasonably diligent competitor or salesman."[161]

Even if the customer list is not a trade secret, the list may still be a protected property right of the defendant's former employer. For example, if the employee copied, physically removed, or intently studied the list, the employee's subsequent use of the list will be enjoined on the theory the list had been converted.[162] But if only "casual memory" is involved, no breach exists if the customers are solicited soon after the employee resigns.[163] As a rule of thumb, the smaller the list, the lower the percentage solicited, or the more widely known are the customers all make less likely the finding of a breach.

The fiduciary may not use the corporation's facilities to compete or prepare to compete,[164] and it is a breach to use corporate trips to evaluate prospective sites for a competing factory or to learn how to design and build a factory similar to the current employer's factory.[165]

Courts deciding whether a director, officer, or employee has unfairly competed frequently do so on the basis of the fiduciary having misappropriated his employer's trade secret. A trade secret is "a plan or process, tool, mechanism or compound known to its owner and those of his employees to whom it is necessary to confide it. In order for the business information to be a trade secret, it must have value to the business; it must take a form different from ordinarily acquired general information."[166] Some factors used to determine if something is a trade secret are: (1) the extent to which the information is known outside the business; (2) the extent to which it is known by employees and others involved in the business; (3) the extent of measures taken by the owner to guard the secrecy of the information; (4) the value of the information to the owner and to its competitor; (5) the amount of effort or money expended in developing the information; and (6) the ease or difficulty with which the information can be properly acquired or duplicated by others.[167] Public disclosure of the information destroys its confidentiality and hence the information's protection in equity.[168]

When misconduct is found, courts have applied a variety of sanctions and remedies. The employee may be enjoined[169] and a constructive trust imposed on the competing business and profits therefrom.[170] Courts also invoke their equitable powers to substitute the former employer as a party to a contract that the employee wrongfully caused the former employer to lose.[171] The employee can also be required to return any compensation he received from the employer during the period of his breach.[172] In addition, any consequential damages suffered by the employer can be recovered from the employee.[173]

PART C. CONTROLLING STOCKHOLDER'S FIDUCIARY OBLIGATIONS

§ 11.11 FIDUCIARY DUTIES OF MAJORITY SHAREHOLDERS TO THE MINORITY

Courts and legal scholars have given much attention to the scope of the controlling stockholder's[174] fiduciary duty to the corporation and its minority shareholders.[175] Typically, the duty is breached because of the effects of a corporate activity instituted in response to the controlling stockholder's influence.[176] Unlike the directors' and officers' fiduciary obligations, where the breach can be found for nonfeasance as well as misfeasance, cases finding breaches by controlling stockholders involve affirmative action that can be traced to the controlling stockholder. Thus, it can be said that the controlling stockholder's fiduciary duty does not require that the controlling stockholder act as a guardian charged with the duty to act affirmatively by encouraging or driving the corporation to take action that will increase the value of the shares.[177]

The basis for the controlling stockholder's fiduciary obligation is the sound policy that, just as directors are bound by certain fiduciary obligations, one who has the potential to control the board's actions should be subject to an obligation as rigorous as those applied to the directors. Quite separate is the belief that control in a corporation, whether publicly or closely held, carries with it the potential that the controlling stockholder may choose to exercise control to reap disproportionate benefits at the expense of the corporation or noncontrolling shareholders such that protection of their interests is desirable. That protection arises by imposing the fiduciary standards on the controlling stockholder exercising the controlling influence. The overall objective of the controlling stockholder's fiduciary obligation is not to bar the controlling stockholder from acting in his own self-interest but to assure that when so acting the interests of the corporation are also served.[178]

In the public corporation, the threshold question is invariably whether the challenged activity or transaction is to be judged by the business judgment rule or the "inherent fairness" test. This is essentially a question of whether the activity or transaction is to be viewed somewhat neutrally so that it carries a presumption of propriety, or whether the court will approach the activity or transaction skeptically by placing the burden of proving its overall fairness on the controlling stockholder.[179]

Outside of Delaware, courts adhere to the dichotomy between a presumption of propriety (that is, the business judgment rule) and imposing the burden of proving fairness (that is, the intrinsic fairness standard) but do not have the same rigorous and narrow test for their application as embodied in Delaware. Evidence of disproportionate gains to the controlling stockholder is prima facie evidence of a breach.[180]

In broad overview, transactions shown to produce disproportionate gains to the controlling stockholders are typically judged by a standard of fairness, and the burden of proof is on the controlling stockholder. Thus, the burden of establishing the fairness of the transaction is placed upon the controlling stockholder when it is transacting business with the corporation and when the plaintiff has made a threshold showing that the transaction disproportionately benefits the controlling stockholder.[181] None of these standards applied portends exactness, so the results in individual cases are difficult to predict *ex ante*, and the cases frequently appear in conflict.

There is no easy reference point to decide what would be a fair sharing in benefits that can occur only in control relationships. Certainly it is too abstract to judge such transactions by what would occur in arm's-length dealings, because the filing of consolidated tax returns by definition does not involve arm's-length transactions.[182] Moreover, reference to what allocations occur in other parent-subsidiary relationships will only invoke a standard that itself is likely to embody dominance and control. California appears to provide the most certainty by holding that fairness requires the benefit be shared proportionately.[183] There is a good deal of appeal to the view that if the controlling stockholder garners more than its proportionate share, it should at least have the burden of proving circumstances justifying why the allocation was fair to the controlled company.

Much like what occurs when directors contract with their corporation, contracts between the corporation and its controlling stockholder invoke critical review. Absent disinterested approval or ratification, the controlling stockholder has the burden of proving the transaction's overall fairness to the corporation.[184] It is well recognized that disinterested minority shareholder approval of a transaction between the controlling stockholder and the corporation places the burden on the challenging party to prove the transaction's unfairness.[185] There is authority that the same presumption of propriety can attach if the independent body of directors approves the transaction.[186]

The American Law Institute's Corporate Governance Project deals specifically with transactions between the corporation and its controlling stockholder,[187] the controlling stockholder's use of corporate assets, information, and influence,[188] and the controlling stockholder's usurpation of a corporate opportunity.[189] In broad overview, the scheme of the American Law Institute places the burden of proving fairness on the controlling stockholder with respect to any challenge to a transaction between the corporation and its controlling stockholder and allegations that the controlling stockholder has usurped a corporate opportunity unless the particular transaction has received disinterested director approval, shareholder approval, or ratification. When the controlling stockholder uses corporate assets or information or otherwise exercises influence over the corporation with the effect of securing an economic benefit, the American Law Institute demands either that value be given to the corporation or that any benefit the controlling shareholder secures is proportionally available to other shareholders similarly situated.[190] In sum, the American Law Institute follows a course that is more protective of stockholder rights on these questions than does Delaware but is well within the approach that appears to apply in most jurisdictions.

In the closely held corporation setting, the breach can be established on a more personal basis, such as by proving that the controlling stockholder had an abrasive or intimidating manner toward the minority stockholders[191] or that the controlling stockholder foreclosed the minority from the opportunity to participate in meetings or receive information about corporate transactions.[192] In the closely held corporation, the controlling stockholder's fiduciary obligation is increasingly viewed as being akin to the obligation that partners owe to one another.[193] The close corporation's controlling stockholder owes a duty of "utmost good faith and fairness" to the controlled corporation and its stockholders.[194] To be sure, such a standard is inherently devoid of specifics but nevertheless embodies a tone that carries with it the view that challenges transactions between the controlling stockholder and the corporation, or merely the exercise of influence over corporate activities; each will be subjected to close review for overall fairness and proper motivation.[195]

§ 11.12 UNEQUAL TREATMENT AMONG DIFFERENT CLASSES OF SECURITIES OR HOLDERS OF THE SAME CLASS OF SECURITY

Disputes regarding the controlling stockholder's obligations sometimes occur in the context of the conflicting rights between different classes of stock where the focus of the dispute is the power of one class (that is, that held by the controlling stockholder) over the rights of another class of stock (that is, the class held by the minority shareholders) and also among holders of the same class of security where disparate treatment among holders arises as a result of actions by those in control of company. In this context, courts frequently support fiduciary obligations by officers, directors, and controlling stockholders to all classes of stockholders, preferred as well as common.[196]

Fiduciary duties in the corporate context exist to fill gaps where the parties have not otherwise set forth their rights and relationships. Fiduciary duties are therefore similar to corporate statutes in that they provide convenient off-the-rack rules to simplify the process of contracting, and permit deviations from corporate provisions when the interests of third parties (most notably, creditors) will not be harmed. Though there is much concern and uncertainty regarding the duty owed minority stockholders, the burdens of the directors' and controlling stockholders' fiduciary duties are not great. The commands of corporate fiduciary duties provide a fairly low threshold for what constitutes appropriate behavior in the corporation. Indeed, the most notable feature of corporate fiduciary duty law is the lack of rigor found in its prescriptions.

Far more important than the broad standards by which the courts purport to judge defendants' behavior is whether the court will deprive the challenged transaction of the deferential presumptions dictated by the business judgment rule.[197] The all-important burden of persuasion follows from whether the defendants' conduct falls within the business judgment rule. So viewed, the single most important issue in considering the content of fiduciary duty obligations among stockholders is the threshold consideration whether the challenged transaction enjoys the presumption of propriety.[198] In this context, the question of the content of the fiduciary duty among stockholders is answered by inquiring into what assumptions we should make regarding the rights, privileges, and preferences among stockholders who have not otherwise chosen to deviate from the recognized norm. Armed with this standard, courts can then take the next step of determining what showing is necessary to consider whether the parties before it have chosen to depart from that norm.[199]

NOTES

1. *See* Subcommittee on Executive Compensation of the ABA Section on Corporation, Banking and Business Law, *Executive Compensation: A 1987 Road Map for the Corporate Advisor,* 43 BUS. LAW. 185 (1987). *See also Report of the National Association of Corporate Directors Blue Ribbon Commission on Director Compensation* 12 (1995) (recommending that the board establish a substantial target of stock ownership for directors and that director fees be paid in stock or cash; also, the report expresses the view that benefits such as pension and health plans are likely to make directors less independent because they are more like employees who seek longevity).
2. *See* Detlev F. Vagts, *Challenges to Executive Compensation: For the Markets or the Courts?*, 8 J. CORP. L. 231 (1983).
3. Corinne Mill, Canal & Stock Co. v. Toponce, 152 U.S. 405 (1894); Vernars v. Young, 539 F.2d 966 (3d Cir. 1976).
4. Savage v. Lorraine Corp., 217 F.2d 378 (9th Cir. 1954) (director-president).
5. Air Traffic & Serv. Corp. v. Fay, 196 F.2d 40 (D.C. Cir. 1952).
6. *See* McDonald v. Sealift Terminals, Inc., 505 So. 2d 675 (Fla. Ct. App. 1987).
7. "It is almost universally held that directors acting as such at their meetings, have no power to vote themselves salaries or compensation for their services, either before or after such services have been rendered." Palmer v. Scheftel, 170 N.Y.S. 588, 590 (N.Y. App. Div. 1918).
8. Former MODEL BUS. CORP. ACT § 4(k) (1969) (officers and agents) [hereinafter Former MBCA]; *id.* § 35 ("The board of directors shall have the authority to fix the compensation of directors unless otherwise provided in the articles of incorporation."). *Accord*, MODEL BUS. CORP. ACT §§ 3.02(11), 8.11 (2008) [hereinafter MBCA].
9. National Oil Co. v. Reeves, 310 S.W.2d 242 (Ark. 1958); Godley v. Crandall & Godley Co., 105 N.E. 818 (N.Y. 1914).
10. *See, e.g., In re* 3Com Corp. Shareholders Litig., 1999 WL 1009210 (Del. Ch. 1999) (no waste plead for stockholder approved plan whereby each director received options valued at $650,000 pursuant to stockholder approved plan).
11. In *Schraft v. Leis*, 686 P.2d 865 (Kan. 1984), bylaws required officers' salaries to be approved by the board of directors but court held that agreement between sole owners of company as to salary constituted implied ratification of establishing salaries in manner not authorized in bylaws.
12. Rocky Mtn. Powder Co. v. Hamlin, 310 P.2d 404 (Nev. 1957) (sales manager not a director or officer).
13. Bellehurst Syndicate v. Commissioner, 83 F.2d 801, 803 (9th Cir. 1936).
14. Neidert v. Neidert, 637 S.W.2d 296 (Mo. Ct. App. 1982); Rocky Mtn. Powder Co. v. Hamlin, 310 P.2d 404 (Nev. 1957).
15. Roach v. Bynum, 403 So. 2d 187 (Ala. 1981).
16. Pub. L. No. 93-406, 88 STAT. 829 (1974).

17. *See, e.g.*, Hurt v. Cotton States Fertilizer Co., 159 F.2d 52 (5th Cir.), *cert. denied*, 331 U.S. 828 (1947).
18. *See, e.g.*, Blish v. Thompson Automatic Arms Corp., 64 A.2d 581, 606–07 (Del. 1948) (exception to retroactive compensation arises when the payment is pursuant to an earlier implied contract or the amount is not unreasonable in view of the services rendered).
19. *See, e.g.*, Estate of Bogley v. United States, 514 F.2d 1027 (Ct. Cl. 1975).
20. *See* Wolf v. Fried, 373 A.2d 734, 736 (Pa. 1977) (board's judgment that manager was "unique and knowledgeable" and worthy of additional compensation is evidence there was adequate consideration supporting additional pay).
21. Wis. Stat. Ann. § 180.0302(12) (West 2002); Va. Code Ann. § 13.1-627(11) (LexisNexis 2006 Replacement). *Cf.* Former MBCA § 41 (1969) (a corporation has power to "pay pensions and establish pension plans, pension trusts, . . . stock bonus plans . . . and other incentive plans for any or all of its directors, officers and employees").
22. *See, e.g.*, Giannotti v. Hamway, 387 S.E.2d 725, 731 (Va. 1990) (in absence of showing of fraud or bad faith, presumption of propriety applies). In some states, shareholder approval is required by statute for specified kinds of compensation such as employee stock option or stock purchase plans. *See* Former MBCA § 20 (1969); MBCA § 6.24 (2008).
23. *See, e.g.*, Morrissey v. Curran, 650 F.2d 1267 (2d Cir. 1981).
24. *See, e.g.*, Moran v. Edson, 493 F.2d 400 (3d Cir. 1974).
25. Angelus Sec. Corp. v. Ball, 67 P.2d 152 (Cal. Ct. App. 1937).
26. *See* Royal Crown Companies, Inc. v. McMahon, 359 S.E.2d 379 (Ga. App. 1987); Koenings v. Joseph Schlitz Brewing Co., 377 N.W.2d 593 (Wis. 1985) (viewing payment as a type of liquidated damage).
27. *See, e.g.*, Cramer v. General Tel. & Elec. Corp., 582 F.2d 259 (3d Cir. 1978), *cert. denied*, 439 U.S. 1129 (1979); Klaus v. Hi-Shear Corp., 528 F.2d 225 (9th Cir. 1975).
28. Galler v. Galler, 316 N.E.2d 114 (Ill. App. Ct. 1974).
29. *See, e.g.*, Rogers v. Hill, 289 U.S. 582 (1933); Delta Star, Inc. v. Patton, 76 F. Supp. 3d 617 (W.D. Pa. 1999) (president and chairman set salaries, including for himself, without consulting the board of directors); Michelson v. Duncan, 407 A.2d 211 (Del. 1979).
30. Aronson v. Lewis, 473 A.2d 805 (Del. 1984).
31. Brehm v. Eisner, 746 A.2d 244, 263 (Del. 2000).
32. *See* Segall v. Shore, 236 S.E.2d 316 (S.C. 1977).
33. *See also* Barrett v. Smith, 242 N.W. 392, 394 (Minn. 1932) (salaries of corporate officers may be so high as to evidence fraud and oppression of minority).
34. Brehm v. Eisner, 746 A.2d 244, 263–64 (Del. 2000) (although executive compensation is inherently a matter of board's business judgment, directors may not irrationally squander or give away corporate assets).
35. Security-First Nat'l Bank v. Lutz, 322 F.2d 348, 354 (9th Cir. 1963) (executives entitled to receive as salary for services to corporation what those services are reasonably worth).
36. Glenmore Distilleries Co. v. Seideman, 267 F. Supp. 915 (E.D.N.Y. 1967) (judgment creditor of corporation recovered from shareholder-officers as

fraudulent conveyances the amounts of excessive salary payments; court considered corporation's ability to pay as well as value of officer's services); Baker v. Cohn, 42 N.Y.S.2d 159 (Sup. Ct. 1942), *modified*, 40 N.Y.S.2d 623 (App. Div. 1943), *aff'd*, 54 N.E.2d 689 (N.Y. 1944).

37. Valeant Pharmaceuticals Int'l v. Jerney, 921 A.2d 732 (Del. Ch. 2007) (applying entire fairness standard to require return of a $3 million bonus).

38. Pacific Grains, Inc. v. Commissioner, 399 F.2d 603 (9th Cir. 1968).

39. *E.g.*, McQuillen v. National Cash Register Co., 112 F.2d 877, 883 (4th Cir.), *cert. denied*, 311 U.S. 695 (1940).

40. *See, e.g.*, Wilderman v. Wilderman, 315 A.2d 610 (Del. Ch. 1974).

41. *See, e.g.*, Neidert v. Neidert, 637 S.W.2d 296 (Mo. Ct. App. 1982).

42. *See* Murphy v. Washington Am. League Base Ball Club, 324 F.2d 394 (D.C. Cir. 1963) (salaries found in line with what other baseball companies were paying).

43. *See* Fendelman v. Fenco Handbag Mfg. Co., 482 S.W.2d 461 (Mo. 1972) (that director-officer received less in first years with company than for previous similar work at another company important in determining that salary not excessive).

44. Hurt v. Cotton States Fertilizer Co., 159 F.2d 52 (5th Cir.), *cert. denied*, 331 U.S. 828 (1947); *Wilderman*, 315 A.2d 610 (listing eight factors including IRS determination of permissible salary deduction).

45. *See, e.g.*, Cohen v. Ayers, 596 F.2d 733 (7th Cir. 1979).

46. *Id.*

47. *See, e.g.*, Gallin v. National City Bank, 273 N.Y.S. 87, 113, 114 (N.Y. Sup. Ct. 1934) (describing the rationale behind the managing officers' claim to a share of the profits).

48. 289 U.S. 582 (1933). *See also* its companion case, Rogers v. Guaranty Trust Co., 288 U.S. 123 (1933).

49. Rogers v. Hill, 289 U.S. 582, 590 (1933); Rogers v. Guaranty Trust Co., 288 U.S. 123 (1933).

50. 160 A.2d 731 (Del. 1960).

51. *See* Michelson v. Duncan, 407 A.2d 211 (Del. 1979).

52. *Id.*

53. *See generally* Douglas C. Michael, *The Corporate Officer's Independent Duty as a Tonic for the Anemic Law of Executive Compensation*, 17 J. CORP. L. 785 (1992).

54. I.R.C. § 162(m) (2000).

55. *See generally* Joseph Antenucci & Peter Woodlock, *Types of Compensation Qualified As "Performance Based" Under Code Section 162(m)*, 76 TAXES 27 (Sept. 1998).

56. *See* Susan J. Stabile, *Is There a Role for Tax Law in Policing Executive Compensation*, 72 ST. JOHN'S L. REV. 91, 89 (1998) (reporting that executive pay grew 29 percent faster in the year after the enactment of section 162(m) than was the rate of growth in the previous 14 years).

57. I.R.C. §§ 280G & 4999.

58. *See* I.R.C. § 162(a)(1) (2000); Treas. Reg. § 1.162-7(a) (2009).

59. For an illustrative case on the taxation issue *see* Rapco, Inc. v. Commissioner, 85 F.3d 950, 955 (2d Cir. 1996) (salary of $900,000 to 95

percent owner disallowed where it was not supported by expert testimony, ignored the bylaw's bonus compensation scheme, and was set by its recipient).

60. *See, e.g.,* Eberl's Claim Service, Inc. v. Commissioner, 249 F.3d 994 (10th Cir. 2001).

61. *See, e.g.,* Exacto Spring Corp. v. Commissioner, 196 F.3d 833 (7th Cir. 1999).

62. *Id.*

63. *See, e.g.,* HEIDRICK & STRUGGLES, THE CHANGING BOARD TABLE 11, 13 (93 percent of surveyed corporations in 1989 had compensation committees). Even as early as 1981, some 72 percent of the proxies surveyed by the SEC revealed the presence of a compensation committee. SEC STAFF REPORT, CORPORATE ACCOUNTABILITY 612–14 (1981).

64. ALI, PRINCIPLES OF CORPORATE GOVERNANCE: RESTATEMENT AND RECOMMENDATIONS § 3A.05(b) (1992).

65. *See Executive Compensation Disclosure,* SECURITIES ACT RELEASE No. 6962 [1992 Transfer Binder] FED. SEC. L. REP. (CCH) ¶ 85,056 (Oct. 16, 1992).

66. LOUIS D. BRANDEIS, OTHER PEOPLE'S MONEY 92 (Stokes 1932).

67. Item 402(k)(1) of Regulation S-K, 17 C.F.R. § 229.402(k)(1) (2009).

68. *See, e.g.,* Item 402(a)(4) and Item 402(k)(2) of Regulation S-K, 17 C.F.R. § 229.402(a)(4) & (k)(2) (2009).

69. *See* Item 402(j)(3) of Regulation S-K, 17 C.F.R. § 228.402(j)(3) (2009).

70. Item 402(k)(3), Regulation S-K § 228.402(k)(3) (2009).

71. 17 C.F.R. § 229.402 (2009).

72. H.R. 1257, 110th Cong. (2007) (sponsored by Rep. Barney Frank (D. Mass.)).

73. *See generally* L.C.B. GOWER & PAUL L. DAVIES, THE PRINCIPLES OF MODERN COMPANY LAW §§ 14-16 to 14-17, 14-22 to 14-23 (8th ed. 2008).

74. *See, e.g.,* FABRIZIO FERRI & DAVID MABER, SAY ON PAY VOTES AND CEO COMPENSATION: EVIDENCE FROM THE U.K. (March 2009) (CEO compensation significantly more sensitive to performance post the introduction of say-on-pay requirement and sensitivity increased as vote in opposition to pay increased).

75. *See, e.g.,* Pepper v. Litton, 308 U.S. 295 (1939); Gulledge v. Frosty Land Foods Int'l, 414 So. 2d 60 (Ala. 1982).

76. *See, e.g.,* Thorpe by Castleman v. CERBCO, Inc., 676 A.2d 436 (Del. 1996); Lyon v. Campbell, 707 A.2d 850, 864 (Md. App. 1998); A. Teixeira & Co., Inc. v. Teixeira, 699 A.2d 1383 (R.I. 1997) (members of close corporation are analogous to partners in a partnership and hence, as fiduciaries, owe duty not to usurp opportunities).

77. *See* United Teachers Assoc. Ins. Co. v. MacKeen & Bailey, Inc., 99 F.3d 645 (5th Cir. 1996) (actuary retained by the firm deemed a fiduciary who usurped opportunity to acquire another firm).

78. *E.g.,* Weigel v. Shapiro, 608 F.2d 268 (7th Cir. 1979).

79. Triple Five of Minnesota, Inc. v. Simon, 280 F. Supp. 2d 895 (D. Minn. 2003) (partner usurped partnership opportunity).

80. *See, e.g.,* Rapistan Corp. v. Michaels, 511 N.W.2d 918 (Mich. Ct. App. 1994) (wrongful usurpation of corporate opportunity arises when (1) the

opportunity is essential to the corporation, (2) the corporation has an interest or expectancy, or (3) fiduciary has used corporate assets to acquire or develop).

81. Lagarde v. Anniston Lime & Stone Company, 28 So. 199 (Ala. 1899).

82. *Id.* at 201.

83. Southeast Consultants, Inc. v. McCrary Engg. Corp., 273 S.E.2d 112 (Ga. 1980).

84. Farber v. Servan Land Co., 662 F.2d 371 (5th Cir. 1981).

85. *See, e.g.,* Design Strategies, Inc. v. Davis, 384 F. Supp. 2d 649, 672 (S.D.N.Y. 2005) (stating the test is "whether the consequences of deprivation are so severe as to threaten the viability of the enterprise") (quoting, Alexander & Alexander of New York, Inc. v. Fritzen, 542 N.Y.S.2d 530, 534–35 (Sup. Ct. App. Div. 1989)).

86. *See, e.g.,* Levy v. Markal Sales Corp., 643 N.E.2d 1206 (Ill. App. Ct. 1994) (also evidence that opportunity first offered in expectation it would be of interest to employer and there was use of company resources in developing opportunity).

87. 5 A.2d 503 (Del. 1939).

88. *Id.*

89. *See, e.g.,* Autocount, Inc. v. Automated Prescription Sys., Inc., 651 So. 2d 308 (La. Ct. App. 1995) (developing a modified version of a device that company was negotiating to acquire not within the same line of business).

90. *See* Imperial Group (Texas), Inc. v. Scholnick, 709 S.W.2d 358 (Tex. Ct. App. 1986).

91. *See* American Inv. Co. v. Lichtenstein, 134 F. Supp. 857 (E.D. Mo. 1955).

92. *See, e.g.,* DEL. CODE ANN. tit. 8, § 122(17) (2001); ALI, 1 PRINCIPLES OF CORPORATE GOVERNANCE: ANALYSIS AND RECOMMENDATIONS § 5.09 (1992).

93. Broz v. Cellular Information Systems, Inc., 673 A.2d 148, 155 (Del. 1996).

94. *See, e.g.,* Central Ry. Signal Co. v. Longden, 194 F.2d 310 (7th Cir. 1952).

95. *See, e.g., Broz,* 673 A.2d at 155 (not dispositive that fiduciary learned of opportunity in individual capacity).

96. *See, e.g.,* Burg v. Horn, 380 F.2d 897 (2d Cir. 1967).

97. *See, e.g., id.*

98. *See, e.g., Central Ry. Signal Co.,* 194 F.2d 310.

99. *See, e.g.,* American Fed. Group, Ltd. v. Rothenberg, 136 F.3d 897 (2d Cir. 1998).

100. *See, e.g., Burg,* 380 F.2d 897; Southeast Consultants, Inc. v. McCrary Eng'g Corp., 273 S.E.2d 112 (Ga. 1980).

101. *See, e.g.,* A. C. Petters v. St. Cloud Enter., 222 N.W.2d 83 (Minn. 1974); Ellzey v. Fyr-Pruf, Inc., 376 So. 2d 1328 (Miss. 1979).

102. In *Miller v. Miller,* 222 N.W.2d 71 (Minn. 1974), the Minnesota Supreme Court attempted to introduce some rigor to the equitable-factors test by combining it with the line-of-business test in a two-step approach. The first question is whether the business opportunity is a corporate opportunity—that is, whether it is of sufficient importance and is so closely related to the existing or prospective activity of the corporation as to warrant judicial sanctions against its personal acquisition.

103. *See* Northeast Harbor Golf Club, Inc. v. Harris, 661 A.2d 1146 (Me. 1995).

104. This is the crucial factor in *Northeast Harbor Golf Club*, 661 A.2d 1146, where the court appears to emphasize more the intent of the broker offering the opportunity than the reasonable belief of the purchasing company official.

105. Thus, in adopting the ALI approach, the case was remanded to determine how a golf club's president learned of the opportunity to acquire land adjacent to the course. *See Northeast Harbor Golf Club*, 661 A.2d 1146.

106. ALI, PRINCIPLES OF CORPORATE GOVERNANCE: ANALYSIS AND RECOMMENDATIONS § 512 (1992). As to controlling stockholders, "corporate opportunity" is defined in terms of the property having been "developed or received by the corporation," or having come to the controlling stockholder because of his relationship to the company, or is of the type that was held out to the stockholder as being an activity within the scope of the company's business. *Id.* § 5.12(b)(1)(2). The absence of case law on whether controlling shareholders can usurp a corporate opportunity may be partly a semantic distinction. *See* Thorpe v. CERBCO, Inc., 676 A.2d 436 (Del. 1996) (controlling shareholders not liable for having usurped a corporate opportunity by diverting an offer to buy the corporation so that they instead sold their majority interest in the corporation; however, they would be liable for any damages caused by their breach of duty of loyalty).

107. *See* Klinicki v. Lundgren, 695 P.2d 906 (Or. 1985).

108. ALI, PRINCIPLES OF CORPORATE GOVERNANCE: ANALYSIS AND RECOMMENDATIONS § 5.05(a)(1) (1992). Subsection (e) does allow approval after the fact by the directors where the director or senior executive officer failed to get earlier approval because of a good faith belief the business activity was not a corporate opportunity.

109. *Id.* §§ 5.05(a)(3)(C), 5.05(c). Courts also place the burden of proving no usurpation of a corporate opportunity on the officer or director. *See* Independent Distributors, Inc. v. Katz, 637 A.2d 886 (Md. App. Ct. 1994).

110. Leavitt v. Leisure Sports, Inc., 734 P.2d 1221, 1225 (Nev. 1987).

111. *See* Noble v. Lubrin, 60 P.3d 1224, 1226 (Wash. Ct. App. 2003).

112. Graham v. Mimms, 444 N.E.2d 549 (Ill. App. Ct. 1982). In their thoughtful article, Professors Brudney and Chirelstein suggest that the appropriate basis for defining corporate opportunities in close corporations is to consider the reasonable expectations of the parties. Victor Brudney & Robert C. Clark, A New Look at Corporate Opportunities, 94. HARV. L. REV. 997 (1981).

113. *See In re* Safety Intl., Inc., 775 F.2d 660 (5th Cir. 1985) (invoking a theory of ratification).

114. *See, e.g.*, Lange v. Lange, 520 N.W.2d 113 (Iowa 1994).

115. Irving Trust Co. v. Deutsch, 73 F.2d 121 (2d Cir. 1934), *cert. denied*, 294 U.S. 708 (1935).

116. Jenkins v. Jenkins, 64 P.3d 953, 957 (Id. 2003) (listing factors to be considered for the defense).

117. *See Noble*, 60 P.3d at 1229.

118. Demoulas v. Demoulas Super Markets, Inc., 677 N.E.2d 159, 181 (Mass. 1997) (the defense to creating separate retail company without the

plaintiff's participation was that state law limited the number of licenses for beer and wine that could be held by a single entity).

119. *Compare* Production Finishing Corp. v. Shields, 405 N.W.2d 171 (Mich. Ct. App. 1987) (not a consideration) *and* Owen v. Hamilton, 843 N.Y.S.2d 298, 301 (Sup. Ct. App. Div. 2007) *with* Moser v. Devine Real Estate, Inc., 839 N.Y.S.2d 843, 848 (Sup. Ct. App. Div. 2007) (is a consideration).

120. Energy Resources Corp. v. Porter, 438 N.E.2d 391 (Mass. App. Ct. 1982). *See also, e.g.,* Imperial Group (Texas), Inc. v. Scholnick, 709 S.W.2d 358, 363 (Tex. Ct. App. 1986).

121. *See* Science Accessories v. Summagraphics, 425 A.2d 957 (Del. 1980); *Demoulas*, 677 N.E.2d at 180 (citing to this treatise).

122. *See, e.g.,* Northeast Harbor Golf Club, Inc. v. Harris, 661 A.2d 1146 (Me. 1995).

123. Red Top Cab Co. v. Hanchett, 48 F.2d 236 (N.D. Cal. 1931); Broz v. Cellular Info. Systems, Inc., 673 A.2d 148 (Del. 1996) (the interest is that of the corporation on whose board the outside director served and not that of its prospective acquiror).

124. Comedy Cottage, Inc. v. Berk, 495 N.E.2d 1006 (Ill. App. Ct. 1986).

125. Massachusetts states this most forcefully. *See Demoulas*, 677 N.E.2d at 183 ("the nondisclosure of a corporate opportunity is, *in itself,* unfair to a corporation and a breach of fiduciary duty") (emphasis added).

126. CST, Inc. v. Mark, 520 A.2d 469 (Pa. Super. Ct. 1987).

127. Jundt v. Jurassic Resources Dev., 656 N.W.2d 15, 24 (N.D. 2003).

128. *See, e.g.,* Ostrowski v. Avery, 703 A.2d 117 (Conn. 1997); Yiannatsis v. Stephanis, 653 A.2d 275 (Del. 1995); *Demoulas*, 677 N.E.2d at 181.

129. *Production Finishing Corp.,* 405 N.W.2d 171.

130. *See, e.g., Ostrowskiery,* 703 A.2d 117.

131. *See, e.g., Science Accessories,* 425 A.2d 957.

132. *See* RESTATEMENT OF RESTITUTION §§ 194, 195 (1937).

133. *See* CST, Inc. v. Mark, 520 A.2d 469 (Pa. Super. Ct. 1987).

134. Delano v. Kitch, 542 F.2d 550 (10th Cir. 1976) (bare disclosure of commission received by director on sale of stock is not sufficient under Kansas law).

135. D'Addario v. Geller, 129 Fed. Appx. 1, 2 (4th Cir. 2005) (allegation that officers and directors received kickbacks from third person's receipt of valuable shares in exchange for worthless treasure maps sets forth breach of fiduciary duty claim).

136. *See, e.g.,* Wilshire Oil Co. of Texas v. Riffe, 381 F.2d 646, 651 (10th Cir. 1967).

137. *See generally* Berkman v. Rust Craft Greeting Cards, Inc., 454 F. Supp. 787 (S.D.N.Y. 1978) (failure of a some directors to disclose to other board members that investment banker held an interest in firm's acquisition partner).

138. RESTATEMENT (THIRD) OF AGENCY § 8.02 (2006) provides:

> An Agent has a duty not to acquire a material benefit from a third party in connection with transactions conducted or other actions taken on behalf of the principal or otherwise through the agent's use of the agent's position.

139. Blum v. Fleishhacker, 21 F. Supp. 527 (N.D. Cal. 1937), *aff'd in part, rev'd in part*, 109 F.2d 543 (9th Cir. 1940), *cert. denied*, 311 U.S. 665 (1940).
140. Reid v. Robinson, 220 P. 676, 681 (Cal. Ct. App. 1923).
141. 1 ALI, PRINCIPLES OF CORPORATE GOVERNANCE: ANALYSIS AND RECOMMENDATIONS § 5.04 (1992).
142. *Id.* § 5.04(a)(3).
143. *Id.* § 5.04(a)(4).
144. *See, e.g.*, Maryland Metals, Inc. v. Metzner, 382 A.2d 564, 568 (Md. 1978); Anderson v. Bellino, 658 N.W.2d 645 (Neb. 2003).
145. This principle has long been recognized. *See* Nichol v. Martyn, 2 Esp. 732, 734 (N.P. 1799).
146. *See* Bancroft-Whitney Co. v. Glen, 411 P.2d 921, 935 (Cal. 1966).
147. *See* FoodComm Intern. v. Barry, 328 F.3d 300, 303 (7th Cir. 2003) (under most circumstances an employee can incorporate a rival company and procure assets for future operation).
148. *See* Chelsea Indus. v. Gaffney, 449 N.E.2d 320 (Mass. 1983); Scanwell Freight Express STL, Inc. v. Chan, 162 S.W.3d 477, 480–81 (Mo. 2005).
149. *See, e.g.*, American Fed. Group, Ltd. v. Rothenberg, 136 F.3d 897 (2d Cir. 1998) (solicited customers of firm); Patmon v. Hobbs, 280 S.W.3d 589, 596 (Ky. Ct. App. 2009).
150. Vernon Library Supplies, Inc. v. Ard, 550 S.E.2d 108 (Ga. Ct. App. 2001).
151. The easiest case for finding no breach is when co-workers approach the defendant to inquire if they can also join the new venture. *See* The McCallister Co. v. Lynn Kastella, 825 P.2d 980 (Ariz. Ct. App. 1992).
152. *See* Foodcomm Intern. v. Barry, 328 F.3d 300, 303 (7th Cir. 2003).
153. The McCallister Co. v. Lynn Kastella, 825 P.2d 980 (Ariz. Ct. App. 1992).
154. C-E-I-R, Inc. v. Computer Dynamics Corp., 183 A.2d 374, 379 (Md. 1962).
155. *See* ABC Trans Nat'l Transp., Inc. v. Aeronautics Forwarders, Inc., 379 N.E.2d 1228, 1239 (Ill. App. Ct. 1978).
156. Ellis & Marshall Assocs. v. Marshall, 306 N.E.2d 712, 714 (Ill. App. Ct. 1973).
157. *Foodcomm. Intern.*, 328 F.3d at 303; Hanson Staple Co., Inc. v. Eckelberry, 677 S.E.2d 321, 324 (Ga. Ct. App. 2009) (informing customers of unhappiness and intent to seek new employment not a breach); Hartung v. Architects Hartung/Odle/Burke, Inc., 301 N.E.2d 240, 245 (Ind. Ct. App. 1973).
158. Cross Wood Prods., Inc. v. Suter, 422 N.E.2d 953 (Ill. App. Ct. 1981).
159. *See* J Bar H, Inc. v. Joanna Johnson, 822 P.2d 849, 861 (Wyo. 1991) (former fifty-percent owner who was squeezed out of the business can commence a competing business).
160. Raines v. Toney, 313 S.W.2d 802, 809 (Ark. 1958). Criminal sanctions are now available under the Economic Espionage Act of 1996, 18 U.S.C. §§ 1831 *et seq.* (1994), for the misappropriation of trade secrets.
161. Hollingsworth Solderless Terminal v. Turley, 622 F.2d 1324, 1332 (9th Cir. 1980).
162. *See* Leo Silfen, Inc. v. Cream, 278 N.E.2d 636 (N.Y. 1972) (no violation because only 47 of 1100 customers were solicited).

163. *Leo Silfen, Inc.*, 278 N.E.2d at 641.
164. *Foodcomm Intern.*, 328 F.3d at 303.
165. Chelsea Indus. v. Gaffney, 449 N.E.2d 320, 323 (Mass. 1983).
166. Bimba Mfg. Co. v. Starz Cylinder Co., 256 N.E.2d 357, 363 (Ill. App. Ct. 1969).
167. *See* RESTATEMENT OF TORTS § 757, Comment (1939).
168. Bacon v. Volvo Service Center, Inc., 597 S.E.2d 440, 443–44 (Ga. Ct. App. 2004).
169. C-E-I-R, Inc. v. Computer Dynamics Corp., 183 A.2d 374 (Md. 1962); Lawter Int'l, Inc. v. Carroll, 451 N.E.2d 1338, 1347 (Ill. App. Ct. 1983).
170. *See* Genesis Technical and Fin. v. Cast Navigation, 905 N.E.2d 569, 576–77 (Mass. App. Ct. 2009).
171. Sialkot Importing Corp. v. Berlin, 68 N.E.2d 501 (N.Y. 1946).
172. Phansalkar v. Andersen Weinroth & Co., L.P., 344 F.3d 184, 205 (2nd Cir. 2003).
173. *Id.*
174. In corporate law, "controlling interest" refers to dominant ownership of a corporation's stock. Dixon v. Pro Image Inc., 987 P.2d 48, 54 (Utah 1999).
175. *See* Thomas L. Hazen, *Transfers of Corporate Control and Duties of Controlling Shareholders—Common Law, Tender Offers, Investment Companies—and a Proposal for Reform*, 125 U. PA. L. REV. 1023, 1027 (1977).
176. *See, e.g.*, Crowley v. Communications for Hosps., Inc., 573 N.E.2d 996 (Mass. App. Ct.), *rev. denied*, 577 N.E.2d 309 (Mass. 1991).
177. *See, e.g.*, Jones v. H. F. Ahmanson & Co., 460 P.2d 464 (Cal. 1969) (controlling stockholder under no duty to have caused company to split company's shares so all shares were more marketable, but when did act to increase marketability had a duty to assure equal treatment for all shareholders).
178. *See, e.g.*, Chiles v. Robertson, 767 P.2d 903, 912 (Or. Ct. App. 1989) ("The fiduciary best fulfills its duties if it approaches them with the attitude of seeking the beneficiary's interests rather than the personal interests of the fiduciary.").
179. Sinclair Oil Corporation v. Levien, 280 A.2d 717 (Del. 1971). *See also, e.g.*, Thorpe by Castleman v. CERBCO, Inc., 676 A.2d 436 (Del. 1996).
180. *See, e.g.*, *Chiles*, 767 P.2d 903 (relying upon Sections 5.04 and 5.11 of the ALI PRINCIPLES OF CORPORATE GOVERNANCE: ANALYSIS AND RECOMMENDATIONS (1992), holds the duty is owed to "use their power to control the corporation in a way that would benefit all shareholders proportionately"). *See also, e.g.*, Jones v. H. F. Ahmanson & Co., 460 P.2d 464 (Cal. 1969).
181. *See* Locati v. Johnson, 980 P.2d 173 (Or. Ct. App. 1999).
182. Meyerson v. El Paso Natural Gas Co., 246 A.2d 789, 794 (Del. Ch. 1967) (allocation of entire tax savings to the parent upheld where court found nature of the issues so problematic that the wisest policy is to commit the allocation to the business judgment rule unless the plaintiff established "gross and palpable overreaching").
183. Smith v. Tele-Communication, Inc., 184 Cal. Rptr. 571 (Cal. Ct. App. 1982).

184. Efron v. Kalmanovitz, 38 Cal. Rptr. 148 (Ct. App. 1964).

185. *See, e.g.*, Rosenblatt v. Getty Oil Co., 493 A.2d 929 (Del. 1985).

186. *See, e.g.*, Odyssey Partners v. Fleming Companies, 735 A.2d 386 (Del. Ch. 1999) (noting director fees of $24,000 per year not so great as to compromise independence and a director who formerly was employee of, and who had a consulting arrangement with, controlling stockholder deemed independent where his membership on board was requested by directors who were clearly independent).

187. ALI, PRINCIPLES OF CORPORATE GOVERNANCE: ANALYSIS AND RECOMMENDATIONS § 5.10 (1992).

188. *Id.* § 5.11.

189. *Id.* § 5.12.

190. *Id.* § 5.11(a)(1) & (2).

191. *See, e.g.*, Evans v. Blesi, 345 N.W.2d 775 (Minn. Ct. App. 1984).

192. *See, e.g.*, Duncan v. Lichtenberger, 671 S.W.2d 948 (Tex. Ct. App. 1984).

193. Estate of Schroer v. Stamco Supply, Inc., 482 N.E.2d 975 (Ohio Ct. App. 1984).

194. Crowley v. Communications for Hosps., Inc., 573 N.E.2d 996 (Mass. App. Ct.), *review denied*, 577 N.E.2d 309 (Mass. 1991).

195. *E.g.*, Knaebel v. Heiner, 663 P.2d 551 (Alaska 1983).

196. *See, e.g.*, Eisenberg v. Chicago Milwaukee Corp., 537 A.2d 1051, 1062 (Del. Ch. 1987). *See also, e.g.*, Zahn v. Transamerica Corporation, 162 F.2d 36 (3d Cir. 1947); Mansfield Hardwood Lumber Co. v. Johnson, 268 F.2d 317 (5th Cir. 1959), *cert. denied*, 361 U.S. 885 (1959); Judah v. Delaware Trust Co., 378 A.2d 624 (Del. 1977).

197. *See* Cede & Co. v. Technicolor, 634 A.2d 345 (Del. 1993).

198. *See* Levien v. Sinclair Oil Corp., 261 A.2d 911 (Del. Ch. 1969), *rev'd*, Sinclair Oil Corp. v. Levien, 280 A.2d 717 (Del. 1971).

199. *See* Jones v. H. F. Ahmanson & Co., 460 P.2d 464 (Cal. 1969).

CHAPTER 12

OBLIGATIONS ARISING OUT OF TRANSACTIONS IN SHARES

PART A. STATE LAW

§ 12.1 THE SALE OF CORPORATE CONTROL

A purchaser of a controlling interest in a corporation often pays a premium above the prevailing market price for the stock.[1] Courts generally hold that any premium paid to acquire controlling stock is merely a reflection of the greater value of that stock due to its control potential, and as such it is a natural consequence of stock ownership and cannot be considered a corporate asset.[2] More generally, every stockholder, including the controlling stockholder, is at liberty to dispose of her shares at any price as long as there is no cause to believe or suspect the sale will proximately harm the corporation or its stockholders, or will necessarily interfere or mislead the other stockholders in exercising their same right to sell.[3]

§ 12.2 FIDUCIARY DUTIES OF SELLERS OF CORPORATE CONTROL

Numerous courts have held that a seller of control may become liable in certain circumstances for the harm to the corporation caused by the purchaser. Clearly, however, the liability is far from absolute.[4] In a leading case[5] after the transfer of a controlling interest, the purchasers proceeded to loot the corporation. The court held the control sellers liable and reasoned that, at a minimum, the transferor of a controlling block of shares owes a duty to the corporation to protect it when "the circumstances surrounding the proposed transfer are such as to awaken suspicion and put a *prudent* man on his guard—unless a *reasonably adequate* investigation discloses such facts as would convince a *reasonable person* that no fraud is intended or likely to result."[6] When the circumstances do awaken suspicion in the reasonably prudent person, the seller of control has a duty to make such inquiry as a reasonably prudent person would make.[7] Liability does not attach, however, merely for the exercise of poor business judgment.[8] A minority view requires proof that the controlling stockholder had actual knowledge, not inquiry notice.[9]

The cases illustrate the highly factual nature of a court's determination in sale of control litigation. This orientation is embraced by the American Law Institute, whose provision makes the controlling stockholders' fiduciary obligation depend in part on the transfer not occurring when "it is apparent from the circumstances that the purchaser is likely" to violate the purchaser's fiduciary obligations so as to acquire a substantial financial benefit for himself.[10]

Looting and mismanagement by the purchaser of control are classic types of misbehavior that form the backdrop for inquiring whether the seller's suspicions were sufficiently piqued for there to have been a breach in disposing of control. Many cases do not involve looting or mismanagement by the new controlling stockholder but rather the diversion of a potential premium from the noncontrolling stockholders by the former controlling stockholder. This occurs when the purchaser offers to acquire at a substantial premium an asset of the company[11] or all the shares of the company,[12] and the controlling stockholder diverts most or all of the premium to himself by converting the offer for the asset or all the shares to a transaction in which the controlling stockholder sells only his shares to the third party at a substantial premium. In these situations, the courts embrace the idea that the fiduciary obligation of controlling stockholders is not to divert or appropriate for themselves an offer or opportunity that a third-party purchaser is prepared to extend that would benefit all the stockholders proportionally. The language of the American Law Institute's provisions is broad enough to proscribe the controlling stockholder's appropriation of the corporation's opportunity to sell its asset at a premium,[13] but these provisions appear to proscribe the conversion of an offer for all the stockholders' shares only if the controlling stockholder secretly acquires shares from the noncontrolling shareholders as part of his disposition of a control block to a third party.[14]

No case has held, however, that the controlling stockholder breaches its duty by failing actively to initiate transactions that are likely to yield a premium for the noncontrolling stockholders' shares.[15] The controlling stockholder's fiduciary duty with respect to dispositions of control is breached by commission, not omission.[16]

When there has been a breach of duty in the transfer of control, the more frequently invoked remedy is to require the vendor of control to disgorge the control premium.[17] It is also possible to recover for any assets or profits lost because of the misbehavior of the new controlling stockholder.[18] The purchaser of control is liable for his seller's breach on a theory of civil conspiracy.[19]

§ 12.3 RESIGNATION OF DIRECTORS IN CONNECTION WITH THE SALE OF CONTROL

In general, a director or other officer, even though elected for a fixed term, may resign at any time with definite notice.[20] Unless a future date or acceptance by the corporation is specified, resignation takes effect at once, and no acceptance is necessary.[21] There are occasions, however, when directors and officers are not free to quit with impunity. Today it continues to be true that directors cannot accept payment in any form or guise for their resignations and delivery of control or for the substitution of others in their place, and they are accountable for any monies so received.[22]

If directors agree to sell their shares, resign from their offices, procure other shareholders to sell their shares, and hand over control to irresponsible persons, they may be liable under various theories. For example, the directors may be liable to fellow shareholders for the profit or excess price that they received over other shareholders whom they persuaded to sell their shares, or to the corporation for secret profits that were obtained by their official acts and for damages caused by the wrongful acts of their transferees and successors.

§ 12.4 THE SALE OF A CORPORATE OFFICE

The seller of a block of shares may lawfully arrange for sitting directors to resign seriatim and for the nominees of her purchaser to be appointed to the board vacancies created by the resignations, provided the block so transferred represents working control. To be sure, it is always possible for one who purchases control between the annual election of directors to simply wait until the next annual meeting or to seek a special meeting at which the new controlling stockholder's nominees can be elected. This rarely occurs, because the new holder of control wishes her influence to be felt immediately. There are sound policy reasons supporting this desire.[23] Even with a sale of less than a majority of the shares, directors' agreements to resign were not invalid if they accompanied the transfer of a block that had effective working control, meaning the power to see that a majority of directors were the nominees of the holder of that block of shares.[24] In contrast, courts have had little problem holding that the premium paid for shares representing only 3 percent[25] or 4 percent[26] was in payment for the directors' resignations and not for working control.

§ 12.5 STATUTORY PROVISIONS AFFECTING CONTROL TRANSACTIONS

Several states have provisions that empower a stockholder to petition for an election of the directors whenever a majority of the sitting directors have been appointed rather than elected by the stockholders.[27] Such provisions can provide a mechanism for testing whether seriatim resignations and appointments in fact are coupled with a block of shares that represents working control.[28] The true significance of such provisions is that they provide the means for stockholders to reestablish their bond to the board. As a practical matter, such provisions are likely to be invoked only when there is no clear group that represents working control, so that the election can be seen as reestablishing the board as the stockholders' representatives.

Section 14(f) of the Securities Exchange Act of 1934 requires extensive disclosures of the new directors' backgrounds whenever a majority of the board of directors is appointed as a consequence of an arrangement with a person required to make the filings required by the Williams Act amendments to the Securities Exchange Act by virtue of its purchases of, or tender offer for, a corporation's shares.[29] The information must be circulated to all voting stockholders not less than 10 days before the directors are to take office.

§ 12.6 OTHER SHARE TRANSFERS THAT TRIGGER FIDUCIARY OBLIGATIONS—GREENMAIL AND EQUAL OPPORTUNITY CONCERNS

"Greenmail" has been defined as the purchase at a premium price of a takeover bidder's or dissident's stock that is not available to other stockholders.[30] Several studies have found that the payment of greenmail causes a net decline in the value of the corporation, a decline that can be attributed to the above-market price paid for the shares as well as providing the unmistakable message that the board of directors does not welcome bids for control of the firm. A traditional analysis examines the board's payment of greenmail for evidence the directors have acted unreasonably or in bad faith and places a slightly higher burden on those directors with a direct financial interest served by the preservation of the status quo.[31] The facts that a board's decision to pay greenmail is made in haste and with little evidence that there has been a genuine threat posed by the dissident shareholder provide powerful circumstantial evidence that the true motive of the directors in paying greenmail is to preserve their control.[32] On the other hand, evidence that the dissidents pose a threat to the corporation or its stockholders overcomes any suggestion that the greenmail payment was prompted solely by managerial self-interest.[33] A few states have enacted anti-greenmail provisions that, for example, condition repurchase of shares above a certain percentage upon stockholder approval.[34] Since 1987, greenmail payments have become much less attractive because section 5881 of the Internal Revenue Code of 1986 imposes a 50 percent excise tax of the gain on the shares' resale to the corporation. For the purpose of this provision, "greenmail" is defined as (1) the payment of any consideration by a corporation to acquire its shares from a stockholder when the shares have been held for less than two years; (2) within two years of their purchase the stockholder or those associated with the stockholder made or threatened to make a tender offer for the company's shares; and (3) the buyback offer is not made to all the stockholders. A few states have prohibited greenmail payments unless approved by the stockholders.[35]

Hostile takeovers are a phenomenon only of publicly traded corporations; greenmail does not arise in closely held corporations. When a close corporation purchases shares at a premium, the corporation has a very different and unique concern: whether all the stockholders should have an opportunity to sell their shares to the corporation at the same price.[36]

As discussed in Chapter 10, transactions between a director and the corporation will be subject to a fairness scrutiny. Transactions in shares between a controlling shareholder and the corporation will be subject to a similar intrinsic fairness requirement.[37]

§ 12.7 COMMON LAW FIDUCIARY DUTY OF DIRECTORS AND OFFICERS WHEN TRADING IN THEIR CORPORATION'S SHARES

State courts are in conflict as to how far and when directors and officers come under a fiduciary duty to disclose inside information to individual shareholders before purchasing their shares. There is a growing tendency to hold officials responsible for taking unfair advantage of the ignorance of selling shareholders by failing to disclose to them non-public corporate information affecting the value of the shares.[38] Nonetheless, the common law has had some difficulty, however, in consistently imposing liability on unscrupulous directors and officers dealing in a faceless market behind the screen of a stock exchange.

What Is Insider Trading? The insider trading problem can be pointed up by the following example. *D*, a director and president of the *C* Oil Company, knows by virtue of his official position that the corporation, after long efforts, has discovered oil on its land, increasing the value of its assets and its shares manyfold. The management carefully conceals this discovery so that the directors themselves can acquire adjoining lands and they and other insiders can buy up as many shares of the company's stock as possible. The shares are listed on a local stock exchange. *D* locates *P*, who is not an insider, and buys certain shares from her privately at the market price, which *D* knows is much less than their actual value. *P* asks no questions, and *D* volunteers no hint of any unusual development. *D* also purchases additional shares from *P* through brokers on the stock exchange before any report of the discovery has been made to the shareholders. Soon the news of the discovery becomes public, and the shares at once quadruple in value. *P*, who would not have sold if she had been informed of the discovery, seeks to have the sales that she made to *D* rescinded or to hold *D* accountable for the profits that *D* gained by his nondisclosure.[39]

Corporate officers and directors, when trading in their corporation's shares, must refrain from any designed or active misrepresentation by word or act. Pursuant to a view that was once the weight of authority, directors and officers are deemed not to stand in a fiduciary relationship to their opposite traders when trading in their corporation's shares, because individual dealing in shares is not corporate business.[40] Formally, the director's or officer's fiduciary relationship is, under this view, seen as being with the corporation and not its shareholders, and certainly not with someone who will not become a shareholder until the challenged transaction is completed. Absent a fiduciary duty to the insider's opposite trader, there is no basis upon which to premise a duty to disclose material non-public information known to the insider. On the other hand, a director who acts for the *corporation purchasing its own stock* does have a fiduciary relationship to the selling shareholder.[41]

"Special Facts" Doctrine. Not all courts have found it necessary to choose between the rule that officers and directors are always subject to a strict fiduciary duty to the shareholders to volunteer all information and the former view that they are always free to trade in their corporation's shares without revealing non-public information. The tendency has been to break down the harsh not-a-fiduciary rule by recognizing exceptions to it in "special facts" or "special circumstances" that give rise to a duty to make disclosure. Circumstances or developments that have been held to constitute "special circumstances" include knowledge by officers or directors of important transactions, such as prospective mergers, probable sales of the entire assets or business, agreements by third parties to buy large blocks of stock at a high price, and impending declarations of unusual dividends.[42] Under such circumstances, it clearly is reasonable to require officials to refrain from taking advantage of the ignorance of the shareholders whom they are supposed to represent and protect. The New York courts, once leaders in maintaining the older position, after first giving cautious recognition of the possibility of imposing an affirmative fiduciary duty of disclosure if the special circumstances are sufficiently strong,[43] now count among their jurisprudence a far-reaching decision recognizing a strict fiduciary duty.[44]

Under the "special facts" doctrine, uncertainties exist as to what developments are sufficiently important to call for disclosure of information if the selling shareholder makes no inquiry about developments that affect the value of the shares. Some courts say that an officer or director need not volunteer information as to the prospects of the company or the probability of dividends, but that the official must give truthful answers to such questions as the shareholder asks. At common law, if the official undertakes to inform the selling shareholder, he must speak fully and truthfully and is liable for misleading the seller even by expressions of his opinion.[45] It would seem, however, that the official should also be obliged to speak fully if he seeks out the shareholder and is active in inducing the sale or if he knows of overtures to purchase the corporate property or shares or any other matter that ought in all fairness to be disclosed.[46] Under SEC Rule 10b-5[47] and the federal securities acts' antifraud provisions generally, the test of materiality for both misstatements and omissions is whether the reasonable investor would have considered the fact important if the defendant had disclosed the information to him.[48]

Corporate Recovery of Ill-Gotten Gains. The preceding discussion has focused on the duty of candor that officers and directors owe to their sellers or buyers when trading on non-public information. A very distinct duty question is whether the fiduciary breaches his duty *to his corporate employer* when he trades on material non-public information acquired by virtue of his relationship to the corporation. This question was addressed in an early Delaware decision[49] involving a "confidential secretary" who had advance knowledge of a corporation's plans to purchase its own stock on the open market. Armed with this knowledge, on his own account the secretary purchased stock, which he resold at a profit when the information became public. The court allowed the corporation to recover the secretary's profit and explicitly stated that no loss or damage to the corporation by the secretary's trading needed to be alleged.[50] The fiduciary obligation so recognized is broad enough to include trading in another corporation's shares, as long as the information used in so trading was acquired through the defendant's relationship to the plaintiff corporation.[51] The key to understanding the corporation's recovery of its fiduciary's insider trading profits is that the fiduciary has acted in a manner inconsistent with the trust placed in him by the corporation that the information be used for corporate and not private purposes. Or, stated somewhat differently, disgorgement to the corporation is a necessary disincentive to the fiduciary not to compromise the relationship of trust by extracting non-consented-to benefits from the relationship. Note that the source of the fiduciary obligation is not just the defendant's position in the company, but the access that position provides him to confidential corporate information. Once the defendant has achieved access to such information, he should be bound not to compromise either its confidentiality or the trust placed in him by trading on the basis of that information.[52] In contrast, there is no breach of duty, however, when the board of directors has authorized a selective disclosure of material non-public information for the purpose of encouraging a third party to purchase the company's securities.[53]

As a practical matter, the state insider trading law is today largely eclipsed by the extensive development of insider trading regulation that has occurred under the federal securities laws. The same can be said of state Blue Sky laws' application to insider trading.[54] Commentators have noted, for example, that state common law has been "overshadowed if not superseded" by Section 10(b) of the Securities Exchange Act of 1934.

PART B. FEDERAL LAW

§ 12.8 SHORT-SWING PROFITS UNDER SECTION 16 OF THE SECURITIES EXCHANGE ACT

Directors and officers of publicly traded companies are not ordinarily held accountable to the corporation for profits made in the purchase and sale of its shares, unless they have taken unfair advantage of information that equitably belonged to the corporation.[55] To prevent the unfair use of inside information for the purpose of speculation, Congress has provided in section 16 of the Securities Exchange Act of 1934 (as amended),[56] that every person who is a director, officer, or beneficial owner of more than 10 percent of any class of "equity security" that is registered pursuant to section 12 of that Act[57] must file a statement and report the changes of ownership that have occurred during that month as to such securities.[58] Any profit[59] realized from any "purchase and sale" or "sale and purchases" of any such equity security within a period of less than six months is recoverable by the issuer without the need of proving unfair use of official information.[60] Section 16(b) is intended to be a prophylaxis for such trading. The remedy provided in Section 16(b) in no way restricts the sanction or recovery that can be obtained pursuant to state law or other provisions of the federal securities law.

Under the early cases, the federal courts consistently interpreted 16(b) to require an objective and mechanical application. The statute continues to be read literally, without a pragmatic eye toward its purpose, except when the transaction is other than a standard securities transaction. When the transaction is of an extraordinary nature in the sense that it does not, for example, fall literally within the common definition of "sale" or "purchase," the courts apply a subjective, pragmatic test pursuant to which they inquire whether the circumstances were such that the defendant might have had access to inside information when she traded. The courts have thus employed a more subjective analysis in such non-cash, non-garden variety transactions as mergers, share exchanges, and exercises of stock options. Similarly, a case-by-case analysis has also been used when trying to determine whether someone who is denominated an officer in fact should be given officer status within the context of section 16(b)'s prophylactic provisions. In such cases, before applying 16(b) liability, the courts have looked to the potential for speculative abuse. Section 16(b) was aimed at a particular type of abuse—namely, those instances in which an insider could make a sure-thing short-swing profit by entering into transactions in anticipation of price changes that would lead to a profit at the second stage of the short-swing transaction. In other words, the section was aimed at discouraging insiders from speculating in their own company's stock, especially when such speculation is based on special knowledge of facts soon to be made public. Notwithstanding the section's apparent objectivity and supposed ease of application, a number of section 16(b) issues have resulted in protracted litigation. Thus, the statute falls far short of providing a predictable rule of thumb.

Section 16(b)'s provisions are enforceable solely by means of private litigation, pursuant to the section's self-contained cause of action, a hybrid cause of action that lies somewhere between a derivative suit and a direct action. There is exclusive federal jurisdiction over such suits. The plaintiff shareholder must demand that the corporation sue, and the corporation can bring suit. However, if the corporation fails to respond within 60 days, the shareholder can initiate the suit, with any recovery going to the corporation. Unlike the standard derivative suit, a good faith determination by the board of directors that the suit should not be prosecuted cannot bar the shareholder from maintaining the suit to recover short-swing profits. Moreover, the section does not contain a requirement that the plaintiff have been a shareholder at the time of the trading transactions in question.[61] Since the suit can be either at equity or in law, the plaintiff has a choice of whether or not to have a jury trial.[62]

One of the more perplexing 16(b) issues has revolved around the statutory definitions of "purchase" and "sale." For example, an early case[63] held that the exercise of conversion rights constituted a 16(b) purchase. Two courts of appeal subsequently took the contrary position and held 16(b) inapplicable.[64] The question of the status of conversions remained in doubt[65] until the adoption of SEC Rule 16b-9, which provides that generally a conversion constitutes neither a sale nor a purchase.[66] Absent a clear SEC rule, courts today take a subjective or pragmatic approach in determining whether the defendant had access to the types of information that have the potential for the speculative abuse that section 16(b) was designed to prevent.[67]

Another significant 16(b) issue is the question of who is a statutory insider. For example, where a corporation appoints or deputizes one of its officers or directors to sit on another corporation's board, that individual's insider status may be attributed to the deputizing body.[68] Similarly, notwithstanding the maintenance of separate brokerage accounts and different investment advisers, a spouse's sale may be matched with an insider's purchase to find a 16(b) profit.[69] Similarly, questions arise about what constitutes a "class" of securities for the purpose of calculating whether the defendant is an owner of more than 10 percent of a class.[70]

The SEC has invoked its rule-making power to clarify the meaning of "beneficial ownership." The rules are directed at those persons who can exercise sufficient control over the company's management to justify presuming access to inside information. The tests of beneficial ownership the SEC uses for determining reporting obligations are different from those it uses to decide whether purchases and sales should be matched for the purpose of requiring the disgorgement of short-swing profits. Once 10 percent beneficial holder status is determined, section 16's reporting and short-swing profit provisions apply only to securities in which the insider has a direct or indirect pecuniary interest.[71]

Rule 16a-2(a)(2)[72] begins by setting forth the basic rule that for reporting purposes beneficial ownership hinges on the direct or indirect pecuniary interest in the shares, and that interest may be the result of "any contract, arrangement, understanding, relationship, or otherwise." This includes the opportunity to participate, directly or indirectly, in any profit attributable to transactions in the shares in question. The rule then goes on to list examples of "indirect pecuniary interest" that trigger section 16. Securities held by immediate family members sharing the same household are included. A general partner's proportional interest in securities held by a general or limited partnership is similarly included. In contrast, a shareholder does not have a pecuniary interest in the portfolio securities held by a corporation, limited partnership, or similar entity, as long as he is not a controlling shareholder of the entity and neither has nor shares investment control over the entity's portfolio securities.

Because of the breadth of the beneficial ownership rules, section 16 problems arise when X joins with Y and Z to sell their Alpha shares for Beta shares pursuant to a lock up agreement imposed by Beta whereby for a period of two years they were barred from disposing of the shares. Though X's interest in the Beta shares was less than 2.5 percent, the combined Beta holdings of the three constituted 18 percent of Beta's outstanding shares. While the shares were subject to the agreement, X individually engaged in a number of trades in Beta shares. The Second Circuit,[73] rejecting the view that beneficial ownership by a group required proof of an intent to acquire control, remanded the case for further findings as to whether X, Y, and Z had combined for the common objective of "acquiring" or "holding" shares, as provided by the beneficial ownership rule that is applicable to groups.[74] If so, Section 16(b) liability would arise from X's trades.

The question of who is an "officer" or "director" may also lead to a fact inquiry insofar as those terms include persons performing similar functions. An analysis of the relevant cases reveals that when an employee, although denominated an officer, does not possess the type of executive power or decision-making authority likely to give him or her access to inside information, section 16(b) will not be held applicable.[75] This pragmatic analysis is supported by SEC rule-making that provides that section 16 applies to executive officers[76]—that is, those who are clothed with policymaking authority. The focus thus is not on a person's title but whether in discharging his or her duties the individual is likely to obtain information that would be helpful in avoiding the risks ordinarily associated with short-swing speculation.[77]

§ 12.9 RULE 10B-5 AND INSIDER TRADING

Rule 10b-5 prohibits certain individuals—insiders, misappropriators, and tippees—from engaging in transactions in their company's stock if they do so on the basis of information not available to the investing public. This prohibition has been extended to tipping such information when doing so is a breach of a fiduciary duty.

Origins of "Disclose or Abstain" Rule. The first step toward making Rule 10b-5 the major enforcement weapon for the regulation of insider trading occurred in 1961, in *In re Cady, Roberts & Co.*,[78] an SEC administrative proceeding. Seven years after the *Cady, Roberts* ruling, a highly significant Rule 10b-5 decision was handed down by the United States Court of Appeals for the Second Circuit.[79] The facts in that case raised a number of questions, including (1) the accountability of those insiders who profited from their disclosure purchases and (2) the posture of the "tippees," who were not corporate officers but had advance notice of the material nonpublic information.

Misappropriation Theory. The misappropriation theory first expands Rule 10b-5 to situations in which a defendant can properly be said to be under a fraud-based duty to disclose or abstain from trading, because of a fiduciary relationship not to use confidential information for private gain. The Supreme Court held that a Rule 10b-5 violation can be based on a breach of a duty to the sources of the information even when the violator is not an insider of the company whose securities are being traded. The necessary deception is present by virtue of the defendant failing to disclose her plans to trade in the securities, i.e., "feigning fidelity" to the source of the information.[80] Furthermore, this deception is "in connection with the purchase or sale of any security" even though it cannot be linked to identifiable purchasers or sellers.[81] In other words, the duty underlying the Rule 10b-5 violation need not be owed to a purchaser or seller of securities.

Problems abound in determining what constitutes a fiduciary relationship. Thus, for example, the Second Circuit, sitting en banc, held that the marital relationship was not itself a sufficient basis upon which the misappropriation theory would operate.[82] Much-needed guidance to the courts is now provided by Rule 10b5-2, which provides a nonexclusive definition of the types of relationships and circumstances that impose a duty of "trust and confidence for the purpose of the misappropriation theory."[83] Rule 10b5-2 provides that trust and confidence can arise by agreement or a history or practice of sharing confidences with reason to believe the confidentiality of the information is to be maintained. Also, information shared among certain family members is similarly deemed confidential, unless the opposite is proven that the person receiving the information did not know and could not reasonably expect that the source of the information expected confidentiality in light of the parties' past practices. Questions have been raised, however, as to whether Rule 10b5-2 goes beyond the scope of the statute in attempting to bring persons under Rule 10b-5's insider trading prohibitions. For example, in one case, it was indicated that a mutual expectation of confidentiality is not sufficient to trigger Rule 10b-5's disclose or abstain rule.[84] The SEC takes the position that a contractual duty of confidentiality is sufficient, but that view has been challenged.[85]

Tippers and Tippees. The Supreme Court underscored the importance of a preexisting fiduciary relationship when it held that outsiders may freely trade on an insider's selective disclosure (that is, a "tip") as long as the disclosure was not "improper."[86] The case law restrains the scope of the disclose-or-abstain rule. First, it provides an extremely narrow definition of what constitutes an *improper* tip. Second, even though a tip is improper, only those who are aware the disclosure was improper are subject to Rule 10b-5 liability if they trade or pass the tip on to another. The bystander who overhears another discussing material non-public information may freely trade, provided he is not a friend or relative, or conferred or could confer a pecuniary benefit upon the speaker.[87] But if the parties are not perfect strangers, it is easier to establish that the selective disclosure was improper.[88] The tippee liability does not require proof that his tipper knew his tippee would trade; it is enough that the tippee knew that the selective disclosure to him was a breach of the tipper's duty to the employer.[89] When, however, tipping is prosecuted under Rule 14e-3, there is not the same requirement for the selective disclosure to constitute a breach of fiduciary obligation, so that the inquiry instead is whether the tippee knew the information was material, non-public, and selectively disclosed after a substantial step had been undertaken toward a tender offer.[90] And, when the act of tipping is within the scope of, for example, the senior officer's employment, the employer can be liable.[91] In most instances, however, tipping and insider trading are outside the scope of one's employment and, hence, do not subject their employer to vicarious liability.[92]

The ability to make selective disclosures has been negated by the SEC's adoption in late 2000 of Regulation FD.[93] In broad overview, Regulation FD (the acronym for "fair disclosure") greatly restricts the freedom public companies formerly enjoyed to make selective disclosures of material non-public information to market professionals or shareholders. The scope of its requirements is examined in a later section of this chapter.[94]

Possession Versus Use. There has been ongoing debate as to whether a case for improper insider trading under Rule 10b-5 can be made by showing that the defendant traded while in *possession* of material non-public information or whether it must be established that he or she in fact *used* the information in making the trades in question.[95] In a 1998 decision, the Eleventh Circuit adopted an "on the basis" rather than "mere possession" test of liability.[96] The court went on to point out, however, that trades while in possession of such information can be used to create a "strong inference" that the defendant in fact used the information.[97] In contrast is the reasoning of Judge Richard Posner that proof that the defendant traded when he had knowledge of insider information should place upon him the burden of establishing that he did not trade on the basis of that information.[98] The SEC has addressed the split in the circuits in its Rule 10b5-1,[99] which essentially equates the meaning of "on the basis" to "in possession."[100] Rule 10b5-1, however, provides a safe harbor for trading when aware of material non-public information if the trade is strictly pursuant to a binding written contract to purchase or sale that was entered into before the defendant became aware of the inside information.[101]

Government Enforcement Actions. Willful violations of the federal securities laws may give rise to a criminal prosecution by the Department of Justice, resulting in fines and/or imprisonment. Furthermore, violations may result in sanctions from the SEC. For example, the Commission may impose administrative sanctions: if the violator is a broker-dealer or other market professional, her license can be suspended or revoked. The SEC is authorized to seek either temporary or permanent injunctive relief in the courts "whenever it shall appear to the Commission that any person is engaged or is about to engage in any acts or practices which constitute or will constitute a violation."[102] More frequently, the SEC seeks some form of monetary recovery in addition to a prospective injunction against future violations.

In the wake of Supreme Court decisions, Congress enacted even stronger insider trading penalties, available for use by the SEC. The Insider Trading Sanctions Act of 1984 (ITSA) increased civil and criminal penalties for trading while in possession of material nonpublic information: The SEC is authorized to seek disgorgement of profits[103] and a civil penalty of up to three times the profits gained or the loss avoided by the defendant,[104] and the criminal penalty was increased from $10,000 to $100,000. However, while facially applicable to transactions involving misuse of non-public material information, ITSA does not define the scope of permissible conduct. Thus, ITSA does not alter the availability of a cause of action, but merely the penalties that may be imposed.

ITSA has proved to be an effective enforcement weapon. Following its enactment, the SEC was increasingly vigorous in enforcing insider trading prohibitions and has reached some lucrative settlements. Beyond the increased penalties in ITSA, in October 1990, Congress enacted the Securities Enforcement Remedies and Penny Stock Reform Act, which, among other things, gave the SEC the power in an administrative proceeding to require disgorgement of illegal profits.

The SEC, but not private plaintiffs, can also pursue those who knowingly provide assistance to insiders in carrying out their violation. Thus, the attorney was an aider and abettor to another when he instructed the insider how to open a Swiss bank account through which the unlawful trading was carried out.[105]

Private Rights of Action for Insider Trading. In a face-to-face transaction, an action will lie against someone who sells or purchases while in possession of material inside non-public information.[106] However, in an open-market context, standing to sue is more problematic and, therefore, at one time posed ticklish standing questions.[107] Congress stepped in to change this result. The Insider Trading and Securities Fraud Enforcement Act (ITSFEA) was enacted by Congress in 1988 to supplement any remedy that may exist under Rule 10b-5. The Act provides an express private right of action by contemporaneous traders against persons making improper use of material non-public information.[108] Damages in such an action are limited to the profit (or loss avoided) that is attributable to the defendant's illegal conduct, reduced to the extent that the SEC has secured disgorgement (as opposed to a penalty) under the 1984 ITSA legislation.

§ 12.10 SECTION 10(b) AND RULE 10b-5 OF THE SECURITIES EXCHANGE ACT OF 1934

The Exchange Act contains several provisions that are of importance to a corporate attorney who does not specialize in securities law. For example, as has been discussed in the preceding section, the Act provides that insider short-swing profits "shall inure to and be recoverable by the issuer."[109] The Act also regulates practices with respect to the solicitation of proxies.[110] Section 10(b) of the Act[111] contains a general antifraud provision that renders unlawful manipulative and deceptive acts and practices in connection with the sale or purchase of a security. This section specifically empowers the SEC to promulgate rules in order to define the prohibited conduct. Rule 10b-5,[112] which was drawn under this authority, constitutes a catch-all antifraud provision. In addition to prohibiting fraudulent acts and practices in connection with the purchase of a security, this rule expressly renders it unlawful "to make any untrue statement of material fact or to omit to state a material fact" in connection with the purchase or sale of a security.[113] The rule's breadth is great, as it applies to *any* security, regardless of whether the security is subject to the Act's registration and reporting requirements.[114] Further, the rule applies to any transaction utilizing an instrumentality of interstate commerce, including the mails and even intrastate telephone conversations.[115]

Rule 10b-5's broad language has been applied in a wide variety of fact contexts. Picking up where section 16(b) leaves off, Rule 10b-5 has an impact on trading in securities based on inside information.[116] The rule can be used to regulate the flow of information to the investing public and in many instances to compel corporate disclosure of material facts. The rule has also proved to be a weapon against certain types of corporate mismanagement. This versatility is due to the breadth of the statute's and rule's language.[117] In addition to material misstatements or omissions reasonably calculated to affect an investor's decision in ordinary sales or purchases of securities,[118] Rule 10b-5 applies to a corporation's issuance of stock or bonds,[119] mergers and other organic changes,[120] a corporation's purchase or sale of its own or another company's securities,[121] and the sale of a controlling interest in a corporation.

Because the cause of action is implied, there was not, until 2002, any expressly provided statute of limitations, although at one time courts used the analogous limitations period in the state or securities law.[122] In 2002, the Congress enacted a statute-of-limitations period requiring that private suits be filed within discovery and not later than five years of the commission of the violation.[123]

Federal jurisdiction over suits based on Rule 10b-5 is exclusive.[124] When, as is frequently the case, a particular set of facts gives rise to both a 10b-5 claim and a cause of action under state law, the aggrieved buyer or seller of securities is generally able to combine both in federal court under the doctrine of pendent jurisdiction.[125] As discussed later, in most securities class action state securities fraud claims are preempted.

[1] Materiality

In order for a misstatement or omission to be actionable under Rule 10b-5, it must be a material one. The Supreme Court has defined "materiality" in terms of the type of information that a reasonable investor would consider significant in making an investment decision.[126] Materiality is highly contextual and bright-line tests are not appropriate in determining materiality.[127] Instead courts must look at the misstatements and omissions in light of the total mix of available information. The test of materiality is an objective one and not one that turns upon the unique information needs of the particular investor. When the misstated or omitted fact is contingent or speculative, such as a prediction, a forecast, or even an appraisal of the value of an asset, the standard definition of materiality must account not solely for the probability that the forecasted event or item will in fact occur. In such a case, the Supreme Court holds that there is to be a balancing of the probability of the event's occurrence and its expected magnitude to make the materiality determination.[128] In such an instance, even though an event might be accorded a low probability of occurrence, a very substantial magnitude should it occur can result in the item being deemed material.[129] Even though an opinion is not a "fact" as such, misrepresenting one's opinion, such as stating that "loan reserves are adequate," can violate Rule 10b-5 if the speaker is aware there is objective evidence that contradicts her opinion.[130] The Supreme Court holds that opinion statements can be materially misleading only when they are "objectively" false, i.e., when the plaintiff can establish by objective evidence that the opinion statement was false.[131] Hence, directors who opine that $40 is a "high" price commit fraud if they have before them evidence that the fair price is $60. However, no violation occurs if the directors have been advised that $40 is the fair price, but the directors' personal belief is that the shares' intrinsic value is higher.

The materiality of a particular item is determined within the "total mix" of information that is publicly available. Through the total mix lens a statement is assessed in light of the other information available to investors. As seen below, this invites defenses such as "truth on the market" and "bespeaks caution." As materiality questions are highly fact-specific, summary judgment is rarely appropriate. Because of the breadth of the definition of materiality, there are many categories of information that can, under the right set of circumstances, be deemed materiality. Courts have held material the following broad categories of information: past business failures of the promoters,[132] ongoing criminal investigation of the firm's president,[133] and directors' concealment of a bribery and kickback schemes.[134]

Whether a fact is material is a joint question of law and fact, and in theory is poorly suited for resolution on the pleadings. However, the courts with some regularity dismiss actions after concluding the alleged omission or misstatement was not material. Aside from their willingness to weigh the likely importance to the objectively qualified investor of an omitted or misstated item, there are several other heuristics that have developed that empower the court to determine the plaintiff has failed to allege a material misrepresentation. The first is the doctrine of "puffing." A puffing statement is a generalized statement of optimism that, in the court's eye, is not material to the investor because the investor would never attribute any importance to such statements as "the business is proceeding well."[135] As Judge Richard Posner observed about statements that the quest for a buyer for the firm was going well (when in fact it was going badly): "*Everyone* knows that someone trying to sell something is going to look and talk on the bright side. You don't sell a product by bad mouthing it."[136]

A second tool for addressing whether a statement is materially misleading is the so-called truth-on-the-market defense. This defense arises when the court is persuaded that, even though the defendant's representations in isolation were materially misleading, they could not have misled investors in an efficient market because truthful information was publicly available. For example, a company, when touting the contribution its new product lines would make, did not commit a material omission by failing to disclose that its established product lines were approaching obsolescence and, hence, would yield smaller and smaller profits; the court noted that the omitted information was set forth in numerous analysts' reports.[137]

The third tool is the "Bespeaks Caution" doctrine that applies only to forward-looking statements, such as a forecast or prediction. Pursuant to this doctrine an erroneous forward-looking statement is not materially misleading if accompanied by "meaningful cautionary language."[138] Not only is the Bespeaks Caution doctrine well established among the various federal circuits,[139] the doctrine is also now part of the statutory safe harbor for forward-looking statements. The statutory safe harbor was added to the Securities Act[140] and Securities Exchange Act[141] in 1995 by the Private Securities Litigation Reform Act. These provisions each provide essentially two distinct safe harbors for forward-looking statements (in addition, they each provide their own definition for what constitutes a forward-looking statement). The first safe harbor essentially codifies the Bespeaks Caution doctrine, since it provides that a forward-looking statement is not actionable if accompanied by meaningful cautionary language. The Conference Committee Report accompanying this provision clarifies that there can be meaningful cautionary language even though the cautionary statements do not include the particular factor that ultimately causes the forward-looking statement not to come true.[142] Second, the Conference Report emphasizes that the cautionary statements "must convey substantive information about factors that realistically could cause results to differ materially from those projected," mere boilerplate is insufficient.[143] Neither the Bespeaks Caution doctrine nor the statutory safe harbor protects misrepresentations of historical fact—each applies only to protect forward-looking statements.

The second safe harbor arises if the plaintiff fails to prove that the forward-looking statement was made with knowledge of its falsity. Juxtaposing this second safe harbor with the first reveals that the first safe harbor applies even if management knows the forward-looking statement is false, provided they have surrounded the knowingly false forecast with meaningful cautionary language. Under the Bespeaks Caution doctrine, courts, when it is clear the forecast was knowingly false, have either found that the cautionary language was deficient or that the defendants had committed material misrepresentations of fact, i.e., non-forward-looking statements.[144] The statutory safe harbor does not apply to forward-looking statements made in certain types of transactions, such as initial public offerings or tender offers, although the Bespeaks Caution doctrine would apply in those contexts.

[2] Scienter and Its Pleading

The Supreme Court has definitively held that the enabling language of Section 10(b) that authorizes the SEC to proscribe through rule making "deceptive or manipulative devices or contrivances" forecloses Section 10(b) and, hence, Rule 10b-5 from reaching conduct that involves no greater fault than mere negligence.[145] Though the Supreme Court has yet to speak on the subject, reckless disregard of the truthfulness, as well as knowledge of the falsity, of the representation are widely recognized by the lower courts as permissible standards for fault, i.e., scienter, in both private and SEC actions under Rule 10b-5. Scienter under the "knowledge" formula does not require, as does the common law action of deceit, that the defendant have intended that the misrepresentation induced the plaintiff to trade. It is enough that the defendant was aware of the untruth and its likelihood of influencing investor behavior.[146] The area of the greatest uncertainty regarding possible future Supreme Court action is whether representations and statements made with reckless disregard of their truthfulness are actionable under Rule 10b-5. Presently all the circuits recognize recklessness as a permissible standard of fault. There are various formulations of what constitutes recklessness under Rule 10b-5. Recklessness falls obviously somewhere between intent and negligence. One court has explained its location as "a lesser form of intent [rather] than a merely greater degree of ordinary negligence."[147] Though a somewhat weaker version of recklessness is a standard of "carelessness approaching indifference" to the truth of the representation,[148] courts more frequently impose a somewhat higher hurdle of what could be called "severe recklessness." However recklessness is defined, and even in a case not involving an allegation of recklessness, the true hurdle facing the plaintiff is the heightened pleading requirements that now apply to securities fraud actions.

The passage of the Private Securities Litigation Reform Act of 1995 (PSLRA) (amending the Securities Act and the Securities and Exchange Act) ended the liberal notice pleading requirements for securities litigation. To discourage what Congress believed was frequent baseless securities fraud litigation,[149] the PSLRA requires that the private plaintiff's complaint not only continue in its other portions to meet the specificity requirements of Federal Rule of Civil Procedure 9(b), but also that the complaint "state with particularity facts giving rise to a *strong inference* that the defendant acted with the requisite state of mind."[150] Adding to the plaintiff's difficulties is that the PSLRA bars any discovery until the resolution of any pending motion to dismiss. Consequently, the plaintiff cannot use discovery, as she once could, to obtain the necessary information to amend her earlier complaint so as to meet the particularity requirements that would be in issue following the defendant's motion to dismiss. Not surprisingly, there is a wide variance among the circuits, and one can even find variances among the district court judges within a single circuit, on just what facts or circumstances give rise to a "strong inference." Indeed, following the PSLRA, the question of pleading scienter is the single most litigated issue in a Rule 10b-5 case. Many courts believe that the template for what constitutes a "strong inference" was the pre-PSLRA Second Circuit decision in *In re Time Warner Securities Litigation*,[151] where a majority of the panel held that scienter was plead with particularity by facts supporting a "motive or opportunity" to commit fraud on the part of the company's officers. In *Time Warner* such facts were found in the managers' likely desire to prop up the price of the company's shares to facilitate a public offering of the securities. The Conference Report accompanying the PSLRA expressly states that it did not intend to codify the Second Circuit's case law, although the new standard was there stated to have been based in part on the Second Circuit's standard.[152] Other courts, following what can be seen as an intermediate approach, though finding that motive and opportunity relevant, considered the facts of the particular case.

The Supreme Court elaborated on the requirements for pleading scienter in *Tellabs, Inc. v. Makor Issues & Rights Ltd.*,[153] which although rejecting a stricter standard urged by the defendants, required that the court take into consideration other plausible inferences negating any alleged inferences of scienter.[154] The strong inference of scienter must be more than a plausible one, it must be "cogent."[155] This means that the inference of scienter must be more than merely reasonable and must be persuasive in light of the particular facts of the case.[156] The inference of scienter must be at least as likely as other reasonable inferences that could be drawn from the facts as pleaded. The court's analysis is far from a bright-line test but appears to strike a balance in requiring more than speculative or reasonable inferences but at the same time not imposing a requirement of firmly requiring unequivocal allegations of a "smoking gun."[157]

[3] Standing—The Purchaser or Seller Requirement

The SEC's standing to sue under the antifraud provision is never in serious doubt since under Section 21(d)(1)[158] the agency is authorized to initiate an enforcement action in the federal district court and can proceed internally pursuant to its cease and desist powers under Section 21C of the Exchange Act.[159] Private investors seeking a monetary recovery must, however, be either a purchaser or seller of a security in connection with the fraud alleged to have been committed by the defendant. Once known as the *Birnbaum* doctrine,[160] a reference to the leading case first enshrining it within the Rule 10b-5 jurisprudence, it was not until three decades after *Birnbaum* was decided that the Supreme Court in *Blue Chip Stamps v. Manor Drug Stores*[161] affirmed the practice that had been uniformly followed in the circuits. *Blue Chip Stamps*, above all other cases, denotes the change in attitude toward private securities suits from the earlier more liberal approaches of the Warren Court. It was not just that *Blue Chip Stamps* opted for a technical standing requirement that signaled a new balance within what was then the Burger Court, but it was the Court's reasons for opting for the technical rule. The Court was not guided by what it thought were logical inferences to be drawn from legislative history. Rather the basis for its mandating a purchaser-seller requirement was its belief of the need for a rule that would insulate companies and their officers from what the court described as "vexatious litigation."[162]

The purchaser-seller requirement is by far the most rigid fixture of Rule 10b-5 litigation. This requires an executed purchase or sale, not merely a speculative opportunity to trade. Even where the defendant's successful intent to prevent the plaintiff from selling by purposefully misrepresenting material facts is beyond peradventure, suit to recover for the losses suffered is barred, even if the sale occurs later after the true facts are known.[163] The sale that is in connection with the fraud does not have to arise by volition so long as the losses are causally related to the sale. Thus, when control of a company was acquired by fraud practiced upon all its shareholders and thereafter the remaining stockholders are cashed out in a squeeze-out merger, the so-called forced seller doctrine applies to confer standing.[164] Somewhat related to the forced seller is the "aborted purchaser-seller." This arises when the defendant's fraud aborts a formal plan involving the sale or exchange of shares.[165] Following the lead of a leading pre-*Blue Chip Stamps* case,[166] most courts that have been called upon to decide the matter have held that the plaintiff seeking injunctive relief need not be a purchaser or seller of shares.[167] There seems to be little cause to deny standing for prospective injunctive relief to a plaintiff who has neither purchased nor sold if the plaintiff sustains the burden of proving that, if equitable relief is not awarded, the defendant's violation likely will cause the plaintiff to suffer a loss through the purchase or sale of a security.

[4] "In Connection With"

Not only must there be a purchase or sale of a security, but also Rule 10b-5, reflecting the operative language of Section 10(b), itself requires that the violation, i.e., the deception, must be "in connection with" the purchase or sale of a security. The language does not, however, require that the defendant be engaged in a security transaction. Thus, companies that release false financial information into a marketplace are liable under Rule 10b-5, even though the company itself does not purchase or sell securities.[168] Correlatively, there is no need to prove in a private suit that the plaintiff is in privity of contract through his purchase or sale with the defendants. Indeed, the in connection with requirement is satisfied even if the target of the fraud is someone other than the purchasing or selling plaintiff.[169] Consequently, untruthful statements about a company's products, certainly in the technology sector where investors can be expected to accord product features on a level akin to earnings per share, can subject such announcements to Rule 10b-5 exposure.[170]

[5] Causal Relationship and Damages

Causation is an element of a Rule 10b-5 action. Many courts have divided causation into two subparts: transaction causation and loss causation. Transaction causation requires a showing that but for the violations in question, the transaction would not have occurred (at least in the form that it took).[171] Loss causation requires a showing of a causal nexus between the transaction and the plaintiff's loss.[172]

Inquiry into transaction causation in many instances occurs by inquiring whether the plaintiff relied upon the deception. When this occurs, the plaintiff must not only prove that the misstated or omitted fact would have assumed actual significance in the deliberations of the reasonable investors under circumstances similar to those that the plaintiff operated within (this of course is the materiality element), but also that the misstated or omitted fact assumed such significance for the plaintiff that it caused the plaintiff to purchase (or to sell, as the case may be), which the plaintiff would not have done had the defendant not misrepresented the facts.[173] This approach gets tricky, if not ethereal, if the plaintiff is required to prove reliance upon a material fact that was omitted. In such a case, the plaintiff is assisted by the holding of *Affiliated Ute Citizens v. United States*,[174] whose facts are narrower than the language the court used to express its holding; in a non-disclosure case (i.e., pure omission case) reliance can be presumed from a showing that the omitted fact was material.[175] The presumption, however, can be rebutted. Courts adhering strictly to the unique facts of *Affiliated Ute*, where there was a fiduciary relationship between the plaintiff and defendant, accord this presumption only when there is a preexisting relationship between the plaintiff and defendant.[176] In cases of misstatements or a combination of misstatements and omissions, proof of reliance by the plaintiff is required.[177]

The major exception to proving the investor's reliance upon the defendant's misrepresentation is the "fraud on the market" theory that was upheld by the Supreme Court in *Basic Inc. v. Levinson*.[178] The theory provides a presumption of reliance and thereby relieves the plaintiff of proving reliance upon the particular false announcement or representation that is the focus of her claim. The theory applies only for securities trading that occurs in a market believed to be efficient.[179]

[6] Primary Participants, Aiders and Abettors, and Control Persons

As discussed above, through the mid-1970s, the Supreme Court acquiesced in the circuit and district courts' expansive view of Rule 10b-5. That trend has not continued. For example, in *Central Bank of Denver v. First Interstate Bank of Denver*, by a five-to-four decision the Court held that there is no implied right of action to redress aiding and abetting a Rule 10b-5 violation.[180] The Court's holding is limited to private rights of action. After *Central Bank*, there no longer is liability in private suits for aiding and abetting. One must be a primary participant, the scope of which is discussed below, or fall within one of the now narrower instances (i.e., vicarious liability or control person liability, discussed below) for secondary liability. Aiding and abetting may still be charged in SEC injunctive and other enforcement actions, as well as in criminal prosecutions.

In *Stoneridge Investment Partners, LLC v. Scientific-Atlanta, Inc.*,[181] the Supreme Court rejected the theory of "scheme liability" in private securities fraud cases, addressing a conflict among the circuits over whether an injured investor may recover from a party that neither makes a public misstatement nor breaches a duty to disclose but does participate in a "scheme" to violate Rule 10b-5. In this case, investors who alleged losses after purchasing a company's common stock sought to impose liability on the company's customers and suppliers that had agreed to arrangements allowing the company to mislead its auditor and issue a false financial statement affecting the stock price. Traditional reliance was missing, because these third parties had no role in preparing or disseminating the statement that the investors used, and their own deceptive acts were never communicated to the public. Nonetheless, the plaintiffs posited that investors in an efficient market rely not only on the public statements relating to a security but also on the transactions that those statements reflect. The Court, applying the general rule tying reliance to causation, thought that the third parties' acts were too remote to satisfy the reliance requirement. In reaching this conclusion, it expressed reluctance to extend the private cause of action beyond the securities markets into the realm of ordinary business operations governed by state law. Recently, the Supreme Court, affirmed the view that only those understood by investors to have made the statement, not those who prepare misleading statements that are attributed to others, are primary participants.[182]

Section 20(a) of the Exchange Act[183] imposes secondary liability upon those who are deemed control persons of the primary violator. Most circuits apply a two-prong test to determine whether a person is a control person subject to Section 20(a) liability. First, the defendant must have actually exercised general control over the operations or activities of the primary participant. Second, the control person must have had the power or the ability—even if not exercised—to control the specific transaction or activity that gave rise to the violation. Thus, outside directors who serve on the audit committee, and in that capacity approved accounting practices, are control persons with respect to recognizing sales prematurely.[184] However, other outside directors would not be so held, unless involved in the review or release of the misleading information.[185] Control liability, however, is not absolute. Section 20(a) provides the control person is liable to the same extent as the primary participant, "unless the controlling person acted in good faith and did not directly or indirectly induce the act or acts constituting the violation or cause of action." Quite separate from controlling person liability is vicarious liability premised upon the doctrine of respondeat superior. Recall that respondeat superior liability is the means for holding the master responsible for torts committed by the servant within the scope of the servant's employment. Under respondeat superior liability, it is the employing organization that is liable. Whereas, under control person liability, responsibility can be imposed upon the supervisor of the primary participant, even though the supervisor is not the employing organization.

[7] Statutory Restraints on Private Actions via PSLRA and SLUSA

The 103rd Congress bestowed a unique honor on securities fraud actions by enacting the Private Securities Litigation Reform Act of 1995[186] and thereby accorded *securities* class actions their own procedural rules. To date, no other area of private suit has earned its own set of special procedural rules, or more accurately, impediments to the private litigant. At the core of the PSLRA was tweaking the incentives that surround the initiation, prosecution, and settlement of securities class actions. Overall, the concern was the relative lack of restraint that Congress believed characterized class action litigation.

An important contribution of the PSLRA to securities class actions is its embrace of the "lead plaintiff," which the Act provides presumptively is the class member with the "largest financial" loss.[187] The lead plaintiff is authorized to make recommendations to the court regarding the selection and dismissal of the suit's counsel. Congress's obvious intent is to harness to the class action's oversight the economic self-interest of such a large claimant. After the PSLRA, being the first lawyer to file a complaint no longer provides a leg up to becoming lead counsel. The evidence to date suggests that securities class actions still are lawyer driven, albeit not of the magnitude as before the PSLRA. A good deal of effort is spent by the lawyers wooing investors with large losses, particularly financial institutions, to petition the court to be a lead plaintiff (all with the understanding that if selected as lead plaintiff the requesting investor would then retain the law firm that recruited the investor).[188] Among the issues posed by the lead plaintiff are whether an aggregation of individual investors who in combination have a larger loss than a single institutional investor is the preferable choice[189] and whether the selection of a lead plaintiff prevents the use of an auction to choose counsel for the class action.[190]

The PSLRA introduced something of a "double whammy" by tightening the pleading requirement beyond the standard particularity requirement and barring any discovery until the exhaustion of the defendant's motion to dismiss. The plaintiff "with respect to each act or omission alleged to" be a violation "must plead with particularity facts giving rise to a strong inference that the defendant acted with the required state of mind" to be liable.[191] And, the misrepresentation must be pled with particularity as well as setting forth the facts that support any allegation of misrepresentation that is based upon information or belief.[192] Discovery is not available to assist the plaintiff in satisfying meeting the tightened pleading requirement.[193] The intent of the discovery bar is to revoke the former license the plaintiff's counsel had to conduct a "fishing expedition" into the defendants' files solely by leveling bald accusations of fraud in the complaint.

The PSLRA mandates that the notice of settlement provided class members set forth an estimate of the average recoverable amount per share.[194] A further provision to chasten any bold class action counsel willing to push a questionable case is the PSLRA's mandating that the trial judge at the conclusion of each case make a finding whether the litigants have complied with Rule 11.[195] If so, then appropriate sanctions are to be imposed upon the violating party. Outside of securities litigation, Rule 11 sanctions arise customarily by a motion of one of the parties. The new provision introduced by the PSLRA avoids the possibility of the plaintiff's and defendant's counsel agreeing as part of the settlement that neither will raise Rule 11 sanctions.

Many substantive changes were also introduced by the PSLRA. There is a safe harbor for forward-looking statements,[196] a provision for proportionate liability that extends to contribution claims,[197] the elimination of securities claims from being a predicate act that satisfies RICO (unless there has been a prior criminal conviction),[198] and a statute of limitations for contribution claims.[199]

Soon after the PSLRA's passage, there was a noticeable increase in securities fraud filings in state courts. The concern arose that resourceful plaintiffs were, by filing their actions in state courts, circumventing the PSLRA's procedural and substantive provisions. Thus, the second shoe to drop in Congress's focus on securities litigation was the passage in 1998 of Securities Litigation Uniform Standards Act (SLUSA).[200] To counter the migration to the state courts, SLUSA preempts state court jurisdictions in *class actions* for certain "covered securities."[201] Class actions are defined as suits seeking damages on behalf of more than 50 persons.[202] Suits arising from misrepresentations made in acquisitions or involving a vote of the stockholders, as well as by state pension funds or political subdivisions of the state, are among the narrow set cases that are expressly exempted from SLUSA.[203] The most notable of its exclusions is the so-called Delaware carve-out that preserves the state court's jurisdiction to hear certain claims based upon fiduciary principles of the issuer's state of incorporation.[204]

§ 12.11 Rule 10b-5 and the Duty to Disclose

Rule 10b-5 plays a major role in ensuring the flow of corporate information to the investing public. The 1934 Exchange Act imposes an affirmative disclosure requirement on corporations that are sufficiently large to fall within the Act's registration and reporting requirements. These provisions require, inter alia, complete financial disclosure, descriptions of the company's operations and future plans, and detailing of management activities, as well as dealing with the more specialized problems of shareholder suffrage, tender offers, and insider trading.[205] Even beyond these express disclosure provisions, the broad prophylactic language of Rule 10b-5 has had a significant impact in the disclosure area.

The duty to not misstate material facts applies regardless of the medium or the intended audience of the misstatement. Thus, a document issued with regard to one type of securities, such as bonds, can have 10b-5 ramifications as to the common stock where the misstatements are material to both.[206] Similarly, statements made in connection with shareholder votes are subject to Rule 10b-5 scrutiny where there is a securities transaction, as is the case, for example, in a merger[207] or in the issuance of additional shares.[208] A purposeful understatement of profits so as not to run afoul of government contracting requirements exposes those releasing the depressed earnings report to liability under Rule 10b-5.[209] Furthermore, a suit exists for investors who purchase the company's shares based on bouncy overstatements regarding the capabilities of the company's new product.[210] The point is that information mediums are seamless so that information intended for one audience can be expected to be accessed by investors whose appetite is insatiable for information bearing on the company's position, performance, and future.

The truly challenging issue under Rule 10b-5 and the securities laws generally arises in providing definitive guidance of when there is a duty to speak. That is, omissions, not misstatements, pose the greatest intellectual challenge under Rule 10b-5. Duty is an element in a Rule 10b-5 action only in the case of the omission of a material fact since a matter in issue is the defendant's obligation to disclose the omitted fact. Note here that the securities laws are quite selective in the instances when there is an express duty to speak. Corporations subject to the registration requirements of Section 12 of the Exchange Act[211] must periodically file reports with the SEC.[212] The Exchange Act does not, however, expressly require a corporation to report material information that is not otherwise required by the periodic reporting and shareholder information requirements. The reporting called for by the Exchange Act is periodic, as contrasted with continuous reporting, in part because of the great difficulty in defining when there should be a duty to speak. Hence, there is no affirmative duty to disclose the types of material developments and information mandated by the SEC's periodic disclosure requirements until the corporation's next quarterly or annual report is due. And, those disclosure requirements are relatively focused in terms of the precise types of information that are required to be disclosed. Furthermore, the listing requirements of the major stock exchanges expressly require corporations to make timely disclosure of all information that would be material to the reasonable investor, but nevertheless accord the issuer business discretion to withhold information when non-disclosure best serves the corporate interest.[213] Thus, the instances in which Rule 10b-5 imposes a duty to speak are fairly limited. The courts are particularly firm in holding that there is no duty to disclose internal projections or business strategies that may be pursued.[214]

Thus, the starting point in examining the duty to speak is a fairly broad principle that the issuer and others are under no duty to speak absent an independent basis for the duty to disclose.[215] This view is supported by the Supreme Court ruling in insider trading cases that the mere possession of confidential inside information is not sufficient to trigger the duty to disclose or abstain from trading.[216]

The most frequent instances of finding a breach of the duty to disclose material information are where the plaintiff alleges the defendant has committed a half-truth by withholding information that thus rendered what the defendant has disclosed materially misleading.[217] Disclosures made pursuant to the requirements of either the Securities Act of 1933 or the Exchange Act of 1934 not only require that there be disclosed the information set forth specifically in the SEC's disclosure guides, but also expressly require that SEC registrants' include in their filings "such further material information . . . as may be necessary to make the required statement, in light of all of the circumstances . . . not misleading."[218] Entangled with the defendant's duty to avoid half-truths is the relative certainty of the information known to the defendant but not disclosed to the plaintiff. This is best illustrated by the issue of whether the issuer must disclose adverse developments that the business is incurring during the fiscal quarter that it is offering its securities to the public.

Notwithstanding the absence of an affirmative duty to disclose, once a statement has been made, there may be a continuing duty to update and/or correct the information that was previously disseminated. The duty to update refers to the situation in which an earlier statement was true when made, but subsequent facts have rendered the earlier statement materially misleading. In contrast, the duty to correct arises when the earlier statement was false when made, but the party making it did so innocently, i.e., without scienter, but later has knowledge (or is reckless) of the untruthfulness of the earlier statement. Both the duty to update and the duty to correct assume that the earlier-made statement is still influencing investor behavior. If the court is persuaded that the earlier representation is stale, being eclipsed by subsequent information reaching the plaintiff, there is no basis to believe investors are being harmed by the earlier information and, hence, there is no basis for either a duty to update or correct.

The duty to correct is not absolute, because it is triggered only when failure to do so would make the statement made materially misleading.[219] Certainly, there is no duty to correct rumors or forecasts that cannot be attributed to the issuer.[220] However, if management confirms the forecast to be made by an analyst or otherwise entangles the issuer with another's statements, there is a duty to correct on the part of the issuer.[221]

Public companies are placed in a difficult position when there are rumors about the company's securities, its fundamental condition, or possible takeover activity.[222] When approached by the press, market researchers, or securities analysts,[223] corporations are faced with a dilemma. They cannot issue a denial if to do so would be materially misleading. Thus, for example, the Supreme Court reaffirmed a materiality standard determined by those facts that a reasonable investor would deem significant in making an investment decision, thus precluding denials of existing merger negotiations.[224]

In such situations, issuers have two alternatives. The issuer can, of course, make full disclosure. Alternatively, the issuer can issue a "no comment" response if the response is given pursuant to an established no-comment policy. There are instances in which the "no comment" response is inappropriate. For example, the SEC has taken the position that if the company or its agents are responsible for leaks of sensitive information or market rumors, there is a duty to correct any misinformation.[225] It follows that public companies should manage their proprietary information, not only for insider trading reasons but also to prevent being forced into premature disclosures by the existence of market rumors due to leaked information. Caution dictates that public companies develop information policies, including the creation of an information ombudsman, as well as limiting the issuer's personnel who are authorized to divulge information or respond to outside questions.

As a corollary to the absence of an affirmative duty to disclose, the mere possibility of an event occurring does not trigger a duty to predict or project information that is positive; yet the SEC has long taken the view that material information that is negative must be disclosed. For example, item 303 of Regulation S-K (the SEC's general disclosure guide) requires periodic management discussion and analysis (MD&A) of financial condition operations. As part of this requirement, management is required to disclose and discuss negative trends and uncertainties.[226] The SEC has taken a vigorous enforcement stance on these disclosures.[227] The MD&A disclosures, of course, may also result in material misstatements or omissions that will form the basis of civil liability in a private action.

The SEC has also imposed pursuant to its Regulation FD[228] a duty on domestic companies that are subject to the Exchange Act's reporting requirements to assure that when it does make certain disclosures that they are not made selectively. In broad overview, Regulation FD greatly restricts the freedom public companies formerly enjoyed to make selective disclosures of material nonpublic information to securities market professionals or their shareholders. Rule 100 of Regulation FD provides that whenever a company or a person acting on its behalf discloses material nonpublic information to securities market professionals or holders of the issuer's securities who the issuer believes may trade on the basis of the information, the company must make simultaneous public disclosure of that same information. If such a selective disclosure was "nonintentional," then the issuer should thereafter "promptly"[229] disclose the information publicly. The rule's prohibitions are sufficiently broad to include revelations of non-public information in a luncheon speech or

investment forum. Public disclosure can occur by filing the information with the Commission,[230] issuing a press release, or providing public
notice and opportunity to the meeting, phone call, or other medium at
which the disclosure occurs.

Rule 100(b) enumerates the types of market professionals swept
within its prohibition, including broker-dealers, investment advisers,
and investment companies. Significantly, the ban on selective disclosures also extends to any holder of the issuer's security for whom under
the circumstances it is reasonably foreseeable that the holder will trade
on the basis of the information. A violation of Regulation FD is actionable only by the SEC. The overall effect of Regulation FD has been to
force the issuer and its attorneys to consider the type of interaction the
issuer's personnel have with financial analysts. One step has been more
frequent webcasting of meetings with analysts.

§ 12.12 RULE 10b-5 AND CONTROL OF CORPORATE MISMANAGEMENT

Rule 10b-5's implied private remedy has even played an important role
in the regulation of internal corporate affairs,[231] due in large part to the
expansive reading that has been given to the rule's "in connection with"
requirement. Even in the face of a restrictive Supreme Court decision,[232]
the federal mismanagement remedy continues to flourish.[233] However, a
remedy for corporate skullduggery exists under the antifraud provision
only if accompanied by deception committed in connection with the
purchase or sale of a security.[234]

NOTES

1. How many shares constitute a "controlling" interest must often be
   determined by a factual inquiry in the particular case. *See, e.g.,* Kings
   Cnty. Dev. Co. v. Buell, 709 F.2d 1516 (9th Cir. 1983) (court held that sale
   of 14 percent of corporation's outstanding stock to purchaser who already
   owned 20 percent was not a sale of control).
2. Martin v. Marlin, 529 So. 2d 1174, 1176 (Fla. Dist. Ct. App. 1988).
3. *See* Doleman v. Meiji Mut. Life Ins. Co., 727 F.2d 1480 (9th Cir. 1984).
4. Clagett v. Hutchison, 583 F.2d 1259 (4th Cir. 1978).
5. Insuranshares Corp. v. N. Fiscal Corp., 35 F. Supp. 22 (E.D. Pa. 1940).
6. *Id.* at 25 (emphasis supplied).
7. Harman v. Willbern, 374 F. Supp. 1149 (D. Kan. 1974), *aff'd,* 520 F.2d
   1333 (10th Cir. 1975).
8. *See id.* at 1161–63.

9. The leading case for this view is Levy v. Am. Beverage Corp., 38 N.Y.S.2d 517, 526 (App. Div. 1942).

10. ALI, PRINCIPLES OF CORPORATE GOVERNANCE: ANALYSIS AND RECOMMENDATIONS § 5.16(b) (1994) [hereinafter ALI, PRINCIPLES OF CORPORATE GOVERNANCE].

11. *See, e.g.*, Dunnett v. Arn, 71 F.2d 912 (10th Cir. 1934) (officers who owned controlling block of stock sold their shares at price not available to noncontrol shares after earlier refusing to sell company assets to purchaser of shares).

12. Brown v. Halbert, 76 Cal. Rptr. 781 (Ct. App. 1969); Thorpe v. CERBCO, Inc., 676 A.2d 436 (Del. 1996).

13. ALI, PRINCIPLES OF CORPORATE GOVERNANCE, *supra* note 10, § 5.12(b)(1) (1994).

14. *Id.* § 5.16(a) (1992):

> [T]he controlling stockholder does not satisfy the duty of fair dealing . . . if (a) the controlling stockholder does not make disclosure concerning the transaction . . . to other shareholders with whom the controlling shareholder deals in connection with the transaction.

15. There is no duty to obtain a premium for the minority's shares, even if the controlling stockholder successfully negotiates for a few of the minority to dispose of their shares at the same premium that the controlling stockholder receives. *See* Shoaf v. Warlick, 298 S.C. 415, 419, 380 S.E.2d 865 (1989) (citing *Martin*, 529 So. 2d 1179).

16. Jones v. H.F. Ahmanson & Co., 460 P.2d 464 (Cal. 1969).

17. *See, e.g.*, Perlman v. Feldmann, 219 F.2d 173, *cert. denied*, 349 U.S. 952 (1955), where it was necessary to also determine the fair value of the shares without their "appurtenant control" over the company's production and marketing. *See* Perlman v. Feldmann, 154 F. Supp. 436 (D. Conn. 1957).

18. *See* DeBaun v. First W. Bank & Trust Co., 120 Cal. Rptr. 354, 362 (Ct. App. 1975).

19. *Doleman*, 727 F.2d 1480 (no duty owned directly by purchaser of control for misconduct in transfer of control).

20. *See* MODEL BUS. CORP. ACT § 8.07(a) (2007) (resignation of directors).

21. Du Bois v. Century Cement Prods. Co., 183 A. 188 (N.J. 1936).

22. Mitchell v. Dilbeck, 74 P.2d 233 (Cal. 1937).

23. Essex Universal Corp. v. Yates, 305 F.2d 572, 578–79 (2d Cir. 1962).

24. *Id.*

25. *In re* Caplan, 246 N.Y.S.2d 913 (App. Div.), *aff'd*, 198 N.E.2d 908 (N.Y. 1964).

26. Brecher v. Gregg, 392 N.Y.S.2d 776 (Sup. Ct. 1975).

27. CAL. CORP. CODE § 305(c) (West 1990); DEL. CODE ANN. tit. 8, § 223 (2001).

28. *See* Carter v. Muscat, 251 N.Y.S.2d 378 (App. Div. 1964).

29. The Williams Act is triggered when market purchases or a tender offer will bring one's ownership of a class of a reporting company's equity securities above 5 percent.

30. Unocal Corp. v. Mesa Petrol. Co., 493 A.2d 946 (Del. 1985).

31. *See, e.g.*, Polk v. Good, 507 A.2d 531 (Del. 1986).

32. *See* Heckmann v. Ahmanson, 214 Cal. Rptr. 177 (Ct. App. 1985).

33. *See* Polk v. Texaco Inc., 507 A.2d 531 (Del. 1986).

34. *See, e.g.,* MINN. STAT. ANN. § 302A.553(3) (West Supp. 2002); ARIZ. REV. STAT. ANN. § 10-2704 (West 1996).

35. *See, e.g.,* MINN. STAT. ANN. § 302A.553(3) (West Supp. 2002); ARIZ. REV. STAT. ANN. § 10-2704 (West 1996).

36. Donahue v. Rodd Electrotype Co., 328 N.E.2d 505 (Mass. 1975), *noted in* 61 CORNELL L. REV. 986; 89 HARV. L. REV. 423 (1975).

37. Kahn v. Tremont Corp., 694 A.2d 422 (Del. 1997) (existence of special negotiating committee did not relieve the burden of proving intrinsic fairness where one of the committee members had commercial ties to the controlling shareholder).

38. Though the violation is premised on the defendant's position, such as being an officer or director, with the company, the violation itself is not an act committed in the defendant's capacity as, for example, an officer or director, but in her individual capacity. As such the conduct is properly seen as being outside the standard coverage of the liability policy for "acts performed in the capacity of an officer or director." *See, e.g.,* Cincinnati Ins. Co. v. Irwin Co., 2000 WL 1867297 (Ohio Ct. App. 2000).

39. An analogous situation arose in SEC v. Tex. Gulf Sulphur Co., 401 F.2d 833 (2d Cir. 1968), *cert. denied,* 394 U.S. 976 (1969), where the defendant insiders had advance knowledge of ore discoveries.

40. *See* Goode v. Powers, 397 P.2d 56 (Ariz. 1964) (director has same right as other shareholders to sell stock as long as director acts in good faith and sale does not injure corporation); Tryon v. Smith, 229 P.2d 251, 254 (Ore. 1951) (same).

41. Fleetwood Corp. v. Mirich, 404 N.E.2d 38 (Ind. Ct. App. 1980).

42. *See, e.g.,* Jernberg v. Mann, 358 F.3d 131 (1st Cir. 2004) (applying Massachusetts law) (director or officer who approaches stockholder for purpose of buying shares has duty to disclose material facts within his or her peculiar knowledge). *See also, e.g.,* Strong v. Repide, 213 U.S. 419 (1909).

43. Fischer v. Guar. Trust Co., 18 N.Y.S.2d 328, 333, 334 (App. Div. 1940). *See* Lesnik v. Pub. Indus. Corp., 144 F.2d 968, 977 (2d Cir. 1944); Goodwin v. Agassiz, 186 N.E. 659 (Mass. 1933).

44. Diamond v. Oreamuno, 248 N.E.2d 910 (N.Y. 1969). *See also, e.g.,* Blakesley v. Johnson, 608 P.2d 908 (Kan. 1980); Hotchkiss v. Fisher, 16 P.2d 531 (Kan. 1932), *noted in* 46 HARV. L. REV. 847 (1933), s.c., 31 P.2d 37 (Kan. 1934); 2 ALI, PRINCIPLES OF CORPORATE GOVERNANCE, *supra* note 10, § 5.04(a) (1992).

45. Ragsdale v. Kennedy, 209 S.E.2d 494 (N.C. 1974); Poole v. Camden, 92 S.E. 454 (W. Va. 1916); Schroeder v. Carroll, 212 N.W. 299 (Wis. 1927).

46. *See* Hayes v. Kelley, 112 F.2d 897, 901 (9th Cir. 1940).

47. 17 C.F.R. § 240.10b-5, discussed *infra.*

48. *See* TSC Indus. v. Northway, Inc., 426 U.S. 438, 449 (1976) (decided under federal proxy rules).

49. Brophy v. Cities Serv. Co., 70 A.2d 5 (Del. Ch. 1949). *See, e.g.,* Kahn v. Kohlberg Kravis Roberts & Co., 23 A.3d 1831 (Del. 2011) (sweeping affirmation of *Brophy*). *See generally* Douglas M. Branson, *Choosing the Appropriate Default Rule—Insider Trading Under State Law,* 45 ALA. L. REV. 753 (1994).

50. In so ruling, the court relied on RESTATEMENT OF RESTITUTION § 200 comment a (1937) and AUSTIN WAKEMAN SCOTT, THE LAW OF TRUSTS § 505.1 (1939).

51. *See, e.g.*, Cambridge Fund v. Abella, 501 F. Supp. 598 (S.D.N.Y. 1980); Gottlieb v. McKee, 107 A.2d 240 (Del. Ch. 1954).

52. *See, e.g, Diamond*, 248 N.E.2d 910. *See* RESTATEMENT (THIRD) OF AGENCY § 8.02 cmt. b (2006) (noting that although it is not necessary to show harm to the principal since the benefit realized by the agent can be more easily calculated, if there *is* harm the principal may also recover compensatory damages from the agent); RESTATEMENT (SECOND) OF AGENCY § 388 cmt. c (1958) (expanding the liability to selling confidential information to a third party even if the principal is not harmed). The Third Restatement took a more general approach to liability than the Second Restatement in order "to make it explicit that a principal's remedies are not limited to recovery of profit from the agent." RESTATEMENT (THIRD) OF AGENCY § 8.02 Reporter's Notes a (2006). *But cf.* Freeman v. Decio, 584 F.2d 186 (7th Cir. 1978) (challenge failed due to damage requirement for shareholder derivative suit); Schein v. Chasen, 313 So. 2d 739 (Fla. 1975) (same).

53. *See* Frigitemp Corp. v. Fin. Dynamics Fund, Inc., 524 F.2d 275 (2d Cir. 1975).

54. *See, e.g.*, CAL. CORP. CODE §§ 25402, 25502, 25502.5 (West 2001).

55. *E.g.*, Weigel v. Shapiro, 608 F.2d 268 (7th Cir. 1979); Bisbee v. Midland Linseed Prods. Co., 19 F.2d 24 (8th Cir.), *cert. denied*, 275 U.S. 564 (1927).

56. 15 U.S.C.A. §§ 78p(a), 78p(b) (2009).

57. The Securities Exchange Act, as amended, requires that an issuer register its securities pursuant to section 12 of that act if the issuer is listed on a national exchange or has total assets exceeding $10 million and a class of equity securities with 2,000 shareholders of record but retains the former 500 record holder threshold with respect to investors who are not accredited investors. Section 12(g)(1)(A), 15 U.S.C. § 78l(g)(1)(A) as amended by the Jumpstart Our Business Startups Act (JOBS Act), H.R. 3606, 112 Cong. 2d sess. § 501 (2012). The record holder calculation excludes shareholders who receive shares as part of an employee compensation plan that is exempt from 1933 Act registration. Section 12(g) was also amended to exclude from the shareholder calculation holders of shares issued pursuant to an exempt crowdfunding offering.

58. These filings have to be made on the second business day following the transaction in shares. 15 U.S.C.A. § 78p(a) (2009). Prior to amendments in 2002, the section 16(a) reports had to be filed in the month following the trades in question.

59. Courts generally take a broad view of defining "profit" under section 16(b). Which can capture a "profit" even in situations where an out-of-pocket loss for all transactions entered into during the six-month period may exist when there have been a series of transactions within a six-month period. The apparent majority view is to match the lowest purchase price against the highest sales price within that period. Gratz v. Claughton, 187 F.2d 46 (2d Cir.1951); Smolowe v. Delendo Corp., 136 F.2d 231 (2d Cir. 1943), *cert. denied*, 320 U.S. 751 (1943); Dreiling v. Jain, 281 F. Supp. 2d 1234, 1238–39 (W.D. Wash. 2003).

60. 15 U.S.C.A. § 78p(b).

61. In contrast, such a contemporaneous ownership rule generally applies to shareholder derivative suits—*e.g.*, FED. R. CIV. P. 23.1. See Chapter 15.

62. Arbetman v. Playford & Alaska Airlines, Inc., 83 F. Supp. 335 (S.D.N.Y. 1949); Dottenheim v. Emerson Elec. Mfg. Co., 7 F.R.D. 343 (E.D.N.Y. 1947).

63. Park & Tilford, Inc. v. Schulte, 160 F.2d 984 (2d Cir.), *cert. denied*, 332 U.S. 761 (1947).

64. Petteys v. Butler, 367 F.2d 528 (8th Cir. 1966), *cert. denied*, 385 U.S. 1006 (1967); Feraiolo v. Newman, 259 F.2d 342 (6th Cir. 1958), *cert. denied*, 359 U.S. 927 (1959). Potter Stewart's opinion in the *Feraiolo* case has been identified as the first of the so-called pragmatic decisions.

65. *See* Blau v. Lamb, 363 F.2d 507 (2d Cir.), *cert. denied*, 385 U.S. 1002 (1967) (conversion not a sale); Heli-Coil Corp. v. Webster, 352 F.2d 156 (3d Cir. 1965) (conversion is sale of convertible security and purchase of underlying security); Blau v. Max Factor & Co., 342 F.2d 304 (9th Cir.), *cert. denied*, 382 U.S. 892 (1965) (conversion not a purchase).

66. 17 C.F.R. § 240.16b-9 (2009).

67. *See, e.g.*, Kern Cnty. Land Co. v. Occidental Petrol. Corp., 411 U.S. 582 (1973); Gold v. Sloan, 486 F.2d 340 (4th Cir. 1973), noted in 42 FORDHAM L. REV. 852 (1974).

68. Feder v. Martin Marietta Corp., 406 F.2d 260 (2d Cir. 1969).

69. Whiting v. Dow Chem. Co., 523 F.2d 680 (2d Cir. 1975).

70. *See, e.g.*, Morales v. Freund, 163 F.3d 763 (2d Cir. 1999) (class A preferred shares were separate class where their vote would have been sufficient to block company's reorganization).

71. SEC, Release No. 34-28869, Ownership Reports and Trading by Officers, Directors, and Principal Security Holders, Fed. Sec. L. Rep. (CCH) No. 1434 (Feb. 13, 1991).

72. 17 C.F.R. § 240.16a-2(a)(2) (2009).

73. *See* Morales v. Quintel Entm't, Inc., 249 F.3d 115 (2d Cir. 2001).

74. Rule 13d-5, 17 C.F.R. § 240.13d-5 (2009). *See generally* Gen. Aircraft Corp. v. Lampert, 556 F.2d 90 (1st Cir. 1977) (finding a group for section 13d-3 purposes).

75. Merrill Lynch, Pierce, Fenner & Smith, Inc. v. Livingston, 566 F.2d 1119, 1122 (9th Cir. 1978).

76. Rule 16a-1(f) includes in the definition of "executive officer" the president, any vice president in charge of a principal unit or division, and the principal financial and accounting officers, as well as any other officer who performs a policymaking function. 17 C.F.R. § 240.16a-1(f) (2009).

77. EXCHANGE ACT Release No. 34-28869 [1990–1991 Transfer Binder] Fed. Sec. L. Rep. (CCH) ¶ 84,709 (Feb. 8, 1991), *relying on* Colby v. Klune, 178 F.2d 872, 873 (2d Cir. 1949).

78. 1961 WL 60638, 40 S.E.C. 907 (1961).

79. SEC v. Tex. Gulf Sulphur Co., 401 F.2d 833 (2d Cir. 1968), *cert. denied*, 394 U.S. 976 (1969), s.c., 446 F.2d 1301 (2d Cir. 1971).

80. 521 U.S. 642 at 655.

81. *Id.* at 652.

82. United States v. Chestman, 903 F.2d 75 (2d Cir. 1990), *reh'g en banc*, 947 F.2d 551 (2d Cir. 1991), *cert. denied*, 503 U.S. 1004 (1992).

83. 17 C.F.R. § 240.10b5-2 (2009).

84. United States v. Kim, 184 F. Supp. 2d 1006 (N.D. Cal.2002) (membership in young executives organization did not create a duty even though there was an expectation of confidentiality, since there was not binding obligation to keep information confidential).

85. The SEC brought charges against Mark Cuban, claiming that he had agreed to keep confidential certain information obtained in connection with a private placement. Among other things, the defense contended that even if such a contractual obligation existed, it is not sufficient to trigger Rule 10b-5's disclose or abstain obligation. *See SEC's Case Against Cuban Looks Set for Long Fight as Academics Join Fray*, 41 SEC. REG. & L. REP. (BNA) 295 (Feb. 23, 2009). The district court agreed with the SEC that the duty need not be fiduciary in nature but went on to distinguish between a contractual duty of confidentiality and a contractual non-use agreement. The court dismissed the complaint, granting the SEC leave to amend the pleadings to provide a basis for implying a non-use agreement. SEC v. Cuban, 634 F. Supp. 2d 713 (N.D. Tex. 2009). Rather than file an amended complaint, the SEC chose to appeal the dismissal and won on appeal. SEC v. Cuban, 620 F.3d 551 (5th Cir. 2010). The Second Circuit has held that a fiduciary duty is not required so long as the information was wrongfully acquired via deception. SEC v. Dorozhko, 574 F.3d 42 (2d Cir. 2009) (defendant hacked computer to obtain non-public information and violated Rule 10b-5 when he traded to his advantage if the information had been obtained via deception).

86. Dirks v. SEC, 463 U.S. 646 (1983).

87. A paradigm illustration involves a famous football coach who, while attending his son's track meet, overheard another proud parent discussing an upcoming "deal." *See* SEC v. Switzer, 590 F. Supp. 756 (W.D. Okla. 1984); SEC v. Platt, 565 F. Supp. 1244 (W.D. Okla. 1983).

88. *See, e.g.*, United States v. Falcone, 257 F.3d 226 (2d Cir. 2001) (conspirators traded on advance knowledge of what companies would be discussed in forthcoming issues of BUSINESS WEEK).

89. *See* United States v. Libera, 989 F.2d 596 (2d Cir. 1993).

90. *See* SEC v. Mayhew, 121 F.3d 44 (2d Cir. 1997).

91. *See* SEC v. Geon Indus., Inc., 381 F. Supp. 1063 (S.D.N.Y. 1974), *modified*, 531 F.2d 39 (2d Cir. 1976).

92. *See, e.g.*, Moss v. Morgan Stanley, Inc., 553 F. Supp. 1347 (S.D.N.Y.), *aff'd*, 719 F.2d 5 (2d Cir. 1983).

93. Rule 100, 17 C.F.R. § 243.100 (2009).

94. See *infra* § 12.11.

95. *See, e.g.*, 2 ALLAN BROMBERG & LOUIS LOWENFELS, SECURITIES FRAUD & COMMODITIES FRAUD, § 7.4(600), at 7:159, 7:160.14 (1996) (a corporate insider can introduce evidence of nonuse of material non-public information as an affirmative defense); ARNOLD S. JACOBS, 5A DISCLOSURE AND REMEDIES UNDER THE SECURITIES LAWS, § 4.148 (2000) (an insider's decision to buy or sell must be based on his inside information).

96. SEC v. Adler, 137 F.3d 1325 (11th Cir. 1998).

97. 137 F.3d at 1337.

98. *See* SEC v. Lipson, 278 F.3d 656, 661 (7th Cir. 2002).

99. 17 C.F.R. § 240.10b5-1 (2009).
100. Rule 10b5-1(b) provides that "on the basis" means "if the person making the purchase or sale was aware of the material nonpublic information when the person made the purchase or sale." 17 C.F.R. § 240.10b5-1 (2009).
101. Rule 10b5-1(c), 17 C.F.R. § 240.10b5-1(c) (2009).
102. 15 U.S.C.A. § 78t. The SEC's power extends to those who provide substantial assistance to insiders such that they are deemed aiders and abettors of the insider trading offense. *See, e.g.*, SEC v. Naegeli, 1993 WL 15126 (S.D.N.Y. 1993) (attorney aided and abetted client by counseling how to establish a Swiss account through which securities were purchased on the basis of material nonpublic information).
103. On the measurement of the amount of profits to be disgorged, *see* SEC v. MacDonald, 699 F.2d 47 (1st Cir. 1983) (*en banc*) (need disgorge only profits up to the market's reaction to initial disclosure and not the later higher price reached by the security).
104. Both disgorgement and treble profits can be recovered, as the purpose of ITSA was not to reduce the scope of other relief the SEC may obtain. *See* SEC v. Lipson, 278 F.3d 656 (7th Cir. 2002).
105. *See Naegeli*, 1993 WL 15126.
106. Affiliated Ute Citizens of Utah v. United States, 406 U.S. 128 (1972), *reh'g denied*, 407 U.S. 916 (1972). Causation was not a problem because the purchaser dealt directly with the seller. Further, the Court held that reliance on the nondisclosure could be presumed from the materiality of the information.
107. Although some courts have imposed liability, most recent decisions have not. The "fraud on the market" theory, however, is far from unanimously accepted in the insider trading context. The Sixth Circuit has held that any duty that is breached is owed to the person from whom the information is appropriated, not to someone in a faceless market. Fridrich v. Bradford, 542 F.2d 307 (6th Cir. 1976), *cert. denied*, 429 U.S. 1053 (1977). Similarly, the Second Circuit has held that a tippee of inside information who is convicted of having violated Rule 10b-5 is not liable to people who are selling their stock at the same time that the defendant is buying on inside information; instead, the person trading on the information must be a corporate official who owes an independent dues to the shareholders who trade on opposite sides of the insiders' transactions. Moss v. Morgan Stanley, 719 F.2d 5 (2d Cir. 1983), *cert. denied*, 465 U.S. 1025 (1984).
108. 15 U.S.C.A. § 78t-1 (2009).
109. *Id.* at § 78p(b) (2009), discussed *supra* § 12.8.
110. *Id.* at § 78n(a) (2009) and Reg. 14A promulgated thereunder.
111. *Id.* at § 78j(b) (2009).
112. 17 C.F.R. § 240-10b-5 (2009).
113. *Id.*
114. *Compare, e.g.*, 15 U.S.C.A. §§ 78p(a) (proxy regulation) and 78m(d) (tender offer regulation) *with id.* § 78p(b) (insider short-swing profits).
115. *E.g.*, Dupuy v. Dupuy, 511 F.2d 641 (5th Cir. 1975).
116. See *supra* § 12.8. This fills a significant void in the law of many states. See *supra* § 12.7.
117. 17 C.F.R. § 230.10b-5 (2009).

118. Zweig v. Hearst Corp., 594 F.2d 1261 (9th Cir. 1979) (sustaining complaint against financial columnist for alleged material misinformation).
119. Lanza v. Drexel & Co., 479 F.2d 1277 (2d Cir. 1973).
120. *E.g.*, Goldberg v. Meridor, 567 F.2d 209 (2d Cir. 1977), *cert. denied*, 434 U.S. 1069 (1978).
121. Superintendent of Ins. v. Bankers Life & Cas. Co., 404 U.S. 6 (1971) (sale of other issuers' securities).
122. Stull v. Bayard, 561 F.2d 429, 431 (2d Cir. 1977), *cert. denied*, 434 U.S. 1035 (1978).
123. *See* Section 804 of the Sarbanes-Oxley Act of 2002, Pub. L. 107–204 (July 20, 2002), amending 28 U.S.C.A. § 1658.
124. 15 U.S.C.A. § 78aa.
125. *See* Lewis D. Lowenfels, *Pendent Jurisdiction and the Federal Securities Acts*, 67 Colum. L. Rev. 474 (1967); Note, *The Evolution and Scope of the Doctrine of Pendent Jurisdiction in the Federal Courts*, 62 Colum. L. Rev. 1018 (1962).
126. The standard for materiality is the same for the antifraud provision as it is for other provisions of the securities laws, such as the proxy solicitations. Thus, the leading case for materiality is *TSC Indus. v. Northway, Inc.*, 426 U.S. 438, 449 (1976) (decided under the proxy rules).
127. Matrixx Initiatives, Inc. v. Siracusano, __ U.S. __, 131 S. Ct. 1309 (2011) (refusing to require that pharmaceutical study that was omitted be statically significant); Basic, Inc. v. Levinson, 485 U.S. 224 (1988) (rejecting bright-line test to determine materiality of preliminary merger negotiations).
128. *See Basic Inc.*, 485 U.S. 224 (decided under Rule 10b-5 involving the denial of merger negotiations). The Supreme Court, in applying the probability-magnitude test, held that omissions of potential side effects of a drug company's major product can be materiality even though the side effects are not yet reflected in medical studies that are statistically significant. *See Matrixx Initiatives, Inc.*, 131 S. Ct. 1309.
129. *See, e.g.*, Kronfeld v. Trans World Airlines, Inc., 832 F.2d 726 (2d Cir. 1987).
130. *See, e.g.*, Shapiro v. U.J.B. Fin. Corp., 964 F.2d 272 (3d Cir. 1992).
131. *See* Virginia Bankshares, Inc. v. Sandberg, 501 U.S. 1083 (1991).
132. *See, e.g.*, SEC v. Carriba Air, Inc., 681 F.2d 1318 (11th Cir. 1981).
133. *See, e.g.*, SEC v. Electronics Warehouse, Inc., 689 F. Supp. 53 (D. Conn. 1988), *aff'd*, 891 F.2d 457 (2d Cir. 1989).
134. *See, e.g.*, Weisberg v. Coastal States Gas Corp., 609 F.2d 650 (2d Cir. 1979). But absent evidence of self-dealing behavior, a leading case holds social character of directors' decisions is not material. *See* Gaines v. Haughton, 645 F.2d 761, 778 (9th Cir. 1981).
135. *See, e.g.*, Makor Issues & Rights, Ltd. v. Tellabs, Inc., 437 F.3d 588 (7th Cir. 2006) (statement that amounts to vague aspiration or unspecific puffery is not material).
136. Eisenstadt v. Centel Corp., 113 F.3d 738, 745 (7th Cir. 1997).
137. *See In re* Convergent Technologies Sec. Litig., 948 F.2d 507, 513 (9th Cir. 1991).
138. *See, e.g., In re* Stone & Webster, Inc., 414 F.3d 187 (1st Cir. 2005); Kaufman v. Trump's Castle Funding, 7 F.3d 357 (3d Cir. 1993).
139. *See, e.g.*, Romani v. Shearson Lehman Hutton, 929 F.2d 875 (1st Cir. 1991); I. Meyer Pincus & Assoc. v. Oppenheimer & Co., 936 F.2d 759 (2d Cir.

1991); Sinay v. Lamson & Sessions Co., 948 F.2d 1037 (6th Cir. 1991); *In re* Convergent Technologies Sec. Litig., 948 F.2d 507 (9th Cir. 1991).

140. *See* Section 27A, 15 U.S.C.A. § 77z-2 (2009).

141. *See* Section 21E, 15 U.S.C.A. § 78uu-1 (2009).

142. H.R. Conf. Rep. No. 369, 104th Cong., 2d Sess. 11 (1995).

143. *Id.*

144. *See, e.g.*, Franklin High Yield v. Cnty. of Martin Minnesota, 152 F.3d 736 (8th Cir. 1998).

145. This holding was first reached in *Ernst & Ernst v. Hochfelder*, 425 U.S. 185 (1976) for private actions and was soon applied to SEC enforcement actions in *Aaron v. SEC*, 446 U.S. 680 (1980).

146. *See, e.g.*, AUSA Life Ins. Co. v. Ernst & Young, 206 F.3d 202 (2d Cir. 2000); SEC v. Falstaff Brewing Co., 629 F.2d 62, 76 (D.C. Cir. 1980).

147. Sanders v. John Nuveen & Co., 554 F.2d 790, 793 (7th Cir. 1977).

148. *See* Hoffman v. Estabrook & Co., 587 F.2d 509, 516 (1st Cir. 1978).

149. There are numerous studies on the impact of the PSLRA. One study focusing on the pleading requirements found that the Ninth Circuit's decision substantially tightening the pleading requirements was greeted favorably by investors, suggesting that investor sentiment believed lax standards that permitted more suits were harmful. *See* Johnson, Nelson & Pritchard, In re *Silicon Graphics Inc.: Shareholder Wealth Effects Resulting from the Interpretation of the Private Securities Litigation Reform Act's Pleading Standard*, 73 So. Cal. L. Rev. 773 (2000). *See also* Elam v. Neidorff, 544 F.3d 921 (8th Cir. 2008) (PSLRA's heightened pleading requirement was intended to eliminate abusive securities litigation and prevent pleading fraud by hindsight).

150. 15 U.S.C.A. § 78u-4(b)(2) (emphasis added).

151. 9 F.3d 259 (2d Cir. 1993).

152. S. 1260, H.R. Conf. Rep. No. 105-803, 104th Cong., 1st Sess. at 41. For an excellent review of the legislative history on this topic, *see* Joseph A. Grundfest & A.C. Pritchard, *Statutes with Multiple Personality Disorders: The Value of Ambiguity in Statutory Design and Interpretation*, 54 Stan. L. Rev. 627, 650–65 (2002).

153. 551 U.S. 308 (2007).

154. *Id.*

155. *Id.*

156. *Id.*

157. *Id.*

158. 15 U.S.C.A. § 78u(d)(1) (2009).

159. *Id.* at § 78u-3 (2009).

160. *See* Birnbaum v. Newport Steel Corp., 193 F.2d 461 (2d Cir.), *cert. denied*, 343 U.S. 956 (1952).

161. 421 U.S. 723 (1975).

162. 421 U.S. at 743.

163. *See* Gurley v. Documation, Inc., 674 F.2d 253 (4th Cir. 1982).

164. The leading case for this doctrine is *Vine v. Beneficial Finance Co.*, 374 F.2d 627 (2d Cir.), *cert. denied*, 389 U.S. 970 (1967). For post *Blue Chip Stamps* decisions recognizing the doctrine, *see* 7547 Corp. v. Parker & Parsley Dev. Partners L.P., 38 F.3d 211 (5th Cir. 1994) (however, proof that there

was a substantial change in the rights, privileges, or preferences of the plaintiff's securities is needed to establish a sale).

165. *See* Mosher v. Kane, 784 F.2d 1385 (9th Cir. 1986).

166. *See* Mutual Shares Corp. v. Genesco, Inc., 384 F.2d 540 (2d Cir. 1967).

167. *Compare* Tully v. Mott Supermarkets, Inc., 540 F.2d 187 (3d Cir. 1976) (upholding injunctive action by a non seller/purchaser) *with* Cowin v. Bresler, 741 F.2d 410 (D.C. Cir. 1984) (strictly applying *Blue Chip Stamps'* reasoning to deny standing to non-trading plaintiff).

168. This point was expressly addressed in a landmark insider trading case; *see* SEC v. Tex. Gulf Sulphur Co., 401 F.2d 833, 860 (2d Cir. 1968) (en banc), *cert. denied*, 394 U.S. 976 (1969) ("We do not believe that Congress intended that the proscriptions of the Act would not be violated unless the makers of a misleading statement also participated in pertinent securities transactions in connection therewith. . . .").

169. *See, e.g., In re* Ames Dept. Stores Inc. Stock Litig., 991 F.2d 953 (2d Cir. 1993); Heit v. Weitzen, 402 F.2d 909 (2d Cir. 1968).

170. *See generally* Robert A. Prentice and John H. Langmore, *Beware of Vaporware: Product Hype and the Securities Fraud Liability of High Tech Companies*, 8 HARV. J. L. & TECH. 1 (1994).

171. Reliance is often equated with "transaction causation." Dura Pharm., Inc. v. Broudo, 544 U.S. 336, 341 (2005). Reliance may well affect one's decision to trade or the price at which the plaintiff would have traded had the true facts been known. It can include other steps as well. For example, even if the plaintiff had taken some steps to protect himself in the event of an IPO, had the true facts been disclosed he might well have sought even greater protection. *See* Castellano v. Young & Rubicam, Inc., 257 F.3d 171 (2d Cir. 2001).

172. *See Dura Pharm., Inc.*, 544 U.S. 336, 125 S. Ct. 1627, 161 L. Ed. 2d 577 (2005). *Loss* causation is a separate element from transaction causation, and the two cannot be collapsed into each other. AUSA Life Ins. Co. v. Ernst and Young, 206 F.3d 202, 216 (2d Cir. 2000). Loss causation is comparable to the tort law concept of proximate cause. Thus, the damages suffered by the plaintiff must be a foreseeable consequence of any misrepresentation or material omission. Emergent Capital Inv. Mgmt., LLC v. Stonepath Group, Inc., 343 F.3d 189 (2d Cir. 2003). A misstatement is the proximate cause of an investment loss if the risk that caused the loss was within the zone of risks concealed by the misrepresentations. Lattanzio v. Deloitte & Touche LLP, 476 F.3d 147 (2d Cir. 2007). A plaintiff must plead loss causation with sufficient specificity to enable the court to evaluate whether the necessary causal link exists. Teachers' Ret. Sys. of La. v. Hunter, 477 F.3d 162 (4th Cir. 2007).

173. *See* Tricontinental Indus. Ltd. v. PricewaterhouseCoopers, LLP, 475 F.3d 824 (7th Cir. 2007) (plaintiff must allege that it would not have invested in securities if defendant had stated material facts truthfully at time of sale).

174. 406 U.S. 128 (1972).

175. *Id.*

176. *See, e.g.*, Cavalier Carpets, Inc. v. Caylor, 746 F.2d 749 (11th Cir. 1984) (court denied the presumption to a plaintiff who carried out his own investigation).

177. *See, e.g.,* Cox v. Collins, 7 F.3d 394 (4th Cir. 1993).
178. Basic Inc. v. Levinson, 485 U.S. 224 (1988).
179. *See, e.g.,* Regents of Univ. of Cal. v. Credit Suisse First Boston (USA), Inc., 482 F.3d 372 (5th Cir. 2007).
180. 511 U.S. 164 (1994). *See also, e.g.,* Stoneridge Inv. Partners, LLC v. Scientific Atlanta, Inc., 552 U.S. 148 (2008) (defendants were secondary actors and thus could not be held liable as primary violators).
181. 552 U.S. 148 (2008).
182. Janus Capital Group, Inc. v. First Derivative Traders, __ U.S. __, 131 S. Ct. 2296 (2011).
183. 15 U.S.C.A. § 78t(a).
184. *See In re* Gupta Sec. Litig., 1995 WL 338893 (N.D. Cal. 1995); Jacobs v. Coopers & Lybrand LLP, 1999 WL 101772 (S.D.N.Y. 1999).
185. *See* Bomarko, Inc. v. Hemodynamics, Inc., 848 F. Supp. 1335 (W.D. Mich. 1993) (excusing outside directors from liability but not director who served as firm's general counsel and had reviewed the misleading announcement).
186. Pub. L. No. 104-67, 109 Stat. 737 (codified in scattered sections in 15 U.S.C.A.) [hereinafter PSLRA].
187. EXCHANGE ACT Section 21D(a)(3)(B)(iii)(bb), 15 U.S.C.A. § 78u-4 (2009). For provisions parallel to those described here for Exchange Act based suits that are applicable to suits brought under the Securities Act of 1933, *see* Section 27, 15 U.S.C.A. § 77z-1 (2009).
188. *See, e.g., In re* Razorfish, Inc. Sec. Litig., 143 F. Supp. 2d 304 (S.D.N.Y. 2001).
189. *See* A. Chris Heck, Comment, *Conflict and Aggregation: Appointing Institutional Investors as Sole Lead Plaintiffs Under the PSLRA*, 66 U. CHI. L. REV. 1199 (1999).
190. *See In re* Cendant Corp. Litig., 264 F.3d 201 (3d Cir. 2001).
191. EXCHANGE ACT Section 21D(b)(2), 15 U.S.C.A. § 78u-4(b)(2) (2009).
192. *Id.* at Section 21D(b)(1), 15 U.S.C.A. § 78u-4(b)(1) (2009).
193. *Id.* at Section 21D(b)(3), 15 U.S.C.A. § 78u-4(b)(3).
194. *Id.* at Section 21D(a)(7)(B), 15 U.S.C.A. § 78u-4(a)(7)(B).
195. *Id.* at Section 21D(c)(1), 15 U.S.C.A. § 78u-4(c)(1).
196. *Id.* at Section 21E, 15 U.S.C.A. § 78u-5. Also this provision exists in the SECURITIES ACT Section 27A, 15 U.S.C.A. § 77z-2 (2009).
197. EXCHANGE ACT Section 21D(f), 15 U.S.C.A. § 78u-4(f) (2009).
198. RACKETEER INFLUENCE AND CORRUPT ORGANIZATIONS ACT Section 1964(c) (2009), 18 U.S.C.A. § 1964(c).
199. EXCHANGE ACT Section 21D(f)(9) (2009), 15 U.S.C.A. § 78u-4(f)(9) (2009).
200. *Id.* at Section 28(f), 15 U.S.C.A. § 78bb(f).
201. Covered securities are defined in Section 18(b) of the Securities Act, 15 U.S.C.A. § 77r(b) (2009), and include securities traded on the New York Stock Exchange, American Exchange, and Nasdaq, and certain other exchanges that have been designated by the SEC, issued by a company subject to the periodic reporting requirements of the Exchange Act, as well as securities offered pursuant to certain exemptions from the registration requirements of the Securities Act.
202. EXCHANGE ACT Section 28(f)(5)(B), 15 U.S.C.A. § 78bb(f)(5)(B) (2009).

203. *Id.* at Section 28(f)(3), 15 U.S.C.A. § 78bb(f)(3).
204. *Id.* at Section 28(f)(3)(A)(i), 15 U.S.C.A. § 78bb(f)(3)(i).
205. *See generally* Homer Kripke, *Rule 10b-5 Liability and "Material Facts,"* 46 N.Y.U. L. REV. 1061 (1971).
206. Lanza v. Drexel & Co., 479 F.2d 1277 (2d Cir. 1973).
207. *E.g.,* Schlick v. Penn-Dixie Cement Corp., 507 F.2d 374 (2d Cir. 1974), *cert. denied,* 421 U.S. 976 (1975).
208. *E.g.,* Hooper v. Mountain States Sec. Corp., 282 F.2d 195 (5th Cir. 1960), *cert. denied,* 365 U.S. 814 (1961).
209. *See* Heit v. Weitzen, 402 F.2d 909 (2d Cir. 1968).
210. *See, e.g.,* Stac Electronics Sec. Litig., 82 F.3d 1480 (9th Cir. 1996).
211. 15 U.S.C.A. § 78l (2009).
212. *Id.* at § 78m. Section 12 requires registration of issuers who have securities traded on a national securities exchange, as well as those having more than $10 million in assets and a class of equity securities with 2,000 or more shareholders of record but retains the former 500 record holder threshold with respect to investors who are not accredited investors. Section 12(g)(1)(A), 15 U.S.C.A. § 78l(g)(1)(A) as amended by the Jumpstart Our Business Startups Act (JOBS Act), H.R. 3606, 112 Cong. 2d sess. § 501 (2012). The record holder calculation excludes shareholders who receive shares as part of an employee compensation plan that is exempt from 1933 Act registration. Section 12(g) was also amended to exclude from the shareholder calculation holders of shares issued pursuant to an exempt crowdfunding offering. In addition, issuers who do not come within the registration requirements but have issued securities pursuant to a 1933 Act registration statement and that have at least 300 holders of those securities are subject to the periodic reporting requirements by virtue of section 15(d) of the Act. 15 U.S.C.A. § 78o(d) (2009). Section 15(d) issuers have to file the periodic reports but are not subject to proxy regulation (§ 14(a) to (c), 15 U.S.C.A. § 78n(a) to (c) (2009)); the Williams Act tender offer disclosure requirements (§§ 13(d), (e), and 14(d), (f); 15 U.S.C.A. §§ 78m(d), (e), 78n(d), (f) (2009)); or the reporting requirements for officers, directors, and 10% beneficial owners (§ 16(a), 15 U.S.C.A. § 78p(a) (2009)).
213. NYSE Co. Manual, 3 Fed. Sec. L. Rep. (CCH) ¶ 23,121; Am. Stock Exchange Co. Guide (CCH) ¶ 10,121; EXCHANGE ACT Rel. No. 34-8995 [1970–71 Transfer Binder], (CCH) ¶ 77,915 (Oct. 15, 1970).
214. *See, e.g.,* San Leandro Emergency Med. Grp. Profit Sharing Plan v. Philip Morris Co., 75 F.3d 801 (2d Cir. 1996).
215. *See, e.g.,* Murphy v. Sofamor Danek Grp. Inc., 123 F.3d 394 (6th Cir. 1997).
216. Dirks v. SEC, 463 U.S. 646 (1983); Chiarella v. United States, 445 U.S. 222 (1980).
217. *See, e.g.,* Ansin v. River Oaks Furniture Inc., 105 F.3d 745 (1st Cir. 1997) (failure to disclose when repurchasing shares from some of its stockholders that it would engage in IPO was material omission).
218. SECURITIES ACT Rule 408, 17 C.F.R. § 230.408 (2009). A similar requirement appears in EXCHANGE ACT Rule 12b-20, 17 C.F.R. § 240.12b-20 (2009).

219. Moss v. Healthcare Compare Corp., 75 F.3d 276 (7th Cir. 1996) (no duty to correct what is merely a tentative estimate); Backman v. Polaroid Corp., 910 F.2d 10 (1st Cir. 1990).

220. *See, e.g.,* Elkind v. Liggett & Myers, Inc., 635 F.2d 156 (2d Cir. 1980).

221. *See, e.g., In re* Cypress Semiconductor Sec. Litig., 891 F. Supp. 1369 (N.D. Cal. 1995), *aff'd sub nom.,* Eisenstadt v. Allen, 113 F.3d 1240 (9th Cir. 1997).

222. *See* Symposium, *Affirmative Disclosure Obligations Under the Securities Laws,* 46 Md. L. Rev. 907 (1987); John H. Matheson, *Corporate Disclosure Obligations and the Parameters of Rule 10b-5;* Basic, Inc. v. Levinson and Beyond, 14 J. Corp. L. 1 (1988).

223. *See, e.g.,* Helwig v. Vencor, Inc., 210 F.3d 612, 620–21 (6th Cir. 2000) (corporation cannot be held responsible for analysts' statements about its financial health unless corporation takes some affirmative action other than simply providing information to analysts).

224. *Basic,* Inc. v. Levinson, 485 U.S. 224 (1988).

225. *See In re* Carnation Co., 1985 WL 547371 (SEC 1985).

226. *See Management Discussion and Analysis of Financial Condition,* Exchange Act Release No. 33-6835 (SEC May 18, 1989).

227. *See In re* Caterpillar, Inc., 1992 WL 71907 (SEC 1992) (settlement order involving MD&A analysis and failure to adequately discuss the possible risk of lower earnings in the future). *Compare* Ferber v. Travelers Corp., 802 F. Supp. 698 (D. Conn. 1992) (finding adequate discussion in MD&A of "known trends" and "uncertainties" relating to problems with issuer's real estate portfolios).

228. 17 C.F.R. §§ 243.100 *et seq.* (2009).

229. Rule 101(d), 17 C.F.R. § 243.101(d), defines "promptly" to be as soon as "practicable" but not later than 24 hours or the commencement of the next day's trading on the NYSE after a senior official of the issuer learns of the non-intentional disclosure.

230. The filing is on Form 8-K; *see* Rule 101(e)(2), 17 C.F.R. § 243.101(e)(2) (2009).

231. *See* James D. Cox, *Fraud Is in the Eyes of the Beholder: Rule 10b-5's Applications to Acts of Corporate Mismanagement,* 47 N.Y.U. L. Rev. 674 (1972); Thomas Lee Hazen, Treatise on the Law of Securities Regulation § 12.9 (6th ed. 2009).

232. Santa Fe Indus. v. Green, 430 U.S. 462 (1977).

233. Healey v. Catalyst Recovery of Pa., Inc., 616 F.2d 641 (3d Cir. 1980); Kidwell v. Meikle, 597 F.2d 1273 (9th Cir. 1979); Ala. Farm Bureau Mut. Cas. Ins. Co. v. Am. Fid. Life Ins. Co., 606 F.2d 602 (5th Cir. 1979); Wright v. Heizer Corp., 560 F.2d 236 (7th Cir. 1977), *cert. denied,* 434 U.S. 1066 (1978); Goldberg v. Meridor, 567 F.2d 209 (2d Cir. 1977), *cert. denied,* 434 U.S. 1069 (1978).

234. Similarly, no action lies under the antifraud provision of the proxy rules for mismanagement if the shareholders were not asked to vote via a proxy on the matters giving rise to their loss. *See, e.g.,* Gen. Elec. Co. v. Cathcart, 980 F.2d 927 (3d Cir. 1992).

CHAPTER 13

RIGHTS AND POWERS OF SHAREHOLDERS: INSPECTION RIGHTS, VOTING, AND PROXIES

TABLE OF SECTIONS

PART A. SHAREHOLDERS' RIGHTS

§ 13.1 THE NATURE OF THE SHAREHOLDERS' INTEREST

Under their share contract and by virtue of their status as owners of shares, shareholders have three classes of rights against the corporation: (1) rights as to control and management, (2) proprietary rights, and (3) remedial and ancillary rights.

The first class of shareholder rights includes: (a) voting rights for the election—and usually for the removal—of directors, in addition to the incidental right to the holding of annual and special meetings and due notice thereof; (b) voting rights as to the making of amendments to the charter and other fundamental changes in the corporate existence and setup; (c) voting rights as to the making and amending of bylaws, which regulate many matters, including the authority of directors and officers and their compensation; and (d) the right to have the corporation managed honestly and prudently for the benefit and profit of the shareholders within the scope of the authorized business.

The second class of shareholder rights, designated as proprietary rights, includes: (a) the right to participate ratably in dividend distributions when declared by the management; (b) the right to participate in the distribution of assets in total or partial liquidation; (c) the right to equality and honesty of treatment by the management and by majority shareholders in corporate transactions affecting share interests, such as new issues of shares or amendments of the articles; (d) the right to be registered as a shareholder on the corporate books, subject only to valid and authorized transfers of the shares; and (e) immunity from personal liability for corporate debts, subject to judicial limitations against abuse of this privilege.

Remedial rights of shareholders include: (a) the right to information and inspection of the corporate records; (b) the right to bring representative or derivative suits on corporate causes of action to prevent or remedy mismanagement and unauthorized acts and compel the corporation to enforce its rights; and (c) common law, equitable, and statutory remedies for infringement of individual rights.

PART B. RIGHT TO INFORMATION

§ 13.2 BASIS OF SHAREHOLDERS' RIGHT TO INFORMATION

A shareholder[1] has a common law right to inspect corporate books and records, in person or by an agent, for a proper purpose in order to protect the shareholder's interest. Most states also provide shareholders a statutory right of inspection, which is generally viewed as supplementing rather than supplanting the common law right.[2] Many states permit reasonable charter and bylaw provisions regulating inspection.

The shareholder's right to ascertain how the affairs of the business are being conducted by the officers and directors has traditionally been founded on the ownership interest and the necessity of protecting that interest.[3] The common law right of inspection rests on the underlying rights of ownership of the corporate property.

There has been much litigation over the proper scope of the shareholder's right to inspect corporate books, files, and records. Thus a statute authorizing inspection of "books and records of account" has been held not to authorize inspection of quarterly financial statements,[4] but the statute does reach recordations and contracts of ongoing business transactions.[5] A court may limit the scope of a shareholder's inspection to those records that are necessary to protect the shareholder's interest in the corporation.[6]

§ 13.3 PROPER PURPOSES FOR INSPECTION

Shareholders today generally have the right of inspection only for legitimate purposes related to their interest as investors. The common law privilege, however, is not absolute, and the corporation may show in defense that the applicant is acting out of wrongful motives, or that the information sought is not germane or necessary for the stated purpose.[7]

An examination of modern decisions reveals that among the purposes held to justify an inspection demand are to ascertain (1) the financial condition of the company or the propriety of dividends;[8] (2) the value of shares for sale or investment;[9] (3) whether there has been mismanagement;[10] (4) to obtain, in anticipation of a shareholders' meeting, a mailing list of shareholders to solicit proxies or otherwise influence voting;[11] or (5) information in aid of litigation with the corporation or its officers involving corporate transactions.[12] A purpose is proper even though it yields no direct benefit to the corporation, but it should not be adverse to the corporation's interest.[13] Among the improper purposes that may justify management denial of a shareholder's claimed right of inspection are: (1) to obtain information as to business secrets or to aid a competitor;[14] (2) to secure business prospects or investment or advertising lists;[15] and (3) to find technical defects in corporation transactions in order to bring strike suits for purposes of blackmail or extortion.[16] In general, a demand is improper if it is motivated merely by idle curiosity or to annoy or harass management.[17] In Delaware, a motive to further social goals does not appear to render the proposal improper.

The majority common law rule does not seem to place the burden on petitioners to show the propriety of examination, nor that the refusal by the officers or directors was wrongful.[18] Similarly, most modern statutes place the burden on the corporation.[19]

§ 13.4 STATUTORY REGULATION OF INSPECTION RIGHTS

In most jurisdictions, the shareholders' right to inspect and examine the books and records of a corporation is not left entirely to the common law but is declared in whole or in part by statutes. Statutory provisions often define the right of inspection only of certain books, such as the stock ledger or list of shareholders. Under this type of statute, the right of inspection of other records, such as books of account, minutes of the meetings of directors and shareholders, and corporate documents, which may be of the greatest importance, are thus left to the common law.[20] Under a statute that provides in general terms that the shareholders of all corporations shall "have the right of access to, inspection and examination of the books, records and papers of the corporation at all reasonable and proper times," it is generally held that inspection will not be allowed for purposes hostile to the interests of the corporation.[21] Ulterior motives may thus be shown by a corporation as a matter of defense.

§ 13.5 REMEDIES IF INSPECTION IS DENIED

If the officers of a corporation wrongfully deny a shareholder the right to inspect its books or papers, the traditional remedy to enforce the shareholder's right was a common law proceeding known as mandamus.[22] Because mandamus was historically used to enforce public rights and duties, the petition was presented in the name of the state on the "relation" or complaint of the party beneficially interested.[23] In a number of states, the real party in interest was named as plaintiff, and the state was not mentioned even as a formal party.[24]

There is a conflict of authority whether a statute appearing to make the right of inspection absolute takes away a court's discretion to refuse the writ of mandamus where inspection is sought for an improper purpose. Most decisions favor the exercise of sound discretion to withhold the writ to protect the just interests of the corporation and the other shareholders against abuse.[25] This discretion is spoken of as inherent in the remedy of mandamus, but it is generally applied in giving equitable relief of a specific nature to avoid injustice and remit the suitor to other forms of relief. There are comparatively few reported cases in which the courts have enforced the right of inspection in equity by injunction. In some jurisdictions, it has been held, however, under statutory provisions or otherwise, especially when ancillary to other equitable relief, that enforcement by an injunction (that is, a mandatory injunction or specific performance) is available.[26]

Modern corporation statutes specifically set forth remedies for enforcing inspection rights. Thus the Delaware statute states that if a corporation does not grant inspection within five business days of a demand, the shareholder may commence an action in the Court of Chancery to enforce the demand.[27] The Model Business Corporation Act as revised in 1984 provides that a court of the county in which the corporation's principal office is located (or, if none in the state, its registered office) may summarily order inspection and copying of the records.[28]

§ 13.6 ACCESSING CORPORATE REPORTS, FINANCIAL STATEMENTS, AND NOBO LIST

The great burden and expense to an individual shareholder of exercising the right of inspection of corporate books and records, not to mention bringing suit to enforce that right, make this a poor method of getting needed information. Although the response of state legislatures was not favorable, the federal securities laws filled the need with respect to publicly held corporations.

The Securities Exchange Act of 1934 requires registration and periodic reporting by publicly held companies.[29] Further, the SEC's proxy regulations under that Act require that proxy statements be mailed to shareholders in connection with the solicitation of proxies. These proxy statements must include much financial information as to proposed corporate changes and proceedings. The making of reports and the rendition of financial statements by corporations, however, are generally held not to be substitutes for the shareholders' right of inspection and are no excuse for management's refusal to permit a shareholder to examine corporate books and records.[30]

An important constraint on the utility of obtaining a list of the stockholders for a public corporation is that in most instances the list does not identify who votes the shares. The stockholders' list identifies only the names and addresses of the stockholders of record. Most stock in public corporations is held not in the name of the owner of the shares but in the name of the brokerage house where the owner maintains an account. Holding shares in the brokerage house's "street name" greatly facilitates purchases and sales of securities, because the owner of the shares does not have to endorse the shares and deliver them to the broker before selling the shares. Indeed, most ownership in public companies is not represented by a certificate but appears only as an electronic entry in the share registry. This is, in part, because holding shares via street names facilitates trading in the shares of public corporations. On purchasing shares investors do not take delivery of any share certificates, but receive only a statement that the shares they have purchased are held in a trust depositary that maintains its own records regarding the identity of the owners of the shares that are on deposit with the trust depositary. The dominant trust depositary in the United States is CEDE & Co.

An examination of the list of stockholders for a public corporation, such as IBM Corporation, will show that a substantial portion of the shares is recorded in the name of CEDE & Co. Separately, CEDE makes available to the corporations whose shares are on deposit with it a list of the brokerage firms holding stock in the CEDE name. This is called the "CEDE breakdown" list. This document, however, does not reveal the names and addresses of customers for whom the broker holds the shares in its street name. The SEC requires brokers to ask each customer who holds stock in a street name if she objects to her name and address being disclosed to the corporation in which she has invested. Those who do not object are then identified to the corporation on the NOBO (non-objecting beneficial owners) list. Thus, it is through the NOBO list that one can determine who the beneficial shareholders are for some of the outstanding shares held in street names (i.e., those in the hands of non-objecting shareholders).

Given the pervasiveness of holding public shares in street names and, hence, the importance of the NOBO list, the question arises whether a shareholder seeking inspection of the list of shareholders is also entitled to the NOBO list. The courts have been unwilling to build upon the principles that underlie the general rights of stockholders to access company records and their power to communicate with their fellow stockholders by conferring upon the stockholders the power to compel the corporation to acquire a NOBO list. Most courts that have engaged this subject conclude that the requesting shareholder can obtain the NOBO list only if such list is already in the corporation's possession,[31] but the shareholder cannot compel the corporation to obtain or otherwise prepare a NOBO list.[32]

§ 13.7 DIRECTORS' RIGHT OF INSPECTION

By both case law[33] and statute,[34] the right of a director to inspect corporate books and records is more extensive than that of a shareholder.[35] The director's right has often been said to be absolute and unqualified.[36] It has been held that the right may not be denied on the ground that the director is hostile to the corporation and that his only object is to promote a claim against it; if the hostility goes to the extent of justifying his removal from office, that remedy is to be followed.[37] Even a claim the documents are protected by the attorney-client privilege is not an absolute bar to the director's access.[38]

Inspection should be denied, however, when necessary to prevent abuse by the director or his representative.[39] It has been declared that directors must act in good faith and therefore may not exercise their right of examination for purposes that conflict with their fiduciary obligations.[40] The duties of their positions require directors to keep themselves informed of the business and to be familiar with the affairs of the company.[41] Inspection by a shareholder is primarily for the purpose of protecting her individual interests. Inspection by a director is with a view to enabling him to perform his duties intelligently.

In making an examination of corporate records, a director, like the shareholder, is entitled to expert assistance in order to exercise the privilege effectively and may use attorneys and accountants to help.[42] Wrongful denial of the request allows the director to the sanction provided by law.[43]

PART C. SHAREHOLDERS' MEETINGS AND VOTING

§ 13.8 SHAREHOLDERS ACT AT MEETINGS OR BY WRITTEN CONSENT

The stockholders' meeting is an important feature of corporate law, but we might well question whether the ritual of a meeting where owners physically come together is a relic of the past. Certainly in the public company we might even question whether the annual meeting has the same importance as it did in the past in terms of providing a medium for management to sense the concerns of the firm's owners. The growing concentration of institutional holders, combined with their increasing activism outside the annual meeting context, support the view that the annual meeting is not necessary for such companies to assure interaction between owners and managers. Also, the sheer number of individual investors in many public companies renders the annual meeting setting a weak medium. As the number of owners increases, the collective action problem becomes an ever increasing obstacle to an effective exercise of their judgment. As seen later in this chapter, the Internet is now being harnessed to corporate governance mechanisms so that the day of the virtual meeting may well not be far away.

As is the case with directors, according to traditional doctrine, a majority of the shareholders have no power to vote or act for the corporation except at a meeting, duly called on proper notice, at which a quorum is present. Absent statutory authorization, written or oral consent to a corporate act by the shareholders or members individually, even though a majority may agree, is not binding on the corporation.[44]

Most corporate statutes authorize shareholder action to be taken or approved without a meeting by the written consents of shareholders holding shares with voting power.[45] The Model Business Corporation Act provides for action without a meeting only on unanimous written consent unless voting by majority consent is authorized in the articles.[46] The statutes vary in their requirements from state to state.[47] For example, Delaware permits a majority of the shareholders to act by consent.[48] A provision common to statutes authorizing action outside a meeting via the consent of less than all the stockholders is a requirement of prompt notice to all the non-consenting shareholders.[49] Consents are analogous to proxies and are revocable.[50]

§ 13.9 NECESSITY OF ANNUAL MEETING AND CONVENING SPECIAL MEETINGS

Subject to statutory authorization for shareholder action by majority consent, each shareholder has a right to have an annual meeting called and held to elect directors.[51] Modern statutes expressly confer this right.[52] A statutory, charter, or bylaw provision stating that a meeting shall be held every year for the election of directors confers a right on each individual shareholder to have an annual meeting called and held at the time specified or at some later reasonable time.[53] Indeed, statutes commonly provide stockholders with a procedure to compel an annual meeting to be convened when a certain number of months have elapsed since the last annual meeting.

The time and place for a regular annual meeting of the shareholders are usually fixed in the bylaws. In a few jurisdictions, if the charter or bylaws fix the place, the day, and the hour at which regular meetings shall be held, no further notice may be legally necessary.[54] However, under most modern statutes, notice must be given a minimum and a maximum number of days before the meeting to every registered shareholder entitled to vote.[55] The notice must specify the time and place of the meeting, but there is no requirement that it elaborate on the purpose of the meeting unless the articles of incorporation require otherwise.[56]

In the absence of an express provision in the charter or bylaws, special meetings may be called by the board of directors whenever deemed necessary or on demand of the shareholders or a certain percentage of them.[57] Once granted by statute, the shareholders' right to call a special meeting presumably cannot be abridged or altered unless permitted by statute.[58] Statutes generally confer a right upon 10 percent of the shareholders to convene a special meeting.[59] The Model Act now permits the articles of incorporation to fix a lower percentage as well as a higher percentage, but not to exceed 25 percent.[60] The shareholders' right to call a special meeting provides an important check on the powers of the directors.[61] However, the requested meeting must be for a matter that is a proper subject for stockholder action.[62]

§ 13.10 THE TIME, PLACE, AND NOTICE OF THE MEETING

Charter or bylaw provisions authorizing corporate meetings at a certain time are not intended to prevent meetings at other times on proper notice.[63] The matter of notice is now governed by statute, although statutes permit deviation by the articles of incorporation or bylaws.[64] In response to pressure from the Uniform Electronic Transmissions Act (UETA) and the federal Electronic Signatures in Global and National Commerce Act (E–Sign), state laws are rapidly embracing wider mediums for notice to be imparted so that increasingly reference to the requirement of a writing refers to a message that is in electronic form that can be produced to a tangible written form.[65] Proper notice includes mention of the time and place. As against absent shareholders or members, a meeting is not legal if held before the day or hour specified in the notice of the meeting.[66] And when the hour for a meeting is fixed by the notice, the meeting should be opened at that hour or within a reasonable time thereafter.[67] As against shareholders who are not present and who do not consent, a meeting held at a different place from that specified in the notice of the meeting is a nullity.[68]

Generally, there is no geographical restriction on the location at which a shareholders' meeting may be held, provided proper notice is given. Delaware allows shareholder meetings by means of remote communication if the directors so choose.[69] Meetings outside the state may be binding on the participants even if unauthorized.[70]

Insufficient notice, which deprives any shareholders of the opportunity to attend, argue, and vote on proposed measures renders action taken at a shareholders' meeting voidable at the instance of those who did not participate.[71] If all the shareholders who did not receive notice attend a meeting and participate, this constitutes a waiver of notice, and neither they nor the corporation can question the validity of a corporate act authorized at the meeting.[72] Mere attendance for the purpose of objecting to notice does not constitute waiver of notice.[73] The minutes of a shareholders' meeting should show the proper notice, provide proof of mailing or otherwise that gives notice, or show a waiver of notice either in the minutes themselves or in attached exhibits to which reference is made in the minutes.

Most state statutes authorize shareholders to waive any required notice. Such a waiver must be in writing and can be executed at any time, and the meeting is not invalid because of the lack of notice if all shareholders entitled to notice but who did not receive it either execute a written waiver or attend and participate in the meeting.[74] To be effective, the waiver must be executed by the holder of record, not by the share's beneficial owner.[75]

Notice is given to the shareholders of record. Statutes now authorize the board of directors or the bylaws to fix a record date for the purpose of determining who is entitled to notice of and to vote at the meeting.[76]

§ 13.11 QUORUM AND VOTING AT SHAREHOLDERS' MEETINGS

Nearly all states require the corporation to make available for inspection a list of shareholders entitled to vote.[77] Most states further specify the number of days preceding the meeting that the list must be available for inspection.

At common law, absent a provision to the contrary in statute, charter, or bylaw, a quorum was met by any number of shareholders, provided there were at least two and any required notice of the meeting had been given.[78] However, generally by express provision of the statute, charter, or bylaws, a majority of the shares entitled to vote (or sometimes less if so provided in the charter or bylaws) must be present in person or by proxy to constitute a quorum for the transaction of business; if there are less than the number of shares so present required for a quorum, the meeting is not validly convened.[79] The articles of incorporation and corporate statute must be closely examined not only to determine what classes of shares are entitled to vote, but also whether the voting power is equal among all shares of the same class. Considering the contractual nature of the corporation, the articles of incorporation can impose voting restrictions provided they do not conflict with the provisions of the state law. Thus, a provision placing a ceiling on the total number of votes any stockholder could cast, regardless that otherwise her shareholdings would entitle her to a greater vote, was upheld as a permissible variation from the typical one-share, one-vote principle.[80] In the typical setting, each share entitled to vote has one voting right. However, many corporations are adopting "tenure voting" whereby holders of shares have greater voting rights the longer they have owned their shares.[81]

The applicable corporate statute, articles of incorporation, and bylaws should be read carefully to determine whether a separate quorum determination is required for each item coming before the stockholders, especially when a corporation has more than one class of stock and the meeting's agenda includes a matter that requires the approval of more than one class of stock. A similar close reading is called for to determine if a greater than majority vote is required. States following the Model Business Corporation Act require a separate quorum determination be made for each matter to be acted on at the meeting.[82]

Most courts have held that where a quorum is once present at a shareholders' meeting, the quorum is not broken by the subsequent withdrawal of some of the shareholders, whether present in person or by their proxies.[83] Some courts, however, have held to the contrary, ruling that a withdrawal that leaves the number of shareholders present or represented below the required number destroys the quorum and precludes any further action except a motion to adjourn.[84]

A validly convened meeting can be adjourned to a later date. Many state statutes expressly deal with the question of whether notice of the date and place of the adjourned meeting must be given. Their treatment of this issue varies widely. Some require no notice of the adjourned meeting so long as it is held within a certain number of days;[85] others require notice if a new record date is set.[86] The statutes further condition avoiding the need for any new notice of the adjourned meeting on the new meeting's time and location being announced at the meeting that is being adjourned.[87]

When a quorum is present, the vote of a majority of those present is sufficient to elect directors or to decide any questions, although it need not be a majority of all the shareholders or members, or a majority of the voting power.[88] By the weight of authority, a plurality of the votes actually cast will be decisive, although some of the shareholders or members who are present may abstain and the majority of the votes cast may not be a majority of the persons present or stock represented.[89] A bylaw or charter provision requiring the affirmative vote of a majority of the shareholders at a corporate meeting means a majority in interest (that is, one vote per share) rather than a majority in number only.[90] These rules are codified in most state corporation statutes, which also generally permit higher voting requirements if specified in the articles.[91] A few statutes still require an extraordinary majority—that is, two-thirds—for approval of charter amendments, mergers, and other organic changes.[92] Also, there may be statutory, charter, or bylaw requirements for class voting by different classes of shares.[93]

§ 13.12 STOCKHOLDERS' MEETINGS IN A DIGITAL AGE

The states slowly, but at a quickening rate, adapting to the digital age by amending various provisions of their corporate statutes to authorize the use of the Internet, e-mail, etc. in connection with stockholders' meeting. Delaware has the most advanced statute in terms of liberating functions such as notice, voting, and even deliberations from the traditional format for stockholders' meeting. Delaware corporations can take advantage of advances in communications technology.[94] More than half the states now have provisions that authorize the board of directors either to authorize "remote participation" by shareholders or more sweepingly to convene the stockholders' meeting solely "by means of remote communication," a "remote only" meeting.[95] There is a split among the states as to whether only the directors can authorize remote participation or whether such authorization can be provided generally in the bylaws or the articles of incorporation.[96]

States impose various conditions for shareholders to enjoy remote participation. Many states follow Delaware's conditions: the corporation shall employ reasonable measures to verify that each person participating remotely is a stockholder or proxyholder; the corporation shall implement reasonable measures to facilitate one participating remotely to read, hear, and vote at the meeting, and the corporation shall have the ability to record the vote or action of the remotely participating party.[97] An equal number of states require only that shareholders be able to hear one another.[98]

A common corporate provision permits notice of the forthcoming stockholders' meeting to be imparted electronically.[99] However, the statute may condition the effectiveness of such delivery upon the shareholder first consenting to delivery of notice in this form.[100] This would appear to permit email messages to stockholders, but it would be no more appropriate to treat merely placing an announcement on the company's website as notice, as it would have been in a paper-based society to impart notice by a classified advertisement.

A clear majority of the states permit proxies to be executed and transmitted electronically. Though there is broad authorization for the electronic execution and transmission of proxies, this is somewhat qualified by the need for determining the validity of the authorization.[101] There are also provisions for actions without a meeting, a parallel to the written consent procedures discussed earlier, to occur electronically.[102]

The NYSE listing requirements permit proxy materials to be delivered by electronic means. The SEC rules governing the delivery of proxy materials have gone electronic. Reporting companies now can provide a URL address where holders can access the documents and vote; nonetheless, holders still retain the option of a paper copy of the proxy statement to holders who desire such a copy.[103]

§ 13.13 Conduct of Shareholders' Meetings

Section 7.08 of the Model Act envisions a strong, but fair, chair. The meetings' decorum and overall order can be assured as well by attention to the rules of parliamentary procedure, although those not versed in the technical niceties of the rules may well prefer the informality of a fair-minded chair.[104]

In many states, the provision of the corporation statute that details the procedure for amending the charter indicates that before shareholders can vote on an amendment, the directors must adopt a resolution setting forth the proposed amendment and directing that it be submitted to a vote at a meeting of the shareholders.[105] No provision is made in these states for a shareholder-initiated amendment of the charter. In a distinct minority of states, the statutory procedure for amending the charter seems to provide leeway for shareholder amendment without director approval,[106] and in a few instances shareholders appear to have successfully utilized a charter amendment to increase the number of directors over the opposition of a majority of the board.[107]

§ 13.14 Shares Entitled to Vote

The general rule is that all legal owners of voting shares in a corporation have a right to be present and vote at all corporate meetings.[108] In the interest of certainty as to voting rights and of the right and duty as to notice of meetings, corporations are universally permitted by statute and charter provisions to look to the corporate records of registered shareholders to determine who is a shareholder entitled to vote, to notice of meetings, to dividends, and to other rights of shareholders.[109] The practice of closing the transfer books for a period of 40 days, more or less, before a meeting is frequently authorized in order to give ample time to make up voting lists of shareholders. In recent years, however, instead of this crude expedient of closing the books against recording transfers, statutes and bylaws have authorized the alternative method of fixing record dates for voting, dividends, and other purposes, so that stock transfers may be continually entered into the books. Those who are registered on the books on the record date remain the shareholders of record for the given purpose, although they may cease to be owners after the record date and before the activity takes place.[110] The Former Model Act, which was typical of modern statutes, permitted the closing of the transfer books at the corporation's discretion for no fewer than 10 nor more than 50 days or the fixing of the record date by bylaw or directors' resolution to be not less than 10 nor more than 50 days before the meeting.[111] The Revised Model Act extends the maximum to 70 days.[112]

The right to vote is an incident of stock ownership except insofar as the corporation needs protection by its records against incurring liability to adverse claimants.[113] In some states, the books are prima facie evidence of the right to vote.[114] Other statutes have provided that the transfer of stock is conclusive evidence of the right to vote as to inspectors of the election, but such statutes are not conclusive on the courts as to share ownership, and rival claimants may litigate their rights.[115] The unregistered or equitable owner of shares has the right to compel the holder of the naked legal title to give her a proxy to vote or to vote at her direction.[116]

Most statutes provide that a shareholder who has pledged shares has the right to vote until the shares have been transferred to the name of the pledgee.[117] The person whose name appears on the books of a corporation (or otherwise is designated as the absolute owner of stock) clearly has the right to vote those shares, even though he in fact may hold the shares as trustee. And even when shares are in the name of a person as a "dry" trustee, he or she is entitled to vote them unless the *cestui que* trust objects and takes steps to have them registered in her own name.[118] The Model Act provides that the trustee is entitled to vote as long as the shares are registered in her name.[119] An executor or administrator has the right to vote shares belonging to the estate even though they stand on the books of the corporation in the decedent's name.[120]

If shares are owned by two or more persons jointly, the right to vote is in them jointly, and they must agree in order to vote the shares.[121] This rule of joint action applies to stock held by several executors or trustees unless there is a provision for majority vote on disagreement.[122] Depending on the statutory authority, fractional shares of stock may or may not be used as the basis of voting, cumulatively or otherwise.[123]

§ 13.15 Power to Vote Treasury Shares and Shares Held by a Subsidiary

Shares of its own stock acquired by a corporation are no longer outstanding and are denominated "treasury shares" unless subject to cancellation.[124] Since shares are contracts with the corporation, on surrender to the corporation they can have only a potential or fictitious existence and cannot have voting rights.[125] Shares acquired by the corporation that issued them cannot be voted even when they are held in the name of a trustee[126] or have been pledged by the corporation.[127] It does not violate this principle to permit the parent corporation's directors to constitute a majority of the subsidiary's board, even though this has the indirect effect of allowing individuals who are directors of the subsidiary to decide how to vote the shares issued by the subsidiary.[128] Moreover, the shares held by the issuer as trustee for another can be voted by the issuer in its capacity as trustee.[129]

Shares of a parent company's stock purchased by a wholly owned subsidiary do not *ipso facto* become treasury shares,[130] but shares of a parent corporation held by its subsidiary should be treated as equivalent to treasury shares at least as far as voting rights are concerned.[131] Otherwise, such shares could be voted by the directors of the parent corporation to continue themselves in office almost as freely as treasury shares could be so voted. The Model Act and most state corporation statutes impose a voting disability on shares a subsidiary holds in its parent.[132]

§ 13.16 Cumulative Voting

Cumulative voting is the privilege of multiplying the number of shares held by the number of directors to be elected and casting the product for a single candidate or distributing the product among two or more candidates. With cumulative voting, shareholders can distribute their votes among some of the vacancies to be filled instead of using "straight voting"—that is, casting votes according to the number of shares held for each vacancy. If five vacancies are to be filled, each share of stock may be voted five times for one individual to fill one position, instead of casting one vote per share for each of the five positions. In other words, a person or persons holding 100 shares may cast 500 votes in favor of one candidate or may distribute the votes in favor of one or more persons for the five vacancies.

The aim of cumulative voting is to allow a minority to secure representation on the board of directors.[133] Without cumulative voting, holders of a bare majority of the shares may elect the full board and thus control the corporation without any representatives of other interests being present at board meetings.

Under cumulative voting, unwary majority shareholders, if they spread their votes over too many offices, may find that a vigilant minority has deprived the majority of control. If there are 1,000 shares outstanding and 10 directors to be elected, and one person holds 600 shares, he should be able to elect the majority of the directors. If, however, he casts 600 votes straight for each one of 10 candidates, and if the 400 minority shareholders cumulate their 4,000 votes on six candidates, the minority will elect six directors and the majority will elect only four.[134] To be safe under a cumulative system, where there is a substantial block of minority shares, majority shareholders must often abandon the attempt to elect a complete board and must cumulate their votes on such a portion of the members of the board as the number of their shares bears to the total number of shares that will be voted at the election. Thus each group, majority and minority, should ascertain the portion that the number of shares it holds bears to the number of shares it expects to be voted at the election, and then vote its shares cumulatively for that portion of the number of directors to be elected. If, after casting his vote, a shareholder sees he has made a mistake, he may recall his ballot and change his vote before the presiding officer finally announces the result of the voting.[135]

For cumulative voting to work, all the directors to be elected in a given year must be voted for at one time; each director position cannot be voted on separately.[136] The more directors there are to be elected, the smaller the minority needed to secure a representative. Where the directors are classified, with only one-half or one-third to be elected annually, the benefits to the minority of cumulative voting are greatly diminished.[137] For example, if there are five directors to be chosen and one-fifth of the shares are voted for one nominee, that nominee is practically assured of getting a place on the board, while if only three directors are to be chosen, one-third of the shares would be required for the same assurance.

§ 13.17 Plurality, Majority and Empty Voting; Advance Notice Bylaws

Plurality Voting

The prevailing default rule for the election of directors is that directors are elected under a plurality voting system whereby in director elections the nominees receiving the highest number of affirmative votes are elected, without regard to the number of votes withheld. While this sounds perfectly democratic, plurality voting is not the same as conditioning election on the will of a majority. With plurality voting, if there are five vacancies and five directors nominated, each director will be assured of election, even though none of the directors receive an absolute majority of the votes cast. Thus, under plurality voting, the unopposed nominees who have been chosen by the board are guaranteed a seat as long as they receive at least one vote in their favor, regardless of how many shareholders withhold their votes. When there are fewer vacancies than nominees, the nominees elected are those receiving the most votes to the extent there are vacancies. As can be seen, with plurality voting a dominant consideration in the control of the corporation is the process whereby directors are nominated; whoever dominates that process ultimately controls the composition of the board of directors and, quite likely, the corporation itself. Due to shareholder dispersion and the obstacles to collective action, the nomination process historically has been outside the control of the stockholders as a group, except in the closely held corporation. This is because rarely will shareholders be willing to incur a burdensome, expensive, and uncertain process to nominate an alternate slate of directors. Hence, board elections are generally uncontested and the slate of nominees is not customarily formulated in consultation with the public stockholders. And, with the number of nominees being equal to the number of seats up for election, nomination and not voting is where the important event.

Majority Voting

Activist stockholders in 2004 pushed majority voting via bylaw proposals to replace the minimalist plurality vote requirement with a majority vote requirement.[138] Today, majority voting, in its various forms, is prevalent among the S&P 500 and the trend is trickling down to mid- and small-cap companies.

One form of majority voting is to provide, either by a bylaw or even board-established policy, that a director elected under a plurality standard who does not receive a majority of the votes to tender his resignation to the board, which will then decide whether or not to accept the resignation. A firmer embrace of majority voting are bylaw or charter provisions that change the legal standard for director elections from a plurality to a majority.

One downside to majority voting is that it may result in a failed election, with one or more seats on the board going unfilled, if a candidate does not receive a majority of the votes. That is, when there is a contested election governed by a majority vote provision and the number of nominees exceed the number of board seats pursuant to a majority vote requirement, it is possible that none of the candidates will receive a majority vote. Most majority vote provisions condition the director's election upon receiving a majority of the votes *cast*, rather than a majority of the votes outstanding. So formulated, non-voted shares do not count as part of the denominator in determining whether the director has received a majority vote. An additional protection arises in contested elections; most majority vote provisions contain an exception in contested elections, since to do otherwise likely would mean no director is duly elected as none would receive a majority of the votes cast if there were multiple candidates for the same seat. In the event of a failed election, state statutes generally contain holdover provisions which permit incumbent directors to remain in place until a successor can be elected.[139]

Several states have responded to the majority vote movement by adopting legislation that makes it easier to implement majority voting. For example, in 2006 Delaware amended its statute to provide that, "[a] bylaw amendment adopted by stockholders which specifies the votes that shall be necessary for the election of directors shall not be further amended or repealed by the board of directors."[140]

Advance Notice

Advance notice bylaws require a shareholder who intends to nominate directors or introduce other business at the shareholder meeting to submit notice in advance.[141] The courts of many jurisdictions enforce reasonable advance notice provisions.[142]

Hedged Voting

In recent years, there has been an increase in proposals by shareholders who have hedged their interest in the company. Investors can effectively buy votes by becoming shareholders on the record date so that they have voting rights, but hedging their position so that they have no corresponding economic interest in the shares. Indeed, derivatives and other capital market developments enable investors to decouple economic ownership from voting rights. Because these shareholders have minimal to sometimes even no economic stake in the firm through share ownership, their interests can be seen as not aligned with those held by fully invested shareholders. Advance notice provisions can address this problem by requiring a shareholder making a proposal to disclose its investment strategy and whether it has entered into any hedging transactions. These provisions provide boards and shareholders with valuable information about whether a stockholder proponent's interest is in line with the interests of other shareholders.

§ 13.18 INTERFERENCE WITH THE STOCKHOLDERS' FRANCHISE

Sometimes, when their control is threatened by an outsider, directors manipulate the timing of a stockholders' meeting to gain a strategic advantage. For example, in a leading Delaware case[143] the directors, who were engaged in a proxy contest, advanced the date of the stockholders' meeting from the date initially established for the meeting. The directors acted in response to the on-going proxy campaign by an insurgent group and the effect of advancing the date was to reduce considerably the time the insurgents would have to persuade other stockholders to grant their proxies to the insurgents and not management. The court enjoined the convening of the meeting on the ground that the directors acted solely to obstruct the legitimate efforts of dissident shareholders to oust the board.[144] It was not until later, in *Blasius Industries v. Atlas Corp.*,[145] that this approach became fully articulated such that it is now an important principle of corporate law. At a time that Blasius Industries was soliciting written consents to expand Atlas's board and fill the newly created seats with nominees who would support a recapitalization plan, Atlas's board quickly met and added three additional board members. The effect of this was to prevent Blasius's on-going efforts to result in it obtaining a majority of the board seats. Chancellor Allen concluded that the board's actions were taken in good faith and were undertaken in the the reasonable belief that the recapitalization plan would not be in the best interests of Atlas or its stockholders. However, he reasoned that good faith alone does not justify the board intentionally interfering with the exercise of the stockholders' franchise. By placing the matter within principal-agent context, where the agent is deemed to act inequitably when taking steps to frustrate the principal's control of the agent, *Blasius* thus imposed upon management the burden of proving a "compelling justification" for acts taken to thwart the exercise of stockholder franchise. *Blasius* is about the validity of directorial power and not an abstract affirmation of shareholder voting rights.

The distinction made in the cases serves the justifiable purpose of subjecting to extremely rigorous review those board actions that are taken in order to thwart the efforts of aroused shareholders. We might well question why *Blasius* should be limited to thwarting the stockholders when engaged in the exercise of their governance rights. Indeed, some flexibility in the doctrine's application appears from time to time. For example, management may well take such steps as calling the meeting where an item known to be controversial will be discussed and purposefully give such short notice as to effectively foreclose any possible opposition from mounting a proxy contest. In this situation, and it would seem others, the fundamental principle should be not whether the opposition is currently taking steps to exercise their shareholder franchise, but whether management has taken steps that prevent such steps from even being commenced. Such an approach does get into difficult factual and problematic factual inquiries. For this reason, having a bright-line test of whether the insurgents are then engaged in steps to oppose management or its position is useful. But it seems that exceptions to this standard can be made where on its face the steps taken by management clearly thwart any possibility of opposition exercising their shareholder franchise.[146]

§ 13.19 Vote-Buying and Coercion

Vote-buying and coercion are two separate but related concepts. Each involves a shareholder voting for or against a matter for reasons other than its intrinsic merits. In vote-buying, a shareholder is enticed with extra benefits that the shareholder would not have received otherwise. Wrongful coercion is where shareholders are threatened through statements that the controlling stockholder, directors, or others will take action that may harm the stockholders' interest.

For the past two decades, vote-buying has been a matter litigated exclusively in Delaware and without success by the party invoking the argument as the foil to prevent the implementation of a transaction requiring stockholder approval. At one time the mere presence of any consideration bestowed for a stockholder's vote was invalid. The rationale for this result was twofold. First, the courts believed that each stockholder owed his fellow stockholders a fiduciary duty when voting to exercise his own independent judgment.[147] This view no longer prevails; only controlling stockholders are held to have a fiduciary duty to other stockholders.[148] Second, during corporate law's formative years analogies to other contexts were made, some analogies, of course, being stronger references than others. Thus, courts reasoned that just as vote-buying by politicians was harmful, so it should be for the purchase of the stockholder's vote.

In 1982, Delaware put an end to vote-buying being per se void. *Schreiber v. Carney*,[149] arose in the context of a corporate restructuring of Texas International Airlines, which required approval of each class of its outstanding securities. One of the three outstanding classes of shares was convertible preferred shares and a majority of those shares were held by Jet Capital, who also held warrants covering 800,000 Texas International common shares. Jet Capital was not favorable to the restructuring because upon its occurrence it would incur a substantial tax liability with respect to the warrants. To secure its approval, Texas International agreed to lend $3.4 million to Jet Capital to enable it to exercise the warrants. In a derivative suit challenging this arrangement on the grounds of unlawful vote-buying, the Delaware Chancery Court voiced a more tolerant approach to vote-buying, reasoning that the despite its unsavory connotation, vote-buying "is simply a voting agreement supported by consideration personal to the stockholder."[150] Instead of being void per se, the court set forth the following two-part approach:

> [V]oting agreements in whatever form . . . should not be considered to be illegal *per se* unless the object or purpose is to defraud or in some way disenfranchise the other stockholders. That is not to say, however, that vote-buying for some laudable purpose is automatically free from challenge. Because vote-buying is so easily susceptible of abuse it must be viewed as a voidable transaction subject to a test of intrinsic fairness.[151]

In *Schreiber*, the court found no harm to the other stockholders because the entire purpose of the restructuring was to benefit the other stockholders and the arrangement with Jet Capital was necessary to secure for them the advantages provided by the restructuring. Moreover, the court concluded the loan transaction was intrinsically fair because it was subsequently ratified by the stockholders. After *Schreiber* vote-buying arrangements have with great regularity been upheld.[152]

At one time, many state statutes proscribed vote-buying. Today, remnants of the former hostility to vote-buying can be found among a few corporate statutes that prohibit vote-buying.[153]

Coercion[154] claims have arisen in but a few cases.[155] What constitutes coercion is not only a factual inquiry, but one for which at least the Delaware Chancery Court appears to have a fairly high level of tolerance of the type of pressure minority stockholders can withstand and still act independently of that pressure.[156] The equitable doctrine against coercion protects preferred as well as common stockholders.[157] It remains to be seen whether other courts will be more willing to find coercion than has Delaware.

PART D. STATE REGULATION OF THE PROXY MACHINERY

§ 13.20 THE NATURE OF A PROXY

A "proxy" is the authority given by one shareholder to another to vote her shares at a shareholders' meeting.[158] The term is also used to refer to the instrument or paper that is evidence of the authority of the agent, as well as to the agent or proxy holder who is authorized to vote.[159] The proxy holder is an agent whose authority may be general or limited. Being an agent, the proxy holder is thus, in the eye of the law, a fiduciary.[160] As the Delaware court has said: "A person acting as proxy for another is but the latter's agent and owes to the latter the duty of acting in strict accord with those requirements of a fiduciary relationship which inhere in the conception of agency."[161] It was accordingly held in that case that the proxy holder, as agent, could not bind his principal by an act done with an interest adverse to that of the shareholder, such as the proxy holder's ratification of an issue of stock to himself for an illegal consideration.[162]

At common law, all votes at shareholders' meetings had to be given in person; there was no right to vote by proxy.[163] This is still the rule for directors' meetings.[164] However, as a result of statutory provision, charter, or bylaw provision, the shareholders' privilege of voting by proxy is universal in stock corporations.[165] When the right is given by statute or charter, a shareholder cannot be deprived of it, nor can it be unreasonably restricted by a bylaw.[166]

A general unrestricted proxy or authorization to attend and vote at an annual meeting, "with all the powers the undersigned would possess if personally present," gives a general discretionary power of attorney to vote for directors and on all ordinary matters that may properly come before a regular meeting, even though specific mention of them is not made in the notice of the meeting.[167] Courts distinguish sharply between what business may be transacted at a regular meeting without notice of specified purposes and what may be transacted at a special meeting. A general proxy is no authority to vote for a fundamental change in the corporate charter or for dissolution or a transfer of all of the property to another corporation, or other unusual transactions, at least where the shareholder has not received proper statutory notice.[168]

A limited proxy may restrict the authority to vote to specified matters only and may direct the manner in which the vote shall be cast.[169] Shares represented by proxy are deemed "present" at a meeting, even though the proxy is granted for the express purpose to "withhold approval" of the slate of directors being put forth by management (when there is no opposing slate of nominees).[170] Failure of proxy holders to produce and file the written evidence of authority will not prevent the votes being counted to make up a quorum to organize a meeting.

There must be satisfactory proof that a proxy has been executed, which minimally requires written evidence of the proxy holder's authority,[171] but courts have recognized proxies executed by a rubber stamp facsimile of the owner's signature[172] as well as by only the owner's initials.[173] When there is a dispute regarding a proxy, in the interest of certainty and expediency courts regularly exclude extrinsic evidence so that only corrections that can be resolved on the face of the proxy will be addressed.[174] Keeping up with technological advances, proxies can be given by electronic transmission and also by telephone so long as certain procedures are followed.[175]

§ 13.21 REVOCATION, DURATION, AND TERMINATION OF PROXIES

A proxy, like an agency in general, is revocable unless "coupled with an interest." Most state statutes provide a proxy's duration cannot extend beyond 11 months, unless the proxy provides a longer period.[176] One who has given a proxy or power of attorney to another to vote her shares may revoke the agency at any time if it is not coupled with an interest, even though it is expressly declared to be irrevocable or a consideration for the appointment is stated.[177] It was formerly against the general policy of the law governing corporate control that an irrevocable power of voting, or of directing the vote of stock, should be created even by contract of the shareholder.

Revocation of a proxy need not be made by formal notice in writing to the corporation unless so required by statute. Revocation may be expressed to the proxy holder or to the election judges or may be indicated by a subsequent proxy to another or by sale of the shares.[178] Appearing and asserting the right to vote at a meeting revokes a proxy previously given.[179] Thus a proxy may be revoked orally or by conduct. Just like any other agency, a proxy is terminated by the death of the principal or of the agent or by the loss of capacity by either party, unless this rule is changed by statute.[180]

Even though it is not so stated, a proxy is generally viewed as irrevocable when it is "coupled with an interest" in the shares.[181] What constitutes a sufficient interest in the shares to make a power to vote them irrevocable is an unsettled question.[182] According to the conventional view, the interest must be either (1) a charge, lien, or some property right in the shares themselves; or (2) a security interest given to protect the proxy holder for money advanced or obligations incurred.[183] Under this view, a "recognizable property or financial interest in the stock in respect of which the voting power is to be exercised," which renders the proxy irrevocable, is said to be distinguishable from "an interest in the corporation generally" and from "an interest in the bare voting power or the results to be accomplished by the use of it," neither of which has that effect.[184]

The more recent liberal view holds that the proxy is also irrevocable when the interest protected is in the corporation for which the shares are held as additional security.[185] It seems that modern courts usually find an interest where the proxy is given for the protection of a right of the proxy holder or a third person or to ensure the performance of a duty. Under either view, payment to the shares' owner as compensation for being allowed to vote the owner's shares violates the common law rule against vote-selling such that the arrangement confers no authority on the proxy holder.[186] More recently, the Delaware courts have shifted from viewing vote-buying as *per se* invalid, to being *voidable*, subject to a test for intrinsic fairness. Thus, consideration paid by a corporation that was approved by its outside directors as being in the best interests of the corporation was not invalid.[187] An irrevocable proxy is not terminated by revocation or by death of the creator of the proxy or by his loss of capacity.

A number of states have either tried by statute to avoid the ambiguous term "coupled with an interest" by specifying the circumstances in which a proxy can be made irrevocable. The Model Business Corporation Act more comprehensively defines "coupled with an interest" as including appointment of: (1) a pledgee; (2) a person who purchased or agreed to purchase the shares; (3) a creditor of the corporation who extended it credit under terms requiring the appointment; (4) an employee of the corporation whose employment contract requires the appointment; or (5) a party to a voting agreement.[188]

Management customarily solicits proxies seeking authority to vote not only on matters that management knows will arise at the meeting, but also discretionary authority to vote the shares on any other matter that may be proposed at the meeting. In the time between soliciting or even obtaining proxies and the meeting, management may become aware of a matter a stockholder intends to propose for stockholder action at the meeting. Under state law this does not by itself revoke the proxy obtained by management. However, the SEC's position, which applies to companies that are covered by the Securities Exchange Act's proxy rules, is that management cannot exercise its discretionary authority if after obtaining the proxy it learns that a matter will be proposed for stockholder action at the meeting and the proponent intends to solicit proxies in support of that proposal from the holders of at least a majority of the shares.[189]

§ 13.22 The Proxy Voting System

The presence in person or by proxy of holders of a majority of a corporation's shares is generally required to constitute a quorum. It is accordingly of great importance that shareholders unable to attend in person appoint suitable agents to represent them so that elections can be held and other necessary business transacted. As a New Jersey court said of a large steel corporation, "[i]t would be stupid indeed to assume that the 80,000 stockholders may possibly attend the meeting in person."[190]

It has similarly been observed: "[I]n the larger corporations the stock-holders' meeting is now only a necessary formality; that stockholders' expression can only be had by the statutory device of proxy. As a result, within limitations, realistically the solicitation of proxies is today the stockholders' meeting."[191] In other words, the proxy system is usually a species of absentee voting by mail for the slate of directors and the proposals suggested by the management.

Management has a great advantage in the solicitation of proxies because it is lawful for the directors to send out blank proxies printed at the expense of the company and to provide postage paid for by the company, at least if it is not purely a personal contest.[192] The ordinary holder of a relatively small number of shares has practically no alternative, other than not voting at all, to delegating his vote to a proxy committee of persons whom he does not know, over whom he has no control, and as to whose intended action he is very poorly informed, except as these matters are regulated by the federal rules on proxy solicitation.

Although proxy contests are usually limited to closely held businesses, there have been a number of bitterly fought proxy fights in publicly held corporations, in large part due to Securities and Exchange Commission regulation of shareholder suffrage. Notwithstanding the resultant increased emphasis on fairness in shareholder suffrage, the success of groups opposing incumbent management and its policies unless within the context of a takeover attempt has not been great when measured in terms of victories at the ballot box. The primary reasons for the continued success of incumbent management are its control of the proxy machinery and shareholder inertia in voting.

§ 13.23 PROXY CONTEST EXPENSES

In addition to having control of the voting process, management's ability to use company funds during a proxy contest assures its success in most cases. Through its board of directors a corporation may spend reasonable sums in a contested election where the expenditures further the intelligent exercise of judgment by the shareholders.[193] In a contest over policy, as distinguished from purely personal struggles for power, the board may authorize reasonable corporate expenditures to support policies that the directors believe in good faith to be in the corporation's best interest.[194] On the other hand, it has been held that shareholders may vote to reimburse successful insurgents for their expenses.[195] In *CA Inc. v. AFSCME Employers Pension Plan*,[196] the Delaware Supreme Court held that a proposal to amend the bylaws to provide for reimbursement of an insurgent's proxy campaign expenses, was a proper subject for shareholder action. However, the precise proposal before the court was not valid because it could cause the directors to provide reimbursement in violation of their fiduciary obligations. It is likely that the proposal would have been appropriate had it included a so-called fiduciary out clause whereby reimbursement would not be required if doing so would have violated the directors' fiduciary obligation. Delaware and the Model Business Corporation Act have since amended its statute to expressly authorize bylaw provisions authorizing procedures to be followed to allow shareholder nominations of directors;[197] and both Delaware and the Model Act expressly authorize bylaws that will provide reimbursement by the corporation of proxy solicitation expenses incurred by a stockholder in connection with the election of directors, subject to such procedures and conditions as the bylaws may prescribe.[198]

PART E. FEDERAL REGULATION OF PROXIES

§ 13.24 SECTION 14 OF THE SECURITIES EXCHANGE ACT OF 1934: AN OVERVIEW

Nondisclosure of needed information and other abuses foisted on the corporate election system led to federal regulation of proxy solicitation. Section 14(a) of the Securities Exchange Act of 1934[199] declares it unlawful to solicit any proxy or consent or authorization from the holder of any security subject to the act's registration and reporting provisions[200] in violation of such rules as may be prescribed by the Securities and Exchange Commission. Pursuant to this authority, the SEC has promulgated extensive requirements regarding the disclosures that must be made in connection with the solicitation of proxies.[201]

With rare exceptions the only way in which shareholders in a large corporation with shares widely diffused can participate in the election of directors and in voting on fundamental changes in the corporate structure is by the use of proxies. Thus to participate effectively, shareholders must be informed by the management, or by others soliciting proxies, about the director candidates and measures for which their authorization is solicited. The general purpose of the federal proxy rules is to require that security holders be provided with sufficient information bearing upon and explanation of the matters on which the persons to whom they give proxies are authorized to cast their votes, so that they may know what they are authorizing. Under the proxy rules, shareholders are also afforded an opportunity to limit the authorization and indicate disapproval as well as approval of management proposals—that is, to specify whether their proxies shall be voted for or against each proposal submitted. Rule 14a-4(c) authorizes the proxy to include discretion to vote on any matter the company's management did not have notice of at least 45 days before the meeting.[202] To avoid the problem of managers coupling unpopular proposals with so-called "sweeteners," the proxy rules now prohibit a group of related proposals to be bundled as a single resolution.[203] This change avoids the problem of stockholders having their natural choice distorted by an artful coupling of value-decreasing proposals with a change that shareholders desire.

The fundamental requirement of the proxy rules is disclosure of accurate and adequate information by those who solicit a proxy, consent, or authorization. The rules and Schedule 14A must be consulted to determine what information is required for each different item requiring shareholder action, such as election of directors, a plan of remuneration of directors and officers, an amendment of the charter or bylaws, a proposal for merger, consolidation, or sale of assets, or modifications of the corporation's securities.[204] An area of concern is corporate governance in publicly held corporations; the Securities and Exchange Commission has responded with detailed disclosure requirements concerning the activities of directors, including the composition and functioning of the various committees of the board as well as the directors' individual attendance records.[205]

If fraud or noncompliance with the rules occurs, that constitutes grounds for an injunction against using the proxies and holding the meeting until the proxies have been resolicited.[206] Nothing in Section 14 makes action taken at any meeting invalid, even though the action is taken pursuant to proxies obtained in violation of the rules. The only express remedy the Securities and Exchange Commission has for violations of the proxy rules is to seek injunctive relief before the meeting or to give the matter to the Justice Department for criminal proceedings after the meeting. However, as is the case with SEC Rule 10b-5,[207] the most powerful impact of section 14(a) and, in particular, Rule 14a-9, is the antifraud provision, since it provides an implied cause of action available to the corporation or an aggrieved shareholder.[208]

The formal proxy solicitation material to be used in a solicitation must be filed with the commission for inspection at least 10 days before the beginning of the solicitation. All other proxy material, such as letters, advertisements, and supplementary material, need not be filed in advance. The material filed is examined by the commission. On request, informal suggestions may be made by the commission in advance of the filing date. In many instances, corporations have been required to issue corrected proxies and statements, and meetings have had to be postponed. Full disclosure requirements, of course, have a discouraging effect on the presentation of unfair proposals to the shareholders. The provision of proxy materials to stockholders beginning in 2008 has gone electronic. Reporting companies now can provide a URL address where holders can access the documents and vote; nonetheless holders still retain the option of a paper copy of the proxy statement to holders who desire such a copy.[209]

Under the federal proxy rules, if a security holder wishes to solicit proxies himself, he may require that the management mail to those who are solicited by the management a form of proxy and other material furnished by the applicant/security holder, provided the applicant makes provision for expenses in connection with the mailing. Thus management is required to cooperate in mailing solicitation literature of dissident groups, and shareholders are given a medium of communication with fellow investors. Provision is also made in the proxy rules for a shareholder who desires to present proposals at the annual shareholders' meeting to have her proposal submitted and explained in a management proxy solicitation if she gives timely notice to management of her intention to present the proposal at the meeting.[210]

§ 13.25 DEFINITION OF "SOLICITATION" AND "PROXY"

The vast majority of the Securities Exchange Act's disclosure provisions are directed toward requiring full information in the marketplace so that informed and intelligent investment decisions can be made. In contrast, in its concern for shareholder suffrage, section 14(a)'s proxy regulation approaches very closely the fine line separating proxy regulation from the chartering function of the state's general corporation laws. The basic rationale for federal involvement in the internal affairs of large corporations through the Exchange Act's reporting and disclosure requirements is that informing the marketplace of significant corporate developments is necessary to investor confidence and protection. The SEC, although lacking authority to weigh in directly on corporate governance issues,[211] nevertheless does so discretely through its disclosure requirements.

To begin with, the Commission has laid down a broad definition of "proxy solicitation."[212] "Solicitation" includes all communications directed to shareholders that are reasonably calculated to affect a voting decision. The regulation has been extended to cover many kinds of communications that are not garden-variety vote solicitations. For example, in the course of a merger between two railroads, management's open letter to the Interstate Commerce Commission extolling the virtues of the proposed transaction and urging its administrative approval was held to be subject to the SEC's filing and disclosure requirements, because the shareholder vote had not yet been taken and the letter contained statements that were likely to influence a voting decision.[213]

The courts continue to adhere to the early standard that a communication that itself does not request the giving of any authorization is nevertheless a proxy solicitation when it is "part of a 'continuous plan' intended to end in solicitation and to prepare the way for success."[214] Thus a letter asking several other stockholders to join the request to access the company's list of stockholders was deemed a proxy solicitation because the letter's author intended to use the list in his campaign to solicit proxies. Moreover, a letter to the stockholders that discussed recent activities at the corporation can be deemed a proxy solicitation because the definition includes communications that are designed to discourage stockholders from giving a proxy to someone else.[215]

In 1992, the SEC amended the proxy rules to reduce in important ways the earlier restrictions on stockholders to communicate among themselves.[216] Rule 14a-2(b)(1) broadly (but somewhat ambiguously)[217] exempts from the filing and format requirements communications with stockholders by a person who himself is not seeking proxies and who does not have a "substantial interest" in the subject matter. This exemption is not available to certain classes of individuals, such as officers, directors, director nominees, or one who has in a Williams Act filing disclosed a possible intent to control the issuer. Moreover, a communication by a holder of more than $5 million of the company's stock must file the communication within three days of its use. A further relaxation appears in new Rule 14a-1(l)(2)(iv), which permits holders to announce how they will vote on any matter. A further innovation allows proxy contestants to solicit proxies for less than a full slate of dissident nominees—that is, the dissident can seek proxies for some of its nominees as well as some of the incumbent management's nominees. The function of allowing such "short slates" is to facilitate minority representation on the board.

Overall, the 1992 proxy rule amendments go a long way toward answering the criticism that the former proxy rules prevented institutions and other sophisticated investors from effectively coordinating their actions to improve the performance and governance of their portfolio companies. Under the new rules, investors can more easily coordinate their actions to maximize their influence at the stockholders' meeting because they are no longer subject to the costly and burdensome prefiling and format requirements. However, their communications continue to be subject to Rule 14a-9's prohibition against misleading communications in connection with a proxy solicitation. However, in late 1999 the SEC did relax the pre-filing obligations of management with respect to announcements related to acquisitions, even though the announcement contained deal related information. Under new Rule 14a-12 the company (or those acting on its behalf) can release announcements related to an acquisition without first filing the information or deliver a proxy statement, provided there is not then a request for a proxy.[218] SEC rules provide that the issuer or a shareholder, as well as a third party acting on behalf of either, can operate an electronic forum that facilitates shareholder interaction[219] and participation in such a forum does not constitute solicitation requiring compliance with the format, pre-filing, etc. requirements for proxies so long as the participant does not solicit personally on behalf of another person.[220]

The Securities Exchange Act also provides for SEC regulation of broker-dealer involvement in the proxy process, including the problem of voting or giving proxies for securities held for investors by stock brokerage firms "in street name."[221] Further, the Act requires management disclosure prior to an annual meeting even if management does not solicit proxies.[222]

§ 13.26 SHAREHOLDER PROPOSALS UNDER THE PROXY RULES

Shareholders have made frequent use of Rule 14a-8, which requires management to submit appropriate shareholder proposals to the shareholders for a vote. Among the proposals based on economic or business considerations that shareholders have asked management to submit for consideration at shareholder meetings are the following: (1) to inaugurate a system of cumulative voting for directors; (2) to place a ceiling on the amount of compensation the corporation can pay to any one executive or to the officers as a group or to subject executive compensation to an advisory stockholders vote; (3) to move the location of shareholders' meetings to a place more convenient for shareholders or to provide for the rotation of meeting places; (4) to make available to the shareholders various types of reports, such as a post-meeting report on the annual stockholders' meeting, goals related to company's charitable giving; and (5) requesting management to establish quantitative goals for reducing greenhouse gases.

"Public interest" and "public responsibility" groups have also resorted to Rule 14a-8 to bring social and political issues before the shareholders at annual meetings and thus give those issues publicity. Among commonly recurring proposals of the recent past have been the following: to terminate a corporation's business activities in South Africa (when apartheid was practiced); to prohibit a corporation from participating in the Arab boycott of Israel; to prohibit a corporation from making political contributions here or abroad; to terminate a corporation's manufacture or sale of armaments or other war materials; and to terminate a corporation's sponsorship of television programs featuring violence or sex. Each proxy solicitation season has its "in" topics.

Although shareholders submitting proposals opposed by management infrequently garner a substantial vote at the annual meeting, managements have often modified corporate policies or practices to obtain the withdrawal of a shareholder proposal or simply to remove irritants to good shareholder relations.[223] Management may rule a proposal not appropriate for shareholder action or otherwise improper under the proxy rules and thus excludible from the proxy materials. Although the ultimate question of a proposal's propriety for shareholder action is often a matter of state law, it is a violation of Rule 14a–8 not to include a proper proposal in the proxy materials.[224]

While the SEC's rule provides numerous grounds for a proposal's omission, the overriding concern is "[i]f the proposal is not a proper subject for action by shareholders under the laws of the jurisdiction of the company's organization."[225] Because there is very little judicial authority on this topic, the staff of the SEC has over the years been the primary generator of guidance on what is or is not a proper subject for stockholder action. The Delaware legislature in 2008 addressed this awkward situation by authoring the Delaware Supreme Court to receive questions certified to it on the question of the scope of Delaware general corporation law. Thus, in the first use of its expanded jurisdiction, *CA Inc. v. AFSCME Employers Pension Plan,*[226] the Delaware Supreme Court, responding to a certification filed by the SEC seeking guidance, opined that a proposal to amend the bylaws to provide for reimbursement of an insurgent's proxy campaign expenses, although a proper subject for shareholder action, the precise proposal before the court was not valid because it could cause the directors to provide reimbursement in violation of their fiduciary obligations. It is likely that the proposal would have been appropriate had it included a so-called fiduciary out clause whereby reimbursement would not be required if doing so would have violated the directors' fiduciary obligation.

A Commission enforcement action under the shareholder proposal rules resulted in the Third Circuit[227] compelling management to include in its proxy materials a shareholder proposal (1) to amend the corporate bylaws to provide for independent public auditors, (2) to require notice of all proposed bylaw amendments, and (3) to require that a report of the annual shareholders' meeting be sent to shareholders. In contrast, a federal district court has upheld management's decision to exclude a shareholder's resolution that the company intensify its offshore drilling efforts.[228] The court pointed to the standard statutory mandate that the directors manage the business and affairs of a corporation and then upheld the Commission's finding that the proposal "related to . . . the ordinary business" and "was made 'primarily for the purpose of promoting a general economic or political cause.'"[229] It would appear that any proposal that deals with the *timing* of an act the corporation is already committed to is likely to be deemed as related to "ordinary business."[230]

From the inception of the shareholder proposal rule, a frequently invoked basis for management to exclude a shareholder proposal is on the grounds, now embodied in subsection (i)(7) of Rule 14a-8, which authorizes exclusion of proposals "relating to the company's ordinary business operations."[231] Just where ordinary business operations cease and fundamental corporate policy issues that affect the character of the enterprise begin is difficult to discern. For example, in one decision, the Court of Appeals for the District of Columbia reasoned that capital expenditures may reach such a level that they no longer merely involve "ordinary business."[232]

Since 1976 the SEC's position has been that a proposal could be excluded whenever it involves business matters "that are mundane in nature and do not involve any substantial policy or other considerations."[233] Under this standard, the SEC consistently held that proposals concerning equal employment opportunities could not be excluded on the basis that they involve ordinary business because they involve important policy questions and were not, under its 1976 interpretative guidelines, merely mundane.[234] In 1992, in the *Cracker Barrel* no-action letter,[235] the SEC retreated from the special treatment accorded proposals involving equal employment opportunities, so that the mere fact that a proposal is tied to a social issue no longer protected it from being omitted if the proposal otherwise focuses on the conduct of ordinary business.[236] Not surprisingly, its retreat stirred a great deal of controversy. Thus, in 1997, the SEC announced it was considering reverting to its prior practice of reviewing each employment-related proposal to determine if it relates to the ordinary business of the company or to more far-reaching social issues, in which case it would not be excludable from management's proxy statement.[237] In 1998, the Commission officially announced this change in position and the reversal of the position that had been taken in the controversial *Cracker Barrel* no-action letter.[238]

More recently the battleground for shareholder proposals, reflecting the increasing activism of institutional investors, has been proposals focused on changes in corporate governance. SEC no-action letters have rejected company pleas that they be permitted to omit proposals for bylaw changes calling for the redemption of an existing poison pill, stockholder approval of the initiation of a poison pill, separation of the position of board chair and chief executive officers, cumulative voting, and supplanting the plurality vote with a majority vote requirement as a condition for a director's reelection. By far the initiative that has generated the greatest reaction from management and institutional investors has been proposals to amend the company bylaws that would empower stockholders to nominate directors.

Today, Delaware and the Model Business Corporation Act each expressly authorize bylaw provisions regarding procedures for shareholder nomination of directors as well as reimbursement of the nominee's expenses.[239] The SEC in 2010 amended Rule 14a-8(i)(8) to permit proposals related to the nomination of directors. The final act on the long road to shareholder access is approaching. In July 2010, The Dodd-Frank Wall Street Reform and Consumer Protection Act was enacted. Section 971 of the Act amends section 14(a) to authorize the SEC to promulgate rules enabling a shareholder to include its nominee on the public company's ballot. In reliance on this authority the SEC adopted Rule 14a-11 empowering holders of 3 percent of a company's shares to nominate up to one-fourth of a company's directors, provided the shares have been held for at least three years. But the rule was invalidated by the D.C. Circuit Court of Appeals.[240]

§ 13.27 IMPLIED PRIVATE ACTION UNDER RULE 14a-9

The first time that the Supreme Court gave its imprimatur to an implied cause of action under the securities acts was with regard to Rule 14a-9's antifraud limitations on the use of the proxy machinery.[241] It is important to bear in mind that the coverage of the proxy rules is limited. In addition to applying only to solicitation of proxies by Exchange Act reporting issuers,[242] section 14(a) necessarily applies only to issues that are brought before the shareholders for a shareholder vote.

Materiality. The dominant concern in any action under Rule 14a-9 is whether the proxy solicitation contained a *material* omission or misstatement of fact. A fact's materiality is a mixed question of law and fact that arises in pretrial motions as well as at trial. As explained by the Supreme Court, "An omitted fact is material if there is a substantial likelihood that a reasonable shareholder would consider it important in deciding how to vote.[243] Subsequent Supreme Court decisions have refined without limiting this standard of materiality. Thus, for example, the standard for determining materiality for soft information, such as financial forecasts, appraisals, and future financial expenditures, that "materiality will depend at any given time upon a balancing of both the indicated probability that the event will occur and the anticipated magnitude of the event in light of the totality of the company activity."[244]

Contrary to a literal reading of both Rule 14a-9 and *prior cases*, the Supreme Court held in *Virginia Bankshares, Inc. v. Sandberg*[245] that opinion statements can be the bases of a materiality claim under Rule 14a-9. In *Virginia Bankshares*, management's proxy statement described the merger's terms as providing the stockholders with a "high" value and elsewhere described the price as "fair." The court held that opinion statements could be materially misleading and just as harmful as misrepresentations of fact. However, *Virginia Bankshares* held that more must be alleged than that the defendant misrepresented their motives, true intentions, or beliefs; otherwise vexatious litigation would arise. The Supreme Court thus conditioned that any suit for materially misleading opinion statements must bear on the substance of the transaction for which approval was sought. This additional requirement was satisfied in *Virginia Bankshares* because the plaintiff alleged the merger's terms were unfair.

It should be apparent that the standard of materiality makes it especially difficult for many matters to be resolved on the basis of pretrial motions.

Causation. Questions of causation are especially difficult in the context of misleading proxy solicitations. Therefore, in one case, the failure to disclose details of earlier discussions with a possible merger partner, though concluded by the court to be material, were nonetheless not believed to rise to the level of materiality as to have had a causal impact on the vote of the stockholders.[246] For most issues, the proxy solicitation involves a collective, rather than an individual, decision. Stockholders decide as a group whether to amend the articles, to elect a director, or to merge with another company. Structural decisions, such as the merger or sale of a company, frequently allow dissenters a right to have their shares appraised, so in this regard the decision has both a collective and an individual character. In either case, the causation question is whether the particular omission or misstatement must be shown to have misled the individual stockholder or group of stockholders.

At the same time, it must be recognized that because the decisions are collective decisions and all stockholders are generally bound by the will of a majority, each stockholder's interest is impacted by a misrepresentation that causes her fellow stockholders to approve or forgo a transaction to the extent that transaction impacts the company. Causation is further complicated by the *TSC Industries* standard of materiality, quoted above, which holds that a fact is material without proof "of a substantial likelihood that disclosure of the omitted fact would have caused the reasonable investor to change his vote."[247] Thus, a fact is material even though it does not have a dispositive impact on how the individual stockholder votes.

One major requirement of causation is that the alleged omission or misstatement in the proxy statement must pertain to a transaction for which stockholder approval was sought. This is the so-called transaction-causation requirement that is sometimes used in the courts' language.[248] To illustrate, consider the court's treatment of numerous cases brought in the 1970s, alleging the board of directors failed to disclose in the proxy statement in which they sought election that they had acquiesced in foreign bribery payments carried out by management. With great consistency, the courts dismissed Rule 14a-9 actions seeking to hold the directors liable for the bribery payments. The courts ruled that because the bribery payments were not submitted to the stockholders for their approval, transaction causation was lacking—that is, there was no causal relationship between the failure to disclose in the proxy statement the directors' misbehavior and the bribes themselves.[249] There is a more direct link between the nondisclosure of the directors' acquiescence in foreign bribery and their own election. In a leading case, the Supreme Court held that causation was not established because the vote was not necessary for approval of the challenged transaction.[250]

Remedies. A panoply of remedies is available in Rule 14a-9 actions. The Supreme Court in *Mills* conditioned damages being available to the extent that the transaction's unfairness can be established.[251] On remand, the lower court reviewed the terms of the merger and concluded they were fair, so no damages were awarded.[252] Injunctive relief is especially appropriate where matters have not been pursued so far as to be beyond the prospective relief of a court of equity. Rescission is possible but is inappropriate where the rights of third parties or excessive transaction costs will be incurred.[253]

PART F. CORPORATE CONTROL DEVICES

§ 13.28 VARIOUS VOTING CONTROL DEVICES

The operation of the proxy system has led to almost universal "management control" and a situation in which "ownership of corporate shares without appreciable ownership has become a natural phenomenon of our economic system."[254] Various devices have been used to obtain control of publicly held corporations with their valuable patronage for little or no investment. On the other hand, many of these same devices have proved to be useful and legitimate tools in meeting the special needs of close corporations and the desires of the owners of such corporations.[255]

The principal control devices by which groups may seek to gain or retain control of corporations by a combination of voting power or otherwise are as follows: (1) voting agreements entered into by a group of shareholders to assure their voting control; (2) voting trusts; (3) pyramiding, the use of holding companies or a series of holding companies to hold controlling shares of their subsidiaries; (4) classification of common shares into voting and nonvoting, with the voting power vested in a small class of "management stock"; (5) management contracts, often with a parent or affiliated corporation; and (6) classification of directors, with staggered elections of only some of the directors each year. Another device is to provide for per capita rather than per share voting.[256]

§ 13.29 Nonvoting Shares and Voting-Only Shares

Preferred shares are frequently given only contingent rights to vote for directors and on other matters in the event of nonpayment of dividends for a specified period. Under most statutes, a corporation may issue nonvoting common stock.[257] The common stock may thus be divided into Class A nonvoting and Class B voting shares. Frequently in such cases, the Class A shares will be widely sold to the public, and Class B, the voting shares, will be closely held by promoters or managers. It is argued that vesting such control in the active promoters and managers so that no other group can dislodge them is for the benefit of the enterprise. But it may be questioned whether such an arrangement does not deprive investors in the nonvoting shares of potential participation in control, which should be their means of self-defense.[258] At least in close corporations, however, controlling shareholders, while perhaps not fiduciaries to the same extent as directors, are not free to exercise control for their own selfish interests and to oppress or defraud holders of minority or nonvoting shares who have no voice in the selection of management. And notwithstanding their denomination as nonvoting or conditional voting stock, holders of preferred as well as nonvoting common shares are entitled under most modern corporation statutes to vote for organic changes that directly affect their ownership interests.[259]

Control arrangements may also take the form of the corporation issuing shares that have voting rights with few or no accompanying financial interests in the company.[260]

§ 13.30 THE VOTING TRUST

To meet business needs, adroit lawyers invented the voting trust to give what is in essence a joint irrevocable proxy for a term of years the protective coloring of a trust, thus enabling the trustees to vote as owners rather than as mere agents. The voting trust meets the formal objections to an irrevocable proxy and, subject to certain formalities and limitations on duration, is now validated by statute.[261]

Corporate statutes provide broad validation of the voting trust.[262] These statutes typically state that the trust agreement must be in writing and filed with the corporation; they also usually limit the duration of the voting trust, most often to ten years.[263] The voting-trust formalities are considered mandatory,[264] and courts have invalidated voting trusts that exceed the statutory duration[265] as well as for other types of noncompliance with the statute.[266] The modern attitude is to uphold arrangements that do not comply with all the requirements of the state voting-trust statute as long as the arrangement does not otherwise violate public policy.[267] Most statutes today are not intended to invalidate all other voting agreements, and in 1969 the Model Act was amended to reflect this.[268]

§ 13.31 VOTING TRUSTS—SCOPE OF TRUSTEE'S POWERS

One object of forming a voting trust is to ensure permanency of tenure for the directors and to take from the shareholders the power to change management. Such an arrangement sometimes is a response to some special business need, and good reason can be shown for this drastic change in the rights of the shareholders, who by law and by the corporation's charter have the right to vote on the selection of directors and on fundamental corporate changes. Obviously, it is not a legitimate function of a voting trust to capture the voting power of the shareholders for those who propose to use it in their own selfish interest[269] or for purposes hostile to the corporation or its shareholders.[270] A voting trust offers to promoters of a corporation the temptation of seizing and retaining dictatorial control over the investments of others with little or no investment and keeping all the patronage and perquisites of control.[271]

The following are among the purposes usually regarded as legitimate for voting trusts: (1) to aid in reorganization plans and adjustments with creditors in bankruptcy or financial difficulty; (2) to assist financing, to procure loans, and to protect bondholders and preferred shareholders; (3) to accomplish some definite plan or policy for the benefit of the company and to assure stability and continuity of management for this purpose; (4) to prevent rival concerns or competitors from gaining control; (5) to apportion representation and protect minority interests by putting the selection of directors in impartial hands; and (6) as a device in connection with mergers, consolidations, or purchases of a business to assure that the predecessors or constituents, though in the minority, may have representation.[272]

The trustee of a voting trust is a fiduciary to the beneficiaries of the trust.[273] The voting of the trusts shares to support a transaction in which the trustee has a direct financial interest calls for close scrutiny of the transaction and the trustee's motives.[274]

§ 13.32 THE VOTING TRUST IN OPERATION

The voting trust involves a more complete and formal surrender of the shareholder's legal rights and remedies than any other control device. Voting-trust procedures commonly require that the shares' ownership be transferred to the voting trustee, that there be a formal voting-trust agreement signed by the shareholders creating the trust, and that a copy of that agreement must be filed with the corporation's principal officer.[275] The failure to comply with these provisions at one time led to the arrangement being viewed as invalid.[276] More recent decisions have upheld arrangements under state voting-trust statutes when there was less than literal compliance with the statute.[277]

The beneficial owners may cease to be recognized as shareholders of record and may be deprived not only of any right to vote but also of any right of inspection, notice, or information from the corporation or any voice in fundamental changes, such as mergers and consolidations, sales of entire assets, increase and reduction of capital, and bylaw and charter amendments that may adversely affect them. There is ordinarily no justification for such a complete stripping of the shareholders of all the safeguards provided by law for their protection. Persons who have put their shares in a voting trust—that is, the holders of voting-trust certificates—are often spoken of as "equitable owners" of shares of stock. They become in effect equitable tenants in common in the mass of shares transferred to the trustees, with a contract right to receive dividends and retransfer of the shares on termination of the trust. The remedies of the holder of a voting-trust certificate are primarily against the trustees to cancel the trust for fraud, to remove the trustees if guilty of misconduct or for conflicting interests, or to sue for an accounting for secret profits.[278] Voting trustees are subject to the usual fiduciary principles of a trust.[279]

A voting-trust certificate is a profit-sharing security or contract issued by the trustees as a kind of association or holding company, of which the "charter" is the voting agreement. Since voting-trust certificates in effect represent shares in such an association, the transfer thereof can result in a taxable event.[280] Under both state[281] and federal[282] securities legislation, voting-trust certificates are securities and thus are subject to those acts' antifraud and registration provisions.

NOTES

1. *See, e.g.*, Deephaven Risk Arb Trading Ltd. v. UnitedGlobalCom, Inc., 2005 WL 1713067 (Del. Ch. 2005) (inspecting granted even though shareholder had a net short position).
2. *See* Scattered Corp. v. Chicago Stock Exch., Inc., 671 A.2d 874 (Del. Ch. 1994).
3. Otis-Hidden Co. v. Scheirich, 219 S.W. 191 (Ky. 1920).
4. Bitters v. Milcut, Inc., 343 N.W.2d 418 (Wis. App. 1983).
5. *See* Meyer v. Ford Indus., 538 P.2d 353 (Or. 1975) (reaches contracts, records, and correspondence).
6. *See, e.g.*, Wells v. League of Am. Theatres & Producers, Inc., 706 N.Y.S.2d 599, 604 (Sup. Ct. 2000); Troccoli v. L&B Contract Indus., Inc., 687 N.Y.S.2d 400, 401 (App. Div. 1999).
7. Sec. First Corp. v. U.S. Die Casting & Dev. Co., 687 A.2d 563 (Del. 1997) (inspection proper to investigate mismanagement during merger negotiations, but denied for records before merger negotiations).
8. Gregson v. Packings & Insulations Corp., 708 A.2d 533 (R.I. 1998) (even though financial statements not prepared, access to books granted to determine propriety of bonuses and extraordinary dividend).
9. Friedman v. Altoona Pipe & Steel Supply Co., 460 F.2d 1212 (3d Cir. 1972); Pagett v. Westport Precision, Inc., 845 A.2d 455 (Conn. App. Ct. 2004).

10. Seinfeld v. Verizon Comm., Inc., 909 A.2d 117 (Del. 2006) (stockholder as a predicate must allege some "credible basis" for inferring possible misconduct).

11. E.L. Bruce Co. v. State *ex rel.* Gilbert, 144 A.2d 533 (Del. 1958); Kalanges v. Champlain Valley Exposition, Inc., 632 A.2d 357 (Vt. 1993) (corporation did not meet its burden in proving that request to examine list of stockholders to facilitate attempt to gain control was improper purpose).

12. Saito v. McKesson HBOC Inc., 806 A.2d 113 (Del. 2002) (inspection extended to records before shareholder maintaining derivative suit became a holder).

13. COMPAQ Computer Corp. v. Horton, 631 A.2d 1 (Del. 1993) (focusing on whether stated purpose is related to the interests of the shareholder that should not be adverse to interests of the corporation).

14. Morton v. Rogers, 514 P.2d 752 (Ariz. Ct. App. 1973).

15. *E.L. Bruce Co.*, 144 A.2d 533.

16. Shabshelowitz v. Fall River Gas Co., 588 N.E.2d 630 (Mass. 1992) (improper purpose to seek list to solicit existing shareholders to sell their shares to plaintiff).

17. Carpenter v. Tex. Air Corp., 1985 WL 11548 (Del. Ch. 1985).

18. NVF Co. v. Sharon Steel Corp., 294 F. Supp. 1091 (W.D. Pa. 1969).

19. *E.g.*, Del. Code Ann. tit. 8, § 220 (2009).

20. Tucson Gas & Elec. Co. v. Schantz, 428 P.2d 686 (Ariz. Ct. App. 1967).

21. State v. Honeywell, Inc., 191 N.W.2d 406 (Minn. 1971). *But see* Lewis v. J&K Plumbing & Heating Co., 418 N.Y.S.2d 244 (App. Div. 1979) (absolute right to inspect balance sheets under N.Y. Bus. Corp. Law § 624(e) (McKinney 1986)).

22. Stern v. S. Chester Tube Co., 390 U.S. 606 (1968) (construing Pa. statute); Miles v. Bank of Heflin, 349 So. 2d 1072 (Ala. 1977).

23. *E.g.*, State *ex rel.* Foster v. Standard Oil Co. of Kan., 18 A.2d 235, 240 (Del. Super. 1941).

24. *See, e.g.*, People v. Pacheco, 29 Cal. 210 (1865).

25. *In re* De Vengoechea, 91 A. 314 (N.J. Sup. Ct. 1914) (mandamus denied due to petitioner's hostile motive).

26. *Otis-Hidden*, 219 S.W. 191.

27. Del. Code Ann. tit. 8, § 220(c) (2009).

28. Model Business Corp. Act § 16.04(a), (b) (2008).

29. The Public Utility Holding Company Act of 2005, 42 U.S.C. § 16451 (2009).

30. Kerkorian v. W. Air Lines, Inc., 253 A.2d 221, 225 (Del. Ch.), *aff'd*, 254 A.2d 240 (Del. 1969).

31. Shamrock Assoc. v. Tex. Am. Energy Corp., 517 A.2d 658 (Del. Ch. 1986).

32. Luxottica Group S.p.A. v. U.S. Shoe Corp., 919 F. Supp. 1091 (S.D. Ohio 1995).

33. *See, e.g.*, Cohen v. Cocoline Prods., Inc., 127 N.E.2d 906 (N.Y. 1955). *See* William C. McLaughlin, *Director's Right to Inspect the Corporate Books and Records—Absolute or Otherwise*, 22 Bus. Law. 413 (1967).

34. *E.g.*, Cal. Corp. Code § 1602 (2009).

35. Kortum v. Webasto Sunroofs, Inc., 769 A.2d 113 (Del. Ch. 2000).

36. *See, e.g., id.* (prima facie showing of entitlement to documents made by allegation requesting party is a director).
37. Wilkins v. M. Ascher Silk Corp., 201 N.Y.S. 739 (App. Div. 1923), *aff'd*, 143 N.E. 748 (N.Y. 1924).
38. *See* Saline v. Super. Ct. of Orange Cnty., 122 Cal. Rptr. 2d 813 (Cal. App. 2002).
39. *See, e.g., Kortum*, 769 A.2d 113 (Del Ch. 2000) (reasonable limits may be imposed if proven director's agent's interests conflict with those of the corporation and the corporation failed to meet its burden of proving that the director or agent has such a conflict; the court was satisfied that the director was not competing with the corporation *when* the request was made).
40. Chappel v. Applied Control Sys., Inc., 39 Pa. D. & C. 4th 168 (Com. Pl. 1998) (access would be denied if established requesting director was employee of competitor).
41. *See, e.g.,* Kelley v. Heritage Nat'l Bank, 897 S.W.2d 96 (Mo. Ct. App. 1995) (director's inspection rights based on necessity for knowledge to discharge duties and, therefore, *former* director's access was denied).
42. *See, e.g., Saline*, 122 Cal. Rptr. 2d 813 (Cal. App. 2002).
43. *See, e.g.,* McGowan v. Empress Entm't, Inc., 791 A.2d 1 (Del. Ch. 2000) (equitable to permit recovery of attorneys fees upon showing of bad faith denial of request).
44. De La Vergne Refrigerating Mach. Co. v. German Sav. Inst., 175 U.S. 40 (1899).
45. Cal. Corp. Code § 603(a) (2009); Del. Code Ann. tit. 8, §§ 228, 275(c) (2009); N.Y. Bus. Corp. Law § 615 (McKinney 1986); Tex. Bus. Corp. Act Ann. art 9.10 (2009).
46. Model Business Corp. Act § 7.04(a) (2008) [hereinafter MBCA]; Former Model Business Corp. Act § 145 (1969) [hereinafter Former MBCA].
47. Cal. Corp. Code § 603(a) (2009) (authorizes action by consent of as many shareholders as would be needed to pass the action at a meeting unless the articles of incorporation provide otherwise); Del. Code Ann. tit. 8, §§ 228, 275(c) (2001) (same as California except that unanimous consent is necessary for dissolution).
48. Del. Code Ann. tit. 8, § 228 (2009). *See also* Ark. Code Ann. § 4-27-704 (2009); Fla. Stat. Ann. § 607.0704 (West 2001); Wis. Stat. Ann. § 180.0704 (2009).
49. *See* Cal. Corp. Code § 603 (2009); Del. Code Ann. tit. 8, § 228 (2009); Ill. Comp. Stat. Ann. ch. 805, ¶ 5/7.10 (2009).
50. Calumet Indus. v. MacClure, 464 F. Supp. 19 (N.D. Ill. 1978).
51. *See, e.g.,* Saxon Indus. v. NKFW, 488 A.2d 1298 (Del. 1984) (even though corporation was in Chapter 11 bankruptcy, reorganization does not override strong public policy of annual stockholders' meetings).
52. Former MBCA § 28 (1969) (the right is not absolute in that the shareholder cannot demand that the meeting be held on the bylaw date because the statute gives a 13-month period); Model Business Corp. Act § 7.01 (2008) (no express 13-month period). *See also* Cal. Corp. Code § 600(b) (2009); Del. Code Ann. tit. 8, § 211(b) (2009); N.Y. Bus. Corp. Law § 602(b) (2009).

53. *See, e.g.,* Morris v. Thomason, 672 So. 2d 433 (La. Ct. App. 1996) (directors could not be elected at a special meeting when articles call for their election at annual meeting).
54. *See* Morrill v. Little Falls Mfg. Co., 55 N.W. 547 (Minn. 1893).
55. MBCA § 7.05 (no fewer than 10, nor more than 60 days before the meeting) (2008); Former MBCA § 29 (1969) (no fewer than 10 nor more than 60 days before the meeting). In counting the number of days, it is proper to exclude either the date of mailing or the date of the meeting, but not both. *See* Hebert v. Stansbury, 248 So. 2d 873 (La. Ct. App.), *writ ref'd*, 253 So. 2d 61 (La. 1971).
56. MBCA § 7.05(b) (2008).
57. "Special meetings of the shareholders may be called by the board of directors, the holders of not less than one-tenth of all the shares entitled to vote at the meeting, or such other persons as may be authorized in the articles of incorporation or the bylaws." MBCA § 7.02 (2008); Former MBCA § 28 (1969).
58. The Model Act as enacted in most states permits the call of a special meeting by holders of 10 precent of the votes entitled to be cast. In 1995, the Model Act was amended to permit the articles of incorporation to provide for a lower percentage or a higher percentage up to 25 percent. MBCA § 7.02(a)(2).
59. *E.g.,* MBCA § 7.02(a)(2) (2008).
60. *Id.*
61. *See, e.g.,* Cullen v. Milligan, 575 N.E.2d 123 (Ohio 1991) (proper to call a meeting for shareholders to consider an offer to acquire company's assets as well as to fill vacancies on the board).
62. *See, e.g.,* Siegman v. Palomar Med. Techs., Inc., 1998 WL 51736 (Del. Ch. 1998) (denying request for meeting to approve settlement of litigation on terms proposed by the petitioner).
63. *In re* Hammond, 139 F. 898 (S.D.N.Y. 1905); Scanlan v. Snow, 2 App. D.C. 137 (1894).
64. For a case intimating that notice may even arise by custom, *see* State *ex rel.* East Cleveland Democratic Club, Inc. v. Bibb, 470 N.E.2d 257 (Ohio Ct. App. 1984).
65. *See, e.g.,* ABA Section of Bus. Law, Committee on Corporate Laws, *Changes in the Model Business Corporation Act—Proposed Amendments to Incorporate Electronic Technology Amendments*, 64 BUS. LAW. 1129 (2009) (defining in section 1.40(6A), (7A), and (28) that a "writing" includes an electronic record which in turn means "information stored in an electronic or other medium and is retrievable in paper form through an automated process used in conventional commercial practice").
66. People v. Albany & Susquehanna R.R., 55 Barb. 344 (1869), *aff'd*, 12 Sickels 161, 57 N.Y. 161 (1874).
67. S. School Dist. v. Blakeslee, 13 Conn. 227 (1839); State v. Bonnell, 35 Ohio St. 10 (1879).
68. Miller v. English, 21 N.J.L. 317 (1848); Am. Primitive Soc'y v. Pilling, 24 N.J.L. 653 (1855).

69. Del. Code Ann. tit. 8, § 211(a) (2009).
70. Handley v. Stutz, 139 U.S. 417 (1891).
71. Dolan v. Airpack, Inc., 513 N.E.2d 213 (Mass. App. Ct.), *aff'd*, 513 N.E.2d 217 (Mass. 1987).
72. Lofland v. Di Sabatino, 1991 WL 138505 (Del. Ch. 1991).
73. Darvin v. Belmont Indus., Inc., 199 N.W.2d 542 (Mich. Ct. App. 1972); Block v. Magee, 537 N.Y.S.2d 215 (Sup. Ct. App. Div. 1989) (attended meeting, voted no and conspicuous absence from minutes of shareholder's signature).
74. *See* Cal. Corp. Code § 601 (2009); Ill. Comp. Stat. Ann., ch. 805, ¶ 5/7.20 (2009); N.Y. Bus. Corp. Law § 606 (2009); MBCA § 7.06 (2008).
75. Gim v. Jan Chin, Inc., 362 A.2d 143 (R.I. 1976).
76. *See, e.g.*, Ark. Code Ann. § 4-27-707 (2009); Del. Code Ann. tit 8, § 213 (2009); N.Y. Bus. Corp. Law § 604 (2009); MBCA § 7.07 (2008) (no greater than 70 days before meeting).
77. *See, e.g.*, Del. Code Ann. tit 8, § 219 (2009); Ill. Comp. Stat. Ann. ch. 805, ¶ 5/7.30 (2009); N.J. Stat. Ann. § 14A:5–8 (2009); MBCA § 7.20 (2008).
78. Sylvania & G. R.R. v. Hoge, 59 S.E. 806 (Ga. 1907); Morrill v. Little Falls Mfg. Co., 55 N.W. 547, 549 (Minn. 1893) ("[I]t is immaterial whether the number present is only one or more than one").
79. Former MBCA § 32 (1969) ("Unless otherwise provided in the articles of incorporation, a majority of the shares entitled to vote . . . shall constitute a quorum at a meeting of shareholders, but in no event shall a quorum consist of less than one-third . . ."); MBCA § 7.25 (2008) (same minimum requirements).
80. *See* Providence & Worcester Co. v. Baker, 378 A.2d 121 (Del. 1977).
81. *See, e.g.*, Williams v. Geier, 671 A.2d 1368 (Del. 1996).
82. Model Business Corp. Act § 7.25(a) (2008).
83. Testa v. Jarvis, 1994 WL 30517, 19 Del. J. Corp. L. 1321 (Del. Ch. 1994).
84. *Id.* (withdrawal from meeting of one of two 50 percent holders is tantamount to adjournment).
85. *See* Me. Rev. Stat. Ann. tit. 13-C, § 705 (2009) (requiring notice if there is a new record date); Cal. Corp. Code § 601 (2009) (45 days).
86. *See* Del. Code Ann. tit. 8, § 222 (2009); Fla. Stat. Ann. § 607.0705 (2009); Wash. Rev. Code Ann. § 23B.07.050 (2009).
87. Woodward & Lothrop, Inc. v. Schnabel, 593 F. Supp. 1385 (D.D.C. 1984).
88. Hill v. Town, 138 N.W. 334 (Mich. 1912).
89. Inhabitants of First Parish in Sudbury v. Stearns, 38 Mass. (21 Pick.) 148 (1838).
90. Delaware has upheld an arrangement one vote per 20 shares for all additional shares of a single holder. *Providence & Worcester Co.*, 378 A.2d 121.
91. MBCA § 7.01(b) (2008); Former MBCA § 32 (1969). Extraordinary voting and quorum requirements are frequent control devices in the closely held enterprise.
92. *E.g.*, Neb. Rev. Stat. Ann. §§ 21-2057, 2072 (2009). *See* Chapter 25.

93. *See* Elliott Assoc., L.P. v. Avatex Corp., 715 A.2d 843 (Del. 1998) (class vote when rights adversely affected by "merger, consolidation or otherwise" arises when firm is acquired).

94. Delaware also provides a sweeping definition of what constitutes "electronic transmission." *See* Del. Code Ann. tit. 8, § 232(c) (2001) (defining to cover any form of communication that does not directly involve the physical transmission of paper, so long as a record of the communication is such that it can be retained, retrieved, and reviewed by its recipient and as long as the recipient can reproduce the communication in paper form by automated process).

95. Del. Code Ann. tit. 8, § 211(a) (2009).

96. *See, e.g.*, Ariz. Rev. Stat. § 10-708 (2009) ("sole" discretion of board); Cal. Corp. Code § 600(a) (2009) ("sole" discretion of board); Colo. Rev. Stat. Ann. § 7-107-108 (2009) (as authorized in articles of incorporation or bylaws) Del. Code Ann. tit. 8, § 211(a)(2) ("sole" discretion of the board); Fla. Stat. § 607.0701(4) (discretion of the board).

97. Del. Code Ann. tit. 8, § 211(b) (2009).

98. *See, e.g.*, 805 ILCS 5/705 (2009); Ind. Code § 23-1-29-1(d) (2009).

99. *See, e.g.*, Conn. Gen. Stat. Ann. § 33-603(a) (2009) ("Notice by electronic transmission is written notice"); Fla. Stat. Ann. § 607.0141 (2009) ("notice may be communicated . . . by . . . other electronic means").

100. *See* Del. Code Ann. tit. 8, § 232 (2009).

101. *See, e.g.*, Mich. Comp. L. Ann. § 450.1421 (2009); Nev. Rev. Stat. Ann. § 78.355(2)(b) (2009); N.Y. Bus. Corp. L. § 609 (2009); N.C. Gen. Stat. Ann. § 55-7-22(b) (2009).

102. *See* Del. Code Ann. tit. 8, § 228(d) (2009) (authorizing electronically executed written consents).

103. Rule 14a-16, 17 C.F.R. § 240.14a-16. adopted in SEC Securities Exchange Act Rel. No. 34-56135 (July 26, 2007).

104. *See* ABA Corporate Governance Committee, Handbook for the Conduct of Meetings (2001) (calling for parliamentary procedures to be replaced by a strong concentration of authority in a chair who must operate pursuant a fairness standard).

105. *See, e.g.*, Del. Code Ann. tit. 8, § 242(b)(1) (2009) (specifying that every amendment "shall be made and effected" in the manner described); MBCA §§ 10.02, 10.03 (2008); Former MBCA § 59 (1969).

106. *See, e.g.*, Mass. Ann. Laws ch. 156, § 42 (2009) (amendment may be authorized by a vote of two-thirds of each class of outstanding stock entitled to vote, or by a larger vote as provided in the charter).

107. *See* Republic Corp. v. Carter, 253 N.Y.S.2d 280 (App. Div. 1964), *aff'd*, 204 N.E.2d 206 (N.Y. 1964).

108. *In re* Giant Portland Cement Co., 21 A.2d 697, 701 (Del. Ch. 1941).

109. Bryan v. Western Pac. Ry., 35 A.2d 909 (Del. Ch. 1944).

110. *See, e.g.*, Mariner LDC v. Stone Container Corp., 729 A.2d 267, 273 (Del. Ch. 1998) (preferred shares not entitled to vote on acquisition though the articles of incorporation were amended to accord preferred full voting rights prior to merger because the date of record was set before the amendment).

111. Former MBCA § 30 (1969). *See* DEL. CODE ANN. tit. 8, § 213 (2009) (no more than 60 days in advance); ILL. COMP. STAT. ANN. ch. 805, ¶ 5/7.25 (2009) (no more than 60 days in advance); N.Y. BUS. CORP. LAW § 604 (2009).
112. MBCA § 7.07 (2008).
113. *In re* Algonquin Elec. Co., 61 F.2d 779 (2d Cir. 1932).
114. Bernheim v. Louisville Property Co., 221 F. 273 (W.D. Ky. 1914) (Ky. law).
115. Lawrence v. I.N. Parlier Estate Co., 100 P.2d 765 (1940).
116. *Gim*, 362 A.2d 143 (R.I. 1976).
117. *See* Former MODEL BUSINESS CORP. ACT § 33 (1969). *Cf.* MODEL BUSINESS CORP. ACT §§ 7.21, 7.24 (2008).
118. Sutliff v. Aydelott, 27 N.E.2d 529 (Ill. 1940).
119. MBCA § 7.24(b)(5) (2008); Former MBCA § 33 (1969).
120. MBCA § 7.24(b)(5) (2008).
121. Tornga v. Mich. Gas & Elec. Co., 144 N.W.2d 640 (Mich. Ct. App. 1966).
122. People *ex rel.* Courtney v. Botts, 34 N.E.2d 403 (Ill. 1941).
123. Commonwealth *ex rel.* Cartwright v. Cartwright, 40 A.2d 30 (Pa. 1944) (decided under Pa. statute: PA. STAT. ANN. tit. 15, § 1608 (1967)).
124. Former MBCA § 2(h) (1969). Recent amendments to the Model Act abolish the concept of Treasury shares. See §§ 21.9 to 21.11. A corporation's acquisition of its own shares is discussed in Chapter 21.
125. Atterbury v. Consol. Coppermines Corp., 20 A.2d 743, 747 (Del. Ch. 1941).
126. Tapper v. Boston Chamber of Commerce, 126 N.E. 464 (Mass. 1920).
127. Granite Brick Co. v. Titus, 226 F. 557 (4th Cir. 1915).
128. State *ex rel.* Washington Indus., Inc. v. Shacklett, 512 S.W.2d 284 (Tenn. 1974).
129. *See* Graves v. Sec. Trust Co., 369 S.W.2d 114 (Ky. 1963).
130. Golden State Theatre & Realty Corp. v. C.I.R., 125 F.2d 641, 642–43 (9th Cir. 1942). See § 21.9.
131. Speiser v. Baker, 525 A.2d 1001 (Del. Ch. 1987) (subsidiary barred from voting shares of its parent though parent owned less than majority of the subsidiary's shares).
132. *See* MBCA § 7.21(b) (2008); MINN. STAT. ANN. § 302A.447(2) (2008).
133. Maddock v. Vorclone Corp., 147 A. 255 (Del. Ch. 1929).
134. Dulin v. Pac. Wood & Coal Co., 35 P. 1045 (Cal.), *aff'd per curiam*, 37 P. 207 (Cal. 1894).
135. Zierath Combination Drill Co. v. Croake, 131 P. 335 (Cal. Ct. App. 1913).
136. Wright v. Cent. Cal. Colony Water Co., 8 P. 70 (Cal. 1885).
137. Reducing the number of directors to be voted for reduces the chances of minority representation. Accordingly, some corporations, in an attempt to dilute minority representation, have staggered the terms of directors. *See, e.g.*, McDonough v. Copeland Refrigeration Corp., 277 F. Supp. 6 (E.D. Mich. 1967).
138. Claudia H. Allen, *Majority Voting in Director Elections: The New Prevailing Standard*, 22 No. 9 CORP. COUNS. (2008) (in the first year, 12 stockholder proposals were filed asking boards to adopt majority voting for director elections).

139. *See, e.g.*, MBCA § 8.05(e) (2005); DEL. CODE ANN. tit. 8, § 141(b) (2009).

140. 75 DEL. LAWS, c. 306, § 5 (2006) (codified at DEL. CODE ANN. tit. 8, § 216 (2009)).

141. MD. CODE ANN., Corps. & Ass'ns § 2-504(f) (2009).

142. *See, e.g.*, IBS Fin. Corp. v. Seidman & Assocs., LLC, 136 F.3d 940, 944–45 (3d Cir. 1998); Accipiter Life Sciences Fund, L.P. v. Helfer, 905 A.2d 115, 125 (Del. Ch. 2006).

143. Schnell v. Chris-Craft Indus., Inc., 285 A.2d 437 (Del. 1971).

144. *Id.*

145. 564 A.2d 651 (Del. Ch. 1988) (Chancellor Wm. Allen).

146. *See, e.g.*, Linton v. Everett, 1997 WL 441189 (Del. Ch. 1997) (after failing to convene stockholders' meeting for three years, called meeting with only 30 days' notice that, in granting injunction, court reasoned effectively prevented opposition slate being put forth).

147. *See, e.g.*, Cone's Ex'rs v. Russell, 21 A. 847, 849 (N.J. Ch. 1891).

148. *See, e.g.*, Priddy v. Edelman, 883 F.2d 438, 445 (6th Cir. 1989) Waters v. Double L, Inc., 769 P.2d 582, 583–84 (Idaho 1989).

149. 447 A.2d 17 (Del. Ch. 1982).

150. *Id.*

151. *Id.*

152. *See, e.g.*, Portnoy v. Cryo-Cell Intern., Inc., 940 A.2d 43 (Del. Ch. 2008) (adding stockholder to management's slate of nominees in exchange for his support in a proxy fight did not constitute illegal vote-buying).

153. *See* N.Y. BUS. CORP. L. § 609(e) (2009) ("A shareholder shall not sell his vote or issue a proxy to vote to any person for a sum of money or anything of value."); MONT. CODE ANN. § 35-1-525(9) (2009).

154. Delaware provides the following definition of coercion:

> Wrongful coercion may exist where the board or some other party takes actions which have the effect of causing the stockholders to vote in favor of the proposed transaction for some reason other than the merits of that transaction. . . . [T]he determination whether a particular stockholder vote has been robbed of its effectiveness by impermissible coercion depends on the facts of the case.

Williams v. Geier, 671 A.2d 1368, 1382–83 (Del. 1996).

155. Coercion is a major consideration for evaluating defensive tactics and claims that shareholders were coerced arise frequently in the broader context of defensive measures. *See, e.g.* Omnicare, Inc. v. NCS Healthcare, Inc., 818 A.2d 914 (Del. 2003) (merger became coercive when directors agreed to submit matter to stockholders for approval and the holders of a majority of the shares had contractually bound themselves to vote in favor of the merger); Orman v. Cullman, 2004 WL 2348395 (Del. Ch. 2004). *See also* Lacos Land Co. v. Arden Grp., Inc., 517 A.2d 271 (Del. Ch. 1986).

156. *See Williams*, 671 A.2d at 1383–84 (announcing that majority stockholder will approve recapitalization so that result is assured is not coercive); Gradient OC Master LTD v. NBC Universal, Inc., 930 A.2d 104 (Del.

Ch. 2007) (not coercive to condition exchange of preferred shares on their waiving protective covenants and providing as well that junior preferred shares would be converted to debt if less than 90 percent of the preferred accepted the exchange offer).

157. Eisenberg v. Chicago Milwaukee Corp., 537 A.2d 1051, 1061 (Del. Ch. 1987).
158. *See* Reynolds Health Care Services, Inc. v. HMNH, Inc., 217 S.W.3d 797 (Ark. 2005) (distinguishing proxy from voting agreement by the latter commanding how the shares are to be voted whereas the former merely grants the power to vote the shares).
159. *E.g.*, Eliason v. Englehart, 733 A.2d 944, 946 (Del. 1999).
160. *See* Preston v. Allison, 650 A.2d 646 (Del. 1994) (trustee of ESOP breached fiduciary obligations to plan participants by voting shares counter to participants' wishes).
161. Rice & Hutchins, Inc. v. Triplex Shoe Co., 147 A. 317, 322 (Del. Ch. 1929), *aff'd*, 152 A. 342 (Del. 1930).
162. *Id.* 317.
163. Taylor v. Griswold, 14 N.J.L. 222 (1834); Pohl v. R.I. Food Dealers Ass'n, 7 A.2d 267 (R.I. 1939).
164. See Chapter 9, §§ 9.7 to 9.10.
165. *See* MBCA § 7.22(a) (2008); Former MBCA § 33 (1969).
166. People's Home Sav. Bank v. Super. Ct., 38 P. 452 (Cal. 1894). A bylaw providing that no proxy shall be voted by one not a shareholder is unreasonable and invalid.
167. McClean v. Bradley, 282 F. 1011 (N.D. Ohio 1922), *aff'd*, 299 F. 379 (6th Cir. 1924).
168. Raible v. Puerto Rico Ind. Dev. Co., 392 F.2d 424 (1st Cir. 1968) (reducing par value with the effect of reducing foreclosure costs to pledge).
169. Bache v. Cent. Leather Co., 81 A. 571 (N.J. Ch. 1911).
170. *See* North Fork Bancorp., Inc. v. Toal, 825 A.2d 860 (Del. Ch. 2000).
171. *See* Dynamics Corp. of Am. v. CTS Corp., 643 F. Supp. 215 (N.D. Ill. 1986) (recognizing strong presumption of proxy validity so that accepted telegraphed proxy even though signature was absent).
172. Schott v. Climax Molybdenum Co., 154 A.2d 221 (Del. Ch. 1959).
173. Atterbury v. Consol. Coppermines Corp., 20 A.2d 743 (Del. Ch. 1941).
174. *See, e.g.*, Mainiero v. Microbyx Corp., 699 A.2d 320 (Del. Ch. 1996).
175. MBCA § 7.22(b) (2008).
176. *See, e.g.*, ILL. COMP. STAT. ANN. ch. 805, § 5/7.50 (2009); N.Y. BUS. CORP. L. § 609 (2009); MBCA § 7.22(c) (2008).
177. *In re* Chilson, 168 A. 82 (Del. Ch. 1933).
178. Concord Fin. Grp., Inc. v. Tri-State Motor Transit Co., 567 A.2d 1 (Del. Ch. 1989) (proxies having same date of execution, the proxy with the later postmark was counted).
179. *See* State *ex rel.* Breger v. Rusche, 39 N.E.2d 433 (Ind. 1942).
180. Restatement (Third) of Agency § 3.12 (2006); Restatement (Second) of Agency, §§ 120 to 123 (1988).
181. Smith v. San Francisco & N.P. Ry., 47 P. 582 (Cal. 1897).
182. Abercrombie v. Davies, 123 A.2d 893, 906–07 (Del. Ch. 1956), *rev'd on other grounds*, 130 A.2d 338 (Del. 1957).

183. *See* Calumet Ind., Inc. v. MacClure, 464 F. Supp. 19 (N.D. Ill. 1978).

184. *See In re* Chilson, 168 A. 82, 86 (Del. Ch. 1933). *Cf.* Smith v. Biggs Boiler Works Co., 82 A.2d 372 (Del. Ch. 1951).

185. *See* Deibler v. Chas. H. Elliot Co., 81 A.2d 557 (Pa. 1951).

186. *See* Chew v. Inverness Mgmt. Corp., 352 A.2d 426 (Del. Ch. 1976).

187. Schreiber v. Carney, 447 A.2d 17 (Del. Ch. 1982).

188. MBCA § 7.22(d) (2008).

189. *See* Idaho Power Co., SEC No-Action Letter, Fed. Sec. L. Rep. (CCH) ¶ 77,224 (Mar. 13, 1996) (interpreting Rule 14a-4(c)(1)).

190. Berendt v. Bethlehem Steel Corp., 154 A. 321, 322 (N.J. Ch. 1931).

191. Sheldon E. Bernstein & Henry G. Fischer, *The Regulation of the Solicitation of Proxies: Some Reflections on Corporate Democracy*, 7 U. Chi. L. Rev. 226, 227 (1940).

192. Rascovor v. Am. Linseed Co., 135 F. 341 (2d Cir. 1905) (newspaper advertisement of proposal for exchange of stock).

193. In practice this enables management to perpetuate itself and control the corporation.

194. Levin v. Metro-Goldwyn-Mayer, Inc., 264 F. Supp. 797 (S.D.N.Y. 1967); Rosenfield v. Fairchild Eng'g & Airplane Corp., 128 N.E.2d 291 (N.Y. 1955).

195. Steinberg v. Adams, 90 F. Supp. 604 (S.D.N.Y. 1950).

196. CA Inc. v. AFSCME Employees Pension Plan, 953 A.2d 227 (Del. 2008).

197. *See* Del. Code Ann. tit. 8, § 112; MBCA § 2.06(c) (2009). *See generally* Committee on Corporate Laws, ABA Section of Business Law, *Changes in the Model Business Corporation Act–Proposed Shareholder Proxy Access Amendments to Chapters 2 and 10*, 64 Bus. Law. 1157 (2009). The official comment provides that section (d) of the provision "allows directors to ensure that such bylaws adequately provide for a reasonable, practicable, and orderly process, but is not intended to allow the board of directors to frustrate the purpose of a shareholder-adopted proxy access or expense reimbursement provision." *Id.* at 1159.

198. *See* Del. Code Ann. tit. 8, § 113; MBCA § 2.06(c) (2009).

199. 15 U.S.C. § 78n(a) (2009).

200. This includes any security traded on a national exchange as well as any class of equity securities with 2,000 or more shareholders of record but retains the former 500 record holder threshold with respect to investors who are not accredited investors. Section 12(g)(1)(A), 15 U.S.C.A. § 78l(g)(1)(A) as amended by the Jumpstart Our Business Startups Act (JOBS Act), H.R. 3606, 112 Cong. 2d sess. § 501 (2012). The record holder calculation excludes shareholders who receive shares as part of an employee compensation plan that is exempt from 1933 Act registration. Section 12(g) was also amended to exclude from the shareholder calculation holders of shares issued pursuant to an exempt crowdfunding offering. *See also* § 12(g), 15 U.S.C. § 781(g), Rule 3a12-3, 17 C.F.R. § 240.3a12-3, exempts foreign issuers from the proxy rules.

201. *See, e.g.*, Schedule 14A, 17 C.F.R. § 240.14a-101 (2009).

202. Rule 14a-4(c), 17 C.F.R. § 240.14a-4(c).

203. 17 C.F.R. § 240.14a-4 (2009). The standing of shareholders to privately enforce Rule 14a-4's proscription of the impermissible grouping of voting items was recognized in *Koppel v. 4987 Corp.*, 167 F.3d 125 (2d Cir. 1999).

204. The Commission specifies in great detail the types of information, both financial and otherwise, that must be disclosed. General Rules & Regulations, Securities Exchange Act of 1934, 17 C.F.R. §§ 240.14a-1 *et seq.* (2002).

205. A director's track record, including remuneration and potential conflicts of interest, is relevant to the shareholder's election decision. Berkman v. Rust Craft Greeting Cards, Inc., 454 F. Supp. 787, 789 (S.D.N.Y. 1978).

206. 15 U.S.C. §§ 78n, 78u (2009).

207. 17 C.F.R. § 240.10b-5 (2009).

208. J.I. Case Co. v. Borak, 377 U.S. 426 (1964). See *infra* § 13.32.

209. Rule 14a-16, 17 CFR § 240.14a-16 (2009).

210. 17 C.F.R. § 240.14a-8 (2009).

211. Business Roundtable v. SEC, 905 F.2d 406, 410–12 (D.C. Cir. 1990).

212. General Rules & Regulations, Securities Exchange Act of 1934, 17 C.F.R. § 240.14a-1 (2009).

213. *See* Union Pac. R.R. v. Chicago & N.W. Ry., 226 F. Supp. 400 (N.D. Ill. 1964).

214. Studebaker Corp. v. Gittlin, 360 F.2d 692, 696 (2d Cir. 1966), citing SEC v. Okin, 132 F.2d 784 (2d Cir. 1943).

215. *See* Sargent v. Genesco, Inc., 492 F.2d 750 (5th Cir. 1974).

216. *See* EXCHANGE ACT Release No. 34-31326 (Oct. 16, 1992).

217. In *MONY Grp., Inc. v. Highfields Capital Mgmt., LP*, 368 F.3d 138 (2d Cir. 2004), a shareholder who opposed merger wrote to other shareholders asking them to oppose the merger, including in the communication a duplicate copy of the proxy card earlier circulated by management.

218. 17 C.F.R. § 240.14a-12 (2009).

219. Rule 14a-17, 17 C.F.R. § 240.14a-17.

220. Rule 14a-2(b)(6), 17 C.F.R. § 240.14a-2(b)(6).

221. Section 14(b) of the EXCHANGE ACT, 15 U.S.C. § 78n(b) (2009). *See, e.g.*, SEC, STREET NAME STUDY (1976).

222. 15 U.S.C. § 78n(c) (2009).

223. *See generally* Randall S. Thomas & James F. Cotter, *Shareholder Proposals in the New Millennium: Shareholder Support, Board Response and Market Reaction*, 13 J. CORP. FIN. 368 (2007).

224. General Rules & Regulations, Securities Exchange Act of 1934, 17 C.F.R. § 240.14a-8(c)(1) (2009). Under the most recent version of the rule, a shareholder must be the beneficial owner for at least one year of at least one percent or of $2,000 in market value of the securities entitled to vote. General Rules & Regulations, Securities Exchange Act of 1934, 17 C.F.R. § 240.14a-8(b)(1) (2009). The shareholder may submit no more than one proposal with a supporting statement; there is a maximum 500-word limit. *Id.* § 240.14a-8(d). If these requirements are not met, management may exclude the proposal from its proxy statement even if it is a proper subject for shareholder action under state law.

225. Rule 14a-8(i)(1), 17 C.F.R. § 240.14a-1(i), (j).

226. 953 A.2d 227 (Del. 2008).

227. SEC v. Transamerica Corp., 163 F.2d 511 (3d Cir. 1947), *cert. denied*, 332 U.S. 847 (1948). *See, e.g.*, Bayless Manning, Book Review, 67 YALE L.J. 1477, 1490 (1958).

228. Brooks v. Standard Oil Co., 308 F. Supp. 810 (S.D.N.Y. 1969).

229. *Id.* at 814.
230. *See* Roosevelt v. E.I. Du Pont de Nemours & Co., 958 F.2d 416 (D.C. Cir. 1992).
231. The current version is found in Rule 14a-8(i)(7), 17 C.F.R. § 240-14a-8(i)(7) (2002).
232. Grimes v. Centerior Energy Corp., 909 F.2d 529 (D.C. Cir. 1990). And, a proposal that requires all capital expenditures in excess of $300 million can be excluded because it would require submission to the shareholders of routine expenditures incurred after the $300 million level was met. *See* Grimes v. Ohio Edison Co., 992 F.2d 455 (2d Cir. 1993).
233. Adoption of Amendments Relating to Proposals by Security Holders, Exchange Act Rel. No. 12,999, 41 Fed. Reg. 52,994, 52,998 (Dec. 3, 1976).
234. For a review of the SEC's course after 1976, *see* Amalgamated Clothing & Textile Workers v. Wal–Mart Stores, Inc., 821 F. Supp. 877 (S.D.N.Y. 1993).
235. Cracker Barrel Old Country Stores, Inc. No-Action Letter, 1992 SEC No-Act. LEXIS 984 at *43 (Oct. 13, 1992).
236. *Id.* The SEC's power to make this interpretative change was upheld in *New York City Employees' Retirement Sys. v. SEC*, 45 F.3d 7 (2d Cir. 1995).
237. Amendments to Rules on Shareholder Proposals, Exchange Act Release No. 34-39093, 62 Fed. Reg. 50682-01 (SEC Sept. 26, 1997).
238. Amendments to Rules on Shareholder Proposals, Exchange Act Release No. 34-40018, 1998 WL 254809 (SEC May 21, 1998).
239. Del. Code Ann. tit. 8, § 112 (2009).
240. Business Roundtable v. SEC, 647 F.3d 1144 (D.C. Cir. 2011) ("Here the Commission inconsistently and opportunistically framed the costs and benefits of the rule; failed adequately to quantify the certain costs or to explain why those costs could not be quantified; neglected to support its predictive judgments; contradicted itself; and failed to respond to substantial problems raised by commenters.").
241. J.I. Case Co. v. Borak, 377 U.S. 426 (1964).
242. *See* 15 U.S.C. § 78l (2009).
243. TSC Indus., Inc. v. Northway, Inc., 426 U.S. 438 (1976).
244. Basic, Inc. v. Levinson, 485 U.S. 224, 238 (1988), *quoting with approval* SEC v. Tex. Gulf Sulphur Co., 401 F.2d 833, 849 (2d Cir. 1968) *(en banc)*, *cert. denied*, 394 U.S. 976 (1969).
245. 501 U.S. 1083 (1991).
246. *See* Minzer v. Keegan, 218 F.3d 144 (2d Cir. 2000).
247. *TSC Indus.*, 426 U.S. at 449.
248. *See* Rosenbaum v. Klein, 547 F. Supp. 586 (E.D. Pa. 1982).
249. *See, e.g.*, Abbey v. Control Data Corp., 603 F.2d 724 (8th Cir. 1979); Gaines v. Haughton, 645 F.2d 761 (9th Cir. 1981).
250. *Virginia Bankshares*, 501 U.S. 1083.
251. Mills v. Electric Auto-Lite Co., 396 U.S. 375 (1970).
252. Mills v. Electric Auto-Lite Co., 552 F.2d 1239 (7th Cir. 1977).
253. For a decision refusing to compel a new proxy solicitation even though the earlier consents were obtained by material misrepresentations, *see* Yamamoto v. Omiya, 564 F.2d 1319 (9th Cir. 1977) (such a cancellation

believed to give innocent third party buyer a right to recover damages in an amount greater than the likely loss caused by the omission itself).

254. Detroit Edison Co. v. SEC, 119 F.2d 730, 739 (6th Cir. 1941).

255. See Chapter 14.

256. Sagusa, Inc. v. Magellan Petrol. Corp., 1993 WL 512487, 19 Del. J. Corp. L. 1304 (Del. Ch. 1993), *aff'd without opinion*, 650 A.2d 1306 (Del. 1994) (upholding per capita voting).

257. *E.g.*, DEL. CODE ANN. tit. 8, § 151(a) (2009); MBCA § 6.01(c)(1) (2008).

258. William Zebina Ripley, Main Street and Wall Street 86 (1929).

259. MBCA § 10.04(d) (2008); see *infra* Chapter 21, §§ 22.1, 22.13.

260. For example, in *Lehrman v. Cohen*, the Lehrman and Cohen families each held a separate class of stock that enabled each family to elect two directors. A third class of stock with no equity in the company but the power to elect the fifth director was issued to the firm's attorney. The arrangement was intended to avoid deadlocks at the board meetings but was challenged when Cohen was replaced as president by the attorney. The validity of the "voting-only" class of shares was challenged. The Delaware Supreme Court held that the arrangement was not a voting trust subject to a ten-year limit because the shares' holder exercised all voting power; the arrangement was not an unlawful delegation of directors' powers; and public policy was not violated by shares having no proprietary interest. *Lehrman*, 222 A.2d 800 (Del. 1966). See Stroh v. Blackhawk Holding Corp., 272 N.E.2d 1 (Ill. 1971).

261. *E.g.*, DEL. CODE ANN., tit. 8, § 218 (2009); N.Y. BUS. CORP. LAW § 621 (2009); MBCA §§ 7.30, 7.31 (2008).

262. MBCA §§ 7.30, 7.31 (2008).

263. *See* 1 F. HODGE O'NEAL & ROBERT B. THOMPSON, O'NEAL AND THOMPSON'S CLOSE CORPORATIONS AND LLCS: LAW AND PRACTICE §§ 4.17 to 4.18, 4.32, 4.36 to 4.37 & 4.41 (rev. 3d ed. 2009); John J. Woloszyn, *A Practical Guide to Voting Trusts*, 4 U. BALT. L. REV. 245 (1975).

264. *See e.g.*, State *ex rel.* Babione v. Martin, 647 N.E.2d 169 (Ohio Ct. App. 1994), *appeal dismissed*, 646 N.E.2d 178 (Ohio 1995) (agreement did not have formalities necessary for enforceable voting trust nor was it a shareholder pooling agreement).

265. Hall v. Staha, 800 S.W.2d 396 (Ark. 1990).

266. *Id.*; Abercrombie v. Davies, 130 A.2d 338 (Del. 1957).

267. *See* Oceanic Exploration Co. v. Grynberg, 428 A.2d 1 (Del. Super. Ct. 1981) (public policy offended only if noncomplying arrangement was mechanism to secretly acquire control).

268. 1 MODEL BUSINESS CORP. ACT ANN. § 34 comment (2d ed. 1971).

269. *See* Sanchez v. Guerrero, 2000 WL 298910 (N.D. Cal.) (reformation of trust appropriate if purpose is no longer to provide stability to company's operations but to perpetuate control of trustee).

270. *See* Warehime v. Warehime, 761 A.2d 1138 (Pa. 2000).

271. *See* SEC Report, Investment Trusts and Investment Companies, Part III, ch. V, at 1913 (1940).

272. Seward v. Am. Hardware Co., 171 S.E. 650, 659–60 (Va. 1932).

273. An interesting question is whether the voting trusts agreement's requirements with respect to how the trust's shares are to be voted are

binding on the trustee in his dual capacity as a director of the corporation. *See* Anchel v. Shea, 762 A.2d 346, 357 (Pa. Super. 2000) (director acting consistent with his fiduciary obligations as a director is not restrained by express terms of voting trust agreement that apply to his status as a trustee).

274. *See, e.g.*, Regnery v. Meyers, 679 N.E.2d 74 (Ill. Ct. App. 1997) (trustee breached obligation by voting trust's shares to approve company's issuance of shares to him at less than their fair market value; also breach by his co-conspirators).

275. Cal. Corp. Code §§ 706, 711 (2009); Del. Code Ann. tit. 8, § 218(a), (b) (2009); N.Y. Bus. Corp. Law § 621 (2009). *See* MBCA § 7.30 (2008); Former MBCA § 34 (1969).

276. *See Abercrombie*, 130 A.2d 338. *But see* Del. Code Ann. tit. 8, § 218(c) (2009) (inviting enforcement of voting agreements generally according to their terms).

277. *See* Reserve Life Ins. Co. v. Provident Life Ins. Co., 499 F.2d 715 (8th Cir. 1974) (omitted address of trustee); Oceanic Exploration Co. v. Grynberg, 428 A.2d 1 (Del. Super. Ct. 1981) (agreement would be struck down as illegal voting trust only if noncomplying arrangement offended public policy as a mechanism to secretly acquire control).

278. Earle R. Hanson Assocs. v. Farmers' Coop. Creamery Co., 403 F.2d 65 (8th Cir. 1968).

279. *See* Tankersley v. Albright, 514 F.2d 956 (7th Cir. 1975).

280. Orpheum Bldg. Co. v. Anglim, 127 F.2d 478, 484 (9th Cir. 1942).

281. *See, e.g.*, Uniform Securities Act § 202(28) (2002).

282. 15 U.S.C. §§ 77b(a)(1), 78c(a)(10) (2009).

CHAPTER 14

CLOSELY HELD ENTITIES

TABLE OF SECTIONS

§ 14.1 Close Corporations: Definitions and Distinctive Needs

"Close corporation" (or "closely held corporation") is defined in a number of ways. The term is often used to refer to a corporation with only a few shareholders to distinguish a corporation of that kind from a publicly held company. Summing up the characteristics of a close corporation, a Massachusetts court commented that such a corporation is typified by: "(1) a small number of stockholders; (2) no ready market for the corporate stock; and (3) substantial majority stockholder participation in the management, direction and operations of the corporations."[1]

A number of states have enacted special legislation to define and govern the close corporation. In Delaware and several other states, for example, this special statutory regulation states that a close corporation's charter must provide that (1) its stock shall be held by not more than a specified number of persons; (2) its stock is subject to transfer restrictions; and (3) it shall not engage in public offerings of its stock.[2] In a few states, the special close corporation statute defines "close corporation" simply as any corporation that elects close corporation status for purposes of the statute.[3] As discussed throughout this chapter, courts recognize the special needs of close corporations even in the absence of statute. This special treatment applies even if a corporation elects not to incorporate under a state's special close corporation statute. However, there is authority in Delaware that corporations desiring to be treated as close corporations must elect to do so under the Delaware Close Corporation Act.[4]

A person taking a minority position in a close corporation may desire and therefore bargain for protection against the power of those holding a majority of a corporation's voting stock to make decisions that will prejudice minority interests. Participants may use some kind of contractual arrangement to set up a control pattern for the corporation that differs from the traditional corporation control structure. The arrangement may take the form of a pre-incorporation agreement among the participants, a shareholders' agreement after the corporation has been organized, a voting trust, special charter and bylaw provisions, irrevocable proxies, or employment contracts between the corporation and the shareholder-employees of the corporation. Most of these arrangements and the laws applicable to them are discussed briefly in the sections that follow.

§ 14.2 Shareholders' Agreements: Contents

Participants in close corporations frequently enter into agreements among themselves to provide protection to minority shareholders against the principle of majority rule or to tailor the corporate structure to the participants' particular desires and the needs of the enterprise. Minority shareholders often seek agreements that will provide them with representation on the board of directors or will otherwise give them input in the management of the corporation.[5] Although board membership may give the minority access to information on some decisions being made for the corporation, membership alone provides the minority with very little protection against the power vested in the majority by the principle of majority rule. Consequently, the minority may bargain for power to veto some or all corporate decisions or for some other effective participation in corporate affairs. The majority may agree to share their power with the minority in order to encourage potential shareholders to invest in the enterprise, bring into the enterprise valuable patents or know-how, or provide needed executives or scientifically skilled employees as key members of the company. Shareholders' agreements to which minority shareholders are parties typically cover selection of the members of the board of directors, the naming of corporate officers, employment of shareholders and their salaries, and the amount of time each participant is to devote to the business.[6]

§ 14.3 Forms and Execution of Shareholders' Agreements

A shareholders' agreement may take a number of forms. In a simple shareholders' pooling agreement, the parties agree to vote their shares in the manner set forth in the agreement. The shareholders retain title to their shares and the right to vote them; however, they are contractually bound to vote pursuant to a prearranged plan. A pooling agreement is to be distinguished from a shareholders' management agreement, in which the parties attempt to control corporate decisions that otherwise would be made by the board of directors, such as determining corporate policy, selecting officers, fixing salaries, and declaring dividends.

An agreement among shareholders may involve more than a simple contract binding the parties to vote their shares in a specified way. It may, for example, set up irrevocable proxies for the voting of stock or establish a voting trust whereby the stock held in trust is voted by the trustees in the manner determined by the trust instrument. Further, an agreement among shareholders may be embodied in the corporation's charter or bylaws in addition to or instead of being evidenced by a separate document.[7] More frequently, the objective of a shareholders' agreement is to restrict the freedom of its parties or to arrange their economic rights in a manner different than would follow their proportionate share ownership. A shareholders' agreement is frequently the document that imposes restrictions on the transfer of shares or even contains covenants not to compete. As would be expected, covenants not to compete are subjected to close scrutiny on policy grounds,[8] and transfer restrictions are subjected to a lower level of review, being upheld in the absence of fraud, duress, or undue influence.[9] A shareholders' agreement can also be the device that accords rights on non-shareholders, such as giving a creditor veto power over board financial decisions.[10]

The Delaware Supreme Court in *Nixon v. Blackwell*,[11] expressed less flexibility for its close corporation provisions than most other states. The specific issue before the Delaware court was whether non-employee-shareholders could require the corporation to purchase their shares because the shares held by certain employee-shareholders had been purchased. In ruling against the petitioning minority shareholders, the Delaware Supreme Court expressed its unwillingness to create special ad hoc rules for the participants of a small corporation that had not followed the formal procedures to qualify as a close corporation under Subchapter 14 of the Delaware General Corporation Law. The court concluded that a corporation failing to so qualify is not governed by Delaware's close corporation provisions.

§ 14.4 VALIDITY OF SHAREHOLDERS' AGREEMENTS ATTACKED BECAUSE THEY LIMIT THE BOARD OF DIRECTORS' DISCRETION OR AUTHORITY

In the past, courts looked with much distrust on shareholders' agreements and often condemned not only dishonest schemes but also any agreement that might conceivably have been injurious to noncontracting shareholders or corporate creditors. Indeed, in some instances courts were overly strict and rejected shareholders' agreements that served a useful purpose and were in the best interest of the corporation and all shareholders and creditors. They applied their concepts of public policy unrealistically, oblivious to the fact that a party to a shareholders' agreement who sets up the illegality of the agreement as a defense often does so simply to escape an honest bargain that has become burdensome.

Most modern statutes provide that shareholders' agreements may stipulate the manner in which the parties will vote their shares,[12] but this does not preclude attacks based on violation of other statutory norms. A common basis for attacking shareholders' control agreements is that they are incompatible with the statutory scheme of corporate management and operation.[13] The statutory section providing that the business of a corporation shall be managed by (or under the supervision of) its board of directors is frequently used to attack the validity of a shareholders' agreement if the agreement purports to control matters within the traditional powers of the directors.[14]

Shareholders' agreements that tend to control directors' actions have often been held invalid even though the agreements were made in good faith and actually were beneficial to the company and its shareholders.[15] Numerous early decisions held that shareholders' agreements, especially agreements by less than all of a corporation's shareholders that restricted the discretion of the directors were invalid as contrary to public policy.[16] The courts reasoned that since the corporation statute provided that the business of a corporation shall be managed by or under the direction of its board of directors,[17] the directors' power of control existed for the benefit of all the shareholders, and they could not bargain away in advance the free exercise of director discretion. Thus shareholders' agreements calling for the election of "sterilized" or dummy directors who would place or maintain designated persons in the corporation's employment were generally held void.[18] Today courts in most states will enforce agreements restricting or eliminating director discretion where the agreement is unanimous and does not violate a public policy. When the agreement is less than unanimous, a court may consider the interests of the non-consenting shareholders.[19]

§ 14.5 Shareholders' Reciprocal Pooling Agreements Controlling Voting for Directors

Agreements to vote for specified persons as directors, or to vote as the holders of a majority of the shares in a pool may direct, are valid and binding if they do not contemplate limiting the discretion of the directors or the committing of any fraud, oppression, or wrong against other shareholders. The validity of voting agreements therefore depends on their purposes, effects, and tendencies.[20]

Courts consider a variety of factors when determining the validity of a shareholders' agreement.[21] Before such agreements received based approval in most state statutes, a variety of factors were considered in judging their validity: (1) the purpose or object of the agreement, (2) the statutes in force in the particular jurisdiction in which the agreement is made, (3) the conceptions of public policy prevailing in the courts of the jurisdiction regarding the separation of voting power from the beneficial ownership of shares, (4) the situation of the corporation and the shareholders at the time the agreement was made, (5) whether or not all of the shareholders in the corporation are parties to the agreement, (6) whether the contracting shareholders are also directors or expect to be at the time of the performance of the contract, (7) the length of time during which the agreement will control the shareholders' right to vote their shares, (8) whether the person challenging the validity of the agreement is a party to it or is a creditor or shareholder not party to the agreement, (9) whether the person challenging the agreement is simply trying to "welch" on his undertaking, (10) whether or not there is consideration, other than the mutual promises of the parties to support the undertakings, to vote in accordance with the terms of the agreement, (11) how long the contract has been in operation and the extent to which action has been taken or positions have changed in reliance on it, and (12) the kind of corporation whose stock is subject to the voting arrangement.

Although most modern statutes declare that voting agreements are enforceable according to their terms,[22] this declaration is far from an unlimited validation of all shareholders' agreements. For example, in a famous Delaware case,[23] the court refused to specifically enforce the agreement but instead simply invalidated the votes voted contrary to the agreement. Many states have statutes recognizing a shareholder agreement as a sufficient interest to support an irrevocable proxy. A shareholders' agreement containing a valid irrevocable proxy has the same effect functionally as an ordinary shareholders' pooling agreement that the courts will specifically enforce; it follows that considerations governing the validity of the two should be the same. In either instance, if the agreement has a legitimate business purpose, it should be given effect in accordance with the intentions of the parties. A few states, including Delaware, do not expressly sanction irrevocable proxies tied to a shareholder agreement. In those states, specific enforcement is not guaranteed.

§ 14.6 USE OF CHARTER OR BYLAW PROVISIONS IN LIEU OF SHAREHOLDERS' AGREEMENTS

Objectives sought in shareholders' agreements can sometimes be achieved by using special charter or bylaw provisions. For example, charter or bylaw clauses imposing an extraordinarily high quorum or voting requirement for shareholder and director action have frequently been employed to allocate control within a close corporation. Such provisions have the effect of giving minority shareholders a veto power over corporate decisions. Almost all states now permit a corporation to insert in its charter a provision setting a high vote for shareholder and director action,[24] and some states permit high vote requirements to be placed in either the charter or the bylaws.[25] In addition, some courts hold that a charter or bylaw provision unanimously adopted by the shareholders may be treated as a contract among the shareholders and thus enforceable as long as there are no new nonapproving shareholders.[26] Even though high vote requirements are clearly permitted, their tendency to lead to deadlock has led some courts to construe them strictly so as to minimize their restrictive effect.[27]

Other special charter and bylaw provisions can be used to depart from the traditional corporate management pattern or to grant protection to minority shareholders. Among special provisions that may be found useful in particular circumstances are the following: clauses requiring cumulative voting for directors; clauses abolishing the board of directors or restricting its powers; clauses authorizing or prohibiting informal operation of the corporation; clauses strengthening shareholders' rights to inspect corporate books and records; clauses controlling dividends and other distributions to shareholders; clauses defining shareholders' preemptive rights; clauses dealing with deadlocks among shareholders and directors; clauses imposing restrictions on the transfer of shares; clauses requiring shareholder approval of officer compensation; clauses giving a shareholder power to dissolve the corporation; clauses prohibiting corporate loans to officers or directors; and clauses providing for arbitration or some other method for resolving disputes among the shareholders.

§ 14.7 RESTRICTIONS ON THE TRANSFERABILITY OF SHARES; REASONS FOR RESTRICTIONS; TYPES OF RESTRICTIONS

In the absence of valid restrictions on their transferability, corporate shares are freely transferable, and the corporation may not refuse to accept a bona fide transferee as a shareholder.[28] In publicly held corporations, free transferability of shares is a valuable attribute in that it encourages contributions to corporate capital by a multitude of investors. In closely held corporations, on the other hand, the participants usually do not want shares to be freely transferable. Considerable latitude is allowed the participants in imposing share transfer restrictions; restrictions will usually be sustained unless palpably unreasonable under the circumstances.[29] Restrictions may be imposed by the articles of incorporation, the bylaws,[30] or a shareholders' agreement.

Participants in a close corporation may want to restrict the transferability of shares for a number of reasons. Because of the close working relationship that often exists among owners and managers, they may want to retain power to select future associates and thus be able to exclude persons who will not be congenial or will not fit into the management team. Further, the participants may desire to restrict the transferability of shares to prevent their purchase by competitors or other persons unfriendly to the corporation.[31] They may also impose transfer restrictions to prevent any one shareholder from gaining absolute control of the corporation by purchasing colleagues' stock. Another reason for restricting the transferability of shares is to preserve the corporation's eligibility to elect the tax status provided by Subchapter S of the Internal Revenue Code[32] or its eligibility to elect to be governed by special close corporation legislation in a number of states requiring close corporations to restrict the transfer of their stock.

There are many different types of share transfer restrictions. The most widely used is the so-called first-option or refusal,[33] which grants the corporation or the other shareholders a right to purchase shares at a set price or at the price offered by a third party, respectively, if a holder decides to sell or otherwise transfer her shares.[34] Other types of transfer restrictions are as follows: (1) absolute prohibitions against transfer; (2) prohibitions against transfer to designated classes of persons, such as competitors;[35] (3) limitation of transfers to stated classes of persons—for example, descendants of the corporation's founders or residents of a designated American state; (4) "consent restraints" that prohibit the disposition of stock without approval of the corporation's directors or shareholders or a stated percentage of one of those groups;[36] and (5) options giving the corporation or the other shareholders the right to purchase the shares of a holder on his death or disability,[37] on the termination of his employment with the corporation,[38] or on the occurrence of some other event.[39] Somewhat related functionally to restrictions on the transfer of stock are buyout agreements, whereby the shareholder agrees to sell stock, and the corporation or the other shareholders agree to buy it, on the occurrence of a stated contingency, such as the shareholder's death or retirement. Such an agreement stipulates a transfer price or sets out a formula for determining price.[40] Mention should also be made of charter provisions that empower the corporation to redeem ("call") a holder's stock either generally at the corporation's option or on termination of the holder's employment with the corporation.[41] Courts have often been called on to pass on the validity of transfer restrictions against a claim that the restrictions constitute unreasonable restraints on the alienation of property.

§ 14.8 LEGAL LIMITS ON THE USE OF TRANSFER RESTRICTIONS

Courts have always looked with disfavor on absolute stock transfer restrictions unlimited in time, regardless of whether they are included in a corporation's articles or bylaws, or in a shareholders' agreement.[42] The courts have, however, generally upheld restraints that they consider reasonable in light of all the circumstances.[43] In passing on the validity of transfer restrictions, the courts have considered a number of factors, including the following: the corporation's size, the extent of the restraint on the holder's power to alienate the shares, the length of time the restriction is to remain in effect, and whether the restriction is conducive to the attainment of corporate objectives and otherwise promotes the corporation's best interests. Generally, courts are more willing to recognize the validity of stock transfer restrictions in close corporations than in publicly held enterprises.[44] However, there are limits on the enforceability of clearly unreasonable restrictions.[45]

The validity of transfer restrictions has frequently been challenged where a great disparity exists between the transfer price provided in the restrictions and the value of the shares. A few courts have held that a restriction, such as a first-option provision, which requires the transfer of shares for considerably less than their value, is an unreasonable restraint on alienation and is thus invalid.[46] Shareholders are not likely to sell their shares if they must first offer them to the corporation or other shareholders at a price that is far below their fair value. Thus a large gap between the option price in a first-option arrangement and the current value of shares may for practical purposes effectively create what is virtually an absolute restraint on alienation.[47] Nevertheless, the great majority of the courts have not invalidated transfer restrictions on the basis that they required the transfer of shares at a price below their value. Even when the value of shares has appeared to be 10, 20, or even 1,000 times greater than the transfer price, courts have sustained the restrictions.[48]

Most states have enacted legislation governing the validity of stock transfer restrictions. The wording and the substance of the legislation varies from state to state. The Delaware statute provides that stock transfer restrictions or restrictions on the amount of securities that may be owned by any person or group may be imposed either by a corporation's certificate of incorporation, its bylaws, or an agreement among its security holders or among such holders and the corporation, but that a restriction will not be binding with respect to securities issued before adoption of the restriction unless the holders of the securities are parties to an agreement or voted in favor of the restriction.[49]

§ 14.9 DISSENSION IN THE CLOSE CORPORATION

Dissension among the owners of a close corporation has a heavy impact on the enterprise. Because of the participants' intimately close working relationship, in most close corporations, once dissatisfaction or distrust has developed, intracorporate friction is likely to continue to grow. Dissatisfied shareholders of a publicly held corporation have a ready market for their shares, whereas an interest in a closely held corporation does not have a readily available market, at least if the interest is not a controlling one. The marketability of a minority interest in a close corporation is further narrowed if the corporation is racked by dissension. Even if a buyer can be found for a minority interest, the price may be sharply discounted.[50] Furthermore, the existence of transfer restrictions may enable an antagonistic associate to thwart an unhappy shareholder's sale of close corporation shares. Dissension and the inability of unhappy shareholders to get out sometimes result in serious and continuing strife among the shareholders and managers,[51] and may result in extensive litigation and serious harm to the corporation and the shareholders.[52]

Deadlocks among the shareholders and in the directorates of closely held corporations may occur because of the way voting shares and positions on the board are distributed. Shares are sometimes divided equally among two or more shareholders or groups of shareholders.[53] And it is not unusual for a close corporation to have an even number of directors; thus a deadlock of directors is likely to occur. Further, in an effort to protect themselves against the power generally vested in shareholders and directors to determine corporate policy by simple majority vote, minority shareholders often bargain for and obtain a veto over corporate policies and decisions or condition their approval upon a greater than majority vote.[54] Such a veto power increases the risk of corporate paralysis.[55] As one Virginia court eloquently stated, "A recalcitrant . . . shareholder may embalm his corporation and hold it helpless . . . in a state of suspended animation."[56]

Despite the frequency of dissension and deadlock in close corporations, in some states neither legislatures nor courts have provided satisfactory solutions. Therefore, during the organization of a close corporation, counsel must anticipate such problems and may need to provide special contractual arrangements to resolve them. These arrangements usually are set up in the corporation's charter or bylaws or in a shareholders' agreement. They typically take one or more of the following forms: (a) provisions for the buyout of the interests of aggrieved shareholders, (b) the creation of special dissolution rights and procedures, or (c) undertakings to arbitrate disputes. Further possibilities to consider to avoid locking unhappy shareholders into a corporation for an indefinite period of time are: (d) limiting the life of the corporation rather than giving it perpetual existence, (e) setting up a voting trust that gives trustees the power to vote for dissolution, and, where legal, (f) issuing stock that is convertible into notes or debentures.[57]

§ 14.10 Dissolution for Deadlock

Among the several bases for involuntary dissolution, most corporate statutes include deadlock within the board of directors or among the shareholders. The various statutory expressions are but imprecise attempts to capture the true basis on which courts appear to order dissolution under their provisions—namely, that irreconcilable differences exist between the contesting owners. Deadlock is truly a phenomenon of the closely held corporation; it would not long exist within the public corporation. Thus, when equal owners of a corporation are divided over whether the sole corporate asset should be sold or developed, there is little room for compromise. It is ironic that the remedy available in such a case, an order of dissolution, leads to the very result that the shareholder seeking the asset's sale has sought.[58] Essentially, what is required is proof that the differences between the shareholders are such that it is no longer reasonable to expect that they will be able to resolve their differences.[59] Acrimony is not required, though it may be present.[60]

Statutory requirements such as "irreparable harm" or that the corporation is "unable to conduct business to the shareholders' advantage" are somewhat irrelevant to the courts' inquiry. Courts instead emphasize the deep divisions between the shareholders, the length of those divisions, and the unlikelihood of the division being corrected.[61] Courts do not inquire as to whether a business is going badly or is not expanding. Certainly the latter inquiry is at best problematic. Just how successful would a business be if cohesion existed among its managers and owners? Thus, one can find more to commend in those statutes that authorize dissolution merely on proof of deadlock, believing this is harm enough.

§ 14.11 Oppression; Protecting Reasonable Expectations

When dissension or deadlock occurs in a corporation, the shareholders can voluntarily dissolve the enterprise, but voluntary dissolution requires the affirmative vote of holders of a majority of the shares in some jurisdictions and a two-thirds vote in others.[62] At one time, the courts generally held that unless authority is conferred by statute, courts of equity had no authority over the suit of a minority shareholder to order dissolution of a solvent corporation or to appoint a receiver to distribute its assets and liquidate its affairs.[63] A number of courts, however, recognized that, in the absence of other adequate remedy, there are circumstances under which a court of equity should afford relief to shareholders against fraud and gross mismanagement by appointing a receiver and winding up a solvent corporation.[64] The remedy for deadlock may be used in limited liability companies as well. This is true for oppression by those in control of the LLC.

In many states, modern corporation statutes now expressly give the courts power to dissolve a corporation in a suit by a minority shareholder if the directors and majority shareholders are guilty of fraud, illegality, gross mismanagement, or oppression of minority shareholders, or if such dissension exists among the shareholders that the corporate business cannot be carried on or it appears that a winding up of the corporate affairs is necessary to protect the rights of the complaining shareholder.[65] The corporation statutes vary greatly from state to state both on the kinds of situations that trigger a court's power to dissolve and in the percentage of shares a person must hold to be entitled to petition for dissolution.[66] In some states, the statutory grounds for involuntary dissolution are rather narrow and specific, such as a deadlock in the board of directors that the shareholders cannot break; in other states, the grounds for involuntary dissolution are stated in broad terms, such as for "just or sufficient cause" or "where reasonably necessary for the protection of shareholders."[67]

In a close corporation disgruntled minority shareholders frequently file an action seeking the corporation's dissolution as a means to salvage their investment in the venture. It is therefore safe to say that over the past several decades there has been an extensive and significant melding of fiduciary standards to state involuntary dissolution statutes such that it is difficult to isolate the doctrine of fiduciary obligation in close corporations from involuntary dissolution. Much of the focus in this activity has been on the phrase common to dissolution provisions, "oppression." Difficult though it be to so isolate the two areas, the materials in this chapter will nevertheless make an attempt at doing so. The material in the balance of this section focuses almost entirely on how the courts have used the "reasonable expectations" of the shareholders to guide the court in deciding whether grounds for invoking the state's dissolution statute have been established.

In the typical case, the "reasonable expectation" doctrine emerges in a suit by the minority shareholder seeking a close corporation's dissolution under a statute that authorizes involuntary dissolution when those in control of the company have acted in an oppressive manner, or dissolution is necessary to protect the rights or interests of the petitioning stockholder or stockholders generally. Frequently, the specific dissolution provision is limited to close corporations or corporations with a small number of stockholders. In broad overview, the courts that have embraced the talisman of the shareholder's reasonable expectations consider conduct that defeats those expectations as being oppressive or as grounds for concluding dissolution is necessary for the protection of that shareholder.

To be protectable, expectations should be part of an understanding, explicit or implicit, between the participants in the corporation.[68] In a leading case,[69] the North Carolina Supreme Court held that reasonable expectations should be determined on a case-by-case basis, using the full history of the relationship in question—from inception through any later developments.[70] The expectations must be compared with and known to the other stockholders, so privately held expectations are not reasonable.[71] Furthermore, a minority shareholder's reasonable expectations must be balanced against what is reasonably believed to be in the best interests of the corporation.[72]

The breadth of the reasonable-expectations standard is that, within the close corporation, participation in management—and certainly the receipt of a salary—are the rewards shareholders customarily seek when investing in a close corporation. This therefore conditions the power of the majority to sever the minority stockholder from the firm's payroll on there being either an adequate return to the owners through dividends or just cause for the employee's termination.[73] Even just cause for terminating an employee-owner may not be sufficient to avoid a court's intervention, even though the court refused to protect the salaried position of a co-owner who had engaged in embezzlement, the court nevertheless required the majority to devise some means to provide a financial return commensurate with the petitioning stockholder's investment in the firm.[74] The protection of minority shareholders' interests are not limited to the closely held corporation principles discussed herein. Protectable expectations may exist on the simple basis of an enforceable agreement, even if not in writing.[75]

§ 14.12 FIDUCIARY DUTIES IN THE CLOSE CORPORATION

As the preceding sections of this chapter illustrate, both the legislatures and the courts have recognized the unique needs of the close corporation. In allowing special control devices, such as high vote requirements for shareholder and director action, and shareholders' agreements that control action within the traditional province of the board of directors, the law has increasingly recognized the so-called "incorporated partnership." A concurrent development in recent years has been the recognition of partnership-like fiduciary obligations running between the participants in close corporations.[76] The fiduciary duty exists among the close corporation's stockholders, and in appropriate cases, continues even though the minority stockholder has been frozen out of his position as an officer of the corporation.[77] When dealing with other closely held limited liability entities, such as the limited liability corporation, it is appropriate for courts to look to the fiduciary duties applicable in closely held corporations and partnerships.[78]

Not all jurisdictions, however, embrace the view that participants in a close corporation are subject to "heightened fiduciary responsibilities" or that those responsibilities are necessarily founded on a liberal construction of their reasonable expectations.[79] The Delaware Supreme Court reasoned that it was inappropriate to fashion ad hoc rules according minority shareholders rights not provided them by statute and which were not otherwise contracted for by the shareholders.[80]

NOTES

1. Donahue v. Rodd Electrotype Co., 328 N.E.2d 505, 511 (Mass. 1975).
2. DEL. CODE ANN. tit. 8, § 342(a)(1)–(3) (2001) (30 nominal shareholders).
3. *See, e.g.,* MD. CODE ANN., Corps. & Ass'n § 4-101 (Michie 2007).
4. Nixon v. Blackwell, 626 A.2d 1366 (Del. 1993).
5. *See e.g.,* Anchel v. Shea, 762 A.2d 346, 359–60 (Pa. Super. 2000) (shareholder agreement calling for each employee to be a director prevented voting trust trustee from removing an employee as a director).

6. *See* Sternheimer v. Sternheimer, 155 S.E.2d 41 (Va. 1967) (failure to include provision dealing with amount of time participants are to work for corporation and extent to which outside part-time activities are allowed can lead to dissension and litigation).

7. *See* Hall v. Tenn. Dressed Beef Co., 957 S.W.2d 536 (Tenn. 1997) (bylaw provision treated as contract among shareholders of closely held corporation).

8. *Cf.* State v. Nichols, 683 P.2d 565 (Or. Ct. App. 1984) (client's right to choose counsel would be frustrated by transfer restriction on attorney's shares, which provided a lower price in mandatory buyout provision than if attorney had signed covenant not to compete).

9. *See, e.g.,* Shortridge v. Platis, 458 N.E.2d 301 (Ind. Ct. App. 1984).

10. *See* Westland Capital Corp. v. Lucht Eng'g, Inc., 308 N.W.2d 709 (Minn. 1981) (venture capitalists granted power to overrule capital expenditures in excess of $25,000).

11. 626 A.2d 1366 (Del. 1993).

12. *See* Model Business Corp. Act §§ 7.30, 7.31 (2008) [hereinafter MBCA]; Former Model Business Corp. Act § 34 (1969) [hereinafter Former MBCA].

13. *See* Benintendi v. Kenton Hotel, Inc., 60 N.E.2d 829 (N.Y. 1945) (invalidating bylaws).

14. *See, e.g.,* Conn. Gen. Stat. Ann. § 33–735(b) (2005); Pa. Stat. Ann. tit. 15, § 1721 (Supp. 2009).

15. *E.g.,* Kennerson v. Burbank Amusement Co., 260 P.2d 823 (Cal. Ct. App. 1953).

16. West v. Camden, 135 U.S. 507 (1890).

17. *E.g.,* MBCA § 8.01(b) (1984).

18. *See, e.g.,* Long Park, Inc. v. Trenton-New Brunswick Theatres Co., 77 N.E.2d 633 (N.Y. 1948).

19. *See* Galler v. Galler, 203 N.E.2d 577 (Ill. 1964) (upholding agreement providing for election of certain persons to specified offices for a period of years). *See also, e.g.,* Zion v. Kurtz, 405 N.E.2d 681 (N.Y. 1980); Clark v. Dodge, 199 N.E. 641 (N.Y. 1936).

20. Smith v. San Francisco & N.P. R.R., 47 P. 582 (Cal. 1897).

21. The distinction between a mere proxy and a voting agreement is that the latter sets forth the manner in which the shares are to be voted whereas the former simply gives the holder the authority to vote the shares. *See, e.g.,* Reynolds Health Care Servs., Inc. v. HMNH, Inc., 217 S.W.3d 797 (Ark. 2005).

22. *See* MBCA § 7.31 (2008).

23. Ringling Bros.-Barnum & Bailey Combined Shows, Inc. v. Ringling, 53 A.2d 441 (Del. Supr. 1947), *modifying* 49 A.2d 603 (Del. Ch. 1946).

24. *See, e.g.,* Cal. Corp. Code §§ 204 (West 1990), 602 (West Supp. 2009); Ill. Ann. Stat. ch. 805, §§ 5/7.60, 5/8.15 (Smith-Hurd 2004).

25. *See, e.g.,* Del. Code Ann. tit. 8, § 141(b), 216 (2001); MBCA § 8.24(c) (1984).

26. E.K. Buck Retail Stores v. Harkert, 62 N.W.2d 288 (Neb. 1954).

27. *See* Blount v. Taft, 246 S.E.2d 763 (N.C. 1978) (finding that bylaws calling for across the board unanimity could be repealed or amended by a simple majority in conformance with the statutory norm).

28. MARK S. RHODES, TRANSFER OF STOCK § 5.1 (6th ed. 1985).

29. Goldberg v. United Parcel Serv., 605 F. Supp. 588 (E.D.N.Y. 1985).

30. *See* Kansas Heart Hosp., L.L.C. v. Badr, 184 P.3d 866 (Kan. 2008) (bylaw provision empowering board to redeem shares if any holder invested in a competing company was enforceable and not invalid right of redemption of the type that must be included in the articles to be a feature of the shares).

31. This can be a useful device to prevent competitors from acquiring control of a corporation. *See* Joseph E. Seagram & Sons, Inc. v. Conoco, Inc., 519 F. Supp. 506 (D.C. Del. 1981).

32. By preventing transfer to a shareholder who does not qualify under Subchapter S or who will refuse to consent to the corporation's election of Subchapter S. *See* I.R.C. §§ 1371 to 1373 (1988).

33. *See, e.g.,* Hall v. Tenn. Dressed Beef Co., 957 S.W.2d 536 (Tenn. 1997) (implying notice requirement from right of first refusal).

34. *See, e.g.,* Coury v. Moss, 529 F.3d 579 (5th Cir. 2008) (transfer restriction in articles forms a contract and no right to purchase minority holder's shares until he offers to sell the shares).

35. *See, e.g.,* Martin v. Villa Roma, Inc., 182 Cal. Rptr. 382 (Ct. App. 1982) (shares in housing cooperative transferable only to persons meeting requirements).

36. *See* Ogden v. Culpepper, 474 So. 2d 1346 (La. Ct. App. 1985); Hill v. Warner, Berman & Spitz, 484 A.2d 344 (N.J. Super. Ct. 1984).

37. *See In re* Dissolution of Penepent Corp., 96 N.Y.2d 186, 192, 726 N.Y.S.2d 345, 750 N.E.2d 47, 50 (2001) (shareholder agreement giving the corporation the right to purchase a deceased shareholder's shares at a fixed price was not controlling since another shareholder had elected to purchase those shares at fair value in lieu of dissolution prior to shareholder's death).

38. *See, e.g.,* Stephenson v. Drever, 947 P.2d 1301 (Cal. 1997) (shares were to be repurchased upon termination of employment; shareholder rights are not extinguished upon termination but rather continue until the repurchase has been consummated and the former employee is no longer a shareholder of record).

39. *See* Kansas Heart Hosp. L.L.C. v. Badr, 184 P.3d 866 (Kan. 2008) (bylaw provision empowering board to redeem shares if any holder invested in a competing company was enforceable and not invalid right of redemption of the type that must be included in the articles to be a feature of the shares).

40. *See* Horne v. Drachman, 280 S.E.2d 338 (Ga. 1981) (repurchase on termination of employment); Avritt v. O'Daniel, 689 S.W.2d 36 (Ky. Ct. App. 1985) (repurchase on death of shareholder).

41. Hamel v. White Wave, Inc., 689 P.2d 709 (Colo. Ct. App. 1984).

42. *See* Hill v. Warner, Berman & Spitz, 484 A.2d 344 (N.J. Super. Ct. A.D. 1984).

43. *See, e.g.*, Groves v. Prickett, 420 F.2d 1119, 1122 (9th Cir. 1970).

44. *See* B&H Warehouse, Inc. v. Atlas Van Lines, Inc., 490 F.2d 818 (5th Cir. 1974).

45. *See, e.g.*, Man O War Rests., Inc. v. Martin, 932 S.W.2d 366 (Ky. 1996) (provision in employment contract requiring employee to sell stock back to the corporation for the price originally paid was voided based on the court's strong public policy against forfeiture).

46. *B&H Warehouse, Inc.*, 490 F.2d 818 (applying Delaware law, concluded requirement that shares be sold to corporation at set price at one-fifth market price could not be applied to shares not voted in favor of the restriction); Systematics, Inc. v. Mitchell, 491 S.W.2d 40 (1973) (agreement requiring resale to corporation at 20 percent of market value is unfair and fails to comply with statute authorizing restrictions for purchase at "fair" price).

47. *Cf. Man O War Rests., Inc.*, 932 S.W.2d 366 (provision in employment contract requiring employee to sell stock back to the corporation for the price originally paid was voided based on the court's strong public policy against forfeiture).

48. *See, e.g.*, Helms v. Duckworth, 249 F.2d 482 (D.C. Cir. 1957) (upholding agreement whereby deceased shareholder's estate received only $10 per share for stock worth $80 per share).

49. Del. Code Ann. tit. 8, § 202(b) (2001).

50. The New Jersey Supreme Court has addressed the issue of whether to apply a marketability discount when a court orders a shareholder to sell his or her stock, concluding that the court must take into account what is fair and equitable. More specifically, a marketability discount cannot be used by the controlling or oppressing shareholders to benefit themselves to the detriment of the minority or oppressed shareholders. Lawson Mardon Wheaton, Inc. v. Smith, 734 A.2d 738, 752 (N.J. 1999).

51. *See, e.g.*, Hall v. John S. Isaacs & Sons Farms, Inc., 163 A.2d 288 (Del. 1960).

52. *See, e.g.*, *In re* Radom & Neidorff, Inc., 119 N.E.2d 563 (N.Y. 1954).

53. *See, e.g.*, Black v. Graham, 464 S.E.2d 814, 815 (Ga. 1996) (having shown deadlock it was not necessary to further establish any related misconduct).

54. Roach v. Bynum, 403 So. 2d 187, 192 (Ala. 1981).

55. Veto arrangements are popular. In most jurisdictions, a valid way of setting up effective veto arrangements is available. *See, e.g.*, Zion v. Kurtz, 405 N.E.2d 681 (N.Y. 1980).

56. Kaplan v. Block, 31 S.E.2d 893, 896–97 (Va. 1944).

57. MBCA § 14.30(2)(i), (iii) (2008).

58. *See* Gillingham v. Swan Falls Land & Cattle Co., 683 P.2d 895 (Idaho Ct. App. 1984).

59. *See* Behrens Co. v. B.D. Rawls, 518 So. 2d 945 (Fla. Ct. App. 1987) (divisions between shareholders had existed for years).

60. *See In re* Hedberg-Freidheim & Co., 47 N.W.2d 424 (Minn. 1951) (director-owner constructed partition around desk to avoid conversation with fellow director-owners).

61. *See Behrens Co.*, 518 So. 2d 945.

62. *E.g.*, MBCA § 14.02(e) (2008) (majority); DEL. CODE ANN. tit. 8, § 275(b) (2001) (majority); N.Y. BUS. CORP. LAW § 1001 (McKinney 2003) (two-thirds vote).

63. *See* Grocery Supply, Inc. v. McKinley Park Serv., Inc., 128 F. Supp. 694 (D.C. Alaska Terr. 1955).

64. *See* Ross v. Am. Banana Co., 43 So. 817 (Ala. 1907).

65. *See, e.g.*, CAL. CORP. CODE § 1800 (West 1990); DEL. CODE ANN. tit. 8, § 226 (2001).

66. *See* Sutter v. Sutter Ranching Corp., 14 P.3d 58 (Okla. 2000) (supervote requirement in articles for certain "action by the corporation," including dissolution, did not deprive minority holder of standing to petition for involuntary dissolution which is not action by the corporation).

67. *See, e.g.*, Gruenberg v. Goldmine Plantation, Inc., 360 So. 2d 884 (La. Ct. App. 1978) (minority shareholders can force a corporation into involuntary dissolution when accomplishment of corporate objectives is "impracticable").

68. *See* Longwell v. Custom Benefit Programs Midwest, Inc., 627 N.W.2d 396, 399–400 (S.D. 2001) (reasonable expectations should be analyzed in light of the entire history of the parties' relationship; the court must balance the minority shareholder's reasonable expectations against the corporation's ability to exercise its business judgment).

69. Meiselman v. Meiselman, 307 S.E.2d 551 (N.C. 1983). *See also, e.g., In re* Kemp & Beatley, 473 N.E.2d 1173 (N.Y. 1984).

70. *Meiselman*, 307 S.E.2d at 563. *See also, e.g.*, Royals v. Piedmont Elec. Repair Co., 529 S.E.2d 515 (N.C. App. 2000).

71. *Meiselman*, 307 S.E.2d at 563.

72. *See, e.g.*, Willis v. Bydalek, 997 S.W.2d 798 (Tex. App. 1999) (wrongful lockout did not establish oppression).

73. *See, e.g., In re* Wiedy's Furniture Clearance Ctr. Co., 487 N.Y.S.2d 901 (App. Div. 1985).

74. Gimpel v. Bolstein, 477 N.Y.S.2d 1014 (1984).

75. *See, e.g.*, Penley v. Penley, 332 S.E.2d 51, 64 (N.C. 1985) (protecting interests based on contract principles).

76. *See, e.g.*, Donahue v. Rodd Electrotype Co., 328 N.E.2d 505 (Mass. 1975). *See also, e.g.*, Hollis v. Hill, 232 F.3d 460 (5th Cir. 2000) (applying Nevada law; cofounder owed fiduciary duty to other cofounder); Orchard v. Covelli, 590 F. Supp. 1548 (W.D. Pa. 1984) (adherence by majority shareholders to their fiduciary duties is particularly critical in context of closely held corporation).

77. *See* Rexford Rand Corp. v. Ancel, 58 F.3d 1215, 1221 (7th Cir. 1995) (minority shareholder who two years earlier had been frozen out of the corporation breached duty by acquiring corporation's name after the corporation had been administratively dissolved).

78. *See, e.g.*, Purcell v. Southern Hills Invs., LLC, 847 N.E.2d 991 (Ind. App. 2006).

79. Merner v. Merner, 129 Fed. Appx. 342 (9th Cir. 2005).

80. *Nixon*, 626 A.2d 1366, 1379 (Del. 1993). *See* Riblet Products Corp. v. Nagy, 683 A.2d 37 (Del. 1996).

CHAPTER 15

THE DERIVATIVE SUIT

TABLE OF SECTIONS

§ 15.1 NATURE AND BASIS OF DERIVATIVE ACTION

An almost necessary consequence of a wrong to a corporation is some impairment of the value of each shareholder's stock interest. As a general rule, however, shareholders are considered to have no direct individual right of action for corporation wrongs that impair the value of their investment. Injuries to the corporation, such as those resulting from negligence, mismanagement, or fraud of its directors or officers, normally are not dealt with as wrongs to the whole group of shareholders in their corporate capacity but rather as a violation of the corporation itself, which can be redressed in a suit by or derivatively on behalf of the corporation.[1]

There are at least three sound reasons that continue to support the continuing distinction between direct and derivative actions. To permit shareholders to sue separately whenever the value of their shares is diminished by a wrong to the corporation would conflict with (1) the separate-corporate-entity concept, (2) the prior rights of creditors, and (3) the duty of management to sue for the protection of all concerned. A single action by the corporation, or by a shareholder in a derivative suit on its behalf, at least in theory obtains redress for all the shareholders and also protects the priorities of creditors, who may be unable to collect their claims if corporate assets are recovered by the shareholders individually.

The derivative suit plaintiff is self-selected; without election or appointment, he presents himself as spokesman for the corporate interest. Because the plaintiff usually has no significant financial interest in the corporation, the possible harmful economic effects of prosecuting the suit cannot be expected to guide his decision to litigate. The derivative suit plaintiff has a fiduciary relationship to the other stockholders of the corporation,[2] yet such a person is not a worthy candidate to decide by himself whether the corporate interest is served by suing on a contract the corporation has entered, a tort allegedly committed to the corporation's property, or any other matter whose initial impact was on the corporation. These are the types of decisions for which the discretionary judgment of the board of directors or its delegates are readily called into play.

As will be seen in succeeding sections, a faint aura of legitimacy accrues to the plaintiff's authority to represent the corporate interest when the demand requirement is excused or otherwise satisfied because the board of directors, due to its own failings or misconduct, is incapacitated from carrying out an independent assessment of the corporate interest served by the suit. To be sure, that aura is not nearly as bright as it would be had the corporation's board of directors, after an assessment from the corporation's perspective of the costs and benefits, crisply resolved to pursue the cause of action. Nevertheless, within the narrow band of factual settings in which the corporate cause of action is today allowed to proceed at the instance of the derivative suit plaintiff, there is a highly recognizable legitimacy to the right of the plaintiff and her lawyer, under the watchful eye of the derivative suit court, to vindicate the corporation's injury.

A shareholder's derivative suit should not be confused with a class suit, in which shareholders having *individual* rights and causes of action against the corporation are represented by a member of the class of shareholders having the rights and causes of action; the transactions and the questions of law and fact involved in the suit are common to all members of the class. In other words, a class action is used for direct shareholder claims against the corporation.

§ 15.2 DISTINGUISHING THE SHAREHOLDER'S INDIVIDUAL SUIT FROM THE DERIVATIVE SUIT

As a rule, the shareholder's judicial remedy for mismanagement or other wrongful acts of directors, officers, or third parties is by a derivative or representative suit on behalf of the corporation. This result reflects not only the practical assessment that the misconduct's initial impact is on the corporation itself, with any stockholder harm being consequential to that impact, but also that the duty breached is one owed directly to the corporation such that it is the corporation's right that is violated by the breaching conduct.[3] In some instances, however, a personal right of action is recognized even for corporate wrongs, if a separate duty is owing to the individual or a collective proceeding on behalf of the corporation does not give the shareholder redress.[4] In some circumstances, either a derivative suit or a direct action may be brought at the shareholder's election. The characterization of a particular cause of action as derivative or direct (which in appropriate cases may be brought as a class action) brings significant procedural differences, which are explored in succeeding sections. Because of these differences, the initial characterization of a suit can be of critical significance.[5]

Courts frequently have great difficulty in classifying a plaintiff's claim as individual or derivative. For example, there has been a conflict as to the proper classification of a suit to compel dividends. In a federal case applying Pennsylvania law, the court held such a suit to be direct and individual, reasoning that because "[t]he right to dividends is an incident of [stock] ownership," the shareholder has been injured directly, and recovery "will benefit only the shareholders."[6] In contrast, a New York court held, over a strong dissent, that a suit to compel dividends must be brought derivatively because it is grounded on a duty owed by the directors to the corporation, but the New York rule has since been changed by statute.[7] It is possible to justify both views. Another some-times litigated question is the proper classification of a shareholder suit to enforce a shareholder's preemptive rights to a new issuance of shares. Under the better view, the action is direct, as it is based on the share-holder's contractual claim against the corporation.[8]

A source of the inconsistency among the courts on their treatment of suits as individual or derivative is a misunderstanding of the effect the court should accord the fact that a class of shareholders has been similarly harmed. Some courts have reasoned that a derivative action is the only basis for a shareholder to complain unless the shareholder has suffered a loss or other injury different from that of the other minority stockholders.[9] This is erroneous.[10]

The difference between individual and derivative actions can be illustrated by examples. The following actions have been held to be indi-vidual (direct) actions:

1. A claim founded on a contract between the corporation and the shareholder as an individual[11] or based on the holder's preferred stock rights.[12]
2. A claim based on false and misleading proxy solicitation.[13]
3. An action to compel dissolution of the corporation.[14] However, dissolution may also be sought in a derivative suit.[15]
4. A suit against directors for fraud in the sale or purchase of the individual shareholder's stock.[16]
5. A claim founded in tort for injury directly upon the shareholder's person or property.[17]
6. An action against a director for disseminating false reports about the validity or value of shareholder's stock that harms the shareholder in his individual capacity as an investor.[18]
7. A claim against a voting trustee for a breach of her obligations.[19]

8. An action to protect the shareholder's relative voting power.[20]
9. A suit to protect a shareholder's inspection rights.[21]
10. A suit against takeover maneuvers, such as adopting a poison pill or issuing stock for the purpose of wrongfully perpetuating or shifting control.[22]
11. An action to enjoin a threatened *ultra vires* act.[23]
12. An action to compel payment of a declared dividend.[24]
13. An action to vindicate a wrong to the individual shareholder, although the same wrongful act may also create a separate corporate cause of action.[25]
14. A suit against the only other shareholder(s) for injuring the corporation's business where a judgment in a derivative suit would benefit the wrongdoer.[26]
15. Suit alleging board abdicated its powers to the CEO.[27]
16. A suit alleging directors breached fiduciary duty when negotiating to sell company.[28]
17. Suit based on oppressive action designed to force the minority shareholder(s) from the corporation or other coercive action directed at the minority.[29]

The following claims have been held to be derivative:

1. An action seeking recovery due to managerial misconduct, producing a proportionate decline in the company's shares, such as the waste of corporate assets or usurpation of corporate opportunities.[30]
2. An action against the purchaser of corporate assets seeking rescission of the sale.[31]
3. An action under section 10(b) of the Securities Exchange Act of 1934 and SEC Rule 10b-5, where the corporation has purchased or sold securities and the individual shareholder is precluded from relief because he is neither a purchaser nor seller of securities.[32]
4. An action to recover for injuries to corporate assets caused by fraud or by third parties.[33]
5. An action to recover damages for an *ultra vires* act.[34]
6. A suit to compel the directors to dissolve the corporation due to director misconduct.[35]

7. An action on a contract between the corporation and a third party.[36]

8. Managerial decisions designed to thwart a takeover and thereby deprive the stockholders of an opportunity to dispose of their shares at a premium.[37]

9. Breach of fiduciary duty during a merger transaction.[38]

10. Malpractice or misfeasance by consultants and experts to the corporation.[39]

There are situations in which a claim can be framed either as a derivative or as a direct claim.[40]

§ 15.3 INDIVIDUAL RECOVERY IN DERIVATIVE SUITS

As a general rule, recovery in derivative suits inures to the corporation, with the proceeds becoming a part of the corporate assets. In some situations, however, the shareholder-plaintiff in a derivative suit on a corporate right of action may recover individual damages in lieu of a corporate recovery. For example, where only few stockholders are injured by the breach, there is no fear that creditors may be disadvantaged if recovery does not go to the corporation, and the wrongdoers are still in control of the corporation, recovery may go directly to the shareholder or shareholders who complain.[41] If a corporate recovery will not cure the injury or if granting equitable relief to the corporation by way of rescission would unsettle and disturb significant interests of innocent third parties, the court should be able to give relief according to the needs of the case.

§ 15.4 NECESSITY OF DEMAND ON THE SHAREHOLDERS

The authority to sue for corporate injuries is vested primarily in corporate management. For a shareholder to show a right to sue on behalf of the corporation, he must allege with some particularity in his complaint that he has exhausted his remedies within the corporation by making a demand on the directors or other officers to sue, or he must allege sufficient reason for not doing so.[42] At one time, the requirement that a shareholder exhaust her intracorporate remedies meant that it was insufficient for a shareholder merely to make a demand on the directors that they institute suit; he must also make a similar demand upon the shareholders as a body. It is rare today to find a demand on the shareholders required, in part because most derivative suits allege misconduct that cannot be ratified by a majority vote of the stockholders.[43] However, the derivative suit plaintiff must take care to plead the basis for excusing the demand or otherwise incur the likelihood of dismissal in those jurisdictions that have not abolished this requirement.[44]

Federal Rule of Civil Procedure 23.1 provides that the plaintiff's complaint must set forth her efforts to obtain action from the stockholders "if necessary." As such, the demand on the stockholders becomes a question in the first instance of substantive state law, save where making a demand would prove inconsistent with federal policy underlying any federal question raised in the derivative suit.[45] As noted above, where state law continues to embody a demand on the shareholders, modern decisions have been most willing to excuse the requirement on one of several possible bases, such as the alleged misconduct being of the type that cannot be approved by a majority vote of the stockholders,[46] or that the defendant holds a majority or controlling block of the voting power,[47] or there is such a large number of stockholders that the plaintiff would incur unreasonable expenses, burdens, and delays in fulfilling the requirement.[48]

§ 15.5 THE DEMAND ON THE DIRECTORS REQUIREMENT

The derivative suit complaint must plead with particularity the efforts the plaintiff has made to seek the board of directors to prosecute the cause of action the plaintiff seeks to initiate or set forth the reasons for not seeking such action by the board of directors.[49] This is the demand requirement and is the single most challenging hurdle that lies in the path of the derivative suit plaintiff.

In general, the directors have discretion to refuse to sue if they decide in good faith not to do so and do not exceed the scope of the business judgment rule.[50] Even if the directors believe that the corporation has a good cause of action for an injury committed by officers or third parties, that fact does not necessarily make it incumbent on them to bring suit. If in the honest and impartial opinion of the directors, the best interests of the company are served by not bringing suit, the directors' decision not to sue is a bar to a shareholder's bringing a derivative suit. In making the decision whether to enforce a corporate cause of action, management generally invokes a cost-benefit analysis. Courts have often said that the question of whether to sue is within the directors' discretion, and that if they act in good faith, their refusal is binding.[51]

The demand requirement gives the board of directors the opportunity to assume control of the decision to litigate.[52] Once a demand is made, the response of the board of directors must be within a reasonable time; if not so forthcoming, the demand required is deemed satisfied.[53] If the directors accede to the shareholder's demands, the corporation supplants the derivative plaintiff for the purpose of enforcing its corporate rights. If the directors refuse to sue despite a proper demand, a few courts have stated that the shareholder is not automatically entitled to pursue the derivative claim.[54] Most courts hold that, if an independent board decides in good faith against the demand (that is, rejects the demand), the directors' refusal to sue falls within the business judgment rule, and the suit must be dismissed.[55] The standard of review of a dismissal recommendation in a demand required case is the same whether the recommendation is proffered by the board or a committee of the board.[56] Only in rare cases will a derivative suit be allowed to proceed after the board of directors has rejected the demand.[57] In essence, the inquiry into whether the board lacks the capacity to make the decision not to sue is much like the inquiry into whether the demand should be excused because it would be futile.[58] Because instances are rare when the board of directors approves of the action *and* does not authorize the corporation's counsel to take over the suit, most derivative suits arise where the plaintiff has successfully pleaded facts that excuse any demand on the board of directors. (Common bases for excusing a demand on the board of directors are discussed below.) A plaintiff who has made a demand on the board of directors cannot reverse course and seek to proceed with the suit on the ground that the demand should have been excused.[59]

Whether a demand is excused for futility is determined at the time the complaint is filed.[60] The courts express in various ways their overall standard for finding futility, but the unique facts of the individual case and the judicial philosophy of the court appear to dominate the outcome more than the general standard that is to guide any finding of futility. When a complaint alleges with particularity that a majority of the board has engaged in fraud, self-dealing, or solely out of self-interest, most courts excuse the demand on the theory that it would be futile, because directors cannot be expected to sue themselves in order to enforce corporate rights.[61] The leading Delaware case on demand futility is *Aronson v. Lewis*,[62] which holds that a demand is excused for futility under one of two alternate standards: (1) whether a reasonable doubt as to the director's disinterest or independence is raised by well-pleaded facts;[63] and, if not, (2) whether the complaint pleads particularized facts sufficient to create a reasonable doubt that the challenged transaction was the product of a valid exercise of business judgment.[64]

As the foregoing indicates, courts are not willing to lightly excuse the demand requirement. In fact, as noted by a recent federal decision, there has been a trend toward strengthening the demand requirement.[65] Furthermore, there appears to be a strong movement at the state level toward a universal demand requirement; a good many states have modified their statutes to adopt the universal demand requirement put forth in the Model Act.[66] This shift is noted by the Seventh Circuit, which observed that the American Law Institute's Corporate Governance principles have prompted a trend of "both the case law and academic commentary moving strongly in that direction as well."[67]

If the board of directors responds to the suit by appointing a special litigation committee that has the sole authority to evaluate whether to pursue the litigation, the court can conclude that the board has conceded its disqualification to entertain a demand.[68]

§ 15.6 Special Litigation Committees

A practice that began in the 1970s has been for the board of directors to delegate the decision of whether to sue on a corporate claim to an independent committee of directors, sometimes with special counsel appointed to assist the committee.[69] Today, it is becoming a common practice for the corporation, either in a demand required or a demand excused case, to establish a committee of independent directors to assess whether continuance of a suit against directors or officers is in the best interests of the corporation.[70] Such committees generally have concluded that continuation of the suit would not promote the best interests of the corporation. Occasionally, a committee will propose a settlement of the action to the derivative suit court.[71] The judicial decisions are in conflict regarding the appropriate standard for reviewing a recommendation of a special litigation committee and a distinct minority of the cases have held such committee action does not merit the attention of the court.

The special litigation committee was created by a melding of the business judgment rule, the demand requirement, and statutory authority for the delegation of board powers. It was intended to provide an efficient means of judging the corporate interest served by a derivative suit when the full board is otherwise disabled by self-interest from gaining the court's attention. The defendant board members' ability to handpick the members of the special litigation committee and defendants' perfect record before these committees, however, have provoked questions about both a committee's ability to render an unbiased assessment of the suit's impact on the corporate interest and the broader issue of whether directors can be impartial in any context when judging their colleagues' actions. The standards for review of the special litigation committee recommendations are evolving, and there continues to be a good deal of uncertainty surrounding these standards.

Presuming Impartiality. The most skeptical judicial response to the charge that directors are afflicted by structural bias is *Auerbach v. Bennett*,[72] which holds that it is inappropriate for a court to evaluate a special litigation committee's weighing of the legal, ethical, commercial, public relations, or fiscal grounds that support its recommendation that a derivative suit be dismissed.[73] In this way, *Auerbach* effectively confines judicial review to two narrow areas that have traditionally been open to attack by the plaintiff under the business judgment rule: the directors' independence and good faith.[74] These two areas permit plaintiff challenges to the adequacy and appropriateness of the committee's procedures; the substantive bases for the committee's recommendation, however, are shielded by the business judgment rule and according to *Auerbach* are removed from judicial scrutiny.[75]

Questioning the Appointive Process. In contrast to *Auerbach*, The Iowa Supreme Court[76] expressed the fear that even the most finely tuned adversarial inquiry could not clearly distinguish rationally drawn conclusions from collegial bias.[77]

Dispatching Skepticism Through Judicial Review. A leading case concerning the review standards for special litigation committee recommendations is *Zapata Corp. v. Maldonado*,[78] which clearly expresses its concern for the directors' potential bias. While recognizing a serious threat of director bias, *Zapata* did not include *Miller*'s sweeping solution. The *Zapata* court reasoned that judicial review of a committee's recommendation should not eviscerate the valuable role the directors' judgments of a suit's worth can play in derivative suit litigation. The court charted what it believed to be a middle course between allowing committee recommendations so much deference that the derivative suit is mortally wounded, on the one hand, and being so skeptical of the committee that the corporation is totally unable to rid itself of a harmful suit, on the other. Into this breach, the Delaware Supreme Court placed a two-step test. Under *Zapata*'s first step, the court evaluates the committee members' independence, good faith, and bases for their recommendation.[79] *Zapata* reinforced these requirements by demanding a detailed report of the committee's investigation procedures and findings, by placing the burden of establishing these factors on the committee, and by subjecting the committee's reasoning to close scrutiny.[80] This scrutiny represents the court's most sweeping response to the threat of structural bias. In its second step, *Zapata* invited the reviewing court to exercise its independent judgment in determining whether the corporate interest is served by the derivative suit's continuance.[81] This discretion is to be exercised only in limited instances, however.

The Independence and Good Faith Inquiries. Independence, whether for considering whether a demand should be required or whether a recommendation of a special litigation committee or, for that matter, the board of directors in a demand required case, should cause the suit's dismissal, turns on the ultimate question whether the opining directors have a relationship with the individual defendant or the suit itself that would reasonably be expected to affect the directors' judgment with respect to the litigation.[82] The threshold requirement for the independence of committee members is that they are not themselves defendants in the derivative suit.[83] A committee does not lack independence solely because its members were appointed by the defendants.[84] There is little doubt that the number of committee members is a factor to consider in evaluating its independence from the defendants,[85] specifically that single-person committees raise interesting flags.[86]

Independence has successfully been questioned on a showing that the committee member has a material financial relationship with the corporation.[87] A committee was found to lack independence where just prior to its formation all the directors, including those later appointed to the committee, voted to resist the derivative suit.[88] Moreover, the committee's recommendation lacks the force of an independent body where it is purely advisory to the full board of directors, most of whose members are defendants in the derivative action.[89]

Close personal friendships naturally raise eyebrows regarding the degree of detachment an individual can be expected to maintain in assessing a suit against his friend. However, the Delaware Supreme Court concluded that standing alone, this is not sufficient to rebut the presumption of independence.[90]

An important consideration, indeed it can be regarded as a separate requirement, for the committee's independence is that the committee be advised by counsel with no historical relationship with the firm.[91] Underlying this requirement is concern that the committee's independent judgment may be compromised whenever the committee's chief legal advisor has a long-standing professional representation of the firm that in no small part depends upon personal relations with the derivative suit defendants. There also is concern that dual representation of the committee and former and ongoing representation of the corporation may seriously compromise the confidentiality requirements of the attorney-client relationship.

A thoughtful, systematic and probing investigation of the facts and report of the findings and conclusions significantly bolster the belief the committee has acted in good faith.[92] Investigations, however, need not be with the formalities of a court proceeding so that stenographic records or testimony under oath are not required to establish the committee's good faith inquiry.[93] The committee's reliance on its independent counsel to perform most of the investigation and the avenues of inquiry that the committee reasonably explained for not exploring is not a basis for finding that its inquiry was so flawed as to constitute a bad faith investigation.[94]

Federalism and the Special Litigation Committee. The U.S. Supreme Court in *Burks v. Lasker* held that in federal question litigation, when confronted with a dismissal recommended by a special litigation committee, the federal district court must follow a two-stage analysis.[95] The first inquiry is to determine the extent to which the committee has the power under state law to cause the derivative suit to be dismissed. If the committee has such power under the facts before the court, the court must determine, second, whether dismissal of the suit would be inconsistent with the policy underlying the federal cause of action. The courts have consistently held that this does not bar a dismissal at the recommendation of a special litigation committee under the antifraud provisions of the federal securities laws.[96]

§ 15.7 STANDING TO BRING A DERIVATIVE SUIT

In order to maintain a derivative suit to redress or prevent injuries to the corporation, the plaintiff must be either an owner of shares or have some beneficial interest therein when the suit is brought.[97] As a general rule, the plaintiff must continue to be a stockholder throughout the life of the suit so that the plaintiff stands to benefit derivatively by the relief given; if the plaintiff ceases to be a shareholder by reason of a transfer of shares, he loses standing to complain.[98] The purpose of the rule is to align the plaintiff's economic interests with the corporate interest to be advanced by the diligent prosecution of the suit.[99] But as is true with any rule whose rigid enforcement can lead to unfair or inequitable results, notable exceptions to this continuous-ownership requirement are recognized in many jurisdictions.[100]

A creditor has no proprietary interest and thus cannot maintain a derivative suit.[101] The authorities are split on whether holders of debentures convertible into stock may bring a derivative suit.[102] The standing of holders of American Depositary Receipts to bring a derivative can be affected by provisions of the deposit agreement.[103] With the exception of the rare corporate statute that provides otherwise, directors and officers who cannot satisfy the share-ownership requirement do not have standing to bring a derivative suit solely because of their capacity as directors or officers.[104] A derivative suit may, however, be brought by a deceased shareholder's administrator or executor having the title to shares in such capacity, by the beneficial owner of shares if a trustee refuses to sue and is made a party defendant,[105] by a pledgee of shares,[106] or by a pledgor of shares, such as a margin customer of a stockbroker holding the stock in the street name for the customer's account.[107]

Under the federal rules[108] and most state statutes,[109] the plaintiff in a shareholder's derivative suit must have been a shareholder of record, a holder of voting trust certificates, or a beneficial owner *at the time of the transaction* that is the subject of the suit. This requirement is also met if the suit's plaintiff acquired her shares by operation of law from one who held the shares at the time of the transaction giving rise to the derivative suit complaint. This requirement is commonly referred to as the "contemporaneous ownership" rule. Where it exists,[110] the contemporaneous ownership rule bars suit by those who acquired their shares or beneficial ownership *after* the misconduct that is the subject of the derivative suit.[111] The rule harmonizes with the basic standing principle that a plaintiff must have sustained a real injury in order to have the right to sue.[112] Most modern courts also agree that a justification for the contemporaneous ownership rule is the prevention of strike suits and speculative litigation.[113]

§ 15.8 DOUBLE DERIVATIVE SUITS

A parent corporation as a shareholder of a subsidiary can bring a derivative action to redress injury to the subsidiary.[114] In turn, a shareholder of a parent company can maintain a "double derivative" suit to enforce a cause of action in favor of a subsidiary company if the directors of both companies have refused after due request to institute an action in the name of either camp.[115] The parent company has a duty to use its control of the subsidiary to compel the subsidiary to sue to right wrongs done to it, and a shareholder of the parent may in effect compel specific performance of this duty in a double derivative suit.[116] A necessary predicate to a double derivative suit is that the parent has not less than operating control of the subsidiary.[117] It is still an open question whether a shareholder in a corporation that holds less than a controlling interest in a company against which a wrong has been committed is entitled to sue on a double derivative basis,[118] although one court has answered the question affirmatively.[119]

§ 15.9 THE PLAINTIFF AS AN ADEQUATE REPRESENTATIVE

The plaintiff in a derivative suit must fairly and adequately represent similarly situated shareholders.[120] Properly interpreted, this means that the plaintiff must be representative of the shareholders who have been injured.[121] The better view is the defendant has the burden of proving the plaintiff is an inadequate representative.[122]

To meet the fair and adequate representation requirement, a plaintiff must have the same interests as the other shareholders and must be free of interests that conflict with theirs.[123] A plaintiff in a derivative action must also show that he will pursue the claim vigorously and competently.[124] The most frequent basis for finding that a plaintiff is not an adequate representative is when the transparent purpose of the derivative suit is to enable the plaintiff to gain leverage in his personal claims or transactions with the defendants or the corporation.[125]

The courts are badly divided as to whether the bidder for control of a corporation is an adequate representative for a suit brought against the incumbent management for misdeeds they allegedly committed in seeking to thwart the bidder's attempt to obtain control. In this area, the courts are presented with the tough choice between a bidder who seeks to serve its private agenda through the successful prosecution of the derivative suit and a plaintiff who can surely be expected to be tenacious in pursuing whatever causes of action the corporation has.

§ 15.10 SECURITY-FOR-EXPENSE STATUTES

The current Model Business Corporation Act does not contain a security-for-expense provision but does authorize the court to require the plaintiff to "pay any of the defendant's reasonable expenses . . . if it finds that the proceeding was commenced or maintained without reasonable cause or for an improper purpose."[126] The primary purpose of a security-for-expense requirement is to reduce strike suits.[127] If plaintiff fails to post security as ordered by the court, the result is dismissal of the derivative suit. Courts generally conduct a fairly close review of the pleadings and any supporting affidavits before requiring the plaintiff to post security. On the whole, security-for-expense statutes have not been a major impediment to the initiation and continuation of derivative suits.

§ 15.11 CONTROL AND SETTLEMENT
OF A DERIVATIVE SUIT

A shareholder's authority to enforce a corporation's cause of action arises from the failure of the official managers to act on its behalf. Assuming the shareholder is a proper representative, the plaintiff does not have absolute control of the litigation but instead has a stewardship function that is exercised under the watchful eye of the derivative suit court to assure that the action's continuation, dismissal, or settlement is in the best interests of the corporation. The final authority to determine whether the action shall be dismissed is the court;[128] a paramount consideration in the court's review is the strength of the plaintiff's case relative to the settlement's terms.[129] Under both statutory and judicially imposed court supervision, the scope of judicial control is not limited to achieving fairness to the particular plaintiff; it extends to the interests of other shareholders, to the corporation as an entity, and to the effect of a settlement on other pending actions. Thus, courts frequently consider the continuing costs to the corporation if the suit continues,[130] but a court will have a difficult time accepting a settlement of a viable cause of action when the only tangible benefit to the corporation is avoidance of further costs to the corporation and inconvenience to its employees.[131] The courts, however, rarely provide a close analysis of the costs and benefits of the settlement's terms; they content themselves with broad incantations sounding in fairness to all the interests before them.[132]

§ 15.12 THE CORPORATION AS A PASSIVE PARTY IN DERIVATIVE SUITS; DEFENSES

The corporation for whose benefit a derivative suit is brought must be joined as a party defendant. Not only is the corporation an indispensable party, but also the suit will be dismissed if the corporation is not served with process, as if it were an actual defendant, or if it does not voluntarily appear by counsel.[133]

The corporation is commonly referred to as a "nominal" defendant.[134] In general, it is required to adopt a neutral or passive role, with only a limited power to defend itself while the shareholder plaintiff— its volunteer representative—conducts for the corporation's benefit the litigation that its management has failed or refused to bring. The corporation need not file an answer to the complaint or take any steps in the proceedings. It cannot assume the status of a co-plaintiff—the complaining shareholder has the right to control the litigation.[135] If the defendants are corporate directors and officers, and control corporate funds, they may well be tempted to exercise their corporate powers to aid their defense. However, apart from reimbursements and advances under indemnification statutes and agreements, it is improper to use corporate funds to give financial aid or to assist in the defense of directors, officers, or other defendants in a derivative suit brought on the corporation's behalf.[136] The plaintiff shareholder is entitled to an opportunity to prosecute the suit without having the resources of the corporation turned against him.

How far the corporation may go in raising defenses to protect its own interests is not entirely settled. Whether the corporate defendant may raise a particular defense depends on the nature of the defense and the interest that the defense is designed to protect.[137] The corporation is allowed to defend when its interests are brought into issue by the suit.[138] Potential defenses can be divided into three groups. First, there are conventional defenses that defeat the corporate right of recovery and are designed to protect the real defendants from liability. The corporation may not assert this type of defense in a derivative suit[139] unless it is a real defendant as to an issue in the litigation.[140] Second are conventional defenses such as laches and ratification. As these defenses are usually designed to protect the alleged wrongdoers, the corporate defendant as a general rule is not allowed to assert these defenses.[141] Third, there are certain defenses that are peculiar to a derivative suit, such as failure to make demand on the board of directors and the necessity for plaintiff to show contemporaneous ownership. These defenses are designed to protect the corporate interest and are therefore ordinarily available to the corporate defendant.

§ 15.13 THE ROLE OF COUNSEL IN A DERIVATIVE SUIT

The individual defendants in derivative litigation frequently seek representation by counsel who also represent the corporation.[142] Questions arise as to the ability of counsel to represent both the corporate and individual defendants. The corporation's true interest in a derivative suit is as a real party plaintiff. Thus where common counsel simultaneously represents in a derivative suit the alleged wrongdoers and the corporation, conflicts of interest may arise.[143] Disqualification of counsel will be ordered where sufficient conflict exists.[144] Courts have held, however, that no conflict exists where the charge is that directors have breached their duty of care in the discharge of their office; the courts reason that this is an attack on the corporation's decisions, and there is no substantial conflict in such a case.[145] Separate attorneys for individual defendants and the corporations are generally desirable. Also, in the special litigation committee context, the courts customarily assess the committee's "good faith" by considering whether it was represented by counsel who was independent from the officers or directors who are the focus of the derivative suit; hence, counsel that has not historically represented the corporation (and hence developed rapport, and perhaps even economic dependence on the suit's defendants) is called for in such instances.[146]

§ 15.14 THE ATTORNEY-CLIENT PRIVILEGE IN DERIVATIVE SUITS

Although a corporation, just as any other client, is entitled to the attorney-client privilege, sensitive questions arise if the corporation attempts to assert the privilege in a derivative suit or other action that is initiated by one of its shareholders against the corporation or even its directors or officers. In the leading case of *Garner v. Wolfinbarger*,[147] the court ruled that on a showing of "good cause" that the plaintiff in a derivative suit may discover relevant facts and documents that would otherwise be covered by the privilege.[148] Among the "indicia" that the court stated bear on whether good cause exists are the following:

> the number of shareholders [requesting the information] and the percentage of stock they represent; the bona fides of the shareholders; the nature of the shareholders' claim and whether it is obviously colorable; the apparent necessity or desirability of the shareholders having the information and the availability of it from other sources; whether, if the shareholders' claim is of wrongful action by the corporation, it is of action criminal, or illegal but not criminal, or of doubtful legality; whether the communication is of advice concerning the litigation itself; the extent to which the communication is identified versus the extent to which the shareholders are blindly fishing; and the risk of revelation of trade secrets or other information in whose confidentiality the corporation has an interest for independent reasons.[149]

There is little doubt that as a consequence of *Garner* and its progeny, clients who are aware of *Garner*'s holding are likely to be much less forthcoming in their communications with the corporation's lawyers. And, although *Garner* is invoked in cases involving the derivative suit plaintiff's discovery of documents, evidence, etc. produced by a special litigation committee, the essential guiding principle in addressing such a request is not *Garner* but the bases upon which the plaintiff can challenge the dismissal recommendation of a special litigation committee.[150]

The attorney-client privilege applies to some, but not all, the communications of the general counsel who also has several other corporate roles; the privilege applies to communications that were created solely in the person's capacity as counsel.[151]

§ 15.15 Indemnification and Insurance for Directors and Officers

Indemnification

When an officer or director is named as a defendant in a lawsuit charging misconduct in office, is he entitled to indemnification for expenses if the defense is successful? Further, may he be reimbursed for his costs even in the event that the plaintiff prevails? All states have indemnification statutes.[152] The former Model Business Corporation Act,[153] as well as the current Model Business Corporation Act,[154] have greatly influenced the overall structure and philosophy of state indemnification statutes. Approximately one-half the state indemnity provisions are substantially similar to the 1969 version of the former Model Business Corporation Act,[155] and all but a handful of the remaining states pattern their indemnification statutes after the current Model Business Corporation Act.[156] The major difference between the two model acts is that the current Model Business Corporation Act makes its provisions the exclusive means for indemnifying directors, empowers the court to approve indemnification in certain instances, precludes indemnification when the defendant receives an improper personal benefit, and requires notice to the shareholders when directors are indemnified.[157] Important variations exist among the states regardless of which particular initiative that state chose as the model for its own indemnification provision.

Both at common law and by statute, the indemnification rules that apply to derivative suits differ from those applicable to suits brought against officers, directors, or corporate agents (outsiders) by third parties. It is well-established agency law that, subject to illegality and in the absence of an agreement to the contrary, a principal is bound to indemnify his agent for "expenses of defending actions by third parties brought because of the agent's authorized conduct...."[158]

An important threshold consideration is the breadth of corporate personnel covered by the state's corporate indemnity statute. For example, the Delaware and New York statutes apply to the "director and officers,"[159] whereas a few states extend their statutes to others, such as employees, agents, or other representatives of the corporation.[160]

Most statutes provide for indemnification as a matter of right "to the extent" the director or officer is "successful" in his defense and, subject to varying standards and limitations, authorize permissive (that is, discretionary with a body such as the independent directors, independent counsel, or the court) indemnification in other cases. The "to the extent . . . successful" language thus overrules those common law decisions that followed the *New York Dock Company* decision denying the successful director indemnification. In determining whether there has been success, it is important whether the statute envisions a decision on the suit's merits or whether a prejudicial dismissal on procedural grounds entitles the corporate official to indemnification. The statute's inclusion of language such as "on the merits *or otherwise*"[161] obviously invites a broad construction of the meaning of "success." Indemnification as a matter of right may also arise by virtue of supplementary indemnification provisions in the employee's contract with the corporation or by virtue of the bylaws of the corporation that, as discussed below, are authorized in most states.[162]

In a leading case,[163] the Delaware Supreme Court held that the directors were successful within the meaning of the Delaware indemnification statute for their expenses related to the criminal counts, which were dropped as a result of their plea bargaining, entered into after their convictions were reversed on appeal. The current Model Business Corporation Act requires that the defendant have been "wholly successful."[164] A defendant is wholly successful "only if the entire proceeding is disposed of on a basis which involves a finding of nonliability."[165] Courts have also held that a dismissal because of the statute of limitations is deemed a successful defense.[166]

The policy choices within indemnity statutes become more numerous in the case of the unsuccessful corporate officer or director. It is at this point that the greatest variation in approaches and language appears among the state statutes. The former Model Business Corporation Act,[167] following the architecture of the Delaware statute,[168] treats separately indemnification arising from actions by or on behalf of the corporation and all other types of actions. The concern that drives treatment of actions that are by or on behalf of the corporation as separate from others is that of the circularity of otherwise allowing the director or officer to be reimbursed for a recovery that the derivative suit obtained on behalf of the corporation. To allow indemnification for actions by or on behalf of the corporation, mocks the therapeutic purposes of the suit, because it will be the corporation, not the real defendant, who will be the worse off as a consequence of the suit. The current Model Business Corporation Act takes a different path by barring indemnification in actions by or on behalf of the corporation where the request arises from any proceeding in which the director has received an improper personal benefit or in any proceeding by or on behalf of the corporation in which she has been adjudged liable.[169]

The Delaware statute distinguishes between actions by or on behalf of the corporation and all other actions in that indemnification is allowed for the former only for the defendant's reasonable expenses, but not for any resulting settlement or judgment.[170] Similarly, the current Model Business Corporation Act allows indemnification of the defendant's expenses but not for any amount paid as a fine, judgment, or settlement, provided a court orders such indemnification on a finding that he is "reasonably and fairly entitled to indemnification."[171]

The unsuccessful corporate director or officer is not entitled to indemnification as a matter of right; she must persuade a designated decision-maker to exercise her discretion to indemnify the director or officer. Statutes generally confine the decision-maker to a body of independent directors, independent counsel, or a court.[172] The route the statute lays out for the decision-maker, however, is not a two-way street. There appears in the statute no restraint on the decision-maker refusing to indemnify the unsuccessful director or officer. That is, the petitioner who seeks indemnification for her unsuccessful defense is not entitled to indemnification as a matter of right; the indemnification authorized by the statute for the unsuccessful defendant is permissive.

Moreover, the decision-maker cannot indemnify the unsuccessful defendant unless satisfied that the defendant's conduct meets the standards set forth in the statute. Indemnification provided without meeting the standards is improper, and the amounts can be recovered by the corporation.[173] The most frequent standards to be satisfied are that the defendant "acted in good faith and in a manner he reasonably believed to be or not opposed to the best interests of the corporation."[174] The New York Court of Appeals interpreted good faith to require that the officer or director acted for a purpose she reasonably believed to be in the best interests of the corporation.[175] The standard was not met by an officer who engaged in racial discrimination.[176] Good faith can also be interpreted more broadly to be violated by an intentional violation of the law. Thus, in an interesting bribery case, this standard for indemnification was not satisfied, even though the bribe was made to advance what the defendant genuinely believed was his employer's interest, because the defendant was believed not to have acted in good faith because he consciously violated the law.[177] And, steps taken by executives to prevent federal regulators from exercising control over the company, even though undertaken for what the executives believed furthered the interests of the company, were nonetheless deemed in bad faith because they sought to undermine the government's regulatory authority.[178] Under statutes that condition reimbursement on whether the executive was "adjudged liable" one court applying this standard upheld indemnification, even though the jury found that the officer had breached his fiduciary duty; since the breach produced no damages the court held that the officer had not been adjudged liable.[179]

When the defendant in an earlier proceeding was found to have breached a fiduciary duty to the corporation and now seeks indemnification, generally the court is the sole decision-maker applying these standards,[180] and the court is under the additional obligation to find that the defendant is "fairly and reasonably entitled to indemnification."[181] Thus, in a decision that makes good sense but no doubt is not politically correct, the court found indemnification of directors was in order where the defendant directors of an all-male club sought indemnification for their continued defense of what they believed the desirable policy for the club.[182] An additional standard is applicable when the defendant seeks indemnification after an unsuccessful defense in a criminal proceeding; the decision-maker must also determine that the defendant "had no reasonable cause to believe his conduct was unlawful."[183]

Most indemnification statutes authorize the corporation to advance expenses to its officers or directors. Advances are especially important when any applicable insurance coverage does not include litigation expenses or, if such coverage exists, the policy has a fairly large deductible before the insurance carrier becomes obligated to assume the defense costs. Even though corporation's power to advance expenses is not unrestrained by the statute, the propriety of making such advances should not depend on the merits of the claim against the officer or director but rather the nature of the underlying claim.[184] For example, the Model Business Corporation Act requires: (1) the director furnish the corporation a written affirmation of his good faith belief that he has met the standard of conduct described in section 8:51; (2) the director furnishes the corporation a written undertaking, executed personally or on his behalf, to repay the advance if it is ultimately determined that he did not meet the standard of conduct; and (3) a determination is made that the facts then known to those making the determination would not preclude indemnification under this chapter.[185]

D&O Insurance

With the virtual universal acceptance by courts and legislature of at least a limited right to indemnification, the next legal development was liability insurance for corporate officers and directors. The typical directors' and officers' (D&O) policy has two distinct parts.[186] The first part provides coverage to reimburse the corporation for its costs in indemnifying its directors and officers. The second part extends coverage directly to the individual officer or director for which indemnification from the corporation is not available or forthcoming. The latter is sometimes referred to as "Side A" or "last resort" coverage; it comes into effect only when the corporation cannot or will not indemnify the officer or director. Such a denial of indemnification is most frequently the result of a change of control. The standard D&O policy rarely requires the insurer to defend the officer or director[187] and operates on a claims-made basis—that is, the policy covers only those actions brought during the period of the policy.[188] The policy may obligate the insurer to advance sums for the insured's defense.[189] However, if the policyholder gives proper notice to the insurer of a transaction or event that could give rise to a claim at some future date, the claim if made will be covered by the policy even if outside the stated policy period. A 5 percent deductible is not uncommon among policies, and the policies generally exclude from their coverage fines and penalties arising from criminal actions, as well as reimbursements for liability arising in civil actions for dishonesty or where the officer or director has personally gained as a consequence of her breach.[190] The standard policy covers non-intentional violations and customarily has many other exclusions, most of which are items likely to be covered by a different type of corporate policy, such as its general liability policy (for the D&O exclusions for libel, slander, environmental liabilities, and other forms of property damage).[191] The key provisions of the policy's coverage are its definition of "wrongful act" and its numerous exclusions. It is standard for the policy to prohibit covered executives from incurring defense costs without the consent of the insurer.

The Model Act empowers a corporation to purchase insurance for any director, officer, employee, or agent for any liability arising out of their corporate capacity "whether or not the corporation would have the power to indemnify or advance expenses to him against the same liability. . . ."[192] Some states, such as New York,[193] place statutory limits on the type of insurance that corporations may provide directors and officers, and, despite the broad language of the Model Act, decisions such as *Waltuch* remind us that liability insurance for gross misconduct may be void as against public policy.[194] This, however, is largely a theoretical proposition because, as discussed below, insurers exclude from their coverage intentional conduct of the type that poses such public policy considerations.

NOTES

1. Dodge v. Woolsey, 59 U.S. (18 How.) 331 (1855); Stevens v. Lowder, 643 F.2d 1078 (5th Cir. 1981), *reh'g denied*, 652 F.2d 1001 (1981); EMI Ltd. v. Bennett, 738 F.2d 994 (9th Cir. 1984).
2. *See* Seeburg-Commonwealth Litig. [1974–1975 Transfer Binder], Fed. Sec. L. Rep. (CCH) ¶ 94,969 (S.D.N.Y. 1975).
3. *See* Flynn v. Merrick, 881 F.2d 446 (7th Cir. 1989).
4. *See, e.g.*, Citibank N.A. v. Data Lease Fin. Corp., 828 F.2d 686 (11th Cir. 1987).
5. *See* Note, DEBORAH A. DEMOTT, SHAREHOLDER DERIVATIVE ACTIONS LAW & PRACTICE, §§ 2.1 to 2.7.
6. Knapp v. Bankers Sec. Corp., 230 F.2d 717, 722 (3d Cir. 1956). This is the preferable view.
7. Gordon v. Elliman, 119 N.E.2d 331 (N.Y. 1954). *See* Eisenberg v. Flying Tiger Line, Inc., 451 F.2d 267 (2d Cir. 1971).
8. Shaw v. Empire Sav. & Loan Ass'n, 9 Cal. Rptr. 204 (Ct. App. 1960).
9. *See, e.g.*, Grace Bros. Ltd. v. Farley Ind., Inc., 450 S.E.2d 814 (Ga. 1994) (barring direct claim by minority stockholders who complained of unfair treatment in a cash-out merger).
10. Jones v. H.F. Ahmanson & Co., 460 P.2d 464, 470–71 (Cal. 1969).
11. *See, e.g.*, Buschmann v. Prof'l Men's Ass'n, 405 F.2d 659 (7th Cir. 1969).
12. Blue Chip Capital Fund II LP v. Tubergen, 906 A.2d 827 (Del. Ch. 2006).
13. *See* Yamamoto v. Omiya, 564 F.2d 1319 (9th Cir. 1977). However, both cases left open the possibility that a derivative action may also have been appropriate.

14. Fontheim v. Walker, 141 N.Y.S.2d 62 (Sup. Ct. 1955).
15. *See, e.g.*, Gottfried v. Gottfried, 50 N.Y.S.2d 951 (Sup. Ct. 1944). See *infra* note 44.
16. *See, e.g.*, Siegel v. Engelmann, 143 N.Y.S.2d 193 (Sup. Ct. 1955); Von Au v. Magenheimer, 110 N.Y.S. 629 (App. Div. 1908), *aff'd*, 89 N.E. 1114 (N.Y. 1909).
17. *See, e.g.*, Gieselmann v. Stegeman, 443 S.W.2d 127 (Mo. 1969).
18. *See, e.g.*, Grogan v. Garner, 806 F.2d 829 (8th Cir. 1986).
19. *See, e.g.*, Lurie v. Rupe, 201 N.E.2d 158 (Ill. App. Ct. 1964), *cert. denied*, 380 U.S. 964 (1965).
20. *See, e.g.*, Lochhead v. Alacano, 697 F. Supp. 406 (D. Utah 1988).
21. *See, e.g.*, *Gieselmann*, 443 S.W.2d 127.
22. *See, e.g.*, *In re* Gaylord Container Corp. Shareholders Litig., 747 A.2d 71 (Del. Ch. 1999).
23. *See, e.g.*, Independence Lead Mines Co. v. Kingsbury, 175 F.2d 983 (9th Cir.), *cert. denied*, 338 U.S. 900 (1949).
24. *Id.*
25. *See, e.g.*, Snyder v. Epstein, 290 F. Supp. 652 (E.D. Wis. 1968).
26. *See, e.g.*, Fischer v. Fischer, 1999 WL 1032768 (Del. Ch. 1999) (complaint over unfair sale of company's only asset that benefited all stockholders other than the plaintiff).
27. Grimes v. Donald, 673 A.2d 1207, 1213 (Del. 1996).
28. Parnes v. Bally Entm't Corp., 722 A.2d 1243 (Del. 1999) (allegations included charge the directors drove off would-be suitors by demanding side payments to themselves for suitor's offer to be considered).
29. Strougo v. Bassini, 282 F.3d 162 (2d Cir. 2002).
30. *See, e.g.*, Phoenix Airline Serv., Inc. v. Metro Airlines, Inc., 403 S.E.2d 832 (Ga. App. 1991).
31. *See, e.g.*, Bassett v. Battle, 1 N.Y.S.2d 869 (App. Div. 1938).
32. *See, e.g.*, Ray v. Karris, 780 F.2d 636, 641 (7th Cir. 1985).
33. *See, e.g.*, Green v. Victor Talking Mach. Co., 24 F.2d 378 (2d Cir.) (misappropriation of corporate assets).
34. *See, e.g.*, Lee Moving & Storage, Inc. v. Bourgeois, 343 So. 2d 1192 (La. Ct. App. 1977) (with good faith and due diligence).
35. *See, e.g.*, Parks v. Multimedia Technologies, Inc., 520 S.E.2d 517, 523 (Ga. Ct. App. 1999).
36. *See* Boothe v. Baker Indus., 262 F. Supp. 168 (D. Del. 1966) (where right of action existed as to both derivative and nonderivative causes, adjudication of state court nonderivative class action held bar to federal derivative suit).
37. *See, e.g.*, Nowling v. Aero Serv. Int'l, 752 F. Supp. 1304 (E.D. La. 1990).
38. *See, e.g.*, *In re* First Interstate Bancorp Litig., 729 A.2d 851 (Del. Ch. 1998).
39. PricewaterhouseCoopers, LLP v. Massey, 860 N.E.2d 1252 (Ind. Ct. App. 2007).
40. *See Boothe*, 262 F. Supp. 168 (where right of action existed as to both derivative and nonderivative causes, adjudication of state court nonderivative class action held bar to federal derivative suit).
41. *See, e.g.*, Jannes v. Microwave Commc'ns, Inc., 385 F. Supp. 759 (N.D. Ill. 1974).

42. *E.g.*, Hawes v. Oakland, 104 U.S. 450, 460–61 (1882); Smith v. Sperling, 354 U.S. 91 (1957); Lewis v. Curtis, 671 F.2d 779 (3d Cir. 1982).
43. *See, e.g.*, Gibbs v. Macari, 1997 WL 1261225 (Mass. Super. 1997) (dismissing suit for failure to allege basis to excuse a demand).
44. *See, e.g.*, McLeese v. J.C. Nichols Co., 842 S.W.2d 115 (Mo. Ct. App. 1992).
45. *See* Burks v. Lasker, 441 U.S. 471 (1979).
46. *See, e.g.*, Mayer v. Adams, 141 A.2d 458 (Del. 1958).
47. *See, e.g.*, Gottesman v. Gen. Motors Corp., 268 F.2d 194 (2d Cir. 1959).
48. *See, e.g.*, Weiss v. Sunasco Inc., 316 F. Supp. 1197 (E.D. Pa. 1970).
49. *See, e.g.*, FED. R. CIV. P. 23.1; CAL. CORP. CODE § 800 (2009); DEL. CH. CT. R. 23.1; N.Y. BUS. CORP. LAW § 626(c) (2009); MODEL BUS. CORP. ACT § 7.42 (2008).
50. United Copper Sec. Co. v. Amalgamated Copper Co., 244 U.S. 261, 264 (1917).
51. *Burks*, 441 U.S. 471 (1979).
52. *See* Brody v. Chem. Bank, 517 F.2d 932, 934 (2d Cir. 1975).
53. Lewis v. Sporck, 646 F. Supp. 574 (N.D. Cal. 1986) (three-month delay assured that board had sufficient time); Rubin v. Posner, 701 F. Supp. 1041 (D. Del. 1988) (30 days sufficient where no complex issues posed).
54. *See* Papilsky v. Berndt, 503 F.2d 554, 556 (2d Cir. 1974), *cert. denied*, 419 U.S. 1048 (1974) (dicta).
55. *See, e.g.*, Atkins v. Hibernia Corp., 182 F.3d 320, 324 (5th Cir. 1999) (citing Louisiana law, concludes rejection of demand upheld unless plaintiff sustains burden of proving that rejection was not rational, honest, and disinterested).
56. *See* Allied Ready Mix Co., Inc. v. Allen, 994 S.W.2d 4 (Ky. Ct. App. 1998); Harhen v. Brown, 730 N.E.2d 859 (Mass. 2000).
57. *See* Ashwander v. Tenn. Valley Auth., 297 U.S. 288 (1936); Stepak v. Addison, 20 F.3d 398 (11th Cir. 1994) (directors in rejecting demand acted with gross negligence when they relied on same law firm that represented defendants in related criminal proceeding).
58. Grimes v. DSC Commc'ns Corp., 724 A.2d 561 (Del. Ch. 1998) (when demand rejected, plaintiff must bear the burden of proof with particular facts to create a reasonable doubt that the corporation's board wrongfully refused the demand).
59. *See* Spiegel v. Buntrock, 571 A.2d 767 (Del. 1990) (the making of demand concedes board's independence).
60. *Brody*, 482 F.2d 1111.
61. Nussbacher v. Cont'l Ill. Nat'l Bank & Trust. Co., 518 F.2d 873, 877 (7th Cir. 1975), *cert. denied*, 424 U.S. 928 (1976).
62. 473 A.2d 805 (Del. 1984).
63. *See, e.g.*, Conrad v. Blank, 940 A.2d 28 (Del. Ch. 2007) (demand excused in part on basis that after learning through its own investigation of misconduct, the board took no action).
64. *Aronson*, 473 A.2d at 814.
65. Boland v. Engle, 113 F.3d 706 (7th Cir. 1997).
66. A majority of the states now statutorily impose a universal demand requirement.

67. *Boland*, 113 F.3d at 712–13 (relying on Kamen v. Kemper Fin. Servs., Inc., 939 F.2d 458, 461–63 (7th Cir. 1991)); Cuker v. Mikalauskas, 692 A.2d 1042 (Pa. 1997), *on remand*, 35 Pa. D. & C. 4th 87 (1998).
68. *See* Peller v. S. Co., 911 F.2d 1532 (11th Cir. 1990) (the court intimates different result may occur if corporation filed motion to dismiss for failure to make demand and after filing that motion established special litigation committee).
69. Lewis v. Anderson, 615 F.2d 778 (9th Cir. 1979), *cert. denied*, 449 U.S. 869 (1980) (under California law, board of directors may delegate to disinterested independent committee business judgment authority to dismiss derivative action against some of directors).
70. *See, e.g.*, Gaines v. Haughton, 645 F.2d 761 (9th Cir. 1981), *cert. denied*, 454 U.S. 1145 (1982) (committee's determination that not in best interests of corporation to pursue derivative action required dismissal of stockholder's claims).
71. *See, e.g.*, Carlton Invs. v. TLC Beatrice Int'l Holdings, Inc., 1997 WL 305829 (Del. Ch. 1997) (reviewing the settlement proposed by a special litigation committee pursuant to the two-step review process set forth in *Zapata*, discussed below, and not the "fair and reasonable" standard that is customarily used in reviewing derivative suit settlements).
72. 393 N.E.2d 994 (N.Y. 1979).
73. *Id.* at 1002. *See also* Desaigoudar v. Meyercord, 133 Cal. Rptr. 2d 408, 418–19 (Ct. App. 2003).
74. *Auerbach*, 393 N.E.2d at 996.
75. *See id.*
76. Miller v. Register & Tribune Syndicate, Inc., 336 N.W.2d 709 (Iowa 1983).
77. *Id.* at 718.
78. 430 A.2d 779 (Del. 1981).
79. *Id.* at 788–89.
80. *See id.*
81. *Id.* at 789. One court has referred to *Zapata*'s second step as invoking an "imprecise smell test." *See* Strougo v. Padegs, 27 F. Supp. 2d 442, 454 (S.D.N.Y. 1998).
82. *See* Einhorn v. Culea, 612 N.W.2d 78, 98 (Wis. 2000) (listing the following factors to be considered: whether the director has potential liability in the underlying action including being a defendant therein; director's participation or approval or receipt of benefits from the challenged transaction; director's past or present business dealings with individual defendant; director's family, personal, or social relationships with defendant; director's past or present financial relations with the corporation; number of members of the committee; and roles of corporate counsel and independent counsel).
83. *See, e.g.*, *Gaines*, 645 F.2d 761, *cert. denied*, 454 U.S. 1145.
84. *See, e.g.*, Strougo v. Padegs, 27 F. Supp. 2d 442 (S.D.N.Y. 1998).
85. *See* Houle v. Low, 556 N.E.2d 51, 59 (Mass. 1990).
86. *See* Hasan v. Clevetrust Realty Investors, 729 F.2d 372 (6th Cir. 1984).
87. *See id.* (single person committee who owned 25% of firm that received substantial fees from corporation managed by derivative suit defendant and also owned two percent of real estate partnership with defendant).

88. *See* Swenson v. Thibaut, 250 S.E.2d 279 (N.C. Ct. App. 1978).
89. *In re* Par Pharm. Inc. Derivative Litig., 750 F. Supp. 641 (S.D.N.Y. 1990).
90. Beam v. Stewart, 845 A.2d 1040, 1050–51 (Del. Super. 2004).
91. *In re* Perrigo Co., 128 F.3d 430 (6th Cir. 1997).
92. For excellent descriptions of steps committees have taken, *see* Strougo v. Padegs, 27 F. Supp. 2d 442, 451–53 (S.D.N.Y. 1998). *See also, e.g.*, Boland v. Boland Trane Associates, Inc., 423 Md. 296, 31 A.3d 529 (Md. 2011).
93. *See, e.g., Strougo*, 27 F. Supp. 2d at 452.
94. *See, e.g.*, Maldonado v. Flynn, 485 F. Supp. 274, 284 (S.D.N.Y. 1980). *See also, e.g., Hasan*, 729 F.2d 372.
95. *Burks*, 441 U.S. at 480.
96. *See, e.g.*, Lewis v. Anderson, 615 F.2d 778 (9th Cir. 1979).
97. A distinct minority of the states require the derivative suit plaintiff to be an "owner of record." *See* W. Va. Code Ann. § 31-1-103 (2009).
98. *See, e.g.*, Lewis v. Chiles, 719 F.2d 1044 (9th Cir. 1983) (continuing interest protects against plaintiff failing to vigorously prosecute action or accepting an insubstantial settlement because she will not be able to share in any recovery as she no longer is owner of firm).
99. *See* Schupack v. Covelli, 498 F. Supp. 704 (W.D. Pa. 1980) (only party with present interest in corporation will adequately represent corporation's interests in derivative action).
100. *Compare* Timko v. Triarsi, 898 So. 2d 89 (Fl. Dist. Ct. App. 2005) (standing lost when defendant exercised his right to buyout the plaintiff in a separate proceeding brought by the plaintiff to dissolve the company) *with* Brown v. Brown, 731 A.2d 1212 (N.J. Super. App. Div. 1999) (standing to continue to maintain suit accorded where shares had been transferred to spouse as part of divorce settlement but reserving right to continue the derivative suit).
101. *See, e.g.*, Darrow v. Southdown, Inc., 574 F.2d 1333 (5th Cir. 1978).
102. *Compare* Kusner v. First Pa. Corp., 395 F. Supp. 276 (E.D. Pa. 1975), *aff'd in part and rev'd in part on other grounds*, 531 F.2d 1234 (3d Cir. 1976); Simon v. Cogan, 549 A.2d 300 (Del. 1988) (denying standing to convertible debenture holders).
103. Batchelder v. Kawamoto, 147 F.3d 915 (9th Cir. 1998) (standing denied because deposit agreement provided holders' rights would be determined according to Japanese law, which does not treat holders of ADR's as shareholders).
104. Schoon v. Smith, 953 A.2d 196 (Del. 2008).
105. Cal. Corp. Code § 800 (2009); N.Y. Bus. Corp. Law § 626(a) (2009); MBCA § 7.40 (2008); Former MBCA § 49 (1980). *See also* Demoulas v. Demoulas Super Markets, Inc., 677 N.E.2d 159, 172 (Mass. 1997) (beneficiary of trust can bring action because trustee may face conflicts in doing so).
106. Green v. Hedenberg, 42 N.E. 851 (Ill. 1896).
107. Braasch v. Goldschmidt, 199 A.2d 760 (Del. Ch. 1964).
108. Fed. R. Civ. P. 23.1.
109. Del. Code Ann. tit. 8, § 627 (2009); N.Y. Bus. Corp. Law § 626(b) (2009). *See* DeMott, *supra* note 5, § 4.02.

110. The requirement appears in Fed. R. Civ. P. 23.1 and exists in a majority of the states either by statute, case law, or court rule.
111. *See, e.g.*, Int'l Broad. Corp. v. Turner, 734 F. Supp. 383 (D. Minn. 1990).
112. This reasoning comes from *Home Fire Ins. Co. v. Barber*, 93 N.W. 1024, 1029 (Neb. 1903) (one who does not own stock at the time of mismanagement is not injured unless the effects continue and are injurious to him), which is generally credited with giving impetus to the force with which the doctrine is applied today.
113. Phillips v. Bradford, 62 F.R.D. 681, 685 (S.D.N.Y. 1974).
114. FED. R. CIV. PROC. 23.1.
115. An individual shareholder can sue derivatively on a corporation's behalf to enforce its right to enforce the subsidiary's right. *See* Bazata v. National Ins. Co. of Washington, 400 A.2d 313 (D.C. Ct. App. 1979).
116. *See* Saltzman v. Birrell, 78 F. Supp. 778 (S.D.N.Y. 1955).
117. *See* Brown v. Tenney, 532 N.E.2d 230 (Ill. 1988).
118. William H. Painter, *Double Derivative Suits and Other Remedies with Regard to Damaged Subsidiaries*, 36 Ind. L. J. 143, 152 (1961).
119. Issner v. Aldrich, 254 F. Supp. 696 (D. Del. 1966).
120. FED. R. CIV. P. 23.1.
121. *See* Eye Site, Inc. v. Blackburn, 750 S.W.2d 274 (Tex. Ct. App. 1988) (suit barred when all other stockholders are either defendants or have affirmatively stated the plaintiff does not represent their interests).
122. *See, e.g.*, Smallwood v. Pearl Brewing Co., 489 F.2d 579, 582 (5th Cir.), *cert. denied*, 419 U.S. 873 (1974).
123. *See, e.g.*, Davis v. Comed, Inc., 619 F.2d 588 (6th Cir. 1980) (providing six factors bearing on adequacy).
124. Barrett v. S. Conn. Gas Co., 172 Conn. 362, 373, 374 A.2d 1051, 1057 (1977).
125. *See, e.g.*, Blum v. Morgan Guar. Trust Co., 539 F.2d 1388 (5th Cir. 1976) (plaintiff initiated suit after corporation sued him for defaulting on loan). *See also, e.g.*, Owen v. Modern Diversified Indus., 643 F.2d 441 (6th Cir. 1981).
126. MBCA ANN. § 7.46(2) (Supp. 1992).
127. Former MBCA § 49 Comment (1969).
128. Whitten v. Dabney, 154 P. 312, 316 (Cal. 1944).
129. *See, e.g.*, *In re* Traffic Executive Ass'n E. R.R., 627 F.2d 631 (2d Cir. 1980).
130. *See* Shlensky v. Dorsey, 574 F.2d 131, 147 (3d Cir. 1978).
131. *See In re* Pittsburgh & Lake Erie R.R. Sec. & Antitrust Litig., 543 F.2d 1058 (3d Cir. 1976) (district court's approval of such a settlement reversed).
132. Polk v. Good, 507 A.2d 531, 536 (Del. 1986).
133. *See, e.g.*, Ross v. Bernhard, 396 U.S. 531 (1970).
134. *See, e.g.*, Miller v. Am. Tel. & Tel. Co., 394 F. Supp. 58 (E.D. Pa. 1975), *aff'd mem.*, 530 F.2d 964 (3d Cir. 1976).
135. Otis & Co. v. Pa. R.R., 57 F. Supp. 680, 682 (E.D. Pa. 1944), *aff'd*, 155 F.2d 522 (3d Cir. 1946), *citing* Groel v. United Elec. Co. of N.J., 61 A. 1061, 1064–65 (N.J. Ch. 1905).
136. Meyers v. Smith, 251 N.W. 20 (Minn. 1933).
137. Foust v. Transamerica Corp., 391 F. Supp. 312 (N.D. Cal. 1975).

138. *See, e.g., Otis*, 57 F. Supp. 680, *aff'd*, 155 F.2d 522.
139. *See, e.g.*, Kartub v. Optical Fashions, Inc., 158 F. Supp. 757 (S.D.N.Y. 1958).
140. *See Otis*, 57 F. Supp. 680, *aff'd*, 155 F.2d 522.
141. *See* Barrett v. S. Conn. Gas Co., 374 A.2d 1051 (Conn. 1977).
142. *See* Westinghouse Elec. Corp. v. Kerr-McGee Corp., 580 F.2d 1311 (7th Cir. 1978).
143. *See* Murphy v. Washington Am. League Base Ball Club, Inc., 324 F.2d 394 (D.C. Cir. 1963); Cannon v. U.S. Acoustics, 398 F. Supp. 209 (N.D. Ill. 1975), *aff'd in part*, 532 F.2d 1118 (7th Cir. 1976).
144. Messing v. F.D.I., Inc., 439 F. Supp. 776 (D.N.J. 1977).
145. *See, e.g.*, Bell Atl. Corp. v. Bolger, 2 F.3d 1304 (3d Cir. 1993): Campellone v. Cragan, 910 So. 2d 363 (Fl. Ct. App. 2005) (identifying exceptions as patently frivolous suit, suit alleging mismanagement as distinct from fraud, self dealing, or intentional misconduct, or where degree of corporate participation would be very low).
146. *See, e.g.*, Einhorn v. Culea, 612 N.W.2d 78 (Wis. 2000).
147. 280 F. Supp. 1018 (N.D. Ala. 1968), *vacated and remanded*, 430 F.2d 1093 (5th Cir. 1970), *cert. denied*, 401 U.S. 974 (1971), *on remand*, 56 F.R.D. 499 (N.D. Ala. 1972).
148. 4430 F.2d at 1103–04.
149. 6430 F.2d at 1104.
150. *See* Carlton Invs. v. TLC Beatrice Int'l Holdings, Inc., 1997 WL 38130 (Del. Ch. 1997) (deposing the committee's counsel denied).
151. *See* Grimes v. LLC Int'l Inc., 1999 WL 252381 (Del. Ch. 1999).
152. *See* MODEL BUSINESS CORP. ACT § 8.50 (1984) [hereinafter MBCA].
153. *See* Former MBCA § 5 (1969), which was patterned after the Delaware indemnification provisions; *see* DEL. CODE ANN. tit. 8, § 145 (2001).
154. MBCA ANN. §§ 8.50 to 8.58. The MBCA reflects the changes made in the Model Business Corporation Act in 1980.
155. *Id.* at § 8.50 note on statutory comparison (3d ed. 1994).
156. *Id.*
157. *See Changes in the Model Business Corporation Act Affecting Indemnification of Corporate Personnel*, 34 BUS. LAW. 1595 (1979).
158. RESTATEMENT (SECOND) OF THE LAW OF AGENCY § 439(d) (1958).
159. DEL. CODE ANN. tit. 8, § 145(a), (b) (2009); N.Y. BUS. CORP. LAW § 722(a), (b) (2009).
160. *See, e.g.*, CONN. BUS. CORP. ACT. § 33-777 (2009).
161. *See, e.g.*, DEL. CODE ANN. tit. 8, § 145(c) (2009).
162. VonFeldt v. Stifel Fin. Corp., 714 A.2d 79 (Del. 1998) (individual elected to serve on subsidiary corporation's board of directors is covered by provision of parent company's bylaws that extends indemnification as a matter of right to one who performs a function "at the request" of the parent).
163. Merritt-Chapman & Scott Corp. v. Wolfson, 321 A.2d 138 (Del. Super. 1974).
164. MBCA § 8.52 (2008).

165. MBCA ANN. § 8.52 official comment (3d ed. 1994).
166. *See* Dornan v. Humphrey, 106 N.Y.S.2d 142 (Sup. Ct. 1951), *modified on other grounds*, 112 N.Y.S.2d 585 (App. Div. 1952).
167. *See* Former MBCA § 5(a)(b) (1969).
168. *See* DEL. CODE ANN. tit. 8, § 145(a), (b) (2001).
169. MBCA § 8.51(d) (2008).
170. *See* DEL. CODE ANN. tit. 8, § 145(b) (2001); former MBCA § 5(b) (1969).
171. MBCA § 8.54(a)(2) (2008). *But see* N.C. GEN. STAT. § 55-8-57 (2009) (authorizing more expansive indemnification by optional provisions in articles or bylaws or otherwise by agreement).
172. DEL. CODE ANN. tit. 8, § 145(d) (2001); MBCA §§ 8.54 & 8.55 (1984); former MBCA § 5(b), (d) (1969).
173. *See* Behrstock v. Ace Hose & Rubber Co., 496 N.E.2d 1024 (1986).
174. *See, e.g.,* CAL. CORP. CODE § 317(b) (2009); DEL. CODE ANN. tit. 8, § 145(a), (b) (2001); N.Y. BUS. CORP. LAW § 722(a), (c) (2009); MBCA § 8.51(a) (2008); former MBCA § 5(a), (b) (1969).
175. *See, e.g.,* Biondi v. Beekman Hill House Apartment Corp., 731 N.E.2d 577, 581 (N.Y. 2000) (key to indemnification is director's good faith toward corporation, and mere judgment against director is not dispositive of this issue; in this case, however, director's willful racial discrimination was not in corporation's best interest).
176. *Id.*
177. *See* Associated Milk Producers, Inc. v. Parr, 528 F. Supp. 7, 8 (E.D. Ark. 1979).
178. *See In re* Landmark Land Co. of Carolina, Inc., 76 F.3d 553 (4th Cir. 1996); Pilpiak v. Keyes, 729 N.Y.S.2d 99 (App. Div. 2001) (violates public policy to indemnify executive expenses incurred in unsuccessful defense of grand larceny).
179. *See* Waskel v.Guar. Nat'l Corp., 23 P.3d 1214 (Colo. App. Ct. 2000).
180. *See* MBCA §§ 8.51(d)(1), 8.54(a)(2) (2008).
181. *See, e.g.,* CAL. CORP. CODE § 317(c)(1) (2009); DEL. CODE ANN. tit. 8, § 145(b) (2001); N.Y. BUS. CORP. LAW § 722(c) (2009).
182. *See* Cross v. Midtown Club, Inc., 365 A.2d 1227 (Conn. Super. Ct. 1976).
183. *See, e.g.,* CAL. CORP. CODE § 317(b) (2009) ("had no reasonable cause to believe the conduct of the person was unlawful"); DEL. CODE ANN. tit. 8, § 145(a) (2001); N.Y. BUS. CORP. LAW § 722(a) (2009); MBCA § 8.51(a)(3) (2008); former MBCA § 5(a) (1969).
184. *See* Ridder v. Cityfed Fin. Corp., 47 F.3d 85, 87 (3d Cir. 1995) (interpreting Delaware law).
185. MBCA § 8.53 (1984).
186. Insurance carriers also offer "entity" policies, especially for securities related matters, which provide insurance to the company even though the suit does not name any director or officer. When through the entity coverage the corporation becomes the insured under the D&O coverage, and the corporation enters bankruptcy when claims are to be dispersed from the policy, an issue can arise regarding what portion of the policy belongs to the bankruptcy estate.

187. Courts are fairly consistent in holding that the D&O carrier must pay the attorneys' bill in a timely fashion. *See, e.g.,* Okada v. MGIC Indem. Corp., 823 F.2d 276 (9th Cir. 1986).
188. *See, e.g.,* Foster v. Summit Med. Systems, Inc., 610 N.W.2d 350 (Minn. Ct. App. 2000) (reasoning that misconduct arose in the preparation of disclosure documents, not the offering of the security itself, court upheld denial of coverage for securities class action claims arising from public offering of securities where policy period commenced on date offering to public commenced).
189. *See* Commercial Capital Bankcorp. Inc. v. St. Paul Mercury Ins. Co., 419 F. Supp. 2d 1173 (C.D. Cal. 2006) (in a duty to defend form of coverage insurer must advance sums necessary for defense even though some of the underlying claims involved intentional misconduct and excluded from coverage; whereas in a D&O policy the allocation agreed upon by insurer and the insured applies).
190. *See* Int'l Ins. Co. v. Johns, 874 F.2d 1447 (11th Cir. 1989) (settlement returning to corporation amounts received as "golden parachutes" not within exclusion for "personal gains" where court concludes golden parachute arrangement was protected by business judgment rule).
191. *See, e.g.,* Cincinnati Ins. Co. v. Irwin Co., 2000 WL 1867297 (Ohio Ct. App. 2000) (upholding denial of claim by officers who engaged in inside trading).
192. *See* MBCA § 8.57 (2008). *See also* CAL. CORP. CODE § 317(i) (2009) (with extensive provisions dealing with propriety of such insurance carrier being affiliated with the corporation); DEL. CODE ANN. tit. 8, § 145(g) (2001); former MBCA § 5(g) (1969).
193. *See* N.Y. BUS. CORP. LAW § 726(b) (2009).
194. *See* Vigilant Ins. Co. v. Credit Suisse First Boston Corp., 800 N.Y.S.2d 358 (Supt. Ct. 2003) (denying on public policy grounds claim for sums investment bank was required to disgorge pursuant to an enforcement action by various securities regulators).

CHAPTER 16

ISSUANCE OF SHARES

PART A. SHARE SUBSCRIPTIONS AND UNDERWRITING

§ 16.1 NATURE AND FORM OF SUBSCRIPTION AGREEMENTS

One may become a shareholder either by (1) subscription contract with the corporation for the issue of new shares; (2) purchase from the corporation of treasury shares—that is, shares already issued and reacquired by the corporation; or (3) transfer from an existing holder of outstanding shares, with the new owner being substituted in the place of the transferor.[1] Share subscribers are persons who have agreed to take and pay for the original unissued shares of a corporation, formed or to be formed.[2] A subscription differs from a contract of sale, a subscription being a contract for the corporation to issue or create new shares, as contrasted with an agreement by a stockholder for the transfer of title to issued shares or shares to be issued.[3]

Unless the corporate statute or charter requires otherwise, a subscription can be oral or written, as long as it is sufficiently definite to satisfy the requirements for a valid contract. This minimally requires evidence of an agreement to purchase a given number of shares in the corporation at a specified price.[4] The states are split as to whether a subscription for stock must be in writing and signed by the subscriber to be enforceable. Approximately one half of the states follow the scheme of the current Model Business Corporation Act or its predecessor by not requiring that the subscription be in writing to be enforceable.[5] Even in jurisdictions that do require a written contract, the subscriber's conduct may estop him from raising the absence of a written agreement as a defense.[6] And in one case, the court interpreted the statute's requirement of a written agreement as affording a defense only to the subscriber; the corporation could have had an unwritten agreement enforced against it by the subscriber.[7] However, courts frequently have held a subscription for stock subject to the statute of frauds, like an agreement for the sale of goods, wares, merchandise, or choses in action.[8]

§ 16.2 PRE-INCORPORATION SUBSCRIPTIONS— REVOCABILITY

The subscriber's power to revoke a stock subscription today is circumscribed by state corporation statutes, which generally render pre-incorporation subscriptions irrevocable for a certain period of time, most frequently six months, unless otherwise agreed or unless all other subscribers agree to the release.[9] In the absence of a statute, courts have sometimes found it difficult to determine the legal principles applicable to pre-incorporation subscriptions.

§ 16.3 LIABILITY ON UNPAID SUBSCRIPTIONS TO CORPORATIONS AND CREDITORS

Under modern statutes, a corporation's board of directors may determine the payment terms of pre-incorporation subscriptions if the subscription agreement does not specify them.[10] A subscriber's default creates a debt due to the corporation, which may be accordingly collected.

Unless liability is imposed by statute, neither subscribers nor shareholders are directly accountable to the corporation's creditors.[11] The subscriber's liability is to the corporation and is pursued by its representatives.[12] In the absence of receivership or bankruptcy proceedings, the usual remedies available to corporate creditors to reach the indebtedness of shareholders for partly paid shares is a creditors' bill in equity or garnishment, in which creditors must show they have exhausted their remedies at law or are excused from doing so.[13]

§ 16.4 THE UNDERWRITING SERVICES OF INVESTMENT BANKERS

It is important for business lawyers to understand the nature of the underwriting arrangements commonly used by issuers and investment bankers in bringing out and distributing issues of corporate securities. However, lawyers should also be aware that securities may be "distributed" to the investing public directly by the management of a going corporation or by the promoters of a new enterprise, without the aid of investment bankers or the use of an underwriting agreement. Small concerns often cannot afford underwriting by investment bankers and must rely on corporate officers and agents to sell securities. Large concerns are sometimes able to place large issues of high-grade securities directly with life insurance companies, pension funds, or other institutional investors. In direct private financing, underwriting commissions are saved, as are other expenses such as registration under the securities laws.

The methods for raising corporate capital can be divided into ten basic categories. A corporation—or any other enterprise, for that matter—theoretically at least can raise capital *without an investment banker* by (1) a direct offering of securities to the public or a limited group of people, (2) a direct offering to existing security holders (sometimes called a "rights offering"), (3) a direct private placement, (4) public sealed bidding, or (5) bank loans, mortgage loans, equipment loans, and "leasebacks." The five basic methods *using the services of an investment banker* are (6) a negotiated, underwritten public offering of securities, (7) an underwritten public offering through sealed bids, (8) an underwritten offering to existing security holders, (9) an offering to existing security holders with the investment banker acting as agent, and (10) private placement with the investment banker acting as agent for the issuer. Financial realities and business exigencies frequently limit the actual choices.

"Origination" by underwriters of securities refers to the many steps an investment banker undertakes in preparation for a client company's public offering of securities. These steps include investigating the affairs and needs of would-be issuers, selecting companies that offer good investment opportunities, devising the types and terms of securities to be offered, negotiating with an issuer the spread or discount between the price the underwriters pay the issuer for the securities and the price at which they will be offered to the public or some other arrangement for compensating the underwriters, and arranging for associated underwriters and broker-dealers. "Distribution" involves the managing of selling syndicates, advertising the securities, and presenting them to investors. Largely because of the federal securities laws, there are extraordinarily high due diligence standards for all participants in the distribution process, including underwriters and professionals such as lawyers and accountants.[14]

The relationship between underwriter and issuer generally begins many months before the public offering is commenced. The managing underwriter provides a wide range of services to the issuer preparatory to the offering, including advice on the type and amount of security to be offered, the offering's timing, and the steps the issuer should take to put its financial and operational status in as favorable a light as possible prior to the offering.

An interesting dimension of underwriting is the matching of underwriter reputation with the relative riskiness of the issuer. The risks of a firm commitment underwriting are that investor demand for the security will be weak so that the underwriter's capital is tied up in the offering. Moreover, its reputation is damaged by having misjudged the marketability of that issuer's securities. It is not surprising, therefore, that lower-risk issuers tend to attract more established, higher-reputation underwriters.

Underwriters' services may be valuable to both issuers and investors. Large investment banking firms have prestige and direct access to the best dealers and customers. Leading underwriters develop a clientele that has faith in the underwriter's investigation, judgment, and responsibility. Thus, by using the services of underwriters, an issuing company may obtain needed funds promptly and save on the terms at which the securities are offered, such as the rate of interest on bonds or debentures or the dividend rate on preferred stock.

Investment bankers frequently establish special relationships with a corporation issuing securities. They may, for example, obtain representation on the corporation's board of directors or acquire control of the corporation by requiring the corporation's shareholders to put their shares into a voting trust with trustees the underwriters select. Underwriters' charges may cover origination costs, compensation for the underwriting risk and syndicate management, and selling compensation. Some underwriters have at times taken advantage of their influence to obtain an undue "spread" between the wholesale price that they pay the issuer and the retail price at which they sell the issue to the public.

PART B. THE ISSUANCE OF SHARES

§ 16.5 Issuance, Creation, or Allotment of Shares

Shares of stock are contracts created by mutual assent of the corporation and its shareholders. The shares must first be "authorized" by appropriate provisions in the corporation's charter, which detail the rights attaching to ownership.[15] Once shares are authorized, the power to issue them lies with the board of directors.[16] When shares are sold by the corporation, they are "issued," and those shares are thereafter referred to as "authorized *and* issued." As long as they are not reacquired by the corporation—that is, they remain in the hands of shareholders—they are also "outstanding" (that is, "authorized, issued, and outstanding"); shares that are "authorized, issued, but *not* outstanding" are shares that were previously issued by the corporation but subsequent to their issuance have been reacquired by the corporation. Such shares are more commonly referred to as "treasury shares" or "treasury stock." Shares issued in excess of the amount authorized, or issued that are not of a type authorized, are void.[17]

The word "issue" is generally employed to indicate the making of a share contract—that is, a transaction by which the directors create new shares and a person becomes the owner of the shares.[18] Share ownership can result either from subscription to an original issue of shares by the corporation or from the transfer of shares from a prior owner and the substitution of the transferee in the place of the prior owner. A corporation usually may resell treasury shares—that is, shares that have already been issued and have been reacquired by the corporation but not retired. Such a resale has the same market impact as the issue or creation of new shares, although the transaction generally gives rise to a different accounting treatment by the corporation.

§ 16.6 Flexibility in Terms of Preferred Shares

As with common stock, the rights, preferences, and restrictions of any class of preferred shares generally are fixed in the charter, i.e., articles of incorporation.[19] The financing of an enterprise may go on year after year, as business expands or the needs for capital arise. New issues of securities may be made from time to time; and, if preferred shares are issued, it may be necessary to meet changing market conditions by variations over time in the dividend rate and other terms of the preferred share contract. Thus the rights, privileges, and restrictions of a series of preferred shares issued at an earlier time quite probably are inappropriate for a contemporary issuance of additional shares. Absent flexible corporate enabling statutes, the serial nature of preferred stock issuances, each with the need for their rights, privileges, and restrictions to meet prevailing market conditions that are different from those of earlier issuances, would necessitate serial amendments to the articles of incorporation to authorize each new series of preferred shares. To avoid the expense and delay of such serial charter amendments, most modern corporation statutes permit a corporation's articles of incorporation to authorize the board of directors to fix the dividend rate, liquidation price, voting rights, and other terms of a class or a series within a class as the board of directors believes in the best interests of the corporation.[20] The board of directors' discretion must be exercised within the limits, if any, set forth in the enabling provision of the articles of incorporation, and the articles must set forth the number of shares of the class of shares over which the board of directors has such authority. Such shares are sometimes referred to as "blank stock" preferred shares. Absent such broad authorization, the board of directors lacks authority to so fix the terms of preferred shares.[21]

"Blank stock" preferred assumed a new role beginning with the takeover frenzy of the 1980s as a potentially powerful takeover defensive weapon. Boards of directors seized upon such blank stock authorization as the mechanism to issue "rights" that would confer upon their holders financial or voting rights whose exercise would thwart any hostile takeover of the corporation. The devices, popularly known as "poison pills," are examined extensively later in this treatise.

Most statutes permit enabling charter provisions authorizing the directors to subdivide classes of preferred shares into series.[22]

§ 16.7 SIGNIFICANCE OF PAR VALUE

"Outside of Delaware, par value" is a rapidly vanishing feature of corporate law.[23] In broad overview, par value was at one time believed a workable approach toward assuring that the full price was paid for a corporation's shares and that a financial cushion existed for the benefit of creditors against improvident dividend payments and share repurchases. As will be discussed later, the protections that were believed to arise from the shares' par value were largely illusionary because they could be easily circumvented by, among other approaches, the use of shares having a very low par value or even shares without any par value. California began what has become an accelerating trend within corporate statutes to accord no legal significance to a share's par value.[24] Delaware and New York are two important corporate domiciles whose corporate statutes continue to embrace this otherwise outmoded approach toward creditor protection.[25]

§ 16.8 SALE OF TREASURY SHARES AT LESS THAN PAR

Shares that once were issued as fully paid and have then been reacquired by the corporation and not retired are called "treasury" shares.[26] Such shares are treated as still having the status of "issued" shares for purposes of resale, although they no longer have dividend or voting rights.[27] It has generally been held that the corporation may reissue and sell these treasury shares for less than their par value.[28] Treasury shares are not truly assets to be sold, but merely represent the power to reissue the shares, which is distinguished from the power to create shares by subscription upon original issue.[29] The reason given for this distinction is that the corporation has already received a capital contribution for treasury shares and has thereby created for the corporation a stated capital "liability" with respect to the shares so issued, which was not eliminated upon the corporation's reacquisition of the shares. Upon their subsequent reissue, these shares do not increase the corporation's stated capital.

§ 16.9 Kinds of Consideration That Validate Payment for Shares

A corporation is not limited to a cash payment for its shares; it may receive payment in property or services if they are of a kind recognized as capable of valuation and are properly valued.[30] Most state statutes set forth the types of consideration the corporation can receive for its shares if the shares are to be "fully paid and nonassessable."[31] The types of consideration commonly authorized are money and real and personal property, including intangible property, as well as services rendered. These traditional forms of eligible types of consideration exclude executory forms of consideration, such as promissory notes or a promise of future services. A minority of the states follow the scheme of the Model Business Corporation Act and allow promissory notes and future services, as well as the traditional types of consideration.[32]

§ 16.10 Valuation of Consideration for Shares

At one time, a few jurisdictions adhered to what was known as the "strict value rule." According to this rule, payment for shares in property or services was satisfaction as against creditors only to the extent of the true value of the consideration, notwithstanding the good faith of the directors in fixing the value of the property or services.[33] This attempt to allow review of the directors' determination of value has been abandoned in the jurisdictions that had once adhered to it.[34]

Modern statutes and decisions have established the "good faith rule," under which the judgment of the board of directors, shareholders, or incorporators as to the value of property or services a corporation receives for shares is conclusive unless fraud or intentional over-valuation is shown by the creditor.[35] Statutes frequently express the standard as being "in the absence of fraud" or "absence of *actual* fraud."[36] There are some variations, however, in what amounts to fraud.

There is a great need for careful and impartial valuation, especially where there is a potential conflict of interest.[37] It is proper practice for the board of directors, by resolution entered in its minutes, to state its appraisal, after careful investigation, of the fair dollar value of services or property for which shares with or without par value are being used. An over-valuation without reasonable and impartial investigation into the elements of present value is evidence of lack of good faith. In many situations, the board should seek an independent appraisal.

A determination in dollars of the value of the property or consideration received by the corporation is necessary for accounting purposes in stating the cost or value of its assets and in making up balance sheets showing the corporation's financial condition.[38] In Delaware, New York, and other states that retain the traditional legal capital accounting, it is necessary to designate what part of consideration received for shares is to be attributed to stated capital and what amount, if any, is to be attributed to paid in surplus, particularly in connection with the issue of shares without par value. However, the absence of such a designation should not prevent the shares from being issued, assuming an eligible form of consideration was exchanged for the shares.[39]

Those states following the Model Business Corporation Act's treatment of the issuance of shares, whereby only the *adequacy* of any consideration is determined by the board of directors,[40] do not require that the directors assign a set value to any non-cash consideration received for the shares when the shares are issued. Under this approach the directors can, if they wish, be more reflective and deliberate and can value the non-cash consideration at some later date. A precise value must at some time be assigned to the non-cash consideration because the corporation's accounting records demand that all assets be recorded in dollars on the company's books at their cost. By requiring the board of directors to pass only on the adequacy of the consideration exchanged for shares before the shares are issued, the Model Business Corporation Act separates the legal consequences of the board's issuance of shares from the accounting questions. Such separation should make successful challenges to the issuance of shares less likely. Moreover, requiring a determination only of adequacy of consideration is consistent with the overall deregulatory and facilitating philosophy of the Model Business Corporation Act.

§ 16.11 EQUITABLE LIMITATIONS FOR PRICING SHARES

Directors have a fiduciary duty to fix a reasonable price for issues of shares, both with and without par value. Timing can be a crucial factor in applying the equitable yardstick of reasonableness. If a newly formed corporation issues no-par or low-par shares to its promoters or others, there is ordinarily no legal restriction on the *amount* of consideration the corporation can receive for the shares, as long as there is some lawful consideration. However, insiders have a heavy burden of establishing the fairness of the transactions when they issue shares to themselves at a significant discount from the price available to outsiders.[41] If the corporation has been in business for some time and has demonstrated its earning capacity, the price at which additional shares are issued will have a direct effect on the interests of existing shareholders. Too low a price will dilute the interest of the holders of outstanding shares and unfairly impair the values underlying their holdings. Ideally, if new shares are not offered to the existing shareholders, the shares should be issued at a fair price, based on market conditions and the value of the corporation's assets and prospective earnings—subject, however, to a reasonable range of business discretion. As a practical matter, new offerings to the public are frequently priced at a discount as a means of attracting investors and reducing any exposure of underwriters to liability.

Differences in the prices at which shares, either par or no-par, are issued must be justified by showing fairness in light of the circumstances. Shares of the same class may be issued for different amounts of consideration at the same time if the discrimination in price is justified by adequate business reasons and is not a matter of favoritism.[42]

Disputes regarding the price at which shares are to be sold rarely arise within companies whose shares are publicly traded. For such firms, the shares' market price provides a powerful benchmark for assessing the board of directors' decision; a rational business purpose is needed to justify offering the shares below their current market value.[43]

A more frequent basis of complaint in the public corporation is that the board of directors has issued the shares to entrench the incumbent management team. When this is established, appropriate equitable relief is provided, generally to cancel shares that were issued or to enjoin their pending issuance.[44] But the courts will not intrude when a bona fide business purpose supports the shares' issuance, even though a necessary effect of issuing more shares is to entrench management.[45] Moreover, the decision to place a substantial percentage of the stock in "friendly" hands does not itself condemn the shares' issuance where the board of directors after reasonable investigation determines in good faith that such a defensive maneuver is a reasonable response to the threat the hostile bid for control poses to the corporation or its stockholders.[46] The relative freedom of the board of directors to deflect an unwanted suitor is discussed in Chapter 23.

Equitable challenges to the corporation issuing more shares frequently arises in the close corporation, where delicate balances of power and economic participation can be swiftly upset by a board resolution selling shares to one faction of stockholders. The complaint in this setting is invariably that the shares are being sold for less than their fair value or to dilute substantially the plaintiff's ownership interest, or both. As for the concern that the shares have not been fairly priced by the board of directors, the courts emphasize a variety of considerations in determining the fair value of shares in the individual case.[47] For example, a substantial departure from the shares' book value—a highly conservative benchmark, given that book value assumes that the firm's assets have no greater worth than their historical cost less any recorded depreciation or amortization—removes the pricing decision from the business judgment rule.[48] More frequently yet, equitable relief is awarded in the close corporation when the transparent purpose of issuing additional shares is to substantially dilute the plaintiff's voting power.[49] However, a business purpose for issuing the shares and no effort to exclude the plaintiff from purchasing them insulates the shares' issuance from equitable attack.[50]

§ 16.12 THE SHAREHOLDERS' PREEMPTIVE RIGHT

The directors' power to issue shares is subject to a common law fiduciary duty not to impair the ratable rights and interests of existing shareholders. The recognition of preemptive rights to an offer of an opportunity to subscribe ratably for new issues arose from an attempt by the courts to create a prophylaxis to unfairness and abusive dilution of existing shares.

Originally, the preemptive right was recognized by the courts as mandatory, but now every state by statute allows the corporate charter to limit or deny the common law preemptive right or eliminates the preemptive right unless it is affirmatively granted by corporate charter. By express statutory provision in many states a corporation's article of incorporation may contain provisions limiting or denying preemptive rights.[51] Some such statutes merely refer to the ability to limit or deny the right in a corporation's articles of incorporation, whereas in other states the statute details the scope of the right in the absence of a defining, limiting, or denying provision in the articles.[52] Most frequently, states provide that there are no preemptive rights unless granted in the corporation's articles of incorporation.[53] And even though provided in the articles of incorporation, preemptive rights can be removed through the amendment process.[54] Since preemptive rights are now effectively permissive, drafters of corporate charters should keep in mind the various factors to be weighed as well as the necessity for making clear the extent of any preemptive right.

Preemptive rights aim to safeguard holders against unfairness in the issue of shares, particularly against two possible wrongs: (1) the manipulation of voting control of the corporation by the issuance of shares to one faction of shareholders to the exclusion of other shareholders,[55] and (2) the issue of shares at an inadequate price to favored persons, thereby diluting the proportionate interest of other shareholders to dividends and to corporate assets on dissolution.[56] As the Minnesota high court earlier said, "If a corporation, either through the officers, directors or majority stockholders, may dispose of new stock to whomsoever it will, at whatever price it may fix, then it has the power to diminish the value of each share of old stock, by letting the parties have equal interest in the surplus, and in the goodwill or value of the established business."[57]

Even when not denied in the charter, preemptive rights apply, according to most courts, only to an issue of newly authorized shares and do not extend to a new issue of originally or previously authorized shares, at least not where the issue does not raise funds to expand the business.[58] A few courts, however, have held that preemptive rights extend to original shares that are issued long after the creation of the corporation and a material time after the original offering of shares has come to an end.[59] The latter is the better view because the availability of such an important prophylaxis should not depend on the fortuity of whether less than all the originally authorized shares were issued. This view is even more compelling when the parties have expressly provided for preemptive rights in the articles of incorporation, as they have thereby expressed a desire for affirmative protection against dilution.

The preemptive right is most frequently granted to the holders of common shares.[60] In the absence of a provision in a corporation's articles of incorporation granting holders of a class of stock preemptive rights in issues of another class, it is doubtful to what extent a holder of shares of one class has a preemptive right to an issue of the shares of another class. The cases are in conflict. Should a preemptive right to new issues of common always be given to the holders of preferred shares or only if the preferred shares currently carry voting rights equal to the common shares? Certainly, if preferred is nonvoting and nonparticipating in dividends, there is no basis for dilution of their interest. If preferred shareholders have full voting rights but no participating rights as dividends, or vice versa, the resolution of whether the preferred has a preemptive right is more problematic and should, in the absence of express contractual provisions, turn on the likely intent of the parties.

As the share structure of a corporation becomes more complex, it is very difficult, if not impossible, to grant preemptive rights to a class of preferred shares without some change in the relative rights of other classes.[61] In the absence of a charter provision to the contrary, some jurisdictions limit preemptive rights to holders of shares of the same class as those being issued.[62] Confusion and uncertainty about such matters in a particular jurisdiction may make it desirable to waive or clarify preemptive rights by specific provision in the articles of incorporation.

Preemptive rights do not ordinarily extend to the reissue or resale of treasury shares.[63] This exception is also based on practical grounds, as treasury shares are usually sold from time to time and not reissued in large amounts. The directors' duty of good faith and fairness, however, applies to a corporation's sale of treasury shares and also to other issues of shares in which no preemptive right is recognized.[64]

Preemptive rights generally do not apply to a corporation's issuance of shares under an employee stock option or employee stock purchase plan. If, in a particular state, preemptive rights do apply to shares issued under such a plan, or if that matter is in question, waiver of preemptive rights may have to be submitted to the shareholders, or the corporation's articles of incorporation may have to be amended.[65] The value of the employees' right to purchase under such a plan should, of course, have some reasonable relation to the value of the services rendered or to be rendered by the employees.[66]

When a corporation is issuing shares, market conditions may not allow for delay that would result from honoring preemptive rights by offering shares to all the shareholders. In such a situation, the requirement of a preemptive rights offering may harm the shareholders more than it helps them.[67] Thus, the conclusion of many courts is that preemptive rights do not apply to shares that are part of those originally authorized. In any event, the existence of a preemptive right can impose a serious timing problem on the corporation's needs to raise capital because any preemptive right postpones sales to outsiders until existing stockholders have been approached. Thus, a company that anticipates a future need to raise funds from new investors is well advised to consider removing preemptive rights as a predicate to that offering.

Preemptive rights do not make sense in a public-issue corporation. In fact, their presence can severely hamper future financing. Accordingly, the charters of public companies typically eliminate such rights if the statutes of their domiciles do not do so. If preemptive rights are abrogated or waived, the directors still must not discriminate unfairly in the issue of shares; differences in the issue price of the shares may be made only in the exercise of fair business judgment for the benefit of the corporation.[68] In a close corporation, however, in the interest of preserving the original shareholders' proportionate preemptive rights, they often should not only be retained but also should be extended to cover many of the share-issue transactions that are generally excepted from the rights.[69]

It is thus clear that regardless of preemptive rights, a corporation's directors must observe their fiduciary responsibilities in issuing new shares; otherwise, the shares may be subject to cancellation.[70] In the issuance of shares, however, the directors have the latitude, including pricing, given by the business judgment rule.[71] Even though there is some division in the courts as to whether a shareholder suit based on an alleged violation of preemptive rights is direct or derivative,[72] the better view is that the preemptive right, as a right of the individual stockholder, should give rise to a direct cause of action.

NOTES

1. Corporate capital structure and the various types of ownership interests are discussed in Chapter 18.
2. *See, e.g.,* Ashley v. Coleman, 219 So. 2d 574 (La. Ct. App. 1969).
3. *See* Zukowski v. Dunton, 650 F.2d 30 (4th Cir. 1981).
4. Klapmeier v. Flagg, 677 F.2d 781 (9th Cir. 1982); AIH Acquisition Corp. LLC v. Alaska Ind. Hardware Inc., 306 F. Supp. 2d 455 (S.D.N.Y. 2004) (specifically enforcing written agreement that contained all essential terms but which had not been signed by the seller where there was clear intent that the agreement was final).
5. *See* Bielinski v. Miller, 382 A.2d 357 (NH 1978).
6. *See* Duncan v. Brookview House, Inc., 205 S.E.2d 707 (S.C. 1974).
7. Putnam v. Williams, 652 F.2d 497 (5th Cir. 1981).
8. *See* Cooper v. Vitraco, Inc., 320 F. Supp. 239 (D.V.I. 1970) (decided under U.C.C. § 8-319).
9. *See, e.g.,* ALA. CODE 1975 § 10-2B-6.20 (Michie 1999); COL. REV. STAT. ANN. § 7-106-201 (West 1986 & Supp. 2002); GEO. CODE ANN. § 14-2-620 (Michie 1994).
10. *See, e.g.,* ALA. CODE § 10-2B-6.20 (2009); ARIZ. REV. STAT. ANN. § 10-620 (2009); WASH. REV. CODE ANN. § 23B.06.200 (2009); VA. CODE ANN. § 13.1-642 (2009); MBCA § 6.20 (2008); Former MBCA § 17 (1969).
11. Thomson-Houston Elec. Co. v. Murray, 37 A. 443 (N.J. Sup. Ct. 1897).
12. Kerosec v. Yirga, 230 N.E.2d 587 (Ill. App. Ct. 1967).
13. *See* Denniston & Co., Inc. v. Jackson, 468 So. 2d 170 (Ala. Civ. App. 1985).
14. *See* Section 11(b)(3), 15 U.S.C. § 77k(b)(3) (2009).
15. MBCA § 6.01 (2008); Former MBCA §§ 15, 54(d) (1969). *But see* James J. Hanks, Jr., *Removing the Limits on Authorized Stock*, 73 WASH. U. L.Q. 479 (1995) (questioning whether the concept of "authorized" shares should continue to be a component of corporate law).
16. *See, e.g.,* CAL. CORP. CODE ANN. § 406 (2009); CONN. GEN. STAT. ANN. § 33-672 (2009); 805 ILL. COMP. STAT. ANN. 5/6.05 (2009); MBCA § 6.21 (2008); Former MBCA § 18 (1969). Issuance without board approval is void. *See* Foster v. Blackwell, 747 So. 2d 1203 (La. Ct. App. 1999).
17. *See, e.g.,* Waggoner v. Laster, 581 A.2d 1127, 1137 (Del. 1990).
18. Blythe v. Doheny, 73 F.2d 799, 803 (9th Cir. 1934).
19. *See, e.g.,* CAL. CORP. CODE § 202 (West 1990 & Supp. 2002); FLA. STAT. ANN. § 607.0601 (West 2001); 215 ILL. COMP. STAT. ANN. 5/14.1 (West 2000), 13-A MAINE REV. STAT. ANN. § 403 (1988); MBCA § 6.01 (1984); Former MBCA § 15 (1969).
20. *E.g.,* ALA. CODE 1975 § 10-2B-6.02 (2009); DEL. CODE ANN. tit. 8, § 151 (2009); IND. CODE ANN. § 23-1-34-6 (2009); MISSOURI STAT. ANN. § 375.198 (2009); N.Y. BUS. CORP. LAW § 502 (2009). *See* MBCA § 6.02 (2008).
21. *Waggoner,* 581 A.2d 1127.
22. *See, e.g.,* ALA. CODE 1975 § 10-2B-6.02 (2001); CAL. CORP. CODE § 202 (West 1990 & Supp. 2002); N.C. GEN. STAT. § 55-6-01 (2001).
23. *See* Venture Stores, Inc. v. Ryan, 678 N.E.2d 300, 303 (Ill. Ct. App. 1997) ("Today the concept of par value is an anachronism.").

24. *See* CAL. CORP. CODE § 202(d) (1990) (legislative committee comment).
25. *See* DEL. CODE ANN. tit. 8, §§ 102(a)(4), 153 (2009); N.Y. BUS. CORP. L. § 402(a)(4) (2009).
26. The 1980 revisions to the Model Act abolish treasury shares. Former MBCA § 6 (1980); MBCA § 6.31 (1984).
27. Former MBCA § 2(h) (1969). *See id.* § 18, which provides that treasury shares may be issued at a price fixed by the board without regard to par.
28. Borg v. Int'l Silver Co., 11 F.2d 147, 152 (2d Cir. 1925).
29. *Id.* 147; Americar, Inc. v. Crowley, 282 So. 2d 674 (Fla. Ct. App. 1973) (Carroll, J. dissenting).
30. *E.g.*, West v. Sirian Lamp Co., 44 A.2d 658 (Del. Ch. 1945).
31. *See, e.g.*, ARIZ. REV. STAT. § 10-621(B) (2009); COLO. REV. STAT. § 7-106-202(2) (2009); DEL. CODE ANN., tit. 8, § 152 (2009); N.Y. BUS. CORP. L. § 504(a) (2009).
32. Following the modern trend, New York amended its statute in 1998 to authorize future services, N.Y. BUS. CORP. L. § 504(b) (McKinney 2003) (Historical and Statutory Notes); MBCA § 6.21(b) (1984). For a decision holding that the N.Y. amendment does no apply retroactively, *see* Carr v. Marietta Corp., 211 F.3d 724 (2d Cir. 2000).
33. William E. Dee Co. v. Proviso Coal Co., 125 N.E. 24, 26 (Ill. 1919).
34. *See* Clinton Mining & Mineral Co. v. Jamison, 256 F. 577 (3d Cir. 1919).
35. *See, e.g.*, Arkota Ind., Inc. v. Naekel, 623 S.W.2d 194 (Ark. 1981).
36. Former MBCA § 119 (1969). *See* DEL. CODE ANN. tit. 8, § 152 (2009) ("in the absence of actual fraud").
37. *See, e.g.*, Doyle v. Union Ins. Co., 277 N.W.2d 36 (Neb. 1979) (fraud occurred by board member submitting his own valuation of property and then supervised the employment of an expert to value the property; his obvious self-interest was not mediated by the other directors who evidence supported finding were negligent in approving the transaction).
38. Garbe v. Excel Mold, Inc., 397 N.E.2d 296 (Ind. Ct. App. 1979); Knickerbocker Importation Co. v. Bd. of Assessors, 65 A. 913, 915 (N.J. 1907) ("Neither bookkeeping nor mere recitative language in resolutions of a board of directors creating values can be accepted as the equivalent of the proof of bona fide value required by our statute when stock is issued for property purchased.").
39. *See* Bissias v. Koulovatos, 761 A.2d 47, 49 (Me. 2000) (statute regulating issuance of no-par shares stated the consideration would "be fixed from time to time by the board" interpreted to require only that the "consideration be given for the shares and for such consideration to have a value").
40. Section 6.21(c) of the Model Business Corporation Act provides simply that before the shares are issued "the board of directors must determine that the consideration received or to be received for shares" is adequate.
41. *See* Schwartz v. Marien, 335 N.E.2d 334 (N.Y. 1975). *See also* Dingle v. Xtenit, Inc., 867 N.Y.S.2d 373 (Sup. Ct. 2008) (no business purpose supported issuance of substantial quantity of shares to majority holder that diluted interests of others).
42. Bodell v. Gen. Gas & Elec. Corp., 132 A. 442 (Del. Ch. 1926), *aff'd*, 15 Del. Ch. 420, 140 A. 264 (Del. 1927).
43. *Id.*

44. *See, e.g.,* Klaus v. Hi-Shear Corp., 528 F.2d 225 (9th Cir. 1975).
45. *See* Empire of Carolina, Inc. v. Deltona Corp., 514 A.2d 1091, 1097 (Del. 1985) (finding bona fide purpose though did also have effect of entrenching management).
46. *See* Herald v. Seawell, 472 F.2d 1081 (10th Cir. 1972).
47. *See* Direct Media/DMI, Inc. v. Rubin, 654 N.Y.S.2d 986 (Sup. 1997).
48. *See, e.g.,* Hyman v. Velsicol Corp., 97 N.E.2d 122 (Ill. App. 1951).
49. *See, e.g.,* Gregory v. Correction Connection, Inc., 1991 WL 42992 (E.D. Pa. 1991).
50. Herbik v. Rand, 732 S.W.2d 232 (Mo. Ct. App. 1987); Crosby v. Beam, 548 N.E.2d 217 (Ohio 1989) (recognizing duty of equal opportunity which can be satisfied by proof of a legitimate business purpose or unequal treatment).
51. *See* Alaska Stat. § 10.06.210 (2009); Minn. Stat. Ann. § 302A.413 (2009); MBCA Ann. § 10.01 (3d ed. 1995).
52. *E.g.,* Fla. Stat. Ann. § 607.0202 (2009); N.H. Rev. Stat. Ann. § 293-A:6.30 (2009); N.Y. Bus. Corp. Law § 622 (2009); Former MBCA § 26A (1980).
53. Ariz. Rev. Stat. § 10-630 (2009); Cal. Corp. Code § 204 (2009); Conn. Gen. Stat. Ann. § 33-683 (2009); Del. Code Ann. tit. 8, § 102(b)(3) (2009) ("no stockholder shall have any preemptive right to subscribe to an additional issue . . . unless, and except to the extent that, such right is expressly granted to him in the certificate of incorporation"); Mich. Comp. L. Ann. § 450.1343 (2009).
54. *See* L.L. Minor Co. v. Perkins, 268 S.E.2d 637 (Ga. 1980).
55. Dickson v. Morrison, 187 F.3d 629 (4th Cir. 1999) (recognizing preemptive right there protected shareholders from management entrenching its control of close corporation).
56. *See* Katzowitz v. Sidler, 249 N.E.2d 359, 363 (N.Y. 1969).
57. Jones v. Morrison, 16 N.W. 854, 861 (Minn. 1883).
58. Yasik v. Wachtel, 17 A.2d 309 (Del. Ch. 1941).
59. Titus v. Paul State Bank, 179 P. 514 (Idaho 1919).
60. More specifically, the registered owner of the shares is entitled to exercise the preemptive right such that the owner-pledgor of shares may exercise preemptive rights with respect to shares he has pledged to secure a loan. *See* Peri-Gil Corp. v. Sutton, 442 P.2d 35 (Nov. 1968).
61. *See* Russell v. Am. Gas & Elec. Co., 136 N.Y.S. 602 (App. Div. 1912).
62. *E.g.,* MBCA § 6.30(b)(5) (1984).
63. *Borg,* 11 F.2d 147.
64. Schwab v. Schwab-Wilson Mach. Corp., 55 P.2d 1268 (Cal. Ct. App. 1936).
65. *See, e.g.,* Schwartz v. Custom Printing Co., 926 S.W.2d 490 (Mo. Ct. App. 1996) (denying injunction seeking to enforce right of stockholder to obtain proportionate amount of shares to be issued pursuant to a employee bonus plan).
66. Dickinson v. Auto Ctr. Mfg. Co., 639 F.2d 250 (5th Cir. 1981).
67. Venner v. Am. Tel. & Tel. Co., 181 N.Y.S. 45, 47 (Sup. Ct. 1920); Harry S. Drinker, Jr., *The Preemptive Right of Shareholders to Subscribe to New Shares,* 43 Harv. L. Rev. 586, 615 (1930).
68. Schwartz v. Marien, 335 N.E.2d 334 (N.Y. 1975).

69. *See* Fuller v. Krogh, 113 N.W.2d 25, 32 (Wis. 1962).
70. *See, e.g.*, Mason Shoe Mfg. Co. v. Firstar Bank Eau Claire, N.A., 579 N.W.2d 789 (Wis. Ct. App. 1998).
71. *See Schwab*, 55 P.2d 1268 (Cal. Ct. App. 1936).
72. *See* Bellows v. Porter, 201 F.2d 429 (8th Cir. 1953).

CHAPTER 17

LIABILITY FOR WATERED, BONUS, AND UNDERPAID SHARES

TABLE OF SECTIONS

§ 17.1 Varieties of Watered Stock

"Watered stock" refers to shares issued as fully paid when in fact the consideration agreed to and accepted by the corporation's directors is something known to be much less than the par value of the shares or lawful subscription price. The term is frequently used to cover bonus shares as well as discount shares and those issued for property or services at an overvaluation.

If shares have been issued by a corporation as paid in full when in fact the subscriber has not paid or agreed to pay the full par value or lawful issue price, in either money, property, or services, the shares are said to be watered to the extent to which they have not been, or are not agreed to be, fully paid. There are various ways in which underpaid or watered shares may come into being. They may be issued gratuitously without any consideration passing to the corporation.[1] They may be issued for cash at a discount below par value,[2] or in exchange for property, labor, or services that are known to be worth less than the par value.[3]

Shares may also be issued as a "bonus" or inducement to the purchaser of bonds or preferred shares. Bonus shares are legitimate when viewed as further consideration for the purchase price that has to be apportioned between them and the other securities.[4] It is often difficult to allocate or apportion the credit where bonus stock has been issued. The word "bonus" implies a gift or gratuity and is sometimes used in the sense of shares issued without any consideration.

Another variety of watered stock may be issued in the guise of a stock dividend. In such a case, the stock is issued to existing shareholders as shares that represent a transfer of surplus to capital when in fact there is insufficient surplus to justify their issuance.[5]

§ 17.2 Evils and Abuses of Stock Watering

Flagrant stock watering was common in the promotion and financing of corporations in the latter part of the nineteenth and the early years of the twentieth centuries. The evils of stock watering consist primarily of injuries to the corporation, innocent shareholders, and creditors perpetrated by promoters and those in control by depriving the corporation of needed capital and of the corporation's opportunity to market its securities to its own advantage, thus hurting its business prospects and financial responsibility. Existing and future shareholders are injured due to dilution of the proportionate interests of those who pay full value for their shares.[6] Present and future creditors are injured when the corporation is deprived of the assets to be contributed by all the shareholders as a substitute for individual liability for corporate debts.

Three developments have significantly reduced the frequency of suits under state corporate statutes for watered stock liability. First, the advent of low-par and no-par stock has to a large extent eliminated watered stock problems in the strict definitional sense. By eliminating par value, the present Model Business Corporations Act also does away with watered stock in its strictest meaning.[7] Finally, the prophylactic effects of state blue sky laws and remedial benefits available under the antifraud provisions, section 10(b) and Rule 10b-5, of the Securities Exchange Act of 1934, have largely supplanted the regulatory impact of state corporate statutes for watered stock, at least with respect to protecting the corporation and later-purchasing shareholders. The discussion that follows closely examines the remedies the corporation and its creditors have for watered stock.

NOTES

1. *See, e.g.*, Andrews v. Chase, 49 P.2d 938, 941 (1935), *reh'g denied*, 57 P.2d 702 (1936).
2. *See, e.g.*, Harman v. Himes, 77 F.2d 375 (D.C. Cir. 1935).
3. *E.g.*, Elyton Land Co. v. Birmingham Warehouse & Elevator Co., 9 So. 129 (Ala. 1890).
4. *In re* Associated Oil Co., 289 F. 693 (6th Cir. 1923).
5. Whitlock v. Alexander, 76 S.E. 538 (N.C. 1912).
6. Bodell v. Gen. Gas & Elec. Corp., 132 A. 442 (Del. Ch. 1926), *aff'd*, 140 A. 264 (Del. 1927).
7. However, the same evils can be accomplished by the issuance of shares at a grossly overvalued price.

CHAPTER 18

CAPITAL STRUCTURE, PREFERENCES, AND CLASSES OF SECURITIES

TABLE OF SECTIONS

§ 18.1 CHOICES IN DEBT AND EQUITY FINANCING

The "capitalization," financial structure, or permanent financing of a corporation is based on the issuance of capital securities. Permanent financing includes not only common stock but also senior securities, which can be (1) an equity interest by way of preferred stock or (2) bonds and debentures, which are the long-term or funded debts. Debt obligations are issued against the corporation's actual or prospective earning power even more than against its assets. The power to issue bonds and other debt obligations is not dependent, as stock issues are, on express authorization by the corporate charter. Debt financing thus provides more flexibility because there generally is no need for prior shareholder approval.

A sound and well-balanced capital structure must be carefully planned. The choice between stocks and bonds of different varieties depends on many considerations, including whether the business has an established earnings record, the ratio of property to its obligations, the rate of return that must be paid, probable marketability and attractiveness to investors, advantages under federal and state tax laws, and the effect on the future credit and ability of the corporation to survive business cycles.

The tax laws encourage debt financing by treating interest payments, but not dividends on stock, as deductible from corporate gross income.[1] In order to safeguard against abuse due to thin equity financing, payments on the debt instruments may be treated for tax purposes as disguised dividends.[2] Similarly, too high a debt-to-equity ratio may lead a bankruptcy court to classify debt as stock for the purposes of subordinating claims of shareholder/creditors to those of other creditors.[3]

Attorneys are frequently asked to assist in evaluating the financial soundness of a firm's capital structure. The choice among different kinds of securities should be determined by the organizer and managers, considering the inducements needed to attract different types of investors and the control of management. They must further adequately anticipate the corporation's future financial needs. Questions that inevitably arise include: (1) How can the company raise money at the lowest cost? (2) What are the tax advantages of different forms of securities? (3) How can control be reserved to the organizers without requiring them to invest too large an amount in the corporation? (4) To what extent can the company meet fixed financial charges when its income is fluctuating? (5) How can the company best ensure its credit for future financing to meet expansion and growth?

Preferred shares, which are frequently viewed as a hybrid of debt and equity, may be advisable as an alternative to pure debt because payment of dividends is not a mandatory fixed charge and non-payment will not entail foreclosure or receivership. In addition to the ability to pass on payments without being in default, there is usually no maturity date for retirement of preferred shares, and the redemption provision, if any, is normally an option in favor of the corporation. In the absence of a prohibitory covenant, the corporation has the power to borrow money by issuing notes or bonds that take priority over the preferred shares. Preferred shares may be desirable because they tend to attract a type of investor different from those who invest in pure debt instruments. Special features, such as the right of conversion into a different type of security, further expand the alternative vehicles for raising capital.

The issuance of senior securities such as bonds and preferred shares may be attractive to the issuer for various reasons. First, senior securities create "leverage" for the common shares—that is, a greater chance of possible gain to the common on the total capital investment. Second, senior securities represent money invested for a limited return on the basis of a stable income to the investor; therefore, they have no claim on capital appreciation or increased corporate income. Third, preferred shares facilitate retention of voting control by the initial or current investors, as all senior securities usually have at most only contingent voting rights. This reduces the amount of investment necessary to obtain voting control by way of either initial investment or subsequent acquisition. Fourth, preferred shares and bonds can be used to tap the reservoir of savings of those who seek to avoid the risks of common stocks.

§ 18.2 BONDS AND DEBT FINANCING

Bonds or debentures are essentially promissory notes with more elaborate provisions than ordinary commercial loans. They are generally long-term, but in times of fluctuating interest rates shorter-term instruments are not uncommon. Despite its existence as a corporate debt, the longer-term instrument has led to the view of bondholders as "joint heirs in the corporate fortunes—participants in the success or failure who have been given preferential rights in the common hazard."

There are two parts to every bond issue: (1) the trust indenture and (2) the separate bonds. In broad overview, the trust indenture has two distinct parts: The first part sets forth all the obligations and restrictions on the bonds' issuer; the second part not only sets forth the bondholders' rights on default of the conditions set forth in the first part but also, by tracking the standards embodied in the Trust Indenture Act of 1939, sets forth the relationship between the indenture trustee and the bondholders.[4] There are also provisions related to amendment of the indenture, as well as protection of any conversion privilege.

The bond is the only writing that the bondholder ordinarily sees. Bonds and debentures may be described as a series of instruments or notes representing units of indebtedness, yet regarded as but parts of one entire debt. The rights of all the bondholders are governed by an underlying trust, deed, mortgage, or indenture between the corporation and a trustee, who is the representative of all the different bondholders. Within this framework the remedies of an individual bondholder are limited. The indenture or mortgage has grown to be an extraordinarily complicated and elaborate legal instrument.

The Trust Indenture Act of 1939[5] today applies to corporate debt obligations where the aggregate issue price is $10 million or greater.[6] The focus of the Act is on providing "an effective and independent trustee." It addresses this goal by proscribing nine "conflicting interest" relationships.[7] The Act also prescribes certain provisions to be contained in the indenture.[8] Additionally, the Act mandates certain minimum capital requirements, calls for high standards of conduct and responsibility on the part of the indenture trustee, preludes seeking preferential treatment for the trustee's claims (as distinct from those of the bondholders the trustee represents) when the obligor is in default, mandates that the issuer provide the trustee with evidence of compliance with the indenture's covenants, and requires the trustee to provide reports and notices to the bondholders. The relationship of the trustee to the bondholders has been subject to various classifications:[9] (1) as fiduciary;[10] (2) as founded in principal-agent law,[11] and (3) based on the contract rights, as defined in the indenture agreement.[12] Of interest is that the Act does not bar the trustee from also being a lender to the obligor of the bonds for which the trustee is the indenture trustee. This reflects the commercial reality that has long existed that most indenture trustees are banks and, as such, are not only in the business of lending funds but use their lending relationships to become the indenture trustee for bonds issued by the bank's clients. A leading case held the indenture trustee breached its fiduciary relationship to the bondholders when it advanced its own interests as a lender to the bond's obligor to the detriment of the bondholders for whom it was the indenture trustee.[13] Neither this fiduciary obligation nor a fair construction of the Act implicates a broader obligation than undivided loyalty to the bondholders. Thus, in one case, the indenture trustee did not breach its duty to the bondholders by accepting less than the maximum period of notice called for by the indenture before the bonds could be redeemed, since the trustee derived no personal gain from its decision.[14]

§ 18.3 TYPES OF BONDS

Open and Closed Mortgage Bonds. A serious error in corporate financing can be the failure to consider future needs for additional capital. The best-framed bond mortgages make liberal provision for the increase of indebtedness by future borrowing under the same mortgage, the increase to be made under careful safeguards and restrictions. Such mortgages are known as "open-end" mortgages or bond issues and vary in the degree of openness. A closed bond issue is one in which no more bonds can be issued under a mortgage or deed of trust.

Debentures and Debenture Agreements. There are many varieties of bonds, ranging from those secured by a first mortgage or senior lien on property to those secured by a secondary or junior lien, those secured by a pledge of personal collateral such as stocks or bonds, those secured by the general credit of the corporation and restrictive agreements such as debentures and serial notes, and income bonds, which are sometimes used in reorganizations. Debentures are serial obligations or notes representing indebtedness but not ordinarily secured by any specific mortgage, lien, or pledge of security. They are usually issued under an indenture, in which a trust company agrees to supervise the execution of the covenants of the debtor for the benefit of all the holders. They are usually for a shorter term than mortgage bonds. A prime disadvantage of debenture bonds is that they rest on the credit of the corporation rather than on any specific collateral. The investor must take care to ascertain the protection given by the indenture against excessive dividends and share repurchases as well as against mortgages or future

issues of bonds that might be placed ahead of the outstanding debentures or compete for payment from the same general sources of funds.
Debentures are frequently protected by "negative pledge" clauses—that
is, covenants against new mortgages on the corporate assets or those of
subsidiary companies that do not equally secure the debentures. A further common protective provision is the "successor obligation clause,"
which requires the bonds to be redeemed when the obligor "sells all or
substantially all" of its assets, unless in connection with such disposition
the debt is assumed by a responsible party.

Redemption Privilege/Obligation. Frequently bonds and preferred
stock contain redemption and/or conversion provisions.[15] When a
redemption feature is included, the borrower almost invariably reserves
the option to call or redeem bonds or debentures on any interest-paying
date prior to their maturity after giving appropriate notice to the bondholders. Without provision for redemption, the debtor corporation would
have no right to prepay the bonds, which it may wish to do to free itself
of high interest payments or restrictions of the mortgage or indenture.
A small premium is usually provided in the redemption or prepayment
price; although it is not as large a premium as that commonly given for
the redemption of preferred stock, it adds to the value and marketability
of the bonds.

Conversion Privilege. In order to make a security attractive, corporations often confer upon bond or debenture holders the privilege
of exchanging their securities for a predetermined number of shares of
stock. This is known as a right or privilege of conversion. The bond
indenture will then provide: (1) the kind of security into which the bond
may be converted; (2) the ratio of conversion—that is, the number of
shares that may be called for in exchange; (3) the period or time limits
during which the conversion right extends; and (4) protection against
dilution and capital adjustments. In drafting protection of the value a
conversion feature, the attorney must take care to identify the types of
transactions that can cause dilution[16] as well as whether the objective
is to maintain the right to a set proportionate amount of the issuer or,
instead, to force the choice between converting or incurring whatever
financial consequences flow from the transaction if the bondholder does
not convert. It is most common to make both bonds and preferred shares
convertible into common shares, although in some instances bonds have
been made convertible into preferred shares.[17] Bonds and debentures are

frequently issued with a stock purchase warrant giving the option to purchase a certain number of shares at a designated price; this is somewhat similar in its effect to the privilege of conversion. Unlike the conversion privilege, warrants can be marketed separately from the accompanying debenture. In either case, the option or conversion privilege will be adjusted in case of capital changes, split-ups, or dilution of the stock as to which option is to be exercised.

Sinking Funds. Corporations frequently provide a sinking fund for the purchase or retirement of its bonds, thus increasing their security and salability. There are various types of sinking funds.[18] Payments for debenture sinking funds, which may be conditioned on net earnings, typically must be made to a sinking fund agent, who frequently is the trustee under the indenture. Default in sinking fund payments may be grounds for acceleration of the bonds' maturity. Serial bonds are made to mature from time to time, so there is a gradual retirement of part of the bonds without payment of a premium. It is more common, however, to provide for an annual sinking fund to be applied solely to the purchase or to the call and retirement of bonds. Such periodic purchases support the price of outstanding bonds and provide some additional liquidity for their holders. Further, if the bond market is depressed so that the price has fallen below face value, the issuer's ultimate financial burden in retiring the indebtedness is reduced, and, during the time that the bonds continue to be outstanding, the redemption of other bonds supports their value by reducing the company's future financial burdens so there is less risk associated with the payment of their interest and principal. It is common for the indenture to provide that the trustee select by lot the bonds to be retired out of the sinking fund.

Income Bonds. Income bonds, which are not normally issued except during a corporate reorganization, are obligations that call for interest payments only to the extent that income is earned annually or within specified interest periods. Such interest payments ordinarily are not made cumulative. Income bonds remove the menace of fixed charges and depend for their return on the success of the business.[19] In this respect they are very similar to non-cumulative preferred shares. The indenture should define carefully the method for determining the periodic net earnings from which interest is to be paid.

Rights of Bondholders. Some states recognize that under certain circumstances bondholders may become concerned with the management of the corporation and accordingly provide that the bondholders be given inspection rights and voting rights. Ordinarily these rights are contingent and are triggered by default in interest payments or by earnings falling below a certain relation to interest requirements.[20] Conditional voting rights make bonds look more like shares of stock, and it is questionable whether in the absence of a statute such protections can be put into the indenture agreement or articles of incorporation. Voting protection for bondholders, particularly in reorganization, is sometimes provided through a voting trust for common shares.

§ 18.4 CLASSES OF STOCK

The ideal financial structure would appear to be the simplest: one class of common shares. In large enterprises, however, especially railroads and public utilities, a reasonable amount of short-term borrowings and of long-term or funded debts is usually included in the capitalization of the firm. Bonded debt has unfortunately often become over-extended, without sufficient basis in existing or foreseeable earnings to give debts a safe margin of protection. This over-extension frequently results in receivership and reorganization. In close corporations, classification of securities is frequently a good device for tailoring control arrangements and participation in profits to the particular desires of the participants.

The law does not limit the various classes, varieties, or combinations of preferred shares that may be authorized, as long as the distinction between debt and shares is observed.[21] The organizers and managers of a corporation may wish to subdivide and classify the units of participation in the corporate income, assets, and control. A corporation may thus issue such varieties of preferred shares as the prospects and needs of the enterprise may call for and as the tastes of the investing public may absorb. These classes of shares may differ as to priority of claim on dividends, as to limited or participating dividend rights, as to conversion rights, voting rights, amounts payable on redemption, dissolution, or liquidation, and in protection against dilution and changes of capital structure. A security's precise financial features are driven not only by the prevailing conditions in the market but also by the risk and return objectives of the security's issuer and the various market participants, who can be expected as prospective holders to parcel different components of the security's features among themselves.

Corporations sometimes issue more than one class of "common stock," one being given full voting power and the other either being nonvoting or having only a fractional vote for each share. If the distinction between classes of common stock is not in voting rights but in priority of amount of participation in earnings or assets, the class that has priority is in effect a participating preferred stock as against the other class.[22]

Preferred shares have been called "compromise securities" because they occupy an intermediate position between common shares and debts. It is this intermediate position that causes some to believe they have greater risks than either the common or bondholders. They usually have a specified limited rate of return or dividend and a specified limited redemption and liquidation price. This creates "leverage" because of the greater possible gain to the common shareholders on the total capital invested and the lesser investment necessary to obtain voting control.

§ 18.5 THE PREFERRED SHARE CONTRACT

Preferred stock is distinctive because of its relationship to common stock. As the highest New York court has declared, "Whatever preferential rights and privileges may thus be granted to a stockholder, the law regards them as contractual. 'The certificate of stock is the muniment of the shareholder's title, and evidence of his right. It expresses the contract between the corporation and his co-stockholders and himself. . . .'"[23] As such, the traditional rules of construction and interpretation apply to determine the rights of the preferred shareholders as set forth in their contract with the corporation.[24]

It is not generally true, however, that the certificate of stock is the authoritative source, evidence, or expression of the preferred share contract. The contract is made with the individual shareholders when they agree to become owners of shares and make themselves parties to the charter contract, not necessarily when a certificate of ownership is issued. In most states all the terms of the preferred share contract must be set forth in the articles of incorporation or charter and cannot be added to or changed by the bylaws, stock certificates, or corporate resolutions.[25] This promotes certainty of information as to the terms of the contract from an authoritative document that is a matter of public record.

§ 18.6 FLEXIBILITY THROUGH A "BLANK STOCK" AUTHORIZATION

The rigidity that results from having the dividend rate and certain other preferences on classes or series of preferred shares fixed in the charter is relaxed in several states by permission to authorize the board of directors to set the terms of new series of classes of preferred shares or even to create different classes from time to time. A series is a subdivision of a class. These "blank stock" statutes enable the directors to vary the terms as to dividend rates and certain other rights of new series or classes according to what the condition of the financial market and that of the corporation may seem to require for ready sale. Blank stock can thus provide advantages similar to bonds with regard to flexibility of terms.

§ 18.7 CUMULATIVE DIVIDENDS

If preferred shares are either expressly or impliedly "cumulative" and dividends are not paid in any year or dividend period, the arrears must be made up in subsequent years, whether earned or not, before any dividends can be declared or paid on common shares.[26] Sometimes dividends on preferred shares are in express terms made to depend on the profits of each particular year, so the holders of the shares will not be entitled to any dividends for a particular year if there are not enough profits in that year to pay them, or they will be entitled only insofar as there were profits. These shares are known as "cumulative if earned," and in the absence of sufficient profits the dividends are non-cumulative and are not made up out of the profits of subsequent years.[27] Unless a contrary intention appears, dividends on preferred shares have generally been held to be impliedly cumulative.[28] Careful draftsmanship should not leave questions open for judicial interpretation.

§ 18.8 NON-CUMULATIVE PREFERRED SHARES

The great advantage of non-cumulative preferred shares is that they avoid an undue accumulation of dividend arrearages, particularly for years in which dividends are not earned. Non-cumulative shares are frequently employed in reorganizations, when it is necessary to limit dividend rights and the investors must take what the enterprise can carry,[29] but the non-cumulative shares may not be listed on the New York Stock Exchange.[30] The principal types of non-cumulative preferred share contracts may be divided into three general groups, subject to internal variation: (1) the discretionary dividend type; (2) cumulative if earned, or "mandatory" dividend type; and (3) "dividend credit" type.

Discretionary Dividend Type. An example of a non-cumulative preferred share contract held to be of the discretionary dividend type is found in a leading Supreme Court case holding that even if there are net profits, the preferred stockholder's right to dividends thereon in any year depends on the judgment and discretion of the directors.[31] This right cannot be enlarged beyond the meaning of the contract to give a right to a dividend credit for prior years in which net earnings might have been lawfully distributed. A share contract should not be judicially augmented because the remedies in case of an abuse of discretion in withholding dividends might not be adequate. The dividend right for any particular fiscal year is gone if the directors, without abuse of discretion, withhold a dividend declaration for that year.

The shareholders' protection under such a discretionary non-cumulative contract lies in equitable relief against abuse of discretion rather than in any ability to enforce a series of supposed contract claims.[32] The mere showing that annual profits, accumulated profits, or earned surplus existed from which a dividend might lawfully have been declared is not sufficient to establish a breach of duty on the part of the directors in failing to declare it. No wrong is done unless the withholding of the dividend would be oppressive, fraudulent, or unfairly discriminatory.[33]

Cumulative-if-Earned or "Mandatory Dividend" Type.[34] A non-cumulative preferred share contract may be made a kind of hybrid "cumulative non-cumulative" type by providing in the articles of incorporation that all back dividends, if earned, must be paid ahead of any common stock dividends.[35] A preferred stock provision mandating dividends up to a certain amount so long as there are profits, net earnings, or net income invariably pose important interpretative questions as to the meaning of these expressions. To the extent that terms conditioning the right to dividends have particular significance in the discipline of accounting, as do the terms "profits," "net earnings," and "net income," it is customary to abide by generally accepted accounting principles in applying such terms to a particular situation.[36]

§ 18.9 PARTICIPATION OF PREFERRED SHARES BEYOND THEIR PREFERENCE

By express provision, preferred shares may participate in dividend distributions beyond their fixed dividend priority. One or two courts adopted the view that preferred shares are entitled to participate equally with the common shares in any distribution of profits after the common shares have received in the same year a dividend at the same rate as that stipulated as a preference for the preferred, unless the share contract provides to the contrary.[37] A different view, however, is followed in almost all states to the effect that where there is no express stipulation as to participation in the surplus, the preferred is entitled only to its fixed priority or preference.[38] It seems reasonable to infer that in consideration of preferential rights, the preferred shareholders agree to accept priority in dividends at a fixed rate in lieu of further participation with the common. This is the understanding of the investing public, especially in view of the fact that participating preferred stock is an unusual type of security having a special feature that should be specified and defined.

§ 18.10 PREFERENCE ON LIQUIDATION

When a corporation's assets are distributed among its shareholders as part of dissolution and winding up, the holders of preferred shares have the same, and no greater, right to share proportionately in the net assets as do the holders of common shares unless the holders of preferred shares have a contractual preference.[39] Usually, however, preferred shares contain provisions for not only a dividend preference but also a stated preference in liquidation or winding up. This liquidation preference most often includes a right to receive any arrears of cumulative dividends in priority to any distribution of assets to the common shareholders. It has generally been held that a liquidation preference including accrued dividends is valid, whether or not there are accumulated earnings or surplus available for dividends.[40] The formerly prevalent rule that dividends cannot be paid out of capital is applicable only to a going concern, not on final liquidation and winding up after payment of the corporation's debts.[41] A mere preference as to "payment in full" or as to "assets" in liquidation has been held not to include arrearages of unpaid cumulative dividends.[42]

By the prevailing view, merger or consolidation of a corporation with another is not such a "dissolution" or "liquidation" as to entitle the holder of preferred shares to payment of the liquidation price or preference, unless it is clearly so specified.[43]

§ 18.11 VOTING RIGHTS OF PREFERRED SHARES

In most instances, the participation in corporate governance by preferred stockholders is much the same as for bondholders: they are much like children, to be seen but not heard. Thus the preferred's contract provides for a periodic return through dividends that is either cumulative or non-cumulative, and perhaps a preference on the firm's liquidation. And, like bondholders, rarely do preferred stockholders enjoy voting rights in the election of directors or most other matters requiring a shareholder vote. Under the typical preferred stock arrangement, any voting rights of preferred stockholders arise in those limited situations where the state corporate statute requires the approval of the preferred when an amendment to the articles of incorporation will change or adversely affect the preferred shares. The precise language of the articles of incorporation frequently generally determines whether the preferred get a vote. Thus, in one case the Delaware Supreme Court held the preferred had a right to vote on a recapitalization that was accomplished via a consolidation because the articles provided for a vote when the preferred shares' rights were adversely affected by "amendment" "whether by merger, consolidation or otherwise."[44] However, when the articles more generally provide for a class vote of the preferred by action "to amend" the articles so as to "to alter or change" the rights of the preferred, a merger changing such rights was held not to fall within this provision because the change occurred by virtue of the merger and not by an amendment so that there is no vote by the preferred is required.[45] With their voting rights so narrowly circumscribed, the preferred shareholder generally lacks a means within the traditional corporate governance mechanisms to, for example, assure that their dividends are regularly paid or that the board of directors does not pursue policies that are likely to harm the future returns of the preferred shareholders. To be sure, there is some economic coercion on the directors when the preferred dividends are cumulative because any arrearages delay dividends to the common stockholders who have elected the board of directors. However, the law is replete with cases in which, after many years of failing to pay the preferred their cumulative dividend, the company undergoes a recapitalization that removes the dividend arrearage and allows future participation by the common on a level more favorable than if the preferred dividends had first been satisfied.[46]

A potentially potent force in the hands of the preferred holders is a provision in their contract granting the preferred the right to vote in the election of directors, and perhaps on other matters, if the corporation fails to pay the preferred dividend. Such contingent voting rights, when provided, usually arise only after a certain number of quarterly dividends have not been fully satisfied—for example, four quarters. The listing requirements of the New York Stock Exchange mandate contingent voting rights for preferred shares.[47] The drafter should carefully consider whether such contingent voting rights should extend to the power to elect the entire board of directors or a majority of the board, or merely provide minority representation on the board.

Some have argued that corporations lack the power to issue shares that have only voting rights. The reasoning behind this argument is that implicit in the meaning and status of "shares" is a proprietary interest. In the only reported decision on this point, the court held that preferred shares are valid even though they carry only voting rights.[48]

§ 18.12 THE REDEMPTION PROVISION: VOLUNTARY OR COMPULSORY FOR THE CORPORATION

Corporations frequently reserve the option to redeem preferred shares at a certain redemption price in order to facilitate future financing. Where such a right exists, the board of directors must exercise the power to redeem in a manner consistent with the terms set forth in the articles of incorporation.[49] In closely held corporations, redemption provisions, like options to repurchase, may be used to keep control of the corporation's stock among a limited number of shareholders. The corporation's right to redeem is generally discretionary with the corporation's board of directors. Repurchase is subject to the requirement that full disclosure of all material facts be made to the stockholders as well as to the equitable consideration that the repurchase not be coercive. In *Eisenberg v. Chicago Milwaukee Corporation*,[50] just after the October 1987[51] stock market collapse (which drove the preferred shares to $41), the board of directors sought to purchase at $55 per share preferred shares whose redemption price was $100. The Delaware Chancery Court enjoined the issuer's tender offer because the directors failed to disclose that they stood to gain by the repurchase as common stockholders because the elimination of the preferred would remove an impediment to their receipt of dividends. Also, the court emphasized that the board's action was coercive because they announced their intention to have the preferred shares delisted from the stock exchange.

Since a corporation's power to redeem shares at a set price is part of the preferred share contract, complaints that a redemption price is unfair vis-à-vis the shares' market value should be unsuccessful. The exercise is subject to the standard requirements of the business judgment rule.[52]

Compulsory redemption provisions and repurchase contracts are sometimes included in preferred share contracts and subscription agreements in order to make shares more attractive to timid investors.[53] Under such contracts the corporation is required to redeem or repurchase its preferred shares at a fixed date or at the option of the owner (essentially granting her a "put" option with respect to the shares), thus giving the shareholders a right to demand a return of their initial investment. Serious harm may result from redemption or repurchase of shares under such contracts. If allowed without restriction, redemptions may injure creditors and other shareholders by depriving the corporation of needed capital.[54]

§ 18.13 The Redemption or Sinking Fund for Retirement of Preferred Shares

A redemption fund, often loosely termed a "sinking fund," may be provided for the purchase or retirement of preferred shares; it is thus similar to a sinking fund used for the gradual or partial retirement of bonds. As with bonds, the sinking fund may consist of a separate account where funds are actually deposited or, as is more commonly the case with preferred shares, it may be unfunded, with balance sheet entries reflecting appropriate restrictions on the surplus accounts. The redemption fund may be accumulated by setting aside specified installments either based on a percentage of the net annual profits, payable out of net assets in excess of capital, based on a periodic small flat percentage of the par value of the preferred shares concerned that are outstanding, or derived from some other source.

§ 18.14 CONVERTIBLE SHARES AND WARRANTS

Preferred shares and bonds may be issued with a conversion privilege or with warrants. The conversion privilege confers upon the holder the option of exchanging fixed or limited income securities for shares of common stock at a designated price or prices and within a specified period. A warrant is an option to purchase shares. Corporations issuing convertible shares or bonds or giving stock purchase warrants must be ready to issue the shares and meet the demands of holders who exercise their options at any period within the time frame specified in the contract.[55] The holder of a convertible security does not become the holder of the security acquired through conversion, and that security is not deemed outstanding, until the conversion occurs.[56]

Warrants may be issued accompanying shares of stock or bonds giving the holder the option to subscribe for or to purchase shares of common stock at a stipulated price or prices per share, usually within a limited time. Warrants may be inseparable from the securities with which they are issued. More commonly, however, warrants are separable and are frequently traded on the stock exchanges. Standing alone, a warrant is not an equity interest; the holder's rights are wholly contractual and may expire on dissolution, consolidation, or by lapse of time.[57] Warrants are sometimes issued to shareholders and general creditors in the reorganization of a bankrupt corporation for otherwise unsatisfied claims.[58]

The financial distinction between convertible bonds and warrants is practically nonexistent if one assumes that warrants are issued in connection with their holder's purchase of a senior security, whether that senior security be a bond or preferred stock. The practical distinction between a convertible security and a warrant is that the latter is a separate security, detachable from the senior security that the initial holder was required to purchase in order to obtain the warrants. The warrant also carries with it an exercise price, thus requiring that fresh cash be paid as consideration for the underlying security, whereas the consideration for the underlying security acquired through conversion is the security converted into the underlying security. The value of the warrant and the value of the conversion feature of the senior security are each dependent on the value of the underlying security—that is, the security that can be acquired on exercise of the warrant or conversion of the senior security.

§ 18.15 Equitable Protections of Preferred Stockholders

The principle is well established that any protection bondholders and preferred stockholders enjoy arises from the four corners of their contract with the corporation (that is, indenture or terms set forth in the articles of incorporation). There are, however, rare instances when the preferred can invoke the protection of a fiduciary obligation. For example, the Delaware Chancery court held that preferred stockholders could proceed with claims that the director and controlling shareholder breached a fiduciary duty of candor by failing to disclose certain material facts involved with the forthcoming sale of a significant product line, even though no vote by the stockholders was called for to approve the sale.[59] Furthermore, the court applied a line of Delaware authority holding that directors owe a fiduciary duty to common and preferred stockholders when dividing the consideration received in a merger or other extraordinary transaction.[60] But in most instances, there are no fiduciary obligations that accompany their relationship to the corporation.[61] By far the greatest problems with this classic contract-law approach have arisen when the bond or preferred share enjoys a conversion privilege that places their holder but a step away from full equity ownership.

Following the developments that have touched modern contract law, gaps in the indenture or preferred stock contract have sometimes been filled, however, by attributing to their contract an implied condition of good faith and fair dealing.[62]

Notes

1. I.R.C. §§ 163, 301 (2009).
2. *Id.* at § 385.
3. *See* Costello v. Fazio, 256 F.2d 903 (9th Cir. 1958). The issue here is analogous to the "deep rock" doctrine, which has been used to subordinate shareholder salary claims.

4. *See Model Simplified Indenture*, 38 Bus. Law. 741 (1983).
5. 15 U.S.C. §§ 77aaa *et seq.* (2009).
6. The legislation authorizes the Securities and Exchange Commission to set the dollar level by exercising its rulemaking authority. *See* General Rules and Regulations of the SEC Rule 4a-3, 17 C.F.R. § 240.4a-3 (2009).
7. Trust Indenture Act, 15 U.S.C. § 77jjj (2009).
8. 15 U.S.C. §§ 77jjj to 77rrr (2000).
9. John P. Campbell & Robert Zack, *Put a Bullet in the Poor Beast, His Leg Is Broken and His Use Is Past*, 32 Bus. Law. 1705, 1723 n.56 (1977).
10. York v. Guar. Trust Co., 143 F.2d 503, 512 (2d Cir. 1944), *rev'd on other grounds*, 326 U.S. 99 (1945).
11. *E.g.*, First Trust Co. v. Carlsen, 261 N.W. 333, 337 (Neb. 1935).
12. *E.g.*, Hazzard v. Chase Nat'l Bank, 287 N.Y.S. 541 (Sup. Ct. 1936).
13. *See* Dabney v. Chase Nat'l Bank, 196 F.2d 668 (2d Cir. 1952).
14. Elliott Assoc. v. J. Henry Schroder Bank & Trust Co., 838 F.2d 66 (2d Cir. 1988).
15. *See generally* William A. Klein, C. David Anderson, & Kathleen G. McGuinness, *The Call Provision of Corporate Bonds: A Standard Form in Need of Change*, 18 J. Corp. L. 653 (1993).
16. *See, e.g.*, Stephenson v. Plastics Corp. of Am., 150 N.W.2d 668 (1967) (resolving whether a spin-off is covered by anti-dilution clause).
17. *See, e.g.*, Augusta Trust Co. v. Augusta, H.&G. R.R., 187 A. 1 (Me. 1936).
18. Eugene F. Brigham & Louis C. Gapenski, Financial Management: Theory and Practice 625–28 (6th ed. 1991).
19. *See* Warner Bros. Pictures, Inc. v. Lawton-Byrne-Bruner Ins. Agency Co., 79 F.2d 804, 816, 818 (8th Cir. 1935).
20. *See* Tooley v. Robinson Springs Corp., 660 A.2d 293, 295–96 (Vt. 1995) (receipt of late payment does not bar holders from exercising their rights that are provided for default, but will bar them from seeking interest on the late payment).
21. *See* Model Business Corp. Act § 6.01 Official Comment (1984).
22. *See, e.g.*, Bodell v. Gen. Gas & Elec. Corp., 140 A. 264 (Del. 1927).
23. Strout v. Cross, Austin & Ireland Lumber Co., 28 N.E.2d 890, 893 (N.Y. 1940), *quoting* Kent v. Quicksilver Mining Co., 78 N.Y. 159, 180 (1879). Barry J. Benzing, Commentary, *Getting What You Bargained For: The Contractual Nature of a Preferred Shareholder's Rights*—Korenvaes Investments. L.P. v. Marriott Corp., 19 Del. J. Corp. L. 517 (1994).
24. *See* Dwoskin v. Rollins, 634 F.2d 285 (5th Cir. 1981). *See also, e.g.*, Elliott Assocs., L.P. v. Avatex, 715 A.2d 843 (Del. 1998) (certificate of incorporation gave preferred shareholders a class vote on merger).
25. *See, e.g.*, Doppelt v. Perini Corp., 2002 WL 392289 (S.D.N.Y. 2002) (articles and not the offering prospectus governed meaning of dividend preference).
26. Bank of Am. Nat'l Trust & Sav. Ass'n v. West End Chem. Co., 100 P.2d 318 (Cal. Ct. App. 1940).
27. Wabash Ry. v. Barclay, 280 U.S. 197 (1930).
28. Ariz. Power Co. v. Stuart, 212 F.2d 535 (9th Cir. 1954).
29. *See* New York, L.E. & W. R.R. v. Nickals, 119 U.S. 296 (1886).
30. NYSE Listed Company Manual § A15, ¶ 281.

31. Wabash Ry. v. Barclay, 280 U.S. 197 (1930).
32. *See generally* ADOLF A. BERLE & GARDINER C. MEANS, THE MODERN CORPORATION AND PRIVATE PROPERTY 172–78, 231–32 (rev. ed. 1967).
33. *E.g.*, Levin v. Miss. River Corp., 59 F.R.D. 353 (S.D.N.Y.), *aff'd*, 486 F.2d 1398 (2d Cir.), *cert. denied*, 414 U.S. 1112 (1973).
34. "Mandatory dividend" is a misnomer because, although dividends may accrue if earned, they do not vest and thus become a debt until declared by the board of directors who, except in the most egregious case, have discretion to retain the earnings for the corporation.
35. Wood v. Lary, 47 Hun. 550 (1888), *aff'd*, 124 N.Y. 83, 26 N.E. 338 (1891).
36. *See* Kern v. Chicago & E. Ill. R.R., 285 N.E.2d 501 (Ill. App. Ct. 1972).
37. Niles v. Ludlow Valve Mfg. Co., 202 F. 141 (2d Cir. 1913).
38. Englander v. Osborne, 104 A. 614 (Pa. 1918).
39. Cont'l Ins. Co. v. Reading Co., 259 U.S. 156, 181 (1922).
40. Fawkes v. Farm Lands Inv. Co., 297 P. 47 (Cal. Ct. App. 1931).
41. *In re* Chandler & Co., 230 N.Y.S.2d 1012 (Sup. Ct. 1962).
42. Powell v. Craddock-Terry Co., 7 S.E.2d 143 (Va. 1940).
43. *See, e.g.*, Rothschild Int'l Corp. v. Liggett Grp., Inc., 474 A.2d 133 (Del. 1984). *See also, e.g.*, Robinson v. T.I.M.E.-DC, Inc., 566 F. Supp. 1077 (N.D. Tex. 1983).
44. *See* Elliott Assoc. v. Avatex Corp., 715 A.2d 843 (Del. 1998).
45. *Id.*
46. *See, e.g.*, Goldman v. Postal Tel., Inc., 52 F. Supp. 763 (D. Del. 1943) (common entitled to receive nothing on liquidation, due to arrearages due preferred, received some portion of the reorganized company as an "inducement" for their support).
47. *See* NYSE LISTED COMPANY MANUAL § 313.00(e)(C) (at least six quarterly dividends, but the power need only extend ability to elected two directors; also recommending same rights for unlisted preferred).
48. Stroh v. Blackhawk Holding Corp., 272 N.E.2d 1 (Ill. 1971).
49. *See* White v. Investors Mgnt. Corp., 888 F.2d 1036 (4th Cir. 1989).
50. 537 A.2d 1051 (Del. Ch. 1987).
51. *See* Kahn v. U.S. Sugar Corp., 1985 WL 4449 (Del. Ch. 1985); Cottle v. Standard Brands Paint Co., Fed. Sec. L. Rep. (CCH) ¶ 95,306, 1990 WL 34824 (Del. Ch. 1990).
52. *See* Hendricks v. Mill Eng'g & Supply Co., 413 P.2d 811 (Wash. 1966).
53. *E.g.*, ThoughtWorks, Inc. v. SV Inv. Partners, 902 A.2d 745 (Del. Ch. 2006) (provision allowing board to avoid preferred's put option to the extent funds were necessary for "the" fiscal year's working capital needs did not empower board to accumulate funds over successive years).
54. In the words of the Supreme Court, "[s]tock which has no retirement provisions is the backbone of a corporate structure." Ecker v. W. Pac. R.R., 318 U.S. 448, 477 (1943).
55. *See generally* Hildreth v. Castle Dental Ctrs, Inc., 939 A.2d 1281 (Del. 2007) (failure when convertible preferred shares were authorized to also authorize sufficient common shares to permit full conversion of the preferred shares did not invalidate the authorization or the issuance of the convertible preferred shares).
56. *See* Nerken v. Standard Oil Co., 810 F.2d 1230 (D.C. Cir. 1987).

57. Helvering v. Sw. Consol. Corp., 315 U.S. 194 (1941). However, they do qualify as "equity securities" under the federal securities laws.
58. *Ecker*, 318 U.S. 476.
59. Jackson Nat'l Life Ins. Co. v. Kennedy, 741 A.2d 377, 390–91 (Del. Ch. 1999). The case would be even stronger if a shareholder vote were required; *see* Gilmartin v. Adobe Res. Corp., 1992 WL 71510 (Del. Ch. 1992).
60. *Jackson Nat'l*, 741 A.2d 390–91. The court relied upon *In re* FLS Holdings, Inc. Shareholders Litig., 1993 WL 104562 (Del. Ch. 1993), *aff'd*, 628 A.2d 84 (Del. 1993) (unpublished opinion).
61. *See, e.g.*, Broad v. Rockwell Int'l Corp., 642 F.2d 929, 958–59 (5th Cir.) (*en banc*) (applying New York law), *cert. denied*, 454 U.S. 965 (1981); Metro. Life Ins. Co. v. RJR Nabisco, Inc., 716 F. Supp. 1526 (S.D.N.Y. 1989); Metro. Sec. v. Occidental Petroleum Corp., 705 F. Supp. 134, 141 (S.D.N.Y. 1989).
62. *See* Rossdeutscher v. Viacom, Inc., 768 A.2d 8 (Del. 2001) (applying N.Y. law to hold there was implied duty of good faith and fair dealing not to manipulate stock price so as to reduce the firm's liability to holders of rights that had variable value depending on how well the post-acquisition price of the firm performed). *See also, e.g.*, Van Gemert v. Boeing Co., 520 F.2d 1373 (2d Cir.), *cert. denied*, 423 U.S. 947 (1975).

CHAPTER 19

ACCOUNTING STATEMENTS AND DIVIDEND LAW

TABLE OF SECTIONS

§ 19.1 THE IMPORTANCE OF ACCOUNTING TO CORPORATE LAW

There is a close interplay between accounting and many corporate transactions. For example, in the preceding chapter it was emphasized that accounting principles play a pivotal role in interpreting bond indentures and the preferred stock's contract when those provisions use expressions that have accounting significance. The connection is equally direct in the case of the states' regulation of corporate distributions, a point examined in the next two chapters. Therefore, because of the frequent interplay between corporate law and accounting, a solid understanding is necessary of the major conventions that underlie accounting principles, as well as of the important financial statements produced through the accounting process. This chapter reviews the major conventions on which accounting principles are premised and provides an introduction to the two principal accounting statements: the balance sheet and the income statement.

On certain topics, such as valuation, depreciation, and depletion, the law impliedly adopts what may be termed "good accounting practice" or, as it is commonly and professionally designated, "generally accepted accounting principles" (GAAP). It should be noted, however, that the courts have the final say in interpreting corporation acts and on legal questions, as between conflicting accounting opinions, and tend to follow what will further the legal objective in view.

There have been recent departures from the traditional legal capital system in California and from the 1980 revisions to the Model Act,[1] which were carried forward in the Revised Model Business Corporation Act in 1984. California expressly adopts GAAP and thus places the courts in the somewhat unusual position of final arbiter of proper accounting methods.

§ 19.2 MAJOR CONVENTIONS OF ACCOUNTING

Nearly all generally accepted accounting principles are anchored in a set of major tenets, more commonly referred to as "accounting conventions." These conventions are briefly set forth below.

The Separate-Entity Assumption. Just as corporate law distinguishes the corporate entity from its owners, accounting statements reflect the performance and financial position of a distinct entity. Thus the financial statements of a corporation report its assets and income, not those of its stockholders; and this is also true for a partnership and its partners. To be sure, there are principles for presenting the performance and position of companies that are affiliated, known as consolidated financial statements, discussed below, but the overarching principle is that financial reports are developed from the viewpoint of a specific entity.

Cost Convention. The bedrock of accounting principles is that each purchase of assets, services, or expenses, as well as liabilities and owners' equity, is recorded at an item's historical cost (in contrast to the item's fair market value). Thus a building that was acquired 10 years earlier is today depreciated on the basis of the cost of acquiring it 10 years earlier, even though the building's current fair market value is much above its cost. Similarly, the building is reported on the balance sheet at its historical cost, less depreciation.

To be sure, difficult questions sometimes arise in measuring an item's cost. For example, when stock is issued for Blackacre, there is a need to record a future value for the capital stock account as well as for Blackacre. In this situation, the fair market value of Blackacre, assumed to be $500,000, is the cost for Blackacre and is also reported in the capital stock account to reflect what was received for the shares. From that point forward, however, Blackacre continues to be reported at $500,000, its cost, even though the land greatly appreciates in value. But the cost convention is not a two-way street. Should there be a material and permanent decline in an asset's market value, accounting requires the asset's carrying amount be reduced to its new, and lower, value. Thus, accounting embodies a highly conservative view of the world in which purchases and assets are recorded at cost and any declines are recognized, but upward appreciation in value is not. Hence the old saying among accountants, "anticipate no gain and recognize all losses."

Constant-Dollar Assumption. Financial reports reflect measurements in a given type of currency, usually that of the company's principal domicile. Whether inflation is moderate or high, the true purchasing power of that unit of measurement is reduced over time. Nevertheless, financial reports are prepared on the assumption of a stable monetary unit or, alternatively expressed, that any changes in the monetary unit are not significant. At one time GAAP required public reporting companies to present information in the footnotes of the financial statements reflecting the effects of inflation; however, the recent modest rate of inflation has caused that requirement to be suspended.

Continuity Assumption. Statements are prepared based on the assumption the business will have a continuous existence. This is frequently referred to as the "going-concern assumption." Thus expenditures for such items as future insurance coverage, a new piece of machinery, and inventory are not charged against revenues as an expense if these assets are believed to contribute to the operations in future years. That is, by assuming an indefinite life for the business, the accountant can assign present expenditures to future years on the basis estimates regarding when a purchased item is likely to contribute to operations. If a going concern were not assumed, then all expenditures would be "expensed" in the year the item was purchased.

Discrete Reporting of Time Periods. Even though a business is assumed to have an indefinite life, accounting reports provide periodic measurements of the firm's performance and financial position. Such periods are called fiscal periods and may be a quarter, a year (calendar year or fiscal year), or sometimes even longer. This requires discrete judgments as to what precise time-period revenues are to be reported and their matching expenses are to be identified. Such decisions are not always clear, and judgment calls invariably arise. Nevertheless, a cornerstone of financial reporting is the need for periodic information regarding the firm's health and operations, even though these reports must be understood not to present a perfectly accurate picture of the firm; perfect accuracy of the firm's overall performance and financial position can be known only when the firm terminates its existence and liquidates. But the users of financial information cannot wait until that day. Hence the assumption that the firm's performance can be divided into defined fiscal periods and reported on.

Realization Principle. A further manifestation of accounting conservatism is the realization principle, which is concerned with the timing of when revenue can be recognized. "Recognized" refers to when the financial statements can report an item's disposition as a sale among its revenues. Simply stated, revenue is not recognized until it is earned. With few exceptions, revenue is not realized until the goods that are sold have been transferred to their purchaser or the services that were acquired have been provided. Thus the primary test of revenue recognition is the completion of the seller's performance; in the case of goods, when title to the goods is transferred.

Matching Principle. If statements were prepared solely on a cash basis, there would be no need for a matching principle. In using a cash basis, expenses are reported as liabilities are incurred or as cash is expended, and sales are recognized when payment in cash is received. Most business records are not on a cash basis but on an accrual basis, under which the realization principle guides when revenue is reported and the matching principle determines when expenses are recognized. Under the matching principle, accounting decisions essentially entail a two-step process. First, revenues are determined pursuant to the realization principle. Thus goods shipped to customers on account are recorded as sales, even though the customer's cash payment has not yet been received. The important difference, therefore, between the cash and accrual basis of reporting is that the latter allows revenue recognition even though cash has not been received. The second step is *matching* the revenues to be recognized in the fiscal period with all the expenses incurred to produce those revenues. This process requires numerous judgments and estimates as to the connection between realized revenues and their related expenses.

The Consistency Principle. This principle calls for the consistent use of the same method or standard in recording and reporting transactions over successive periods. The consistent use of the same assumptions, approach, and reporting method assures comparability over time. Nevertheless, GAAP does permit assumptions, estimates, and principles to change, provided there is sufficient collateral disclosure.[2]

§ 19.3 THE BALANCE SHEET

The balance sheet sets forth a company's cumulative financial position as of a specific date. Thus the balance sheet reports on the composition of the company's assets, liabilities, and owners' equity at a fixed point in time, whereas the income statement reports the company's operations over a period of time. In separately stating the amount and composition of all the company's assets, and also reporting the totals of its liabilities and owners' equity, the balance sheet follows the established accounting equation where

Total Assets = Total Liabilities + Total Owners' Equity

As will be seen, the balance sheet is the basic financial report for dividend purposes; most important, it indicates whether, pursuant to an older regulatory pattern, a corporation has sufficient "surplus," or, pursuant to statutes patterned after the current Model Business Corporation Act, its assets are sufficient in light of the firm's liabilities, so that there is a basis for dividends or other distributions to shareholders.

The balance sheet may appear to be inferior to the income statement, the other major financial statement, but when the two are read in tandem, the relationship between them becomes manifest. More specifically, the amount of net income reported on the income statement, together with the amount of dividends, explains the change in net surplus (retained earnings) from the beginning to the end of the accounting period. The balance sheet lists the assets, liabilities, capital, and surplus in two sections or groups: one on the left side—a classified list of the assets with their book values (generally reflecting historical cost less depreciation), the other on the right side—a classified list of the liabilities, capital, and surplus (or shareholders' equity) and their amounts. A vertical arrangement with assets placed at the top may also be used. The capital represented by the different classes of shares and the different kinds of surplus are entered along with the true liabilities on the right side of the balance sheet. The difference between the assets and the liabilities to creditors is sometimes called the net assets or net worth of the enterprise.[3] It is more frequently referred to as the "equity" of the shareholders—their proprietary interest—and indicates the "book value" of the shares.[4] If the value of the assets is less than the sum of the amount of the liabilities plus the legal or stated capital, then there is a capital deficit. If the value of the assets, at a proper valuation, is less than the liabilities to creditors properly estimated, then the corporation is insolvent, at least in the bankruptcy sense.[5]

§ 19.4 CLASSIFICATION OF ASSETS ON THE BALANCE SHEET

Assets are stated at their acquisition cost, less any changes due to depreciation, depletion, or amortization. Owners' equity reports not only the amount invested in the company but also cumulative increases arising from profitable operations (retained earnings) or decreases due to a net loss from operations. These terms are defined according to generally accepted accounting principles.

In addition to being broadly grouped into assets, liabilities, and stockholders' (owners') equity, the balance sheet's individual items are classified into subcategories according to an underlying characteristic. The most basic subcategories are the following:

Assets	Liabilities	Stockholders' Equity
Current Assets	Current Liabilities	Capital Stock
Fixed Assets	Long-Term Liabilities	Capital in Excess of Par Value
Other Assets	Deferred Credits[6]	Retained Earnings

The above classifications are not exclusive. For example, a parent company's investment in a subsidiary will appear on its unconsolidated balance sheet as "Investments" and appears after Fixed Assets and before Other Assets. Also, over time a highly ambiguous fourth category has developed between Liabilities and Stockholders' Equity, entitled "Deferred Income" or "Deferred Credits." Deferred income refers to advance payments for goods that have not yet been shipped or for services to be provided by the company in the future. In such cases, the *recognition* of revenue is held not yet to have been *realized* because of such non-shipment of goods or non-provision of services. Thus the receipt of revenues in connection with a transaction for which realization has not occurred because of the tenets of the realization convention is reported on the balance sheet as deferred income. Deferred credits most frequently arise because many items or transactions are reported differently in determining taxable income than in determining net income on the company's financial statement. The cumulative differences between the tax expense reported on the company's financial statement and the tax liability actually determined on its tax return are reported as deferred tax credits.

Current Assets. Current assets include cash in banks and on hand, accounts receivable, notes receivable, and marketable securities that are readily converted into cash. The current-assets category also includes less liquid assets, such as inventories, finished goods, work in process, raw materials, and factory supplies that may soon be salable. The standard definition of items suitable for inclusion within "current assets" covers items reasonably expected to be converted into cash or consumed within one year or one operating cycle, whichever is longer.[7] The true significance of current assets is their ability to be converted into cash during normal operations. Assets within this category are the first, if not principal, source for satisfying a company's liabilities and other cash needs in the short run. "Working capital" usually refers to the net current assets—that is, the excess of current assets over current liabilities available for use in the business operations.[8] Entries are generally listed at historical cost.

Inventories include goods held for sale, goods in production, or goods that are consumed in the ordinary course of business. Because inventories are constantly being replenished, some assumptions are made regarding the order of their replacement. Common methods used are LIFO (last in, first out) and FIFO (first in, first out). While the latter no doubt reflects the physical flow of most goods, the former more nearly matches cost with actual operations, if one sees the act of replenishing inventory as the cost of the goods that gave rise to the need to replenish the inventory.

The basis of valuation for securities and inventories, however, is frequently indicated "at the lower of cost or market" or "cost or market, whichever is lower." Special provision is generally made for slow and doubtful accounts to reflect their actual or discounted worth. The assets are ordinarily listed in the general order in which they may be turned into cash or, as it is often expressed, in the order of their "liquidity."

An entity's financial status for immediate credit purposes is not indicated merely by the proportion that exists between the total assets and the total liabilities but even more so by the current ratio between them. "The current ratio" represents the proportion of the current assets to the current liabilities—that is, between the more immediate liabilities to be met and the various kinds of assets that will be available for meeting them. Even though total assets far exceed the liabilities, forced liquidation may occur if these assets are "frozen,"—that is, are not a kind that may be relied upon to raise needed cash. Working capital and the current ratio thus provide a better indication of a corporation's financial liquidity. It is not, however, *per se* unlawful to declare a dividend when there is a sufficient surplus of assets over liabilities, although there may not be sufficient cash or liquid assets on hand, and borrowing to pay the dividends may be necessary.[9]

Fixed Assets. Fixed assets comprise those that are held indefinitely for the purpose of conducting the business, as contrasted with those that are intended for sale. Assets within this category contribute to future operations through their use or consumption during a longer time period than one year or operating cycle. They may be tangible or intangible property interests owned by the business and include land, buildings, machinery, and equipment as well as goodwill, patents, trade secrets, and other intangible assets. Overvaluation of tangible or intangible assets has frequently been the cause for skepticism as to whether such assets' fair market value can ever be reliably determined.[10]

The unfortunate term "capital assets" is frequently and incorrectly used as an equivalent to fixed assets. The term is misleading because current assets are just as much capital as are fixed assets and are much more significant to the creditors' security. The astute lawyer should recognize that no particular assets or funds are segregated and earmarked as capital or surplus. That is, the legal capital is an amount of the business, not a res. Impairment of legal capital may result as much from loss of current assets as from loss of fixed assets.[11]

Fixed asset value, as represented on the balance sheet according to GAAP, is not customarily based on a fair market appraisal or realizable value of the asset. Rather, the value is a record of the original cost of the asset, less the estimated depreciation that has accrued to date. In this respect, the balance sheet is largely an historical record, because fixed asset valuations are often greater than any recorded amounts. As a result, the capital and surplus accounts, as far as being dependent on the historical cost of the fixed assets or even on their present appraisal, are usually of little significance as bearing on the ability to pay either debts or dividends. Current assets as opposed to fixed assets are the liquid resources. These assets are customarily (and conservatively) stated on the basis of cost or market, whichever is lower. Generally, the basis of all asset values should be, and is, disclosed more clearly in footnotes to the balance sheet than in its corpus. The Securities and Exchange Commission has formulated extensive policies as to the necessary accounting and valuation bases so as not to make these public disclosures misleading. These standards of reporting are provided by the accounting profession.[12] These recognize that historical cost can no longer be the sole basis of valuation for all purposes.

Deferred Charges and Prepaid Expenses. This special class of debits, seemingly of relatively minor importance, might best not be designated as assets. By definition, a "deferred charge" is an expenditure for a service that will contribute to the generation of revenues in the future. Prepaid expenses, as the name implies, more closely resemble operating expenses but are temporarily designated as assets, until they are consumed by the business. Examples of prepaid expenses are prepaid premiums for insurance covering the protection one or more years in advance, and rent paid in advance. These two examples represent expenses that are not charged against income for the period in which incurred but instead set up as prepayments, to be amortized (or "expensed") as they are used up. In contrast, deferred charges may be described as long-term prepaid expenses. One example is the unamortized debt on bond discount plus the expense of the bond issue. Likewise, legitimate organizational costs may be regarded as creating intangible assets for a going concern, from which the earning capacity of the business will benefit over long periods. Therefore these too are designated as deferred charges and are also amortized periodically.

§ 19.5 CLASSIFICATION OF LIABILITIES

Liabilities are customarily designated as current or long-term. Current liabilities are those debts and obligations that are reasonably expected to be paid during the upcoming year or operating cycle. Liabilities that do not qualify as current liabilities appear under the heading Long-term Liabilities and include such items as mortgages payable and bonds payable. Each class of bonds or debentures should be shown on the balance sheet at the face value of the bonds outstanding, with the maturity date and interest rate included. Any discount or premium on the issuance of the bond should also be shown, but in a separate or "contra" account. These contra accounts are customarily amortized using the straight line or the interest rate method, based on the valuation period and the actual and effective interest rates. The two accounts—the face value and the contra entries—are netted to show the amount owing on the account. Furthermore, serial maturities of long-term liabilities should be transferred to the current liability group within the last year before maturity because these amounts then become current.

Current liabilities are usually sub-classified into three or four accounts, such as accounts payable, notes payable, dividends payable, accrued liabilities, and taxes payable. Customarily, debts maturing within a year are current liabilities, although in rare cases, such as when a business's operating cycle is longer than one calendar year, its current liabilities may not mature within that period.

A demand of any sort against a corporation, even though contingent, unliquidated, or disputed, such as a damage claim or a guaranty of another's obligation, is still characterized as a liability. The accountant thus has a difficult task in estimating the nature and amount of contingent liabilities. Once they are recognized, the accountant must choose between determining whether to make the disclosure in the balance sheet itself or in the accompanying footnotes. This choice is necessary because contingent liabilities not sufficiently certain to be estimable are usually reflected in footnotes to the financial statement, rather than specifically in a balance sheet account. Nevertheless, where possible, a reserve against contingencies should be provided if there is a substantial likelihood of such contingent liabilities accruing. Despite their separate treatment, notes to balance sheets, especially qualifications in the accountant's certification to the financial statement with regard to them, must be read with care, as they too can be a basis for the accountant's liability for malpractice or negligence in performing the audit function.

§ 19.6 STOCKHOLDERS' EQUITY ACCOUNTS

The various classes of shares of stock are all listed in the corporation's balance sheet. The balance sheet displays information as to the number or amount of par value of shares authorized and the number and amount of shares outstanding as well as those shares that have been repurchased and are thus carried on the books as treasury shares.[13] The rights, privileges, and preferences of each class of stock are also presented in summary fashion. In the case of corporations whose shares have a par value, the "capital stock" entry usually sets forth the aggregate par value of the shares authorized and also of those issued and outstanding, each class of shares being shown separately if more than one exists. In the case of no-par shares, the stated capital figure usually represents the aggregate capital contributions of all the issued shares.

Shares of stock outstanding are usually represented at their aggregate par value if they have such, or otherwise at their stated value. Reflecting par value in the capital stock account is more or less mechanical and traditional, for it has little or no reliability as a record of the amount of actual investment of the shareholders in the business. The directors may allocate a larger part of the paid-in capital to stated capital rather than account for it as capital surplus. The customary capital stock entry corresponds more closely to the important concept of stated or legal capital.[14] Therefore, once an amount is designated as legal capital, it acts as a limitation to the capital margin. Thus legal capital limits distributions, rather than representing a figure of any independent financial significance.[15] All corporation laws, except California's and those of states adopting the current Model Business Corporation Act,[16] still adhere to the legal-capital basis of accounting and thus require a working knowledge thereof on the part of corporate counsel.

Legal capital may be best illustrated by way of the following example. Suppose that in the early history of a large mining company, preferred shares of the aggregate par value of $1 million were sold for cash. Common shares were also issued with an aggregate par value of $1 million for some nominal consideration, such as underwriting or promotion services or speculative mining options. The common shares had no market value at the time of issue. Journal entries were made showing a capital stock item of $2 million, based on the total par value of the issued shares, common and preferred. That amount is the legal capital but not the actual capital invested.[17] The corporation prospers. It later becomes advisable to issue additional shares to raise further capital. A registration statement and a prospectus are required by the federal securities acts, including a balance sheet showing the assets and liabilities of the corporation. Suppose further that a regulatory commission inquiring into the history of the original financing orders a radical "write-down" or restatement at a realistic valuation of the assets originally received in payment for the common shares, involving a reduction in the value of assets of some $1 million. What is the effect of these events on the capital stock liability and on surplus?

Accumulated but undistributed profits are reported in earned surplus/retained earnings. A word about the choice of parlance with this item. "Earned surplus" is the term used in the older varieties of corporate statutes; however, the accounting profession eschews using "surplus" correctly seeing it as an ambiguous expression poorly understood by investors. The accounting profession thus prefers the expression "retained earnings." The amount recorded in earned surplus/retained earnings represents the sum of all profits since the company was formed, less any losses or dividends paid to its shareholders since its formation. Sometimes this account is restricted or appropriated to meet future contingencies or expenditures. The effect of such a restriction (frequently referred to as a "reserve") is to reduce the company's future ability to purchase its shares or declare dividends, since both those acts depend on the amount of *unrestricted* earned surplus or retained earnings.

Losses from operations are recorded as reductions in earned surplus (retained earnings) and, should the losses exceed such accumulated earnings, a deficit will thus appear in earned surplus (retained earnings). In no case will the deficit appear other than in the Stockholders' Equity section of the balance sheet.[18] When earned surplus (retained earnings) has a negative balance, it effectively reduces pro tanto the balance for stockholders' equity.

§ 19.7 THE INCOME OR PROFIT AND LOSS STATEMENT

The mission of the income statement is to report the net income or loss for a given fiscal period, such as a quarter or year. In broad overview, it reports the revenues realized less the expenses incurred to produce those revenues plus any other gains or losses during that reporting period. Because the accountant assumes the business will have an infinite life, the task of accounting is to provide reliable measurements within discrete fiscal periods of the firm's performance. As a result of dividing reported operations into successive fiscal periods, it becomes necessary to employ a variety of assumptions, estimates, and judgments in the allocation of revenues and expenses among successive fiscal periods. In combination, these decisions introduce a good deal of uncertainty as to the accuracy of what is actually captured on the financial statements.

The income statement usually reflects "earnings from operations" or "profit from operations" in a general format. The income statement may particularize as to the gross sales and net sales or other revenue, as well as "nonrecurring" income, after deducting the cost of sales and operations, administrative and general expenses, maintenance and repairs, and provision for taxes, depreciation, depletion, amortization, and unusual expenses and losses. The income statement is concerned with the earning results and realized gain or loss for an accounting period. Because it best bears on the financial performance of the firm over a recent fiscal period, it is viewed by many as the most important financial statement. In the income statement, the cost of goods sold, including selling, administrative, and general expenses, are subtracted from sales, thus bearing a net income (or loss) figure. Depreciation, depletion, and amortization taken during the year are also subtracted as normal operating costs or expenses of the business. In a manufacturing operation, such charges become embedded in the cost of the goods manufactured during the fiscal period. Thus the depreciation of an asset, such as the machinery in the company's plant, is first allocated to the products manufactured during that fiscal period. As recorded, it becomes part of the asset "inventory." It is only when the manufactured product is sold that depreciation is effectively charged against revenues, such charge being imbedded in the cost of goods sold for that fiscal period.

As seen earlier, a major accounting convention is that revenues or income is recognized when earned—whether or not received in cash—and expenses are recognized when incurred—whether or not paid in cash.[19] Most businesses and substantially all corporations use the accrual method of ascertaining income or profit and loss instead of the simpler but less informative cash basis. "Accrual accounting" is a system that matches expenses with revenues but does not require the actual receipt of cash as a precondition for revenue recognition.

Depreciation in the Income Statement. As described above, there can be no profits recognized until all expenses, depletions, and depreciation have been deducted. No one would think of computing the profits of a factory by omitting from the cost of the goods sold the value of the fuel consumed in manufacturing. Likewise, the value of the machinery is consumed in the manufacturing process just as truly as is the fuel. Depreciation reflects this decrease in value due to the "wear and tear" of machinery. Depreciation is an inevitable element of operating cost and must therefore be reckoned in determining profits. The federal income tax laws have done much to improve accounting practice in this respect. Depreciation is thus to be treated as an operating expense, or equivalent entry, that is deductible from current or operating revenue before obtaining the net operating income.

Direct Charges of Certain Losses to Surplus. A serious question is whether unusual losses on items not connected with ordinary operations of the period and extraordinary non-recurring charges are to be included in the annual profit-and-loss statement or whether they should be shown elsewhere. An increase in assets due to the additional investment of funds is not entered in the income account. A question also arises as to whether certain losses that have undoubtedly diminished the net value of the corporation should be reflected in the income statement or instead are to be treated as deductions from earned surplus. At one time, an extraordinary loss, say by earthquake or fire, was sometimes accounted for as a loss of earned or paid-in surplus rather than as a deduction from the profits of the period.[20] The accounting profession has greatly restricted such extraordinary items from bypassing the income statement.[21] Today, extraordinary gains and losses are separately reported in the income statement, not in the statement of earned surplus. The income statement is then reconciled with a surplus statement commonly termed the "statement of retained earnings." This statement shows the opening and closing balance of the earned surplus (retained earnings) account and the changes that occurred throughout the fiscal year such as by the payment of dividends or the repurchase of shares. Moreover, the income statement should be reconciled with the balance sheet regarding the increase or decrease of earned surplus shown thereon by reason of unusual sources of gain or loss. An income report for a particular year, like a single balance sheet, should not be relied on to show earning capacity but should be compared with those of preceding years to ascertain the trend of earnings.

Explanatory Comments. Balance sheets and income statements often seem needlessly cryptic and obscure. Supplementary explanatory comments as to the different classes of assets and liabilities, reserves, and surplus are often supplied for the enlightenment of shareholders and investors in connection with the technical financial exhibits. Generally accepted accounting practice mandates the use of footnotes, parenthetical notes, and discussion statements to explain the figures shown on financial statements, especially with regard to foreign investments, contingent liabilities (such as pending lawsuits), bases of valuation, and investments in subsidiary companies.[22] Certain important qualifications, warnings, explanations, or even disclaimers may be called for in the accountant's comments and certificate. This statement, called the auditor's report, consists of a concise report by the auditor or public accountant expressing an opinion on the statement and the representations it contains, and how far the auditor assumes responsibility for its fairness of presentation. Such matters as changes in accounting practice and unusual accounting methods should be disclosed clearly and prominently.

§ 19.8 CONSOLIDATED FINANCIAL STATEMENTS

Where, as often happens, a group of affiliated companies make up one large business enterprise conducted by a parent or holding company, with one or more subsidiaries and affiliates, annual reports generally include consolidated financial statements. The consolidated statements are really an economic concept, valid only as to the creditors and shareholders of the parent corporation. The statements and the financial status of the enterprises, or system as a whole, operate as though they were a single entity. This method does not purport to represent the statements of one particular entity; it is simply a device used for reporting purposes.

A consolidated balance sheet eliminates the parent company's investment in each of its associated companies; the actual assets and liabilities of such companies being substituted therefor. Thus the statement includes assets that legally do not belong to the parent corporation but are instead the property of affiliated corporations. Any minority interest in affiliated companies—that is, the shares held by non-affiliates—must be shown on the right-hand side of the balance sheet, because such outstanding shares, in the public's hands, have an equity interest in the assets of their respective companies. Although the parent company may have an equity interest of only four-fifths of the net assets of its subsidiary companies, the entire complex of assets of all the companies is used in the artificial, consolidated enterprise. As a general rule, consolidated statements will not include a subsidiary unless it is more than 50 percent owned. As noted above, the fact that there is a divided interest in these assets is accounted for by exhibiting on the right-hand side of the balance sheet the portion of the value of the net assets to be allocated to the holdings of the minority or outside shareholders.

Additional modification is necessary in the consolidated balance sheet with regard to intercompany relations where an asset of one of the associated corporations consists of a liability of another member of the group. For financial reporting purposes, the effects of intercorporate transactions must be removed from all consolidated financial statements. Intercompany receivables and payables are also eliminated and should not appear in the consolidated statement. As for liabilities, the consolidated balance sheet shows the combined amounts owing from the parent company and the associated companies to outsiders or public holders. This assures that gain or loss is recognized in consolidated statements only when a member of the consolidated entity has transactions with entities that are not members of the group.

By taking the above-mentioned measures, the consolidated balance sheet thus summarizes the total assets of a group of companies and indicates the parent company's pro rata portion of the cash, inventory, and other assets of the consolidated entities. A consolidated balance sheet thus aims to cut through the artificial legal subdivision of a group of companies and presents the actual assets and liabilities of the entire economic unit. Through this format, consolidated statements provide a comprehensive view of the situation of the combined business as a whole.

NOTES

1. CAL. GEN. CORP. LAW § 500 (West 1990).
2. *See* AICPA APB Op. No. 20, Accounting Changes (August 1971).
3. For a typical statutory definition of net assets, *see* Former MODEL BUSINESS CORP. ACT § 2(i) (1969).
4. The objectives of financial reporting, as set forth in Financial Accounting Standards Board (FASB) Concepts Statement No. 1, do not require accounting information to directly measure the value of the business enterprise. That is, balance sheets are not intended to reflect enterprise market value. This value estimation is the role of investment analysis, not accounting. Accounting provides information useful for the analysis.
5. "Insolvency" as defined in the federal Bankruptcy Code is the excess of liabilities over assets valued at fair value. 11 U.S.C. § 101(31) (2000). This is in contrast to defining "insolvency" in terms of the inability to pay debts as they become due.
6. The term "credit" has its own, indeed arbitrary, meaning in accounting. It is not synonymous with a benefit or privilege owned by the company. "Credit" refers merely to an entry that appears on the right-hand side of an account; the left side being the debit side.
7. The operating cycle is the combined time, on average, to acquire, process, and sell inventory, plus the time necessary to realize cash from any sales made on credit.
8. That is, if all of the current assets were converted into cash at their book value and all of the current liabilities paid at their book value, working capital would be the amount of cash remaining.
9. Steele v. Locke Cotton Mills Co., 58 S.E.2d 620 (N.C. 1950). *See generally* GABRIEL A.D. PREINREICH, THE NATURE OF DIVIDENDS (reprinted ed. 1978).
10. Randall v. Bailey, 23 N.Y.S.2d 173, 177 (Sup. Ct. 1940), *aff'd*, 43 N.E.2d 43 (N.Y. 1942), discussed in Chapter 20, § 20.13.
11. The term "capital losses" is used to distinguish certain unusual losses for accounting purposes from "operating" losses. *See* Stuart Turley, *Accounting Standards and the True and Fair View*, 5 COMPANY LAW 31 (Jan. 1984).
12. The FASB, in its Statement of Financial Accounting Standards No. 33, requires large public enterprises to file supplemental reports with their financial statements to provide, among other information, the increase or decrease in the current costs of inventory and plant and equipment. SEC

Accounting Series Release No. 287 adopts the same position. *See* 6 Fed. Sec. L. Rep. (CCH) ¶ 1172, 309.

13. The stockholder's equity accounts appear under the liabilities of a corporation because both types of accounts are increased by making "credit" entries, as distinguished from assets accounts, which are increased by making "debit" entries. A corporation's "liability" to its shareholders on account of their stock is not a debt; it represents ownership.

14. Legal capital is computed as the number of shares outstanding multiplied by their par value, stated value, or issue price (for no-par shares). The amount of legal capital is properly recorded in the capital stock account. Amounts received in excess of legal capital should be recorded in other appropriately designated accounts.

15. *See generally* Case v. N.Y. Cent. R.R., 232 N.Y.S.2d 702 (Sup. Ct. 1962), *rev'd*, 243 N.Y.S.2d 620, 19 A.D.2d 383 (App. Div. 1963), *rev'd*, 204 N.E.2d 643 (N.Y. 1965).

16. CAL. GEN. CORP. LAW §§ 501 *et seq.* (West 1990).

17. *See* Gulf Oil Corp. v. S.C. Tax Comm'n, 149 S.E.2d 642 (S.C. 1966).

18. *See* First Indus. Loan Co. v. Daugherty, 159 P.2d 921, 930 (Cal. 1945) (Traynor, J. dissenting).

19. The major objective of accounting is the determination of periodic net income by matching appropriate costs against revenues. The timely recognition of income and related expenses reflects this objective, which is called the "matching principle."

20. The effect of an extraordinary item, if material, should be classified separately in the income statement. The Accounting Principles Board, in APB Opinion No. 30 (Oct. 1973), provides, as an authoritative guide, that "extraordinary items" refer to events or transactions that are *both* unusual and infrequent in occurrence. APB Op. No. 30, AICPA, *Professional Standards* §§ 2010.16, 2012.10.

21. *See* APB Op. No. 30, *Reporting Results of Operations* (June 1973).

22. *See* SEC Regulation S-X, Rule 3-16, 17 C.F.R. § 210.3-16 (2009).

CHAPTER 20

DIVIDEND DISTRIBUTIONS: RIGHTS, RESTRICTIONS, AND LIABILITIES

PART A. RIGHTS TO DIVIDENDS

§ 20.1 DECLARATION AND PAYMENT OF DIVIDENDS

A dividend is properly declared by formal resolution of the board of directors specifying the amount, the time of payment, and the "record date," and fixing the date for ascertaining the shareholders of record. Most dividends are distributed to shareholders in the form of cash. Distributions may also be made in property or in the corporation's own shares. Regardless of the method of declaration or payment, the distribution of dividends among shareholders of the same class must be without discrimination and pro rata unless it is otherwise agreed by all.[1]

§ 20.2 DIRECTORS' REFUSAL TO DECLARE DIVIDENDS

A corporation may have a surplus or accumulated profits legally available for dividends, but the right of the shareholders to the making of any distribution is dependent on the exercise of the directors' good faith discretion with regard to financial advisability at the time.[2] An abuse of this discretion may call for equitable relief.

There are two dangers of abuse of the directors' discretion in declaring or withholding dividends. One is a policy of wastefulness or prodigality—improvident distributions that are injurious to present or future creditors and investors reduce working capital and weaken the corporation as a going concern. The converse abuse is undue accumulation beyond the reasonable needs of the business—the arbitrary refusal to pay shareholders a fair return on their investment when it clearly would be possible and wise to divide accumulated profits. Investors purchasing shares in a business often expect to obtain a return in the form of more or less regular dividends according to the corporation's ability to pay. The management's desire for expansion and more compensation instead of dividends in some cases may defeat the shareholders' just expectations.[3] The law has been concerned primarily with restraining dividend distributions that are dangerous to the rights of corporate creditors.

The major source of funds for business expansion is the accumulated but undistributed profits of the business. The board of directors' decision to expand the business opens a host of questions as to how the expansion should be financed—by issuance of equity, by debt, or from undistributed earnings. Even though a school of financial theory counsels that the firm's value is not impacted by whichever of these choices occurs, this "irrelevancy principle" can be seen as placing more emphasis on intangible considerations that are best commended to the board of directors unless an abuse of discretion is otherwise demonstrated. Thus, the courts hesitate to substitute their judgment on complicated questions of business policy for that of the elected managers of the business and have limited the scope of judicial review that they are willing to undertake.

It is accordingly a well-settled doctrine that whether or not dividends shall be paid, and the amount of the distribution at any time, is primarily to be determined in the good faith discretion of the directors.[4] Courts examine directors' decisions regarding dividends through the lens of the business judgment rule. In fact the rhetoric of the cases suggests a slightly more deferential standard, stating the court will not intrude upon the decision to not declare dividends absent "fraud or gross abuse of discretion."[5] In sum, dividend declarations are like other matters within the discretion of the board of directors for which director judgments are presumptively valid. The mere fact that a corporation reports a substantial surplus or large profits out of which a dividend might lawfully be declared is not of itself sufficient ground to compel the directors to make a dividend.[6] Directors are given a great deal of discretion to use corporate resources to expand the business, to increase executive compensation by bonuses and profit-sharing contracts, and to establish various reserves if they consider it to be in the interests of the corporation to do so. Thus, many reasonable bases have successfully been advanced to justify the directors' decision not to declare dividends:

the seasonable nature of the business,[7] new equipment and the possible relocation of a plant,[8] the repurchase of outstanding shares,[9] expansion of business and a contingency for increased competition,[10] and to buffer the corporation against the possible loss of a major account.[11]

In most cases where dividends have been compelled, it has been shown that the directors willfully abused their discretion by withholding distributions because of an adverse interest, a wrongful purpose, or bad faith. More frequently the prevailing minority stockholder is able to link the nonpayment of dividends to a larger scheme to drive the minority out of the corporation.[12]

By far the greatest success plaintiffs have had in challenging the nonpayment of dividends has been within closely held corporations. It would appear that personal hostility is more visible and thus easier to establish in the close corporation. It is also much easier to refute the business justifications advanced for nonpayment in a close corporation. The authority of the directors is usually said to be absolute as long as they act in the exercise of honest judgment. If the refusal to make a distribution of profits is shown to be clearly unjust even though no fraud or intent to harm the shareholders appears, some courts have indicated that relief should be given and that the minority shareholders should not wait indefinitely while profits are needlessly accumulated.[13] Thus, non-payment of dividends in the close corporation invites inquiry whether "oppression" is afoot whereby the directors' decision is assessing in light of the "reasonable expectations" of the minority. It should be noted that the limitation on the discretion of directors of close corporations may not apply to large corporations with listed stock and a ready market that reflects capital appreciation.[14]

§ 20.3 RESCISSION OR REVOCATION OF DIVIDEND DECLARATIONS

A director's resolution declaring a cash dividend probably does not become immediately binding and irrevocable until an announcement to the shareholders or to the public. A leading Massachusetts case held that a directors' vote authorizing a dividend may be revoked if it has not been made public or communicated to the shareholders.[15] But the arguments against the directors' power to rescind dividends after notice of the declaration seem conclusive. It has thus become established that a cash or property dividend, once announced, cannot be revoked.

§ 20.4 RIGHT TO DIVIDENDS DECLARED PRIOR TO TRANSFER OF SHARES

In general, any dividend already declared when shares are transferred belongs to the transferor and does not pass by the transfer, and the fact that the dividend is made payable at a future date does not alter the rule. Frequently this problem is solved by the directors' declaration fixing a record date in order to determine who is entitled to the distribution.

The shareholders' right to a corporate distribution becomes fixed by the dividend declaration in the absence of a record date.[16] This general rule, which is codified in many states,[17] is based on the theory that a dividend declaration automatically makes the corporation a debtor to the shareholder.[18] The right or debt thus does not pass on transfer of the shares. Accordingly, when dividends are made payable at a future date, usually for the convenience of the corporation, a transfer between the date of declaration and the date of payment will not affect the transferor's right to the dividends. The dividends will be payable to the owner at the time of declaration rather than at the time of payment.[19] Dividends declared subsequent to the transfer of ownership belong to the transferee.[20] A share of stock has been compared to a fruit tree: the seller may retain any fallen fruit (declared dividends) on sale of the tree but may not shake the tree to recover more fruit after the sale.[21] If the transferor of the stock receives dividends that were declared after the transfer, he is liable to the transferee for them, whether or not the transfer was recorded or registered with the corporation;[22] however, the corporation is not liable to a transferee without notice.[23]

PART B. RESTRICTIONS ON DIVIDEND DISTRIBUTIONS

§ 20.5 THE PURPOSE OF DIVIDEND RESTRICTIONS

A difficult and complex branch of corporation law deals with legal capital requirements and the limitations on distributions to shareholders. The rule against capital impairment has long been the fundamental restriction on dividends. Historically, statutes have attempted to provide for the establishment, contribution, and maintenance of some margin of asset values over liabilities for the protection of creditors. But because these statutes did not keep up with changes in generally accepted accounting practices and the insights of modern finance, legal capital has become a dated dividend restriction. One mitigating factor has been the addition of an insolvency test in most statutes.

§ 20.6 THE VARIOUS DIVIDEND LIMITATIONS

Every state statutorily restricts the directors' authority to make dividend distributions based on the corporation's financial condition. These statutes contain one or more of the following restrictions: (1) A prohibition of dividends when the corporation is insolvent or that would render it insolvent; (2) The requirement that a general surplus exists from which dividends may be paid and that consists of the value of the net assets or net worth of the corporation over the stated or legal capital margin, determined from the balance sheet and usually excluding any unrealized appreciation of fixed assets; (3) The requirement that an earned surplus exists, which devises its value from accumulated earnings or profits.[24] All legal-capital statutes permit dividends from capital surplus but the availability of capital surplus has been restricted by several acts to preferred shares. (4) As an alternative to surplus, the existence of current earnings usually measured for the year in which the dividend is declared or in the preceding year will permit "nimble dividends" in a few states, regardless of impairment of capital; (5) A certain ratio of certain assets to current liabilities, or assets to liabilities, such as 1 ¼ to 1, may be required to be left after a distribution of dividends in order to avoid impairment of debt-paying ability and working capital position;[25] (6) An exception to the general dividend restrictions permits a "wasting asset corporation," although not formed for the liquidation of specific property, to distribute the proceeds derived from the consumption of wasting assets without deduction for their depletion or exhaustion.[26] This in effect permits liquidating dividends or a distribution of capital, which may be dangerous to creditors and preferred shareholders.

In addition to the foregoing legal capital restrictions, there is the new balance-sheet approach and "distribution" restrictions adopted in the 1980 amendments to the former Model Business Corporation Act, and these are carried forward in the current Model Business Corporation Act.[27] They prohibit a distribution if, after giving effect to such distribution, the corporation's total assets would be less than its total liabilities plus the maximum amount required for the payment of any liquidation preferences. Nearly half the states have patterned their statutes after the model acts, and the remaining states continue to adhere to some form of legal capital restriction.

As will be seen in the next chapter, statutory restrictions on the purchase by a corporation of its own shares are often similar to, or at least related to, those on dividend distributions, because both transactions involve the withdrawal of corporate assets in favor of shareholders.[28]

Dividend restrictions also appear in loan agreements as creditors frequently resort to private contracting for protection to supplement the minimum level provided by corporate statutes and fraudulent transfer acts. Where such a provision exists, the limits found in the agreement entered into with a single creditor are much like rain—the benefits fall upon all the corporation's creditors, since the debtor's reduced discretion to make distributions to its stockholders has the effect of conserving assets that are available to all of its creditors.[29] Because of the frequency of detailed loan agreements among public companies, it is safe to say that the ultimate restriction on distributions to stockholders by public companies is that found in their loan agreements and not corporate statutes or fraudulent transfer provisions.

§ 20.7 THE CAPITAL IMPAIRMENT LIMITATION

The oldest and still prevalent dividend restriction limits dividends to the extent that there is sufficient surplus, which is defined in the statutes as the amount net assets or net worth is in excess of the legal capital.[30] The laws of Delaware, New York, and some other states permit dividends out of surplus of any and all varieties, whether earned or capital surplus.[31] Unlike the pre-1980 Model Business Corporation Act,[32] these states do not draw distinctions between an "earned surplus" and the different kinds of "capital surplus" that may be derived from paid-in surplus or from reduction surplus arising on the reduction of the legal capital. The pre-1980 Model Business Corporation Act distinguishes among different types of surplus, with the result that dividends and share repurchases premised on available earned surplus have much fewer limitations than those premised on other forms of surplus (for example, capital surplus). The pre-1980 Model Business Corporation Act's definitional section divides "surplus" into two components and treats them dissimilarly in important ways. Section 45(a) of the act authorizes dividends in cash or property to the extent of unreserved and unrestricted earned surplus. Because it arises almost invariably from shareholder's investment in the enterprise,[33] capital surplus is burdened with most of the restrictions that surround stated capital. Capital surplus does, however, have some uses accorded earned surplus. For example, even though distributions to the shareholders from capital surplus are allowed, such distributions are conditioned on there being express authorization in the corporation's charter for utilization of capital surplus or approval of a majority of the shares of each outstanding class of stock.[34] Use of capital surplus is prohibited if the corporation's net assets following the distribution are less than the aggregate liquidation preference of a senior class of stock. The prohibition also applies whenever there are any unpaid dividends for any class of stock having a preferential right to dividends. None of these limitations arise when dividends are based on earned surplus. All distributions, whether from earned surplus or capital surplus, must not under the equity test render the corporation insolvent—that is, unable to satisfy its obligations as they mature.

Until the adoption of the current provisions of the Model Business Corporation Act, discussed below, there were few exceptions[35] to the view that unrealized appreciation in value of fixed assets could not be counted in the computation of a surplus as a basis for cash or property dividends.[36] Historically, dividend regulation rested on certain metrics focused on the firm's balance sheet. Since assets under generally accepted accounting principles (GAAP) are recorded at their historical cost, less any depreciation, amortization, or depletion, this approach naturally led to view that unrealized asset appreciation was necessarily foreclosed as a basis of dividends. The presumed intent of the legislature in adopting regulation dependent upon the balance sheet is that the legislature intended the statutory tests to incorporate GAAP for defining the terms used in the statute, that is, terms which historically have significance within the field of accounting should carry forward their meaning from that field. An assumed connection between dividend regulation and GAAP should be powerful because the purposes that underlie GAAP's conservatism and dividend regulation are identical.[37] GAAP's adherence to historical cost and strict rules for the realization of gains and income are based on a number of factors, including: the lack of relevance of market or replacement costs to a fixed asset that is not intended to be sold, the difficulties of valuation, the loss of comparability of financial statements of corporations using different valuation methods, problems of application in depreciation accounting that is intended only to charge asset costs against operations, and the possibilities of employing unrealized appreciation as a purely fictitious basis for dividends.

The leading case for recognizing unrealized gains as a source for dividends is *Randall v. Bailey*,[38] which was decided under an impairment-of-capital statute that permitted dividends as long as "the *value* of its assets remaining after the payment of such dividend, or after such distribution of assets . . . shall be at least equal to the aggregate amount of its debts and liabilities including capital or capital stock as the case may be."[39] When *Randall* was decided, not only did practice vary widely among accountants with respect to what was required to recognize income—that is, the realization convention as we understand it today was not then widely practiced—but also courts were far more willing to exercise their judgment as to the meaning of "significant accounting terms." These distinctions did not, however, enter the Delaware Supreme Court's thinking when the court permitted unrealized appreciation in assets to meet the state's impairment of capital test.[40]

Sound policy supports allowing firms to distribute true economic gains to their owners. Such gains are those that are not needed to replace the facilities and resources either committed or already consumed within the company's current business.[41] If the land on which the company's plant is built increases in value, that is not a true economic gain that can be distributed to the shareholders—any sale of the land or a parcel of it would possibly necessitate an equal expenditure to replace the land so that operations can continue. Thus pure holding gains are rarely a true advance in a company's fortunes if those gains are associated with an asset without which the business cannot operate. However persuasive such arguments are, they are moot in the face of the clear language of the present Model Business Corporation Act.[42] There appears little likelihood that the relaxed method of determining distributable dividends under such a provision will occur within a public corporation where dividend practices, particularly for companies in financial distress, have historically been conservative and have been muffled by external lending agreements. But the freedom permitted by the current Model Business Corporation Act is likely to be irresistible within a close corporation, where the rush to grab the assets within a failing company is all too well documented. Certainly one must ponder whether the very meaning of the standards embodied in statutes intended for the protection of creditors should ever be commended to those whose interests are adverse to creditors.

§ 20.8 The Earned Surplus Test

Following the pre-1980 Model Business Corporation Act,[43] many states restricted dividend distributions to earned surplus except in special cases, such as when expressly authorized in the articles of incorporation, when stockholders vote to use capital surplus, when distributions are used to pay cumulative dividends on preferred shares, or when distributions are made from a wasting asset corporation. The role of GAAP in the construction of earned surplus is not clear under the Model Business Corporation Act or, for that matter, under most other statutes. It is generally believed that the earned-surplus test looks to realized gains and accumulated but undistributed profits as the normal basis of dividends on common shares.[44] Similarly, as an alternative test in California, distributions are permitted to the extent of "retained earnings"; thus the current accounting terminology is substituted for the old.[45]

Earned surplus is generally a far more conservative limitation on common share dividends, and on share purchases also, than surplus generally because it links such distributions directly to the financial performance of the company. But even earned surplus may be based in large part on fixed, unmarketable, and frozen assets, such as investments in machinery or real estate. The ability to pay dividends, as distinct from the legal right to pay dividends, depends largely on the liquidity of the financial position—that is, on the so-called current ratio and the sufficiency of working capital to keep the business going.[46] While the existence of the required surplus over capital may satisfy the statutory prohibition, it is the duty of directors to take many other factors into account in the exercise of prudent management.

The earned-surplus restriction is often coupled with prohibitions against capital impairment and payments that would render the corporation insolvent.[47]

§ 20.9 Capital Surplus as a Source of "Distributions" to Shareholders

In some states, including Delaware and New York, capital surplus is available equally with earned surplus for dividends on all kinds of shares.[48] This can create a danger to preferred shareholders and creditors, because directors are given the authority by many corporation acts to attribute substantially all of the consideration received on the issue of no-or low-par shares, either common or preferred, to paid-in surplus rather than to capital. A dividend paid out of paid-in surplus would then leave an inadequate capital margin for creditor and preferred shareholder protection. Conceivably, dividends could even be paid to common shareholders out of paid-in surplus received from the issue of the preferred shares and thus divert part of the investment of the senior shares to the holders of the junior shares. Any abuse of this discretion by the directors, however, is properly subject to equitable limitations.

Dividends from paid-in surplus and from capital reduction surplus are a return on capital akin to a partial liquidating distribution, because they represent a distribution of part of the price invested by the original share-subscribers in the business, and, as such, they are not taxable as dividend income, but are treated as a capital return.[49] Most statutes require notice to the shareholders of the extent to which the dividend represents capital surplus.[50] It is surprising that only a few states have required that capital surplus be available for dividends only in the absence of an earned surplus.[51]

The former Model Business Corporation Act, like other "earned surplus" statutes, permits "distributions from capital surplus" under certain circumstances.[52] In addition to the insolvency limitation, such distributions must be authorized either in the charter or by a majority shareholder vote on a class basis, including nonvoting shares. This authorization is not necessary, however, in the case of distributions in discharge of cumulative dividend rights, provided there is no earned surplus. Distributions out of capital surplus may not be made in a manner prejudicial to preferred shareholders.[53]

§ 20.10 THE INSOLVENCY LIMITATION

At one time, insolvency was the only statutory restriction on dividends in some jurisdictions. Today virtually all statutes have some form of balance-sheet test in addition to an insolvency limitation.[54] Only Massachusetts, Minnesota, and North Dakota have the insolvency test as their exclusive requirement.[55]

There are two rival definitions of "insolvency": (1) The commercial or equity test of an inability to meet debts and obligations promptly as they fall due;[56] and (2) the bankruptcy or "balance sheet" test, an excess of the amount of liabilities over the total value of the assets.[57] It is not always clear in dividend statutes which of the two possible meanings of "insolvency" should be taken. The rule against impairment of capital should take care of the question of the total assets at least equaling the liabilities,[58] but, if the insolvency limitation is to have any additional force or effect, it should be drawn so as to cover some objective test of reasonable grounds for believing that the corporation will not be rendered unable to pay its debts and liabilities, both long-and short-term, as they fall due. The plaintiff need only set forth allegations under one of the two statutory solvency tests.[59] Probably the most prevalent interpretation of prohibitions against insolvency in dividend statutes is the equity test.

The equity solvency test should be seen as setting forth a context within which traditional manners of inquiry occur as to whether the directors' decision is protected by the business judgment rule.[60] Within this context, a host of considerations are appropriate:

> [I]n determining whether the equity insolvency test has been met, certain judgments and assumptions as to the future course of the corporation's business are customarily justified, absent clear evidence to the contrary. These include the likelihood that (a) based on existing and contemplated demand for the corporation's products or services, it will be able to generate funds over a period of time sufficient to satisfy its existing and reasonably anticipated obligations as they mature, and (b) indebtedness which matures in the near-term will be refinanced where, on the basis of the corporation's financial condition and future prospects and the general availability of credit to business similarly situated, it is reasonable to assume that such refinancing may be accomplished. To the extent the corporation may be subject to asserted or unasserted contingent liabilities, reasonable judgments as to the likelihood, amount, and the time of any recovery against the corporation, after giving consideration to the extent to which the corporation is insured or otherwise protected against loss, may be utilized.[61]

§ 20.11 Nimble Dividends

Some state statutes allow dividends from the net profits or net earnings of the preceding year or other recent specified period in the absence of any surplus and in spite of a capital deficit. These provisions providing for "nimble dividends" have been criticized by many writers as being unduly lax. The privilege may be justified, however, on the ground that the surplus limitation at times becomes unreasonably strict and arbitrary, as it may permit dividends when they are inexpedient and forbid them when their distribution would be financially sound. The purpose of the law is to establish some minimum test of whether the financial condition of a corporation permits a distribution with a view to the safety of creditors and the investment of the shareholders.

§ 20.12 "Wasting Asset" Corporations

A controversial provision in some states permits corporations solely or principally engaged in the exploitation of "wasting assets" to distribute the net proceeds derived from exploitation of their holdings, such as mines, oil wells, patents, and leaseholds, without allowance or deduction for depletion.[62] There may be a vague limitation of making sufficient provision for creditors and the liquidation priorities of preferred shareholders. Such statutes are often accompanied by a requirement of notice that liquidation dividends are being paid without allowance for depletion. The pre-1980 version of the Model Business Corporation Act imposes such limitations in addition to applying them only to corporations engaged principally in the exploration of natural resources.[63] The Act also limits such distributions to depletion reserves and requires authorization in the charter. As a result of the 1980 amendments eliminating legal capital, the wasting asset provision has been deleted.[64] Even in the absence of an express statute, some courts have permitted wasting-asset distributions.[65]

If a corporation is organized to exploit, liquidate, and distribute the proceeds of a particular mineral reserve, estate, or specific lot of assets, the corporation may be described as a "liquidating corporation," which may be excused by statute from making any reserve for depletion or replacement of the assets liquidated. But if the purpose of a corporation that is engaged in the oil or mining or similar business is a continuing one and not the exhaustion and liquidation of a particular property, then, as to keeping its capital intact there is no reason for treating such corporation as different from any other continuing concern, such as a manufacturing corporation.

§ 20.13 The Innovations of the California Statute and the Model Business Corporation Act

Very few parts of the corporate mechanism are more complicated, unworkable, or incomprehensible than the system of legal-capital requirements, with its various attempted restrictions on unsafe distributions of assets to the shareholders.

The formerly prevalent limitations as to capital and surplus rest on vague financial standards that are difficult to ascertain and to apply. The margin of safety measured by the legal capital is an arbitrary limit, established on the issue of shares, that has no relation to the kind of business being conducted, the liquidity of assets, the net current asset position, and the ability to meet or refinance obligations as they fall due.[66]

In discarding long-outmoded legal-capital concepts and adopting GAAP, California took an important step in improving the law's regulation of dividend distributions. An alternative new approach to dividend restrictions is embodied in the previously mentioned 1980 amendments to the Model Business Corporation Act, which are carried forward into the present Model Business Corporation Act.[67]

The current version of the Model Business Corporation Act followed California's lead in jettisoning most of the traditional legal-capital concepts. The treasury share enigma is abolished,[68] and both share repurchases and dividends are covered under the concept of "distributions" to shareholders.[69] Also, the equity insolvency test is retained as a basic restriction.[70] The Model Business Corporation Act diverges significantly from the former California and other current statutory approaches in rejecting a restriction based on earnings.[71] In lieu of retained earnings or earned surplus, the Model Business Corporation Act uses a simpler and more flexible balance-sheet test. The new provision prohibits distributions if, after the distribution, a corporation's total assets are less than its total liabilities plus liquidation preferences, if any.[72] The Model Business Corporation Act further declines dependency on GAAP by placing the method for valuation of assets and liabilities within the directors' discretion, subject to a standard of reasonableness under the circumstances.[73]

§ 20.14 STOCK DIVIDENDS AND STOCK SPLITS

The term "stock dividend" is an unfortunate misnomer. It is a dividend only in the sense that the corporation has made a pro rata distribution among a class of its stockholders. However, it is unlike the other kinds of dividends discussed in this chapter because the corporation is not distributing any of its assets to its shareholders, and in turn its shareholders receive only additional shares to represent their same proportionate ownership interest. The declaration of dividends in new shares is a kind of psychological, constructive, or symbolic benefit that is sometimes used in order to keep investors satisfied with the retention of profits in the business or for purposes of stock market manipulation by those in control. The customary dividend statutes, discussed in the preceding sections, and the surplus and capital impairment limits do not apply to stock dividends. As explained in a leading case,[74] "a stock dividend does not distribute property, but simply dilutes the shares as they existed before. . . ." It is in no sense a distribution of surplus.

Neither stock dividends nor stock split-ups themselves increase or decrease the assets or earnings of the corporation. Nevertheless, these two events are treated quite differently by the accounting profession. As will be seen in the next section, surplus equal to the market value of the shares distributed must be capitalized for stock dividends but not for stock split-ups. What distinguishes the two is not the name assigned to the distribution by the board of directors, but whether a material reduction in the shares' market value is likely to accompany the distribution.[75] Investors associate both events with positive news about the corporation, so that rarely is the market value of the corporation's outstanding shares less after the declaration date of either a stock dividend or stock split than before the declaration.

A corporation's distribution of shares held by it in another corporation is properly referred to, not as a stock dividend, but as a property dividend, an actual distribution of corporate assets[76]—and, as such, is subject to the normal restrictions on cash and property dividends. The ordinary stock dividend—that is, the issuance of new shares, is very different in effect from a distribution of other property or of such shares to a different class. A stock dividend does not give the common shareholders any new or different interest in the corporation than they had before; it simply divides the holdings of each shareholder into a larger number of share units, with each stockholder maintaining the same proportionate interest in the corporation.[77]

A stock split is simply a division of outstanding shares by amendment of the articles of incorporation into a greater number of share units, like changing a five dollar bill into five "ones." It is the reverse of a share consolidation or "reverse stock split."[78] A share split-up does not, however, make any representations as to any accumulation of earnings or other surplus or involve any increase of the legal capital[79] as occurs with a stock dividend. In the case of a stock split, the per share par value or stated capital is decreased in the same proportion as the amount of the stock split. Share split-ups may be used for the legitimate purpose of reducing the market value of share units, which may otherwise be too high for general convenience in trading.

Under generally accepted accounting principles, the distinction between a stock dividend and a stock split is whether a material decline in the price of the shares is likely to occur on their distribution. When such a decline is not expected, the distribution is deemed a stock dividend, and surplus must be capitalized, as discussed in the next section, in an amount equal to the aggregate fair market value of the distributed shares. Under accounting standards, a distribution of less than 20 percent or 25 percent may not produce such an effect.[80] Stock splits are distributions where a material decline in the shares' market value is likely to occur. However, when characterizing a distribution with regard to allocation in trusts between principal and income, some courts have disregarded the dilution effect and instead have looked to the accounting entries made on the corporate balance sheet.

§ 20.15 CAPITALIZATION OF SURPLUS FOR STOCK DIVIDENDS AND STOCK SPLITS

The principal limitation on the issue of the typical stock dividend is a peculiar one—the capitalizing of surplus. Capitalization of surplus refers to the accounting transfer from one of the surplus accounts to the capital stock (stated capital) account. The requirement for such a transfer arises from the commands of the state corporation statute, the listing requirement of the American or New York Stock Exchange, if applicable, and the demands of generally accepted accounting principles. This is more than a mere bookkeeping entry. It decreases surplus and increases the legal-capital margin, which limits dividend distributions. When a share dividend is charged against earned surplus, it has been said that this in effect is the same as a distribution of accumulated profits to the shareholders and a compulsory subscription for shares or reinvestment by them of the amount received in the corporation.[81] The increase of legal capital due to a decrease of surplus restricts the directors' authority to declare dividends payable in cash or property.

By far the least demanding of these is that of the corporation statute that requires that an amount of surplus not less than the aggregate par value of shares distributed as a stock dividend be capitalized.[82] When the shares issued as a dividend are without par value, there is no convenient measure of the amount of surplus to be transferred to capital. Many states leave the amount almost wholly to the directors' discretion.[83]

As seen in the preceding section, there is great concern that investors may misinterpret the true economic effects of a stock dividend. Thus, generally accepted accounting principles require capitalization of surplus equal to the aggregate *fair market value* of the distributed shares in those instances in which a material decline in the per share market value is not believed to accompany the stock dividend's distribution.[84] Since share dividends are usually issued to evidence retention of earnings for reinvestment by the corporation, surplus is transferred and capitalized to give some assurance that such earnings will be retained by the corporation and to prevent misleading investors.[85] It would seem that the padding of the accounts by estimates and conjectures, by reappraising of fixed assets, and by writing up of inventories in order to make a revaluation of surplus for share dividends is undue laxity, which may give a deceptive representation of corporate prosperity to shareholders and to the investing public. GAAP requires transferring earned surplus to the category of permanent capitalization (i.e., "capital stock" and "capital surplus") an amount equal to the fair market value of the additional shares when a material adjustment in market prices is not likely to follow a stock dividend.[86]

Even though California and the Model Business Corporation Act exclude stock splits and stock dividends from the definition of "distributions," accounting standards still apply, so retained earnings must still be reduced if the states are to comply with generally accepted accounting standards and a material decline in the shares' market value is not likely to accompany the distribution.

PART C. LIABILITIES OF DIRECTORS AND SHAREHOLDERS

§ 20.16 DIRECTORS' LIABILITY FOR UNLAWFUL DIVIDENDS

The primary responsibility for protecting capital and keeping dividend distributions within statutory limits rests on the directors by whose authority such distributions are made. Directors' liability is the principal sanction or means of enforcement of dividend restrictions, supplemented by the less effective liability of shareholders and by injunction suits at the instance of shareholders.[87]

Most instances in which directors are held liable for illegal dividends can best be described euphemistically as "bankruptcy planning," through which corporate assets have been purposely deflected by cunning insiders to themselves without satisfying or making provision for outstanding obligations and while the corporation is either insolvent or is winding up its affairs.[88] Absent clear proof that the insiders were aware of their company's financial distress, or otherwise flaunted the statute's restrictions on distributions, director liability is highly unlikely.[89] Simply stated, the cases do not bear out the fear that directors will be hoisted on the petards of arcane principles and technical statutory requirements that so dominate the financial provisions of corporate statutes.[90]

Even in the absence of statutes expressly imposing liability, the directors are liable for participating in violations of the statutory restrictions that are directed to them.[91] All business corporation statutes contain express liability provisions making directors jointly and severally liable to the corporation[92] (or to its shareholders or its creditors) for payment of dividends in violation of statutory restrictions.[93] Drafting a satisfactory liability provision requires a delicate balancing between maintaining protection of creditors and avoiding harsh burdens on directors. One of the most interesting questions of construction and legislative policy is whether good faith and due care should be a defense. On the one hand, the legislature may consider that a drastic absolute liability is essential to prevent directors from declaring improper dividends and to give adequate protection to creditors and shareholders. On the other hand, there appears little reason to accord creditors greater protection and directors less protection in the area of illegal dividends than creditors enjoy derivatively in other areas of the directors' discretionary behavior. It would appear that the policy should protect directors whenever they act in good faith and with the reasonable care that the circumstances require. If greater protection is demanded, this should and does occur through the loan agreements that lenders so frequently require for their protection.

Many state statutes have sections on director liability similar to the Model Business Corporation Act. These sections make specific reference to the directors' general standard of care.[94] Accordingly, the business judgment rule is incorporated by reference, as is good faith reliance on counsel, public accountants, and officers or their financial statements and reports.[95] The Model Business Corporation Act reflects the scheme of most state statutes on this subject. Liability is imposed on any director who "votes for or assents to" an unlawful distribution if it is established that he "did not perform his duties in compliance with section 8.30," the provision that codifies the business judgment rule.[96] Any director so held liable has a right of contribution from other directors who similarly breached their statutory duties[97] and from any shareholder for the amount she received knowing the distribution was in violation of the statute or the articles of incorporation.[98]

There is little basis for believing that statutory liability provisions relating to illegal distributions are the exclusive proscriptions for protecting creditors.[99]

§ 20.17 SHAREHOLDERS' LIABILITY TO RETURN ILLEGAL DIVIDENDS

It has already been pointed out that a dividend distribution in violation of statutory restrictions is primarily a wrong done by the directors who declare it. The liability most frequently imposed by specific statutes is placed on the directors who declare the dividend rather than on the shareholders who receive it, although the directors may seek contribution against the shareholders who received the illegal dividend with knowledge.

The clear trend among statutes is not to impose liability on shareholders unless it can be shown that the dividends were received with knowledge of the company's condition. This is the position taken in the present Model Business Corporation Act, which permits directors to obtain contribution "from each shareholder for the amount the shareholder accepted *knowing* the distribution was made in violation" of the statute.[100] There is no direct shareholder liability to the corporation provided within the Model Business Corporation Act. There is always a question, however, whether a state statute that sets forth rights against shareholders who receive unlawful distributions supplants the common law.[101]

NOTES

1. Stout v. Oates, 234 S.W.2d 506 (Ark. 1950).
2. An obvious justification is that the corporation does not satisfy the minimum statutory requirements for the payment of dividends. *See, e.g.,* Jones v. Jones, 637 N.Y.S.2d 83 (Sup. Ct. App. Div. 1996).
3. Miller v. Magline, Inc., 256 N.W.2d 761 (Mich. Ct. App. 1977).
4. *In re* Reading Co., 711 F.2d 509 (3d Cir. 1983).
5. *See, e.g.,* Baron v. Allied Artists Pictures Corp., 337 A.2d 653, 659 (Del. Ch. 1975).
6. *In re* Estate of Butterfield, 341 N.W.2d 453 (Mich. 1983)
7. Iwasaki v. Iwasaki Bros., 649 P.2d 598 (Or. App. 1982).
8. *In re* Reading Co., 711 F.2d 509 (3d Cir. 1983); Zidell v. Zidell, Inc., 560 P.2d 1086 (Or. 1977).
9. Kohn v. Birmingham Realty Co., 352 So. 2d 834 (Ala. 1977).
10. Gay v. Gay's Super Markets, Inc., 343 A.2d 577 (Me. 1975).
11. Coduti v. Hellwig, 469 N.E.2d 220 (Ill. 1984).
12. *See, e.g.,* Shostak v. Shostak, 851 A.2d 515 (Me. 2004) (bad faith established by evidence close corporation had historically paid dividends from profits at least to the level of income taxes attributable to each member per IRS Form K-1).
13. Stevens v. U.S. Steel Corp., 59 A. 905, 907 (N.J. Ch. 1905).
14. In close corporation cases, the courts are more willing to accord less of a presumption of propriety to decisions to withhold dividends than in cases involving public companies. *See, e.g.,* Santarelli v. Katz, 270 F.2d 762, 768 (7th Cir. 1959) ("if a stockholder is being unjustly deprived of dividends that should be his, a court of equity will not permit management to cloak itself in the immunity of the business judgment rule").
15. Ford v. Easthampton Rubber-Thread Co., 32 N.E. 1036 (Mass. 1893).
16. Ford v. Ford Mfg. Co., 222 Ill. App. 76 (1921).
17. *See* MODEL BUSINESS CORP. ACT § 6.40 (2008) [hereinafter MBCA]; Former MODEL BUSINESS CORP. ACT § 30 (1969) [hereinafter Former MBCA].
18. Caleb & Co. v. E.I. DuPont de Nemours & Co., 615 F. Supp. 96 (S.D.N.Y. 1985).
19. *Id.*
20. *See* Wilcom v. Wilcom, 502 A.2d 1076 (Md. 1986) (purchasers of shares pursuant to stock transfer restriction is equity owner entitled to dividends thereafter, even though transferor refused to transfer title).
21. De Gendre v. Kent, L.R. 4 Eq. 283 (1865).
22. Herzfeld & Stern v. Freidus, 330 N.Y.S.2d 479 (Sup. Ct. App. Term 1971).
23. Richter & Co. v. Light, 116 A. 600 (Conn. 1922).
24. In order to comport with GAAP, the California statute speaks in terms of "retained earnings." CAL. GEN. CORP. LAW § 500(a) (as amended 2012). See Chapter 19, § 19.6 and infra § 20.19.
25. This is now the alternative approach to the use of retained earnings in California. CAL. GEN. CORP. LAW § 500(a) (West 1990).
26. See *infra* § 20.12

27. Former MBCA §§ 2(i), 45(b) (1980); MBCA §§ 1.40(b), 6.40 (2008). The text to the 1980 amendments to the Model Business Corporation Act is reported in 34 Bus. Law. 1867–1889 (1979).

28. *See, e.g.,* Cal. Gen. Corp. Law § 166 (West 1990). *See generally* Chapter 21.

29. For an analysis of whether state-imposed dividend restrictions reflect efficient contracting by creditors, *see* John Armour, *Share Capital and Creditor Protection: Efficient Rules for a Modern Company Law*, 63 Mod. L. Rev. 355 (2000).

30. Del. Code Ann. tit. 8, §§ 170(a), 173, 154 (2001); N.Y. Bus. Corp. Law § 510 (McKinney Supp. 2009).

31. Del. Code Ann. tit. 8, §§ 170(a), 173, 154 (2001).

32. This was the case prior to the 1980 Model Business Corporation Act amendments. Former MBCA § 45(a) (1969). See *infra* § 20.14.

33. Other sources of capital surplus are transfers from earned surplus to capital surplus on approval of the board of directors, Former MBCA § 70 (1969), by a reduction in stated capital, *id.*, or issuances of shares as part of an exchange or conversion of outstanding shares. *Id.* §§ 18, 19.

34. *Id.* § 46.

35. Randall v. Bailey, 43 N.E.2d 43 (N.Y. 1942), *aff'g* 23 N.Y.S.2d 173 (Sup. Ct. 1940). *See* Thomas A. Reynolds, Note, *Cash Dividends Payable from Unrealized Appreciation of Fixed Assets—A Reconsideration of* Randall v. Bailey, 20 U. Pitt. L. Rev. 632 (1959).

36. Klang v. Smith's Food & Drug Centers, 702 A.2d 150, 154 (Del. 1997) (directors have the power to use fair value of assets to determine the firm's surplus).

37. *See Current Issues on the Legality of Dividends from a Law and Accounting Perspective*, 39 Bus. Law. 289, 292–300 (1983).

38. 23 N.Y.S.2d 173 (Sup. Ct. 1940), *aff'd*, 43 N.E.2d 43 (N.Y. 1942).

39. N.Y. Stock Corp. Law § 58, enacted in 1923 (emphasis added).

40. *Klang*, 702 A.2d at 154.

41. This indeed is the notion within the accounting movement calling for current-value accounting.

42. MBCA § 6.40(d) (2008) (emphasis added).

43. Former MBCA §§ 45, 46 (1969).

44. *Id.* at § 2(1).

45. Cal. Gen. Corp. Law § 500(a) (West 1990).

46. See Chapter 19, § 19.4.

47. Former MBCA § 45 (1969). The insolvency test is also used new or in conjunction with other dividend tests in state statutes. *See* Cal. Gen. Corp. Law § 501 (West 1990).

48. Del. Code Ann. tit. 8, §§ 154, 170(a) (2001); N.Y. Bus. Corp. Law § 510 (McKinney Supp. 2009); MBCA Ann. 3d § 640 Statutory Comparison ¶ 1(c) (Supp. 1993).

49. I.R.C. §§ 316, 301(c)(2) (2009).

50. A number of state statutes require notice to shareholders of the source of the distribution if not from earned surplus or if from capital surplus. *See, e.g.,* N.Y. Bus. Corp. Law § 501(c) (McKinney 1986).

51. *See* Ark. Code Ann. § 4-26-619(B) (Michie 2001).

52. Former MBCA § 46 (1969).

53. All cumulative arrearages must have been paid, and the distribution cannot reduce the next assets below the aggregate liquidation preference. *Id.* at § 46(e), (d).

54. *E.g., id.* § 43.

55. Minn. Stat. Ann. § 302A.551(a) (West 2004); N.D. Cent. Code § 10-19.1-92.1 (Michie 2005).

56. *See* Paratransit Risk Retention Grp. Ins. Co. v. Kamins, 160 P.3d 307 (Colo. Ct. App. 2007) (equity solvency test contemplates that corporation continues to generate or attempts to generate profits).

57. *See* Tumarkin v. Gallay, 127 F. Supp. 94 (S.D.N.Y. 1954).

58. Since rules against capital impairment operate on the theory that dividends will be paid out of the excess of net assets over liabilities and stated capital, such a rule requires the total assets to exceed total liabilities. The problem with such determinations is that they are based on the balance sheet values, which do not necessarily correlate with the true market value, particularly in the context of a forced sale. Thus a bankruptcy solvency test may not in fact be incorporated into the capital impairment prohibition and perhaps should be viewed as a distinct limitation, particularly to protect long-term creditors.

59. *In re* Felt Mfg. Co., Inc., 371 B.R. 589 (Bankr. D.N.H. 2007) (applying N.H. Law).

60. This linkage is expressly made in the present Model Business Corporation Act by premising director liability for unlawful distributions only if the director "did not perform his duties in compliance with section 8.30," which codifies the business judgment rule. MBCA § 8.33(a) (1984).

61. *Id.* § 6.40 Comment 2 (2008).

62. *E.g.,* Del. Code Ann. tit. 8, § 170(b) (2001).

63. Former MBCA § 45(b) (1969).

64. *Id.* § 45 (1980); MBCA § 6.40 (1984); Ill. Rev. Stat. ch. 805, § 5/9.10 (West 2004); Minn. Stat. Ann. § 302A.551 (West 2004); Mont. Code Ann. § 35-1-712 (2009); N.M. Stat. Ann. § 53-11-44 (Michie Supp. 2007); Wash. Rev. Code Ann. § 23B.06.400 (West Supp. 2009).

65. The California court in an early decision declared that the then California statute, which forbade withdrawal of capital or "capital stock" and confined dividends to "surplus profits arising from the business," did not preclude a mining corporation from distributing the net proceeds of its mining operations without provision for depletion, although the necessary result was that something was subtracted from the value of its mine and from the net worth of its investment. Excelsior Water & Mining Co. v. Pierce, 27 P. 44 (Cal. 1891).

66. The earning power of a corporation, its ability to pay debts and dividends, may not depend on the amount of its net assets.

67. The text of the 1980 amendments and the Report of the Committee on Corporate Laws may be found in 34 Bus. Law. 1867–1889 (1979).

68. MBCA § 6.40 (and comments) (2008); Cal. Gen. Corp. Law § 510 (West 1990).

69. MBCA § 1.40(6) (2008); Cal. Gen. Corp. Law § 166 (West 1990).

70. Former MBCA § 45(a) (1980); MBCA § 6.40 (2008); CAL. GEN. CORP. LAW § 501 (West 1990).
71. Both the earned-surplus test (Former MBCA § 45 (1969)) and California's retained-earnings test (CAL. GEN. CORP. LAW § 500(a) (as amended 2012)) are based on the concept of paying dividends based on the corporation's earnings or profits rather than on money (capital) paid into the company by the sale of shares. California now allows an assets and liabilities test as an alternative to retained earnings. *Id.*
72. Former MBCA § 45(b) (1969); RMBCA § 6.40 (1984).
73. Former MBCA § 45 (1969). Directors may make asset and liability determinations from financial statements based on accounting practices and principles that are reasonable under the circumstances. *See id.* § 45 Comment. In many cases the reasonableness standard may require use of GAAP.
74. Williams v. W. Union Tel. Co., 57 N.Y.S. 446, 453 (1883).
75. AICPA, ACCT. RES. BULL. No. 43 ch. 7, Stock Dividends and Stock Split-Ups 11 (1953) [hereinafter AICPA, BULL. No. 43].
76. Peabody v. Eisner, 247 U.S. 347 (1918); City Bank Farmers' Trust Co. v. Ernst, 189 N.E. 241 (N.Y. 1934).
77. Eisner v. Macomber, 252 U.S. 189 (1920).
78. *See* Teschner v. Chicago Title & Trust Co., 322 N.E.2d 54 (Ill. 1974).
79. *In re* Trust Estate of Pew, 158 A.2d 552 (Pa. 1960).
80. AICPA, BULL. No. 43, *supra* note 75.
81. Trefry v. Putnam, 116 N.E. 904, 911 (Mass. 1917).
82. Former MBCA § 45(d) (1969).
83. *E.g.*, DEL. CODE ANN. tit. 8, § 173 (2001); N.Y. BUS. CORP. LAW § 511(a)(2) (McKinney 2003); Former MBCA § 45(d)(2) (1969).
84. AICPA, BULL. No. 43, *supra* note 75.
85. *See id.*
86. *See* ARB No. 43, ch. 7, *Stock Dividends and Stock Split-Ups* (AICPA 1953) (suggesting capitalization when the number of shares to be distributed is less than 20–25 percent of the shares outstanding before the stock dividend is declared).
87. In most jurisdictions, remedies to recover illegal dividends from shareholders are limited to cases of insolvency or knowledge of impropriety.
88. *See, e.g.*, Retirement Benefit Plan of Graphic Arts Int'l Union Local 20-B v. Standard Bindery Co., 654 F. Supp. 770 (E.D. Mich. 1986).
89. *See In re* Tufts Elecs., Inc., 746 F.2d 915 (1st Cir. 1984) (no liability for insolvency within one and one-half years of payment to sole shareholder when evidence showed company was solvent immediately after payment made).
90. *See, e.g.*, *Klang*, 702 A.2d 150, 156–57 (Del. 1997) (board resolution need not set forth amount of pre-and post-distribution surplus so that understatement of amount of liabilities does not give rise to directors' liability provided sufficient surplus in fact did exist).
91. A statutory violation is not regarded as being negligence per se or even evidence of negligence, but willful or negligent violation must ordinarily be shown. Directors are not liable for mistakes or errors of judgment if

they act in good faith or with due care, as usually shown by considering and checking balance sheets and relying reasonably on reports of subordinates. *See* Blythe v. Enslen, 95 So. 479 (Ala. 1922).

92. Lerner v. Lerner Corp., 711 A.2d 233, 240–41 (Md. App. 1998) (shareholder lacks standing to complain of illegal dividend, the right of action belongs to the corporation).

93. *See* MBCA ANN. § 8.33 (3d ed. 1994).

94. *See* MBCA § 8.33 (2008); Former MBCA § 48 (1969). *See also, e.g.,* CAL. GEN. CORP. LAW § 316 (West 1990); IDAHO CODE § 30-1-833 (Michie 2005); N.Y. BUS. CORP. LAW § 719 (McKinney 2003).

95. *See* Former MBCA § 35, Comment (1969). *See also, e.g.,* CAL. GEN. CORP. LAW § 309 (West 1990); IDAHO CODE § 30-1-833 (Michie 2005); N.Y. BUS. CORP. LAW § 717 (McKinney 2003).

96. MBCA § 8.33(a) (2008).

97. *Id. at* § 8.33(b).

98. *Id. at* § 8.33(c).

99. A number of cases refute the exclusivity of statutory shareholder liability. *See, e.g., In re* Kettle Fried Chicken of Am., Inc., 513 F.2d 807 (6th Cir. 1975); Reilly v. Segert, 201 N.E.2d 444 (Ill. 1964). Statutes may also leave open other possibilities of director liability. *See* Former MBCA § 48 (1969): "In addition to any other liabilities imposed by law."

100. MBCA § 8.33(b)(2) (2008) (emphasis added).

101. *See* Reilly v. Segert, 201 N.E.2d 444 (Ill. 1964) (statute imposing liability on directors for unlawful distributions with a right of contribution from knowing shareholders does not preclude suit by receiver against shareholders).

CHAPTER 21

REPURCHASES, REDEMPTIONS, AND THE REDUCTION OF CAPITAL

PART A. SHARE PURCHASES AND REDEMPTIONS

§ 21.1 AMERICAN RULES ON SHARE REPURCHASES

It is important to understand the financial difference between a corporation's purchase of its own shares and its purchase of shares issued by an independent enterprise. Shares in another entity are assets of possible value to creditors. On a surrender of a corporation's own shares, the purchase price is simply withdrawn from the issuer's business. Nothing of value to creditors takes its place except what is in reality an unissued share, which cannot profitably be reissued when there is a financial reversal. Today all American jurisdictions permit a corporation to purchase its own shares, subject to various limitations such as impairment of capital.

The underlying reason for limiting share purchases is the same as that of dividends. Safeguards should be imposed against a corporation's depletion of its assets and the impairment of its capital needed for the protection of creditors and other shareholders. This has sometimes been expressed in terms of the trust fund doctrine,[1] which has been used to protect creditors.[2]

Exceptions to a Restrictive Rule. There are certain situations that are considered to give little opportunity for abuse, in which the corporation is generally recognized to have the authority to purchase its own shares even out of capital. Exceptions include: the purchases of preferred shares subject to a redemption provision in the articles of incorporation; purchases to compensate dissenting shareholders under appraisal statutes; employee stock purchase plans that have an option or agreement to repurchase; and purchases pursuant to an authorized statutory method of reduction of legal capital.[3]

The Solvency Limitation. Many statutes retain an insolvency test, however, along with the surplus or capital impairment tests.[4] As will be seen later in this chapter, the timing of these tests assumes special importance when shares are repurchased over a long period, perhaps on an installment basis. The courts are badly divided over whether the surplus and solvency tests are each applied to each installment payment or whether either of these tests should be applied only when the contract of purchase is entered into.

§ 21.2 THE DANGERS AND ABUSES OF DEALING IN THE CORPORATION'S OWN SHARES

The dangers and abuses incident to allowing a corporation, through its management, to make purchases and sales of its own shares are as follows: (1) Stock repurchases make it possible for favored shareholders to withdraw current assets from the business and impair the capital and the financial responsibility on which creditors have a right to rely; (2) Repurchases may be used to undermine the equity or margin of safety of preferred shares, to decrease assets, or to decrease surplus and thereby defeat the reasonable expectations of preferred shareholders as to dividend arrearages, future dividends, and liquidation preferences; (3) Repurchases may be used with similar discriminatory effect against other common shareholders; (4) Repurchases may be used to juggle the voting control of the corporation and to buy off bona fide opponents of the management. In the context of a takeover attempt, this practice is currently known as "greenmail;" (5) Repurchases may be used for speculation by the corporation or by its management and for manipulation of the market price of the corporation's stock.

In recognition of these and other dangers, state laws not only impose legal restrictions but also regulate the fairness of such transactions.[5] Additional protection is found under federal law, which imposes stringent disclosure requirements as a result of the 1968 Williams Act amendments to the Securities Exchange Act of 1934.[6]

§ 21.3 STATUTORY RESTRICTIONS ON REPURCHASES OF SHARES

Dangers incident to the purchase by corporations of their own shares have led to statutory regulation of the practice. Under the pre-1980 Model Business Corporation Act, share repurchases were generally limited to the extent of unrestricted earned surplus or unrestricted capital surplus if specifically authorized by the articles or a majority shareholder vote.[7] The earlier version of the Model Business Corporation Act exempts certain repurchase transactions, such as elimination of fractional shares and retirement of redeemable shares.[8] There is also an insolvency limitation similar to that affecting cash or property dividends.[9] The Act further imposes liability on directors who vote for such illegal share purchases.[10] The 1980 amendments to the Model Business Corporation Act's financial provisions, carried forward to the present Model Business Corporation Act, treat share purchases as a form of distribution to shareholders and apply the same limitations to share purchases as to dividends.[11] As seen in the preceding chapter, the new limitations on distributions after the 1980 amendments do away with traditional legal-capital concepts and are much less restrictive than the former earned-surplus test. California's general corporation statute was the first to use this preferable approach of treating share purchases as a distribution.[12] Because the California statute and, since 1980, the Model Business Corporation Act provide that repurchased shares are restored to the status of authorized but unissued shares, they have each thereby prevented such shares from being reported as treasury shares.[13]

Some state corporation laws expressly authorize corporations to purchase their own shares "out of surplus."[14] The same limitation may be expressed by a prohibition against purchases that cause an impairment of capital.[15]

These "earned surplus" statutes may allow purchases out of capital surplus when approved in the articles of incorporation or by a majority of the shareholders.[16] Many states allow a corporation to purchase or redeem its redeemable preferred shares out of capital as well as out of surplus—subject, however, to a provision that the capital shall not be impaired as to other preferred shares having priority or equality as to liquidation rights.[17] A general insolvency limitation is often added to these statutes. All such statutes invite inquiry into the extent to which generally accepted accounting principles (GAAP) will guide the statute's application with respect to terms that have accounting significance. As seen earlier, some states expressly incorporate GAAP into their statutes,[18] whereas the present Model Business Corporation Act, following the 1980 amendments to the Model Business Corporation Act, allows "fair valuation or other method that is reasonable in the circumstances,"[19] a result that has occasionally been reached by the courts.[20]

The Delaware Supreme Court provides a sweeping embrace of the authority of the board of directors to resort to unrealized appreciation in assets as a source for the repurchase of shares.[21] This interpretation essentially brought the law of Delaware into line with the discretion the board of directors enjoys under the current Model

Business Corporation Act to resort to unrealized gains as a source for distributions to shareholders.

§ 21.4 EXECUTORY AND INSTALLMENT CONTRACTS TO REPURCHASE

Particular problems arise with regard to shares' purchase contracts that are executory in nature or where payment by the corporation is delayed by an installment agreement or by the issuance of a debt obligation. There may be important reasons for a corporation to repurchase some of its shares when it has insufficient funds to do so. Repurchase agreements are also common in close corporations, but the commercial purpose for such repurchases may arise when the corporation lacks sufficient cash with which to make the repurchase.[22] A frequent response to these problems is for the corporation to purchase the shares in exchange for an installment note.[23]

Making installment payments to former shareholders when the corporation is insolvent is problematic in many states whose statutes or court decisions have not yet defined the moment when the statutory restrictions are to apply to the transaction. The question is whether, when applying the statutory restrictions to an installment repurchase of shares, the transaction should be treated as a single purchase, so that the restrictions are applied at the moment the contract is entered into, or whether the installment repurchase should be treated as a series of successive purchases, so that the statutory restrictions are to be satisfied as to each payment. At a time when states had only a solvency test, a highly influential decision held that the state's solvency test should be applied at the moment of payment, not when the parties entered into the installment contract.[24] This so-called insolvency cutoff rule has been widely followed where the question is the timing of a solvency test.[25]

Given the insolvency cutoff rule, with its emphasis on the time of payment and the gradual proliferation of statutory surplus tests for share repurchases, an issue arises as to whether statutory surplus tests should be applied at the time of the purchase or at the time of the actual payments. A tax case held that the surplus test must be met only at the time of payment, not when the repurchase agreement was made.[26] This is the so-called surplus cutoff rule. Thus, under this approach, an installment note for the repurchase of stock was valid even if the corporation did not have sufficient surplus to cover the repurchase at the time the note was given.[27] This surplus cutoff rule, requiring that statutory balance-sheet tests be met at the time of payment, has been accepted in many cases.[28] Even under the stricter surplus cutoff rule, however, where there are no creditors to be protected, a former shareholder may obtain specific enforcement of a note even if it forces the corporation into liquidation.

Not all decisions have followed the surplus cutoff rule. The current Model Business Corporation Act applies the statutory tests to each payment only if the corporation did not earlier issue a note or other evidence of indebtedness to acquire shares.[29] Delaware statutorily rejected a surplus cutoff rule.[30]

The pre-1980 Model Business Corporation Act, which is similar to the statute that was before the Texas court, speaks in terms of purchases out of surplus and then provided that "no purchase or payment" may be made that would render the corporation insolvent.[31] Beginning with the 1980 amendments, the Model Business Corporation Act supplants the surplus test with a requirement that the assets following the distribution not be less than the firm's liabilities and also maintain the solvency test.[32] The statute now applies its own timing standard for the application of both these tests, under which the tests would appear to be applied when the contract to repurchase is entered into, assuming that is the moment when the corporation issues the note embodying its obligation to pay for the shares.[33]

Some courts have also held that former shareholders may enforce the debt, despite insolvency or lack of surplus, where there is an underlying lien.[34] One may wonder why the underlying debt that secures a lien should ever achieve greater dignity because of its existence than the debt it secures. Another view holds that a note given as partial consideration to repurchase shares when the corporation was insolvent is illegal, so that the corporation is not obligated to honor the note.[35]

§ 21.5 Redemption and Purchase of Callable Shares

"Repurchase of shares" is a generic term that includes the narrower concept of redemption pursuant to a contractual right embodied in the share contract and the articles of incorporation. In many cases, it is significant which type of repurchase is involved.

Preferred shares may be made subject not only to redemption that is optional with the corporation but also to compulsory redemption or resale. There are serious objections to compulsory redemption provisions. The normal redemption provision is an option in favor of the corporation to call in and retire preferred shares at a specified redemption price, usually at a premium over the issue price. Any right of redemption, however, must be exercised in strict compliance with the terms of the contract or instrument granting the right.[36] Procedures exercising redemption rights, such as notice to the shareholders and some method of selection by lot, pro rata or otherwise, are usually provided in the charter to prevent discrimination for or against other holders if the entire class of shares is not called. Such provisions have been held by some courts not to preclude a corporation from making independent share repurchases without making a pro rata redemption.[37] Even apart from a pro rata requirement, there are, of course, equitable limitations on both repurchases and redemptions.

The option to redeem is exercised by the board of directors. A resolution adopted in accordance with the charter provisions calling certain shares for redemption creates a contract and, unless expressly conditional, the board's action may not be rescinded or modified.[38]

Traditionally, common shares may not be made redeemable at the option of the corporation.[39] "Stock which has no retirement provisions is the backbone of a corporate structure."[40] The chief function of the provision for redemption in stock or bonds is to facilitate the retirement of senior securities for the benefit of the holders of common shares and to make possible the reduction of capital or refinancing at a lower rate of return on new senior securities by paying off and terminating the old shares that call for a higher dividend. The rule against redeemable common stock must be kept in mind when drafting repurchase agreements.[41] Modern corporation acts make a distinction between the purchase of common shares and the exercise of the right to purchase of callable or redeemable preferred shares. The former is subject to the standard requirement that the purchase can be made to the extent of unrestricted surplus, whereas the acquisition of redeemable shares can rely on the stated capital of the shares to be redeemed, with any additional amount coming from unrestricted surplus. Thus, the stated capital of redeemable shares is of a somewhat temporary character. If shares are redeemed out of capital, this reduces pro tanto the surplus thereafter available for dividends on the common.

Redemptions are subject, of course, to the general restriction in favor of the priority of creditors and may not be made when a corporation is insolvent or when the redemption would result in insolvency or inability to meet debts and liabilities as they accrue.[42] Many modern acts also take into account the liquidation preferences of shares to remain outstanding.[43] A charter provision may protect the dividend rights of preferred shareholders—for example, by providing that dividends shall be paid "before any sum shall be paid or set apart for the purchase or redemption of any stock now or hereafter authorized."[44]

§ 21.6 FIDUCIARY LIMITATIONS ON SHARE REPURCHASES

Share repurchases are subject to abuse to the extent that they provide a facade for an unfair distribution of corporate assets. In a leading Massachusetts case,[45] the majority shareholders caused the directors to repurchase a portion of their holdings at a premium. The court held that the fiduciary duties between shareholders in close corporations demanded equal treatment and a right of the minority to participate on a pro rata basis. Similarly, in a Georgia case,[46] it was held that the corporate right to purchase its own shares is not absolute but is conditioned on good faith. "Good faith is not just a question of what is proper for the corporation. It also requires that the stockholders be treated fairly and that their investments be protected."[47] However, it has been held that the directors may authorize repurchase at a premium in order to protect the corporation against an outside takeover attempt.[48] The Delaware court reached this conclusion by relying on the business judgment rule in the face of a claim that the directors were wasting corporate assets in order to perpetuate their control.[49] This practice, known as "greenmail," is discussed in Chapter 12. Greenmail is a subset of a wide range of concerns that arise when the incumbent management, through the board of directors, causes the corporation to make a defensive purchase of shares as a step toward thwarting a shift in control. Both privately negotiated repurchases[50] and the redemption of a class of shares held by one stockholder[51] have been upheld when used to remove dissident shareholders. The right to redeem shares may be balanced with the shareholder's conversion rights.[52]

The Williams Act amendments to the Securities Exchange Act of 1934[53] impose various substantive and disclosure requirements on tender offerors and issuers repurchasing their own shares. The term "tender offer" is not defined in the act. The term includes many share repurchases that are essentially tender offers by the issuer, in light of the expansive interpretations by the SEC and the courts.[54] Although expressly excluded from most of the Williams Act's disclosure, filing, and substantive provisions,[55] the issuer is subject to section 14(e)'s[56] general antifraud provisions,[57] and section 13(e) expressly empowers the SEC to regulate share repurchases by SEC reporting companies.[58] Pursuant to its authority under this provision, the Commission has promulgated a going-private rule[59] as well as a general disclosure requirement for issuer tender offers.[60] An important provision prohibits the issuer from making any purchases of its shares after someone other than the issuer has commenced a tender offer, unless certain detailed disclosures are made by the issuer.[61] Outside of the Williams Act, SEC Rule 10b-18 provides a safe harbor for a public company's purchases of its own shares.[62]

PART B. STATUS OF TREASURY SHARES

§ 21.7 THE PECULIAR STATUS OF TREASURY SHARES

Treasury shares carry neither voting rights[63] nor rights to dividends or other distributions.[64] Their existence as "issued shares" is a pure fiction, a figure of speech to explain certain special rules and privileges as to their reissue. A share of stock is simply a unit of interest in the corporate enterprise arising from a contract. When holders of a share surrender their rights to the corporation, it is obvious that the contract is in reality terminated. In cases where the presence, vote, or assent of the majority of the shareholders is required, it must be understood to mean shares that are issued and outstanding and that may be voted.[65] If shares in corporation A are purchased or held by corporation B, which is controlled or dominated by corporation A, the prevailing view is that such shares should not be regarded as treasury shares of the parent. But they should not, and generally may not, carry voting rights because the voting power could be controlled by the management of the parent, and this would be indirect voting by the parent.[66] Treasury stock is in essence authorized stock that may be reissued as fully paid without some of the restrictions on an original issue of shares as to consideration and as to preemptive rights, if any.

Due to the fictional nature of treasury shares, the current Model Business Corporation Act, following the 1980 amendments to the Model Business Corporation Act and the California statute, has abolished the need to recognize treasury stock. Under these provisions,[67] all reacquired shares, whether by way of redemption or other purchase, are restored to the status of authorized but unissued, unless the articles prohibit their reissue, in which case their repurchase results in an automatic amendment to the articles of incorporation reducing the number of authorized shares.

§ 21.8 THE REISSUE OR RETIREMENT OF TREASURY SHARES

When treasury shares are reissued and sold by the corporation, the shares are issued to the new purchaser, and the corporation is viewed as an intermediate transferee between the former and new shareholders. In reality, the old share contract has been extinguished and the new shares are new units of interest created in their place.

Retirement and Cancellation. Outside of California and states that have patterned their financial provisions after the Model Business Corporation Act, a corporation usually has the option on reacquisition of shares to treat them as treasury shares or to retire or cancel them.[68] Treasury shares are carried on the books as authorized and still issued but not outstanding.[69] When retired or cancelled, the shares usually retain the status of authorized but unissued shares.[70] Sometimes the terms "retired" or "cancelled" may be used in the articles of incorporation to mean that once a share is reacquired, it may never be reissued. Such a permanent "retirement" results in an automatic reduction in the number of shares authorized by the articles of incorporation. This is common under provisions in the articles in connection with the redemption of preferred shares. To avoid confusion, such provisions in the articles of incorporation should be drafted to expressly prohibit reissue and require reduction of authorized shares where that is desired.[71]

PART C. REMEDIES FOR IMPROPER SHARE PURCHASES

§ 21.9 RECOVERY BY CORPORATION FOR UNLAWFUL SHARE PURCHASES

There appears little reason in theory to distinguish unlawful share repurchases from unlawful dividends when considering whether innocent shareholders should escape liability. In both cases, the danger is the wrongful transfer of assets from the corporation that erodes the creditors' estate. The non-pro-rata nature of a share repurchase raises questions of fairness to nonselling shareholders but does not especially suggest a greater threat to creditors, unless the non-pro-rata repurchase is inherently consistent with a richer factual mosaic in which insiders purposely are transferring assets to themselves, such as at the brink of the company's insolvency. And, even in this context, there appears little gained in the analysis by distinguishing between the treatment of cunning insiders who sell their shares to the corporation and of those who merely pay themselves dividends. Thus, since the 1980 amendments, the former Model Business Corporation Act and the current Model Business Corporation Act impose liability only on guilty shareholders.[72]

Initially, shareholder liability for improper share repurchases was grounded primarily in common law, but today this liability is primarily statutory.[73] Corporation statutes either provide directly for shareholder liability or subject shareholders to the contribution rights of directors.[74] Either form of liability is usually limited to those shareholders acting with knowledge of the impropriety.[75]

In the case of improper share purchases, the directors are liable for causing a corporation to repurchase shares in violation of statutory legal capital requirements.[76] Director liability for improper distributions is usually governed by statutes and is enforced through director liability provisions based on the directors' breach of the duty of care to the corporation.[77] There is some conflict of authority as to whether recovery from directors may be had only for the benefit of existing creditors or also for subsequent creditors. The trend, however, seems to be to allow recovery even to subsequent creditors without notice.[78]

§ 21.10 Right of Recovery by Creditors from Selling Shareholders

The standing of creditors to pursue unlawful share repurchases is no different from their standing to pursue unlawful dividends. When the corporation is insolvent, creditors are usually represented by a receiver or trustee in bankruptcy. However, the individual creditor may bring an action for the improper payments. In this case, rather than suing the shareholder on the creditor's original claim, the creditor usually secures a judgment against the corporation first and then follows the assets of the corporation to the selling shareholders.

Notes

1. *In re* Atl. Printing Co., 60 F.2d 553 (D. Mass. 1932).
2. In the classic English case, for example, more than one-fifth of the capital of the company had been withdrawn, and the company had increased its bank borrowings by a wholesale policy of share-purchasing over a period of years. Trevor v. Whitworth, 12 App. Cas. 409 (1887).
3. *See* RFE Capital Partners, LP v. Weskar, Inc., 652 A.2d 1093 (Del. Super. Ct. 1994) (lender's option to "put" warrant to corporation held outside Delaware repurchase statute, which applied only to "capital stock").
4. *See, e.g.,* Former MBCA § 6 (1969); N.Y. Bus. Corp. Law § 513 (McKinney 2003).
5. *But see* Kohn v. Birmingham Realty Co., 352 So. 2d 834 (Ala. 1977) (court refused to enjoin meeting at which redemption would be approved where evidence demonstrated corporation had adequate surplus and was solvent, so business purpose for redemption not relevant).
6. Pub. L. No. 90-439, 82 Stat. 454 (1968), codified at 15 U.S.C. §§ 78m(d) to (e), 78n(d) to (f) (2009). See § 24.1.
7. Former MBCA § 6 (1969). Most states have adopted similar provisions.
8. *Id.* The former Model Business Corporation Act also appears to exempt transactions compromising indebtedness and payment of dissenting shareholders. *Id.* For more on redemption of redeemable shares, see § 18.13.
9. Former MBCA § 6 (1969). See § 20.16.
10. Former MBCA § 48(b) (1969). See §§ 21.12, 21.13.
11. *See* Model Business Corp. Act § 6.40 (2008) [hereinafter MBCA]; Former MBCA §§ 2(i), 6, 45 (1980).
12. *See* Cal. Corp. Code § 166 (West Supp. 2009); Thomas C. Ackerman, Jr. & James K. Sterrett, III, *California's New Approach to Dividends and Reacquisitions of Shares*, 23 UCLA L. Rev. 1052 (1976).
13. Cal. Corp. Code § 510(a) (West Supp. 2009); Former MBCA § 6 (1969).
14. La. Rev. Stat. Ann. § 12:55(B) (West 2004); N.Y. Bus. Corp. Law § 513 (McKinney 2003).
15. *See* Del. Code Ann. tit. 8, § 160 (2001). *See* Am. Heritage Inv. Corp. v. Ill. Nat'l Bank, 386 N.E.2d 905 (1979).

16. *See* Former MBCA § 6 (1969).
17. *See id.* § 66. The 1980 amendments to the Model Business Corporation Act deleted this section.
18. *See* CAL. CORP. CODE § 114 (West Supp.1990).
19. MBCA § 6.40(d) (2008).
20. *See* Klang v. Smith's Food & Drug Centers, 702 A.2d 150, 154 (Del. 1997).
21. *Id.* at 150.
22. In case of death or disability, the funding problem can be handled with key man insurance.
23. *See In re* Envirodyne Indus., Inc., 79 F.3d 579 (7th Cir. 1996) (unsecured claims of nontendering cashed-out shareholders of corporation subordinated under Bankruptcy Act Section 510(c)).
24. Robinson v. Wangemann, 75 F.2d 756 (5th Cir. 1935). Earlier another court addressed this problem with the same effect.
25. McConnell v. Estate of Butler, 402 F.2d 362 (9th Cir. 1968).
26. Mountain State Steel Foundries, Inc. v. Comm'r, 284 F.2d 737 (4th Cir. 1960).
27. *See also* Rainford v. Rytting, 451 P.2d 769 (Utah 1969).
28. *In re* Nat'l Tile & Terrazzo Co., 537 F.2d 329 (9th Cir. 1976).
29. N.J. BUSINESS CORP. ACT ch. 350, § 14A.7-14.1(4) (2003).
30. DEL. CODE ANN. tit. 8, § 160(a)(1) (2001).
31. Former MBCA § 6 (1969).
32. Former MBCA § 45 (2008). *See also* MBCA § 6.40 (1984).
33. Former MBCA § 45 (1980).
34. *In re* Nat'l Tile & Terrazzo Co., 537 F.2d 329 (9th Cir. 1976).
35. *See* Field v. Haupert, 647 P.2d 952 (Or. Ct. App. 1982).
36. Cotten v. Weatherford Bancshares, Inc., 187 S.W.3d 687 (Tex. Ct. App. 2006).
37. Kansas Heart Hosp., LLC v. Idbeis, 184 P.3d 866 (Kan. 2008) (distinguishing between "redemption" and "purchase" but upholding bylaw that compelled "redemption" of stock held by shareholders who had violated ownership requirements).
38. Taylor v. Axton-Fisher Tobacco Co., 173 S.W.2d 377 (Ky. 1943), noted in *Recent Decisions, Corporations—Power of Directors to Rescind or Modify Action Calling Stock for Redemption,* 42 MICH. L. REV. 530 (1943).
39. Starring v. Am. Hair & Felt Co., 191 A. 887 (Del. Ch.), *aff'd mem.,* 2 A.2d 249 (Del. 1937).
40. Ecker v. W. Pac. R.R., 318 U.S. 448 (1943).
41. *See In re* W. Waterway Lumber Co., 367 P.2d 807 (Wash. 1962) (upholding bylaw requiring sale to corporation on leaving the business).
42. Hurley v. Boston R.R. Holding Co., 54 N.E.2d 183 (Mass. 1944).
43. *See* Former MBCA § 66 (1969).
44. *See* Peterson v. New England Furn. & Carpet Co., 299 N.W. 208 (Minn. 1941).
45. Donahue v. Rodd Electrotype Co., 328 N.E.2d 505 (Mass. 1975).
46. Comolli v. Comolli, 246 S.E.2d 278 (Ga. 1978).
47. *Id.* at 280. The court invalidated a corporate purchase of a deceased brother's shares with borrowed funds in order to perpetuate the control of one of the two surviving brothers, who could not afford to buy the entire holding. The shares had never been offered to the other brother.
48. Cheff v. Mathes, 199 A.2d 548 (Del. 1964).

49. *See* Kors v. Carey, 158 A.2d 136 (Del. Ch. 1960) (upholding corporate repurchase of shares from unsuccessful takeover attempt).
50. Martin v. Am. Potash & Chem. Corp., 92 A.2d 295 (Del. 1952).
51. Hendricks v. Mill Eng'g & Supply Co., 413 P.2d 811 (Wash. 1966).
52. *See, e.g.* Zahn v. Transamerica Corp., 162 F.2d 36 (3d Cir. 1947).
53. Pub. L. No. 90-439, 82 Stat. 454 (1968), codified at 15 U.S.C. §§ 78m(d) to (e), 78n(d) to (f).
54. *See* Wellman v. Dickinson, 475 F. Supp. 783 (S.D.N.Y. 1979).
55. 15 U.S.C. §§ 78m(d)(6)(C), 78n(d)(8)(B) (2009).
56. *Id.* § 78n(e).
57. Since subsection 14(d) contains a specific issuer exclusion and 14(e) contains no exclusion, 14(e) logically should extend to all tender offers, even those by an issuer.
58. 15 U.S.C. § 78m(e) (2009).
59. Rule 13e-3, 17 C.F.R. § 240.13e-3.
60. Rule 13e-4, 17 C.F.R. § 240.13e-4.
61. Rule 13e-1, 17 C.F.R. § 240.13e-4.
62. 17 C.F.R. § 240.10b-18.
63. Former MBCA § 33 (1969).
64. *See, e.g.,* NEV. REV. STAT. § 78.283(2) (1994).
65. Former MBCA § 33 (1969).
66. Italo Petrol. Corp. v. Producers' Oil Corp., 174 A. 276 (Del. Ch. 1934) (99% owned subsidiary); Note, *The Voting of Stock Held in Cross Ownership*, 76 HARV. L. REV. 1642 (1963).
67. CAL. CORP. CODE § 510 (West Supp. 2009).
68. Former MBCA §§ 67, 68 (1969). *See also* N.Y. BUS. CORP. LAW § 515(b), (e) (McKinney 2003); 15 PA. CONS. STAT. § 1552 (1995).
69. Former MBCA § 2(h) (1969).
70. *Id.* §§ 67, 68.
71. The former Model Business Corp. Act § 67 (1969) enables corporations to reduce authorized shares on redemption or repurchase through a provision in the articles. It specifies that reacquired shares have the status of authorized but unissued shares, unless an article's provision prohibits reissue.
72. MBCA § 8.33 (2008); Former MBCA § 48 (1980).
73. There continues to be a question as to whether such statutes are exclusive. *See In re* Kettle Fried Chicken of Am., Inc., 513 F.2d 807 (6th Cir. 1975) (court refused to conclude that Delaware General Corporation Statute § 174's proscription of director liability for unlawful distributions with no reference to shareholder liability exempted shareholders from liability).
74. *Cf.* CAL. CODE § 506(a) (West 1990) (shareholder liability to corporation for benefit of creditors) *with* Former MBCA § 48(d) (1969) (contribution to directors).
75. *See, e.g.,* Palmer v. Justice, 322 F. Supp. 892 (N.D. Tex.), *aff'd per curiam*, 451 F.2d 371 (5th Cir. 1971).
76. *See* MBCA § 8.33 (2008); Former MBCA § 48(b) (1969).
77. *See* Former MBCA § 48(b) (1969).
78. For cases stating that recovery may be had for the benefit of subsequent creditors, *see, e.g.,* Coleman v. Tepel, 230 F. 63 (3d Cir. 1916).

CHAPTER 22

CORPORATE COMBINATIONS

PART C. REMEDIES OF DISSENTING SHAREHOLDERS

§ 22.1 CORPORATE COMBINATIONS OVERVIEW

Sales of assets, mergers, and consolidations present three different methods of corporate fusion, each with its own financial and legal considerations. A fourth method of corporate combination is a share exchange, whereby all the outstanding shares of an approving class of stock are acquired by another corporation. A variation of this form is the purchase of shares of another corporation (called the "target" corporation). Such purchases can occur either through open market purchases or by a solicitation of the shareholders to sell, generally referred to as a "tender offer." Unlike the other methods of corporate fusion, the tender offer commits to the individual shareholders of the target corporation the decision whether to part with their shares. In contrast, the combination that is consummated by a sale of corporate assets, a merger, or a consolidation is authorized by complex statutory procedures, and generally requires shareholder approval by a set percentage of the class voting by each class of shares affected by the class.[1]

Any method of corporate combination or other fundamental change can work to the disadvantage of minority shareholders. The most prevalent mechanism to protect those who oppose the acquisition is the statutory appraisal remedy. This procedure allows dissenting shareholders to receive in cash the fair value of their shares, as determined through an independent appraisal.[2] As will be seen, the so-called dissenters' right is cumbersome and does not always protect the minority's interests. Further, the appraisal remedy does not apply to all types of acquisitions.[3] In recent years, there has been a serious conflict as to the availability of a judicial remedy for unfairness when dissenters' rights were available. The trend of recent decisions is to allow for judicial scrutiny of alleged unfair acquisitions in exceptional cases, independent of any statutory remedy.[4]

The federal securities laws have substantial impact on the law relating to corporate combinations. Many methods of corporate combination involve shareholders exchanging their shares either for another class of shares, for shares of another corporation, or for cash. In each case, the antifraud provisions of SEC Rule 10b-5 come into play, as is equally true when the corporation rather than the individual shareholder acquires or issues securities.[5] Whenever the issuance of securities is involved, the registration provisions of the Securities Act of 1933 must be considered.[6] Moreover, the federal proxy rules heighten the disclosure when carrying out acquisitions involving publicly traded corporations subject to section 14(a) of the Securities Exchange Act of 1934. Finally, significant regulatory protection occurs through the 1968 Williams Act amendments to the Securities Exchange Act of 1934 and subsequent state legislation that regulate tender offers and open market purchases of corporate shares.[7]

§ 22.2 COMPARISON OF METHODS OF COMBINATION OR REORGANIZATION

Although the three traditional methods of reorganization—merger, consolidation, and sale-purchase of assets—are distinct, they have a number of similarities. The essential steps to consolidate or merge[8] are as follows:

(1) A consolidation or merger always involves a transfer of the assets and business of one or more corporations to another corporation in exchange for its securities, cash, or other consideration.[9] A merger results in a transfer of the assets to one of the constituent corporations that absorbs the other. With a consolidation, a new consolidated corporation is created into which each constituent corporation transfers its assets and liabilities. In each case, the transfer is made by operation of law—that is, by force of the statute operating on the agreement of the constituents to merge or consolidate.[10]

(2) A merger or consolidation entails the assumption of the debts and liabilities of the absorbed company or companies by operation of law.[11]

(3) A necessary effect of a merger or consolidation is the dissolution of the absorbed company or companies.[12] As will be seen, a sale of

assets does not constitute a dissolution and does not necessarily call for the liquidation or dissolution of the seller.[13]

(4) A merger or consolidation involves a payment to the shareholders of the absorbed corporation in shares, debt, or cash or securities of the new or surviving corporation. Those who pursue their appraisal remedy can receive cash equal to the appraised value of their shares.

The principal differences between an acquisition by sale of assets and statutory merger or consolidation are:[14]

(1) In case of a sale by one corporation to another, the assets of the selling corporation are transferred by written instruments of conveyance, not by operation of law, as occurs in a merger or consolidation.

(2) There are different statutory requirements as to the vote or consent of shareholders. As will be seen, the shareholders of both the successor/surviving corporation and shareholders of the acquired corporation are generally entitled to vote and, if approved, those who dissent to the merger or consolidation are entitled to their appraisal remedy. In contrast, only the shareholders of the corporation selling its assets are entitled to vote on the transaction,[15] because the purchasing corporation acts only through its board of directors.

(3) In a consolidation or merger, the method and basis of exchanging the shares of the constituent corporations for shares, debt, or cash of the successor corporation are set forth in the consolidation or merger agreement. This becomes binding on all parties except dissenting shareholders who elect to invoke their appraisal remedy. Thus, following approval there is a compulsory exchange of new shares for old. In contrast, authority distinct from the stockholders' approval of the sale must be involved to distribute the sales proceeds to the selling corporation's stockholders. Such authority arises after the stockholders have approved the corporation's dissolution. It is also possible, within the limitations of the local state statute, to distribute the sales proceeds through either a dividend or repurchase of shares. That is, neither the dissolution of the selling corporation nor

the mechanism for distributing the sales proceeds to the selling corporation's shareholders is embodied in the state statutes that authorize corporations to sell all or substantially all their assets. Thus, such a distribution pursuant to the plan is a separate transaction following the actual consummation of the sale itself.

(4) Unlike the rules for a merger or consolidation, the general rule for a sale of corporate assets is that the purchasing corporation is not liable for any of the liabilities of the seller.[16] As will be seen, exceptions to this generality abound. A purchaser of corporate assets will be found to have assumed the seller's liabilities in certain circumstances, such as when (a) the purchaser expressly or impliedly has assumed the seller's obligations, (b) the transaction is determined to be a de facto merger, (c) the purchasing corporation is merely a continuation of the selling corporation, or (d) the transaction involved fraud.

(5) A selling corporation is not dissolved by reason of a sale of its entire assets; this requires separate approval by the stockholders and can occur at the same meeting as their approval of the sale of the company's assets. Generally, after such a sale, the corporation is liquidated pursuant to a vote approving its voluntary dissolution. A dissolution, however, is not the inevitable consequence of a sale, and the corporation may continue in the same or some new business or in a state of suspended animation.[17]

The ultimate choice of the form a corporate combination is to take is generally a function of legal considerations, combined with business and financial realities. One point of primary importance in selecting a method of reorganization is to take advantage of those provisions of the federal tax code that make certain kinds of reorganization exchanges tax-free.[18]

PART A. SALE OF ASSETS

§ 22.3 PURPOSES OF SALE OF SUBSTANTIALLY ALL ASSETS

The power to sell all of a corporation's assets can be a preliminary step to formal dissolution. Simply put, the authority to sell all its assets outside the regular course of business can be the means for the orderly cessation of business, whether going out of business was caused by financial distress or otherwise.

A purchase and sale of assets may be used not only as a method of expansion or acquisition of a business by another corporation, but also as a method of voluntary reorganization or recapitalization. In such cases, a new corporation is organized for the purpose of acquiring the assets and business of the old, and these assets are then transferred to the purchaser in exchange for an issue of its securities to be distributed directly or indirectly to the shareholders of the selling corporation.

§ 22.4 STATUTORY AUTHORIZATION OF SALE OF ASSETS

Every jurisdiction now has a statute expressly authorizing a corporation to sell, mortgage, or pledge, and to convey all or substantially all of its property rights with the vote or consent of its board of directors and a specified majority of its shareholders. These statutory provisions have been adopted in order to relax the strict common law rule in many states requiring unanimous consent and thereby to prevent a small minority of shareholders from thwarting the will of the overwhelming majority.[19] These statutory requirements apply even though the corporation is insolvent,[20] which authorization is commercially desirable when the purpose of reorganization is to continue the business in another corporation rather than to liquidate.[21]

Creditors' protection lies in the statutory restrictions on the corporation's distributing the proceeds of the asset sale. Under these statutes, the sale or transfer of all or substantially all of the corporate assets requires authorization by a majority of the board of directors and also the approval of at least a majority of the shareholders entitled to vote. Failure to obtain shareholder approval may subject the seller to liability for conversion.[22] Under most statutes, shareholder authorization can be given only after prior notice of the time, place, and purpose of the meeting at which the vote will be taken and after distribution of a complete and specific statement of the terms and conditions of the proposed sale to be considered. In some jurisdictions, board approval may follow the shareholder action,[23] although generally the plan must first be adopted by the directors.[24] In a few jurisdictions, a meeting is not necessary to obtain the shareholders' consent.[25] Under most statutes, it is not required that there be final shareholder approval of the complete and final contract of sale;[26] shareholders are considered sufficiently protected if they approve the principal terms of the transaction and the nature and amount of the consideration to be received by the corporation upon the sale. Under the earlier version of the Model Business Corporation Act, even the fixing of consideration can be delegated to the board.[27] When the shareholder vote is subject to the federal proxy rules, there are more stringent requirements of specificity.[28]

Ordinarily, class voting on proposals for the sale of assets is not required. It would seem, however, that a class vote is sound policy whenever the purpose of a sale is to carry out a recapitalization such that as a result of the transaction the relative rights, privileges, and preferences in the share contract will be altered. A class vote of the preferred shares would appear unnecessary when the sale is the prelude to a dissolution and liquidation of the company. In such a case, the entitlements and protection for the preferred shares should be those provided through their contract with the corporation—for example a vote on dissolution or a liquidation privilege.[29] If the purpose of the transaction is to dissolve and liquidate, the same rules as to voting should apply as in cases of dissolution. The holders of common stock may well have the right to decide this question and to pay off the preferred shareholders in winding up if they so desire.

Statutes are not specific as to what constitutes "substantially all" of a corporation's assets. The statutory terminology negates the use of a hard and fast rule; one might use an 80 percent rule of thumb borrowed from the tax laws,[30] although courts have gone below this figure. For example, it has been held that stock in another company totaling more than 75 percent of the selling corporation's assets triggered the statutory requirement of shareholder approval prior to its disposition by the corporation.[31] The test has been said to be both quantitative and qualitative, and thus depends on the entirety of circumstances surrounding the sale.

The vast majority of the states condition the requirement of shareholder approval on both the sale being of "all or substantially all the assets" and the sale being "otherwise than in the usual and regular course of business."[32] Delaware is among those states that do not limit the scope of their statutes to sales outside the regular course of business, but in a leading case the Delaware Supreme Court applied such a limitation: "If the sale is of assets quantitatively vital to the operation of the corporation *and* is out of the ordinary and substantially affects the existence and purpose of the corporation, then it is beyond the power of the Board of Directors."[33]

Thus, the inquiry entails a dynamic interaction between a quantitative and qualitative standard. This approach has long been emphasized.[34] The comment to the Revised Model Business Corporation Act explains: The phrase "substantially all" is synonymous with "nearly all" and was added merely to make it clear that the statutory requirements could not be avoided by retention of some minimal or nominal residue of the original assets. A sale of all the corporate assets other than cash or cash equivalents is normally the sale of "all or substantially all" of the corporation's property. A sale of several distinct manufacturing lines, while retaining one or more lines, is normally not a sale of "all or substantially all" *even though the lines being sold are substantial business.* If the lines retained are viewed only as a temporary operation or as a pretext to avoid the "all or substantially all" requirements, however, the statutory requirements of chapter 12 [of the Model Business Corp. Act] must be complied with.[35]

While the Model Business Corporation Act's comment may appear inconsistent with the statute's language, which has eliminated the "all or substantially all" standard and instead refers to a disposition that would leave the corporation without a "significant continuing business activity,"[36] the comment can best be seen as emphasizing the distinction made earlier between decisions that shift the company assets to new areas,[37] which decisions are committed to the discretion of the board of directors, and decisions that are a prelude to a structural change in the nature of investment, such as sales that are a prelude to liquidation, for which shareholder approval is necessary. Nevertheless, the comment and the statute are far from definitive in their content or scope.

Some courts have held that sales of real estate, even if the company's only asset, is not subject to a statute governing sale of assets.[38] The rationale here is that if the sale of real estate is a purpose for which the company was organized, such a sale is "in the ordinary course of business" and thus within the directors' purview.[39] The sale of property that is the core asset of a real estate investment corporation formed to manage the property's rental is not in the ordinary course of business.[40] There are no exceptions in such statutes for financial exigencies:[41] If the sale of assets is within the ordinary course of business, then no shareholder approval is required.[42]

§ 22.5 SALE OF ASSETS FOR SECURITIES

At one time, there was a conflict as to whether in the absence of a statute a corporation could sell substantially all its assets in exchange for shares or other securities of the purchasing company. Today a corporation may exchange all or part of its assets for securities, but some statutes are silent as to what, other than shares of stock, constitutes legitimate consideration.[43] The statutory authority for these transactions is augmented by tax-free treatment where substantially all of the selling corporation's assets are exchanged solely for all or part of another corporation's voting stock.[44]

§ 22.6 THE DE FACTO MERGER DOCTRINE

In a large majority of jurisdictions, with the important exceptions of Delaware and California, dissenting shareholders are given the right to be paid in cash for the appraised value of their shares in the event of a sale or exchange of all or substantially all of a corporation's assets not in the ordinary course of its business. No showing of fraud, unfairness, or prejudice is required.[45] In Delaware, this statutory remedy arises only in connection with statutory mergers and consolidations.[46] In a few states, such as New York and Ohio, as well as the Model Business Corporation Act, the dissenting shareholder is given "a rather full armory of rights which permit appraisal in most cases of fundamental change."[47] Whether or not the scope of appraisal statutes should be so extended is a question of policy depending on the jurisdiction's assessment of how well the appraisal remedy works and whether it does more harm than good.

In a state that does not grant dissenters' rights for sales of assets, there is a serious gap in the shareholder's protection because an effect the same as a merger can be achieved by a sale of assets.[48] For example, assume corporation *A* sells its assets to corporation *B* and, as part of the deal, *B* assumes *A*'s obligations and *A* dissolves. Thereafter, corporation *A* distributes the proceeds of the sale (the *B* securities) to its shareholders under its plan of dissolution. In reviewing these transactions some courts may determine that there has been a de facto merger, in which dissenters' rights under the merger statute are to be honored. Two significant effects of so treating transactions so the procedural rights that accompany mergers apply are: The shareholders of the "purchasing" corporation will be entitled to vote on the transaction, and an appraisal remedy is available to all shareholders entitled to vote.

The Supreme Court of Pennsylvania held a sale of assets transaction to be a de facto merger, so that the plaintiff shareholder was entitled to an appraisal remedy.[49] The court concluded that whenever one corporation combines with another so as to lose its essential nature and alter the fundamental relationships of the shareholders among themselves and their relationships to the corporation, shareholders who do not wish to continue may treat their membership in the original corporation as terminated and may demand payment for the value of their shares. A far greater number of jurisdictions, including Delaware,[50] refuse to embrace the de facto merger doctrine. This refusal is based on the doctrine of "independent statutory significance" or equal dignity. This doctrine holds that each authorizing provision of the state's corporation statute is entitled to its own independent significance such that the substantive effects and procedural requirements of one provision are not to be harmonized with another provision under which the same objective could have also been accomplished but pursuant to different procedural requirements. Thus, under the doctrine of independent statutory significance, if the formal requirements of the sale-of-assets statute are complied with, the transaction will be considered a sale rather than a merger, at least where the contract of sale does not call for dissolution and the selling corporation remains in existence long enough to receive the proceeds of the sale and distribute them to its shareholders.

The de facto merger doctrine is not limited to suits attempting to assert dissenters' rights. It may arise where creditors object to the failure of one corporation to assume liabilities along with the purchase of assets of another. This has been fertile ground for litigation with regard to attempts to avoid products liability damage awards. The cases for successor liability have not been limited to product liability claims.[51] Further, the de facto merger doctrine is not limited to sales of assets: It may arise from other forms of corporate combination, such as a lease of all the productive assets or acquisition of a corporation's control block of stock[52] without merging or liquidating a subsidiary.

§ 22.7 SUCCESSOR CORPORATION LIABILITY

As was seen earlier, a distinguishing feature of a business combination carried out as a merger or consolidation is that by operation of law the surviving corporation is subject to all the liabilities of the acquired companies. In contrast, when the combination is structured as an asset or stock purchase-sale, absent special circumstances, the acquiring company is subject only to those liabilities it has agreed to assume. Traditionally, there were just four circumstances in which the selling corporation's creditors could successfully proceed against a purchaser who had not so assumed the debt owed to that creditor:

> [T]here are four well-recognized exemptions under which the purchasing corporation becomes liable for the debts and liabilities of the selling corporation. (1) Where the purchaser expressly or impliedly agrees to assume such debts; (2) where the transaction amounts to a consolidation or merger of the corporations; (3) where the purchasing corporation is merely a continuation of the selling corporation; and (4) where the transaction is entered into fraudulently in order to escape liability for such debts.[53]

This traditional approach continues to be the great weight of authority, despite the important inroads, discussed below, that modern tort law trends have made on the subject.[54] The most significant testing of the rigidity of these four exceptions has occurred, not surprisingly, in the context of product liability claims brought against corporations that acquired the assets of a company that during its previous life had produced a defective product, which defect did not cause a plaintiff-creditor's injury until after the acquisition.

Successor liability may also be imposed in the case of an acquisition of a target company's stock. Courts have indicated that successor liability will attach under the de facto merger doctrine when subsequent to the stock acquisition, the target company ceases to have an independent identity and the target's business can only be carried on through the acquiring corporation.[55]

Various federal statutes pose unique obligations for successor corporations. Significant successor liability arises under the "Superfund Law," Comprehensive Environmental Response, Compensation, and Liability Act (CERCLA),[56] which provides that owners as well as operators of property are liable for all costs in cleaning up a site, even though the generator of the waste was a prior owner.[57] Thus, by simply becoming an owner of property on which others have disposed of waste, the new owner can become a "responsible party" under CERCLA.[58] And continuity of the workforce is an important factor under the labor laws, at least with respect to the successor corporation's obligation to bargain with the union that represented the acquired company's employees.[59]

PART B. MERGER AND CONSOLIDATION

§ 22.8 MERGER AND CONSOLIDATION DISTINGUISHED

A consolidation is the uniting or amalgamation of two or more existing corporations to form a new corporation.[60] The firm resulting from the union is called the "consolidated" corporation. A merger is a union effected by the absorbing of one or more existing corporations by another, which survives and continues the combined business.[61] The disappearing corporation is generally referred to as the "merged" corporation, with the other being the "surviving" corporation. The parties to a combination either by consolidation or merger are called the "constituent" corporations. The chief difference between mergers and consolidations is one of form; the procedure, legal effect, and end product are the same.[62]

§ 22.9 ATTRIBUTES AND ADVANTAGES OF MERGER AND CONSOLIDATION

Merger and consolidation are very complex proceedings involving several different transactions affecting many parties, all of which may be accomplished simultaneously by statute. Legislative authority is essential to authorize a true merger or consolidation.[63] These transactions are fundamental changes of the charter contract and the share contracts and also in the rights of creditors. Each constituent corporation must be authorized under the law of its domicile to enter into a union by merger or consolidation.[64] Each constituent corporation must comply with the procedure set forth by the statute of its state of incorporation.[65] A merger may be preferable to a consolidation in combining corporations because one of the corporations may have nonassignable leases, franchises, or employment contracts that by their terms cannot pass to another entity. Another reason may be that one of the constituent corporations may have qualified to do business as a foreign corporation in a large number of other states and it would be burdensome to qualify a new corporation.[66]

As we have seen, selling the entire assets and issuing shares in payment by the purchaser, followed by dissolution and winding up, is often preferable to either merger or consolidation. A sale of assets is particularly helpful when the acquiring corporation is not interested in all of the business of the corporation to be acquired or where it wishes to make a selective assumption of liabilities—subject, of course, to the equitable rights of creditors. Merger or consolidation can be used to acquire some part of the business when preceded or followed by a sale of assets to a third party. Another alternative is to place the unwanted assets in a subsidiary corporation and spin off the shares to the stockholders in the form of a dividend.

The great advantage of a statutory merger or consolidation over combination by sale of assets is that it furnishes a shortcut to accomplishing various transactions and may avoid difficulty, delay, and expense such as that attendant on a dissolution, winding up, and the distribution of securities to its shareholders by the selling corporation. By statute, all of the rights and liabilities of the transferor are assimilated into the transferee corporation.

Merger and consolidation are, in essence, the transfer of the property and business of one corporation to another in exchange for securities or cash issued by the purchaser to shareholders of the seller. Merger and consolidation involve the automatic (that is, by operation of law) assumption of all the debts and liabilities of the transferring corporations and a compulsory novation on the part of the creditors. As we have seen, in a combination by sale of assets there may not be a compulsory exchange or distribution of new shares for old or a compulsory substitution of a new debtor as to the debts and liabilities of the seller. In a sale of assets, sufficient funds must be reserved or adequate provision made to take care of the debts and liabilities of the seller; otherwise the transfer would be a fraudulent conveyance, which could be attacked by the creditors. Merger and consolidation are also highly advantageous forms of reorganization, because they bring the transaction of an exchange of property for shares within the class of tax-free reorganizations under the federal tax laws.

§ 22.10 STATUTORY AUTHORITY FOR MERGER AND CONSOLIDATION

Mergers and consolidations can be effected only under statutory authority.[67] The power of corporations to merge without unanimous shareholder approval does not exist without statutory authorization, so liability can arise for consequential damages from mergers consummated without complying with the applicable statutory requirements.[68] All jurisdictions have liberal provisions for merger, consolidation, sales of assets, and charter amendments, which on enactment were made applicable to existing corporations as well as to those to be formed. In some jurisdictions, constitutional doubts were raised as to the scope of the reserved power to authorize fundamental changes by majority shareholders in preexisting corporations. Although the contrary has long been taken for granted by others, there still may be problems regarding the ability of legislatures to affect the internal rules of existing corporations. The extent to which the authorization of such fundamental changes is dependent on provisions enabling objecting shareholders to demand payment of the fair value of their shares has also been questioned.[69]

§ 22.11 PROCEDURES TO MERGE OR CONSOLIDATE

[1] Procedures Generally

The procedure to accomplish a merger is practically the same as that necessary to effect a consolidation. In general, the essential steps in each involve: (1) the negotiation and approval of an agreement of merger or consolidation by the boards of directors of the constituent companies and the drafting of a formal agreement to combine in accordance with the applicable statute;[70] (2) the submission of the agreement, either in full or in substance, to the shareholders for their approval by the specified majority vote after lawful notice of a shareholders' meeting; and (3) the execution of the formal agreement by the proper corporate officers, with the formal certificates of due authorization, and the filing of the agreement so duly certified with the secretary of state or other designated official.

Once a merger agreement is in place, it will create contractual obligations between the parties to the agreement. Merger agreements typically contain a "material adverse change" or "material adverse effect" provision allowing the contract to be voided when material changes or effects are discovered after the merger agreement is made.[71] The court decisions reveal that a generalized material adverse change provision will not always provide meaningful protection with respect to changed conditions. If the parties foresee specific contingencies, they would be well advised to enumerate them in the merger agreement as examples of what constitutes a material adverse change.[72]

[2] Voting Requirements

Most states now provide for majority approval by the shares entitled to vote,[73] although some adhere to the older practice of a two-thirds requirement.[74] Recent amendments to the Model Act if adopted by state legislatures would dilute the shareholders' power in reducing the required vote from a majority of those entitled to vote, to a plurality of those actually voting.[75]

In view of the fact that the interests of different classes of shares, particularly preferred and common, frequently conflict in a merger or a consolidation (they do as in the case of amendments to the articles of incorporation), a class vote is frequently accorded to each class of stock affected in a proscribed manner by the merger or consolidation. Jurisdictions following the scheme of the Revised Model Business Corporation Act define how the stock is "affected" broadly to include not only by any changes in the existing rights, privileges, and preferences of an outstanding class of stock but also by any dilution in their economic or voting rights through the issuance of additional shares of that class or of a class that will compete for assets with an outstanding class.[76] In contrast, a class vote is not provided in many states, such as Delaware, so that they grant inadequate protection to the holders of preferred shares.[77]

The modern trend among corporate statutes is to include a "small acquisition" exception to the right of shareholders to vote on mergers or consolidations. This exception removes mergers and consolidations from the necessity of any vote of the stockholders of the *surviving* corporation, provided the articles of incorporation are not amended to change their rights, privileges, or preferences, the number of shares each owns is not affected by the merger or consolidation, and the number of voting shares outstanding after the combination is not increased by more than 20 percent from the number of outstanding voting shares before the acquisition.[78] This exemption reflects the drafters' wisdom that some acquisitions are of such small impact to the corporation in terms of their dilutive effects that they should fall exclusively within the discretion of the board of directors to carry out. In a sense, in terms of the shareholders' involvement the transaction is treated no differently than if the board of directors had first sold common shares (not to exceed 20 percent of those already outstanding) for cash and used the cash to acquire another corporation.

[3] The Agreement of Merger or Consolidation

The foundation of a merger or consolidation is an agreement negotiated and approved by the directors of each constituent corporation and approved by the requisite number of the outstanding shares. This agreement yields the "plan of merger" that is approved by the shareholders. In the case of consolidation, the agreement to consolidate or the articles of consolidation contemplates the articles of incorporation of the newly formed corporation. It should set forth matters required by statute to be stated in articles of incorporation. In the case of a merger, the agreement should state any matters as to which the articles of incorporation of the surviving corporation are to be amended. However, in a merger, separate procedures are required to carry out that amendment. In each case, the agreement should set forth the terms and conditions of the union and the mode of carrying it into effect, as well as the basis of converting the shares of the constituent corporations into shares of the consolidated or surviving corporation. Under the Delaware statute, once the directors and officers approve the agreement, it is to be executed and filed publicly.[79] The Model Business Corporation Act requires the filing of "articles of merger or share exchange" with the secretary of state, which must include the articles of incorporation or any amendments thereto.[80] This document sets forth specific information regarding the shareholders' approval of the combination. The merger becomes effective on the effective date specified in the filed articles of merger or exchange.[81] In some states, the plan of merger itself is filed.[82] In some states a "certificate of merger" is filed with the proper state and/or county officials.[83]

[4] Distributions to Shareholders

Statutes commonly provide that the plan of merger submitted to the shareholders for approval must set forth the manner and basis for converting shares of each constituent corporation into shares of the surviving corporation's shares, the shares of a third corporation, or cash or other property.[84]

§ 22.12 "SHORT-FORM" MERGERS

Most states now provide for a simplified procedure in mergers of certain subsidiaries into the parent corporation or vice versa, or into another subsidiary.[85] Since the procedure is less complex than the normal statutory merger, such transactions are referred to as "short-form" mergers. Under these short-form merger statutes, no vote is required by the shareholders of either the surviving parent or the absorbed subsidiary, and the approval of the board of directors of the subsidiary is not required.[86] However, if the parent corporation is merged into the subsidiary, a vote of the parent shareholders will be required.[87] A significant result of the short-form procedure is the denial of dissenters' rights to the shareholders of the surviving parent, although such rights are given to the shareholders of the merged subsidiary.[88] Though the subsidiary's shareholders do not have an opportunity to dissent in a short-form merger, their avenue for appraisal is to give notice of their intent to seek appraisal after receiving notice of the parent's board's approval of the acquisition. In Delaware, California, and those states that have adopted the Model Business Corporation Act, the short-form merger is available for subsidiaries where 90 percent of the outstanding shares of each class are owned by the parent.[89] Some states impose a greater ownership requirement, although most have now adopted the 90 percent rule.[90]

The short-form merger statute avoids the hollow ritual of a 90-percent-plus owner convening a meeting to approve its decision to acquire the subsidiary; although the minority shareholders are disenfranchised, they still have their right to exit through the appraisal remedy.[91] The subsidiary's minority shareholders need not be given an opportunity to receive any interest in the surviving corporation.[92] Instead, they may be forced to accept cash payment as determined by the buy-out terms of a merger plan or, if they dissent, as determined by the statutory appraisal process.

§ 22.13 TRIANGULAR MERGERS AND SHARE EXCHANGES

[1] Triangular and Reverse Triangular Mergers

An ingenious variation that may also take advantage of the federal tax laws is the three-party or triangular merger. There are three principal reasons for utilizing the triangular merger: (1) to avoid the automatic assumption of liabilities,[93] which can be particularly desirable when acquiring a high-risk enterprise; (2) to avoid a vote by the acquiring parent corporation's shareholders and their attendant appraisal rights; and (3) to continue the existence of the acquired corporation as a subsidiary of the parent acquiring corporation.[94] The triangular merger also avoids several disadvantages of a purchase of assets[95] and a straight stock acquisition of another company.[96]

In the straight triangular merger, the acquiring corporation forms a subsidiary[97] for the purpose of merging with the target. A merger then occurs between the subsidiary and the target. Although standard merger law generally requires a vote of each merging corporation's shareholders, this is not a problem in the triangular merger because the subsidiary's shares are held exclusively by its parent (Acquiring Corporation), whose board of directors votes those shares. When Target merges into Subsidiary, Target's shareholders receive the stock of Acquiring Corporation. This can be accomplished by having capitalized Subsidiary with the parent's stock in exchange for the Subsidiary's shares. Alternatively, the stock can be issued directly by Acquiring Corporation to Target's shareholders. One possible pitfall is that the transactions must be structured to avoid the claim that the parent's shares have been issued for invalid consideration. Statutes in most states now authorize the use of shares of another corporation as consideration for mergers. Since the parent is not a party to the merger no parent shareholder vote is required, assuming that there had already been authorized in the charter sufficient shares to be issued pursuant to the merger plan, because directors have the power to issue previously authorized shares. As a bona fide parent-subsidiary structure, the subsidiary, not the parent, assumes the liabilities of the merged target company.

After the transaction described in the preceding paragraph, Acquiring Corporation owns 100 percent of Subsidiary, and Subsidiary has all the assets and liabilities of Target. If the parent corporation does not wish to continue Subsidiary's existence, it can use the short-form merger provision to merge Subsidiary into itself. In so structuring the transaction, the parent corporation's shareholders never have an opportunity to vote on its acquisition of Target. Thus the triangular merger is a straightforward mechanism to avoid the acquiring corporation's shareholders having a direct vote, and, for that matter, an appraisal remedy, in an acquisition of another company.

A variation on the above procedure is the reverse triangular merger. In the reverse transaction, Subsidiary is merged with Target, so Target survives and becomes a subsidiary of the original parent. The advantage to the reverse method is that it allows the acquired company to continue to exist, unlike in a traditional two-party merger or consolidation. The continued existence of the target avoids the necessity of negotiating new labor contracts and making formal transfers of the target's property. Additionally, the target's continued existence may be required by the terms of outstanding bonds or other types of agreements it has with creditors. The triangular and reverse triangular methods of combination are not limited to mergers; they can also be used for a purchase-of-assets acquisition.

[2] Statutory Share Exchange

It sometimes is desirable to structure an acquisition so that the acquired company continues as a separate, albeit wholly owned, subsidiary of the acquiring company or a holding company, rather than ceasing to exist. Ideally suited for this objective is the "share exchange," a procedure now authorized in numerous states that have patterned their own enactments after the Revised Model Business Corporation Act.[98] Following board of director and shareholder approval by each corporation, the shares of the acquired corporation are exchanged for cash or stock of the acquiring corporation or a third corporation. The agreement between the corporations can provide that only designated classes of stock of the acquired company will be exchanged, so that following a share exchange some classes of the acquired corporation are unaffected. In any case, following the share exchange, all the shares of one or more classes of stock are acquired by the acquiring corporation, and the existence of the acquired corporation continues.

§ 22.14 RIGHTS OF CREDITORS OF CONSTITUENT COMPANIES

Absent contractual provisions to the contrary, the creditors of a corporation cannot prevent its consolidation or merger with another corporation even if the new debtor corporation is not as satisfactory to them as the old.[99] Accordingly, it is not uncommon to find express restrictions, such as consent requirements, in credit agreements as well as in debt indentures and preferred-share contracts.[100] In general, the only recourse of the creditors of the constituent corporations is to sue the united corporation directly or to pursue the assets of the constituents into the hands of the new corporation under a theory of fraudulent conveyance.[101]

§ 22.15 Leveraged Buyouts as Fraudulent Conveyances

Fraudulent conveyance provisions trace their roots to the sixteenth century. Their proscriptions remain nearly as simple today as they were then, whether they appear in the state's version of the Uniform Fraudulent Conveyance Act,[102] the Uniform Fraudulent Transfer Act,[103] or the Bankruptcy Act's own version of this avoidance provision.[104] It is in their simplicity that these provisions raise highly troubling questions in the complex leveraged buyout (LBO) transaction.

Leveraged buyouts can take many forms. A most common form involves creating a thinly capitalized corporation to purchase the corporation that is to be acquired. The funds for the purchase are borrowed by the newly formed corporation, usually through bridge loans from a syndicate of financial institutions. The loan's proceeds are used to purchase the shares of the acquired corporation. Upon the merger of the acquired corporation and the newly formed corporation, the acquired corporation's assets can be used to satisfy the loan. Thereafter, the two corporations are combined, permanent financing is arranged, and the earnings and assets of the acquired corporation are used to meet these financial obligations. It is when all the various steps are collapsed together that the issue of the acquisition constituting a fraudulent conveyance arises.[105] In considering a collapse of the various steps of the LBO, courts frequently emphasize the interdependence of the various steps.[106]

§ 22.16 Accounting for Corporate Combinations

For the longest time, there were two alternative methods of accounting for corporate mergers and other forms of combination: the purchase method and the "pooling-of-interest" approach. As discussed more fully below, the purchase method requires a revaluation of the acquired company's assets based on the purchase price in connection with the merger. In contrast, the pooling method simply consolidated the existing balance sheets of the constituent companies.

In 1999, the Federal Accounting Standards Board voted unanimously to abandon the use of the pooling method of accounting for corporate mergers.[107] FASB chairman Jenkins explained that "the purchase method of accounting gives investors a better idea of the initial cost of a transaction and the investment's performance over time than does the pooling-of-interest method."[108] There then ensued many months of intense lobbying to deflect the FASB from its position or to prevent an absolute bar to this popular method for accounting for company acquisitions. All such efforts were to no avail, as the FASB ultimately adopted FASB Statement 141, which bars the pooling method of accounting for acquisitions completed after June 30, 2001.[109]

Statement of Financial Accounting Standard No. 141 was revised in 2007, tightening several aspects, most notably emphasizing the central role of identifying the "identifiable assets" acquired in a business combination, embracing methods for their fair valuation, and imposing a requirement to "re-measure" any assets given as consideration by the acquirer in the business combination including any contingent consideration as of the acquisition date. While the acquirer may—under the 2007 revision—adjust the amounts recorded by using new information acquired up to one year after the acquisition date, this adjustment is limited to reflect new information only to the extent it bears on facts and circumstances that existed as of the acquisition date. Thus, post-acquisition events cannot be the basis to adjust figures. The most controversial portion of the 2007 revision of SFAS No. 141 is its requirement, contrary to the treatment in the preparation of the company's tax return, that acquisition-related costs (e.g., advisory, accounting, valuation, legal) shall be accounted for as expenses in the period in which the costs are incurred and the related services are received. There is an exception to this expensing requirement for costs incurred in connection with the issuance of securities.

Commencing with fiscal years that begin after December 15, 2001, FASB Statement No. 142 requires that goodwill and other tangible assets that appear on the balance sheet must be evaluated annually pursuant to see if their carrying value is impaired. The impairment assessment for goodwill is a two-step process. First, the fair value of the reporting unit for which the goodwill is associated must be determined. This figure is compared to the carrying amount (including goodwill) for that reporting unit on the parent's books. If the overall value of the reporting unit equals or exceeds the carrying amount, there is no impairment. However, if the carrying amount exceeds the fair value so determined, the second step must be taken. This requires that the "implied fair value" of the goodwill must be ascertained and compared with its carrying amount. The implied fair value of goodwill is determined by allocating the aggregate fair value of the reporting unit among its assets with the residual of any unallocated amount being attributed to its goodwill. The amount, if any, that the implied fair value of goodwill that is so determined is less than its carrying amount is the amount of impairment that must then be expenses on the company's financial statements.

In broad overview, under the "purchase method" the acquired companies' assets are listed at their fair market value as determined by the consideration paid by the acquiring company. Because the purchase price will reflect the going-concern value rather than the liquidation or replacement value of the assets, under the purchase method it is necessary to list goodwill as an asset of the surviving corporation. Overvaluation of goodwill can give rise to fraud claims against directors.[110] Under generally accepted accounting practices (GAAP), goodwill must be amortized so that it is charged to earnings on a periodic basis.[111] Under the pooling-of-interests method of accounting, the assets of the constituent companies are pooled and are listed at their pre-combination book values; the constituents' retained earnings are similarly combined.

PART C. REMEDIES OF DISSENTING SHAREHOLDERS

§ 22.17 ALTERNATIVE REMEDIES OF DISSENTING SHAREHOLDERS

Shareholders in constituent corporations are put to a statutory election in merger and consolidation proceedings, and sometimes asset sales and recapitalizations, to take the securities specified in the agreement or withdraw from the enterprise and obtain payment in money for the appraised value of their shares by following the strict statutory appraisal procedure.[112] Dissenters cannot simply retain the old securities and assert any rights under them; if they fail to demand appraisal they are bound by the lawful action of the majority, just as if they had consented to the action taken.[113] In recent years, however, the exclusivity of statutory dissenters' rights has been subject to some isolated erosion, but generally the appraisal remedy displaces other state law remedies, discussed next, except in the case of fraud or illegality.[114] Denial or loss of statutory dissenters' rights is considered to be an injury to the shareholders' property (i.e., their stock) for statute of limitations purposes.[115]

[1] Injunction

Prior to the consummation of a merger, consolidation, or sale of assets, a dissenting shareholder may sue to enjoin its completion either on the ground of lack of authority or compliance with a statute or on the ground of fraud or abuse of power.[116] Similarly, an injunction will lie to prevent violations of the securities laws' disclosure provisions.[117] Dissenting shareholders may lose their right to equitable relief by injunction by laches—that is, by failing to bring suit with the utmost promptitude before the rights of third persons have intervened.[118] Another limitation on injunctive relief is the maxim that equity is not available if an adequate remedy at law exists.[119]

[2] Rescission

Suits are sometimes brought for rescission of a completed merger or consolidation or sale of assets. Theoretically, such a transaction may be voidable on the ground that it is unauthorized or procured by fraud or abuse of power. But, as a practical matter, the only relief granted in such suits is an award of pecuniary compensation or a cash settlement to redress the injury to the dissenting shareholder for loss of his investment. This is on the ground that the task of readjusting the rights and interests of the constituent corporations, the creditors, and perhaps the thousands of shareholders and investors concerned is so insurmountable as to make any attempt to do so, upon a rescission, utterly fantastic.[120] A suit for rescission, therefore, is usually in practical effect treated as simply a suit for the value of the shareholder's interest as fixed by a judicial, non-statutory appraisal.[121]

[3] Individual Shareholder Action for Damages

Where, in voting to dissolve, merge, consolidate, or sell substantially all corporate assets, the majority have exceeded their lawful powers, have failed to comply with statutory conditions, or have been guilty of abuse of powers, objecting shareholders frequently were allowed to sue and recover for the value of their holdings on the theory that their equitable interest in the corporation had been misappropriated, "converted" or destroyed by the wrongful or inequitable action of the corporation.[122] Because the purchase, merger, or transfer under such circumstances is illegal or wrongful, the purchaser or successor may be held personally accountable to the dissenting shareholder for the value of the shares or of his proportional interest either on the ground of participation therein or on the ground that the successor is subject to the liabilities of the predecessor.[123]

[4] Direct Actions under the Securities Laws

Under SEC Rule 10b-5 defrauded purchasers or sellers may sue for damages resulting from misrepresentation or nondisclosure that resulted in their being deceived.[124] Similarly, a business combination consummated through a misleading proxy statement gives rise to individual recoveries under Rule 14a-9 of the Exchange Act, and various express liabilities exist for the purchaser of new securities that may be issued pursuant to the place of merger, consolidation, or sale of assets.[125]

[5] Statutory Dissenters' Rights

The foregoing remedies for dissenting shareholders are available through the courts on appropriate facts. These remedies are supplemented and in many cases replaced by the statutory appraisal remedy. As discussed in the sections that follow, statutory appraisal rights have been adopted in every state although they vary in scope, application, and the extent to which they are the exclusive remedy available to dissenting shareholders.

§ 22.18 THE STATUTORY APPRAISAL REMEDY

Every state has adopted "appraisal" statutes, which give dissenting shareholders a right to demand payment of the fair value of their shares. The statutes vary broadly in their coverage. The right is given in case of certain fundamental changes, such as merger or consolidation, and often in case of sale of the entire assets, and sometimes in case of amendments that change the rights of a certain class of outstanding shares and some other changes.[126] There is a widely adopted but debatable exception for a corporation whose shares are publicly traded.[127]

The states vary as to which shareholders can assert the appraisal remedy. Some require that the shareholder actually voted against the combination or, in some states, have at least abstained.[128] Accordingly, in some states a shareholder not attending the meeting in person or by proxy cannot receive an appraisal regardless of how difficult or useless it may have been for him to comply with this voting requirement. Other states simply require that the dissenting shareholder not have voted in favor of the merger.

Statutes differ as to the status of dissenting shareholders after demand for payment. Under other statutes, the rights cease only after payment of the appraised price.[129] Under the Revised Model Business Corporation Act, a shareholder who has perfected his rights to appraisal loses all rights as a shareholder, unless he withdraws from the appraisal process.[130] The shareholder is thereafter entitled to be paid the amount the corporation believes is the fair value of his shares.[131] And the shareholder can continue to press his claim in a formal appraisal proceeding for any additional amounts above paid by the corporation that the shareholder argues is necessary to raise the total payment to the shares' fair value.[132] Both the shareholder and the corporation have obligations with respect to initiating formal appraisal proceedings under the Revised Model Business Corporation Act. The shareholder must, among other requirements, demand payment of his estimate of the shares' fair value within 30 days,[133] and the corporation must within 60 days of that demand initiate the proceeding or be obligated to pay the shareholder the full amount sought.[134]

In an appraisal proceeding, evidence of value must be taken and a record must be kept.[135] An appraiser's report must usually be filed with the clerk of court, and the parties may take exception to the report.[136] After a hearing as to the exceptions, argument on the report, and the consideration of evidence, the court will confirm, modify, or reject the report.[137]

The expenses of an appraisal proceeding are a factor of serious importance, as they involve appraisers' fees, attorneys' fees, and fees for expert accountants and witnesses before the appraisers. This may be an undue burden on the dissenter, but it may also allow a shareholder acting in bad faith to cause the corporations to spend substantial sums.[138] Only a few statutes make adequate provision for attorneys' fees and other expenses of the petitioner.[139]

§ 22.19 SCOPE OF STATUTORY APPRAISAL RIGHTS

In some states, including Delaware, appraisal rights do not attach to sales of assets or charter amendments; thus this remedy is limited to mergers or consolidations.[140] In most states a corporation's sale of all or substantially all of its assets "not made in the usual and regular course of its business" triggers statutory dissenters' rights.[141] However, even with a sale of assets, dissenters' rights possibly can be avoided if some substantial asset—for example, a tract of real property—is left in the selling corporation.[142] Most statutes do not give dissenters' rights to shareholders of the purchaser of assets, and, subject to the infrequently applied de facto merger doctrine,[143] a transaction can thus be structured to avoid the statutory remedy.[144]

Appraisal rights extend to charter amendments under both the Model Business Corporation Act and the Model Business Corporation Act.[145] There are no states in which dissolution per se triggers dissenters' rights, although in some states a sale of all or substantially all assets in a dissolution proceeding will invoke the statutory right.[146] Under the current Model Business Corporation Act, appraisal rights also apply to a planned exchange of shares to which the corporation is a party if the shareholder is entitled to vote on the exchange.[147]

The Model Business Corporation Act[148] and some states now deny appraisal rights to holders of shares registered on a national securities exchange. In Delaware, for example, where appraisal rights attach only to merger and consolidation, the statute now excludes transactions where shares of any class or series are either listed on a national exchange or held by more than 2,000 stockholders.[149]

§ 22.20 VALUATION OF SHARES IN APPRAISAL PROCEEDINGS

The most difficult task in obtaining relief under appraisal statutes is establishing the fair value of the dissenting shares. The statutes use a variety of terms to describe what the dissenting share is worth. These include "value," "fair value," "fair cash value," or "fair market value." These different expressions in effect mean the same thing. The use of the word "fair" indicates that market quotations for a particular day or even the average over a period of time is not conclusive as to the valuation of the shares.[150] Legislatures and the courts have not been able to establish any definite measure or standard of value. The current Model Business Corporation Act simply provides that fair value should be determined "using customary and current valuation concepts and techniques generally employed for similar businesses in the context of the transaction requiring appraisal."[151] Although varying terms are used, the vague general standard leaves it up to the appraisers to fix a fair price as between the parties. The appraiser is expected to consider all the elements and factors, both positive and negative, that would be considered by practical and experienced business people in estimating the value of the shares as an investment. The process must take into account not only the liquidating value of the corporation's net assets but also the future prospects and earning power of the corporation as a continuing enterprise.[152] The appraisal, whether by an appraiser or the court, must be reasonable and fair.[153]

More important than the adjectives used to express the value that dissenters are to receive are the assumptions regarding the context in which such value is to be realized. One can assume the value of the firm based on its piecemeal liquidation, assuming that the firm is to go out of business and that there will be no purchaser of its assets as an operating economic unit. This assumption, in most cases, will produce the most conservative valuation of the firm, because it does not permit consideration of the synergies the assets produce through their interaction as a going concern. This assumption is frequently referred to as the net asset value of the firm. If one values the corporation, assuming it is a going concern, three different scenarios are possible: (1) the firm is auctioned off to the highest bidder; (2) the sale is at arm's length but without encouraging competing bids; or (3) the role of a third-party buyer is not considered[154] and the business is valued in light of its present income and risks. By far the most liberal valuation occurs under the assumption there is an auction; the more conservative ignores the impact of a third-party buyer on the intrinsic value of the firm.[155] By making the amount obtained through an arm's-length acquisition presumptive of fair value unless the dissenter proves otherwise by clear and convincing evidence, the American Law Institute discreetly reinforces the presumption of propriety that normally accompanies director actions not involving self-dealing. On the other hand, this presumption does not arise in self-dealing acquisitions, so these types of transactions can be put to something akin to a market test by measuring fair value in an auction setting.[156]

In determining the adequacy of particular appraisal prices, many courts, being influenced by the reasoning of earlier Delaware decisions, have used a weighted average of four values: (1) asset value, (2) market value, (3) earnings value, and (4) dividend value, with the relative weight to be decided according to all of the surrounding circumstances.[157] Where there is no ascertainable market value, the courts generally look to the other three factors.[158] The four-factor analysis is generally known as the "Delaware block" method, which is a misnomer today, because the Delaware Supreme Court has now discarded its strict adherence to a weighted-average approach and has instituted a method of valuation based on all relevant factors.[159] In other words, Delaware will now accept as evidence "proof of value by any techniques or methods which are generally considered acceptable in the financial community and otherwise admissible in court."[160]

The determination of value is a factual one[161] and is thus done on a case-by-case basis. Certain principles, however, have been said to govern every valuation: (1) net asset value should not be heavily weighted, unless valuation is being made for liquidation, because the value of corporate assets bears little relation to the value of the stock;[162] (2) extraordinary gains, such as gains from a sale of fixed assets or "gains" achieved by changes in inventory accounting should not be considered, because these gains will not be repeated in the future, and therefore they are not indicative of future earnings potential;[163] (3) market value can be ignored or discounted[164] when shares are so thinly traded as to question the reliability of their market value.[165] In valuing shares of a closely held corporation, reference to comparable public corporations is sometimes appropriate when the comparative group has similar earnings and other financial relationships.[166]

With its decision in *Weinberger v. UOP, Inc.*,[167] Delaware broke free of the rigid adherence to the formulas of the Delaware block method[168] by holding that all relevant factors should be considered when appraising shares.[169] The underlying assumption in an appraisal valuation is that the dissenting shareholders would be willing to maintain their investment position had the merger not occurred. Consequently, the corporation must be valued as an operating entity.[170] This invites the use of modern financial valuation models used in business and finance to be used in appraisal proceedings. For example, a fairly widely used financial technique for valuing businesses is the "discounted cash flow technique," which was sometimes emasculated within the "earnings value" component of the Delaware block method. The discounted-cash technique, a variation on the method's application, is now well accepted in Delaware.[171]

The overall objective of the appraisal process is to determine the dissenter's proportionate value *of the firm*,[172] which is not the same as stating the value of her shares in the firm. In determining the value of the shares, the latter emphasis would consider such intangibles as whether the shares represent majority or minority interests in the firm. If minority shares, they are not nearly as valuable as majority shares because they lack the power to direct the company's operations. This is the so-called minority discount that some courts subtract from the dissenter's shares in determining their value. Some courts have employed a minority discount in valuing shares.[173] However, the great majority of the more recent decisions have emphasized that the appraisal statutes call for a value of the shareholder's proportionate interest in the firm, not simply their shares, so that it is inappropriate to deduct a minority discount.[174] The 1999 amendments to the Model Business Corporation Act follows the majority trend by taking the position that fair value is to be determined on a proportionate basis without considering a minority discount.[175]

A number of courts have disapproved the application of a marketability discount, which adjusts for a lack of liquidity when there is a limited supply of buyers for the stock.[176] A marketability discount reflects the reality that shares that are not marketable likely carry a lower value to their holder and any prospective purchaser.[177] Again, the 1999 amendments to the Model Act provide that in determining "fair value" the appraisal proceeding should not take into consideration a marketability discount.[178]

Under many state statutes, the dissenting shareholder is not to be allowed a value enhanced by the prospective benefits of the merger, consolidation, or sale in which he refuses to participate.[179] Courts more recently have permitted post-transaction benefits to be included in determining the fair value of dissenter's shares.[180]

§ 22.21 EXCLUSIVITY OF STATUTORY APPRAISAL RIGHTS

In some states, the appraisal statutes are silent as to what effect the statutory right of appraisal has on the availability of other remedies.[181] In a few states, the statute expressly provides that appraisal is the exclusive remedy,[182] but this flat restriction is usually tempered by either other statutory language or judicial interpretation.[183]

In 1983, the Delaware Supreme Court indicated that in the absence of fraud or illegality, the appraisal remedy will be exclusive.[184] Failing to provide details related to the exercise of the appraisal remedy, such as when and where to submit the dissenter's shares, as required by the statute, is enforceable outside the appraisal procedure, although the relief is likely constrained to the harm proximately caused by any delay, etc. in pursuing appraisal.[185] Material nondisclosures in connection with the transaction will preclude the exclusivity of the statutory appraisal remedy.[186] The Delaware Supreme Court has not elaborated on what types of unlawful conduct other than fraud will avoid the exclusivity of the statutory appraisal remedy.

The appraisal remedy does not foreclose complaints that the merger never secured the necessary approvals,[187] other procedural improprieties,[188] the corporation's failure to initiate dissenters' rights proceedings,[189] or for misconduct before the merger.[190] Finally, the Delaware Supreme Court held that a shareholder who had begun an appraisal proceeding and thereafter, before that proceeding's conclusion, learned of fraud in the merger, could join in one proceeding the fraud and the appraisal actions, so that if fraud were indeed proved, appraisal would be moot; otherwise, appraisal could be pursued.[191]

NOTES

1. MODEL BUSINESS CORPORATION ACT §§ 71, 72, 72A, 73, 79 (1969) [hereinafter Former MBCA]; REVISED MODEL BUSINESS CORPORATION ACT §§ 11.02, 11.03, 11.04, 12.02 (1984) [hereinafter MBCA] (the revised Act has deleted the section on consolidation).
2. Former MBCA §§ 80, 81 (1969); MBCA §§ 13.02, 13.03, 13.20 to 13.26 (2008). See §§ 22.23 to 22.27.
3. The most striking example is corporate reclassifications, which are covered in only a few jurisdictions, such as N.Y. BUS. CORP. LAW § 806(b) (McKinney 2003). See Former MBCA § 80(a)(4) (1969); MBCA §§ 13.02(a)(4) (2008); Chapter 25.
4. Weinberger v. UOP, Inc., 457 A.2d 701 (Del. 1983) (indicating appraisal remedy is exclusive in absence of fraud). But see Rabkin v. Philip A. Hunt Chem. Corp., 498 A.2d 1099 (Del. 1985) (interpreting Weinberger as allowing for remedies other than appraisal when specific acts of unfairness are alleged).
5. 17 C.F.R. § 240.10b-5 (2009).
6. 15 U.S.C. §§ 77(f), 77(g) (2009).
7. Id. §§ 78m(d), 78m(e), 78n(d), 78n(f).

8. Merger and consolidation are two different forms of combination. In a merger, one corporation merges into another. In contrast, with a consolidation, the two combining companies consolidate into a third.

9. *See, e.g.*, Shannon v. Samuel Langston Co., 379 F. Supp. 797 (W.D. Mich. 1974); Loving & Assoc., Inc. v. Carothers, 619 N.W.2d 782 (Minn. Ct. App. 2000) (merger does not necessarily terminate a loan guaranty arrangement made with entity that disappeared through merger).

10. MBCA § 11.07 (2008); Former MBCA § 76 (1969); *infra* § 22.17.

11. *See* Del. Ins, Guar. Ass'n v. Christiana Care Health Services, Inc., 892 A.2d 1073 (Del. 2006) (duties and liabilities of disappearing corporation are those of the surviving entity).

12. Knapp v. N. Am. Rockwell Corp., 506 F.2d 361, 363 (3d Cir. 1974), *cert. denied*, 421 U.S. 965 (1975).

13. Cleveland Worsted Mills Co. v. Consol. Textile Corp., 292 F. 129 (3d Cir. 1923); Goldman v. Postal Tel., Inc., 52 F. Supp. 763, 771 (D. Del. 1943).

14. *See* George S. Hills, *Consolidation of Corporations by Sale of Assets and Distributions of Shares*, 19 CAL. L. REV. 349, 351–352 (1931) (*quoting from* HENRY W. BALLANTINE, CORPORATIONS (1927)).

15. In Delaware, even the shareholders of the selling corporation do not have statutory dissenters' rights. DEL. CODE ANN. tit. 8, § 262 (2001).

16. *E.g., Knapp*, 506 F.2d 361 (3d Cir. 1974), *cert. denied*, 421 U.S. 965 (1975).

17. *Goldman*, 52 F. Supp. 763, 771 (1943).

18. I.R.C. § 368 (2009). 26 U.S.C.A. § 368 (2009).

19. Voeller v. Neilston Warehouse Co., 311 U.S. 531, 535 n.6 (1941).

20. *E.g.*, Mich. Wolverine Student Coop., Inc. v. Wm. Goodyear & Co., 22 N.W.2d 884 (Mich. 1946). *Contra*, Bassett v. City Bank & Trust Co., 165 A. 557 (Conn. 1933).

21. *See, e.g.*, Mills v. Tiffany's, Inc., 198 A. 185 (Conn. 1938).

22. Trifad Entm't, Inc. v. Anderson, 36 P.3d 363, 369–70 (Mont. 2001).

23. *E.g.*, CAL. CORP. CODE § 1001(a)(2) (West Supp. 2009).

24. MODEL BUS. CORP. ACT ANN. § 11.03 (3d ed. 1994).

25. *E.g.*, MINN. STAT. ANN. §§ 302A.441, 302A.661 (2004) (requires unanimous consent); DEL. CODE ANN. tit. 8, § 228 (2001) (generally allowing consent of a majority of shares without a meeting).

26. *E.g.*, CAL. CORP. CODE § 1001(c) (West Supp. 2009) ("Such sale . . . may be made upon such terms and conditions . . . as the board may deem in the best interests of the corporation").

27. Former MBCA § 79(c) (1969). The Revised Model Business Corporation Act requires the corporation to notify the shareholders of the consideration to be received. MODEL BUS. CORP. ACT § 12.02(d) (2008).

28. SEC Schedule 14A, item 16.

29. *See* MBCA § 10.04 (2008); Former MBCA § 60 (1969). The Model Business Corporation Act provides for class voting only if the transaction affects special rights of that class, which is generally not the case with a sale of corporate assets not followed by dissolution.

30. I.R.C. § 322(b) (2009); 26 U.S.C. § 332(b) (2009); Treas. Reg. § 1.332-2.

31. *See* Philadelphia Nat'l Bank v. B.S.F. Co., 199 A.2d 557 (Del. Ch.), *rev'd on other grounds*, 204 A.2d 746 (Del. 1964). *See* Katz v. Bregman, 431 A.2d

1274 (Del. Ch. 1981) (sale of subsidiary that was parent's sole income-producing asset, was 51% of parent's total assets, and provided 45% of parent's net sales held to be sale of substantially all assets).

32. *See* MBCA § 12.02(a) (2008).

33. Gimbel v. Signal Co., 316 A.2d 599, 606 (Del. Ch.), *aff'd per curiam*, 316 A.2d 619 (Del. 1974).

34. *See, e.g.*, Stiles v. Aluminum Prod. Co., 86 N.E.2d 887 (Ill. App. Ct. 1949) (assets sold were twice value of assets retained but were the essential operating assets as those retained were cash equivalents). *See generally* Siegel, *supra* note 18, 537–44.

35. MBCA § 12.01 Official Comment (2008) (emphasis added).

36. *Id.* § 12.02(a).

37. In this regard, the Model Act's Official Comment's use of "former" takes on added significance because it assumes the corporation's continuation.

38. Roehner v. Gracie Manor, Inc., 160 N.E.2d 519 (N.Y. 1959). *Contra*, Boyer v. Legal Estates, Inc., 255 N.Y.S.2d 955 (Sup. Ct. 1964).

39. Morris v. Washington Med. Ctr., Inc., 331 A.2d 132 (D.C. Ct. App. 1975).

40. *See Boyer*, 255 N.Y.S.2d 955 (Sup. Ct. 1964). *See also* Naas v. Lucas, 739 P.2d 1051 (Or. Ct. App. 1987) (transfer of substantially all assets by president to satisfy bona fide debt not within ordinary course of business).

41. Mich. Wolverines Student Coop., Inc. v. Wm. Goodyear & Co., 22 N.W.2d 884 (Mich. 1946).

42. Jeppi v. Brockman Holding Co., 206 P.2d 847 (Cal. 1949) (real estate).

43. Del. Code Ann. tit. 8, § 271 (2001) ("money or other property, including shares of stock in and/or other securities . . . ").

44. I.R.C. § 368(a)(1)(C) (1988).

45. Homer v. Crown Cork & Seal Co., 141 A. 425, 434 (Md. 1928).

46. Del. Code Ann. tit. 8, § 262 (2001).

47. N.Y. Bus. Corp. Law §§ 806, 910, 1319 (McKinney 1986, Supp. 1994); Former MBCA § 80 (1969, 1979 rev.); MBCA § 13.02 (1984).

48. Even in states granting dissenters' rights, they can be eliminated by leaving some assets or by amending the charter to permit such sales in the ordinary course.

49. Farris v. Glen Alden Corp., 143 A.2d 25 (Pa. 1958).

50. *See* Hariton v. Arco Elec., Inc., 188 A.2d 123 (Del. 1963), *aff'g* 182 A.2d 22 (Del. Ch. 1962).

51. *See, e.g.*, Fitzgerald v. Fahnestock & Co., 730 N.Y.S.2d 70 (App. Div. 2001) (suit by former employee of acquired company).

52. *See id.* (acquisition of stock).

53. W. Tex. Refining & Dev. Co. v. Comm'r, 68 F.2d 77, 81 (10th Cir. 1933).

54. *See, e.g.*, Dayton v. Peck, Stow & Wilcox Co., 739 F.2d 690 (1st Cir. 1984).

55. *See Fitzgerald*, 730 N.Y.S.2d 70 (App. Div. 2001).

56. 42 U.S.C. § 9601 (2009).

57. CERCLA, 42 U.S.C. § 107 (2000).

58. *See, e.g.*, New York v. Shore Realty Corp., 759 F.2d 1032 (2d Cir. 1985).

59. Fall River Dyeing & Finishing Corp. v. NLRB, 482 U.S. 27 (1987) (when majority of successor's employees had been employed by predecessor). More recently, the NLRB took an even broader approach, emphasizing

the representations made by the successor of an "intention" to retain the acquired company's workforce. *See* Canteen Co., 317 NLRB No. 153, 317 NLRB 1052 (1995), *enfd.* 103 F.3d 1355 (7th Cir. 1997).

60. *E.g.*, Metro. Edison Co. v. Comm'r, 98 F.2d 807, 810 (3d Cir.), *aff'd*, 306 U.S. 522 (1939); Former MBCA § 72 (1969).

61. *E.g.*, Ala. Power Co. v. McNinch, 94 F.2d 601, 610 (D.C. Cir. 1937).

62. Delaware retains the distinction between mergers and consolidations. DEL. CODE ANN. tit. 8, § 264 (2001). In contrast, the Model Act has abolished consolidation as a separate form; the transaction can still be accomplished through a share exchange. MBCA § 11.02 (2008).

63. *See* MBCA § 22.13 (2008).

64. *See* Wm. B. Riker & Son Co. v. United Drug Co., 82 A. 930 (N.J. Err. App. 1912).

65. *E.g.*, DEL. CODE ANN. tit. 8, § 252 (2001); N.Y. BUS. CORP. LAW § 907 (McKinney 2003); Former MBCA § 73 (1969); MBCA § 11.04 (1984).

66. *See* Former MBCA § 106 (1969).

67. *E.g.*, *Wm. B. Riker*, 82 A. 930 (N.J. Err. App. 1912); Colgate v. U.S. Leather Co., 72 A. 126 (N.J. Err. App. 1909).

68. Nelson v. All Am. Life & Fin. Corp., 889 F.2d 141 (8th Cir. 1989).

69. *See* Nice Ball Bearing Co. v. Mortg. Bldg. & Loan Ass'n, 166 A. 239 (Pa. 1933).

70. There is no duty under state law to disclose such negotiations. *See, e.g.*, Eldridge v. Tymshare, Inc., 230 Cal. Rptr. 815 (Ct. App. 1986).

71. *E.g.*, Pine State Creamery Co. v. Land-O-Sun Dairies Inc., 201 F.3d 437 (4th Cir. 1999); Great Lakes Chem. Corp. v. Pharmacia Corp., 788 A.2d 544 (Del. Ch. 2001); Raskin v. Birmingham Steel Corp., 1990 WL 193326 (Del. Ch. 1990).

72. IBP Inc. v. Tyson Foods Inc., 789 A.2d 14 (Del. Ch. 2001), *aff'd sub nom.*, Tyson Foods, Inc. v. Aetos Corp., 818 A.2d 145 (Del. 2003).

73. *E.g.*, DEL. CODE ANN. tit. 8, § 251(c) (2001); Former MBCA § 73 (1969); MBCA § 11.03 (2008).

74. MASS. ANN. LAWS ch. 156D, § 11.04(5) (LexisNexis. Supp. 2009) (articles may authorize a lower vote); N.Y. BUS. CORP. LAW § 903(a)(2) (McKinney 2003) (two-thirds of all shares; if class vote required, majority of all shares of each class). The New York statute was amended in 1998 to require only a majority of those shares entitled to vote. The amendment applies prospectively only to corporations incorporated after Feb. 22, 1998. NY BCL § 903 (2001).

75. *See* Committee on Corporate Laws, *Changes in the Model Business Corporation Act Pertaining to Appraisal Rights and to Fundamental Changes— Final Adoption*, 55 BUS. LAW. 405 (1999).

76. *See* MBCA §§ 11.04(f), 10.04 (2008).

77. *See SEC Report on Reorganization Committees Part VII* 329, 376, 388, 397, 411, 530–36 (1938); Comment, 45 YALE L.J. 105, 113–14 (1935).

78. *See, e.g.*, MBCA §§ 6.21(f), 11.04(g) (2008).

79. DEL. CODE ANN. tit. 8, § 251(c) (2001).

80. BCA § 11.06 (2009); Former MBCA § 74 (1969).

81. MBCA § 11.06(b) (2009).

82. Cal. Corp. Code § 1103 (West Supp. 2009); Del. Code Ann. tit. 8, § 251(c) (2001); Kan. Stat. Ann. § 17-6704(d) (2001).
83. *E.g.,* Mass. Ann. Laws ch. 156D § 11.06(d) (LexisNexis Supp. 2009); N.C. Gen. Stat. § 55-11-05 (Supp. 2001); 15 Pa. Stat. Ann. §§ 1926, 1927 (1995).
84. *See* Auserehl v. Jamaica Builders Supply Corp., 404 N.Y.S.2d 421 (App. Div. 1978) (no violation for failure to refer to manner in which ten shares in acquiring corporation are to be converted into same number of shares in surviving corporation).
85. *See* Former MBCA § 75 (1969); MBCA § 11.05 (2008); Comment, *The Short Merger Statute*, 32 U. Chi. L. Rev. 596 (1965).
86. Cal. Corp. Code § 1110 (West Supp. 2009); Del. Code Ann. tit. 8, § 253 (2001).
87. *See* MBCA § 11.05 (2008). *But see* Del. Code Ann. tit. 8, § 253(a) (2001).
88. Del. Code Ann. tit. 8, § 253(d) (2001); Former MBCA § 80(c) (1969); BCA § 13.02(a)(1)(ii) (2008).
89. Cal. Corp. Code § 1110(b) (West Supp. 2009); Del. Code Ann. tit. 8, § 253 (2001); MBCA § 11.05 (2008); Former MBCA § 75 (1969).
90. N.Y. Bus. Corp. Law § 905 (McKinney 2003), (formerly 95%, now 90%); Wis. Stat. Ann. § 180.1104 (West Supp. 2009) (formerly 100%, now 90%).
91. *See* Teschner v. Chicago Title & Trust Co., 322 N.E.2d 54 (Ill. 1974).
92. Stauffer v. Standard Brands, Inc., 187 A.2d 78 (Del. 1962).
93. *See In re* Beck Indus., 479 F.2d 410 (2d Cir. 1973).
94. Among the possible advantages of a continued existence are the opportunity to maintain ongoing agreements with prior creditors and the ability to retain existing labor contracts.
95. The advantages include (1) greater flexibility in the consideration to be paid without jeopardizing tax-free status because a qualifying purchase of assets must be solely for voting stock, I.R.C. § 368(a)(1)(C) (2009); (2) avoidance of transfer-of-title problems; (3) there is no need to liquidate as a second step and the acquired corporation may remain in existence if desired; (4) the avoidance of a shareholder vote in those states requiring such for a purchase of assets.
96. There is greater freedom in the consideration for tax-free acquisitions; (2) the acquiring company is assured of complete control; (3) there is no need to worry about the various tender offer provisions of state and federal securities laws. However, with a triangular merger the shareholders of the acquired company will be given dissenters' rights, but this is equally true of clean-up mergers that frequently follow tender offers.
97. The subsidiary may also be referred to as a "phantom corporation," which has led to the alternative appellation "phantom merger." *See, e.g.,* Marcou v. Fed. Trust Co., 268 A.2d 629 (Me. 1970).
98. *See* MBCA § 11.03 (2009).
99. Western Air Lines, Inc. v. Allegheny Airlines, Inc., 313 A.2d 145, 153 (Del. Ch. 1973).
100. Similarly, noncompliance with statutory requirements for shareholder approval of a sale of assets outside the ordinary course of business is not a

defect creditors can raise. *See* Phillips Petrol. Co. v. Rock Creek Mining Co., 449 F.2d 664 (9th Cir. 1971); McDermott v. Bear Film Co., 33 Cal. Rptr. 486 (Ct. App. 1963).

101. *See, e.g.,* Cameron v. United Traction Co., 73 N.Y.S. 981 (App. Div. 1902); DEL. CODE ANN. tit. 8, § 259(a) (2001); N.Y. BUS. CORP. LAW § 906(b)(3) (McKinney 2003); Former MBCA § 76(e) (1969); MBCA § 11.07(a)(4) (2008).

102. 7A U.L.A. 427 (1985).

103. *Id.* at 639.

104. 11 U.S.C. § 548 (2000).

105. *See* Raymond J. Blackwood, *Applying Fraudulent Conveyance Law to Leveraged Buyouts,* 42 DUKE L.J. 340 (1992).

106. *See* Moody v. Sec. Pac. Bus. Credit, Inc., 127 B.R. 958 (W.D. Pa. 1991).

107. *See* FASB to Bar Pooling Method for Mergers; *Trade Groups Unhappy,* 31 SEC. REG. & L. REP. (BNA) 543 (April 23, 1999).

108. *Id.*

109. Pooling-of-interest accounting, however, can still be used for combinations of companies that are under the common control.

110. *See, e.g.,* Williams v. Bartell, 225 N.Y.S.2d 351 (App. Div. 1962) (Bergan, J. dissenting) (amount of goodwill lowered as a result of SEC letter of consent).

111. *See* APB Op. No. 17 (1970).

112. Porges v. Vadsco Sales Corp., 32 A.2d 148, 1150 (Del. Ch. 1943).

113. Nat'l Supply Co. v. Leland Stanford Jr. Univ., 134 F.2d 689 (9th Cir. 1943), *cert. denied,* 320 U.S. 773 (1943).

114. Umstead v. Durham Hosiery Mills, Inc., 578 F. Supp. 342 (M.D.N.C. 1984).

115. Willard v. Moneta Bldg. Supply, Inc., 551 S.E.2d 596, 599–600 (Va. 2001).

116. *E.g.,* Under some cases the proposed combination may be enjoined on the basis of gross unfairness. *E.g.,* Bryan v. Brock & Blevins Co., 490 F.2d 563 (5th Cir. 1974); Young v. Valhi, Inc., 382 A.2d 1372 (Del. Ch. 1978).

117. *Bryan,* 343 F. Supp. 1062 (N.D. Ga. 1972), *aff'd on other grounds,* 490 F.2d 563 (5th Cir.), *cert. denied,* 419 U.S. 844 (1974).

118. Fed. United Corp. v. Havender, 11 A.2d 331 (Del. 1940).

119. DAN B. DOBBS, LAW OF REMEDIES § 2.5 (2d ed. 1993).

120. McMillan v. Intercargo Corp., 768 A.2d 492, 500 (Del. Ch. 2000) (completed merger cannot be unwound once "the metaphorical merger eggs have been scrambled").

121. *See, e.g.,* Harman v. Masoneilan Int'l, Inc., 418 A.2d 1004 (Del. Ch. 1980).

122. Parnes v. Bally Entm't Corp., 722 A.2d 1243, 1245 (Del. 1999) (permitting direct suit by shareholder challenging merger).

123. Am. Seating Co. v. Bullard, 290 F. 896, 900 (6th Cir. 1923).

124. 17 C.F.R. § 240.10b-5 (2002). *See* §§ 12.9 to 12.12.

125. SECURITIES ACT 1933, §§ 11, 12(a)(1), 12(a)(2), 15 U.S.C. §§ 77k, 78l(a)(1), 78l(a)(2) (2000).

126. Peters Corp. v. N.M. Banquest Investors Corp., 188 P.3d 1185 (N.M. 2008) (appraisal protects minority who object to fundamental corporate

change that was found in case flowing from the company's redemption of the substantial holdings of one of its stockholders).

127. *See, e.g.,* Del. Code Ann. tit. 8, § 262(b)(1) (2001). *See* Note, *A Reconsideration of the Stock Market Exception to the Dissenting Shareholder's Right of Appraisal,* 74 Mich. L. Rev. 1023 (1976).

128. Del. Code Ann. tit. 8, § 262(b) (2001).

129. *See* Johnson v. C. Brigham Co., 136 A. 456 (Me. 1927) (under prior Maine statute requiring specific negative vote).

130. MBCA § 13.23 (2008).

131. *Id.* § 13.24.

132. *Id.* § 13.26(a).

133. *Id.* § 13.26.

134. *Id.* § 13.30(a).

135. *Id.* § 13.30; Former MBCA § 81(h) (1969).

136. *See* Note, *Rights of Dissenting Stockholders Pending Statutory Appraisal Proceedings,* 21 Va. L. Rev. 825 (1935).

137. *See* Francis I. duPont & Co. v. Universal City Studios, Inc., 312 A.2d 344 (Del. Ch. 1973), *aff'd,* 334 A.2d 216 (Del. 1975).

138. *See* Dimmock v. Reichhold Chem., Inc., 360 N.E.2d 1079 (N.Y. 1977) (ten-year proceeding produced an increase in value of $13,000 after expenses of $50,000).

139. *See, e.g.,* Hernando Bank v. Huff, 609 F. Supp. 1124 (N.D. Miss. 1985), *aff'd,* 796 F.2d 803 (5th Cir. 1986) (expense assigned to corporation because appraisal yielded significant increase in amount to be paid by corporation).

140. Del. Code Ann. tit. 8, § 262 (2001); Kan. Stat. Ann. § 17-6712 (2007). A number of states deny dissenters' rights to shareholders in a surviving parent corporation that used a short form procedure to merge with a subsidiary. *See* § 22.14.

141. *E.g.,* 805 Ill. Comp. Stat. 5/11.60 (1994).

142. There is surprisingly little authority on what constitutes "substantially all." *See* F. Hodge O'Neal & Robert B. Thompson, O'Neal and Thompson's Oppression of Minority Shareholders and LLC Members § 5.19 (rev. 2d ed. 2009).

143. *See, e.g.,* Pratt v. Ballman-Cummings Furn. Co., 495 S.W.2d 509 (Ark. 1973), *appeal after remand,* 549 S.W.2d 270 (Ark. 1977) (partnership formed by two corporations held to be a de facto merger entitling minority shareholders to appraisal rights).

144. For another avoidance device, *see* the discussion of triangular mergers *supra.*

145. *E.g.,* N.Y. Bus. Corp. Law § 806(b)(6) (McKinney 2003); Former MBCA § 80(a)(4) (1969); MBCA § 13.02(a)(4), (5) (2008). *See* § 25.5.

146. Flarsheim v. Twenty Five Thirty Two Broadway Corp., 432 S.W.2d 245 (Mo. 1968).

147. MBCA § 13.02(a)(2) (2008); Former MBCA § 80(a)(3) (1969).

148. MBCA § 13.02(b) (2008).

149. Del. Code Ann. tit. 8, § 262(b) (2001).

150. *See, e.g.,* Bell v. Kirby Lumber Corp., 395 A.2d 730 (Del. Ch. 1978), *aff'd in part and rev'd in part,* 413 A.2d 137 (Del. 1980).

151. MBCA § 13.01(4)(ii) (2008).
152. *See also* Cede & Co. v. Technicolor, Inc., 875 A.2d 602 (Del. 2005) (upholding use of forecasts of capital expenditures and depreciation as well as revenue predictions).
153. *See* Gonsalves v. Straight Arrow Publishers, 701 A.2d 357, 361 (Del. 1997) (reversible error for court to choose one party's expert over the other party's expert who espouses one method—capitalization of average earnings for past five years—over another expert's approach who utilizes capitalization of most recent year's earnings without considering some combination of the approaches used by each expert).
154. M.P.M. Enters., Inc. v. Gilbert, 731 A.2d 790 (Del. 1999).
155. *See generally* Lucian Bebchuk & Marcel Kahan, *Fairness Opinions: How Fair Are They and What Can Be Done About It?*, 1989 DUKE L.J. 27, 31–33.
156. *See* ALI, PRINCIPLES OF CORPORATE GOVERNANCE 319–324 (1994).
157. *See, e.g.*, Bell v. Kirby Lumber Corp., 395 A.2d 730 (Del. Ch. 1978), *aff'd in part and rev'd in part*, 413 A.2d 137 (Del. 1980); Gibbons v. Schenley Indus., 339 A.2d 460 (Del. Ch. 1975); *In re* Delaware Racing Ass'n, 213 A.2d 203 (Del. 1965).
158. *E.g.*, Foglesong v. Thurston Nat'l Life Ins. Co., 555 P.2d 606 (Okla. 1976).
159. *Weinberger*, 457 A.2d 701 (Del. 1983).
160. *Id.* at 701, 713. Another case has also taken an unstructured approach to valuation.
161. Piemonte v. New Boston Garden Corp., 387 N.E.2d 1145 (Mass. 1979).
162. *See Hernando*, 796 F.2d 803 (5th Cir. 1986).
163. *In re* Valuation of Common Stock of Libby, McNeill & Libby, 406 A.2d 54 (Me. 1979).
164. Munshower v. Kolbenheyer, 732 So. 2d 385 (Fla. App. 1999) (applying a 20% nonmarketability discount to shares in a closely held corporation).
165. *See* Swope v. Siegel-Robert, Inc., 243 F.3d 486, 493 (8th Cir. 2001) (applying Missouri law; since fair market value is irrelevant in determining fair market value, market forces do not affect ultimate assessment of fair value in appraisal proceeding).
166. *See In re* Radiology Assoc., Inc., 611 A.2d 485 (Del. Ch. 1991).
167. 457 A.2d 701, 713 (Del. 1983).
168. The rigidity of this method is best illustrated by Universal City Studios v. Francis I. duPont & Co., 334 A.2d 216 (Del. 1975), wherein the court mandated use of the five-year earnings average, though the trend line in earnings was steeply rising, countering this ultimate conservatism by imprecisely using lower discount rate with which to capitalize earnings.
169. *Id.*
170. Paskill Corp. v. Alcoma Corp., 747 A.2d 549, 553 (Del. 2000); M.G. Bancorporation, Inc. v. Le Beau, 737 A.2d 513, 525 (Del. 1999).
171. *See Cede & Co.*, 1990 WL 161084 (Del. Ch. 1990).
172. *See, e.g.*, Advanced Commc'n Design, Inc. v. Follett, 615 N.W.2d 285, 290 (Minn. 2000) ("fair value" means pro rata value of corporation's value as a going concern).
173. Offenbecher v. Baron Services, Inc., 2001 WL 527522 (Ala. Civ. App. 2001) (upholding lower court's application of 50% minority discount).

174. *Swope*, 243 F.3d at 495–96 (applying Missouri law; minority status of stock is irrelevant in appraisal proceeding).
175. MBCA § 13.01(4).
176. *Swope*, 243 F.3d 486, 493 (8th Cir. 2001) (applying Missouri law; marketability discount is incompatible with purpose of appraisal, that is, to enable dissenting shareholders to recapture their complete investment when they are unwillingly subjected to substantial corporate changes).
177. Lawson Mardon Wheaton, Inc. v. Smith, 716 A.2d 550, 562 (N.J. Super. App. Div. 1998) (unlike minority discount on the basis that marketability discount reflects illiquidity and should be applied to all shares of stock, not just those of the dissenters).
178. MBCA § 13.01(4).
179. Perlman v. Permonite Mfg. Co., 568 F. Supp. 222 (N.D. Ind. 1983) (Indiana law).
180. *See* M.P.M. Enters., Inc. v. Gilbert, 731 A.2d 790 (Del. 1999).
181. *E.g.*, Del. Code Ann. tit. 8, § 262 (2001). Broadcasting Co. v. Mahurin, 365 S.W.2d 265, 270 (Ark. 1963). Joseph v. Wallace-Murray Corp., 238 N.E.2d 360 (Mass. 1968).
182. *E.g.*, Conn. Gen. Stat. Ann. § 33-373(f) (West 1987). *See In re* Jones & Laughlin Steel Corp., 398 A.2d 186 (Pa. Super. Ct. 1979), *aff'd*, 412 A.2d 1099 (Pa. 1980).
183. *See* Miller v. Steinbach, 268 F. Supp. 255, 270 (S.D.N.Y. 1967) (former Pennsylvania statute's exclusivity limited to "good faith" and transactions that are not "sham or subterfuge").
184. Weinberger v. UOP, Inc., 457 A.2d 701 (Del. 1983).
185. *See, e.g.*, Galligan v. Galligan, 741 N.E.2d 1217 (Ind. 2001).
186. *E.g.*, Nagy v. Bistricer, 770 A.2d 43 (Del. Ch. 2000).
187. *See* Shidler v. All Am. Life & Fin. Corp., 775 F.2d 917 (8th Cir. 1985).
188. *Rabkin*, 498 A.2d 1099 (second step of acquisition purposely delayed to avoid paying higher consideration promised in first stage if merger completed within one year).
189. *Galligan*, 741 N.E.2d 1217, 1225–1226 (Ind. 2001) (shareholders may proceed with separate claim against persons responsible for breach of fiduciary duty to initiate dissenters' rights proceedings).
190. *See* Kademian v. Ladish Co., 792 F.2d 614 (7th Cir. 1986).
191. *See Cede & Co.*, 542 A.2d 1182.

CHAPTER 23

EQUITABLE LIMITS ON ACQUISITIONS AND DEFENSIVE MANEUVERS

TABLE OF SECTIONS

§ 23.1 FIDUCIARY OBLIGATIONS IN ACQUISITION TRANSACTIONS

Acquisitions where the acquiring company owns a majority of the target prior to the merger agreement create the potential of self-dealing by favoring the majority over the minority. The essence of the majority's fiduciary obligations in such acquisitions is the Delaware Supreme Court's "entire fairness" standard.[1] The court embraced the give-get formula for measuring fairness, reasoning that "the test of fairness which we think [is] the correct one [is] that upon a merger the minority stockholder shall receive the substantial equivalent in value of what he had before."[2] The Delaware Supreme Court, and other courts,[3] now recognize that the minority should also participate proportionally in any nonspeculative gains generated by the acquisition.[4]

The procedural context in which the transaction is formulated, proposed, and approved has assumed increasing importance. For example, the Delaware Supreme Court has distinguished between "fair dealing" and "fair price" such that it more readily concludes the appraisal remedy is exclusive as to the latter but not necessarily as to the former.[5] "Fair dealing" is defined to include questions regarding the acquisition's timing, how it was initiated, structured, and negotiated, and the approvals of the directors and stockholders obtained.[6] In essence, fair dealing examines whether the transaction is the product of overreaching misbehavior by which those in a fiduciary relationship to the target corporation use their power to deprive the target corporation of fair and independent representation in the acquisition.[7]

These problems are circumvented by interjecting an independent negotiating committee between the parent and the target corporation.[8] A further means to clothe the controlled corporation with an independent voice is by conditioning the transaction's consummation on the approval of a majority of the disinterested shares. However, the burden of proving the acquisition's entire fairness does not shift if the procedures followed are not truly independent.[9]

§ 23.2 EQUITABLE LIMITATIONS ON THE POWER OF SALE OR MERGER

A controlling shareholder or parent corporation that dominates and controls another corporation is not as a matter of law precluded from purchasing the entire property and assets of the controlled corporation, either when the assets of a going concern are sold or when the corporation is being wound up. However, such a purchase by a controlling person or the company's managers implicates the same concerns examined in Chapter 10 regarding self-dealing such that close or rigorous judicial scrutiny occurs.[10]

When the appraisal remedy is not exclusive, the reviewing court should "carefully scrutinize the board's actions to ascertain whether the board instituted measures to ensure a fair process, and whether the board achieved a fair price for the disinterested stockholder minority."[11] This formula is more frequently stated as the "entire fairness" inquiry with fairness thus having two distinct components: fair dealings and fair price.[12] The court undertakes a unified assessment that involves balancing the process followed and the price received by the minority.[13] In assessing the fairness of the process, the court will consider "the board's composition and independence, the timing, structure and negotiation of the transaction; how the board and shareholder approval were obtained; and the extent to which the board and the shareholders were accurately informed about the transaction."[14]

Delaware has qualified the scope of the entire fairness review standard. In *Glassman v. Unocal Exploration Corporation*, the court held that the parent company that exercises its right under the short-form merger provision to rid itself of the minority shareholders in the subsidiary does not have to establish the entire fairness for its actions.[15] In such a case, the exclusive remedy to the minority, absent fraud or illegality, is the appraisal remedy.[16] Similarly, in *Solomon v. Pathe*,[17] the Delaware Supreme Court held that the entire fairness standard does not apply to tender offers initiated by a controlling stockholder. However, fiduciary limits do apply when the controlling shareholder combines the tender offer and short-form merger with the objective of eliminating the minority shareholders.[18]

§ 23.3 MERGER FREEZE-OUTS OF MINORITY SHAREHOLDERS

Abuses that may accompany a controlled merger or other conflict-of-interest transaction are magnified when the minority shareholder is cashed out and thus is not able to share in the profits of the surviving corporation. These cash-outs, also known as "squeeze-outs" or "freeze-outs," which are not new, have been accomplished in a variety of ways. The short-form merger is the simplest of the various statutory liberalizations and has led to an increase in the use of merger, consolidation, or sale of assets as a freeze-out technique. This is a rapidly developing area in which there has been a great deal of judicial and scholarly energy directed toward the proper treatment of freeze-out transactions. The cases recognizing a freeze-out remedy have focused on two factors: (1) the purpose of the transaction and (2) fairness to the minority shareholders. While some courts require a showing of no valid purpose as a threshold to scrutiny of the transaction's fairness,[19] older Delaware cases, at least in their language, put the burden of proving both on the defendants.[20] While briefly imposing a business purpose requirement for a freeze-out,[21] the Delaware Supreme Court subsequently abandoned the business purpose requirement.[22]

Notwithstanding its subsequent rejection in Delaware, the business purpose test continues to be an issue in many other jurisdictions.[23] Further, the business purpose test is not limited to mergers; it has also been applied, for example, where the directors issued additional shares to themselves to perpetuate their control.[24]

§ 23.4 Going-Private Transactions under the Securities Laws

A subspecies of the freeze-out merger is the going-private transaction.[25] This has been described as any organic corporate change, such as merger, reverse stock split, repurchase of shares, or recapitalization, that results in a publicly traded company being delisted or closely enough held so as no longer to be subject to the 1934 Exchange Act's reporting requirements.[26] There are various possible motives behind going private—for example, a company may decide that the burdens of SEC reporting are too expensive or it may be the final step in a takeover by another company. All of the fairness considerations applicable to any freeze-out transactions necessarily apply with equal force to this special subspecies. In addition, there have been both SEC involvement and state law concern, based on the fact that going-private transactions lessen the standards of corporate conduct. Going-private transactions have been on the rise with respect to smaller public companies, following the increased burdens placed on public companies by the Sarbanes-Oxley Act.

Beyond the state law fiduciary standards for directors and controlling shareholders,[27] relief may be found under SEC Rule 10b-5,[28] the federal proxy rules, if a shareholder vote is involved, and section 14(e) of the 1934 Exchange Act, which deals with tender offers.[29] Issuer tender offers are specifically regulated under Rule 13e-4 of the Exchange Act.[30]

The SEC in Rule 13e-3 promulgated extensive disclosure requirements and a special antifraud rule for going-private transactions.[31] In broad overview, Rule 13e-3 imposes special disclosure obligations on non-arm's-length mergers, recapitalizations, tender offers, and the like by the issuer or its affiliate that either (1) will cause delisting by a securities exchange or Nasdaq of *any* class of the issuer's securities or (2) will reduce the number of its record stockholders below 300 so that it will be exempt from the registration and reporting requirements of the Securities Exchange Act.[32] Several exceptions to the going-private rule are provided, the most significant being (1) the second step of a pre-announced two-step acquisition, provided the consideration is at least equal to that offered in the earlier tender offer, the second step occurs within one year of the earlier tender offer, and the earlier tender offer fully disclosed the intention to undertake a second-step acquisition;[33] (2) the transaction provides that all the issuer's security holders receive only an equity security that has substantially the same rights as the equity security given up and is registered under the Securities Exchange Act;[34] and (3) issuer redemptions, calls, and other acquisitions pursuant to the rights established in the instruments (articles of incorporation) creating that class of security.[35] The term "affiliate" enjoys a fairly broad construction under the rule, so that the issuer's combination with another company indirectly controlling the issuer can trigger the disclosures required by Rule 13e-3.[36]

If an exemption is not available, the issuer or its affiliate involved in a transaction subject to Rule 13e-3 must provide to each affected security holder of record the extensive disclosures required by the rule. This must be provided to the holders not later than 20 days prior to the purchase of the shares or the date when their consent or vote on such transaction will be sought.[37] The disclosure required by Rule 13e-3 is extensive. For example, Item 8(a) of Schedule 13E-3 requires the directors to express their opinion of the transaction's fairness to the frozen-out stockholders.[38] Further, Item 8(b) of Schedule 13E-3 requires a reasonably detailed discussion of the "material factors upon which the belief stated in Item 8(a) is based."[39] In applying these disclosure requirements, the SEC demands more than mere itemization of the factors relied on; it requires their discussion.[40] Thus, a general statement that the board of directors considered $29.50-per-share fair, in light of the company's book value of $3.77-per-share, was held incomplete absent any discussion "of the reasons and extent to which book value is or is not an accurate reflection of the company's value and therefore was accepted or rejected as a criterion for judging the fairness of the transaction."[41] The full force of Rule 13e-3's disclosure demands appear in the Supreme Court's holding that opinion statements, such as those elicited by the going-private rule, can in appropriate circumstances be material misrepresentations that give rise to private recoveries.[42] Violations of Rule 13e-3's disclosure demands subject the violator not only to the full panoply of the SEC's enforcement remedies, but also to the private actions that are available under the rule for affected shareholders.[43]

§ 23.5 DEFENSIVE TACTICS—SHARK REPELLENT PROVISIONS

[1] Introduction to Defensive Tactics

In recent years, tender offers[44] have become a popular alternative means of corporate acquisition. Tender offers are often not as time-consuming as proxy battles and, because they do not involve action by the target company, no dissenters' rights are involved. There are many different tender offer techniques that are often the first part of a multistep acquisition,[45] freeze-out, or going-private transaction. Tender offers may be consummated with the support of the target's management,[46] or can evolve into contested battles for corporate control.[47] Once a tender offer has been made, the target company's management must respond. If management decides to go along amicably with the takeover, it will be bound to adhere to the fiduciary standards that apply to any controlled takeover.

The defense against a takeover attempt is generally covered by the business judgment rule, which allows management the use of reasonable corporate funds to defend its policies.[48] The business judgment rule does not apply, however, to decisions by directors who have a self-interest in the transaction. Often a charge is made that a takeover defense is motivated by the directors' desire to entrench themselves in office.

Accordingly, the courts have to decide in which instances the directors will be insulated by the business judgment rule and in which instances their self-interest will limit their discretion to act.

Defensive tactics vary widely but can be placed in two categories: responsive or preventive. Some of the most popular responsive defensive tactics include arrangements and mergers with "white knights,"[49] the issuance of additional shares to dilute the tender offeror's holdings,[50] or the self-tender for shares from either the raider[51] or the other shareholders.[52] There is, of course, always a characterization issue whether a step taken by the board of directors or the company officers is a defensive maneuver.[53]

There are, of course, many other varieties and combinations of defensive tactics available to the target's management. A common feature of defensive maneuvers such as these is that they can be, and are, taken solely on the authority of the board of directors, without prior authorization or approval by the corporation's shareholders. The most frequently invoked measures are discussed in the next two sections.

[2] Porcupine Provisions

A quite different type of defensive measure is the preventive measure, frequently called a "shark repellent" or "porcupine" provision. These measures place in the corporation's articles of incorporation or bylaws a provision or provisions designed not only to protect the corporation's shareholders from certain harmful effects that may accompany a shift in control but also to discourage attempts to make a hostile bid for control.

Three types of shark repellent or porcupine provisions have been identified. The first type of amendment impedes the transfer of corporate control. This includes a staggering of directors' terms of office, which necessarily increases the time it will take to effect a turnover in management, the use of a classified board, a provision that the removal of directors requires cause, the reservation to the board of the right to fill vacancies or add directors, the limitation of the use of consent and special meetings, and the setting of the date for shareholder meetings.[54] Management may further attempt to lock in these provisions by requiring a supermajority to further amend the charter or bylaws.[55]

The second type of amendment creates barriers to the second step in two-tiered transactions by requiring a supermajority for the authorization of a merger following a tender offer.[56] The percentage required is usually chosen as the average number of shareholders who regularly attend the meetings, so that near unanimity at the meetings is required. Often management collectively controls enough stock to block the required supermajority.

The third type, the fair price amendment, is different from the first two in that, while it may deter a corporate raider, it operates mainly to benefit the shareholders rather than to preserve the management. A fair price amendment may be passed to waive the supermajority requirement for approval of a merger if the second-step buyout price is above a specified amount. Another amendment of this type grants shareholders the right to have their shares redeemed at a certain price after a partial tender offer. This right of redemption is derived from the English Companies Act[57] and was apparently first used in the United States in 1978. It deters tender offers because it removes control from them over how many shares they must purchase and it gives the target shareholders an incentive not to tender their shares at the initial offering.

Much controversy remains over whether the use of various defensive tactics is legal, is within the power of the management at all, or is a breach of management's fiduciary obligations,[58] and whether such use has a positive or negative impact on economic and public policy.[59]

§ 23.6 DEFENSIVE MANEUVERS AND THE BUSINESS JUDGMENT RULE

The most commonly used template for assessing defending control is *Unocal v. Mesa Petroleum Company*,[60] where the Delaware Supreme Court embraced a two-step process for judging defensive maneuvers. Under the first step, incumbents have the burden of proving they acted in good faith after reasonable investigation.[61] *Unocal* calls for the burden of proof to be placed on the target board of directors because of the "omnipresent specter that a board may be acting primarily in its own interests, rather than those of the corporation and its shareholders."[62] The second step of the *Unocal* test demands that the defensive measure "must be reasonable in relation to the threat posed."[63] This standard, interpreted literally, suggests courts are required to balance the particular defensive maneuver against the harm threatened by a particular bid. Such an approach necessarily invites more scrutiny of the directors' decisions than normally occurs when the court has already satisfied itself that the directors have acted in good faith after reasonable investigation. However, this step has been largely eroded in later decisions, discussed below.

At the opposite end of this interpretation of *Unocal* is the belief that the two steps in fact collapse into one, such that a board satisfying its burden of proving it acted in good faith after reasonable investigation can "just say no." In one of the most significant corporate decisions of the twentieth century, *Paramount Communications, Inc. v. Time, Inc.*,[64] the Delaware Supreme Court interpreted *Unocal's* reasonable relationship standard as being much closer to the "just say no" approach than to one inviting acute assessments of the proportionality between the defensive maneuver and the perceived threat. The Delaware Supreme Court deemed the alteration of the acquisition's consideration from stock to cash as a defensive maneuver that should be examined under *Unocal*.[65] In a major victory for target company directors, *Paramount* holds that the nature of the threat for which defensive measures can be crafted transcends questions of fair price or a coercive offer. For example, in *Paramount* the bid posed a threat to Time's preexisting long-range strategic plans as well as running the risk of confusing the shareholders' approval of a stock-for-stock transaction had that plan been submitted to the Time shareholders for their approval.

The Delaware court has since made it clear that even under the enhanced review standard of *Unocal*, a corporation's board has a wide range of discretion in reacting to hostile takeover attempts. Indeed, there is cause to doubt that little additional scrutiny is introduced through the second step of *Unocal*. A showing of preclusion has replaced the earlier proportionality test first embraced in *Unocal*. Moreover, in considering whether a board has acted improperly in refusing to redeem the corporation's poison pill so that a formal takeover of the firm can be considered by the stockholders, the Delaware courts have assumed that the theoretical possibility of a proxy contest renders the pill non-preclusive. Also, under *Unocal's* first step, though the burden of proof is on the target management a good deal of deference still is accorded its decision.[66] Unless the defensive measures are "draconian" or outside a "range of reasonableness," the board's response should be upheld. A defensive measure is draconian when it is either coercive or preclusive.[67] As explained by the Delaware Supreme Court, "[w]hen a corporation is not for sale, the board of directors is the defender of the metaphorical medieval corporate bastion and the protector of the corporation's shareholders."[68] A court should not substitute its judgment for that of the board of directors.[69] Delaware courts place an especially high burden of proving fairness when the primary purpose of the board's defensive action is to interfere with the shareholders' voting franchise. In such a case, the defendants must present a "compelling justification" for the action.[70] As observed by the Delaware Supreme Court, this heightened standard of review "is quite onerous, and is therefore applied rarely."[71] The highly deferential view reflects not just the unwillingness of courts to enter the role of business decision makers, but also their likely awareness that they would not be very good at such inquiries if they chose to be more active. When a corporation is not for sale,[72] the board of directors thus is given considerable discretion in repelling hostile assaults. Thus, as in *Time*, when a proposed acquisition does not coincide with the target company's established long-term business plan, it may reject the offer to merge.[73] A central consideration in the *Unocal* analysis is the perceived "threat" posed by the unwanted suitor.

§ 23.7 SPECIFIC TYPES OF DEFENSIVE MANEUVERS

Nowhere is the lawyer's creativity better documented than in the seemingly endless varieties of defensive maneuvers that have developed and continue to evolve. Moreover, the flexibility—or perhaps the indeterminacy—of the prevailing review standards (as seen in *Unocal*, discussed in the preceding section) becomes quite evident in examining how the very different features that distinguish defensive maneuvers from one another are treated under *Unocal*.

Poison Pills. The most common type of defensive measure is a shareholder rights plan, more commonly known as a "poison pill." The device begins with a corporation's distribution, generally in the form of dividend, of "rights" pro rata among its stockholders. A right entitles its holder to purchase stock or other security upon a certain triggering event. The precise triggering (or activating) event depends on the type of pill. As will be seen, in the "flip-over" variety of pill, the triggering event is a second-step transaction, such as a merger or asset purchase by the bidder of the target corporation. In the "flip-in" variety of pill, the triggering event is usually a first-step transaction, such as the bidder launching a tender offer for, or completing the purchase of, a certain percentage of the corporation's stock—for example, 20 percent of its outstanding stock. The precise right that a holder has upon the triggering event's occurrence depends on the type of poison pill.[74]

A flip-over poison pill allows the target company's shareholders to acquire the bidder's stock at a substantial discount, usually at half price (for example, the purchase of $200 worth of the bidder's common shares by paying only $100) if the two corporations merge. The flip-over pill becomes operative, therefore, when the bidder, after acquiring a substantial ownership interest in the target, merges the target into itself or another entity that it controls. The overall effect of the target shareholders' exercising their flip-over rights is to dilute substantially the value of the bidder's common shares. It is because of this possibility that the flip-over provision acts as a disincentive to unwanted suitors. Its primary benefit to the target shareholders is to protect them against an unfair, coercive second-step merger that forces them to give up their target shares for securities or cash of the bidder.

Another variety of poison pill is the "back-end" plan, under which the target corporation's board of directors designates a price deemed fair for the target shares. Thereafter, the target shareholders have a right to require the target corporation to acquire their shares at that price, provided the bidder has not already acquired the shares at that price. As with the flip-over pill, the primary objective of a back-end pill is to protect stockholders from a coercive second-step merger.

The flip-over pill is not operative, however, if the bidder does not merge with the target. Thus a flip-over provision can be avoided if the bidder operates the target as a controlled subsidiary. Even this arrangement does little to salve the unease that the target management may have for the unwanted bidder. Target management is not without mechanisms to discourage a nonmerging bidder—it may resort to a flip-in poison pill. A flip-in rights plan allows the holders to acquire stock or other securities of the target company at prices substantially below their market value. The triggering event for the flip-in pill is generally the bidder announcing a tender offer for a certain percentage of the target's shares and/or its purchase of a stated percentage of the target's shares. Because the amount specified is generally in the 20 percent to 30 percent range, the flip-in pill can be triggered even though control may not in fact be threatened.[75]

Consequently, if the rights are triggered and thereafter exercised by their holders, the cost of the acquisition to the bidder increases substantially as the value of its holdings is diluted by the ability of other holders to purchase additional shares of the target below their fair market value. The potency of poison pills in dampening the appetite of would-be suitors of target corporations has been documented by several studies that reflect that negative stock effects accompany the adoption of poison pills.

Poison pills have spawned a good deal of litigation regarding their validity under state statutes and the directors' fiduciary obligations with respect to a poison pill defense.[76] A common and necessary feature of any rights plan is that the bidder receives no rights and cannot acquire any rights from another. That is, the dilutive effects vis-à-vis the bidder could easily be overcome by the bidder's purchase of the rights from their holders, if those rights could be so acquired. Thus rights plans commonly provide that the rights are not issued to the bidder and are not transferable. Some courts have invalidated rights plans because of their discriminatory treatment within the same class of shares.[77] Rights plans that do not include the bidder can have unanticipated and unwanted effects even if the rights are nontransferrable.[78]

In the leading case applying *Unocal* to uphold the adoption of a poison pill, the Delaware Supreme Court reasoned that a flip-over provision was analogous to the antidilution provisions that customarily exist to protect holders of senior securities in mergers.[79] With this predicate, the court then reasoned that a poison pill was a reasonable and proportional response to a threat of a harmful second-step coercive merger at a price unfair to the target shareholders. The court emphasized that the rights were redeemable prior to their activation by the triggering event. The rights' redemption feature is a key element to their legal validity as a takeover defense and is central to understanding why poison pills are created in the first place.

The target directors cannot refuse to redeem the pill in the face of an offer that is neither coercive nor unfair on its face.[80] On the other hand, there are a larger number of decisions that evidence the patience and deference courts accord the target board of directors' decision not to redeem the pill, at least to the extent of allowing the target board to devise or execute a plan for a greater return for the target shareholders.[81]

The most draconian form of the poison pill is the "dead hand" poison pill, so named because its distinguishing feature is its continuing director provision, which permits the rights to be redeemed only by the directors who were in office when the rights plan was put into place. Thus, under a dead-hand poison pill a new board of directors, whose members support the firm's acquisition, cannot redeem the rights that stand as an obstacle to the firm being acquired. On its face, such a continuing director provision conflicts directly with the well-established principle that contractual provisions that restrain the discretion of the board of directors are void as against public policy. Emphasizing the strong public policy in the boards' power to manage the affairs of the corporation, the New York Supreme Court invalidated a dead-hand poison pill.[82] The Delaware Supreme Court invalidated what it described as a "no hand" or "delayed redemption provision" of a rights plan.[83] The delayed redemption provision provided that, if the shareholders replace a majority of the directors, the newly elected board could not redeem the rights for six months if the purpose or effect of the redemption were to facilitate a transaction with an "interested person." The court explained that such a provision, by limiting the new directors' ability to redeem a poison pill, could prevent them from authorizing a transaction that their fiduciary duty would otherwise require.[84]

Who has the final word in the adoption of poison pills—the shareholders or directors? The pill comes into existence by the fiat of the board of directors exercising its authority under the "blank stock" provision of the articles of incorporation. Having the general authority to issue shares with such "rights, privileges and preferences" as the board believes is appropriate, no further approval from the stockholders is necessary for the rights to be issued.[85]

Issuer Repurchases and Restructurings. One response that target management can make to a hostile bid, believed to offer an inadequate amount for the target corporation's shares, is to develop a plan that offers a greater amount. The simplest approach is for the target corporation to initiate its own tender offer for a certain percentage of its shares. This is unlikely to thwart the unwanted bid, however, as target shareholders would still be able to tender to the bidder the shares that were not acquired by the target in its self-tender offer. Thus, all that a simply designed self-tender offer accomplishes is to reduce ultimately the number of shares the bidder must purchase to obtain control (that is, after the target corporation's self-tender, there are fewer outstanding shares, so control requires an absolute smaller number of shares to be held). To scuttle an unwanted offer, a self-tender offer must be structured so as to coerce the shareholders to choose the issuer's offer over that of the outside bidder.[86] Such an effect has been held to violate *Unocal* because of its coercive nature and because it likely will not be judged to be reasonably related to the threat posed when the bidder's offer was for all the outstanding shares.[87] Recall that the defensive maneuver upheld in *Unocal* was a self-tender offer that excluded the shares of the hostile bidder; that offer was upheld, however, because the bidder's offer posed the threat of a second-step, unfair cash-out merger of the target shares not acquired in its first-step tender offer. A repurchase is also effective if it causes the insiders' percentage ownership to increase such that they can veto any actions of the unwanted suitor.[88] When the outside bid is for *all* the target shares, the target shareholders have the freedom to compare that offer with what is offered by the target management. Thus, there appears no practical justification to protect the corporation or the shareholders from the coercive features of target management's response.[89]

A means for the target to offer greater value than is being offered in the hostile tender offer is to undertake a restructuring of the corporation. Restructuring includes a variety of ways by which a corporation can generate cash to distribute pro rata among its stockholders by selling major divisions and by borrowing significant amounts of money with the effect of increasing the financial leverage within its capital structure. After these steps are taken, the existing shareholders are offered a package of securities (equity and debt) and cash that in combination have a value greater than that offered by the hostile bid. Many successful restructurings are indistinguishable in their effects from a leverage buyout, as the target corporation borrows to the full extent of is debt capacity, raising concerns for future financial distress that may require additional asset disposals to reduce the crushing burden of its newly incurred debt. Courts have been reluctant to enjoin restructurings, viewing them as alternative means to maximize the value of the firm for the benefit of its shareholders.[90]

Greenmail. Another form a defensive repurchase can take is "greenmail," whereby the target board of directors approves the corporation acquiring the target shares held by a raider at a premium above-market price so as to fend off a takeover.[91] For such a purchase to be protected by the business judgment rule, the record must reveal a good faith, reasonable belief of the target board of directors that the corporate interest is served by the repurchase. In a few instances, the courts have ruled favorably on pretrial motions brought by plaintiffs challenging a greenmail transaction.[92] In response to concern over greenmail, the Tax Reform Act of 1986 included provisions that disallow any deduction "for any amount paid or incurred by a corporation in connection with the redemption of its stock,"[93] and in 1987 Congress imposed a 50 percent excise tax on the gain or other income arising from a payment that is not made on the same terms to all shareholders.[94] The tax laws, therefore, provide a substantial disincentive for greenmail transactions.

Share Issuances and ESOPS. The most direct assault on a hostile bid is by the target board of directors issuing a substantial block of voting shares to a holder who can be depended on to support the incumbent management team.[95] In such a situation, the target board of directors has a heavy burden of proof either that its primary motive in approving the issuance of shares was not related to control of the corporation[96] or that the hostile bid posed a threat to the corporation or its shareholders. A common form this defensive maneuver takes is the target corporation issuing shares to an employee stock ownership plan (ESOP). ESOPs are tax-favored devices[97] designed to provide retirement benefits for a corporation's employees through the collective stock ownership of their employer.

Challenges to ESOPs on the grounds that they are an invalid defensive maneuver have largely depended on whether the reviewing court is persuaded that the primary motive for transferring shares to the ESOP was to entrench management. Absent evidence that the corporate interest is in improving employee morale and productivity, an ESOP adopted in the heat of a takeover will most likely be enjoined.[98]

Lock-up Options and Other Deal Protection Arrangements. When confronted by two or more opposing bids for control, target management sometimes enters into an arrangement with one of the bidders that has the effect of conferring on that bidder a significant strategic advantage in the contest for control vis-à-vis the other bidders. These arrangements can take several forms, such as an option by the preferred bidder to acquire significant target assets at a favorable price (called a "lock-up option"), an agreement not to seek other bidders (called a "no-shop clause"), the payment of a significant fee if that bidder's offer does not result in the bidder obtaining control (called a "termination fee," "hello fee" or "goodbye fee"),[99] or agreeing to share certain proprietary/inside information only with that bidder. Because of their dampening effect on continued bidding for control, these arrangements are correctly characterized as defensive maneuvers and will be examined under *Unocal*. They also are more frequently examined under the special requirements of *Revlon*, discussed in the next section.

Termination fees can be examined either under contract law, where the question is whether it is an enforceable provision for liquidated damages or under corporate law. Under the former the first question is whether damages would be uncertain if the deal were not consummated. If so uncertain, the final test of the provisions validity is whether the amount so stated is reasonable.[100]

Another common provision requires a board to submit the merger proposal to its shareholders or bars the target management from actively pursuing other bidders. Each type of agreement inherently restricts the freedom of a board of directors and meets the historical reluctance of courts to uphold agreements that interfere with the directors' discretion. That is, the board of director's fiduciary obligation is paramount to any contractual obligation.[101] At the same time, the contractual requirements cannot simply be ignored under the guise that the directors are fiduciaries.[102] Hence, there is an interesting dynamic that arises whereby the validity of the contractual restrictions is assessed in terms of whether ex ante entering into the contractual restrictions was pursuant to the directors' fiduciary responsibilities.[103] In a leading case,[104] the Delaware Supreme Court held that merger agreement terms that mandated directors act in a certain fashion or that the directors forbear were invalid. Thus, the Delaware Supreme Court held that a no-shop provision was unenforceable because it unduly restricted the board in fulfilling its fiduciary duties in responding to changing circumstances that typically occur in takeover contests.[105] However, the case is distinctive because the merger posed a change of control such that the company had entered the *Revlon* moment, discussed below, and was not seen as the product of the board acting in a deliberate and open-minded manner.

In another case,[106] the Delaware Supreme Court struck down a deal protection provision because it failed to include a "fiduciary out" provision. The majority opinion reasoned that although the minority holders were not forced to vote in favor of the merger, they were required to accept it because when coupled with the voting agreement with the majority holders the minority holders were effectively presented with a *fait accompli*.[107] Moreover, the court found this deal protection provision was outside the range of reasonableness as absent a fiduciary out provision the measure made "mathematically impossible" for any other proposal to succeed.[108]

The Delaware legislature enacted a limited "force the vote" provision, which provides that a "corporation may agree to submit a matter to a vote of its stockholders whether or not the board of directors determines at any time subsequent to approving such matter that such matter is no longer advisable and recommends that the shareholders reject or vote against the matter."[109] Several other states have also followed Delaware and provide express statutory authority for directors to agree to submit an acquisition proposal to their shareholders.[110] However, none of the enacting states removes the power for the directors to either make no recommendation or to recommend that the stockholders reject the proposal.

Many state provisions permit the board to submit mergers to their shareholders without a board recommendation.[111] Thus, the board, having this statutory option, could withhold its recommendations, make full disclosure of all the facts, and allow the shareholders then to decide whether to approve the acquisition. The crucial variables in determining the validity of such agreements are whether the agreement has the effect of terminating the "bidding process," whether the agreement was important in obtaining a bid from the present suitor or significantly improving its prior bid, and whether the target company has entered the *Revlon* moment, discussed below, because there is a prospective change of control. Standstill agreements entered into by parties exploring their possible combination also raise questions regarding the extent that the directors' discretion can be restrained.[112]

A unique defensive tactic used in recent years is the acquisition of another business by the target company, creating a potential antitrust threat to impending tender offers.[113] A somewhat related strategy of imposing a regulatory obstacle in the suitor's path is to purchase assets of a type such that any change in their ownership requires prior governmental clearance. For example, the purchase of a radio station or some other heavily regulated business can tie up the takeover attempt in any administrative proceedings that may be needed to approve a change of ownership in the regulated business. Another type of asset acquisition that becomes a defensive maneuver is the "Pac-Man" defense, where the target company makes a tender offer for control of the original tender offeror.[114]

§ 23.8 The Directors' Role as Auctioneers— The *"Revlon* Moment"

A significant qualification of *Unocal* was announced by the Delaware Supreme Court in *Revlon Inc. v. MacAndrews & Forbes Holdings, Inc.*,[115] which arose from the competing efforts to acquire control of Revlon Inc. The Delaware Supreme Court, pursuant to the language of the court, set out below, held was inconsistent with the duties of directors under the facts to become "auctioneers." *Revlon* is a qualification of *Unocal* rather than an alternative. It does not prohibit defensive maneuvers but requires that their reasonableness be measured not in terms of the threat to control but by the objective of obtaining the best offer for the target shareholders. Thus *Revlon* does not prohibit lock-up options when the directors have entered the *"Revlon* moment." The court stated "A lock-up is not per se illegal under Delaware law.... Such options can entice other bidders to enter a contest for control of the corporation, creating an auction for the company and maximizing shareholder profit."[116] Because the lock-up did not result in a substantial improvement in the existing bid and did not attract a new bidder to the contest, the court viewed its only impact as bringing the intense bidding contest to a close for an insubstantial benefit to the target shareholders. *Revlon* can be seen as a natural extension of *Unocal* in the sense that both cases set standards for the target board of directors to act in their shareholders' best interest.

The mere commencement of a hostile bid does not trigger *Revlon* duties on the part of the target directors, even though that offer puts the target company into play.[117] In the period immediately following, *Revlon*, Delaware Supreme Court decisions vaguely identified three alternative bases for applying *Revlon*'s auctioneering standard:[118] (1) When the target initiates an active bidding process seeking to sell itself or effect a restructuring that will lead to the break-up of the company;[119] (2) When the target abandons its long-term strategy and seeks an alternative plan that entails the break-up of the company;[120] (3) Where the effect of the plan supported by the target board of directors is to bring about a change in control of the corporation.[121]

Revlon's reach today is in the "change of control" situation.[122] *Revlon* demands that the board's actions in favoring or disfavoring a particular bidder must have a reasonable relation to the advantage sought to be obtained.[123] The target board can enter into arrangements with one bidder that "tilt the playing field," provided doing so is in the shareholders' interest.[124] Thus, an asset lock-up such as that struck down in *Revlon* is valid when undertaken to draw a new bidder into the contest or to entice a present bidder to change materially its prior bid.[125] The auctioneering duty requires a quest of the best offer that, because of timing and valuation considerations, is not synonymous with the highest price.[126] At the same time, there is no duty to seek additional bidders when a company is confronted by a hostile bid or is negotiating a friendly combination.[127] Traditional business judgment rule considerations regarding the director's independence and reasonable investigation continue to assume even greater significance when the target board has entered the *Revlon* moment.[128] Since such judgments are made under the unique circumstances of the case, an important variable in assessing the board's performance is whether rigid deal protective provisions were concurred to which prevented the possibility of other bidders stepping forward.[129]

Quite independent of *Revlon* is the more general question of whether directors can, consistent with their fiduciary duties, enter into an enforceable agreement with a bidder not to actively pursue or support competing offers. An early federal decision held that directors can at least bind themselves not to *accept* a competing merger offer until the shareholders have voted on an initial agreement.[130] The Nebraska Supreme Court held that directors were bound by the fiduciary duties to the shareholders to submit with a favorable recommendation a subsequent higher bid, even though they had agreed with an earlier bidder to support that offer.[131] Importantly, the Delaware Supreme Court has held that contractual provisions that bar the board of directors from actively pursuing another bidder must complement the directors' fiduciary obligations. Thus directors who have entered the *Revlon* moment cannot enter into a no-shop agreement if it is inconsistent with their likelihood of securing a better offer through the pursuit of other bidders and bids.[132]

Outside of Delaware, *Revlon* has had a checkered fate. Persuaded by the experience of the Delaware courts, *Revlon* is frequently adopted as the applicable standard.[133] On the other hand, many courts believe the standard business judgment rule, including its presumption the directors have acted properly, is the appropriate approach.[134] There also is the view that directors are not under a duty to initiate an auction when control is to be transferred;[135] such a view rejects the fundamental tenet of *Revlon*.

Notes

1. Sterling v. Mayflower Hotel Corp., 93 A.2d 107, 109–110 (Del. 1952). *See also* McMullin v. Beran, 765 A.2d 910 (Del. 2000) (directors who approved unfair merger at the insistence of the controlling stockholder and did not adequately inform themselves will be deemed to have breached their fiduciary duty).
2. *Sterling*, 93 A.2d 107, 114 (Del. 1952).
3. *See, e.g.*, Mills v. Electric Auto-Lite Co., 552 F.2d 1239 (7th Cir.), *cert. denied*, 434 U.S. 922 (1977).
4. *See* Weinberger v. UOP, Inc., 457 A.2d 701 (Del. 1983).
5. *See* Rabkin v. Philip A. Hunt Chem. Corp., 498 A.2d 1099 (Del. 1985). *See also* Cede & Co. v. Technicolor, Inc., 542 A.2d 1182 (Del. 1988).
6. *See Weinberger*, 457 A.2d 701, 711 (Del. 1983).
7. *See* Parnes v. Bally Entm't Corp., 722 A.2d 1243 (Del. 1999) (allegations that chairman and controlling stockholder favored his interests over interests of other shareholders tainted entire process such that if established fair dealing part of "entire fairness" standard would not have been satisfied).
8. *See* Rosenblatt v. Getty Oil Co., 493 A.2d 929, 937–939 (Del. 1985).
9. Kahn v. Tremont Corp., 694 A.2d 422 (Del. 1997).
10. Abelow v. Symonds, 173 A.2d 167 (Del. Ch. 1961) (sale of subsidiary's assets to parent required hearing to determine fairness of selling price).
11. Lerner v. Lerner Corp., 750 A.2d 709, 711 (Md. Ct. App. 2000).
12. *See Weinberger*, 457 A.2d 701 (Del. 1983).
13. *See* Cinerama, Inc. v. Technicolor, Inc., 663 A.2d 1156, 1179 (Del. 1995).
14. Ryan v. Tad's Enters., Inc., 709 A.2d 682, 690 (Del. Ch. 1996).
15. Glassman v. Unocal Exploration Corp., 777 A.2d 242 (Del. 2001).
16. *Id.*
17. 672 A.2d 35 (Del. 1996).
18. *In re Pure Resources, Inc. Shareholder Litigation*, 808 A.2d 421 (Del. Ch. 2002).
19. *E.g.*, M&W, Inc. v. Pac. Guardian Life Ins. Co., Ltd., 966 P.2d 1098 (Haw. Ct. 1998); Gabhart v. Gabhart, 370 N.E.2d 345 (Ind. 1977).
20. Roland Int'l Corp. v. Najjar, 407 A.2d 1032 (Del. 1979).
21. Singer v. Magnavox Co., 380 A.2d 969 (Del. 1977).
22. *Weinberger*, 457 A.2d 701 (Del. 1983).
23. *E.g.*, Bryan v. Brock & Blevins Co., Inc., 490 F.2d 563 (5th Cir. 1974) (Georgia law); *Gabhart*, 370 N.E.2d 345 (Ind. 1977).
24. Lichtenberger v. Long Island Mach. Sales Corp., 420 N.Y.S.2d 507 (App. Div. 1979).
25. *See* Lynch v. Vickers Energy Corp., 383 A.2d 278 (Del. 1977).
26. SEC Rule 13e-3, 17 C.F.R. § 240.13e-3 (2009).
27. Bird v. Wirtz, 266 N.W.2d 166 (Minn. 1978); Berkowitz v. Power/Mate Corp., 342 A.2d 566 (N.J. Super. Ch. Ct. 1975).
28. 17 C.F.R. § 240.10b-5 (2009).
29. 15 U.S.C. § 78n(e) (2009).
30. 17 C.F.R. § 240.13e-4 (2009).
31. *Id.* § 240.13e-3.
32. 17 C.F.R. § 240.13e-3(a)(3) (2009).

33. *Id.* § 240.13e-3(g)(1).
34. *Id.* § 240.13e-3(g)(2).
35. *Id.* § 240.13e-3(g)(4).
36. *See, e.g.,* Brewer v. Lincoln Int'l Corp., 148 F. Supp. 2d 792 (W.D. Ky. 2000) (agreement by acquiring company with person controlling 90% of the voting power that the latter would vote in favor of a step necessary for the acquisition to occur in exchange for ultimately receiving 50% of the acquiring company could make the acquiring company an affiliate).
37. Rule 13e-3(f), 17 C.F.R. § 240.13e-3(f) (2009).
38. *See* 17 C.F.R. § 240.13e-100 (Item 8(a)) (2009).
39. *See* § 240.13e-100 (Item 8(b)).
40. *See id.*
41. Meyers Parking Sys., Inc., EXCHANGE ACT Release No. 26,069 [1988–1989 Transfer Binder] FED. SEC. L. REP. (CCH) ¶ 84,333 (1988).
42. *See* Virginia Bankshares, Inc. v. Sandberg, 501 U.S. 1083 (1991).
43. *See* Howing Co. v. Nationwide Corp., 826 F.2d 1470 (6th Cir. 1987), *cert. denied,* 486 U.S. 1059 (1988).
44. Although there is no statutory definition of "tender offer," both the courts and the SEC have taken an expansive approach to include certain privately negotiated control transfers and some open market purchases. *See, e.g.,* Wellman v. Dickinson, 475 F. Supp. 783 (S.D.N.Y. 1979) (privately negotiated "lock-up" of control).
45. *See, e.g.,* Radol v. Thomas, 534 F. Supp. 1302 (S.D. Ohio 1982).
46. *See, e.g.,* Smallwood v. Pearl Brewing Co., 489 F.2d 579 (5th Cir.), *cert. denied,* 419 U.S. 873 (1974).
47. *See, e.g.,* Piper v. Chris-Craft Indus., 430 U.S. 1 (1977).
48. Kaplan v. Goldsamt, 380 A.2d 556 (Del. Ch. 1977).
49. *See, e.g., Piper,* 430 U.S. 1 (1977).
50. A valid business purpose is required for the dilution. It is not allowable if merely a defensive tactic. *See* Norlin Corp. v. Rooney, Pace Inc., 744 F.2d 255 (2d Cir. 1984).
51. This is popularly known as submitting to "greenmail." *See* Cheff v. Mathes, 199 A.2d 548 (Del. 1964).
52. The leading case upholding the self-tender for shares excluding the shares owned by the raider is Unocal Corp. v. Mesa Petrol. Co., 493 A.2d 946 (Del. 1985) (corporate self-tender for shares excluding the shareholder making the hostile tender offer is allowable if there is any rational business purpose for doing so).
53. *See, e.g.,* Williams v. Geier, 671 A.2d 1368 (Del. 1996) (recapitalization that was supported by owners of more than 50% of the voting shares that had the effect of entrenching their control was not defensive maneuver).
54. *See* Mentor Graphics Corp. v. Quickturn Design Sys., Inc., 728 A.2d 25, 40–41 (Del. Ch. 1998) (upholding bylaw amendment providing that special meeting could not be convened in less than 90–100 days).
55. *See* Chesapeake Corp. v. Shore, 771 A.2d 293, 343 (Del. Ch. 2000) (bylaw amendment required a 90% shareholder turnout for approval deemed to be preclusive, and if not preclusive, was unreasonable to the threat posed).
56. Young v. Valhi, Inc., 382 A.2d 1372 (Del. Ch. 1978) (charter provision required approval of 80% of the issued and outstanding common shares in

order to accomplish a merger with any offeror holding at least 5% of the corporation's stock).

57. 11 & 12 GEO. 6, ch. 38, § 209(2) (1948).

58. *See, e.g.,* Asarco Inc. v. Court, 611 F. Supp. 468 (D.N.J. 1985) (blank-check preferred stock defense is *ultra vires* and void. Unlawful discrimination between shareholders of the same class).

59. John C. Coffee, Jr., *Regulating the Market for Corporate Control: A Critical Assessment of the Tender Offer's Role in Corporate Governance,* 84 COLUM. L. REV. 1145 (1984).

60. 493 A.2d 946, 954 (Del. 1985).

61. *Id.*

62. *Id.*

63. *Id.*

64. 571 A.2d 1140 (Del. 1989).

65. *Id.*

66. Unitrin, Inc. v. Am. Gen. Corp., 651 A.2d 1361 (Del. 1995).

67. "This court's choice of the term 'draconian' in *Unocal* was a recognition that the law affords boards of directors substantial latitude in defending the perimeter of the corporate bastion against perceived threats.... [D]epending upon the circumstances, the board may respond to a reasonably perceived threat by adopting individually or sometimes in combination: advance notice bylaws, supermajority voting provisions, shareholder rights plans, repurchase programs, etc." *Id.* at 1388 n.38.

68. *Unitrin,* 651 A.2d 1361, 1388 (Del. 1995).

69. The court in *Unitrin* overturned the Chancery Court's temporary restraining order and remanded for determination of whether the poison pill and repurchase program were within the range of reasonable defensive measures available to the board.

70. Blasius Indus. v. Atlas Corp., 564 A.2d 651 (Del. Ch. 1988).

71. Williams v. Geier, 671 A.2d 1368, 1376 (Del. 1996).

72. When a corporation's board of directors has placed the company up for sale, then the *Unocal* test does not apply and the board's duty is to maximize shareholder value.

73. Kahn v. MSB Bancorp, Inc., 1998 WL 409355 (Del. Ch. 1998), *aff'd,* 734 A.2d 158 (Del. 1999) (bank holding company that was in the process of acquiring another bank was justified in rejecting unsolicited merger proposal from another bank holding company).

74. For an unfortunate unintended result involving a flip-in provision, *see* Emeritus Corp. v. ARV Assisted Living, Inc., Case No. 793420 (Super. Ct. Orange Cnty. 1999) (issuing shares to friendly investment group inadvertently triggered rights plan that hostile bidder could take advantage of).

75. *See* Dynamics Corp. of Am. v. CTS Corp., 794 F.2d 250 (7th Cir. 1986), *rev'd on other grounds,* 481 U.S. 69 (1987) (invalidating flip-in pill where trigger was activated by bidder's purchase of 15% of the target shares, even though that bidder did not intend to seek control of bidder).

76. *See* Gearhart Indus. v. Smith Int'l, Inc., 741 F.2d 707 (5th Cir. 1984) ("springing" feature of warrant was not manipulative under section 14(e)).

77. *See* Avon Prod., Inc. v. Chartwell Assoc. L.P., 907 F.2d 322 (2d Cir. 1990).

78. *See, e.g., Emeritus Corp.*, Case No. 793420 (Super. Ct. Orange Cnty. 1999) (defensive tactic that involved issuing shares to friendly investment group inadvertently triggered rights plan that hostile bidder could take advantage of).

79. Moran v. Household Int'l, Inc., 500 A.2d 1346 (Del. 1985).

80. Grand Metro. Pub. Ltd. v. Pillsbury Co., 558 A.2d 1049 (Del. Ch. 1988) (restructuring response proposed by target management not clearly better than that of bidders because it would require long-term holdings to recoup predicted greater rewards than immediate cash all shares bid).

81. *See, e.g.,* Dynamics Corp. of Am. v. WHX Corp., 967 F. Supp. 59 (D. Conn. 1997) (concluding the plaintiff-bidder continued to have the inferior offer so that pill need not be redeemed to preserve merger with another company offer greater premium).

82. *See* Bank of N.Y. Co. v. Irving Bank Corp., 528 N.Y.S.2d 482 (Sup. Ct. 1988).

83. Quickturn Design Systems, Inc. v. Shapiro, 721 A.2d 1281 (Del. 1998).

84. *Id.*

85. *See* Leonard Loventhal Account v. Hilton Hotels Corp., 780 A.2d 245 (Del. 2001) (power recognized by *Moran* would be meaningless if rights plan required stockholder approval).

86. For a close analysis that defensive repurchases, like third-party tender offers, pressure firm shareholders and accordingly each should be similarly regulated, *see* Michael Bradley & Michael Rozenzweig, *Defensive Stock Repurchases*, 99 HARV. L. REV. 1377 (1986).

87. *See* AC Acquisitions Corp. v. Anderson, Clayton & Co., 519 A.2d 103 (Del. Ch. 1986).

88. *See* Am. Gen. Corp. v. Unitrin, Inc., 1994 WL 698483 (Del. Ch. 1994).

89. This point was recognized in Shamrock Holdings, Inc. v. Polaroid Corp., 559 A.2d 278 (Del. Ch. 1989), but management's coercive self-tender offer was not enjoined because the court was persuaded that shareholders would have difficulty comparing the two choices before them because of the indefiniteness of determining the future value of a significant patent infringement action the issuer had against another major corporation.

90. *See* British Printing & Commc'n Corp. v. Harcourt Brace Jovanovich, Inc., 664 F. Supp. 1519 (S.D.N.Y. 1987).

91. *See* David Manry & D. Strangeland, *Greenmail: A Brief History*, 6 STAN. J. L. & BUS. 217 (2001).

92. Heckman v. Ahmanson, 214 Cal. Rptr. 177 (Ct. App. 1985).

93. 26 U.S.C. § 162 (2000).

94. *Id.* § 5881.

95. *See, e.g.,* Unilever Acquisition Corp. v. Richardson-Vicks, Inc., 618 F. Supp. 407 (S.D.N.Y. 1985) (issuing preliminary injunction against dividend in preferred stock that would dilute the offeror's control).

96. *See, e.g.,* Klaus v. Hi-Shear Corp., 528 F.2d 225 (9th Cir. 1975) (injunction granted where target board failed to establish a compelling business justification for share issuance); Condec Corp. v. Lunkenheimer Co., 230 A.2d 769 (Del. Ch. 1967) (injunction granted where primary purpose was to preserve control).

97. An employer can establish an ESOP in many ways, but the maximum tax advantages arise if the funds for the shares contributed to the ESOP

are borrowed. The lender or employer can exclude from gross income 50% of the interest received from a loan to the employer or ESOP when the loan proceeds are used to acquire employer securities. In any case, employers are allowed to deduct the dividends paid on the ESOP shares when those dividends are distributed by the ESOP or the employer to the plan's participants. Finally, when an ESOP is created by the termination of a qualified plan, any excess assets that existed in the qualified plan that are transferred to the ESOP are exempt from the 10% excise tax that otherwise applies. *See generally* CCH GUIDE TO EMPLOYEE BENEFITS ¶¶ 271–277 (1986).

98. *See, e.g.,* Norlin Corp. v. Rooney, Pace Inc., 744 F.2d 255 (2d Cir. 1984) (requires proof of a basis independent from threat posed by bidder for creation of ESOP).

99. *See, e.g., In re* Lear Corp. Shareholder Litig., 967 A.2d 640 (Del. Ch. 2008) (not outside business judgment rule to approve $25 million termination fee in exchange for suitor increasing bid $1.25 per share when shareholder disapproval looked likely and there were no other suitors).

100. *See* Brazen v. Bell Atl. Corp., 695 A.2d 43, 48 (Del. 1997) (relying upon Lee Builders v. Wells, 103 A.2d 918 (Del. Ch. 1954)).

101. *See* Paramount Commc'ns v. QVC Network Inc., 637 A.2d 34 (Del. 1994).

102. *See* Corwin v. deTrey, 16 DEL. J. CORP. L. 267 (Del. Ch. 1989).

103. *See* Great Western Producers Coop. v. Great Western United Corp., 613 P.2d 873 (Colo. 1980).

104. *Paramount v. QVC,* 637 A.2d 34, 38–41 (Del. 1994).

105. *Id. Compare, eg.,* Ace Ltd. v. Capital Re Corp., 747 A.2d 95 (Del. Ch. 1999).

106. Omnicare, Inc. v. NCS Healthcare, Inc., 818 A.2d 914 (Del. 2003).

107. *Id.* at 936.

108. *Id.*

109. DEL. CODE ANN. tit. 8, § 146.

110. *See* MD. CODE ANN. § 3-105(d) (Michie 2007); MINN. STAT. ANN. § 302A.613 (Supp. 2008) (Repealing earlier provision and authorizing submission to shareholders even if board changes opinion of proposed offer); OKLA. STAT. tit. 18, ch. 22, § 1027(I) (Supp. 2006).

111. *See, e.g.,* DEL. CODE ANN. tit. 8, § 251(c) (2001); MBCA § 11.04(b) (1999). *See* William T. Allen, *Understanding Fiduciary Outs: The What and the Why of an Anomalous Concept,* 55 BUS. LAW. 658 (2000).

112. *See* Crane Co. v. Coltec Ind., Inc., 171 F.3d 733 (2d Cir. 1999) (interpreting notice requirement of a standstill agreement).

113. *See* Consol. Gold Fields PLC v. Minorco, S.A., 871 F.2d 252 (2d Cir. 1989) (affirming the issuance of a preliminary injunction against tender offer on antitrust grounds).

114. *See* Martin Marietta Corp. v. Bendix Corp., 549 F. Supp. 623 (D. Md. 1982).

115. 506 A.2d 173 (Del. 1986).

116. *Id.* at 173, 183.

117. *See* Paramount Commc'ns, Inc. v. Time Inc., 571 A.2d 1140, 1151 (Del. 1989).

118. *See* Odyssey Partners, L.P. v. Fleming Cos., Inc., 735 A.2d 386 (Del. Ch. 1999).
119. Flake v. Hoskins, 55 F. Supp. 2d 1196, 1215 (D. Kan. 1999) (applying Missouri law which stated to parallel Delaware to conclude that seeking a white knight does not constitute shopping the firm such as to trigger *Revlon*).
120. 571 A.2d at 1151.
121. *Paramount v. QVC*, 637 A.2d 34 (Del. 1994).
122. Lyondell Chem. Co. v. Ryan, 970 A.2d 235 (Del. 2009).
123. *See, e.g.,* Black & Decker Corp. v. Am. Standard, Inc., 682 F. Supp. 772, 786 (D. Del. 1988) (triggering of contractual rights in pension plan and officer's if third party acquired control deemed unfair treatment of third party versus the favored MBO participants).
124. *See* West Point-Pepperell, Inc. v. J.P. Stevens Co., 542 A.2d 770 (Del. Ch. 1988).
125. *See, e.g.,* Cottle v. Storer Commc'n, Inc., 849 F.2d 570 (11th Cir. 1988).
126. Citron v. Fairchild Camera & Instrument Corp., 569 A.2d 53 (Del. 1989) (upholding board's preference of $66 cash offer for all shares over $70 cash offer for 42% of the company with the remaining shares to be later acquired in a share-for-share exchange).
127. *See* Barkan v. Amsted Indus., 567 A.2d 1279 (Del. 1989).
128. *See, e.g.,* Hanson Trust PLC v. ML SCM Acquisition, Inc., 781 F.2d 264 (2d Cir. 1986).
129. *In re* Pennaco Energy, Inc. Shareholders Litig., 787 A.2d 691, 705-07 (Del. Ch. 2001).
130. *See* Jewel Co. v. Pay Less Drug Stores Nw., 741 F.2d 1555 (9th Cir. 1984).
131. *See* ConAgra, Inc. v. Cargill, Inc., 382 N.W.2d 576 (Neb. 1986).
132. *See Paramount v. QVC*, 637 A.2d 34 (Del. 1994).
133. *See, e.g.,* Priddy v. Edelman, 883 F.2d 438, 444 (6th Cir. 1989) (believing Michigan would follow *Revlon*, but nevertheless examined the case under the more restrained business judgment rule).
134. *See,* Hudson v. Prime Retail, Inc., 2004 WL 1982383 (Md. Cir. Ct. 2004) (in Maryland *Revlon*-like considerations within the business judgment rule and, thus, places the burden of proof on those challenging the directors' decisions in control transactions).
135. Lewis v. Celina Fin. Corp., 655 N.E.2d 1333 (Ohio. Ct. App. 1995).

CHAPTER 24

FEDERAL AND STATE TAKEOVER LAWS

§ 24.1 FEDERAL REGULATION OF TAKEOVERS

The Williams Act provisions impose disclosure requirements on various persons in connection with tender offers and stock acquisitions.[1] The required disclosures include identification of the entity launching the takeover attempt and a description of the purpose of the proposed action and related future plans. Disclosure is required of any person who acquires more than 5 percent of the outstanding shares of any class of equity security subject to the Act's reporting requirements.[2] This provision serves to prevent secret creeping acquisitions—that is, acquisitions in which the target company learns of the takeover attempt too late to take any action. At the same time, an overall effect of the Williams Act disclosure requirements as well as its many substantive rules regulating the conduct of tender offers is to increase the cost of a takeover, to increase the premiums that are paid to target shareholders, and to raise the uncertainty as to whether a bid for control will be successful.[3]

Under section 14(d), similar disclosure is required for "a tender offer for or request or invitation for tenders of" any equity security subject to the reporting requirements of the Exchange Act.[4] Disclosure and SEC filings must also be made by anyone resisting, opposing, or supporting any tender offer.[5] Section 14(e) of the Exchange Act is not limited to reporting companies; in effect it applies Rule 10b-5 standards to all conduct and statements in connection with a tender offer.[6]

Other rules and regulations that affect tender offers include SEC Rule 14e-5, which prohibits tender offerors from buying shares through means other than the tender offer itself,[7] and Rule 14e-4, which prohibits short tendering and hedged tendering during a tender offer.[8] Rules 14e-1[9] and 14e-2[10] govern the behavior of the tender offeror and the target management, respectively. Rule 14(e)-3 is a general prohibition of insider trading during a tender offer.[11]

While section 14(e) provides an express remedy only for the SEC or criminal enforcement,[12] the bulk of 14(e) litigation has arisen from implied private causes of action.[13] Section 14(e) is the preferred provision to proceed under, as it depends on the plaintiff's status as a target of some deceptive act in connection with a tender offer rather than on the narrower purchaser/seller requirement of Rule 10b-5.[14] There remains some question as to the requirement of scienter.[15] It seems clear, however, that section 14(e) does require detrimental reliance in order to establish a private remedy.[16]

In proceeding under 14(e), the plaintiff may be the tender offeror (but not a defeated tender offeror seeking damages),[17] the target management,[18] or shareholders of the target company.[19] There is no set definition of "manipulation," and there has been much controversy as to what is required for a 14(e) action. The Supreme Court examined this question and held that in order to state a cause of action there must be some element of non-disclosure, misrepresentation, or deception.[20] Accordingly, fully disclosed conduct that may be manipulative will not support an implied cause of action.

§ 24.2 FILING REQUIREMENTS OF SECTION 13(D)

Any person other than the issuer who acquires, directly or indirectly, beneficial ownership[21] of more than 5 percent of a class of equity security registered pursuant to section 12 of the 1934 Act[22] must file appropriate disclosures with the SEC within 10 days after reaching the five percent threshold, pursuant to section 13(d)(1).[23] In 2010, the SEC was given the authority to shorten the 10-day filing window. Somewhat similar disclosures are required of an issuer's purchases of its own shares (or through its affiliate) by virtue of section 13(e).[24]

Any person acquiring 5 percent of a class of equity securities must, within 10 days after reaching the 5 percent threshold, file with the Commission six copies of a statement reflecting the information required by section 13(d)(1).[25] Thus, under section 13(d)(1) the purchaser has a 10-day window between the crossing of the 5 percent threshold and the disclosure date. This gives the hostile bidder some important running space to gain momentum toward acquiring control of the target company. There is no express limitation on the amount of securities that may be purchased prior to filing the required Schedule 13D. An SEC advisory group recommended amending the rules to require filing in advance of the 5 percent purchase,[26] but no such change has taken place.

The appropriate filing under section 13(d)(1) is embodied in Schedule 13D.[27] Holders of less than 20 percent of the class of securities who certify that they do not have an intent to exercise control of the issuer (referred to as a "passive investor"), may use Schedule 13G in place of Schedule 13D.[28] Certain "qualified institutional investors" also may report their holdings on Schedule 13G regardless of whether their holdings are 20 percent or greater of a class of the issuer's securities, provided the institutional investor does not intend to control the issuer.[29] Passive investors must amend the Schedule 13G within 45 days after the end of the calendar year to report any change in information on their previous report.[30] Moreover, amendments to the Schedule 13G must occur "promptly" when the passive investor's holdings exceed 10 percent of the class of securities and thereafter a prompt amendment is required to report an increase or decrease by more than five percent when the passive investor's holdings are greater than 10 percent but less than 20 percent.[31] Finally, upon acquiring 20 percent or more, or, as pointed out below, upon a change of intent to control the issuer, the former passive investor is no longer considered passive and, therefore, must report the acquisition on Schedule 13D within 10 days and is subject to a "cooling off" period. During the cooling off period, the investor is prohibited from voting any securities of the issuer until 10 days after filing of a Schedule 13D.[32] A similar cooling off period applies when the passive investor or qualified institutional investor has a change of intent regarding controlling the issuer.[33]

The failure to make a timely Schedule 13D filing may result in an injunction against future purchases, at least until the violation is cured.[34] The SEC has also obtained disgorgement of profits made on shares acquired during the period between when a filing should have been made and when the defendant filed its Williams Act disclosures.[35]

The long-form Schedule 13D requires the following disclosures.[36] Item One must contain a description of the security purchased and its issuer. Item Two elicits information regarding the beneficial owner, including the principal business of the person making the filing and whether the filer has been convicted within the past five years of criminal violations or has been the subject of a civil order arising out of a violation of the securities laws. Item Three requires detailed disclosures of the source and amount of funds or other considerations being used to acquire the securities.[37] Item Four requires a description of the purpose(s) of the transaction, including any plans the purchaser may have that likely will result in a reorganization or a business combination such as mergers, consolidations, sales or acquisition of substantial assets, tender offers, changes in dividend policies and the like.[38] The level of detail is generally less when the shares are acquired only for investment.[39] Item Five requires the person filing the Schedule 13D to provide detailed information regarding the number of the target company's securities owned by the filer and its affiliates. Item

Six elicits descriptions of all contracts, arrangements, understandings, or relationships between the persons filing the Schedule 13D and any person with respect to the target company's securities.[40]

In addition to the initial filings, the person acquiring the 5 percent threshold must make amendments reflecting any significant changes in the information contained in Schedule 13D or 13G.[41] In determining whether a change in circumstances necessitates an amendment, the general doctrine of materiality is applicable.[42] Under SEC Rule 13d-2(a),[43] a 1 percent or larger change in beneficial ownership is presumptively a material change.

The greatest interpretative problems in completing Schedule 13D arise with respect to Item 4, which requires a description of the control aspirations of the purchasers. For example, a purchaser's intent to acquire a 20 percent equity interest, thereby obtaining some representation on the target company's board, was held to create an obligation to disclose a plan to acquire control.[44] In considering such questions, the courts have applied Rule 12b-2(f)'s definition of "control"[45] to determine when a purchaser's objective is to affect control. In view of the overall objective of the Williams Act amendments, which is to provide an early warning of a potential change in control, it is not surprising that disclosure of a control purpose is required even when the purchaser does not yet have a formalized concrete plan for exercising that control.[46]

By virtue of section 13(d)(3),[47] when two or more people combine their efforts, such as by forming a partnership, limited partnership, syndicate, or other group for the purpose of acquiring, holding, or disposing of a target company's securities, that group is deemed to be a "person" for the purposes of section 13(d).[48] Accordingly, a Schedule 13D must be filed when members of a group aggregately acquire 5 percent of a class of equity securities subject to the Exchange Act's reporting requirements. The Second Circuit has held that the determinative factor is whether a group has been established that holds the securities pursuant to an express or implied agreement, thus presenting the *potential* for a shift in control; no agreement to buy further securities is necessary.[49] Furthermore, it is not necessary that the agreement be in writing.[50] The Second Circuit has also held that the members' agreement to acquire control may be established by purchase of enough securities to reach the 5 percent threshold.[51] On the other hand, discussions by various persons of the possibility of entering into an agreement do not alone establish the formation of a group.[52] The Seventh Circuit requires a greater showing of concerted activity to establish the formation of a group than does the Second Circuit. The Seventh Circuit requires the group to have an agreement not only to exert control, but also to have an agreement to acquire additional shares for the purpose of exerting control.[53] A group may be deemed to exist when parties agree to act in concert to purchase additional shares, regardless of the absence of a common plan with respect to the target corporation beyond the acquisition of additional shares.[54] Quite separate from section 13(d)(1) is the question of whether failure to disclose the existence of a group in Schedule 13D constitutes a material misstatement or omission. Generalizations in this area are difficult since the determination of a group often depends on the facts of the case.

§ 24.3 Definition of "Tender Offer"

Whereas section 13(d)(1)'s filing requirements are aimed at creeping acquisitions and open-market or privately negotiated large block purchases,[55] section 14(d)(1)'s filing and disclosure provisions are called into play when there is a "tender offer." Although "tender offer" is not defined in the act, it is important in that it determines the applicability of section 14(d)(1)'s[56] filing requirements, section 14(e)'s[57] general antifraud proscriptions, and section 14(f)'s[58] disclosure requirements relating to new directors.

The essence of the SEC's position is that "tender offer" covers more than traditional takeover attempts involving public solicitation and may, under appropriate circumstances, include privately negotiated and open-market purchases. In a widely cited decision, *Wellman v. Dickinson,*[59] the court adopted an eight-factor test to determine whether a tender offer exists. The eight factors can be summarized as follows: (1) active and widespread solicitation of public shareholders; (2) solicitation for a substantial percentage of the issuer's stock; (3) whether the offer to purchase is made at a premium over prevailing market price; (4) whether the terms of the offer are firm rather than negotiable; (5) whether the offer is contingent on the tender of a fixed minimum number of shares; (6) whether the offer is open only for a limited period of time; (7) whether the offerees are subject to pressure to sell their stock; and (8) the existence of public announcements of a purchasing program that precede or accompany a rapid accumulation of stock.[60] These factors are simply broad guidelines.

Ordinarily, widespread, open market purchases known as "street sweeps" are not tender offers.[61] A different result might have followed had the withdrawal of the tender offer been part of a plan designed to evade the protections of the Williams Act.[62]

A number of decisions have discussed whether privately negotiated transfers of a controlling block of shares can constitute a tender offer. The cases conflict, but most hold that privately negotiated transactions are susceptible to being categorized as tender offers even though most privately negotiated purchases will not fall within the definition of "tender offer." Any privately negotiated purchase that interferes with a shareholder's "unhurried investment decision" and "fair treatment of ... investors"[63] defeats the protections of the Williams Act and most likely is a tender offer.[64]

§ 24.4 THE WILLIAMS ACT REQUIREMENTS FOR TENDER OFFERS

As discussed more fully below, section 14(d) and applicable SEC rules require filing with the SEC certain mandated disclosures at a tender offer's commencement.[65] In addition, there are certain substantive requirements in Regulations 14D and 14E for any tender offer subject to section 14(d)(1).

[1] Filing Requirements

Section 14(d)(1) of the Exchange Act[66] requires that all "tender offer material" for equity securities subject to the registration requirements of section 12 be filed with the Commission and be accompanied by the appropriate disclosures.[67] Section 14(d)(1) requires disclosures of the type specified in Schedule 13D,[68] in addition to such other information as the SEC may require.[69] As is the case with a Schedule 13D filing for acquisition of 5 percent or more of a class of a target company's stock,[70] section 14(d)(1) filings must be updated to reflect material changes and developments.[71] Section 14(d)(1) does not apply to an issuer's acquisition of its own shares; those transactions are governed by section 13(e), not section 14(d)(1). However, the SEC's regulations for issuer tender offers are comparable to those in Regulation 14D's rules for third-party offers.[72]

Regulation 14D sets forth the Commission's filing and disclosure requirements under section 14(d)(1). Rule 14d-1[73] provides the basic definitions for covered tender offers and incorporates by reference all general definitions applicable under other provisions of the Exchange Act. Rule 14d-3 requires filing Schedule TO with both the SEC and the target company as well as with the exchange on which the target shares are listed and, if not listed, with the National Association of Securities Dealers (NASD). In addition to the long-form filing embodied in Schedule TO,[74] the tender offeror must file 10 copies of all additional tender-offer materials with the Commission no later than the date on which it is first published or disseminated.[75] All documents used in the tender offer and the solicitation must thus be on file with the Commission prior to their use.[76] When the bidder's consideration includes non-exempt securities, the offer must be disseminated to the target shareholders through a prospectus, in compliance with the federal Securities Act of 1933. In all other cases (that is, cash or exempt securities) the bidder has three alternative methods to disseminate its bid: the long-form publication, summary publication, or, using a list of stockholders, through a communication directly to the target shareholders.[77]

[2] Commencement of the Tender Offer

Rule 14d-2[78] provides that a tender offer begins at 12:01 a.m. on the day it is first sent to securities holders or published.[79]

[3] Schedule TO

All bidders must file Schedule TO. "Bidder" is defined as any person who makes a tender offer or on whose behalf a tender offer is made, however, an issuer seeking to acquire its own securities is not within the definition.[80] Schedule TO requires certain basic information regarding the bidder and the bid. For example, Schedule TO requires disclosure of the name of the bidder, the name of the target company, and the title of the class of securities being sought. It also requires that all "persons" reporting under the Schedule provide their names and addresses as well as disclose whether or not they belong to a "group" within the meaning of section 14(d)(2).[81] But the disclosures demanded of the bidder are more extensive than mere background information. There must be disclosure of the source of funds to be used in connection with the tender offer and the identity and background of the person filing the document, including the disclosure of any criminal convictions or civil orders arising out of a securities violation within the past five years of the person presenting the tender offer. The tender-offer document must also disclose all contracts, transactions, or negotiations in the preceding three fiscal years between the bidder and the target company, its directors or its officers, the purpose of the tender offer, and the bidder's plans and proposals for the future with regard to the target company. The Schedule TO must divulge the bidder's current interest and holdings of securities of the target company as well as any contracts, arrangements, understandings, or relationships between the bidder and the target company. Present or proposed contracts, arrangements, understandings, or relationships between the bidder, its officers, directors, controlling persons, or subsidiaries and the target company or any of its officers, directors, controlling persons, or subsidiaries that are material to a stockholder's decision must likewise be disclosed. Schedule TO must identify all persons retained, employed, or compensated in connection with the tender offer. The bidder must also disclose extensive information regarding its financial position if the bidder's financial position is material to an investor's decision regarding whether or not to tender shares in the target company.

Certain prospective information must be disclosed—such as any steps towards compliance, with necessary administrative approval for the offer, the possible impact of the antitrust laws, or the margin requirements,[82] as well as a summary of pending material legal proceedings. When there have been material misstatements in a Schedule TO filing, they can be cured by subsequent correction, provided that adequate prominence is given to the curative changes.[83]

[4] The Bidders' Access to the Target Company's Shareholders

Rule 14d-5 spells out the target company's obligation to respond to requests for a shareholder list in connection with tender offers.[84] Briefly, if the bidder or other person presents the request according to the rule's requirements, the target company's management must comply, but the reasonable cost of compliance can be charged to the bidder. Faced with such a request, the target company has two options. First, within three business days it may deliver the stockholder lists to the bidder making the request.[85] Or second, it can mail the bidder's materials, within three business days of receipt, to the target company's holders.[86] The SEC dictates the proper form for the bidder's written request.[87] Also, a bidder's request for such lists subjects the bidder to certain requirements, including the return of any lists furnished by the target company.[88]

[5] Withdrawal and Duration of Tender Offer

Rule 14d-7[89] provides that withdrawal rights may be exercised throughout the period that the tender offer remains open, which must be for at least 20 business days.[90] Any increase or decrease in the consideration offered under the tender offer requires that the tender offer's duration be extended for an additional 10 business days from the date of change in consideration.[91] The rule also prescribes how the notice of withdrawal is to be given. The overall effect of the SEC's regulations respecting the duration of tender offers and providing withdrawal rights through the life of the tender offer is not only to remove pressure from the target shareholders to rush their acceptance of the bidder's offer but also to create a climate within which competing bids may arise.

[6] Proration and "Best Price" Rules

Rule 14d-8[92] requires pro rata acceptance of shares tendered where the tender offer by its terms does not obligate the tender offeror to accept *all* shares tendered. This takes pressure off the target company's shareholders, who would otherwise have to make a quick decision were acceptance to be on a first-come basis. Proration occurs at the tender offer's close. Thus, target shareholders can delay their acceptance of a bid until near its closing without fear they will be treated differently if the bidder's offer is oversubscribed. A tender offeror may not extend the proration period after expiration of the offer where the effect would be to alter the pro rata acceptance of the shares tendered.[93]

Section 14(d)(7) of the Securities Exchange Act[94] provides that whenever a bidder varies the terms of a tender offer or request before the expiration thereof by increasing the consideration offered to the holders of the securities sought, the bidder must pay to all persons tendering securities pursuant to their requests that same price, whether or not the securities were tendered prior to the variation of the tender offer's terms. This can be especially important if a series of transactions are integrated and held to be parts of a single tender offer.[95] This best price requirement is applicable to both issuer self-tenders and tender offers by third-party bidders.[96] The SEC "best price" requirement applies only to shares purchased during a single tender offer. As such, unlike state "fair price" statutes,[97] the SEC does not regulate two-tiered offers consummated in two distinct steps. The SEC best-price requirements do not prohibit different types of consideration, and the different consideration need not be substantially equivalent in value as long as the tender offer permits the security holders to elect among the types of consideration offered.[98]

When different types of consideration are offered, the tender offeror may limit the availability and offer it to tendering shareholders on a pro rata basis.[99] As is the case with the "all holders" requirements, discussed below, the Commission has given itself the power to grant exemptions from the operation of the best-price requirement.[100] As with the rules respecting the duration of tender offers and the withdrawal rights of tendering shareholders, the liberal proration rules and best-price rules shield the target shareholders from being pressured to tender their shares. In combination, these rules contribute to an auction environment by making competing bids possible by assuring that the target shareholders are free within relative broad time periods to place their shares with the highest bidder. While this may well reduce the incentive for bidders to initiate a takeover, it is equally likely that the bidder that offers the highest price, on average, is the company that can put the target corporation's assets to their highest use. To the extent that this leads to a better allocation of resources, the concomitant greater costs imposed by the Williams Act are not all that bad.

[7] The "All Holders" Requirement

A Delaware decision upheld a tender offer by an issuer that excluded a hostile tender offeror.[101] Since that decision, the SEC has adopted an "all holders" rule, so such an exclusion is now prohibited. Even though there is no explicit statutory requirement that a tender offer be made to all shareholders, the SEC takes the position that the "all holders" requirement is "necessary and appropriate" to implement the Williams Act.[102]

There is an exception in the "all holders" requirement for tender offers that exclude one or more shareholders in compliance with a constitutionally valid state statute.[103] In addition to reserving general exemptive power under the "all holders" rules,[104] the SEC has promulgated a specific but limited exemption for odd-lot tender offers by issuers. An "odd-lot offer" is one that is limited to security holders owning less than a specified number of shares under one hundred.[105]

[8] Exemptions from Regulation 14D; Mini Tender Offers

Section 14(d)(8) of the Act[106] exempts certain tender offers or requests for tenders from the scope of section 14(d)'s requirements. When the acquisition of the securities sought together with all other acquisitions by the same person of securities of the same class within the preceding 12 months does not exceed 2 percent of the outstanding securities of the class, section 14(d) does not apply.[107] Similarly, section 14(d) does not apply where the tender offeror is the issuer of the security.[108] The Securities Exchange Act also gives the SEC exemptive power by rule, regulation, or order from transactions "not entered into for the purpose of, and not having the effect of, changing or influencing the control of the issuer or otherwise as not comprehended within the purposes of this subsection."[109]

Although not couched in terms of an exemption, section 14(d) provides that its provisions do not apply to tender offers when after completion of the offer, the bidder would hold less than five percent of a class of the target company's equity securities.[110] Tender offers falling below this threshold became known as mini tender offers. In the 1990s, various fraudulent practices developed in connection with these largely unregulated mini tender offers, including offering to buy back stock at a price lower than the current market price.[111] In order to prevent the abuses of mini tender offers, the SEC issued guidelines that essentially require full disclosure with respect to mini tender offers.[112]

§ 24.5 THE ANTIFRAUD PROVISION—SECTION 14(e)

Section 14(e) of the Exchange Act[113] prohibits material misstatements, omissions, and fraudulent practices in connection with tender offers. The jurisdictional reach of this antifraud provision is broader than other provisions of the Williams Act because it applies to *any* tender offer in interstate commerce, regardless of whether the target company is subject to the Exchange Act's reporting requirements.[114] Whether a fact is material depends on whether a reasonable investor would consider it significant in making an investment decision.[115] Materiality is based on a highly factual inquiry and thus is difficult to predict. For example, it is not necessary to disclose preliminary merger discussions that may lead to a tender offer.[116] At the same time, a denial of such negotiations, even though they are at a very early stage, is not advisable in light of the Supreme Court's holding that whether a denial of preliminary merger negotiations is material is a question of fact.[117]

As in other areas of the securities laws, courts approach materiality determinations cautiously so as to preserve a healthy balance between the need of investors for information and the fact that too-demanding disclosure requirements ultimately will work against the interests of the corporation's shareholders.[118] Accordingly, subjective motivation behind fully disclosed transactions need not be spelled out as long as all material facts underlying the transaction are disclosed.[119]

The SEC has promulgated a series of rules under section 14(e), which appear as Regulation 14E. Collectively, they regulate certain conduct within tender offers regardless of whether the target corporation is subject to the reporting provisions of the Securities Exchange Act. Rule 14e-1[120] requires that any person making a tender offer must hold the offer open for at least 20 business days from the date on which it is first published. The *Schreiber* decision, discussed above, requires deception as an element of any section 14(e) violation. To the extent that the reasoning carries over to the SEC rule-making power, that decision casts a cloud over the validity of Rule 14e-1 because the rule regulates the duration of the offer and thus goes beyond mandating full disclosure.[121] It can, of course, be argued that the SEC's power to mandate a period during which the tender offer must remain open is justified because it gives investors and the market the time necessary to digest the information mandated by the Williams Act's affirmative disclosure requirements.

Rule 14e-1(b) further provides that the tender offeror may not increase or decrease the terms of the offer, the type of consideration, or the dealer's soliciting fee unless the tender offer remains open for at least 10 business days from the publication of the notice of such change in the terms of the offer.[122] It also declares it to be an unlawful practice for a tender offeror to fail to pay the consideration offered or to return the securities tendered promptly after either the withdrawal or termination of the tender offer.[123] Rule 14e-1(d)[124] makes it unlawful to extend the length of the tender offer without issuing a notice of such extension by press release or other public announcement, and the notice must give sufficient detail of the time period of the tender offer and its extension.

Whenever a tender offer is made for a target company's shares, the target company has 10 business days from the first date on which the tender offer is published to respond.[125] Rule 14e-2[126] requires that the target company's management make one of the following responses within the 10-day period: (1) a recommendation of acceptance or rejection of the tender offer; (2) an expression of no opinion with a decision to remain neutral toward the offer; or (3) a statement that it is not able to take a position with respect to bidder's offer. The Rule 14e-2 statement must also include all reasons for the position taken, or the stance of neutrality, as well as any explanation of the inability to take a position. In setting forth its reasons, the target company's management is, of course, subject to all of the rules concerning materiality[127] as well as to potential civil and criminal liabilities for material misstatements.

Rule 14e-3[128] prohibits insider trading during a tender offer. The Rule 14e-3 prohibitions expressly apply not only to insiders of the target company but also to others possessing nonpublic information about an upcoming tender offer. In 1997, the Supreme Court upheld the validity of Rule 14e-3 but left undecided the question of whether the SEC's rule-making authority is broader under section 14(e) than it is under section 10(b).[129]

An important anti-manipulation rule is Rule 14e-5, which prohibits a tender offeror from purchasing the target securities other than through the tender offer once the offer has commenced and until it is completed.[130] It has been held that violations of Rule 10b-13 (Rule 14e-5's predecessor) supported a private damage action,[131] but not all courts seem to agree.[132]

Rule 14e-4 prohibits short tendering[133]—the practice of tendering or guaranteeing securities not owned by the person making the tender or guarantee.[134]

§ 24.6 DIRECTOR TURNOVER AND WILLIAMS ACT SECTION 14(f)

As is the case with any transfer of corporate control, tender offers will frequently result in a shift in corporate management. Accordingly, it is not uncommon to find tender offers containing agreements relating to management turnover and the election of new directors. These control transfers can raise problems under state law relating to invalid control premiums and other breaches of fiduciary duty.[135] The Williams Act adds certain disclosure obligations when the bidder has arranged for at least a majority of the directorships to change. Under section 14(f) of the Exchange Act,[136] when in connection with a tender offer for equity securities subject to the Act's reporting requirements of section 14(d)(1) or a purchase of shares subject to section 13(d)(1) agreements arise concerning the designation of new directors who will be at least a majority of the target's board of directors and such change will occur otherwise than through a formal vote at a meeting of securities holders, extensive disclosure is required. Essentially, the information that must be disclosed is of a scale equal to that required in connection with a stockholders' meeting at which directors will be elected.[137] Contemplated management turnover, including any arrangement regarding the make-up of the majority of directors, also must be disclosed.[138] Thus, for example, where a stock purchase agreement permits the purchaser to designate a majority of the issuer's directors, section 14(f)'s disclosure obligation is triggered.[139] When the agreed upon shift in control occurs, a second filing obligation arises.[140]

§ 24.7 STATE REGULATION OF TENDER OFFERS

Approximately two-thirds of the states have statutes that regulate tender offers. In less than 20 years, the states went through three generations of takeover statutes.[141] The statutes' effectiveness arise because they impose additional and substantial impediments to a takeover thus inhibiting or at least slowing any transaction.

The vast majority of the state acts base jurisdiction on the target company's incorporation within the state, or on the location within the state of the target company's principal place of business and/or substantial target company assets.[142] Another important variation among the states is how they define "tender offer." The state statutes generally include precise but diverse statutory definitions, including the number of solicited target company shareholders required before the act applies.[143]

State anti-takeover laws have evolved through successive generations. Today, only the second and third generation statutes have survived constitutional challenges.

First Generation Anti-Takeover Statutes. Following the pattern of the state blue sky laws, many of the first generation anti-takeover statutes went beyond the disclosure philosophy of the Williams Act by giving the state administrator the power to review the merits of the tender offer's terms and the adequacy of the bidder's disclosures.[144] These statutes were invalidated under the Commerce Clause.[145]

Second Generation Anti-Takeover Statutes. Relying on some helpful language from the Supreme Court,[146] a number of states enacted second generation takeover statutes, which were designed to overcome the constitutional infirmities of the Illinois statute that was struck down. The basic thrust of many of these second generation statutes is to regulate tender offers through state law rules relating to corporate governance rather than through state securities laws and administrative regulations. That is, adhering to the traditional choice-of-law rule that questions regarding the internal affairs of a corporation are to be resolved according to the state of the company's incorporation, the second generation anti-takeover statutes introduce many corporate law requirements that operate to the serious disadvantage of the bidder for control. Ohio was the first state to adopt second generation legislation.[147]

The most common and effective form of second generation anti-takeover statute is the "control share acquisition" statute.[148] Control share acts classify takeover transactions by the percentage of shares owned by the acquiring person, with each control zone triggering the act's substantive requirements.[149] Acquiring persons must deliver to the target company a disclosure statement describing the proposed acquisition. The target company's board then has 10 days to call a special shareholders' meeting, which must take place within 50 days. At that meeting, the transaction requires approval of a majority of the disinterested shares not owned or controlled by the acquiring person or any affiliate.

An alternative to the "control share acquisition" type of statute is the "fair price" statute. Fair price statutes take a more structural approach in regulating share acquisitions. A fair price statute typically requires that any takeover be approved by at least 80 percent of the shareholders and two-thirds of the disinterested shareholders, unless all shareholders receive the best price paid by the acquiring person within a five-year period.[150] The best-price approach, patterned after fair price charter amendments adopted by many corporations, is designed to fend off two-tiered offers. These statutes ordinarily exclude "friendly" offers from its coverage.

Another form of statute within the second generation is the "constituency" or "stakeholder" statute,[151] which permits management to consider interests other than those of the shareholders in making decisions.[152] These statutes generally make it clear that although management may consider other interests, it does not have to. Still another approach taken in some of the second generation statutes is to give dissenters' rights to a wide variety of control transactions.

Third Generation Anti-Takeover Statutes. Finding few limits in the Supreme Court's analysis,[153] states have spawned a third generation of anti-takeover provisions even more draconian than their predecessors. A version of the third generation takeover statutes is modeled on the New York "freeze" statute,[154] also known as a business-combination statute. The idea behind such statutes is to delay any transaction that would complete the second step of a two-step acquisition where the first step was not agreed to by a target company's management. Thus, for example, the New York statute prohibits a merger or other business acquisition within five years of the control acquisition date unless the transaction was approved by the target company's directors *prior* to the control acquisition date. Other states followed New York's lead, including Delaware, which adopted a three-year-freeze statute.[155] The Delaware statute withstood early challenges to its constitutionality,[156] and the constitutionality of the Wisconsin freeze statute was upheld by the Seventh Circuit.[157] Statutes are still likely to fall victim of the Commerce Clause when they treat foreign bidders more harshly than local bidders.[158]

The varieties of third generation statutes have continued to proliferate. In the spring of 1990, Pennsylvania adopted the most ambitious anti-takeover statute to date. In addition to adopting a control share statute, the Pennsylvania legislature enacted a provision requiring any person owning more than 20 percent of a company's voting shares to disgorge any profit realized within an eighteen-month period.[159] The impact of this provision is to discourage suitors by locking them in as shareholders in the event that their takeover attempt is unsuccessful. Pennsylvania has taken yet another approach by expressly sanctioning use of poison pills as a defensive measure.[160] Also in 1990, Massachusetts enacted a statute that mandates dividing the directors into groups and staggering the election of directors.[161] A corporation's board by a majority vote may choose to opt out of the law, should the directors decide to have all directors elected annually. Shareholders can opt out of staggered elections only on a two-thirds vote.

NOTES

1. Pub. L. No. 90-439, § 2, 82 Stat. 454 (1968) (codified at 15 U.S.C.A. §§ 78m(d) to (c), 78n(d) to (f) (1997 & Supp. 2009)). In the case of an exchange offer, as opposed to a cash tender offer, the new securities will be subject to the 1933 Act's registration requirements. 15 U.S.C.A. §§ 77f, 77g (1997 & Supp. 2009).

2. 15 U.S.C.A. § 78m(d) (1997). *See id.* § 78m(e) (1997 & Supp. 2009), which prohibits misstatements, omissions, and fraud in connection with such SEC filings.

3. *See* Gregg A. Jarrell & Michael Bradley, *The Economic Effects of Federal and State Regulation of Cash Tender Offers*, 23 J.L. & ECON. 371 (1980).
4. 15 U.S.C.A. § 78n(d) (1997). *See also id.* § 78n(f) (1997), which requires disclosure of any agreement concerning management turnover.
5. *Id.* § 78n(d).
6. *Id.* § 78n(e). *See generally* 2 THOMAS LEE HAZEN, TREATISE ON THE LAW OF SECURITIES REGULATION §§ 11.6, 11.10 (4th ed. 2002).
7. 17 C.F.R. § 240.14e-5 (2009), which replaced Rule 10b-13, 17 C.F.R. § 240.10b-13 (2002).
8. *Id.* § 240.14e-4. These practices consist of tendering securities not owned or tendering securities subject to a put or call option.
9. *Id.* § 240.14e-1.
10. *Id.* § 240.14e-2.
11. 17 C.F.R. § 240.14e-3 (2009). The Supreme Court upheld the rule as a valid exercise of the SEC's rule-making power. United States v. O'Hagan, 521 U.S. 642, 117 S. Ct. 2199 (1997).
12. Section 14(e) declares certain conduct unlawful but does not make any mention of a private remedy.
13. It is clear that a defeated tender offeror cannot maintain an action for damages under section 14(e). Piper v. Chris-Craft Indus., Inc., 430 U.S. 1 (1977). *See also* Sedighim v. Donaldson, Lufkin & Jenrette, Inc., 167 F. Supp. 2d 639, 650 (S.D.N.Y. 2001). However, most federal courts recognize an implied cause of action for target shareholders under section 14(e) only to prevent or offset damages incurred in the decision to tender shares during a tender offer.
14. 15 U.S.C.A. § 78n(e) (1997); 17 C.F.R. § 240.10b-5 (2009).
15. *See infra* § 24.5; Schreiber v. Burlington N., Inc., 472 U.S. 1 (1985); Mobil Corp. v. Marathon Oil Co., 669 F.2d 366 (6th Cir. 1981), *cert. denied*, 455 U.S. 982 (1982).
16. *See* Panter v. Marshall Field & Co., 646 F.2d 271 (7th Cir.), *cert. denied*, 454 U.S. 1092 (1981).
17. *Piper*, 430 U.S. 1 (1977).
18. Rondeau v. Mosinee Paper Corp., 422 U.S. 49 (1975).
19. *In re* Digital Island Sec. Litig., 357 F.3d 322, 325 (3d Cir. 2004); *Panter*, 646 F.2d 271, 287 (7th Cir.), *cert. denied*, 454 U.S. 1092 (1981).
20. *Schreiber*, 472 U.S. 1 (1985).
21. Many questions arise as to who is a beneficial owner for the purposes of the Williams Act. For example, a nominee with voting power who may vote only at the instruction of third parties is not the beneficial owner of the shares in question and thus is not subject to the section 13(d) filing requirements. Calvary Holdings, Inc. v. Chandler, 948 F.2d 59 (1st Cir. 1991).
22. Companies with securities listed on a national securities exchange must register by virtue of section 12(a). 15 U.S.C.A. § 78l(a) (1997 & Supp. 2009). Section 12(g) imposes registration requirements on issuers with more than $10 million in assets having a class of equity securities with 2,000 or more shareholders of record but retains the former 500 record holder threshold with respect to investors who are not accredited investors. Section 12(g)(1)(A), 15 U.S.C.A. § 78l(g)(1)(A) as amended

by the Jumpstart Our Business Startups Act (JOBS Act), H.R. 3606, 112 Cong. 2d sess. § 501 (2012). The record holder calculation excludes shareholders who receive shares as part of an employee compensation plan that is exempt from 1933 Act registration. Section 12(g) was also amended to exclude from the shareholder calculation holders of shares issued pursuant to an exempt crowdfunding offering.

23. 15 U.S.C.A. § 78m(d)(1) (1997). Section 12, 15 U.S.C.A. § 78l (1997).
24. 15 U.S.C.A. § 78m(e) (1997 & Supp. 2009); 17 C.F.R. § 240.13e-3 (2009).
25. 15 U.S.C.A. § 78m(d)(1) (1997).
26. *See* 15 Sec. Reg. & L. Rep. (BNA) 156 (June 17, 1983).
27. 17 C.F.R. § 240.13d-1 (2009).
28. *Id.* § 240.13d-1(c). *See also* Edelson v. Ch'ien, 405 F.3d 620, 623 (7th Cir. 2005).
29. 17 C.F.R. § 240.13d-1(b) (2009). Qualified institutional investors are defined as registered broker dealers, banks, insurance companies, registered investment companies, registered investment advisers, employee benefit plans, parent holding companies, control persons, and savings associations. *Id.*
30. *Id.* § 240.13d-2(b).
31. *Id.* § 240.13d-2(d). Qualified institutional investors must file within 10 days after the close of the month in which such change in ownership occurred. 17 C.F.R. § 240.13d-2(c) (2008).
32. 17 C.F.R. § 240.13d-1(e)(2)(i) & (f)(2)(i) (2009).
33. *Id.* § 240.13d-1(e)(2)(i).
34. *See, e.g.*, SEC v. First City Fin. Corp., 890 F.2d 1215 (D.C. Cir. 1989) (enjoining future violations).
35. *E.g., id.*
36. *See* 17 C.F.R. § 240.13d-101 (2009).
37. *See, e.g.*, SEC v. Levy, 706 F. Supp. 61 (D.D.C. 1989).
38. *See, e.g., In re* Phillips Petrol. Sec. Litig., 738 F. Supp. 825 (D. Del. 1990).
39. In some such cases, there may be an exemption from section 13(d)'s filing requirements. *See* 15 U.S.C.A. §§ 78m(d)(6), 78m(f) (1997).
40. *See* CSX Corp. v. Children's Inv. Fund Mgmt. (UK) LLP, 562 F. Supp. 2d 511, 556 (S.D.N.Y. 2008) (failure to disclose actual swap agreements did not amount to a material nondisclosure).
41. 15 U.S.C.A. § 78m(d)(2) (1997); 17 C.F.R. § 240.13d-2 (2009). Once a Schedule 13D has been filed, a sale of the stock so acquired must be disclosed promptly. *In re* Cooper Labs., Inc., 1985 WL 548418 (SEC Release 1985).
42. *See* 17 C.F.R. § 240.12b-2 (2009).
43. *Id.* § 240.13d-2(a).
44. Dan River, Inc. v. Unitex Ltd., 624 F.2d 1216 (4th Cir. 1980), *cert. denied*, 449 U.S. 1101 (1981); Chromalloy Am. Corp. v. Sun Chem. Corp., 611 F.2d 240 (8th Cir. 1979).
45. 17 C.F.R. § 240.12b-2 (2009).
46. Chevron Corp. v. Pennzoil Co., 974 F.2d 1156 (9th Cir. 1992) (triable issue of fact as to whether Schedule 13D was materially misleading in failing to adequately disclose intent to obtain board position and exert degree of management influence over target company).

47. 15 U.S.C.A. § 78m(d)(3) (1997).

48. For a similar provision with regard to tender offers, *see* Section 14(d)(2), 15 U.S.C.A. § 78n(d)(2) (1997).

49. GAF Corp. v. Milstein, 453 F.2d 709 (2d Cir. 1971), *cert. denied*, 406 U.S. 910 (1972).

50. *CSX Corp.'*, 562 F. Supp. 2d 511, 553 (S.D.N.Y. 2008); SEC v. Drexel Burnham Lambert Inc., 837 F. Supp. 587 (S.D.N.Y. 1993).

51. Corenco Corp. v. Schiavone & Sons, Inc., 488 F.2d 207 (2d Cir. 1973).

52. Lane Bryant, Inc. v. Hatleigh Corp., 517 F. Supp. 1196 (S.D.N.Y. 1981).

53. Bath Indus., Inc. v. Blot, 427 F.2d 97 (7th Cir. 1970) (enjoining group acquiring nearly 50% control from ousting incumbent management). *See also* Edelson v. Ch'ien, 405 F.3d 620, 630 (7th Cir. 2005).

54. Mid-Continent Bancshares, Inc. v. O'Brien, 1981 WL 1404 (E.D. Mo. 1981).

55. 15 U.S.C.A. § 78m(d) (1997). *See* § 24.2 *supra.*

56. *Id.* § 78n(d). *See* § 24.4 *infra.*

57. *Id.* § 78n(e). *See* § 24.5 *infra.*

58. *Id.* § 78n(f). *See* § 24.6 *infra.*

59. 475 F. Supp. 783, 823–824 (S.D.N.Y. 1979), *aff'd on other grounds*, 682 F.2d 355 (2d Cir. 1982), *cert. denied*, 460 U.S. 1069 (1983). *See also* SEC v. Carter Hawley Hale Stores, Inc., 760 F.2d 945 (9th Cir. 1985).

60. The eight-factor test, which is not contained in any formal SEC rule, has evolved over a period of time.

61. Hanson Trust PLC v. SCM Corp., 774 F.2d 47 (2d Cir. 1985).

62. *Cf.* Field v. Trump, 850 F.2d 938 (2d Cir. 1988), *cert. denied*, 489 U.S. 1012 (1989), wherein the court found that a privately negotiated purchase sandwiched between the withdrawal of one tender offer and the initiation of a second, both at a lower price, was part of a single tender offer.

63. Cattlemen's Inv. Co. v. Fears, 343 F. Supp. 1248, 1251 (W.D. Okla. 1972) (finding a tender offer to have occurred). *See also, e.g.*, Telenor East Invest AS v. Altimo Holdings & Invs. Ltd., 567 F. Supp. 2d 432, 443 (S.D.N.Y. 2008) (noting the difference between those in need of protection of the Act and those who do not; specifically, "privately negotiated transactions with sophisticated investors do not constitute tender offers").

64. Wellman v. Dickinson, 475 F. Supp. 783 (S.D.N.Y. 1979), *aff'd on other grounds*, 682 F.2d 355 (2d Cir. 1982), *cert. denied*, 460 U.S. 1069 (1983).

65. Filing requirements are not limited to the tender offeror but apply to anyone who is recommending in favor of or against a tender offer covered by the Act. *See* Schedule 14D-9.

66. 15 U.S.C.A. § 78n(d)(1) (1997).

67. *Id.*

68. *Id.* § 78m(d).

69. *See* SEC Schedule TO and Rule 14d-1, 17 C.F.R. § 240.14d-100 (2009). Schedule TO was formerly Schedule 14D-1.

70. 15 U.S.C.A. § 78n(d) (1997). *Cf.* 15 U.S.C.A. § 78m(d) (1997), which is discussed *supra* § 24.2.

71. 15 U.S.C.A. § 78n(d) (1997).

72. 15 U.S.C.A. § 78m(e) (1997 & Supp. 2009).

73. 17 C.F.R. § 240.14d-1 (2009).
74. *Id.* § 240.14d-100.
75. *Id.* § 240.14d-3(b).
76. *Id.* § 240.14d-3.
77. *See* Rule 14d-4, 17 C.F.R. § 240.14d-4 (2009).
78. 17 C.F.R. § 240.14d-2 (2009).
79. Rule 14d-2(a), 17 C.F.R. § 240.14d-2(a) (2009).
80. 17 C.F.R. § 240.14d-1(g)(2) (2009).
81. *Id.* § 240.14d-100.
82. *See, e.g.,* Irving Bank Corp. v. Bank of N.Y. Co., 692 F. Supp. 163 (S.D.N.Y. 1988).
83. *See, e.g.,* Am. Insured Mortg. Investors v. CRI, Inc., 1990 WL 192561 (S.D. N.Y. 1990) (material changes had to be highlighted through the use of boldface and italic typeface).
84. 17 C.F.R. § 240.14d-5 (2009).
85. *Id.* § 240.14d-5(c).
86. *Id.* § 240.14d-5(b). The bidder is to be informed of the progress of any such mailing undertaken by the target company.
87. *Id.* § 240.14d-5(e).
88. *Id.* § 240.14d-5(f).
89. *Id.* § 240.14d-7.
90. *Id.* § 240.14e-1.
91. *Id.* §§ 240.13e-4(f)(1)(ii), 240.14e-1(b).
92. 17 C.F.R. § 240.14d-8 (2008).
93. Pryor v. U.S. Steel Corp., 794 F.2d 52 (2d Cir. 1986); Pryor v. USX Corp., 1991 WL 346368 (S.D.N.Y. 1991) (tender offeror could not accept shares tendered after the deadline when this would affect proration rights of shares previously tendered; tender offeror was liable to shareholders who had wrongfully been denied their tender offer premium), s.c., 806 F. Supp. 460 (S.D.N.Y. 1992) (denying summary judgment because terms of offer were susceptible to differing interpretations as to whether late-tender shares would fall within the proration period).
94. 15 U.S.C.A. § 78n(d)(7) (1997).
95. *See, e.g.,* Gerber v. Computer Assocs. Int'l, 303 F.3d 126, 136 (2d Cir. 2002) (finding the payment to be made during and not after the tender offer since "giving effect to every purported withdrawal that allows a discriminatory premium to be paid to large shareholders would completely undermine the 'best-price rule'" (citing Field v. Trump, 850 F.2d 938, 944 (2d Cir. 1988))).
96. 17 C.F.R. §§ 240.13e-4(f)(8)(ii), 240.14d-10(a)(2) (2009).
97. *E.g.,* Md. Code Ann., Corps. & Ass'ns §§ 3-602, 3-603 (LexisNexis 2007). *See* § 24.8 *infra.*
98. 17 C.F.R. §§ 240.13e-4(f)(9), 240.14d-10(c) (2009).
99. *Id.*
100. *Id.* §§ 240.13e-4(g)(7), 240.14d-10(e) (2009).
101. Unocal Corp. v. Mesa Petrol. Co., 493 A.2d 946 (Del. 1985).
102. *See* Exch. Act Rel. No. 34-23421 [1986–1987 Transfer Binder], Fed. Sec. L. Rep. (CCH) ¶ 84,016 (SEC July 11, 1986).

103. 17 C.F.R. §§ 240.13e-4(f)(9)(ii), 240.14d-10(b)(2) (2009).
104. *Id.* §§ 240.13e-4(f)(7), 240.14d-10(e).
105. *Id.* § 240.13e-4(h)(5).
106. 15 U.S.C.A. § 78n(d)(8) (1997).
107. *Id.* § 78n(d)(8)(A).
108. *Id.* § 78n(d)(8)(B).
109. *Id.* § 78n(d)(8)(C).
110. *Id.* § 78n(d).
111. By labeling the offer a "tender offer," unwary investors were duped into tendering their shares and receiving less than they would have had they sold the shares on the market.
112. *See* Commission Guidance on Mini-Tender Offers and Limited Partnership Tender Offers, Release No. 34-43069, 2000 WL 1190808 (SEC July 24, 2000).
113. 15 U.S.C.A. § 78n(e) (1997).
114. In contrast, the other provisions of the Williams Act are limited to securities of issuers subject to Section 12's registration requirements. 15 U.S.C.A. § 78l (1997 & Supp. 2009).
115. TSC Indus. v. Northway, Inc., 426 U.S. 438 (1976). *See* § 13.32 *supra*.
116. Staffin v. Greenberg, 672 F.2d 1196 (3d Cir. 1982).
117. Basic, Inc. v. Levinson, 485 U.S. 224 (1988).
118. Macfadden Holdings, Inc. v. JB Acquisition Corp., 802 F.2d 62, 71 (2d Cir. 1986), *relying on* Data Probe Acquisition Corp. v. Datatab, Inc., 722 F.2d 1, 5 (2d Cir. 1983), *cert. denied*, 465 U.S. 1052 (1984).
119. Diamond v. Arend, 649 F. Supp. 408, 415-416 (S.D.N.Y. 1986).
120. 17 C.F.R. § 240.14e-1(a) (2009).
121. *But see* Polaroid Corp. v. Disney, 862 F.2d 987 (3d Cir. 1988), which upheld the SEC's "all-holders rule" (Rule 14d-10, 17 C.F.R. § 240.14d-10 (2009)), reasoning that requiring the offer be made to all shareholders furthers the disclosure goals of the Williams Act.
122. 17 C.F.R. § 240.14e-1(b) (2009). *See also* § 240.13e-4(f)(1)(ii) (imposing same requirement for tender offers by issuers).
123. *Id.* § 240.14e-1(c).
124. *Id.* § 240.14e-1(d).
125. *Id.* § 240.14e-2.
126. *Id.* § 240.14e-2.
127. *See, e.g.,* Schwarzschild v. Tse, 1992 WL 448796 (N.D. Cal. 1992) (allegation that directors did not adequately disclose assumptions underlying fairness examination were unsupported by evidence). *See* § 24.1 *supra*.
128. 17 C.F.R. § 240.14e-3 (2009).
129. United States v. O'Hagan, 521 U.S. 642 (1997).
130. 17 C.F.R. § 240.14e-5 (2009).
131. City Nat'l Bank v. Am. Commw. Fin. Corp., 801 F.2d 714 (4th Cir. 1986), *cert. denied*, 479 U.S. 1091 (1987).
132. Beaumont v. Am. Can Co., 797 F.2d 79 (2d Cir. 1986).
133. 17 C.F.R. § 240.14e-4 (2009).

134. *See* Merrill Lynch, Pierce, Fenner & Smith, Inc. v. Bobker, 636 F. Supp. 444 (S.D.N.Y. 1986), *rev'd*, 808 F.2d 930 (2d Cir. 1986) (denying proration to shareholder who sold short while tendering).

135. This subject is discussed in Chapter 12 *supra*.

136. 15 U.S.C.A. § 78n(f) (1997).

137. Rule 14f-1 provides for specific disclosures in the event there is going to be a change in the majority of directors other than at a shareholder meeting, in a transaction subject to either section 13(d) or section 14(d). 17 C.F.R. § 240.14f-1 (2009).

138. 15 U.S.C.A. § 78n(f) (1997). *See* 17 C.F.R. § 240.14f-1 (2008).

139. Drobbin v. Nicolet Instrument Corp., 631 F. Supp. 860 (S.D.N.Y. 1986).

140. *Id.*

141. *See* Thomas Lee Hazen, *State Anti-Takeover Legislation: The Second and Third Generations*, 23 WAKE FOREST L. REV. 77 (1988).

142. *See, e.g.*, CONN. GEN. STAT. ANN. § 36b-41(1) (West 2004 & Supp. 2009); OHIO REV. CODE ANN. § 1707.041(A)(1) (West) (2004, Supp. 2009) (amended 1990).

143. *See, e.g.*, N.H. REV. STAT. ANN. § 421-A:2(VI)(a) (LexisNexis 2009) (" 'Takeover bid' does not include: (3) Any ... offer to acquire an equity security, or the acquisition of such equity security pursuant to such offer ... from not more than 25 persons ...").

144. *E.g.*, LA. REV. STAT. § 51:1501(E) (West 1987) (repealed); 70 PA. CONS. STAT. § 74(d) (Supp. 1993) (repealed).

145. Edgar v. MITE Corp., 457 U.S. 624 (1982).

146. *See Edgar*, 457 U.S. 624 (1982).

147. OHIO REV. CODE ANN. § 1701.832 (2004) (amended 1993).

148. *See* CTS Corp. v. Dynamics Corp. of America, 481 U.S. 69 (1987) (upholding Illinois' control share act).

149. For example, the Pennsylvania statute sets three control thresholds: 20%, 33 1/3, and 50%. 15 PA. CONS. STATS. ANN. § 2562 (West 1995 & Supp. 2009).

150. MD. CODE ANN., Corps. & Assns. §§ 3-602, 3-603 (LexisNexis 2007).

151. IND. CODE ANN. § 23-1-35-1(d) (LexisNexis 1999 & Supp. 2007).

152. *See* CAL. CORP. CODE § 309 (West 1990 & Supp. 2002); IND. CODE ANN. § 23-1-35-1 (LexisNexis 1999 & Supp. 2007).

153. CTS Corp. v. Dynamics Corp. of Am., 481 U.S. 69 (1987).

154. N.Y. BUS. CORP. LAW § 912 (McKinney 2003).

155. DEL. CODE ANN. tit. 8, § 203 (2001 & Supp. 2008).

156. *See* BNS, Inc. v. Koppers Co., 683 F. Supp. 458 (D. Del. 1988).

157. Amanda Acquisition Corp. v. Universal Foods Corp., 877 F.2d 496 (7th Cir. 1989), *cert. denied*, 493 U.S. 955 (1989).

158. Campeau Corp. v. Federated Dept. Stores, 679 F. Supp. 735 (S.D. Ohio 1988).

159. 15 PA. CONS. STAT. ANN. §§ 2571 to 2576 (West 1995).

160. *See Pennsylvania Enacts Law Against Hostile Takeovers*, 20 SEC. REG. & L. REP. (BNA) 502 (April 1, 1988).

161. MASS. ANN. LAWS ch. 149, § 184 (LexisNexis 2008).

CHAPTER 25

AMENDMENTS TO THE CORPORATE CHARTER

§ 25.1 POWER TO AUTHORIZE FUNDAMENTAL CHANGES

Corporation statutes vest the management of corporate business in the board of directors. The board's authority extends to the making of contracts of any kind, incurring indebtedness, and authorizing any other act, unless otherwise limited by the articles of incorporation or by a provision in the state corporation statute.[1] Any statutory limitation on the board of directors' authority to carry out corporate business arises when the transaction is of a type for which the statute requires shareholder approval to be obtained. Shareholder approval is also required in those instances where the transaction poses a fundamental change in the corporation or the stockholders' economic or voting rights.[2] Fundamental corporate transactions are those characterized by their extraordinary nature, as well as by the unusual changes they bring either to the corporate business or to the rights of its shareholders. It is because of their effects on the business and the shareholders that the authority to undertake such transactions is not commended solely to the discretion of the board of directors, but must be authorized by some specified vote or written consent of the shareholders. The shareholders' competence to assess the merits of the proposed fundamental change is found in their self-interest and in the fact that the skills called into practice are analogous to those exercised in investing generally. That is, the type of structural decision for which stockholder approval is required under most corporate statutes bears directly on the risks and returns associated with an ownership interest in the firm.

§ 25.2 THE AMENDMENT PROCESS

In most instances, the amendment of the articles of incorporation requires the approval of both the board of directors and the shareholders entitled to vote. Many states follow the lead of the former Model Business Corporation Act and the current Model Business Corporation Act to permit certain types of amendments solely on the authority of the board of directors.[3] In most instances, such authorization is confined to certain "housekeeping" changes, such as deleting the names or addresses of the initial directors, substituting the full expression "corporation" or "incorporated" for the abbreviated version, or vice versa, or deleting the name or address of the initial registered agent. Some substantive changes are also authorized to be made solely on the authority of the board of directors, such as the power to extend the duration of the corporation if the corporation was formed at a time when a limited duration was required by law,[4] to change the par value of a class or series of shares,[5] or to create a series of shares within an authorized class.[6] In Illinois, a majority vote of the board of directors can authorize a stock split, provided that no class or series of shares is adversely affected.[7]

Subject to appropriate approval by the board of directors and the shareholders entitled to vote, all states expressly authorize amendments to the articles of incorporation if the provisions of the amendment could lawfully be contained in the original articles at the time the amendment is made.[8] However, the extent of the authority to amend the articles of incorporation depends on the wording of the governing provision in the corporation statutes. The most common state statutory approach is to provide a laundry list of amendments that are permissible;[9] other states provide a broad grant of power to amend the articles of incorporation.[10] Regardless of which statutory approach is taken, the power of amendment in most states generally requires approval by a vote of at least a majority of the shares eligible to vote;[11] a handful of states still require a two-thirds vote of the shareholders.[12]

The Model Business Corporation Act has a somewhat more intricate approach to determining the approval required to amend the articles of incorporation. In states adopting the Model Act's approach, the articles of incorporation are amended pursuant to a bare majority of the votes cast affirmatively or negatively at a stockholders' meeting at which a quorum is present; if the amendment is of the type that gives rise to a class vote the required approval (i.e., a majority of the votes cast provided a quorum of that group of shares is satisfied) of such class of shares must also be obtained.[13] The articles of incorporation may specify a greater quorum or voting requirement for resolutions to amend the articles of incorporation.

State statutes commonly require in specific types of amendments to the articles of incorporation that a class or series of shares is entitled to vote and the approval of a requisite percentage of the shares of that class or series must approve.[14] Such class voting is an important right to a class or series of shares. A class vote affords the possibility for a class affected by the amendment to veto the amendment. This power provides them with important bargaining power in assuring that any amendments of their rights, privileges, and preferences are not simply in the best interest of the corporation but that they are also in the economic interest of that class of shareholders. Some states have phrased their statutory provisions to grant a class vote only where the amendment would "adversely affect"[15] a class or series of shares,[16] and then proceed to enumerate a list of amendments that are deemed to adversely affect the rights of holders.[17] Delaware is distinctive in the brevity with which its statute proscribes amendments triggering a class vote.[18]

The Model Business Corporation Act grants appraisal rights when an amendment to the articles of incorporation, with respect to a class or series of shares, reduces the number of shares of a class or series owned by a shareholder to a fraction of a share if the corporation has the obligation or right to repurchase the fractional share.[19] In addition, the Act grants appraisal rights in the event of any other amendment to the articles of incorporation to the extent provided by the articles, bylaws, or board resolution.[20]

NOTES

1. *See* CAL. CORP. CODE § 300 (West 1990 & West Supp. 2009); N.C. GEN. STAT. ANN. 55-2-02 (2002); MBCA §§ 8.01, 8.02, 8.11, 8.30 (1984).
2. Under this traditional pattern of corporate governance, no direct power can be exercised by the shareholders unless by unanimous consent. *See* Manson v. Curtis, 119 N.E. 559 (N.Y. 1918).
3. *See, e.g.*, MBCA §§ 10.02, 10.03 & 10.05 (1999).
4. *See* MBCA § 10.05(1) (1999).
5. *See* FLA. STAT. ANN. § 607.1002 (West 2007).
6. *See* WIS. STAT. ANN. § 180.1002 (West 2002).
7. 805 ILCS § 5/10.15(d) (2004 & West Supp. 2008).
8. *See, e.g.*, DEL. CODE ANN. tit. 8, § 242(a) (2001 & Michie Supp. 2008).
9. *See, e.g., id.*
10. *See, e.g.*, CAL. CORP. CODE § 900(a) (West 1990).
11. *See* DEL. CODE ANN. tit. 8, § 242(b)(1) (2001 & Michie Supp. 2008).
12. *See, e.g.*, 805 ILCS § 5/10.20(c) (West 2004 & West Supp. 2008).
13. The actual means for accomplishing this result is a bit complex. MBCA § 10.03(e) (1999) sets forth the requirement for shareholder approval and refers the reader to MBCA § 10.04 (1999) to determine whether a class vote is required. The actual approval required, absent a charter provision calling for a greater requirement is the general shareholder voting requirements of MBCA §§ 7.25 & 7.26 (1999). *See* MBCA § 10.03 Official Comment (1999).
14. The Model Business Corporation Act introduces new terminology by using "voting groups" in place of a class or series. *See* MBCA § 10.04 (1999).

15. For a case considering whether a class is "adversely affected," *see* Dalton v. Am. Inv. Co., 490 A.2d 574 (Del. Ch. 1985) (not adversely affected by amendment switching from redemption by lot to redeeming via market and negotiated purchases 5 percent each year for 20 years).
16. *See, e.g.,* Mass. Gen. Laws Ann. ch. 156B, § 71 (2005 & LexisNexis Supp. 2009); N.Y. Bus. Corp. Law § 804(b) (McKinney 2003 & West Supp. 2009).
17. *See* Mass. Gen. Laws Ann. ch. 156B § 77(a) to (e) (2005 & LexisNexis Supp. 2009).
18. Delaware provides a class vote only for amendments that (1) increase or decrease the aggregate number of authorized shares of the class, (2) increase or decrease the par value of the shares of the class, or (3) alter or change the powers, preferences, or special rights of the shares of the class. *See* Del. Code Ann. tit. 8, § 242(b)(2) (2001 & Michie Supp. 2008).
19. MBCA § 13.02(a)(4) (1999).
20. *Id.* § 13.02(a)(5).

CHAPTER 26

VOLUNTARY DISSOLUTION, ADMINISTRATIVE DISSOLUTION, AND WINDING UP

TABLE OF SECTIONS

§ 26.1 VOLUNTARY DISSOLUTION VERSUS INFORMAL LIQUIDATION

Voluntary dissolution of a corporation involves two legal steps: (1) the dissolution itself, which involves the termination of the corporate existence, at least as far as the right to continue doing ordinary business is concerned, and (2) the winding up of affairs, payment of debts, and distribution of assets among the shareholders. Winding up may precede or follow the dissolution, depending on the jurisdiction's statutory procedures. For convenience in winding up, the corporate existence is usually continued either indefinitely or for some period limited by law in order to dispose of the corporation's assets and pay creditors.[1] This enables the directors to function as a board with title in the corporation rather than as trustees of the liquidation process.

The pre-1984 Model Business Corporation Act provided a two-step process to dissolve. First, a statement of intent to dissolve that has been approved by the shareholders is filed with the secretary of state. Additionally, notice of the intent to dissolve must be given to known creditors during this step. Second, when the winding up process is completed, the articles of dissolution must be filed. The secretary of state then issues a certificate of dissolution and the corporation is dissolved.[2] The current Model Business Corporation Act and a clear majority of the states have simplified the process by requiring only that the articles of dissolution to be filed, with the dissolution becoming effective as of the date of the filing.[3]

A corporation's legal existence terminates only when it is dissolved by legal authority, expires by limitation of its term of existence, or is dissolved by forfeiture.[4] Although it is not a formal dissolution, an informal liquidation may occur by sale of all the corporate assets, the abandonment of corporate activities, and the distribution of the corporation's property among the creditors and shareholders. This is sometimes referred to as a practical or de facto dissolution. However, a liquidation of assets does not terminate the corporate existence as a matter of law.

There may be reasons for retaining a corporation as a shell, such as for reactivation at a later date or for use in a corporate merger or consolidation. Directors and shareholders should follow the proceedings prescribed by law for voluntary dissolution and the winding up process; otherwise, the directors and shareholders risk liability due to unauthorized return of capital to the shareholders.[5] That is, absent dissolution, distributions to shareholders are lawful only to the extent that they do not exceed the regulatory limits for dividends or share repurchases.

§ 26.2 STATUTORY AUTHORITY FOR VOLUNTARY DISSOLUTION

Every state provides for the voluntary dissolution of a corporation when authorized by a vote of the shareholders. The vote is generally initialized with an adoption of a resolution and a submission of a proposal of dissolution by the directors.[6] Most states require that the resolution to dissolve include a recommendation by the directors to approve the dissolution before the shareholders may vote. Jurisdictions based on the current Model Business Corporation Act require a recommendation, but provide for an exception when there is a conflict of interest.[7] Only a small number of states do not mandate any type of director approval prior to a shareholder vote to dissolve.[8] In all jurisdictions, however, notice of the dissolution vote must be given to the shareholders prior to the meeting at which the vote is to take place.[9] The number of shareholder votes required for approval of the dissolution varies with most requiring a majority of the shares entitled to vote.[10]

Most states authorize dissolution based solely on the approval of the incorporators or the initial board of directors. Each jurisdiction that authorizes this method of dissolution when either one or both of the following two factors are present: (1) the corporation has not issued shares; or (2) the corporation has not commenced business activities. In jurisdictions based on the pre-1984 Model Business Corporation Act both factors must be present,[11] while jurisdictions based on the current Model Business Corporation Act require the presence of either one of the two factors.[12] The remaining jurisdictions that authorize this method of dissolution either require only that the corporation not have issued shares,[13] or require only that business activities have not commenced.[14]

Following the completion of a statutorily approved method of voluntary dissolution, a certificate of dissolution is filed by the corporation and the dissolution becomes effective.[15]

In most states only the voting shares have a voice as to dissolution under many corporation acts.[16] Filing of a certificate of dissolution and, in some states, the publication of notice are required steps. After the statement of intent to dissolve has been duly adopted and filed, notice thereof is generally required to be sent to all known creditors. When a corporation conducts business in several states, it must dissolve according to the law of the state that granted its charter.

§ 26.3 DISSOLUTION BY EXPIRATION OF STATED DURATION AND ADMINISTRATIVE DISSOLUTION

A corporation may be dissolved upon expiration of a certain period of time or the occurrence of a specified event, if provided in its corporate charter.[17] The corporation's right to exist as a *de jure* corporation ceases after that time[18] unless it is extended or renewed by vote of the shareholders or amendment of the articles of incorporation under legislative authority.[19] According to some authorities, there may be an existence by estoppel or a *de facto* corporation as a result of the continuation of corporate activities after the expiration of the charter.[20] By express statutory provision, the existence of a corporation, even when created for a limited time, is usually prolonged for the limited purposes of winding up business affairs, paying debts, distributing assets, and pursuing and defending claims stemming from activities occurring prior to dissolution.[21]

A corporation may be dissolved administratively for failure to fulfill state requirements, such as nonpayment of state taxes and fees, failure to appoint or give timely notice of a change in its registered agent, failure to file the mandated annual report with the secretary of state, or expiration of the period of duration stated in the articles of incorporation.[22]

Usually, when a corporation is dissolved for failure to comply with corporate filing and fee requirements, its corporate powers are suspended but not forfeited. Almost all states have statutes allowing corporations to apply for reinstatement upon compliance with the state requirement that gave rise to the dissolution.[23] The majority of these states' statutes provide that reinstatement relates back to the effective date of the dissolution; therefore, the corporation is free to resume business as if it was never dissolved. Courts interpret these statutory provisions as validating corporate transactions that occurred during the period in which the corporation was dissolved. The relation back provision also retroactively restores a corporation's power to sue, which provides legislative incentive to pay taxes and fees and file annual reports in a timely manner.

§ 26.4 GROUNDS FOR JUDICIAL DISSOLUTION

Judicial dissolution is a remedy that may be sought in an action by individual shareholders, the state, or, in some instances, creditors of the corporation. Although the power to dissolve a corporation is conferred upon the court by statute, dissolution proceedings are fundamentally equitable in nature. Dissolution is generally regarded as an extreme remedy and courts have been reluctant to grant it except as a last resort.

Action by Shareholders. The subject of voluntary dissolution in response to a petition by shareholders is examined in chapter 14. Most statutes provide for judicial dissolution in a suit by minority shareholders in some or all of the following four situations:[24] (1) when the directors are deadlocked, the shareholders cannot break the deadlock, and irreparable injury to the corporation is suffered or threatened; (2) when the directors, controlling managers, or majority shareholders are acting in an illegal, oppressive, or fraudulent manner; (3) when the shareholders are deadlocked and cannot elect directors; and (4) when corporate assets have been misapplied or wasted. The emphasis of such actions is the protection of the interests of the shareholders. The two categories of judicial dissolution discussed below—dissolution by action of the state and dissolution by action of creditors—arise out of concern for the non-stockholder interests if the corporation's existence is not terminated.

Action by the State. Historically, the common law quo warranto action was the only action available to the state to cause the forfeiture of a corporation's existence or to prevent the corporation from continuing its harmful activities.[25] Today nearly all jurisdictions have enacted statutes that permit judicial dissolution in an action brought by the state upon a showing of an established ground for dissolution.[26] Often, certain state officials or a state's attorney generally may initiate judicial dissolution in limited circumstances.[27] Permissible grounds include (1) where "the corporation obtained its articles of incorporation through fraud"; or (2) where the corporation has continued to exceed or abuse the authority conferred upon it by law. Some states provide additional grounds for dissolution, such as nonuse of corporate powers.[28]

Thus, most states have adopted mechanisms by which the state can administratively dissolve corporations for the failure to meet corporate filing and fee requirements.[29] The procedure generally commences with the secretary of state giving notice to the corporation of the particular defect that, if not corrected within a stated length of time—generally 60 days—will cause the corporation's administrative dissolution. Most state statutes provide that, even though a corporation has been administratively dissolved, its existence can be reinstated by curing the defect that gave rise to its dissolution, such as payment of past and current fees that are due the state.[30] The effect of administrative dissolution in most states is to suspend the corporation's powers, not terminate its existence outright. Such suspension bars any action on the corporation's behalf except as necessary to wind up its affairs.[31]

Petition by Creditors. In most states, judicial dissolution proceedings may be initiated by a creditor upon certain conditions.[32] Under statutes modeled after the Model Business Corporation Act, for example, an action may be commenced by a creditor against an insolvent corporation when the creditor has obtained a judgment which is left unsatisfied after an attempt to execute it, or when the corporation has admitted, in writing, that the creditor's claim is due.[33] A small number of states do not provide for judicial dissolution in a suit by creditors. Some of these states, such as Delaware, permit creditors to petition for appointment of a receiver when a corporation is dissolved.[34]

Provisions authorizing dissolution initiated by creditors should not to be confused with involuntary proceedings under the federal bankruptcy act, which may be brought by three or more creditors and may culminate in liquidation or reorganization.[35] Bankruptcy proceedings are a matter of federal law and do not result in dissolution because only the state has the authority to dissolve a corporation.

§ 26.5 WINDING UP AND STATUTORY CONTINUATION OF EXISTENCE AFTER DISSOLUTION

All states now have statutes that provide for the continued existence of a dissolved corporation for winding up purposes.[36] Although the detail in which winding up procedures are described in these statutes varies widely from state to state, all states require that a corporation cease all business activities upon dissolution, except those germane to winding up the affairs of the corporation. The current M.B.C.A. and statutes patterned after it go as far as to provide a list of various steps to be taken during the winding up period. These steps include: (1) collecting the corporation's assets; (2) disposing of properties that will not be distributed in kind to the shareholders; (3) discharging or making provision for the liabilities of the corporation; (4) distributing the remaining property among shareholders; and (5) doing every other act necessary to wind up and liquidate the corporation's business and affairs.[37] A recent amendment to the current M.B.C.A. gives further structure to the winding up process by imposing on the directors of a dissolved corporation the duties of making provision for liabilities and distributing the remaining assets to the shareholders.[38]

Personal liability may be imposed on those who exceed the scope of winding up activities permitted by statute, and continue business as a going concern.[39] This liability may be explicitly stated in statutes that govern administrative dissolution, or derived from statutes that prohibit persons from acting on behalf of a nonexistent corporation.[40] However, liability for continuing to operate a dissolved corporation is generally contingent on personal knowledge that the corporation has been dissolved.

Today, dissolution does not alter the general governance of the corporation. The current Model Act and statutes patterned after it explicitly reverse common law notions by specifying that dissolution does *not*: (1) transfer title to the corporation's property; (2) prevent transfer of its shares or securities; (3) subject directors and officers to different standards of conduct; (4) change quorum or voting requirements for the board or shareholders; (5) prevent commencement of a proceeding by or against the corporation; (6) abate or suspend a proceeding pending by or against the corporation on the effective date of dissolution; or (7) terminate the authority of the registered agent of the corporation.[41]

NOTES

1. *See, e.g.*, CAL. CORP. CODE § 2010 (West Supp. 2009); DEL. CODE ANN. tit. 8, § 278 (2001); 805 ILL. COMP. STAT. ANN. 5/12.75, 12.80 (West 2004); N.Y. BUS. CORP. LAW §§ 1005, 1006 (McKinney 2003); MBCA § 14.05 (1984).
2. Former MBCA §§ 83, 84–87 (1969).
3. MBCA §§ 14.03(b) & 14.06 (1984).
4. *See In re* Clark's Will, 178 N.E. 766 (N.Y. 1931).
5. *See* Cent. Nat'l Bank v. Conn, Mut. Life Ins. Co., 104 U.S. 54 (1881).
6. All states authorize the directors of a corporation to submit a proposal of dissolution to the stockholders. *See, e.g.*, DEL. CODE ANN. tit. 8, § 275(a) (2001).
7. MBCA § 14.06 (1984).

8. *See, e.g.*, CAL. CORP. CODE § 1900(a) (West 1990); 805 ILL. COMP. STAT. ANN. 5/12.15(a)(2) (West 2004) (allowing for a proposal of dissolution to be submitted to the shareholders upon written request by one-fifth of shareholders entitled to vote on dissolution).

9. *See, e.g.*, DEL. CODE ANN. tit. 8, § 275(a) (2001).

10. *See* ARIZ. REV. STAT. ANN. § 10-1402 (2004) (requiring a majority of shares entitled to vote unless articles of incorporation specify a greater percentage).

11. Former MBCA § 82 (1969).

12. MBCA § 14.01 (1984).

13. *E.g.*, CAL. CORP. CODE § 1900.5 (West Supp. 2009).

14. *E.g.*, KAN. STAT. ANN. § 17-6803 (2007); 15 PA. CONS. STAT. ANN. § 1971 (West 1995).

15. The current MBCA as well as a majority of states require only that the articles of dissolution be filed for the dissolution to become effective. However, states based on pre-1984 versions of the MBCA require a two-step process to dissolve, with the articles of dissolution becoming effective only after the winding up period.

16. *See, e.g.*, CAL. CORP. CODE § 1900(a) (West 1990) (50 percent of shares entitled to vote); DEL. CODE ANN. tit. 8, § 275 (2001) (majority of all shares entitled to vote thereon).

17. *See, e.g.*, CAL. CORP. CODE § 200(c) (West 1990); DEL. CODE ANN. tit. 8, § 122(1) (2001).

18. *See, e.g.*, Woodroffe v. Woodroffe (*In re* Estate of Woodroffe), 742 N.W.2d 94 (Iowa 2007).

19. *See, e.g.*, CAL. CORP. CODE § 909 (West 1990); DEL. CODE ANN. tit. 8, § 242 (2001).

20. *See supra* chapter 6.

21. *See, e.g.*, CAL. CORP. CODE § 2010 (West Supp. 2009); DEL. CODE ANN. tit. 8, § 278 (2001).

22. *See, e.g.*, MBCA § 14.20 (1984).

23. *See, e.g.*, DEL. CODE ANN. tit. 8, § 312 (Supp. 2008).

24. *See, e.g.*, MBCA § 14.30(a)(2).

25. *See* People *ex rel.* Carey v. Lincoln Towing Serv., Inc., 369 N.E.2d 94 (Ill. App. Ct. 1977).

26. *See, e.g.*, DEL. CODE ANN. tit. 8, § 284 (2001); MBCA § 14.30(a)(1).

27. *See, e.g.*, MBCA § 14.30(a)(1) (1984); CAL. CORP. CODE § 1801(a) (West 2009); DEL. CODE ANN. tit. 8, § 284(a) (West 2009).

28. *See, e.g.*, CAL. CORP. CODE § 1801(a)(4) (West 1990) (providing for dissolution by state for failure to pay taxes for five years); DEL. CODE ANN. tit. 8, § 284(a) (2001) (providing for dissolution by state for nonuse of corporate powers).

29. *See, e.g.*, DEL. CODE ANN. tit. 8, § 510 (2001).

30. *See, e.g.*, IOWA CODE ANN. § 490.1422 (West 1999) (within two years); R.I. GEN. LAWS § 7-1.1-88.1 (1999) (within five years); N.Y. Tax Laws § 203-a(7) (McKinney Supp. 2002) (within 90 days).

31. *See* Graham, Inc. v. Mountain States Tel. & Tel. Co., 680 P.2d 1334 (Colo. Ct. App. 1984).

32. *See, e.g.,* MBCA § 14.30(a)(3).
33. *Id.*
34. *See, e.g.,* DEL. CODE ANN. tit. 8, § 279 (2001); KAN. STAT. ANN. § 17-6808 (2007); OKLA. STAT. ANN. tit. 18, § 1100 (West 1999).
35. 11 U.S.C. § 303 (2000). Where there are fewer than 12 creditors, any one of them may institute involuntary bankruptcy proceedings. *Id.* § 303(b)(2).
36. *See, e.g.,* DEL CODE ANN. tit. 8, § 278 (2001).
37. MBCA § 14.05 (1984).
38. *Id.* § 14.09 (1984) (added by 2000 amendment). Several states have adopted this provision.
39. *See, e.g.,* OSHRC, 591 F.2d 991 (4th Cir. 1979).
40. *See* ARIZ. REV. STAT ANN. § 10-204 (2004).
41. MBCA § 14.05(b) (1984).

CHAPTER 27

INVESTOR PROTECTION: STATE AND FEDERAL SECURITIES REGULATION

§ 27.1 SECURITIES REGULATION—OVERVIEW

State corporate laws are geared to the chartering function and, for the most part, do not concern themselves with investor protection. The great problems caused by stock watering and other fraudulent promotional schemes at the turn of the century did not result in adequate common law safeguards. The courts' inability to prevent or redress these frauds led to the passage in 1911 of the first state securities regulatory scheme, or blue sky law.[1] Despite the growth of these statutes, frauds continued to flourish in the wake of the Great Crash of 1929. Congress realized that there was a gap in the protection investors needed and accordingly responded by enacting the Securities Act of 1933 and the Securities Exchange Act of 1934.[2] The importance of the state statutes has been dwarfed to a large extent by the impact of federal regulation. Yet, the state laws provide significant protection for investment schemes that are either small or essentially local in nature, as well as supplementing federal law for more widely offered issues. The topic of securities regulation consumes several treatise volumes and thousands of pages in law reviews. What follows is but a general introduction and overview.

PART A. STATE BLUE SKY LAWS

§ 27.2 HISTORY, POLICY, AND PURPOSE OF STATE SECURITIES LAWS

The Kansas legislature in 1911 passed the first American securities act.[3] The law, popularly called a "blue sky law," attracted wide attention. Similar legislation has now been adopted in every state.

§ 27.3 PREEMPTION OF STATE REGISTRATION REQUIREMENTS

Ever since the enactment of the Securities Act of 1933, Congress preserved the power of the states to regulate securities transactions, notwithstanding the coverage of the federal securities laws. In 1996, however, Congress substantially reversed its position by expressly preempting the field with regard to most registration requirements. The National Securities Markets Improvement Act of 1996[4] took away from the states the power to impose registration and reporting requirements with regard to a large number of securities transactions. As amended by the 1996 legislation, Section 18 of the 1933 Act precludes the imposition of registration and reporting requirements in many securities transactions, including securities listed on the New York Stock Exchange, the American Stock Exchange, or the Nasdaq Stock Market.[5] The federal act, however, expressly preserves the states' right to require filing of documents solely for notice purpose,[6] which in effect preserves a state's ability to require registration by coordination with the federal registration. The preemption of state registration and reporting requirements is not limited to publicly traded securities.[7]

§ 27.4 Preemption of State Securities Fraud Class Actions

Federal preemption has continued. Congress largely eliminated the use of state courts for securities class actions when it enacted the Securities Litigation Uniform Standards Act of 1998, which mandates that class actions involving publicly traded securities be brought in federal court.[8] Class actions involving state securities law and common law class actions with regard to these securities are preempted. The Uniform Standards Act is not complete in its elimination of state court class actions, since the Act preempts only those actions involving publicly traded securities. It is important to note further that the Uniform Standards Act applies only to class actions and thus not to individual or derivative suits. There also is an exclusion for actions brought in the state of incorporation involving certain corporate transactions.

The preemptive provisions apply only to "covered securities." Covered securities under the Uniform Standards Act are securities registered with the SEC and traded on the New York Stock Exchange, American Stock Exchange, the Nasdaq National Market, or other national markets designated by the Commission, as well as securities issued by investment companies registered under the Investment Company Act of 1940.[9] The preemption applies to any class action with more than 50 members involving misrepresentations, omissions, deception, or manipulation in connection with the purchase or sale of a covered security.[10] The Act does not preempt individual actions, derivative suits, or suits brought on behalf of 50 or fewer persons from being brought in state

606 | <small>Corporate Counsel Guides: Corporation Law</small>

court. The Uniform Standards Act also preserves state court actions brought in the issuer's state of incorporation by shareholders challenging management's statements or recommendations in connection with corporate transactions or the exercise of appraisal rights.[11] Class actions by states or their political subdivisions, as well as class actions by state pension plans, are not subject to the Uniform Standard Act's preemptive effect.[12]

PART B. FEDERAL PROTECTION OF INVESTORS

§ 27.5 Overview of Federal Securities Regulation

The collapse of the long boom in the stock market in October 1929, the grievous losses suffered by investors, and the lax financial and ethical standards exposed by subsequent public investigations called national attention to the urgent need for comprehensive regulation of the sale of securities and market manipulations by the strong arm of the federal government. As an able New York lawyer wrote, "after the happenings of the 1920's, completely unregulated security markets seem unthinkable."[13] In the period between May 1933 and August 1940, a series of important federal statutes were enacted: (1) the Securities Act of 1933; (2) the Securities Exchange Act of 1934; (3) the Public Utility Holding Company Act of 1935; (4) the Commodity Exchange Act of 1936; (5) the Reorganization acts, Section 77B of the Bankruptcy Act (1934), revised in 1938 as Chapter X of the Chandler Act; (6) the Railroad Reorganization Act; (7) the Trust Indenture Act of 1939; (8) the Investment Company Act of 1940; and (9) the Investment Advisers Act of 1940.[14]

Congress enacted the Sarbanes-Oxley Act[15] in the wake of corporate scandal involving such companies as Enron and Worldcom. The Sarbanes-Oxley Act imposed corporate governance and accounting reforms. The Act focuses on a variety of issues, including accounting and auditing reforms, the role of public corporations' audit committees, and increased accountability of executive officers and corporate attorneys. In focusing on accounting problems, the Act created an accounting oversight board to oversee the accounting profession to police the self-regulatory system that previously existed. The Act also addressed auditor independence requirements. Another feature of the Sarbanes-Oxley

Act is its increased criminalization of corporate conduct involving fraud with respect to publicly held companies. Some of the more important provisions affecting public corporations are described below.

Title III of the Sarbanes-Oxley Act addressed various corporate governance concerns including the audit committee, requiring personal certifications of accuracy by the chief executive and chief financial officers of public companies. The Act further prohibits loans to high-ranking executives, subject to certain exceptions to be elaborated upon in SEC rulemaking. The Act also calls for enhanced financial disclosures by public companies.

Titles VIII and IX of the Sarbanes-Oxley Act provide for enhanced criminal penalties for violations of the Act generally and in particular for frauds perpetrated upon shareholders of public companies. Sarbanes-Oxley provides protection to corporate whistle-blowers. The Act also covers other areas, including heightened controls over securities analysts' conflicts of interest and a sense of the Senate that federal corporate tax returns should be signed by a corporation's chief executive officer.

§ 27.6 FEDERAL SECURITIES ACT OF 1933—OVERVIEW

The heart of the Act is section 5,[16] which is designed to assure an informed market for investments. Section 5, absent an applicable exemption, prohibits the offer and sale of securities unless a registration statement has been filed with the Securities and Exchange Commission. Section 5 further requires the delivery of a prospectus to purchasers as well as to offerees. Section 3[17] exempts from the registration requirements a wide variety of securities, including securities issued by governmental bodies, banks, and insurance companies. Section 4[18] lists categories of transactions that are exempt from the registration and prospectus requirements.[19] Registration procedures are found in sections 6 and 8 of the Act.[20] The disclosure requirements are broadly set forth in sections 7 and 10 and in Schedule A.[21] More detailed disclosure guidelines are found in the applicable SEC forms and regulations. Section 11 provides a private right of action for investors who have purchased securities offered pursuant to a materially misleading registration statement.[22] Section 12 imposes civil liability on persons who sell securities in violation of section 5's registration and prospectus requirements, as well as on anyone who sells a security using materially misleading statements.[23] Section 17 embodies general antifraud proscriptions in connection with the offer or sale of securities.[24] Section 19 gives the SEC broad rule-making power, and section 20 gives the Commission broad enforcement powers.[25]

§ 27.7 The Registration and Prospectus Requirements of the Securities Act of 1933

In the absence of a security or transaction exemption,[26] no security may be publicly offered or sold in interstate or foreign commerce or through the mails until it has been registered with the Securities and Exchange Commission. When new issues are distributed in a public offering by an issuer or underwriter, agent or dealer, complete information must be made publicly available for the benefit of original and subsequent purchasers. The 1933 Act thus closes the mails and other communications in interstate commerce to the sale, offering, or carriage for the purpose of sale or delivery of any security or any prospectus unless a registration statement is filed and is in effect as to such security.[27] Similarly, there can be neither offers to sell nor offers to buy prior to the filing of the registration statement.[28] After the registration statement has been filed, there is no longer any prohibition against offers to buy or oral offers to sell; however, all written offers to sell must conform to the Act's prospectus requirements.[29] Finally, no sales may be made until after the registration statement becomes effective.[30]

The first duty of counsel with reference to an issue of securities is to ascertain whether registration is required. The only way to avoid registration is by reliance on one of the Act's security or transaction exemptions. The lawyer must accordingly be able to answer the following questions: (1) What constitutes a "security"?; (2) What constitutes a sale or "offer to sell"?; and (3) What securities and transactions are exempted?

Section 5 of the 1933 Securities Act breaks down the registration process into three periods. These periods are based on the filing and effective date of the registration statement, which generally will be prepared by a team of lawyers, accountants, issuer's management, and underwriters.

The first is the "prefiling" period, starting months before the filing of the registration statement and lasting until the filing date. The second period, the "waiting" period, runs from the filing date until the effective date.[31] The last period, the "post-effective" period, begins at the effective date and is the first time that sales may take place.

Section 5 of the Act places various restrictions on the dissemination of information throughout the registration process. A violation of section 5 depends on use of the jurisdictional means—an instrumentality of interstate commerce. Section 5 limits the type of selling efforts that may be used. The scope of permissible selling efforts and the type of information that may be disseminated varies depending on whether one is operating during the prefiling period, waiting period, or post-effective period. In general, sections 5(a)(1) and 5(a)(2) are in effect in the prefiling and waiting periods, but not during the post-effective period. Section 5(b)(1) is in effect in the waiting period and post-effective period, but not during the prefiling period. Section 5(b)(2) is in effect only in the post-effective period. Finally, section 5(c) is in effect only in the prefiling period.

Prefiling Period. Section 5(c) of the Act prohibits all offers to sell and buy prior to the filing of the registration statement. An offer to sell is any communication reasonably calculated to generate a buying interest. It applies to oral as well as to written offers. A large body of public information concerning securities is generated by broker-dealers, investment advisers, and other financial analysts. Balanced against the desire to prevent "gun jumping," as expressed by the prohibitions of section 5(c), is the underlying purpose of federal securities regulation: affirmative disclosure. Therefore there are various exemptions from section 5(c)'s prohibitions in the prefiling period. For example, SEC Rules 137, 138, and 139 provide exemptions from gun-jumping prohibitions for certain broker-dealer recommendations in the case of securities of 1934 Act reporting companies.[32] These exemptions apply with equal force to the waiting and post-effective periods. These rules recognize the fact that many investment bankers have research analysts who are separate from the underwriting department. Accordingly, the rules permit the research department to continue with its regular business without violating the prohibitions of section 5 of the 1933 Act. The exemptions are conditioned on certain protections, including the requirements that the issuer of the recommended securities is sufficiently large and subject to the reporting requirements (which ensure that there is sufficient public information already available). At the same time, it is clear that any broker's or dealer's recommendation to purchase a security that does not fall within the parameters of these rules would violate section 5— unless, of course, some other exemption could be found.

Section 2(a)(3)'s definition of the terms "sale" and "offer to sell" excludes preliminary negotiations and agreements between the issuer and the underwriter as well as among underwriters in privity with the issuer.[33] This exclusion permits the formation of the underwriting syndicate. However, generally only a letter of intent is signed at this stage; the final underwriting agreement is usually not executed until the eve of the offering. Although there may be prefiling activity designed to form the underwriting group, contacting too many potential underwriters or potential members of the retail "selling group" may be viewed as improperly preconditioning the market and therefore may result in a finding of illegally jumping the gun. The purpose of the section 2(a)(3) exclusion for underwriter negotiations and agreements is to balance the need for formation of the underwriting group against the desire not to have premature widespread generation of a buying interest.

Section 5(a) of the 1933 Act prohibits sales prior to the effective date and thus operates during both the prefiling and waiting periods. Section 5(a)(1) prohibits the sale (or confirmation of a sale) prior to the effective date; section 5(a)(2) prohibits taking steps toward the sale or delivery of securities pursuant to a sale through instrumentalities of interstate commerce prior to the effective date.

All companies are allowed to publicly disseminate information that does not refer to a securities offering, provided the issuer takes reasonable steps to prevent further distribution of the information during the 30 days immediately preceding the public offering.[34] There is also a more expansive safe harbor for preexisting public companies, or seasoned issuers, that explicitly includes both "factual business information or forward-looking information."[35] As a practical matter, most of section 5(c)'s gun-jumping prohibitions do not apply to the largest public companies that qualify as well-known seasoned issuers (WKSIs). A WKSI is a company that qualifies for registration on 1933 Act Form S-3 or F-3 and meets other specific conditions.[36]

Waiting Period. Section 5(c)'s prohibitions on offers to sell and buy no longer apply once the registration statement has been filed. However, section 5(a)'s prohibitions on sales continue through the waiting period. In addition, section 5(b) of the 1933 Act imposes prospectus requirements that have the effect of controlling the types of written offers to sell that may be made during both the waiting and post-effective periods. Section 5(b)(1) provides that any prospectus must meet the requirements of section 10 of the 1933 Act.[37] Section 2(a)(10)[38] defines "prospectus" as any written or other permanent or widely disseminated offer to sell. For example, a telephone communication is not a prospectus, but a television or radio advertisement is. A written confirmation of a sale is expressly included in the statutory definition of "prospectus."[39]

The combination of these statutory provisions results in a limited variety of permissible written offers to sell that may be used during the waiting period (and post-effective period as well). While section 5 permits offers during the waiting period, section 2(a)(10) makes any offer in writing a prospectus, and section 5(b)(1) makes it unlawful to transmit any prospectus after the filing of the registration statement unless the prospectus contains the information called for by section 10. This information may not be available until the underwriting agreements have been signed and the offering price set. The Act solves this problem by exempting from this path the "tombstone ad" and the preliminary, or "red herring," prospectus. Both are discussed below.

Because section 5(c) does not apply during the waiting period, offers to buy are permissible. However, an offer to buy that leads to a premature or otherwise illegal sale will violate section 5(a). By virtue of section 10(b), which permits certain prospectuses during the waiting period, and section 2(a)(10), which excludes certain communications from the definition of "prospectus," there are five types of permissible waiting period offers to sell.

First, all oral communications are permitted, provided that no sale is consummated (lest there be a violation of section 5(a)).[40] Since an oral communication is not "permanent," it is excluded from the section 2(a)(10) definition of "prospectus."

Second, an "identifying statement" (one variety of which is known as a "tombstone ad"), as defined in section 2(a)(10)(b) and Rule 134, is permissible during the waiting period.[41] This is a relatively narrow category because the type of information that may be included is severely limited. Section 2(a)(10)(b) expressly excludes these communications from the definition of "prospectus" as long as the requirements of Rule 134 are met. Inclusion of any information not specifically permitted by Rule 134 renders the rule unavailable and thus may result in a prospectus that fails to comply with section 10's requirements. This in turn can result in a violation of section 5.

Third, a preliminary (or "red herring") prospectus, as defined in Rule 430,[42] is permissible during the waiting period. The preliminary prospectus must contain the information required in a full-blown statutory prospectus, except that the price and some other terms may be omitted. Furthermore, there must be a legend explaining that it is a preliminary prospectus. This prospectus may be used only during the waiting period; it may not be used after the effective date.

Fourth, a preliminary summary prospectus, as defined in Rule 431,[43] which, like the red herring prospectus, is a section 10(b) prospectus, may be used by certain experienced issuers during the waiting period. The summary prospectus may also be used after the effective date and, like the preliminary version, is available only for an issuer who is a 1934 Act registered reporting company. The Rule 431 prospectus must contain all of the information specified in the official SEC form accompanying the applicable registration statement form as well as a caption stating that a more complete prospectus will be available from designated broker-dealers. The summary prospectus may not include any information not permitted in the registration statement or in a tombstone ad, as spelled out in Rule 134(a). A Rule 431 summary prospectus satisfies only section 5(b)(1);[44] it does not satisfy section 5(b)(2).[45] Thus, when a Rule 431 summary prospectus is used, a full-blown (or statutory) section 10(a) prospectus must still be delivered to all purchasers. This necessarily increases the record-keeping and monitoring activities of the underwriters.

Fifth, under Rules 163 and 164, the SEC now allows qualifying issuers to use a free writing prospectus during the prefiling and waiting periods.[46] A free writing prospectus constitutes an offer to sell and must contain a statement explaining that the offering is being made pursuant to a registration statement. WKSIs are generally able to use a free writing prospectus regardless of whether a registration statement has been filed with the SEC. Other issuers generally must file a registration statement with the SEC first. In some cases dealing with unseasoned reporting companies, the free writing prospectus must be accompanied or preceded by a statutory prospectus.

Post-Effective Period. Once the registration statement becomes effective, section 5(a)'s prohibitions cease to apply, and sales are permitted. Both of section 5(b)'s prospectus requirements apply. Subsection (b)(1) requires that all written or otherwise permanent offers to sell or confirmations of sales must be qualifying prospectuses (that is, a section 10(a) full-blown statutory prospectus or a qualifying section 10(b) prospectus). Section 5(b)(2) provides that no security may be delivered for sale unless accompanied or preceded by a statutory section 10(a) prospectus. As part of the SEC public offering reforms adopted in 2005, the physical delivery requirement was replaced with an "access equals delivery" approach with respect to final prospectuses.[47] In the case of securities held for a customer's account by a broker or other custodian, the customer must still receive the prospectus before delivery.

Under section 2(a)(10), "free writing" is permitted in the post-effective period. Thus, supplemental sales information may be sent to prospective purchasers, provided that the information is preceded or accompanied by a prospectus that meets the requirements of section 10(a). In such a case, free writing is limited only by the antifraud provisions of the securities laws.[48]

§ 27.7 WHAT CONSTITUTES A SECURITY UNDER FEDERAL AND STATE LAW?

The federal securities laws provide jurisdiction, of course, over securities. But what is the definition of "security"? The term has been broadly defined by the statutes; section 2(a)(1) of the Securities Act of 1933 is representative.[49]

The administrative and judicial definition of "security" has developed primarily from the interpretation of the statutory phrase "investment contract." In struggling for an appropriate definition, courts have always been mindful that the bottom-line issue is whether the particular investment or instrument involved needs or demands the investor protection of the federal securities laws.[50]

The landmark case on the definition of "investment contract" is *SEC v. W.J. Howey Co.*[51] Under the test developed in that case, a contract, transaction, or scheme is an investment contract if "a person [1] invests his money [2] in a common enterprise and [3] is led to expect profits [4] solely from the efforts of the promoter or a third party."[52]

The definition of "security" is not limited to investment contracts. For example, stock is explicitly included in the statutory definition.

There is a strong presumption that stock is a security. Nevertheless, under the "economic reality" test, it has been held that some transfers of instruments called stock are not transfers of securities.

Both the 1933 and 1934 Acts provide that "any note" is a security. However, both the statutes themselves and the courts have modified the phrase so that it is not read literally. Special provisions deal with the applicability of the federal securities laws to short-term notes. Section 3(a)(3) of the Securities Act of 1933 exempts from registration (but not from liability imposed by antifraud provisions of the Act) any "note . . . aris[ing] out of a current transaction" with a maturity not exceeding nine months.[53] In contrast, section 3(a)(10) of the Securities Exchange Act of 1934 excludes (even from the antifraud provisions) such notes from the definition of "security."[54] The Supreme Court declared that the phrase "any note" "must be understood against the backdrop of what Congress was attempting to accomplish in enacting the Securities Acts."[55] In the *Reves* case, the Supreme Court adopted the "family resemblance" test for determining whether or not a note is a security. Using this approach, the starting point is a rebuttable presumption that the note is a security. Based on a number of factors, the courts have created a list of instruments that, although they are "notes," do not fall within the definition of "security."[56] The presumption that a note is a security may be rebutted by showing that the note in question fits in a category on the list, bears a strong "family resemblance" to a category on the list, or belongs to another category that should be on the list.

Another common form of investment is a partnership interest. Partnership interests can implicate the definition of "security." Since general partners ordinarily take an active part in the business, interests in a general partnership ordinarily will not be securities.[57] However, when partners are likely to be relying substantially on the efforts of others, the interest may be a security.[58] It is for this reason that limited partnership interests (where investors cannot exercise control) will ordinarily be classified as securities.[59] In the case of the new form of doing business known as a limited liability company, if the enterprise is set up in such a way that the owners will be active participants, the securities laws are not likely to be implicated.[60] However, if the limited liability company is used as a passive investment for its members, then a security is likely to exist.[61]

§ 27.8 SECURITIES AND TRANSACTION EXEMPTIONS UNDER FEDERAL LAW

It is to be recalled that section 5 of the 1933 Act applies to any offer or sale of any security unless an exemption exists.[62] Exemptions may be based on the type of security involved (generally covered by section 3 of the 1933 Act and various SEC rules promulgated thereunder)[63] or on the type of transaction (generally covered by section 4 of the Act and applicable rules). The exemptions granted are exemptions from registration, not from the antifraud provisions. Exemptions are strictly construed, and the burden of proof falls on the person trying to establish the exemption.

Section 3 of the 1933 Act is designed to provide exemptions from section 5 because of the nature of the security involved. For example, section 3(a)(2) exempts bank securities, insurance policies, and government securities. Section 3(a)(11) contains an intrastate exemption for securities offered and sold exclusively within the issuer's state of incorporation.

Section 3(b) of the 1933 Act empowers the SEC to provide additional small issues exemptions by promulgating appropriate rules. This section is not self-executing: It requires "enabling rules" developed and promulgated by the SEC. Thus, the SEC has the freedom to create the exemptions it believes necessary or appropriate in light of the agency's policy considerations. Currently, such exemptions are limited to offerings of $5 million or less.[64] The section 3(b) exemptions emanating from this provision can be found in Regulation A, Regulation B, Rules 504 and 505 of Regulation D. In 1996, Congress gave the SEC broader, virtually unlimited exemptive authority via a new section 28 of the Act, making the raising of section 3(b)'s ceiling far less significant.[65]

Section 4 of the 1933 Act describes the types of transactions that are exempt from the registration requirements of section 5. Transaction exemptions rise and fall with both the form and substance of the transaction and the nature of the participants. These exemptions, once available, can be destroyed when purchasers under the exemption resell the securities. Downstream sales have the potential to eradicate an existing exemption.

Section 4(1) provides a transaction exemption for persons other than an issuer, underwriter, or dealer. "Issuer" and "dealer" are defined in the 1933 Act[66] and have been interpreted as in ordinary parlance, not as terms of art. "Underwriter," by contrast, has become a term of art subject to significant SEC and judicial construction.

Determining who is included in this definition has required substantial interpretation. Someone who is an essential cog in the distribution process is a statutory underwriter even if no remuneration is received.[67] It has been established that, by definition, underwriters include participants in relatively large transactions who may unwittingly become underwriters and thus subject to the proscriptions of section 5.[68] The Act's definition encompasses persons who purchase or otherwise obtain a large amount of securities directly from the issuer (or a control person) and who then resell the securities.[69]

The need for predictability led to SEC promulgation of Rule 144, a safe-harbor rule. Rule 144 applies to all sales for control persons and other affiliates of the issuer,[70] and resales of restricted securities (generally restricted to preserve the original exemption) by anyone.

Section 4(2) exempts private placements and other "transactions by an issuer not involving any public offering."[71] This exemption was enacted to permit offerings by issuers for isolated sales to particularly sophisticated persons wherein there is no need for the Act's protections. Although the statutory language is somewhat vague, after years of SEC decisions, interpretive releases,[72] and judicial scrutiny, certain key factors have been isolated by the Supreme Court.[73] First, the number of offerees: although the Supreme Court expressly refused to adopt a "numbers test" as determinative, the number of offerees remains an important factor—the fewer the number, the greater likelihood that a section 4(2) exemption applies. Likewise, the size of the offering is a factor: the smaller the offering, the greater chance for an exemption. Second, access to information: each offeree should have access to the type of information that would be disclosed should the issuer be required to undertake a full-fledged registration. Third, the sophistication of investors: each offeree should be sophisticated with respect to business and financial matters, as well as with respect to the particular investment being offered.[74] Fourth, the manner of the offering: it should be limited to those who have a privately expressed interest rather than be a general solicitation.

Section 4(3) provides an exemption from the prospectus delivery requirements for certain transactions by dealers. This exemption is directed generally to the aftermarket, after primary distribution has occurred. Section 4(4) of the Act exempts unsolicited brokers' transactions.

Section 4(5) (formerly section 4(6)) exempts offerings made solely to accredited investors where the aggregate amount of securities sold does not exceed the dollar limit of section 3(b) (currently $5 million). "Accredited investor" is defined in section 2(a)(15) of the 1933 Act.[75]

Under the authority of section 3(b)(1) of the 1933 Act, the SEC promulgated Regulation A[76] to exempt certain "small issues." Regulation A is limited to issuers in the United States or Canada that are not investment companies, and it applies to issues with an aggregate offering price of $5 million or less within a one-year period. The Regulation A exemption contains "bad boy" disqualification provisions that render it unavailable in most cases if a participant in the offering has been subject to SEC disciplinary proceedings or has been convicted of a violation of relevant laws in the last five years.[77] In 2012 Congress added a new section 3(b)(2) mandating SEC rulemaking for an exemption for offerings up to $50 million every twelve months.[78]

Regulation D[79] consists of three separate private offering and small offering exemptions: Rule 504, Rule 505, and Rule 506, a safe harbor. Rules 504 and 505 are section 3(b) exemptions, while Rule 506 is promulgated under section 4(2)'s nonpublic offering exemption. These three exemptions are all governed by Rules 501, 502, 503, 507, and 508. The exemptions are, of course, exemptions only from registration, not from the antifraud or civil liability sections of the federal securities laws; nor do the exemptions relieve the issuer of the necessity to comply with state securities laws. Regulation D exemptions are available only to the issuer of securities, not to affiliates or purchasers of securities that were initially acquired under Regulation D offerings.

Under Rule 504, which is an exemption promulgated under section 3(b), an issuer that is not an investment company or a 1934 Act reporting company may have an exemption for small offerings. There is a $1 million limit on the aggregate offering price. All securities offered within the past 12 months under a section 3(b) exemption and all securities offered in violation of section 5 within the past 12 months are included in calculating the aggregate offering price.[80] General solicitations of purchasers are permitted and no resale restrictions are required, but, as a practical matter, only if the offering is registered under applicable state securities law (or blue sky law) provisions.

Rule 505, which is also a section 3(b)(1) exemption, exempts certain offerings up to $5 million by issuers that are not investment companies.[81] The offering must be limited to no more than 35 purchasers, but related purchasers and accredited investors do not count in that limit. No general solicitation is permitted. There are no limitations on the nature of the purchasers; however, there are informational requirements for any of the offerees who are not accredited. As with Regulation A offerings, Rule 505 offerings are subject to the "bad boy" disqualification provisions of Rule 262. Resales of the securities relying on this exemption are subject to restrictions.[82]

Rule 506, the third exemption in Regulation D, is a safe harbor for a section 4(2) exemption.[82] There is no limit on the dollar amount of an offering under Rule 506. General solicitation of purchasers is not permitted, and the offering is limited to 35 unaccredited purchasers.[84] Moreover, all of the unaccredited purchasers must be knowledgeable, sophisticated, and able to evaluate and bear the risks of the prospective investment, or represented by such a person.[85] Additionally, the purchasers must have access to the information as required by Rule 502(b), and affirmative disclosure of such information must be made by the issuer if there are any unaccredited purchasers. Rule 506, like Rule 505, is subject to the limitations on resale imposed by Rule 502(d). Downstream sales are similarly governed by Rule 144.

The "integration" doctrine is to the SEC what the "step transaction" doctrine is to the IRS. It permits the telescoping of two or more purportedly separate transactions into one transaction. Under the integration doctrine, the SEC and the courts examine multiple offerings to determine whether they should be treated as a single, unitary transaction. The SEC has developed the following five-factor test[86] to determine whether the integration doctrine should be applied to two or more transactions: (1) Are the sales part of a single plan of financing?; (2) Do the sales involve issuance of the same class of securities?; (3) Were the sales made at or about the same time?; (4) Is the same type of consideration received?; and (5) Are the sales made for the same general purpose? The Commission has not given much guidance on how these factors should be weighted. Accordingly, it would appear that in a particular case any one or more of the five factors could be determinative.

§ 27.9 CIVIL LIABILITY FOR VIOLATIONS OF THE SECURITIES ACT OF 1933

The 1933 Act creates private rights of action for both fraud-based violations and violations of the Act's registration provisions. The Act has three sections prohibiting fraud and misstatements. Sections 11[87] and 12(a)(2)[88] create remedies based on material misrepresentation. Section 17 does not contain a private remedy but sets forth the Act's general antifraud provision,[89] used primarily by the SEC and by the Department of Justice in criminal actions. In addition to the antifraud provisions mentioned above, section 12(a)(1) of the 1933 Act creates a private right of action for violations of that Act's registration requirements.[90]

[1] Misrepresentations and Omissions in Registration Statements—Section 11

Section 11 imposes express civil liability on persons preparing and signing materially misleading registration statements.[91] Section 11 is the only liability provision limited to registered offerings. It imposes broader liability than other antifraud provisions because aggrieved purchasers need only show that they bought the security traceable to the offering, and there was a material misrepresentation in the registration statement. There is no requirement under section 11 that purchasers show that they relied on the misrepresentation.[92]

There are two standards of liability imposed by section 11. The first standard applies to the issuer, which is, generally, strictly liable once the plaintiffs have proved that they bought the stock and that there was a material misstatement in the registration statement. The only affirmative defenses for the issuer are (1) to show that the person acquiring the security knew of the untruth or omission in the registration statement at the time of the acquisition, (2) lack of materiality, or (3) expiration of the statute of limitations. The second standard of liability applies to nonissuers.

For all persons other than the issuer,[93] section 11(b) provides three additional possible affirmative defenses. The first two defenses relate to someone who discovers the material misstatement or omission and takes appropriate steps to prevent the violation. Potential section 11 defendants may be relieved of liability by either (1) resigning or taking steps toward resignation, and informing the SEC and the issuer in writing that they have taken such action and disclaim all responsibility for the relevant sections of the registration statement; or (2) if the registration statement becomes effective without their knowledge, on becoming aware of the effectiveness they take appropriate steps toward resignation, inform the Commission as above, and give reasonable public notice that the registration statement became effective without their knowledge.

The third defense, contained in section 11(b)(3), is the most frequently used. This absolves defendants from liability if they had reasonable grounds for believing, and did in fact believe, that there was no omission or material misstatement. This accordingly insulates defendants from liability if, after reasonable investigation, they have a reasonable basis to believe and did believe the registration statement was free of any material misstatement or omission when it became effective. As for any portion of a registration statement prepared on the authority of an expert, such as an accountant, others are liable only if they fail to establish they had no reasonable ground to believe and did not believe the registration statement contained a material misstatement or omission when it became effective.

Section 11(c) establishes the appropriate standard of care: "[T]he standard of reasonableness shall be that required of a prudent man in the management of his own property."[94] Thus, this defense is often described as the "due diligence" (although that phrase does not appear in the statute) and "reasonable investigation" defense. The courts have not articulated a bright-line test as to what satisfies the due diligence and reasonable investigation standard of care.[95] What has emerged, however, is a sliding scale of culpability depending on the defendant's knowledge, expertise, and status with regard to the issuer, its affiliates, or its underwriters, as well as the degree of the defendant's actual participation in the registration process and in the preparation of registration materials.[96]

[2] Liability of Sellers for Violations of Section 5 and Material Misstatements or Omissions in the Prospectus or Otherwise— Section 12

Section 12 of the 1933 Act[97] imposes liability in two contexts: when a person sells a security in violation of section 5,[98] or when a security is sold by means of a prospectus or oral communication that contains a material misstatement or omission.[99] Unlike section 11, section 12 by its terms applies to any transaction, whether or not it is subject to the registration provisions of the 1933 Act. A major issue in many section 12 cases is whether the defendant is a permissible one—that is, a "seller" for purposes of section 12. Issuers and underwriters generally are not "sellers" within the meaning of section 12, unless they actively participate in the negotiations with the plaintiff/purchaser.[100] Similarly, an attorney's having worked on the offering circular will not make her a seller.[101] On the other hand, a broker who deals directly with the plaintiff is a seller under section 12.[102] The Supreme Court has delineated two factors that should be considered in identifying a "seller" under section 12: (1) whether the defendant received direct remuneration or benefit as a result of the sale, and (2) whether the defendant's role in the solicitation and purchase was intended to benefit the seller (or owner) of the security.[103]

Civil Liability for Sales in Violation of Section 5—Section 12(a)(1). Anyone who offers or sells a security in violation of section 5 is liable in a civil action under section 12(a)(1) to the person "purchasing such security from him." In order to recover under this section, the plaintiff need only show that the defendant sold the security to him and that it was unregistered. The defendant then carries the burden of either showing that an exemption existed or establishing the in pari delicto (or equal fault) defense.

Liability of Sellers for Material Misstatements or Omissions— Section 12(a)(2). Section 12(a)(2) of the 1933 Act creates an express private remedy for a purchaser against the seller of a security for material misstatements or omissions in connection with the offer and sale. As is the case with section 12(a)(1), section 12(a)(2) is limited to the liability of sellers and thus imposes a privity requirement. Once the privity requirement is satisfied, the plaintiff must establish only that there was a material misstatement or omission in the prospectus or oral communication. There is no requirement that the plaintiff prove reliance; it will be presumed.[104] The plaintiff also need not have read the misstatement in question.[105] However, if the plaintiff knew of the untruth or omission, the section 12(a)(2) claim should be dismissed.[106] The defendant may also be absolved of liability if "he did not know, and in the exercise of reasonable care could not have known, of such untruth or omission."[107] The Supreme Court has limited the section 12(a)(2) actions to sales pursuant to an offering by prospectus.[108]

§ 27.10 THE SECURITIES EXCHANGE ACT OF 1934

The Securities Exchange Act of 1934 deals with a greater variety of subjects than the Securities Act of 1933. The Exchange Act provides for (1) the registration and supervision of national securities exchanges (section 6);[109] (2) margin requirements, which govern the purchase of securities on credit, and restrictions on borrowing by members, brokers, and dealers (sections 7, 8);[110] (3) prohibition of the manipulation of securities prices (sections 9, 10);[111] (4) regulation of functions of brokers, members, and dealers (sections 11, 15(c));[112] (5) registration requirements for securities trading on national exchanges, and reports of companies whose securities are listed (section 12)[113]—the registration and reporting provisions also extend to certain over-the-counter equity securities[114] and the reporting provisions for securities subject to registration under the 1933 Act;[115] (6) registration of over-the-counter brokers and dealers and supervision of their general trade practices (sections 15, 15A);[116] (7) solicitation of proxies, consents, or authorizations as to securities registered on national securities exchanges (to be under rules and regulations prescribed by the Commission) (section 14);[117] (8) regulation of tender offers and other share acquisitions (sections 13, 14);[118] (9) special rules for municipal securities dealers (section 15B); (10) recovery by the corporation of short-swing profits of directors, officers, and large shareholders in securities of their own companies to prevent unfair profits by insiders;[119] and (11) periodic and other reports by issuers subject to the Act (section 13).[120] The Commission has administrative power to expel or suspend members of exchanges whose conduct fails to conform to prescribed standards (section 19(h)(3)). The Commission also has investigatory, adjudicatory, and prosecutorial functions with regard to violations of the Acts' various provisions. Manipulative, deceptive, or fraudulent devices by brokers and dealers, such as the sale of securities in excess of prevalent market prices, are grounds for revocation of registration and license as broker or dealer and forfeiture of all undisclosed profits (section 15). Even beyond these administrative sanctions, the Act contains criminal penalties[121] and a broad spectrum of civil liability provisions.

Issuers of securities are regulated by both the 1933 Act and the 1934 Act. The 1933 Act regulates distribution of securities; the 1934 Act deals with day-to-day trading. While most of the 1934 Act's regulation applies only to registered and/or reporting companies, two important provisions are not so limited: (1) the general antifraud provisions of section 10(b) and, in particular, SEC Rule 10b-5; and (2) the tender offer antifraud provision found in section 14(e).

There are two jurisdictional bases for regulation of securities and their issuers under the 1934 Act. First, some of the regulation is triggered by use of an instrumentality of interstate commerce.[122] The second basis for jurisdiction is found in the registration provisions of section 12 and the periodic reporting provisions of sections 13 and 15.

Section 12 of the 1934 Act requires registration of most publicly traded securities.[123] Under section 12(a), any security that is traded on a national exchange must be registered under the 1934 Act.[124] Section 12(a) thus covers exchange-traded equity securities (stock and securities convertible into stock), exchange-traded options (puts and calls),[125] and exchange-traded debt securities (bonds). The registration provisions of section 12 further apply to equity securities that are publicly traded in over-the-counter markets[126] rather than on an exchange.

Until April 2012, by virtue of section 12(g)(1) of the Exchange Act and Rule 12g–1, 1934 Act registration was required for non-exchange listed companies having both a class of equity securities with 500 or more shareholders of record and have more than ten million dollars in total assets.[127] In 2012, Congress amended section 12(g) to increase the threshold from 500 to 2,000 shareholders of record but retains the lower 500 record holder threshold with respect to investors who are not accredited investors.[128] The registration and consequent periodic reporting obligations cease, if on the last day of each of the issuer's last three fiscal years, the issuer (1) has had fewer than 300 shareholders of record of that class of securities or (2) has had assets not exceeding $5 million.[129] In such cases, the issuer may withdraw its registration.

Registration under the 1934 Act brings with it periodic disclosure obligations. Section 13 of the 1934 Act sets forth the periodic reporting requirements. The basic reports that must be filed with the SEC are (1) Form 10-K, an annual report; (2) Form 10-Q, a quarterly report; and (3) Form 8-K, an interim "current report." Form 8-K's interim reporting requirements are relatively limited, and, as a general rule, companies are not under an affirmative duty to disclose information until the next quarterly report. Section 13 periodic reporting requirements are not limited to companies that register securities. Section 15(d) of the 1934

Act also imposes the same periodic reporting requirements on companies who issue securities pursuant to a 1933 Act registration statement.[130]

The 2012 JOBS act provides some relaxation of reporting requirements for certain companies that have recently gone public. The "on ramp" provisions of the Act set forth establishes a new class of issuers, "emerging growth companies" defining this group as companies with less than $1 billion in total annual revenues (provided the issuer does not have a public float above $700 million); this category encompasses all but the very largest issuers in their initial years after an IPO. The proposal seeks to make a registered public offering more attractive to emerging growth companies by relieving them (for up to five years) of a list of specific obligations that would otherwise follow from their becoming a reporting company after an IPO. To be precise, the dispensations terminate on the earlier of (1) the issuer's revenues reaching $1 billion, the issuer having a public float of $700 million, or (2) the passage of five years since going public.

These on-ramp amendments provide a host of dispensations such as: excusing detailed executive pay disclosures and the non-binding say on pay votes, compliance with any new accounting standards, and any future mandate that firms rotate auditors, and reintroduces the research analysts to the underwriting effort.

§ 27.11 CIVIL LIABILITY UNDER THE SECURITIES EXCHANGE ACT OF 1934

The Securities Exchange Act of 1934 contains both express and implied private rights of action, although the three provisions that expressly create liability are much narrower than those in the Securities Act of 1933. Section 9(e) of the Act confers a private remedy against one who has engaged willfully in market manipulation of securities subject to the Act's reporting requirements.[131] The Supreme Court has pointed out that "manipulation" is a term of art limited to specific types of market conduct designed to manipulate the price, such as artificial bids and wash sales, and thus does not extend to all cases where conduct has the deliberate intent to affect price.[132] Section 18(a) provides a private remedy to an investor defrauded by reliance on documents filed with the SEC.[133] Under the "eyeball" requirement, courts have limited the 18(a) remedy to plaintiffs who have viewed the actual filed document or a copy of it;

thus section 18(a) does not apply to statements that are seen elsewhere.[134] There is no scienter requirement, but a defendant can prevail by proving good faith and lack of knowledge of the misstatement or omission. Under the better view, the section 18(a) remedy is not exclusive.[135] The third express remedy, under section 16(b), which was considered earlier, provides for disgorgement by insiders of short-swing profits on equity securities. Like the other two express remedies, section 16(b) is limited to reporting companies.[136]

The Supreme Court has recognized implied private remedy proxy antifraud prohibitions[137] and Rule 10b-5's general antifraud provisions.[138] Although a competing tender offeror does not have standing to sue for damages,[139] a number of courts have recognized an implied remedy under section 14(e) relating to tender offers.[140]

[1] Conduct Proscribed

As pointed out above, Rule 10b-5 represents delegated rulemaking pursuant to statutory authority giving the SEC the power to prohibit the use of "manipulative or deceptive device[s] or contrivance[s]" "in connection with the purchase or sale of any security."[141] Since the rule represents lawmaking delegated by the legislature, the rule can be only as broad as the delegating statutory provision. Accordingly, the terms of the statute place limits on the permissible scope of the rule. The rule itself has a sparse legislative history but has spawned a great deal of litigation. For example, the conduct prohibited by the rule must have been "deceptive."[142] This in turn has been interpreted to mean that the absence of full disclosure is the essence of the evil addressed. Additionally, the courts have read the deception requirement as limiting section 10(b) to fraudulent conduct.[143] Rule 10b-5 is discussed in Chapter 12.

NOTES

For a more detailed overview, *see* THOMAS LEE HAZEN, SECURITIES REGULATION (ABA Corporate Counsel Series 2011). For a more complete analysis, *see* THOMAS LEE HAZEN, TREATISE ON THE LAW OF SECURITIES REGULATION (6th ed. 2009).

1. Kan. Laws 1911 ch. 133.
2. 15 U.S.C.A. §§ 77a *et seq.*, 78a *et seq.* (2009).
3. Kan. Laws 1911 ch. 133 ("an Act to provide for the regulation and supervision of investment companies and providing penalties for the violation thereof").

4. Pub. L. No. 104-290, 110 Stat. 3416 (1996).
5. Section 18(b)(1)(A), 15 U.S.C.A. § 77r(b)(1)(A) (2009).
6. Section 18(c)(2), 15 U.S.C.A. § 77r(c)(2) (2009).
7. Section 18(b)(4), 15 U.S.C.A. § 77r(b)(4) (2009).
8. *See, e.g.,* THOMAS LEE HAZEN, TREATISE ON THE LAW OF SECURITIES REGULATION §§ 7.17[2], 12.15[2] (6th ed.).
9. 15 U.S.C.A. §§ 77p(f)(3), 78bb(f)(5)(E); 1933 Act § 16(f)(3) (2009). This definition in turn refers to section 18 of the Securities Act of 1933, 15 U.S.C.A. § 77r, which preempts those securities from state registration requirements. Debt securities exempt under section 4(2) of the Investment Company Act are, however, excluded from the definition of covered securities. 15 U.S.C.A. § 77p(f)(3); 1934 Act § 28(f)(5)(E), 15 U.S.C.A. § 78bb(f)(5)(E) (2009).
10. 15 U.S.C.A. § 78bb(f)(1) (2009) (a class action or constructive class action brought "by any private party alleging (1) an untrue statement or omission of a material fact in connection with the purchase or sale of a covered security, or (2) that the defendant employed any manipulative or deceptive device or contrivance in connection with the purchase or sale of a covered security").
11. *Id.* §§ 77p(d)(1), 78pp(f)(3)(A). This has been referred to as the "Delaware carve out," although it is not expressly limited to Delaware. It is designed to preserve remedies under Delaware law involving breaches of fiduciary duty and disclosure to existing shareholders in corporate transactions.
12. 15 *Id.* §§ 77p(d)(2), 78pp(f)(3)(B).
13. Arthur H. Dean, *The Lawyer's Problems in the Registration of Securities,* 4 LAW & CONTEMP. PROBS. 154, 189 (1937).
14. 48 Stat. 74, 15 U.S.C.A. §§ 77a to 77aa (2009) (Securities Act of 1933); 48 Stat. 881, 15 U.S.C.A. §§ 78a *et seq.* (2009) (Securities Exchange Act of 1934); 48 Stat. 912, 11 U.S.C.A. § 207 (2009) (Bankruptcy Act § 77B); 47 Stat. 1474, 11 U.S.C.A. § 205 (2009) (Railroad Reorganization Act); 53 Stat. 1149, 15 U.S.C.A. §§ 77aaa *et seq.* (2009) (Trust Indenture Act of 1939); 49 Stat. 1491, 7 U.S.C.A. (generally disbursed through Chapter 1) (2009) (Commodity Exchange Act); 54 Stat. 79, 15 U.S.C.A. §§ 80a-1 *et seq.* and 80b-1 *et seq.* (1982) (Investment Company and Investment Advisers Acts of 1940).
15. SARBANES-OXLEY ACT OF 2002, PL 107–204 (July 30, 2002).
16. 15 U.S.C.A. § 77e (2009).
17. *Id.* § 77c. See § 27.15.
18. *Id.* § 77d. See § 27.15.
19. See also section 28, which gives the SEC general exemptive authority through its rulemaking process. 15 U.S.C.A. § 77z-3.
20. 15 U.S.C.A. §§ 77f, 77h (2009).
21. *Id.* §§ 77g, 77j, Schedule A.
22. *Id.* § 77k. See § 27.16.
23. 15 U.S.C.A. § 77l (2009). See § 27.16. Section 13 contains the statute of limitations applicable to remedies under sections 11 and 12. 15 U.S.C.A. § 77m (2009).
24. 15 U.S.C.A. § 77q (2009).

25. *Id.* §§ 77s, 77t.
26. *See id.* §§ 77c, 77d.
27. Section 5(a), (b), 15 U.S.C.A. §§ 77e(a), (b) (2009).
28. Section 5(c), 15 U.S.C.A. § 77e(c) (2009). There is some limited prefiling publicity that may be disseminated without violating the Act's gun-jumping prohibitions. *See, e.g.,* 17 C.F.R. § 230.135.
29. 15 U.S.C.A. § 77e(b) (2009). Section 2(a)(10) defines "prospectus," and section 10 sets out the types of disclosures required. *Id.* §§ 77b(a)(10), 77j (2009). After the filing of the last amendment to the registration statement, there is a 20-day waiting period until the effective date. *Id.* § 77h. No sales may be made during the waiting period. *Id.* § 77e(a). The 20-day waiting period is subject to acceleration on application to the SEC. *Id.* § 77h.
30. *Id.* § 77e(a).
31. The waiting period can be several months or longer. Pursuant to section 8 of the 1933 Act (15 U.S.C.A. § 77h), the registration statement becomes effective 20 days from the date of the original filing or the filing of the most recent amendment, whichever is last. The 20-day period is misleading in terms of actual practice. The waiting period is usually much longer than the statutory 20 days for first-time issuers and for complicated offerings because of SEC review practices. Under section 8, the effective date of deficient registration statements can be delayed by a stop order or refusal order. Formal section 8 orders are the exception, as the SEC will generally respond to deficient registration statements with a letter of comment suggesting changes. The letter of comment will frequently be followed by a delaying amendment filed by the prospective issuer, which will put off the effective date until the deficiencies are corrected. When appropriate, the effective date can be accelerated (*see* SEC Rule 461; 17 C.F.R. § 230.461 (2009)).
32. 17 C.F.R. §§ 230.137 to 230.139. Sections 13 and 15(d) of the 1934 Act provide for periodic reporting of issuers whose securities are traded on a national exchange, securities that have been subject to a 1933 Act registration, or issuers with more than $10 million in assets and 2,000 or more shareholders of record but retains the former 500 record holder threshold with respect to investors who are not accredited investors. Section 12(g)(1)(A), 15 U.S.C.A. § 78l(g)(1)(A) as amended by the Jumpstart Our Business Startups Act (JOBS Act), H.R. 3606, 112 Cong. 2d sess. § 501 (2012). The record holder calculation excludes shareholders who receive shares as part of an employee compensation plan that is exempt from 1933 Act registration. Section 12(g) was also amended to exclude from the shareholder calculation holders of shares issued pursuant to an exempt crowdfunding offering.
33. 15 U.S.C.A. § 77b(a)(3) (2009). A letter of intent to underwrite an offering is not a binding contract for the sale of securities. Cafe La France, Inc. v. Schneider Secs., Inc., 281 F. Supp. 2d 361 (D.R.I. 2003).
34. *See* SEC Rule 163A, 17 C.F.R. § 230.163A (2009). This rule provides a safe harbor from a section 5(c) violation provided that the statement is made more than thirty days before the registration statement is filed and the upcoming offering is not mentioned.

35. *See* SEC Rule 168(a), 17 C.F.R. § 230.168 (2009). This exemption applies to the types of information that the company has been disseminating in the regular course of business.

36. *See* SEC Rule 405, 17 C.F.R. § 230.405 (2009) for a complete definition of a WKSI.

37. 15 U.S.C.A. § 77j (2009).

38. *Id.* § 77b(a)(10).

39. Rule 10b-10 of the 1934 Act requires that all sales by broker-dealers be confirmed in writing. 17 C.F.R. § 240.10b-10 (2009).

40. The only prohibition is on written offers to sell, thus any (including written) offers to buy are permissible, provided the sale is not consummated. Furthermore, while there are no section 5 implications, oral offers to sell are, of course, subject to the securities acts' general antifraud provisions.

41. 15 U.S.C.A. § 77b(2)(a)(10)(b) (2009); 17 C.F.R. § 230.134 (2009).

42. 17 C.F.R. § 230.430 (2009).

43. *Id.* § 230.431.

44. Section 5(b)(1) requires any written offer or confirmation to comply with section 10; a summary prospectus is valid for this purpose under section 10(b).

45. Section 5(b)(2), which applies only during the post-effective period, requires every person who purchases a security in the offering to receive a section 10(a) "full-blown" prospectus prior to or with delivery of that security.

46. 17 C.F.R. §§ 230.163 and 230.164 (2009).

47. *Id.* § 230.173(a). Rule 173 provides that notice of the availability of a statutory prospectus will satisfy section 5(b)'s prospectus delivery requirement.

48. Other rules to look at include Rules 137, 138, and 139, which deal with broker-dealer recommendations of securities during the registration process.

49. 15 U.S.C.A. § 77(a)(1) (2009).

50. *E.g.*, Marine Bank v. Weaver, 455 U.S. 551 (1982) (bank-issued certificate of deposit not a security subject to federal securities laws because it is already federally insured and purchasers therefore do not need that extra layer of protection the laws afford).

51. 328 U.S. 293 (1946).

52. *Id.* at 298–299.

53. 15 U.S.C.A. § 77c(a)(3) (2009). The Act further exempts all renewals thereof that are likewise limited in time. *Id.*

54. *Id.* § 78c(a)(10).

55. Reves v. Ernst & Young, 494 U.S. 56, 63 (1990).

56. *See, e.g.*, Chem. Bank v. Arthur Andersen & Co., 726 F.2d 930, 939 (2d Cir.), *cert. denied*, 469 U.S. 884 (1984); Exch. Nat'l Bank v. Touche Ross & Co., 544 F.2d 1126, 1137 (2d Cir. 1976).

57. Holden v. Hagopian, 978 F.2d 1115 (9th Cir. 1992).

58. Koch v. Hankins, 928 F.2d 1471 (9th Cir. 1991).

59. *See, e.g.*, Reeves v. Teuscher, 881 F.2d 1495 (9th Cir. 1989).

60. *See, e.g.*, Great Lakes Chem. Corp. v. Monsanto Co., 96 F. Supp. 2d 376 (D. Del. 2000).
61. SEC v. Shreveport Wireless Cable Television P'ship, 1998 WL 892948 (D.D.C. 1998).
62. See § 27.11, *supra*.
63. 15 U.S.C.A. § 77c (2009). However, as discussed *infra*, §§ 3(a)(9), 3(a)(10), 3(a)(11), 3(b), and 3(c) operate more like transaction exemptions (that is, later downstream resales may need a new exemption or else face registration).
64. Prior to 2012, the dollar limit for section 3(b) was $5 million. Congress retained the existing $5 million ceiling in section 3(b)(1) but added a new section 3(b)(2) with a $50 million ceiling every twelve months and mandating SEC rulemaking to implemented the new exemption. 15 U.S.C.A. § 77c(b), as amended by Jumpstart Our Business Startups Act (JOBS Act) § 401, H.R. 3606, 112 Cong. 2d sess. (2012).
65. 15 U.S.C.A. § 77z-3 (1996).
66. "Issuer" is defined in § 2(a)(4) as "every person who issues or proposes to issue any security." "Dealer" is defined in § 2(a)(12) as "any person who engages either for all or part of his time, directly or indirectly . . . in the business of offering, buying, selling, or otherwise dealing or trading in Securities issued by another person."
67. *See, e.g.*, SEC v. Chinese Consol. Benevolent Assoc., 120 F.2d 738 (2d Cir. 1941), *cert. denied*, 314 U.S. 618 (1941).
68. *See, e.g.*, *In re* Ira Haupt & Co., 23 S.E.C. 589 (1946).
69. *See, e.g.*, United States v. Wolfson, 405 F.2d 779 (2d Cir. 1968), *cert. denied*, 394 U.S. 946 (1969).
70. Rule 144(a)(1) defines "affiliate" as "a person that directly, or indirectly through one or more intermediaries, controls, or is controlled by, or is under common control with, such issuer." 17 C.F.R. § 230.144(a)(1) (2009).
71. 15 U.S.C.A. § 77d(2) (2009).
72. *See, e.g.*, Sec. Act Release No. 33-285 (Jan. 24, 1935); Sec. Act Release No. 33-5487 (Jan. 23, 1974).
73. *See, e.g.*, SEC v. Ralston Purina Co., 346 U.S. 119 (1953).
74. *See, e.g.*, Doran v. Petrol. Mgmt. Corp., 545 F.2d 893 (5th Cir. 1977).
75. 15 U.S.C.A. § 77b(a)(15) (2009).
76. Rules 251 to 263; 17 C.F.R. §§ 230.251 to 230.263 (2009).
77. For example, it is unavailable where the issuer, its predecessors, or affiliates are subject to a pending SEC proceeding or have within the preceding five years been subject to an SEC stop order, court securities injunction, or U.S. Post Office fraud order. Similarly, it is unavailable where any of the issuer's directors, officers, principal security holders, current promoters, or underwriters, or any affiliate of such underwriters has been convicted of any crime under the securities laws (not limited to federal securities laws) within the preceding five years or has been subject to an SEC or Post Office order. 17 C.F.R. § 230.262 (2009). The SEC may waive the disqualification. *Id.*
78. 15 U.S.C.A. § 77c(b), as amended by Jumpstart Our Business Startups Act (JOBS Act) § 401, H.R. 3606, 112 Cong. 2d sess. (2012).

79. *Id.* §§ 230.501 to 230.509.

80. This makes the planning, timing, and ordering of offerings very important. For example, an issuer cannot have a $500,000 Rule 504 offering following within one year of a $4.5 million Regulation A offering, because Rule 504 puts a $1 million ceiling on § 3(b) offerings within the preceding twelve months. On the other hand, an issuer can have a $500,000 Rule 504 offering followed by a $4.5 million Rule 505 offering, because Rule 251 would permit it as within Rule 505's $5 million ceiling on § 3(b) offerings within 12 months.

81. The method of calculation is similar to Rule 504.

82. Rule 502(d) requires that resales be made in compliance with Rule 144. 17 C.F.R. §§ 230.144, 230.502(d) (2009).

83. As such, Rule 506 is limited to the scope of the statutory section 4(2) exemption. However, this may change to the extent that the SEC invokes its general exemptive power under section 28 of the 1933 Act. 15 U.S.C.A. § 77z-2 (2009). See 27.15[3].

84. Closely related purchasers and accredited investors are excluded from the calculation of the number of purchasers.

85. The former safe-harbor rule for § 4(2), Rule 146, used to require this qualification for each offeree. Although this requirement is not specifically stated in Rule 506, disputes over whether a prohibited general solicitation has taken place frequently arise when this qualification is not met. *See, e.g., Doran*, 545 F.2d 893.

86. *E.g.,* SEC ACT Release No. 33-4434 (Dec. 6, 1961).

87. 15 U.S.C.A. § 77k (2009).

88. *Id.* § 77l(a).

89. *Id.* §§ 77k, 77l(a)(2), 77q(a).

90. *Id.* § 77l(a)(1).

91. *Id.* § 77k.

92. *But cf.* the last clause of section 11(a), which requires a showing of reliance with respect to financial statements more than twelve months old.

93. Persons liable include all signers of the registration statement (which must include the principal executive and financial officers, the issuer, and a majority of the directors), all directors (including people not yet directors but agreeing to be named as about to become directors), experts (e.g., the certifying accountant), and underwriters. *See* §§ 11(a)(1) to (5) for a list of these persons, 15 U.S.C.A. § 77k(a) (2009).

94. *Id.* § 77k(c).

95. *See, e.g.,* Escott v. BarChris Constr. Corp., 283 F. Supp. 643 (S.D.N.Y. 1968); Feit v. Leaseco Data Processing Equip. Corp., 332 F. Supp. 544 (E.D.N.Y. 1971).

96. In an effort to clarify its position, the SEC promulgated Rule 176, which sets forth factors to be considered, reinforces the judicial sliding scale of culpability, and further provides for the necessity of a case-by-case, highly fact-specific analysis. 17 C.F.R. § 230.176 (2009).

97. 15 U.S.C.A. § 77l (2009).

98. This is the remedy set forth in section 12(a)(1). 15 U.S.C.A. § 77l(a)(1) (2009). *See* Babst v. Morgan Keegan & Co., 687 F. Supp. 255, 261 (E.D.

La. 1988) (Section 12 is the exclusive basis for an implied right of action for a section 5 violation).
99. Section 12(a)(2). 15 U.S.C.A. § 77l(a)(2) (2009).
100. *See* Foster v. Jesup & Lamont Sec. Co., 759 F.2d 838 (11th Cir. 1985). *See also* Pinter v. Dahl, 486 U.S. 622 (1988) (holding that to be a seller in an action under § 12(a)(1), the defendant must have been both an immediate and direct seller; substantial participation alone will not suffice).
101. *E.g.*, Abell v. Potomac Ins. Co., 858 F.2d 1104 (5th Cir. 1988), *cert. denied*, 492 U.S. 918 (1989); Stokes v. Lokken, 644 F.2d 779 (8th Cir. 1981).
102. *E.g.*, Quincy Coop. Bank v. A.G. Edwards & Sons, Inc., 655 F. Supp. 78 (D. Mass. 1986).
103. *Pinter*, 486 U.S. 622.
104. Currie v. Cayman Resources Corp., 835 F.2d 780 (11th Cir. 1988).
105. Sanders v. John Nuveen & Co., 619 F.2d 1222 (7th Cir. 1980), *cert. denied*, 450 U.S. 1005 (1981).
106. *See* Mayer v. Oil Field Sys. Corp., 803 F.2d 749 (2d Cir. 1986).
107. 15 U.S.C.A. § 77k(a)(2) (2009).
108. Gustafson v. Alloyd Co., 513 U.S. 561 (1995).
109. 15 U.S.C.A. § 78f (2000).
110. 15 U.S.C.A. § 78g, 78h (2009).
111. 15 U.S.C.A. §§ 78i, 78j (1988 & Supp. 1993).
112. *Id.* §§ 78k, 78o(c).
113. 15 U.S.C.A. § 78l (2009). The Act also calls for registration of transfer agents. Section 17A(c), 15 U.S.C.A. § 78q-1 (2009).
114. Section 12(g)(1), as modified by Rule 12g-1, requires registration of any class of equity security with more than 500 shareholders where the issuer has more than $10 million in assets. 15 U.S.C.A. § 78l(g)(1) (2009); 17 C.F.R. § 240.12g-1 (2009).
115. Section 15(d)(1). 15 U.S.C.A. § 78o(d)(1) (2009).
116. 15 U.S.C.A. §§ 78o, 78o-1 (2009).
117. *Id.* § 78n. *See* §§ 13.29 to 13.32.
118. In particular, sections 13(d) to (e), 14(d) to (f). 15 U.S.C.A. §§ 78m(d) to (e), 78n(d) to (f) (2009). See Chapter 24.
119. See § 12.8 *supra*.
120. In particular, section 13(a), 15 U.S.C.A. § 78m(a) (2009).
121. 15 U.S.C.A. § 78o(a) to (c) (2009).
122. *See, e.g.*, Rule 10b-5 and § 14(e); 17 C.F.R. § 240.10b-5 (2009); 15 U.S.C.A. § 78n(e) (2009).
123. Section 15(d) applies periodic reporting requirements to still others— namely, to those companies that had a public offering of securities that was registered under the Securities Act of 1933.
124. The 1934 Act's registration requirement is set forth in 15 U.S.C.A. § 78g (2009). It is quite different from 1933 Act registration; a corporation that has registered a class of securities under the 1934 Act will still have to register each particular offering of that class of securities under the 1933 Act.
125. Options are included in the definition of equity securities because they are convertible into equity securities.

126. The statute required registration for companies with assets of more than one million dollars but Rule 12g–1 exempted issuers with assets under ten million dollars. 15 U.S.C.A. § 78l(g)(1) (2011); 17 C.F.R. § 240.12g–1 (2011).

127. Section 12(g)(1)(A), 15 U.S.C. § 78l(g)(1)(A) as amended by the Jumpstart Our Business Startups Act (JOBS Act), H.R. 3606, 112 Cong. 2d sess. § 501 (2012). The record holder calculation excludes shareholders who receive shares as part of an employee compensation plan that is exempt from 1933 Act registration. Section 12(g) was also amended to exclude from the shareholder calculation holders of shares issued pursuant to an exempt crowdfunding offering.

128. 17 C.F.R. § 240.12g–1 (2009).

129. Rule 12h-3, 17 C.F.R. § 240.12h-3 (2009). To give an example of the numbers, there are approximately 3,000 exchange-listed securities (stocks and bonds, not options) and approximately 6,000 securities traded in the over-the-counter markets.

130. 15 U.S.C.A. § 78o(d) (2009). The 1933 Act registration requirements are discussed in § 27.11.

131. *Id.* § 78i(e). *See* 3 THOMAS L. HAZEN, TREATISE ON THE LAW OF SECURITIES REGULATION § 12.1 (6th ed. 2009).

132. Santa Fe Indus. v. Green, 430 U.S. 462, 476–77 (1977); Ernst & Ernst v. Hochfelder, 425 U.S. 185, 199 (1976).

133. 15 U.S.C.A. § 78r(a) (2009).

134. *See* Heit v. Weitzen, 402 F.2d 909 (2d Cir. 1968), *cert. denied*, 395 U.S. 903 (1969).

135. *See* Herman & MacLean v. Huddleston, 459 U.S. 375 (1983).

136. 15 U.S.C.A. § 78p(b) (2009). See § 12.8 *supra*.

137. *E.g.*, J.I. Case Co. v. Borak, 377 U.S. 426 (1964). See § 13.32.

138. *E.g.*, *Herman*, 459 U.S. 375; Superintendent of Ins. v. Bankers Life & Cas. Co., 404 U.S. 6 (1971).

139. Piper v. Chris-Craft Indus., 430 U.S. 1 (1977). Most courts have held that even the bidder can sue for injunctive relief.

140. See Chapter 24.

141. 15 U.S.C.A. § 78j(b) (2009).

142. *E.g.*, Schreiber v. Burlington N., 472 U.S. 1 (1985); *Santa Fe Indus.*, 430 U.S. 462; *Ernst & Ernst*, 425 U.S. 185.

143. *Schreiber*, 472 U.S. 1.

INDEX

ABOUT THE AUTHORS

James D. Cox is the Brainerd Currie Professor of Law at Duke University. In addition to his texts *Financial Information, Accounting and the Law*; *Cox and Hazen on Corporations*; and *Securities Regulations Cases and Materials* (with Hillman & Langevoort), Professor Cox has published extensively in the areas of market regulation and corporate governance, as well as having testified before the U.S. House and Senate on insider trading, class actions, and market reform issues. In 2001 he was awarded an Honorary Doctorate of Mercature from the University of Southern Denmark for his work in international securities law.

Thomas Lee Hazen is the Cary C. Boshamer Distinguished Professor of Law at the University of North Carolina, Chapel Hill. His books include *Corporate Counsel Guides: Securities Regulation*, a seven-volume treatise on the law of securities regulation (plus a one-volume student edition), and he is coauthor of a three-volume treatise on corporate law, a two-volume treatise on broker-dealer law, and a three-volume treatise on derivatives regulation.